# American Political Economy in Global Perspective

This book is a guide to claims about the proper role of government and markets in a global economy. Moving deftly between systematic comparison of 19 rich democracies and debate about what the United States can do to restore a more civilized, egalitarian, and fair society, Harold L. Wilensky tells us how 6 of these countries got on a low road to economic progress. He specifies which components of their labor-crunch strategy are uniquely American. He provides an overview of the impact of major dimensions of globalization, only one of which – the interaction of the internationalization of finance and the rapid increase in the autonomy of central banks – undermines either national sovereignty or job security, labor standards, and the welfare state. Although he views American policy and politics through the lens of globalization, he concludes that the nation-state remains the center of personal identity, social solidarity, and political action. The book concentrates on what national differences mean for the well-being of nations and their people.

Drawing on lessons from abroad and from America's own past successes, Wilensky shows how we can reverse our three-decade decline. He argues that, in order to get off the low road, we must overcome the myths of "moderation," the rise of the "independent voter," and a rightward shift of the electorate. He specifies a feasible domestic agenda that matches majority sentiments in all rich democracies.

Harold L. Wilensky was Professor Emeritus of Political Science at the University of California, Berkeley. He was a Fellow of the American Academy of Arts and Sciences and was twice a Fellow at the Center for Advanced Study in the Behavioral Sciences. He is the author of 75 articles and 13 books, including *Industrial Society and Social Welfare* (1958, 1965), *Organizational Intelligence: Knowledge and Policy in Government and Industry* (1967, 1969), *The Welfare State and Equality* (1975), and *Rich Democracies* (2002). Before joining the University of California in 1963, he taught at the University of Michigan and the University of Chicago.

# Advance Praise for *American Political Economy in Global Perspective*

"Wilensky's book is a major contribution to comparative politics. It is ideal for researchers and teachers on the impact of globalization. Written with analytical clarity and passion, the book comes across as a voice of sanity in the dysfunctional U.S. elite-political discourse – especially to European friends of America and outside observers."

– Einar Øverbye, Oslo University College

"The United States must get beyond polarization of the Left and Right, and nobody is better equipped to tell us how to do it than Hal Wilensky, with his 40 years of in-depth research on 19 rich democracies. In this brilliant summation of his life's work, Wilensky shows that neither the Left nor the Right is correct: globalization is not the culprit, and neoliberalism is not the solution. Centrist, activist, market-enabling, and work-facilitating governmental policies make rich democracies richer, and by enacting them, the United States can get on the high road to greater employment, growth, and social welfare."

– Henry E. Brady, University of California, Berkeley

"What is groundbreaking in this book is the detailed application of comparative policy analysis to a wide range of social and economic problems of the United States in a global economy. No treatment of the 'varieties of capitalism' presents data as rich and comprehensive as Wilensky offers, or provides the depth of understanding of the U.S. political economy and the possibilities for reform. His sections on education reform alone are worth the price of the book; they are superb, provocative, and timely. I would gladly use this book in graduate and upper-division undergraduate courses."

– Lowell Turner, Cornell University

"Wilensky offers a powerful message for the United States at a critical moment: we must get off the low road of underinvestment in human and physical capital, low wages, and high inequality, and we *can* do it. He combines careful research with incisive analysis and clear policy prescriptions. And he builds on a remarkable breadth of evidence – extensive data from 19 countries over 60 years – that gives his conclusions considerable weight."

– Steve Vogel, University of California, Berkeley

"The late Hal Wilensky was the dean of social scientists working on the political economy of the welfare state. The present volume is a powerful summary of that life's work and a practical road map to reforming public policies for the 21st century. The focus here may be on the United States, but the implications are much broader."

– Barry Eichengreen, University of California, Berkeley

# American Political Economy
# in Global Perspective

HAROLD L. WILENSKY

*Formerly of University of California, Berkeley*

 **CAMBRIDGE**
UNIVERSITY PRESS

CAMBRIDGE UNIVERSITY PRESS
Cambridge, New York, Melbourne, Madrid, Cape Town,
Singapore, São Paulo, Delhi, Mexico City

Cambridge University Press
32 Avenue of the Americas, New York, NY 10013-2473, USA

www.cambridge.org
Information on this title: www.cambridge.org/9781107638952

First published 2012

Printed in the United States of America

*A catalog record for this publication is available from the British Library.*

*Library of Congress Cataloging in Publication data*
Wilensky, Harold L.
American political economy in global perspective / Harold L. Wilensky.
    p.   cm.
Includes bibliographical references and index.
ISBN 978-1-107-01809-9 (hardback) – ISBN 978-1-107-63895-2 (paperback)
1. United States – Economic policy.   2. United States – Economic conditions.
3. Economic policy.   4. Comparative government.   5. Political sociology.
6. Welfare state.   7. Globalization.   I. Title.
HC103.W52    2012
330.973–dc23                                            2011025693

ISBN 978-1-107-01809-9 Hardback
ISBN 978-1-107-63895-2 Paperback

# Contents

# Figures

# Tables

# Preface and Introduction

> One should really never say, "the state does this or that." It is always important to recognize who or whose interest it is that sets the machine of the state in motion and speaks through it.
>
> Joseph Schumpeter (1918)

> Practical men, who believe themselves to be quite exempt from any intellectual influences, are usually the slaves of some defunct economist. Soon or late, it is ideas, not vested interests, which are dangerous for good or evil.
>
> John Maynard Keynes (1936)

"Globalization" has become the all-purpose cause of our troubles and opportunities. Among the basic questions about its impact on public policy and human welfare, two are of great interest to both scholars and policy makers:

1. Is the nation-state eroding as a unit of social-science analysis and as the center of political action?
2. Do capital and labor flows across national boundaries threaten the social and labor policies of the rich democracies – especially job protection and good earnings and welfare-state benefits, such as government-guaranteed universal pensions and health insurance?

Because these questions assume that globalization gives countries with low labor costs and lean social policies a competitive advantage over their rivals, we must give an estimate regarding a third question:

3. Leaving aside the net contribution of the welfare state and labor policies to such values as dignity, security, equality, family well-being, social integration, and political legitimacy, what are the net effects of the welfare state, social policies, and job protection on productivity and economic performance?

Here is a preview of answers to these questions. First, every chapter in this book provides evidence of the persistence of striking national differences in domestic policy and politics from 1950 to today, before and after the changes labeled globalization are supposed to have weakened national sovereignty. At the outset of my 40 years of research on 19 rich democracies, prepared to uncover significant change whatever its causes and pace, I found instead amazing continuity in the contrasting institutions and paths of development of these countries. Of course, there is change, including some convergence in policies and politics, but not as much as most scholars and observers of globalization claim. The most important question for me (and the focus of more than half of this book) is this: In view of continuing national differences among rich democracies, what lessons can the United States learn from abroad about domestic politics and policies to cope with its mounting political and social problems, and which successful policies are transferable? Although I see these problems through the lens of global developments, I keep my eye on the primary arena for action, the nation-state.

If there is any problem that should be handled globally, it is energy policy and the environment. Yet Chapter 2, which deals in detail with global climate change and the environment, underlines the poor record of international agencies and organizations in this area. It suggests that each nation needs to take responsibility for its own energy policy now, looking to the life-cycle emissions of greenhouse gases from each of its energy uses. No rich democracy, least of all the United States, can delay action with the excuse that international agreements among 30 or 200 countries have not been consummated or that China, a large emitter of greenhouse gases, is not joining such agreements. The great day when scores of nations might adopt binding agreements with common enforceable standards is far, far away. That is why Chapter 2 covers the politics and policies of all 19 nation-states and shows which ones are performing best and worst and what we can learn now from the recent history of national and international policies. It begins with the contrasting strategies of the only two rich democracies that since 1980 have sharply reduced their vulnerability to external energy shocks while greatly improving their economic performance and leading in the reduction of greenhouse gas emissions – Denmark and Sweden. It then assesses alternative energy options, policies, and politics.

The second question – about the impact of capital and labor flows across national boundaries – is answered in detail in Chapter 6, an overview of six dimensions of globalization: capital flows, migration, deregulation of the labor market, outsourcing of jobs, the rise of multinational corporations, and the increased autonomy of central banks as related to the internationalization of finance. Capital and labor flows (including migration and immigration rates) are not new nor do they undermine the institutional and policy differences among the countries I compare. Similarly, the deregulation of the labor market in order to increase international competitiveness occurs in some countries and not in others. To demonstrate this by the relevant comparisons, I contrast countries with deregulated "flexible" labor markets and countries with "rigid" labor markets ("Eurosclerosis"), that is, strong job protection or job security. Then I explore the question, What jobs are now or can be outsourced with what effect? The conclusion: the greater job security of the more consensual democracies is a positive advantage for enterprise productivity and for national well-being. And outsourcing is not yet a major threat to labor standards or jobs, although much of this analysis, handicapped by deficiencies of data, remains speculative.

The fifth dimension of globalization is the growth of multinational corporations (MNCs). Regarding its impact, there is no support for the popular argument that MNCs undermine labor standards and collective bargaining if we compare nationals with multinationals and trace recent trends in the MNCs' investment targets; their ready adaptation to national laws and practices; and their policies on wages, union recognition, and consultation. In other words, Wal-Mart's sins cannot be generalized to the thousands of multinationals.

If the emergence of multinationals, the movement of migrants across national borders, and even the international flow of capital, as well as varied attempts to deregulate the labor market and the outsourcing of jobs, are only a moderate to small influence on the national bargaining patterns between labor, professions, management, government, and political parties, then what is there about globalization that *does* undermine national policy, politics, and well-being? The real culprit is the rapid rise in the power and ideology of the leaders of central banks, investment banks, insurance companies, and other financial institutions. This change is the one major force that threatens the collaborative bargaining through which labor and center-left and center-right party coalitions have tamed the "free market" for more than a century, thereby enhancing the real welfare of large majorities through decent labor standards, some job security, and a universalistic welfare state. Sections on the deregulation of finance and the financial meltdown of recent years conclude with a discussion of the Great Recession of 2007–2009 and the continuing near-Depression level of unemployment and underemployment in several rich democracies, including the United States.

The third question concerns the net effects of social policies, labor policies, and the welfare state on economic performance; it is answered in Chapter 1 (The Welfare State as the Center of Public Finance and Political Conflict) and Chapter 3 (What Trade-Offs Are Good and Bad for the Economy?).

Among the most solid generalizations from my project is that for the past 60 years the welfare state has been either good for economic performance or neutral, depending on the period analyzed. Even if we examine the impact of social spending or aggregate total government spending on debt and deficits, we find that the welfare-state leaders, the lavish spenders, are not spending themselves into the grave. Chapter 1 examines these connections and explains why among these 19 rich democracies there is little or no relation between spending and debt, except at great extremes of debt, rare among modern countries.

The record of the past 60 years offers little support for the argument that there is a sharp trade-off between job security, labor standards, social security, equality, and poverty reduction, on the one hand, and worker productivity, economic growth, and other measures of economic performance, on the other. What is often left out of the discussions of these alleged trade-offs are (1) systematic empirical observations of the economic performance of big spenders and lean spenders at a similar economic level; (2) the contrasting economic and political effects of particular types of spending and the types of taxes used to finance public spending; and (3) analysis of the impact of various economic and social policies on consensus or political legitimacy, as these in turn shape economic performance. The interplay between economic and political policies is evident in the recent history of the United States. For instance, the tax-cutting mania from Reagan to Bush II ultimately paralyzed government at every level, reducing the capacity to use fiscal policy for public purposes other than military, alienating citizens who had been educated to believe in free lunches, and putting too great a burden on monetary policy. Its radical escalation under President George W. Bush resulted in an explosion of deficits and debt. It polarized politics to its greatest intensity since the 19th century. As we have seen again in 2009, that makes it much more difficult to take timely action to deal with the health-care crisis and the climate change crisis, and to gradually reform Social Security (see Chapters 3, 7, and 8).

Mass resistance to cuts in the core programs of the welfare state combined with the universal popularity of government-guaranteed health care, pensions, disability insurance, family policies, and decent labor standards suggests that political elites so inclined can build on majority sentiments while they make these programs more efficient and fair. Chapter 4 analyzes the unhappy fate of politicians who are serious about cutback budgeting and the shape of issue-specific public opinion about taxing and spending – two forces that explain the recurrent success of a center-left agenda, sometimes embraced or at least tolerated by the center-right. Chapter 5 gives special attention to the convergence and reform of pension systems and explains why the peculiar U.S. health-care system is a lesson in what not to do. Proposals for reform of both of these big-ticket items often take the form of solutions in search of a problem. It is wise to start with diagnosis of the disease before plunging in with cures.

Regarding OASDI (government-guaranteed pensions, disability insurance, and survivors' benefits), where the United States has no crisis, the problem is two century-long trends: a decline in the age of exit of men from the labor force and an increase in healthy displaced older workers. Chapter 5 analyzes what the United States can learn from other rich democracies that have recently created flexible retirement systems to cope with this problem: how to provide incentives and opportunities for healthy older workers to continue to work without pressuring the worn-out workers to postpone retirement.

It is the same with health-care reform, where the United States does have an urgent need to act. The basic problem to be solved: increase mass access to doctors, drugs, hospitals, clinics, and public-health services and at the same time contain exploding costs and improve health performance. To do this we must follow the lead of every other rich democracy and move toward national health insurance. Among the 19 rich democracies, the United States is the odd-man-out in its health-care spending, organization, and results. In the past hundred years, with the exception of the United States, the currently rich democracies have all converged in the broad outlines of health care. They all developed central control of budgets with financing from compulsory individual and employer contributions and/or government revenues. All have permitted the insured to supplement government services with additional care, privately purchased. All, including the United States, have rationed health care. All have experienced a growth in doctor density and the ratio of specialists to primary-care personnel. All evidence a trend toward public funding. Our deviance consists of no national health insurance, a huge private sector, a very high ratio of specialists to primary-care physicians and nurses, and a uniquely expensive (non)system with a poor cost-benefit ratio. The cure: increase the public share to more than 65 percent from its present level of 45 percent. About two-thirds of the public is the lowest public dominance in the other 18 countries. Regarding funding the transition cost and the permanent cost of guaranteed universal coverage: no rich democracy has funded national health insurance without relying on mass taxes, especially payroll and consumption taxes. Whatever we do to begin, broad-based taxes will be the outcome. Three explanations of why there is no national health insurance in the United States are examined. The weakest and most misleading is the claim that American public opinion opposes it (see Chapters 4 and 5). The persuasive explanations accent the history of public policy choices since World War II and, most important, the fragmented decentralized structure and operation of the U.S. government.

The problem we face is how to stop two games played by commercial providers in a system where they account for 55 percent of total health-care costs: *cost shifting* and *risk selection*. Without a substantial increase in public-sector bargaining power, those games and the extraordinary administrative overhead they necessitate will continue to escalate spending while decreasing coverage and the quality of care for an increasing majority of Americans. As Chapter 5 shows, the runaway costs are not from Medicare; they are mainly commercial. Without containing the reach and political power of the medical-industrial complex, the United States will never be able to join the rest of the affluent democracies that have national health insurance with better health performance at much lower cost. Here is a case where fixing a broken system by avoiding the problem of public vs. private power – let's have more efficiency, tell doctors what the best practices are, tell the insurance companies and big consumers of health care to behave themselves, squeeze a third of a trillion dollars out of Medicaid and Medicare – will merely make things worse, ultimately undermining support for any serious reform. Discussion of the politics of health care appears in Chapters 5, 7, and 8 (National Health Insurance).

In sum, analysis of the impact of globalization on these national variations is captured in the phrase "the nation-state is alive and well"; it remains the ultimate object of allegiance and the main source of personal identity, social solidarity, and political action. National institutions continue to make a big difference for real welfare. After reviewing the impact of each of the six dimensions of globalization, Chapter 6 concludes that only the interaction of central bank autonomy and the internationalization of finance is a significant threat to job security, labor standards, and the welfare state. Even here, national responses vary depending on the institutions in place when these trends became dominant.

Although I continue to search for an understanding of the differences and similarities among rich democracies, more than half of this book is about American politics and policies as they shape the well-being of the nation and its people. Part II (Chapters 7 and 8) lists 13 ways in which the United States has adopted a low-wage, inegalitarian, labor-crunch strategy for economic growth. I compare extremes: the confrontational "low road" pursued by the United States and the "high road" pursued by the strongest consensual democracies of continental Europe, where social partners have negotiated real reforms in expensive social policies while preserving social cohesion. Both paths of development are compatible with good economic performance, but they have a drastically different impact on the lives of people. In the final chapter, I consider what the United States can learn from the experience of the more centralized, more consensual democracies and, most important, which of their successful policies can be transferred to the United States without major changes in the structure of our government and constitution. To address this issue, I specify the political conditions and coalitions necessary for adoption of policies that would get the United States off the low road toward a more civilized, equitable, and just society. After examining feasibility of alternative policies and political history from Truman through Obama's first two years, I conclude that on the basis of its dismal record of governing in recent decades, the Republican Party offers little hope for moving America off the low road (see discussion of Table 11 for a summary of the evidence) and turn my attention to the possible revitalization of the Democratic Party. I examine the myth of the rise of "moderation" and the related myth of the "independent voter," as well as the myth of the rightward drift of the American electorate. I then suggest a center-left agenda that reflects the issue-specific preferences of vast majorities of the electorate, with close attention to practical limits and possibilities.

I am convinced that the United States, despite its parochialism, is capable of learning from and adapting lessons from abroad. That new knowledge of issues discussed in this book makes its way in the long run is evident from the intellectual history of the past century or so. Both our past experience and our present crisis provide examples of successful borrowing and adaptation of social-science findings from academia transcending national boundaries. Consider these examples from comparative research in economics, industrial relations, sociology, and political science:

- The theories of John Maynard Keynes penetrated high policy in every modern country from the 1930s until now. Fiscal policy was greatly shaped by this basic research. Although FDR, elected on a budget-balancing platform, did not pay attention to Keynes and failed to extricate himself from the recession of 1937–1938, subsequent presidents benefited from the institutionalization of academic economics in the Council of Economic Advisers and, on average, did better. In addition, comparable advisory institutions in other modem democracies provided a channel for steady professional economic advice, thereby improving economic performance (Wilensky, 1967a: ch. 5).

- The labor economists and labor historians of the "Wisconsin School" during the first third of the 20th century mightily shaped U.S. social security laws and the National Labor Relations Act (Wagner Act) and related labor legislation. Again, the ideas emerged long before they were embodied in legislation. For instance, the early impetus for the Social Security Act of 1935 came from social scientists – economists, political scientists, and others – who were familiar with European social and labor policies; they were the original founders and leaders of the American Association for Labor Legislation (AALL), which was established in 1906 as a section of the International Association for Labor Legislation. Among the most active scholars in or around this association who shaped the public agenda of the 1930s were John R. Commons, labor economist of Wisconsin, who wrote eleven volumes under the title *Industrial Society* and advised Senator LaFollette on progressive social legislation before World War I; Commons's student and collaborator John B. Andrews, AALL's executive secretary from 1908 until his death in 1943; Edwin E. Witte, chief of Wisconsin's Legislative Reference Library when he taught economics at the university in the 1920s; and Arthur J. Altmeyer, former student and research assistant of Commons. Both Witte and Altmeyer helped Commons move the issue of unemployment insurance to state debates in the 1920s (Lubove, 1968: 29–34; Chambers, 1963: 174–175; Altmeyer, 1968: 7; Cohen and Lampman, 1962: xv–xvi). During the three decades before the New Deal, these scholarly advocates researched collective bargaining, labor law, industrial regulation, income maintenance, workers' compensation, unemployment insurance, and health insurance. They crafted laws, some of which were debated in the legislatures of Wisconsin, Ohio, and New York; later they directly shaped New Deal social legislation.[1] The persistence of the influence of these intellectuals on social legislation of the 1930s is symbolized by Wilbur Cohen's appointment as secretary of Health, Education, and Welfare (HEW) in the Johnson administration thirty years later. He studied at Wisconsin in the early 1930s, where he was fully exposed to the lively academic debates about labor and social legislation. From 1935 to 1969 he rose from research positions in the Social Security Administration to secretary of HEW in 1968–1969.

- Morris Janowitz's work on the military – his 1961 book, for instance – was unusual in the context of a discipline that was dominated by a vague pacifism and therefore ignored the serious study of the military. The related sociological research of Charles Moskos (1988) had considerable influence on the reorganization of the military. Their 1960s ideas about a national youth service corps directly shaped the political debate of the 1990s, with Senator Nunn and Governor Clinton embracing the idea – again, about a thirty-year time lag from sociological analysis to national public policy debate that loosely corresponds to political cycles.

Similarly, when political and economic conditions were favorable for the adoption of national health insurance in 2008–2009, many a congressional staffer and academic consultant dug out old memos, articles, and position papers based not only on the work of medical economists but also on research in the sociology of medicine and the professions and on comparative studies of the financing, organization, and delivery of medical services in other countries from several disciplines. Of course, after long neglect, Keynes was once again resurrected in the Great Recession, to good effect. Perhaps Ronald Reagan's social policies are a less benign example of the impact of theory coming many decades after its formulation; those policies were inspired not by the painstaking research on the roots of poverty but by the social Darwinism of Herbert Spencer. Sometimes ideas take a very long time to penetrate the higher circles of power – from Spencer to Reagan in one hundred years.

My research has shown that today the most easily transferable policies that have achieved much success abroad include the family policies of Sweden, Belgium, and France; the active labor-market policy of Sweden, Finland, and Germany; the rehabilitation emphasis of disability policies in Sweden; and the flexible retirement system of Finland. Chapters 5, 7, and 8 tell why these policies are likely candidates for transfer to the United States, whether they come from the little countries of Scandinavia that we can view as laboratories for socioeconomic experimentation or from large countries such as Germany and France.

This book summarizes and updates the main results of a long-term research project focused on the causes and effects of national variation in labor and social policies among all of the 19 rich democracies with a population of at least 3.5 million. By 1966 they had achieved a GNP per capita that put them in the upper sixth of the world's distribution – very rich, indeed. How rich can be grasped by looking at how much money to play around with each year comes from various GDP growth rates in the United States. An anemic growth rate of 1 percent in 2009 dollars when the GDP was $14.3 trillion yields $143 billion extra; a below-average growth of 2 percent brings $286 billion; 3 percent growth yields $429 billion, more than the annual Pentagon budget before the escalation of the George W. Bush years; 4 percent brings $572 billion in one year.

Current debates in the United States about major issues – the stimulus package of 2009; reforms of health care, energy, and the environment; labor law; education and job creation – often take the form "We can't afford this; it will explode the debt, ruin our children's future" and the like. Perhaps a single figure of the foregone income lost in the Great Recession (officially the four quarters of 2008 plus the first two quarters of 2009) will put these claims in perspective. The average real growth from 1975 through 2007 – after the first oil shock and worldwide recession and before the most recent meltdown – was 3.2 percent. With a more modest "normal" growth rate of 3 percent, the foregone real (inflation-adjusted) figure for the year and a half of the Great Recession is $1.16 trillion (calculated from Bureau of Economic Analysis, 2009: table 1.1.1). That is more than the entire Congressional Budget Office guesstimated cost of the final health-care bill over 10 years, including extra administrative costs. In short, restoring growth and investing in the productivity-enhancing social and labor-market policies discussed herein are far more effective ways to put debt on a sustainable track than an obsession with debt alone. Chapter 1 compares government spending in our 19 rich democracies with both deficits and debt/GDP and explains why the big spenders are not running up unsustainable debt levels, if we assume that the world recession of 2007–2009 is not permanent.

I have found two complementary theories useful in explaining the similarities and differences among these 19 rich democracies. First is convergence theory or "modernization" theory. It suggests that as the currently rich countries got richer, as they achieved high levels of technological and economic development, they became more alike in social structure, culture, and politics. It specifies the consequences of advanced and continuing industrialization (the increasing use of high-energy technology and inanimate sources of energy). The second set of theories suggests that rich nations, whatever their similarities, still vary greatly in their problems of consensus and conflict, the Madisonian problem of containing factional war, and the Durkheimian problem of threats to social integration. Everyone knows that Sweden is not the United States is not Japan. Plainly the 19 rich democracies discussed here, as they cope with the problem of aggregating interests and resolving conflict, differ greatly in their labor relations and in the interplay of politics, markets, and the nonprofit sector. They differ in the size and shape of their welfare states, in their patterns of taxing and spending, in the clusters of public policies they pursue, and in their effectiveness in implementing policies. Most important, they differ greatly in their system outputs – what all the taxing and spending, all the policy choices mean for the well-being of their people. Throughout the 40 years of this project, I have used convergence theory to explain similarities among rich democracies and types of political economy to explain national differences. This current work concentrates more on explaining the differences but attends to areas of obvious convergence.

Drawing on research analyzing similarities and differences among 19 rich democracies, this book compares the economic performance of big spenders and lean spenders at a similar economic level from 1950 to 2007. Going beyond aggregate public spending, it shows the contrasting effects of particular types of spending and taxing and specific social, labor, and environmental policies. I highlight the extraordinary continuity of the contrasting institutions and policy directions of these countries, finding that there is not one road to good economic performance but several. I specify five types of political economy, each with its own costs and gains in people's well-being, both economic and noneconomic. The types begin with national differences in the structure and interplay of government, political parties, the mass media, industry, labor, the professions, and religious institutions. Differences in degrees of centralization and bargaining arrangements among these groups generate three types of national bargaining. My classification ranks them as follows (Wilensky, 1976, 1981, 2002: ch. 2):

- Democratic corporatist: Austria, Netherlands, Belgium, Sweden, Norway, and Finland and, less strongly, Denmark, Italy, and Israel, with Germany a marginal case
- Corporatism without labor: Japan and, less strongly, France, with Switzerland a marginal case
- Least corporatist or most fragmented and decentralized: United States, United Kingdom, Ireland, Canada, Australia, and New Zealand

For variety, I shall use several labels interchangeably: "corporatist democracies" are consensual democracies; "least corporatist" are fragmented and decentralized or confrontational or noncorporatist. The types of political economy are completed by combining these variations in national bargaining arrangements with the power of mass-based political parties of long and continuous standing, principally left (typically labeled Socialist, Labor, Social Democratic) and Catholic (typically labeled Christian Democratic, Social Christian, Christian Socialist). The resulting five types are listed in Table 2; they are used to explain national outcomes throughout the book, both economic and noneconomic. Their historical origins are discussed in Chapter 3. Sources, concepts, and measures are further elaborated in the Appendix.

I have emphasized the advantages of more centralized systems of bargaining over the highly fragmented and decentralized system of the United States. Despite its radical federalism, an overview of the most successful policies of the United States shows that they are almost entirely financed by the central government, for instance, Social Security, Medicare, the GI bill, the racial integration of the armed forces, the electrification of the South via the Tennessee Valley Authority, progress in the cleanup of air and water and in the control of local vigilantes; while the most botched problems, the most inefficient and ineffective and periodically underfunded policies are fully or partly state and local – education, especially K–12 schooling, welfare reform, Medicaid, criminal justice, prisons, and policing.

There is no more complex problem in organizational theory than ideas about decentralization (Wilensky, 1967a: 58–62). If we go beyond the ideologies of populist Right and Left about the joys of decentralization and limited central government, we find that all rich democracies have large doses of both centralization and decentralization. They all have central financing of many programs; they all necessarily rely on regional or communal units for delivery of personal social services such as job training, education, and health care. The great variations are in exactly what is centralized or decentralized in what degree – functions, location, authority, financing, records, intelligence, loyalty – and with what effect on equity, equality, efficiency, service, citizen response, and degrees of corruption. Throughout this book I discuss these matters, emphasizing the differences between the moderately or highly centralized bargaining arrangements of corporatist democracies and the more-decentralized political economies.

Although the text discusses the main ideas and indexes used in this study, the Appendix provides convenient definitions, measures, and sources of such concepts as democracy, pluralism, cumulative party power, electoral systems, export dependence, and democratic corporatism (or negotiated political economies or consensual democracies) vs. fragmented and decentralized (or confrontational democracies). It also suggests the severe limitations of forecasts that are common in economics and demography and widely used in scoring the costs and gains of proposed public policies.

The project used both quantitative and qualitative methods: simple cross-tabulations of averages by types and periods; regressions or path diagrams where appropriate; studies of deviant or extreme cases; comparative historical context; and more than 400 interviews I conducted with top decision makers and their advisers. I concentrate on what governments do, not what they say. This does not mean that I ignore ideology as a source of government behavior. I show, however, that if ideology is not anchored in organizations and political parties that achieve substantial power, it has little effect on public policy. In other words, if I have to choose between the two quotations at the beginning of this introduction, I favor Schumpeter's accent on the interests of powerful groups more than Keynes's accent on ideology, although both capture part of the truth.

Because all of my research combines the perspectives of political economy (the interplay of markets and politics) and political sociology (the social bases of politics), because I maintain a deep concern with the public-policy implications of my findings, I hope that this book will be useful to both scholars and practitioners. It should not only interest students of globalization but should also find its way into courses in comparative political economy, comparative politics, European politics, public policy, social problems, political sociology, American government, political behavior, advanced industrial society, and labor and industrial relations.

This book was written well before the Republican gains of November 2010. Nothing I could see in the early reports of exit polls, election results, and subsequent economic performance changes any of my analysis, including Part II on American politics, economics, and policies.

# Acknowledgments

The current work is based in part on my book, *Rich Democracies: Political Economy, Public Policy, and Performance* (Berkeley: University of California Press, 2002), especially chapters 2, 12, 13, 16, 17, and 18, extensively revised and updated. New material dealing with current issues and the period 1980–2009 is presented throughout. The 941 pages of *Rich Democracies* include 108 tables and figures covering various periods, policies, and measures of well-being in 19 countries; they support my conclusions in this book wherever I do not provide new data or discuss new topics. *American Political Economy in Global Perspective* is designed to be more easily accessible than *Rich Democracies* with more direct policy relevance. In fact, most of this book is about the recent politics, public policies, and peculiarities of the United States, including my analysis of how we might more effectively deal with our long-neglected social, political, and economic problems.

I thank Steven Vogel for his thorough reading of the whole manuscript and his reflections on its central themes. Barry Eichengreen's comments on the economic sections of an early draft improved the final version. I am grateful to Mark Vail, Bartholomew Watson, and Roselyn Hsueh for research assistance. In the final stages of the work, Bart Watson's tenacious detective work online and in the library was indispensable as was his help in proofreading. In an earlier phase of the project special thanks are due to Fred Shaffer, Karen Adelberger, John Talbott, and Betsy Carter. Part of Chapter 8 benefited from many long conversations with the late Nelson Polsby, colleague and friend, an ethnographer of Congress. Fred Crews's insistence on precision shocked me into still another revision of sections on threats to higher education. Alan Silver made sure I read opposing arguments on research vs. teaching and a national program of civic and military service. I am also grateful for the small research grants that came from the Department of Political Science, the Institute for Research on Labor and Employment, the Institute of Governmental Studies, and the Committee on Research, despite the severe budget crunch of UCB. Other sources of support over the 40-year life of the project are recorded in previous publications.

Finally, my gratitude and love goes to Mary Sharman. In between her concerts and her piano practice, she put up with a political junkie who talks back to C-SPAN and, worse, incessantly tested the ideas in this project in daily conversation. I am sure that I loved her music more than she could love my book, and she therefore deserves special appreciation for her steady help.

Harold L. Wilensky
*Berkeley, California*
*October 2010*

PART I

# GLOBALIZATION, PUBLIC POLICY, AND THE WELL-BEING OF PEOPLE

# The Welfare State as the Center of Public Finance and Political Conflict

The essence of the welfare state is government-protected minimum standards of income, nutrition, health and safety, education, and housing assured to every citizen as a social right, not as charity (Wilensky, 1965: xii). In the abstract this is an ideal embraced by both political leaders and the mass of people in every affluent country, but in practice it becomes expensive enough and evokes enough ambivalence to become the center of political combat about taxes, spending, and the proper role of government in the economy. In public expenditures, the welfare state is about half to three-quarters of what modern governments do. The core programs of the welfare state, often subsumed under the general heading of "social security," have taken the form of social insurance against the basic risks of modern life: job injury, sickness, unemployment, disability, old age, and income lost because of illness, shifts in family composition, or other random shocks (wars, depression, recessions). Because the welfare state is about shared risks crosscutting generations, localities, classes, ethnic and racial groups, and educational levels, it is a major source of social integration in modern society. Because it lends a measure of stability to household income, it has also been an important stabilizer of the economy in the downswings of the business cycle especially since World War II.

Because the welfare state is the center of efforts to rein in public spending and because many economists and public officials assume that social spending is the root of our economic troubles, I shall first concentrate on its economic effects, with special attention to why reform efforts are most successful where social partners negotiate realistic compromises. Later I broaden the analysis to include noneconomic effects.

Much recent public discussion is about a "crisis of the welfare state." Plainly such rhetoric is overdone. By any measure, social spending as a fraction of GDP has evidenced slower growth since 1975 or 1980, in some cases leveling off. Moreover, the burden of social spending in these countries varies in both level and trend (Wilensky, 2002, 2006; Lindert, 2004).

If the welfare-state crisis means that the social budget is heavy and growing, that the welfare state is the root of public deficits, and deficits are dangerous, then again there is no general crisis. Results are the same whether we consider total government spending or confine analysis to social spending and whether we are talking about deficits or debt. Thorough studies of gross debt-to-GDP ratios from 1961 to 2003 among 13 of our rich democracies show that although types of taxing and spending matter – a theme I elaborate at length later in this chapter – the ratio of aggregate government expenditures to GDP is unrelated to the gross debt ratio and that rising deficits are not the result of growing expenditures (von Hagen, 1992: 12–13, 2003; Hallet, Lewis, and von Hagen, 2003; cf. Cameron, 1982; Wilensky, 2002: ch. 13).[1] Similarly, the annual net government deficit in 1993–1994 among big spenders ranged from Sweden's 8.3 percent of GDP (down to 5.2 percent in 1996), Belgium's 3.7 percent, the Netherlands' 1.2 percent, and Norway's 2.4 percent surplus, while among welfare-state laggards the annual deficits ranged from Japan's 6.0 percent, the United States' 4.1 percent, and Ireland's low 1.6 percent (OECD National Accounts).

TABLE 1. *Social Spending 2005, Total Government Spending 2005, and Government Debt 2007 as Percentage of GDP*

|  | Social Sp./GDP % | Govt. Sp./GDP % | Govt. Debt/GDP % |
|---|---|---|---|
| **High Soc. Sp./GDP** | | | |
| Sweden | 29.4 | 52.8 | 40.9 |
| Denmark | 29.2 | 51.0 | 27.7 |
| Austria | 27.2 | 48.4 | 60.0 |
| France | 27.1 | 52.4 | 71.0 |
| **High-Medium** | | | |
| Germany | 26.7 | 43.8 | 64.2 |
| Belgium | 26.4 | 48.4 | 86.2 |
| Finland | 26.1 | 47.3 | 40.0 |
| Italy | 25.0 | 48.2 | 117.1 |
| **Medium-Low** | | | |
| Norway | 21.6 | 40.9 | 89.4 |
| United Kingdom | 21.3 | 44.4 | 49.8 |
| Netherlands | 20.9 | 45.3 | 49.3 |
| Switzerland | 20.3 | 33.7 | 56.7 |
| **Low** | | | |
| New Zealand | 18.5 | 39.9 | 22.1 |
| Japan | 18.5 | 36.0 | 170.9 |
| Australia | 17.1 | 34.9 | 14.9 |
| Ireland | 16.7 | 35.4 | 32.4 |
| Canada | 16.5 | 39.1 | 64.4 |
| United States | 15.9 | 37.3 | 65.8 |

*Note:* Government expenditures data for Australia, Japan, and Switzerland are for 2006. The correlations of either social spending or total government spending with gross government debt/GDP are near zero, whether we include or exclude the two debt outliers, Japan and Italy. The correlation of total government spending and social spending as percentage of GDP is .89. Education spending is excluded.

*Source:* OECD (2009–2010).

Assuming a two-year lag between spending and debt, Table 1 shows the same pattern for more recent years among 18 of the 19 rich democracies – no consistent relationship between either government social expenditures in 2005 and the gross debt ratios in 2007 or total government spending and debt ratios.

In fact, the countries with the most lavish social spending (Sweden, Denmark, Austria, and France, with a median of about 28% of GDP) have about the same debt ratios (median debt about 50% of GDP) as the leanest social spenders (New Zealand, Japan, Australia, Ireland, Canada, and last, the United States (median social expenditure of about 17% of GDP but a median debt ratio of about 48%) (OECD.stat, 2009–2010). Japan, a lean social spender, has the very highest government debt ratio in Table 1.

Here is a summary of the median values of the data in that table (note that social spending excludes spending on education):

|  | Soc. Sp./GDP % | Govt. Sp./GDP % | Govt. Debt/GDP % |
| --- | --- | --- | --- |
| High Soc. Sp./GDP | 28.2 | 51.7 | 50.5 |
| High-Medium | 26.3 | 47.7 | 75.2 |
| Medium-Low | 21.1 | 42.7 | 53.3 |
| Low | 16.9 | 36.7 | 48.4 |

The explanation is straightforward: debt ratios depend not on government spending but on what else these countries do – whether they tax enough to pay for the services their citizens demand, the kind of labor and social policies they pursue, their economic performance, the structure of their government (e.g., degrees of decentralization, the strategic dominance of the prime minister or finance or treasury minister over the spending ministers), and the structure of the budgetary process (cf. von Hagen, 1992: 38ff.).

Finally, if the heavy burden of the welfare state inevitably subverts good economic performance, that might justify "crisis" talk. The evidence is to the contrary. Welfare-state spending (excluding housing and education)[2] up to 1973 was a positive contribution to the combination of low-to-moderate inflation, good real GDP growth per capita, and low unemployment. Since the first oil shock, aggregate social spending has been on average neutral. Why is the welfare state as a whole *not* a drag on economic performance?

First, some major sectors of social policy are plainly productivity enhancing. Mass access to medical care and health education via schools, clinics, and child care facilities reduces long-term medical costs and in some measure enhances real health and lifetime productivity (see Chapter 4); preventative occupational health and safety programs in the workplace reduce absenteeism and turnover and other labor costs; active labor-market policies supplement and in some countries reduce reliance on passive unemployment insurance and public assistance and improve the quality of labor (Chapters 7 and 8); innovative family policies reduce the cost of both mayhem and poverty, they also reduce income inequality and gender inequality, which are a drag on economic growth.[3] These are substantial offsets for the cost of welfare-state benefits to the nonworking poor, handicapped, and the aged. The net economic effect of all the programs labeled the "welfare state" is therefore either positive (before 1974) or neutral (since 1974).

If we compare types of political economy, we find a second explanation of why the welfare state and decent labor standards are not a drag on the economy. Some rich democracies facilitate productive trade-offs among the government, mass-based political parties, and broad-based interest groups (labor, management, professions, established churches, farmers, and other associations), whereas other equally rich democracies do not. Three types of national bargaining arrangements are labeled democratic corporatist, corporatist without labor, and "least corporatist" (most fragmented and decentralized). My model of democratic corporatism (Wilensky, 1976, 2002: ch. 2) accents four interrelated criteria: (1) bargaining channels for the interaction of strongly organized, usually centralized economic blocs, especially labor, employer, and professional associations with a centralized or moderately centralized government obliged to consider their advice; (2) a blurring of old distinctions between public and private; (3) a broad scope of national bargaining going beyond labor-market issues resulting in (4) the integration of social and economic policy and a greater chance to reach consensus and implement policy. A variant is corporatism without labor, epitomized by Japan. Germany is an ambiguous case of corporatism; Switzerland, a marginal case of corporatism without labor. These national bargaining types are contrasted with decentralized, fragmented political economies ("least corporatist"). Although students of comparative political economy disagree on 2 or 3 of the 19 rich democracies, they generally agree on the rest. By combining the cumulative power of two mass-based political parties of long and continuous standing – Catholic (e.g., Christian Democratic, Social Christian, and Christian Socialist) and Left (e.g., Labor, Socialist, Social Democratic) – with these types of bargaining among the social partners, I generate five types of political economy. Details on the historical origins of these types of political economy are in Chapter 3 with further elaboration of sources and measures in the Appendix.

Table 2 classifies the 19 rich democracies. These five types predict the well-being of nations and their people in the descending order indicated in Table 2 with the democratic corporatist countries at the top and the fragmented and decentralized political economies ("least corporatist") at the bottom. Table 3 shows how spending and these types relate to the economic performance of the 19 countries from 1950 to 1989, taking account of differences in vulnerability to external shocks. Table 4 does the same for 1990 to 2007. Other scholars have also brought analysis to 2000 or other dates with the same conclusions (e.g., Lindert, 2004).

Table 2 shows that the consensual corporatist democracies, especially those with strong left or competing left and Catholic parties – all of which are big spenders – outpace the more-fragmented and decentralized political economies

TABLE 2. *Types of Political Economy, Recent Growth in Labor Productivity, and Household Income Inequality*

| | Labor Productivity Growth, 1980–2002 (%)[a] | Household Disposable Income Inequality (90/10 ratio), Most Recent Year[b] |
|---|---|---|
| Left corporatist | | |
| Sweden | 2.0 (3) | 2.96 (16) 2000 |
| Norway | 1.3 (13) | 2.80 (18) 2000 |
| Finland | 2.9 (2) | 2.90 (17) 2000 |
| Denmark | 1.8 (5) | 3.15 (14) 1997 |
| Cell average | 2.0 | 2.96 |
| Left-Catholic corporatist | | |
| Netherlands | 1.1 (16) | 2.98 (15) 1999 |
| Belgium | 1.5 (10) | 3.19 (13) 1997 |
| Austria | 2.0 (3) | 3.37 (11) 1997 |
| Cell average | 1.5 | 3.18 |
| Catholic corporatist | | |
| Italy | 1.3 (13) | 4.48 (3) 2000 |
| Germany | 0.8 (17) | 3.29 (12) 2000 |
| Cell average | 1.1 | 3.89 |
| Corporatist without labor | | |
| France | 1.7 (6) | 3.54 (9) 1994 |
| Japan | 1.6 (8) | 4.17[c] (6) 1992 |
| Switzerland | 0.4 (18) | 3.62 (8) 1992 |
| Cell average | 1.2 | 3.78 |
| | 1.7 minus Switzerland | |
| Least corporatist | | |
| United States | 1.5 (10) | 5.45 (1) 2000 |
| United Kingdom | 1.6 (8) | 4.58 (2) 1999 |
| New Zealand | 1.2 (15) | 3.46[d] (10) 1987–1988 |
| Australia | 1.6 (8) | 4.33 (4) 1994 |
| Canada | 1.3 (13) | 4.13 (7) 1998 |
| Ireland | 3.2 (1) | 4.33 (4) 1996 |
| Cell average | 1.7 | 4.38 |
| | 1.4 minus Ireland | |
| 18-country average | 1.9 | 3.71 |

*Note:* For types of political economy, see discussion in text.

[a] Business sector average percent increase per year. *Source*: OECD, 2003: table 1.A.1.1., p. 60. Numbers in parentheses indicate rank. The Irish exception is discussed in Wilensky, 2002: ch. 2.

[b] Luxembourg Income Survey, "LIS Key Figures: Income Inequality Measures," http://www. lisproject.org/keyfigures/ineqtable.htm. Low rank = egalitarian.

[c] Gottschalk and Smeeding, 1999b: 42.

[d] Ibid. Timothy M. Smeeding (2001: 12) suggests that New Zealand has become significantly less egalitarian since the late 1980s. See Chapter 4 for my account of the neoconservative experiment of New Zealand, late 1980–1999, which sharply increased inequality.

TABLE 3. *The Interaction of Political Economy, Vulnerability to Energy Shocks, Welfare Effort, and Economic Performance, 1950–1989*

## High vulnerability to energy shocks, 1970

### Corporatist without labor; lean spenders

| | Econ. perf. index | | | | |
|---|---|---|---|---|---|
| | 1950–74 | 1965–74 | 1974–79 | 1980–84 | 1985–89 |
| Japan | 4 | 4 | 6 | 6 | 6 |
| Switz. | 4 | 3 | 4 | 5 | 5 |
| Ave. | 4.0 | 3.6 | 5.0 | 5.5 | 5.5 |

### Corporatist big spenders

| | Econ. perf. index | | | | |
|---|---|---|---|---|---|
| | 1950–74 | 1965–74 | 1974–79 | 1980–84 | 1985–89 |
| Sweden | 4 | 3 | 3 | 4 | 3 |
| Finland | 4 | 3 | 5 | 4 | 3 |
| Belgium | 4 | 5 | 3 | 3 | 4 |
| Denmark | 3 | 2 | 2 | 2 | 2 |
| Italy | 3 | 2 | 2 | 1 | 2 |
| Ave. | 3.6 | 3.0 | 2.2 | 2.8 | 2.8 |

### Corporatist without labor; big spenders

| | Econ. perf. index | | | | |
|---|---|---|---|---|---|
| | 1950–74 | 1965–74 | 1974–79 | 1980–84 | 1985–89 |
| France | 3 | 5 | 4 | 1 | 2 |
| Ave. | 3.0 | 5.0 | 4.0 | 1.0 | 2.0 |

## Low to medium vulnerability to energy shocks, 1970

### Corporatist big spenders[a]

| | Econ. perf. index | | | | |
|---|---|---|---|---|---|
| | 1950–74 | 1965–74 | 1974–79 | 1980–84 | 1985–89 |
| GFR | 5 | 4 | 5 | 4 | 4 |
| Norway* | 4 | 3 | 6 | 5 | 3 |
| Austria | 4 | 6 | 6 | 5 | 5 |
| Nld.* | 4 | 3 | 4 | 2 | 2 |
| Israel | 2 | 2 | 1 | - | - |
| Ave. | 3.8 | 3.6 | 4.4 | 4.0 | 3.5 |

### Least corporatist lean spenders

| | Econ. perf. index | | | | |
|---|---|---|---|---|---|
| | 1950–74 | 1965–74 | 1974–79 | 1980–84 | 1985–89 |
| NZ | 3 | 3 | 2 | 3 | 1 |
| Australia* | 3 | 3 | 1 | 3 | 2 |
| USA* | 2 | 2 | 2 | 4 | 4 |
| Canada* | 2 | 3 | 2 | 1 | 2 |
| UK* | 2 | 1 | 1 | 1 | 2 |
| Ireland | 1 | 1 | 2 | 1 | 3 |
| Ave. | 2.2 | 2.2 | 1.7 | 2.2 | 2.3 |

*Note:* The economic performance index equally weights average annual real growth per capita, standardized unemployment and inflation (GDP deflator). Except for four countries the averages are for the 24 years 1951–1974. For Belgium and Japan the averages cover 1954–1974. For New Zealand and Finland the averages cover 1955–1974.

[a] Germany a marginal case of corporatism; Israel a lean spender.

* Least vulnerable to energy shocks.

*Sources:* UN, *Yearbook of National Accounts Statistics* (Geneva, various years); "International Tables," table 4a, except for Australia and New Zealand, where data are from OECD, *National Accounts Statistics of OECD Countries* (Paris, various years). See footnotes to Wilensky, 2002: tables 12.1, 12.3, and 12.4 and appendix G, pp. 743–765. Possible total scores: 6 (best) to 0 (worst). The index of vulnerability to energy shocks equally weights liquid fuels (almost all oil) as a percentage of total energy consumption in 1970 and energy production as a percentage of total energy consumption. See ibid., appendix G, pp. 746–747.

TABLE 4. *The Interaction of Political Economy, Vulnerability to Energy Shocks, Welfare Effort, and Economic Performance, 1990–2007*

| High vulnerability to energy shocks, 2005 | | | | | | Low to medium vulnerability to energy shocks, 2005 | | | | | | | | | |
| --- | --- | --- | --- | --- | --- | --- | --- | --- | --- | --- | --- | --- | --- | --- | --- |
| Corporatist without labor; lean spenders | | | Corporatist big spenders | | | Corporatist without labor; big spenders | | | Corporatist big spenders | | | Least corporatist lean spenders | | | |
| | Econ. perf. index | | | Econ. perf index | | | Econ. perf. index | | | Econ. perf. index | | | Econ. perf. index | |
| | 1990–99 | 2000–7^a | | 1990–99 | 2000–7 | | 1990–99 | 2000–7 | | 1990–99 | 2000–7 | | 1990–99 | 2000–7 |
| Japan^b | 2.0 | 1.5 | Finland^c | 1.0 | 4.0 | France | 2.0 | 3.0 | Germany^d | 4.5 | 2.0 | New Zealand | 4.0 | 4.0 |
| Switzerland | 3.5 | 5.0 | Belgium | 3.5 | 3.0 | | | | Norway | 5.0 | 3.5 | Australia | 4.5 | 3.0 |
| | | | Italy | 1.5 | 1.0 | | | | Austria | 6.0 | 5.0 | United States | 5.0 | 4.0 |
| | | | Netherlands | 5.5 | 3.5 | | | | Sweden | 3.0 | 4.5 | Canada | 2.5 | 2.0 |
| | | | | | | | | | Denmark | 4.5 | 3.5 | United Kingdom | 3.0 | 4.0 |
| | | | | | | | | | | | | Ireland^e | 2.0 | 4.0 |
| Averages | 2.8 | 3.3 | Averages | 2.9 | 2.9 | Averages | 2.0 | 3.0 | Averages | 4.6 | 3.7 | Averages | 3.5 | 3.5 |

*Note:* The economic performance index equally weights real GDP growth per capita, unemployment (standardized), and inflation (GDP deflator), scored from 0 to 2 for each component. Possible total scores: 6 best, 0 worst. See text.

[a] Unemployment data for the EPI index run through 2006, both growth and inflation data run through 2007.

[b] Scored zero for inflation for 1990–1999 because of disastrous deflation in four of the years. The average – low inflation – is misleading.

[c] Finland's loss of Soviet markets and consequent restructuring, despite increases in productivity, makes the 1990s a bad period: unemployment above average, deep recession 1991–1992, offsetting subsequent strong growth. Ten-year average relatively poor.

[d] German high average for the 1990s obscures major fluctuations: strong West German performance from 1990 to 1992. In July 1991 the statistics cover reunified Germany, with much poorer East Germany such a drag on growth from 1993 to 1999 that Germany was labeled "the sick man of Europe." From 2005 to 2008, however, Germany experienced a strong upswing.

[e] Ireland now has high vulnerability to energy shocks.

*Source:* OECD.stat. GDP deflator data unavailable from 1990 to 1993 so CPI data used for inflation for these years. The index measures relative, not absolute, performance, so this should not change the results.

as well as corporatist democracies that keep labor at a distance. They have an edge in labor productivity growth (1980–2002) and shine in the achievement of more household equality (ca. late 1990s). Recent research confirms my findings. For instance, using measures and econometric methods different from mine, Peter Lindert (2004: vol. 1, ch. 10; vol. 2, chs. 18 and 19) shows that from 1980 to 2000 among modern democracies the net impact of social spending on the economy (i.e., GDP/person and growth) is close to zero. Similarly, Mishel, Bernstein, and Allegretto (2007: tables 8.1 and 8.2) show that for 18 of our 19 rich democracies (Israel missing) the average growth in annual per capita GDP in the period 1989 to 2004 (using purchasing-power parity – PPP – in 2004 dollars) for the big-spending corporatist democracies is 1.8 percent. The average for the lean-spending fragmented and decentralized political economies is only slightly better, 2.0. These averages eliminate two extreme cases (Ireland with annual growth of 5.7% and Italy 1.3%). In Mishel et al.'s research (p. 327), results are similar regardless of whether PPPs or market exchange rates are used.[4] For instance, much of the slight edge of the United States in growth in that 15-year period would disappear if we eliminated the best six years of the Clinton administration, an aberration in both policy and performance. Again, as I found throughout my 19-country analysis, the greater earnings and income equality, job security, welfare-state protections, and poverty reductions of the more consensual democracies have *not* retarded their productivity and income growth and other measures of relative economic performance either in the 40 years preceding 1990 or even in the 17 years following 1990.

The Clinton years are instructive for students of social and economic policies. There is disagreement about the relative weight of public policy and productivity (rooted in technological-organizational change) in the good performance of the United States in the 1990s and, indeed, up until the 2007–2008 housing collapse and financial meltdown, when the United States lagged the EU-15. It is clear, however, that the United States not only did well in economic performance but also during Clinton's best years reduced both poverty and inequality. Among the reasons: a reversal of some public policies that prevailed in Republican-dominated governments before and after 1992–2000. Among the most important measures were successive increases in the minimum wage and in the Earned Income Tax Credit (EITC) for the working poor, as well as some expansion of the Children's Health Insurance Program (SCHIP), federally funded and income-tested; by 2001 it covered about 3.4 million children and 300,000 adults.

In addition to these modest shifts in social policy, Clinton accepted a bargain worked out between his chairman of the National Economic Council, Robert Rubin, and Fed Chairman Alan Greenspan. The Fed would lower interest rates if Clinton would put the federal deficit on a downward path by restraining spending. Secretary of Labor Robert Reich reports that Clinton was livid about having to abandon his big-ticket domestic priorities (e.g., education, job training, child nutrition, mass transit) but reluctantly caved in (Reich, 1997: 104ff.).[5]

The Fed did indeed lower interest rates to the point where a borrowing binge began. Together with the policy changes that created a modest redistribution of income downward that created an explosion of household and consumer debt, a consumption-driven boom took hold. (Historically, two-thirds to three-quarters of growth is consumption led.) On Clinton's watch more than 22 million jobs were created. The net effect is seen in Table 3: the United States is one of the three best economic performers of the 1990s along with Austria and Norway.

At the same time, if we confine analysis to the budgets Clinton was responsible for, we see that he presided over a stagnant real discretionary domestic budget (in 1991 dollars). While the real GDP climbed an average of 3.8 percent per year from 1991 to 2001, real spending on transportation, education, training, unemployment compensation, Supplementary Security Income, child tax credits, and scores of other programs targeted to the poor and near poor only inched up (CBO, 2008a, 2008b; OECD, 2008a) – a continued neglect of physical and human capital, which accelerated under his Republican successors. In the long-run perspective of 1973–2008, Clinton's few years of reduction in poverty and inequality were an aberration. The low road to growth remained the American Way (see Chapter 7).

The effects of the Fed's loose policy of the 1990s were greatly intensified by the 1999 deregulation of financial institutions. Chairman Greenspan, a disciple of Ayn Rand, vigorously opposed financial regulations that might have limited the economic meltdown of 2008. He also denied that either arcane derivatives or the long-developing housing bubble were threats to the economy.[6] Lax oversight by all regulatory agencies during President Bush's eight years exacerbated speculative fervor and deepened and prolonged the inevitable crash.

Table 3 contains an overview of the economic performance of various types of political economy in five periods from 1950 to 1989. Table 4 covers the period 1990–2007.

The measure is a 6-point index that equally weights real GDP growth per capita, inflation, and unemployment – scoring high to low growth from 2 to 0, high to low inflation from 0 to 2, and high to low unemployment from 0 to 2. The best performers score 6 on this index; the worst score 1. This index avoids arguments about what is most important – the control of inflation, good growth, or low unemployment. To take account of each country's vulnerability to the oil shock of 1973–1974, I examine performance in the five years 1974–1979 and then consider their 1980–84 response to the worst oil shock combined with multiple shocks of 1979–1981 (worldwide recession and the export by the United States of the self-administered Volker interest-rate shock). Table 3 also controls for energy vulnerability – relevant since January 2002 when the steep increase in oil prices began, with a further acceleration after January 2007 (by January 2008 inflation-adjusted oil prices had reached the shock level of 1979–1982 and then declined during the subsequent worldwide recession). The equally weighted components of my index of vulnerability to energy shocks are liquid fuels (almost all oil) as a percentage of total energy consumption and energy production as a percentage of energy consumption in 1970 and 2005, for Tables 2 and 3, respectively.[7] Think of energy vulnerability as a handicap race. If the United States, United Kingdom, Canada, Australia, Norway, and the

Netherlands do well in the years after each oil shock, we should take a little credit away from them because they are least vulnerable; if the most vulnerable countries – Japan, Switzerland, Finland, and Belgium – score medium to high in economic performance as they do, we should be impressed that they leaped over the high hurdles with such gusto.

Using Table 3 and 12 other tables, including disaggregated results and explanations of deviant cases (not reported here), we find the following:

1. Corporatist democracies – with a couple of possible exceptions (Japan and Switzerland, both with systems that do not fully integrate labor into social and economic policy making and implementation) – tend to devote more of their resources to social security and related social spending and labor-market programs.
2. Corporatist democracies pursue tax policies that strike a balance between painfully visible taxes (income taxes and property taxes on households), hefty social-security contributions, and heavy consumption taxes (e.g., VAT), thereby permitting high levels of taxation with minimal political uproar.
3. Such social spending and taxing, far from constituting a brake on good economic performance, is a positive contribution or, at times, neutral. Corporatist big spenders and taxers on average had an edge in economic performance. They definitely led before 1975, and if we take account of differences in their exposure to the oil shock of 1973–1974 and the multiple shocks of 1979–1982, even up to 1992, clearly in low inflation and low unemployment, less clearly in economic growth. After the first energy shock, corporatist democracies, with or without labor, far from evidencing the rigidity of "Eurosclerosis," adapted better and quicker than the more "free marketeer" democracies did. This pattern becomes stronger after the second bigger shock. The only noncorporatist country that makes the top eight in 1980–1984 is the United States.
4. From 1990 through 1996, types of political economy were unrelated to average economic performance measured by my index; but corporatist democracies, with or without labor, continued to outperform the fragmented and decentralized democracies in holding down unemployment. The average for corporatism without labor was 5.5 percent with Japan and Switzerland leading, for democratic corporatist countries 7.8 percent, and for least-consensual (or least-corporatist) democracies 9.3. Least-corporatist democracies, however, had a slight edge in controlling inflation (2.6% vs. 2.9% for noncorporatist democracies, with the best performance again going to corporatism without labor). The real GDP per capita growth per year was 2.3 percent for least-corporatist and 2.0 for corporatist democracies; the worst performance goes to corporatism without labor, 0.4 percent, with Switzerland and France at the bottom and Japan with an above-average 1.5 percent.

5. For some recent years, major policy mistakes in Japan, the Netherlands, and Sweden explain why Japan and the United States traded places as "Number One" while the economies of Sweden and the Netherlands sputtered. A classic burst of a speculative bubble combined with some erosion of centralized bargaining in Sweden account for the short period of poor performance (mainly 1984–1992). Similarly, the economy of the Netherlands stalled (mainly 1984–1991). Then, as Tables 2 and 3 show, both countries recovered smartly. (See Wilensky, 2002: 110–116, for full explanations for Sweden and the Netherlands; 445–450, for why Japan and the United States traded places after 1992; and Vogel, 2006, for a detailed account of continuity and change in Japan.)

Further evidence that corporatist democracies with big welfare state burdens nevertheless adapt flexibly to external shocks comes from Table 3, which brings the story up to date.

Comparing Table 3 (1950–1989) and Table 4 (1990–2007), we see that two left corporatist countries, Denmark and Sweden, moved from most vulnerable to energy shocks to least vulnerable, with quite good economic performance. The main reason: they made dramatic changes in both energy conservation and the development of alternative fuels. In general, however, the older pattern remains. In economic performance the corporatist big spenders with left power or alternating left and Catholic power outshined the fragmented and decentralized political economies (the only clear exceptions are the poor performance of Japan and Italy in both of which cumulative left party power is very weak). Energy dependence was a bit of a drag among corporatist big spenders, although if the deviant case of Italy is dropped, the most vulnerable consensual big spenders almost matched the averages of the least corporatist, least vulnerable, lean spenders. And clearly the best performers in Table 4 are the five corporatist big spenders with low to medium vulnerability to energy shocks. Again we see striking evidence of the adaptability of countries with consensual bargaining.

If we disaggregate the three components of my economic performance index and look at the entire period from 1990 through 2007, we find that corporatist democracies, with or without labor, continued to outperform noncorporatist democracies in holding down unemployment (the average for corporatism without labor, 5.8% with Japan and Switzerland leading; the average for democratic corporatist countries was 7.0%, and for least-corporatist democracies it was 7.3). Overall, corporatist democracies also had a slight edge in controlling inflation (2.3% vs. 2.8% for the least corporatist democracies – these figures exclude Japan because of its damaging deflation). The real GDP per capita growth per year, however, was 4.1 percent for least-corporatist (3.5% excluding Ireland) and 2.8 for big-spending corporatist democracies; the worst performance goes to corporatism-without-labor, 2.2 percent, with Japan at 2.0 percent having the lowest average growth during the period.

In short, with few exceptions for few years, big-spending democracies with the more or less centralized bargaining structures I have outlined have evidenced remarkably good economic performance through thick and thin for more than half a century. This is a product of the corporatist trade-offs most positive for economic performance. Before specifying these positive trade-offs, we need an answer to the question, Why were Denmark and Sweden the only countries that moved from most vulnerable to energy shocks to least vulnerable in Tables 3 and 4?

# 2

# Energy Policy and Performance
## *The United States and the World*

> I am involved in mankind and therefore never send to know for whom the bell tolls; it tolls for thee.
>
> John Donne (1624)

To report the current consensus of climate scientists is to risk sounding alarmist. Only 25 or so years ago a substantial minority of serious scientists doubted that emissions of heat-trapping gases by human activity would lead to irreversible global warming. But not all alarms are false. And successive research reports by such agencies as the National Academy of Sciences, the National Oceanic and Atmospheric Administration, the U.S. Geological Survey, the International Energy Agency, NASA's Goddard Institute for Space Studies, and the UN's Intergovernmental Panel on Climate Change have grown more urgent about an approaching tipping point. For instance, there is now agreement that when and if the atmospheric concentration of carbon dioxide – the principal heat-trapping gas emission – reaches 450 to 600 parts per million, up from about 385 ppm today, irreversible planetary damage will occur. Before the summer of 2007 scientists underestimated the speed with which warming temperatures would melt the polar regions' permafrost that caps large deposits of methane, another potent greenhouse gas. So if we add methane emissions, the new tipping point may be even less than 450 ppm of $CO_2$. Because of the way $CO_2$ persists in the atmosphere and in the oceans and the interaction of the two, the result will include rising seas that threaten coastal regions. Southern Europe, North Africa, the Southwestern United States, and West Australia could expect 10 percent less rainfall. That means reduced crop yields and fiercer storms alternating with Dust Bowl levels of drought (Solomon et al., 2009; Hansen et al., 2008). Too little discussed is a tsunami of climate refugees numbering perhaps one or two hundred million pouring into nations and regions on higher ground searching for water, food, shelter, and safety. Such migration would make the current flow from Mexico into the United States look like a trickle.

The question is not, Is there a crisis? It is how to deal with a crisis that within 40 to 60 years will destroy civilization as we know it, if we do little to reduce our use of fossil fuels and allow climate change to take its course.

This chapter reviews the record of action and inaction among nations and international organizations regarding energy policy and performance. Because so much of the political opposition to sensible clean-energy policies claims that they undermine economic progress and threaten decent standards of living, I begin with the two most successful cases among our 19 countries.

## A. ECONOMIC PERFORMANCE AND ENERGY INDEPENDENCE, 1980–2005

Denmark and Sweden exemplify two strategies for sustaining good to excellent economic performance while increasing energy efficiency and reducing greenhouse gas emissions – current policy goals of all rich democracies. They both substantially reduced their vulnerability to energy shocks from 1980 to 2006 but adopted quite different policy packages. Table 5 summarizes the policy differences and their effects.

### 1. Denmark: Wind, Biofuels, and the Best Reduction of Greenhouse Gases

Over the past 25 years Denmark's economy has grown by about 75 percent with nearly stable energy consumption, reduced $CO_2$ emissions, and reduced dependence on fossil fuels (oil, coal, and gas). Energy intensity (energy consumption relative to GDP) is the lowest in the EU. This accomplishment is a product of an active, persistent, and integrated energy policy. Among the most important measures: the spread of combined heat and power production (the share of district heating produced by CHP plants has increased from about 40% to more than 80%); end-use energy efficiency via "high energy standards for buildings, energy labeling schemes for electrical appliances, public campaigns for energy savings in households, energy savings agreements with industry, and not least, taxes on energy consumption" (Danish Ministry of Climate and Energy, 2008: 2–3). By April 2010 Denmark had added 29 waste-to-energy plants that use new technology for clean burning of garbage and industrial waste. (Germany and the Netherlands also lead in the number of such plants.)

A Danish general tax on electricity promotes energy efficiency. Three separate taxes also foster the use of renewables: (1) a tax that varies for natural gas, unleaded gasoline, diesel fuel, and other energy; (2) a carbon dioxide tax; and (3) a sulfur dioxide tax. Energy taxes account for about 7 percent of domestic revenues (Global Energy Network Institute, 2008). In 2008 the government adopted a plan for renewable energy in transportation, for example, hydrogen cars and electric cars are exempt from taxes and charges until 2012 (Danish Ministry of Climate and Energy, 2008: 5). Note the expiration date: some students of taxes as a regulatory strategy argue that to be effective they must be temporary so that politicians do not count on them as a new cash cow; the aim

TABLE 5. *Why Did Denmark and Sweden Decline So Much in Vulnerability to Energy Shocks, 1980–2005?*

| Category | Denmark | Sweden |
|---|---|---|
| Energy index component #1 (production / consumption) | Biggest change in production/consumption ratio of any of the 19 rich democracies. Slightly decreased consumption (4%) and greatly increased energy production. From virtually no energy in 1980 to 156% of the energy needed for domestic consumption in 2005. | Sweden improved production/consumption ratio. From 1980 to 2005 consumption increased only slightly while production increased almost 72%. |
| Energy index component #2 (liquid fuels consumption / total consumption) | Danish liquid fuels consumption as a % of total consumption improved since 1980. Decreased liquid consumption (despite the discovery of North Sea oil). Total consumption dropped only 4% through 2005, but alternative sources helped liquid fuels ratio to drop 38%. | Swedish ratio of liquid fuel consumption as a % of total consumption modestly improved. Petroleum consumption decreased by 33% while total energy consumption has dropped only 12% since 1980. |
| Energy sources / total energy production, 2005 | Petroleum (60%), natural gas (32%), renewables (8%) | Early commitment to hydroelectric power, later commitment to nuclear. Renewables less developed than in Denmark. Hydroelectric (48%), nuclear (46%), renewables (6%) |
| Nuclear energy production | Denmark has no nuclear power. | Sweden leads in nuclear energy development, producing nearly half of total energy production by 1986. |
| Alternative and renewable energy production / consumption | Since the mid-1980s, renewable energy has been the focus of energy policy. A comprehensive long-range program, including early commitment to wind power, led to a renewable energy share of total consumption of over 15% by 2006. | An early commitment to hydroelectric and a later commitment to nuclear. Renewables less developed than in Denmark. In 2005 renewable production other than hydroelectric was only 4% of domestic consumption. |

*(continued)*

TABLE 5 *(continued)*

| Category | Denmark | Sweden |
|---|---|---|
| Alternative and renewable energy (nonhydro) / total consumption, 2005 | 12% | 4% |
| Carbon emissions, % change since 1980 | Denmark has reduced carbon emissions by 24% since 1980. | Sweden has reduced carbon emissions by 32% since 1980. |
| Per capita carbon emissions | In 2005, Denmark ranked 6th best of the 19 rich democracies with 9.38 metric tons of carbon dioxide per capita. | Given its heavy reliance on nuclear and hydroelectric energy, in 2005 Sweden ranked 2nd best of the 19 rich democracies with 6.53 metric tons of carbon dioxide per capita. |
| Petroleum production and consumption | Since the discovery of North Sea oil, Denmark ramped up its crude oil production, currently down from its peak in 2004. In 2007 Denmark produced 163% of the crude oil needed for consumption, but had refinery capacity for only 92% of consumption; it exports crude oil and relies on imports of finished products. Oil consumption declined 34% between 1980 and 2007. | Sweden currently has no crude oil production or proven reserves of petroleum. Nevertheless, Sweden has a large refinery capacity, totaling 123% of consumption needs; Sweden is an importer of oil and an exporter of finished petroleum products. Oil consumption declined by 33% between 1980 and 2007. |

of a carbon tax, for instance, would be to prompt producers to change behavior, not to allow them to continue polluting while handing over cash to the government (Prasad, 2008). Danish planners seem to be aware of this problem. Moreover, Denmark has used the revenue from energy taxes to subsidize further environmental innovation, not for general use.

Denmark has almost no hydroelectric power resources and no long tradition of using biomass. Yet by 2005 it became one of the leading nations in renewable energy as a share of energy consumption – up from 3 percent in 1980 to 15 percent in 2005 – joining Sweden, Latvia, Finland, and Austria as best performers (Danish Ministry of Climate and Energy, 2008: 3). The largest share of renewable energy came from biomass, especially wood and biodegradable waste and straw. In February 2008, with all parties but one endorsing it, the Danish government adopted a plan to increase renewable energy to 20 percent of consumption in 2011 (Danish Energy Agency, 2008: 2). Regarding domestic energy production, Denmark now derives 27 percent of its electricity supply from renewable energy, with the introduction of wind energy contributing to the increase, though biomass is still the largest share of renewable energy in the electricity supply. After much debate, in 1985 the government made a deliberate decision to avoid controversial nuclear power.

All this did cost a lot initially but rising prices of fossil fuels and the steadily falling costs of renewables have made them more competitive. Heavy R&D investment has been crucial in bringing new energy technologies to market. Denmark, having pioneered in such research since the 1890s, is now the leader in wind turbine production, with about one-third of the global market (Danish Energy Agency, 2008: 62; Rassmussen, 1987). Success in wind power is based on subsidies to individual entrepreneurs, early official certification of wind turbines, and systematic government support. Government policy includes stable, favorable incentive systems with long-term contracts, easy grid connection, resource mapping and assessment, quality control, and the promotion of cooperative private ownership of wind turbines and offshore wind farms (Meyer, 2007: 349–353; Danish Energy Agency, 2008).

Attitude surveys show that about 8 in 10 Danes support wind power. Acceptance of specific projects is widespread; the NIMBY (not-in-my-back-yard) syndrome is minimal. The main reason is reliance on local neighborhood cooperatives as part owners of shares in wind turbines. Beginning in 1979 private citizens who installed certified wind turbines received 30 percent of the purchase price from the central government. By 2001 about 150,000 Danish households had registered as owners. As Niels Meyer (2007: 351) suggests, "It is easier to accept some extra noise and the view of a turbine if it reminds you that the turbine gives you money when the wind blows." The government now plans to pay neighbors of onshore wind turbines for losses in property values from wind turbine installation and to increase subsidies for new wind turbines during peak loads (Danish Energy Agency, 2008: 8). In any case, newer technologies as well as minimum separation from dwellings and careful siting and design have already overcome remaining public opposition. Offshore wind farms, recently developed by Denmark, are further solutions for countries with long coastlines and shallow waters.

The only potential threat to this success is future regulatory uncertainty rooted in free-market ideology. The new Danish energy act of 1999 proposed a market for trade in green certificates combined with quotas for green electricity. Because of high transaction costs in a small national market, however, the trading system never got off the ground. One motivation of the incoming Conservative-Liberal government of 2001 for promoting this policy shift was its assumption that the EU Commission preferred more market-oriented support systems harmonized across countries. But the EU itself has postponed this harmonization (Meyer, 2007). The main effect of the threatened move to a cumbersome green certificate system has been uncertainty for private investors. In fact, the installation of new land-based capacity in Denmark dropped sharply in 2000 and continued to slide until the net increase was close to zero between 2003 and 2007 (p. 353).[1]

Denmark is a model for those countries without hydro resources that want to avoid the nuclear power option and rely instead on energy conservation, the wind, biomass, and other renewables. It has achieved strong economic growth while keeping energy consumption nearly constant and reducing greenhouse emissions.

## 2. Sweden: Hydropower, Nuclear Power, and Tops in Reducing $CO_2$ Emissions

Sweden, the only other country that moved to the least vulnerability column in Table 4, achieved roughly the same outcome with a quite different policy package.[2] Sweden's change in vulnerability is largely the result of increased production, first through nuclear power and more recently through alternative sources. This has improved Sweden's consumption-production ratio and reduced its dependence on liquid fuels consumption (mostly oil plus liquid hydrocarbon mixtures).

While total domestic production of energy has increased 72 percent from 1980 to 2005, total consumption increased less than 13 percent despite economic growth of about 75 percent (inflation adjusted). Energy intensity (energy consumption in relation to GDP), while not matching Denmark's low ratio, improved markedly during the same time period, decreasing by 34 percent. In addition, the increase of nuclear energy production allowed its liquid fuel consumption to fall from about 55 percent of total consumption to about 31 percent – a drop of 43 percent in 25 years.

Like Denmark, Sweden reduced $CO_2$ emissions from energy production through fossil fuels dramatically; Sweden's 32 percent decrease from 1980 to 2005 was the largest among my 19 rich democracies. Among the most important measures: an early commitment to and expansion of hydroelectric power and a strategic move to nuclear power. The 10 nuclear power plants currently active in Sweden came on line from 1972 to 1985, producing more than half of Sweden's total energy consumption by 1986, where it stayed for the next 20 years.

## 3. The Nuclear Option: Comparing Sweden, France, and the United States

The nuclear option in Sweden triggered vigorous opposition within and between political parties, mounting over time. How the government handled this reflects the consensual style of Swedish governance and reveals the problems and ambiguities of nuclear power.[3] As in France, there was state bureaucratic dominance, highly competent utility managers, and highly trained workers – essential for passable performance of nuclear plants. In contrast to France, where local protesters have been gassed and beaten (in 1977 the police killed one), the system was much more open and participatory. Swedish planners and regulators relied on continuous informal communication and persuasion with the usual social partners, industry, labor, professional groups, government agencies, and the Riksdag. Royal commissions helped forge consensus. In contrast to the American AEC, Swedish nuclear regulators and inspectors work closely with owners and operators in studying the technicalities of operations and safety; they are therefore both more trained and effective.

The oil shock of 1974–1975 lifted nuclear energy to a new level of contention. The mounting antinuclear movement anchored in the Center Party's women's and youth groups expressed moral outrage against what they saw as the blind faith of the Social Democrats in technology and economic growth. In the narrow victory of the Center Party and its coalition partners in 1976 an antinuclear moralist, Thorbjörn Fälldin, became prime minister. Now was their time. What is notable is that despite this victory, Fälldin's coalition partners argued that it would be irresponsible to abandon nuclear plants already well along. The antinuclear position was gradually abandoned.

The Three Mile Island accident of 1979 produced contrasting responses in countries that had pursued the nuclear option. The French claimed it meant nothing. The United States, with great media fanfare, drifted into further delays, instituted a few safety precautions, and discouraged future construction (new investments had already ceased, anyway) but adopted no alternative energy policy. Swedish political elites decided to devote themselves to forging a new consensus, hoping for the long-term maintenance of nuclear plants while alternatives could be developed. In 1980 the Social Democrats launched a rare referendum – surely one of the largest-scale national issue debates in the history of postwar democratic politics (if the measure is expenditure per voter and voter participation in political discussion). In contrast to American advocates of nuclear energy who dismissed antinuclear activists as ignorant, irrational, and hopelessly romantic, their counterparts at the top of Swedish society made a heroic effort to educate their opponents and the public by including them in policy deliberations. In an unprecedented, intensive educational effort over four months, including Parliament- and party-financed reading, talking, and campaigning by all sides, the Swedish voters became what could be the most informed electorate on Earth about this technical-political issue. Here is how they divided on the three ballot choices, much condensed: 19 percent said use the 12 plants now operating, completed, or under construction, and close them down only if there is no threat to the supply of electricity, jobs, and welfare; 39 percent endorsed the "middle way" of the Social Democrats and Liberals, that is, the above "Conservative" position with additions – promote energy conservation, protect the weakest groups, expand R&D on renewable energy, improve safety rules, and put responsibility for production and distribution in public hands; and 39 percent voted for the Center Party and Communist alternative: stop continued expansion of nuclear power, shut down existing plants immediately if safety analysis proves them unsafe,[4] and phase out the six reactors currently in operation within 10 years. In short, about three in five voters were saying, "We have some doubts but let's not rush." Even Line 3 advocates were not urging a blanket shutdown. The major parties soon agreed to phase out nuclear energy in 30 years, by 2010. However, having no alternative energy that could fill the gap if half of total production accounted for by nuclear was eliminated, the phase-out was repeatedly delayed, and by 2008 only 1 of the 11 plants on line had been shut down. In February 2009 the government presented a bill to stop the phase-out officially and allow new nuclear construction.

The nagging issues of operational safety and the disposal of nuclear waste are perhaps handled best by Sweden, although I am skeptical that either issue can be fully resolved. The best studies that compare national efforts to dispose of nuclear waste conclude that the cautious Swedish approach is better designed and executed than that of any other country (Carter, 1987; Cook, Emel, and Kasperson, 1991–1992: 106). The current Swedish plan for disposal of spent nuclear fuel is a repository where the waste is placed in copper capsules, surrounded by a bentonite layer and buried 500 meters deep in the crystalline bedrock. Site investigations have started in two municipalities with local acceptance (International Energy Agency, 2008; Swedish Ministry of Enterprise, Energy, and Communications, 2007). Regarding operational safety, James Jasper (1990) concludes that Sweden is slightly better than France and the plants in both countries are much safer than plants in the United States. The reasons: high levels of management and worker competence combined with close, cooperative interaction between industry, science, and government.

In all three of these cases of nuclear development since World War II, the powerful actors were insiders – top politicians and bureaucrats constrained only a little by protest movements and public attitudes, which they shaped by their policies, successes, and failures. The French case is characterized by elite and expert dominance, the exclusion of all countervailing forces, and centralized decision making by a small group of top bureaucrats belonging mainly to the Corps des Mines and the Corps des Ponts et Chaussées. These technocrats are scattered among the main managing and operating company, Electricité de France (EDF) and the planning agency, Commissariat à L'Énergie Atomique (CEA), the Ministry of Industry, and other government agencies as well as nuclear manufacturers. The prestigious Corps des Mines, which dominates CEA, and the Corps des Ponts et Chaussées, dominant at EDF, recruit the "best and brightest" from the grands écoles. The top 5 or 10 graduates of École Polytechnique go to the most prestigious technical corps, Corps des Mines; next in line for top recruits is the Corps des Ponts et Chaussées.

These technological enthusiasts articulated a vision of a France awash in cheap energy, independent of any other nation. Polytecniciens are a tight-knit group. As their careers develop, they fan out about evenly in the state apparatus, nationalized industry, and private business. Of 28 "nucleocrats" identified as top managers of public or private organizations involved in nuclear energy, 20 are graduates of École Polytechnique (9 in Mines, 7 in Ponts) (Simonnot, 1978: 24–25). As one of them told Jasper (1990: 85), polytechniciens "speak only to Mines, and Mines speak only to God."

EDF, which produces and distributes electricity, is one of the world's best-run companies. It is autonomous, state-owned, and (after 1970) profit making. Its combination of service, autonomy, prestige, and competence attracts able managers, who recruit and train skilled workers. Although EDF has a governing board with representatives from the state ministries, labor unions, consumers, and others, there is no doubt that members of Corps des Mines and Corps des Ponts were in effective control of EDF and, indeed, of the whole nuclear energy program.

France is a case of the triumph of technological planning. The combination of centralized decision making by a cohesive group of strategically placed, elite technocrats in both government and industry resulted in standardized construction processes, plant layouts, and control rooms. The state underwrote many costs. Large economies of scale were achieved. As one might expect from the recruitment pattern, levels of competence were high throughout nuclear-energy planning and operation. Because the French polytechniciens, unlike most American nuclear enthusiasts, admitted that error and even accidents were inevitable, they carried out more preventive maintenance, more careful design, and established strong safety teams at each plant. The CEA perfected those aspects of safety that had been swept under the rug in the United States (Jasper, 1990: 86). The key to both safety and cost control appears to be the training and competence of managers and workers, as much as the technology (p. 253). By the mid-1980s, French electricity costs were 20 percent cheaper than German costs, 30 percent cheaper than British, 40 percent cheaper than the Dutch; they were competitive with coal. Today the nuclear industry has become a "national champion" of French industrial policy. France is an aggressive salesman for its nuclear reactors around the world; it has targeted China, the United States, Finland, Brazil, and India (*Economist*, Dec. 6, 2008: 81–82). In short, although the French may have ended up with too many reactors and less flexibility in the use of alternative sources of energy, the outcome so far has been a cheaper, more efficient, and probably safer nuclear program than those of its competitors, except Sweden.[5]

At the other extreme, nuclear energy development in the United States was characterized by dispersed authority, the premature deployment of plants, lax supervision of operators, and sloppy management, followed by cost escalation and safety problems that ultimately stopped further expansion. The dominant actors were private utility companies, reactor manufacturers such as GE and Westinghouse, banks and the federal government, especially the Atomic Energy Commission (AEC, later the NRC) and, at times, the Bureau of the Budget (later OMB). The regulatory regime was at once legalistic and indulgent. The AEC issued lengthy specifications and lists of procedures and was strict about conforming to the letter of the law in licensing but careless regarding the actual operation of the plants. Hands-off private enterprise was the main theme.

Matching the casual commitment of the government was the casual attitude of the utility companies ("nuclear reactors are just another way to boil water"). As the commercialization of the light-water reactor proceeded apace after 1963, inept management and the poor training and supervision of operators led to much greater costs than anyone expected.

In its structure and mission, the AEC embodied fatal contradictions: it was simultaneously to promote new nuclear technologies but not to interfere with private companies running existing reactors; it was to promote the commercialization of nuclear energy and at the same time regulate and protect public safety. Promotion without close supervision was the continual resolution of these dilemmas. AEC promotion was matched by successes of the nuclear lobby in

Washington. Successive bills of the past 20 years gave the industry large public subsidies, including tax breaks and loan guarantees (Representative Ed Markey's Hearing, U.S. House of Representatives, Apr. 24, 2009). For critics concerned with safety and cost, it is notable that commercial companies refuse to write loss guarantees for nuclear plants. Specifically, as Henry Sokolski (2008) observes, no private bank in the world has yet chosen to fully finance the building of a new nuclear reactor and no private insurer has yet chosen to insure a nuclear plant against third-party off-site damages.

By Three Mile Island, economics had already buried the prospects of the industry. Cost explosions and denial of risks coupled with well-publicized surprise accidents were a poor formula for inspiring confidence of investors or the public. With the benefit of hindsight and comparative analysis, we can conclude that the American nuclear program was relatively costly, amazingly sloppy in management, poorly regulated, and unsafe. America is not alone. Established and experienced nuclear powers ranging from efficient Japan to least efficient Russia have also had accidents in their nuclear facilities.

In the United States today, as energy demand climbs and environmental concerns spread, the nuclear industry lobby has been given new life. Because America leads in greenhouse emissions, the industry can accurately claim that at the moment 20 percent of electricity and 70 percent of "clean" energy in the United States comes from nuclear. Most policy makers, even in the science-friendly Obama administration, hesitate to accent its limitations. These include dangers in plant operation and disposal of toxic nuclear waste, which has a half-life even longer than that of $CO_2$; the heavy costs and long lead times for new nuclear power plants, costs impossible to calculate without knowing the future prices of alternatives such as oil, natural gas, coal, and renewables; and the drain of public and private resources away from alternative energy solutions.[6] Finally, "clean" nuclear depends on perfect systems, a utopian goal. The United States lacks the political and economic structures that made Sweden and France relatively safe, and even they have not fully solved the problems posed by nuclear power.

Nuclear power goes forward only with very heavy government subsidies. Thus in June 2009 the Senate Energy and Natural Resources Committee voted for a bill that provides massive incentives for both nuclear and coal-fired plants. And in his January 2010 budget President Obama announced a tripling of federal loan guarantees for new nuclear projects from $18 billion to $54 billion. A new Energy Department panel commission will study what to do with nuclear waste.

The history of nuclear development in Sweden suggests that whatever the level of safety, the political and economic resources required for a large nuclear effort may block the development of alternatives. Although its wind resources are comparable to Denmark's, Sweden came to wind power late. In the 1970s it went for large turbines developed by two large utility companies. Promotion was divided among several agencies and institutions. The effort was largely unsuccessful. New support for renewables, however, including solar, wind, wood, ocean waves, and biomass, was introduced in 2003. Public policy was based on a complex trading of green electricity certificates that constitute incentives for the production and use of renewable energy (Swedish Ministry of Sustainable Development, 2006). The Swedish Renewables Association (SERO) calls the tradable green certificates "a catastrophe for wind power and small hydro-power." And the Danish Wind Industry Association comments, "Since the same basic flaws which led to the collapse of the Danish certificate scheme are present in the Swedish scheme, we expect the Swedish system to be put on ice, at least until a potential EU-wide system has been properly analyzed and discussed" (Krohn, 2003). The EU has explored the development of a harmonized trading system with little progress so far. Sweden and Norway have undertaken negotiations for a joint market, and although Norway went its own way in 2006, negotiations were resumed in 2008 (Meyer, 2007; Reuters, 2008).

Sweden aims to free itself from fossil fuel use by 2020. In 2005, however, renewables were only 5.9 percent of total energy production. The main reason for the limited move toward renewables is the early commitment to hydroelectric power (in 1980 about 70% of total production, it went down to about half in 1986 and thereafter) and the later full-scale commitment to the development of nuclear power (30% of production in 1980, it climbed to about half in 1986 and thereafter). This again suggests that *countries that go far down the nuclear road will retard the development of alternative green-energy solutions.* Confirming this hypothesis, France, a country that fully followed the nuclear path, produced only 1.2 percent of total energy production from alternative or renewable sources; in 2005 it produced about half as much total renewable energy as tiny Denmark.[7]

In addition, Swedish wind development has been hampered by technical problems, such as the inability of local grids to handle higher levels of wind power electricity (Reiche and Bechberger, 2004).

Another factor limiting Sweden's transition away from nuclear power is its limited natural resources in fossil fuels. Sweden produces no natural gas or crude oil and has no proven reserves. Although Sweden's consumption of petroleum has decreased 34 percent from 537,000 barrels a day in 1980 to 354,000 in 2007, it still relies on imports for more than 99 percent of this consumption.

Contributing to the Swedish preference for large nuclear plants and a couple of big wind turbines while Denmark chose many small turbines with highly decentralized delivery are sharp contrasts in industrial concentration. By 1986, 61 percent of Swedish workers were employed in firms with 500 or more employees; the figure was only 18 percent of Danish workers. Government planning tends to reflect the structure of the economy (Wilensky, 2002: 122 and 130, n. 24).

A final skeptical question about the Swedish and French full-scale commitment to the nuclear option asks, How green is it? A careful survey of 103 life-cycle studies of greenhouse gas equivalent emissions for a variety of nuclear plants concentrated on a subset of the most current, original, and transparent studies (Sovacool, 2008). The aim: to assess the great range of estimates of their emissions. The conclusion: although nuclear power plants are not directly emitting greenhouse gases, their life-cycle emissions are substantial through plant construction, operation, uranium mining and milling, and plant decommissioning. "Nuclear energy is in no way 'carbon free' or 'emissions free,' even though it is much better (from purely a carbon-equivalent emissions standpoint) than coal, oil, and natural gas electricity generators." Nuclear is worse than renewable and small-scale distributed generators (p. 2960 and table 8). And it cannot match the world potential of hydropower and biofuels (Goldemberg, 2009: 73).[8]

The life cycle of these plants lasts about 30 to 40 years but they produce electricity at full power for no more than 24 years. The heaviest emissions occur at the front end and back end of the nuclear life cycle. The back end involves fuel processing, interim storage, and permanent sequestration of nuclear wastes. The half-life of uranium-238 is about 4.5 billion years.

Aside from the issue of climate change (and even if nuclear power were bright green), the obvious danger of nuclear proliferation in the hands of terrorists or rogue states is clear and present. Today 30 nations operate one or more nuclear power plants, and some 50 others have requested technical assistance from the International Atomic Energy Agency (IAEA) to develop their own nuclear energy programs. There are 436 nuclear power reactors around the globe, more than half in the United States, France, Japan, and Russia (International Atomic Energy Agency, 2009). The 436 provide 16 percent of the world's supply of electricity (Lester and Rosner, 2009: 24). It is important to note that nuclear power and atomic weapons are interconnected: uranium enrichment and plutonium reprocessing capabilities are relevant to both. Many of the states that already have plants or are planning to build them are politically unstable. They lack the kind of governance that could stop the theft or sales of fissile materials to terrorist networks or states (Miller and Sagan, 2009: 9–11).[9] For analysis of proposals for enhancing the nuclear safety regime, see volumes 1 and 2 of *The Global Nuclear Future* (*Daedalus*, Fall 2009 and Winter 2010).

### B. CAP-AND-TRADE OR CARBON TAX?

In discussion of how to limit global warming, everyone acknowledges that there is no one solution, no quick fix. The most successful efforts to reduce greenhouse gases so far are evident in countries like Denmark and Sweden that act on many fronts simultaneously – not just taxes, but generous investment in R&D, strong regulatory standards, and incentives for renewables and for energy efficiency (in cars and buildings). Nevertheless, perhaps the most favorably discussed single solution worldwide is financial – a cap-and-trade system (or "carbon trading"). This is favored in many countries, including the United States (Jay, 2008), even China, and is promoted by the EU Commission under industry pressure. A skeptical note based on experience to date is therefore useful.

Such systems in theory limit how much greenhouse gas (e.g., carbon dioxide) producers can emit and lets them buy and sell emissions credits. Critics suggest three major reasons for restraining our enthusiasm for this "market-based" solution. First, producers who have blocked a broad range of environmental regulations in the past can easily game the system. Where cap-and-trade has been tried, as in the European Emissions Trading System (ETS) begun in 2005, the reductions are severely limited or nil. In fact, emissions under ETS have crept up about 1 percent per year since 2005 (*Wall Street Journal*, May 30, 2008). Industry leaders make sure that the regulators do not set the cap too low while they exploit opportunities for cheating and collect an excessive number of credits, pretending they are cleaner than they are. If, when regulatory agencies pass out credits, corporate interests can gain a seat at the table, they maximize their credits. Carbon traders also can game the system; banks and brokers jump in to collect commissions on carbon trades as they have with many other commodities and derivatives, Citigroup style.

Besides the power of industry lobbyists, the second limitation of cap-and-trade is that it is too complicated and costly to administer, regulate, and verify (see note 1). The third major limitation is that it puts a value on pollution: at best, the most ardent polluters who game the system maintain or even worsen whole areas of intensive pollution. The victims are hapless communities that are unlucky enough to be located in the wrong place. And it does nothing to limit the burden of electricity costs for consumers. Power companies in Europe receive most carbon permits free in the startup phase but raise rates anyway. Thus: "In Germany heavy industrial companies saw their electricity costs jump, while major power producers' profits soared" (*Wall Street Journal*, May 30, 2008; Bohringer, Voß, and Rutherford, 1998). It is no surprise that big American firms such as Duke Energy are now much less hostile to cap-and-trade than they were before the European system started up, while American politicians, including President Obama (Obama and Biden, 2008), accommodate industry preferences as the line of least resistance. If, however, governments do not give power companies free permits to pollute at the startup phase but instead require up-front payment through an auction, then industry abandons the cause. This auction idea is a major source of the strong resistance of Germany, Italy, and Poland and other countries in Central and Eastern Europe to the 2008 proposed climate change package of EU. To reach agreement, EU leaders succumbed to industry pressure. The steel industry and other business lobbies welcomed the watered-down climate-change deal of December 12, 2008 (*Wall Street Journal*, Dec. 13–14, 2008). This process of accommodating industry interests under the banner of free-market solutions was repeated in the Obama administration. Beginning with the rejection of a carbon tax and advocating instead a cap-and-trade system favored by big energy producers, the president then suggested that he might push a bill with 100 percent auctions. Industry lobbyists and coal-state senators combined to demand a large number of free emission permits outside of auctions and the president backed down (*New York Times*, Apr. 1, 2009, A19; *Wall Street Journal*, Apr. 9, 2009, A4; cf. Metcalf, 2008).[10] Washington was repeating the cycle of successive compromises that watered down the European system and undermined its effectiveness.

If the United States and China and India are not subject to emission caps and those European countries that do face cap-and-trade have not meaningfully curbed greenhouse gases, it is hard to share the enthusiasm of its advocates. There is merit, however, in a straightforward carbon tax (and taxes on nitrogen oxide or sulfur dioxide) as one among the whole range of measures I have discussed. Such a tax is simpler to administer, less subject to corporate gaming, and offers no incentive to pollute. For these reasons critics, on the left, right, and center, ranging from Ralph Nader to Jeffrey Sachs to Greg Mankiw, former chief economic adviser to President Bush, and including Nobel Prize winners such as Al Gore, Paul Krugman, and Joe Stiglitz all favor simpler carbon taxes (see Nader and Heaps, 2008; Sachs, 2009; Mankiw, 2007; Krugman, 2000; Stiglitz, 2006a).[11]

That taxes are a disincentive to energy consumption and carbon emissions is evident in cross-national variation in per capita gasoline consumption (as shown in data circa 2007 from *Foreign Policy Magazine*, Sept.–Oct., 2008):

| Country | Tax per Gallon | Total Price | Gallons/Person/Day |
|---|---|---|---|
| Netherlands | $4.18 | $6.33 | .18 |
| Italy | $3.59 | $5.73 | .20 |
| United Kingdom | $4.11 | $5.94 | .24 |
| Japan | $2.37 | $4.94 | .26 |
| Australia | $1.38 | $3.21 | .50 |
| Canada | $0.96 | $2.86 | .68 |
| United States | $0.39 | $2.49 | .81 |

Taxing all carbon emissions, the generation of garbage (landfill taxes), and cars driven in cities – shifting taxes from labor to energy – has been effective in several European countries and in California; such taxes have at once cut greenhouse gases, created green jobs, and accelerated the growth of renewables. As nations adopt environmental taxes on emissions, international organizations such as the EU and UN can work toward a universal global carbon tax without interfering with specific national decisions about either the means to comply or what to do with the revenue. As former Mexican president Ernesto Zedillo suggests, universal participation is critical to avoid calls for the imposition of tariffs on carbon-intensive imports, a new trade war of the environmentally observant countries against all others (*Forbes*, Mar. 24, 2008). Until the happy day when universality is achieved, the national efforts I have discussed have been and remain quite effective.

That global solutions are still a dream is illustrated by the failure of the UN to coax developing countries even to discuss emissions targets at recent meetings (Aguilar et al., 2005) and the failure of the summit of July 2009 to get 17 nations that account for 80 percent of the world's greenhouse gases even to set serious goals for emission reductions. These failures are an added argument against a cap-and-trade system, which inevitably involves large transfers from the rich countries to developing countries. In contrast, a carbon tax, as with rules shaping auto emissions, can be imposed by each government now without the need for politically difficult transfers added to the other limitations of cap-and-trade – corporate gaming, complexity, and the folly of permission slips to spew carbon dioxide. (For further discussion of these alternatives, see Gilbert E. Metcalf, 2008, who discusses ways to make a carbon tax revenue neutral and distributionally fair; Lackner and Sachs, 2005: 215–269; Brookings Papers on Economic Activity, 2005: 270–284; and *Foreign Policy Magazine*, Sept.–Oct. 2008: 73.)

Advocates of cap-and-trade often point to the success of the U.S. Environmental Protection Agency's 1990 market-based regulation of sulfur dioxide. The EPA set a limit on $SO_2$ emissions from the few big sources (e.g., coal-fired plants) and allowed those who emit less than their quota to trade excess allowances. Regional acid deposits were dramatically reduced. As William Schlesinger notes (2006: 1217), the biogeochemistry and sources of $SO_2$ differ so much from those of $CO_2$ that the success of $SO_2$ cap-and-trade regulation is virtually irrelevant to the control of carbon dioxide emissions. $CO_2$, in contrast to $SO_2$, comes from many distributed sources, some sensitive to climate, others sensitive to human disturbance such as cutting forests, electric power generation, industry, home heating, and transportation. Further, $SO_2$ has a short lifetime in the atmosphere; $CO_2$ lives on for hundreds of years.

Estimates of the emissions reductions with a carbon tax suggest that even in the short run (a \$15 per metric ton of $CO_2$ from 2003 to 2015) greenhouse emissions would fall about 14 percent ($CO_2$, 8.4%; other GHG – methane, nitrous oxide, and fluorinated gases – 47%); the use of coal drops 15 percent, petroleum products 5.6 percent, and natural gas 3.4 percent (Metcalf, 2008: 2–8). Tax revenues estimated at \$90–100 billion could be used for innovative energy technology to increase renewables and improve carbon capture and storage as well as environmentally friendly transportation, as Denmark has done, or for tax reductions favored by "conservatives." Either way, if the carbon tax starts at this modest level and is slowly increased every year, its long-run effects will be substantial. As Gilbert Metcalf suggests (2008: 6–8), administrative costs can be reduced and political acceptability increased if the carbon tax is levied upstream on fuel producers rather than downstream on fuel users. For instance, the tax is paid by such polluters as coal producers, petroleum refineries, natural gas distribution centers, and fossil fuel importers. In the United States the taxed firms are already reporting to the IRS and paying taxes; no extra layer of bureaucracy is necessary. If all greenhouse gases are included, the tax rate can start quite low. As success is achieved revenue declines and the rate can gradually rise until still more of the polluters clean up their act (Metcalf et al., 2008: 27–30).

In short, a well-designed carbon tax, in contrast to cap-and-trade arrangements, is far more effective in coping with the climate change challenge. Standing alone, however, no tax strategy can have sufficient impact in view of the size and urgency of the problem. As the cases of Denmark and Sweden show, taxes must be combined with a broad range of policies including combined heat and power production, high energy standards for buildings and transportation, investment to improve existing infrastructure (including transit, rail, and electrical grids), the development and use of renewables from biomass (e.g., wood and bio-degradable waste and straw), enhanced geothermal systems, wind, solar, and more.[12] Underlying any effective policy package is a serious public commitment to research and development to bring new energy technologies to market. Finally, as a comparison of Sweden and France with Denmark suggests, going far down the nuclear energy road, even if the problems of waste disposal and nuclear proliferation are solved, diverts resources and political energy away from alternative green technologies.

## C. WHAT TO DO ABOUT THE GLOBAL LOVE AFFAIR WITH CARS

The world car population is exploding. Dwindling oil supplies assure long-term increases in fuel prices, whatever the short-term fluctuations. The result is increasing dependence of almost all nations on the kindness and stability of

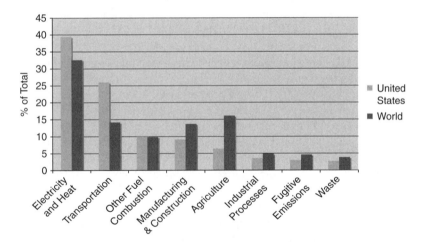

FIGURE 1. Greenhouse gas emissions by sector, 2005. Gases included in GHG emissions are carbon dioxide, methane, nitrous oxide, perfluorocarbons, hydrofluorocarbons, and sulfur hexafluoride. Sector categories come from the Intergovernmental Panel on Climate Change (IPCC) Common Reporting Framework. They are mutually exclusive, with emissions totaling 100 percent. *Electricity and heat* equals public heat and power production (e.g., coal-fired power plants and other utilities). *Transportation* equals emissions from domestic transportation. *Other fuel combustion* equals emissions from electricity and heat in industry, exclusive of *manufacturing and construction* (bar 4). *Agriculture* equals human emissions from agricultural activities. *Industrial processes* equals emissions from by-products from industrial processes. *Fugitive emissions* equals residual emissions (e.g., international transport and flaring in production). *Waste emissions* equals waste disposal and management activity.

oil-rich regimes of the Middle East and elsewhere. Reducing that dependence requires a drastic change in transportation systems and infrastructures of both rich democracies and developing countries such as Brazil, Russia, India, and China – all large, rapidly developing auto consumers and carbon emitters. A few facts for context:

- The proportion of global greenhouse gases that came from all transportation in 2005 was about 14 percent. In contrast, transportation in the United States alone in 2005 accounted for about 26 percent of $CO_2$ equivalent emissions, almost twice the world emissions (World Resources Institute, 2008). Beyond $CO_2$, vehicles using gasoline also emit such pollutants as sulfur oxides and particulates. Figure 1 shows that transportation in the U.S. is second only to "electricity and heat" (at 39%, including utilities, homes, and buildings) as a source of greenhouse emissions.
- The International Monetary Fund (Chamon, Mauro, and Okawa, 2008: 271–272) estimates that the number of cars worldwide will grow from 600 million in 2005 to 2.9 billion in 2050 – in less than two generations. Or in the very short run, by 2030 China's car fleet alone will overtake that of the United States even while American car ownership climbs by 60 percent.
- In the face of a worldwide recession annual car sales in 2008 reached an all-time record of about 59 million cars (*Economist*, Nov. 15, 2008: 3). The *Stern Review on the Economics of Climate Change* (2006: 173) estimates that if car emissions were to grow in line with ownership, the global $CO_2$ emissions from cars in 2006 will skyrocket by 2050. Greenhouse gas emissions from total transportation are expected to double by 2050. (The transportation share of all emissions is expected to remain roughly the same [14%], however, because every other source will increase, too; "electricity and heat" emissions in Figure 1 will more than double its share.)
- The United States has 900 cars (including trucks) for every 1,000 people of driving age with Europe and Japan at only 600, largely because public transportation is much better in both and population density is greater. Or put another way, fuel efficiency in the United States is about two-thirds of the level in the EU (An and Sauer, 2004: 24). Although the less developed countries' ownership rate is much lower than that of rich countries, their car use is rising at an exponential rate.

How did the United States become the leader in dependence on autos and trucks?[13] It began with a strategic decision in the mid-1950s. Americans were already restive about the rush-hour crush, but they were delighted by Eisenhower's 1956 $41 billion plan to build nonstop, limited-access, high-speed freeways that would permit them to go anywhere just by hopping into the car – that is, if not too many others have the same idea at the same time. (That $41 billion is equivalent to $317 billion in 2008 inflation-adjusted dollars.) Mobilizing these sentiments was a potent nationwide highway lobby with roots in every local community: auto manufacturers and their 64,000 local car dealers, gasoline companies, tire producers, the state motor clubs, highway contractors and highway department officials in city halls and state capitols, the trucking industry, the cement and asphalt companies, and the many businesses and industries that profit from cars and roads. In 1956 this formidable combination led to a fateful choice – the adoption of the Interstate Highway System embracing both rural and urban areas, the line of least resistance. Described as "old fashioned" were plans to rebuild rapid transit facilities; ignored was the unwritten law that added roads demand added parking space and the two together merely invite a new overflow of automobiles.[14]

Ignored too, was the knowledge that increasing the overflow of autos and parking structures invariably uses up land, especially in dense urban areas, thereby increasing urban housing costs and accelerating a half-century trend (1900 to 1950) toward deconcentration of population and economic activity (suburbs, exurbs). In turn, all this increases the time it takes for the journey to work with escalating traffic jams, decreases the tax base of cities and thereby their capacity to finance essential services and build affordable housing, creating both central-city slums and urban sprawl.

Combining all levels of government, by the early 1960s the United States was spending about $1.00 per capita every week on building and maintaining roads and highways (excluding outlays on bond retirements, administration, interest, and law enforcement). That is about $6.50 in 2006 dollars, which by 2006 had climbed to $7.68. Finally, when the worst recession since the Great Depression confronted the new Obama administration, the politics of the financial-industrial bailout package meant that Congress had to include $17.4 billion for the auto manufacturing complex because it accounted for 1 in 10 of all American jobs (McAlinden, Hill, and Swiecki, 2003).

The $789.2 billion stimulus package passed by Congress February 14, 2009 (reported in *Wall Street Journal*, Feb. 13, 2009, A6; *New York Times*, Feb. 14, 2009) allocated $29 billion to "road and bridge infrastructure." In contrast, "public transit improvements" got only $8.4 billion and "high-speed rail," $8 billion. Thus, alternatives to roads received a little more than half the amount devoted to roads and bridges. That was a big improvement over previous budgets but still reflected the legacy of 1956 and the power of the auto manufacturing/highway complex.[15] Eight billion dollars for high-speed rail, about 1 percent of the stimulus package (or .06 of 1 percent of GDP), is tiny for a country with the population and geography of the United States. For instance, just one proposed project for a high-speed line in California from San Francisco to Los Angeles is estimated to cost almost six times that, $45 billion. Similarly, in 2007, after a Democratic center-left victory, Congress approved the first increase in U.S. fuel efficiency standards in 32 years. Nevertheless, U.S. fleetwide standard of 25.3 miles per gallon (27.5 for cars and 22.2 for trucks) is still well below Japan's 43, the EU's 43, and China's 36 (International Council on Clean Transportation, 2009).

It is tragic for the planet and the environment that some developing countries are repeating some of the worst transportation infrastructure mistakes of the United States and other rich democracies.

The sheer scale of demand in only four of the rapidly developing countries – Brazil, Russia, India, and China – means that in 2008, the worst year of car sales in America since 1992, these countries will buy 17.5 million vehicles, more than U.S. vehicle sales within the United States of approximately 15.7 million (*Business Monitor International Online Database*, 2008). Brazil's sales have increased by nearly 30 percent a year in 2007 and again in 2008. When the world economy recovers, China, the world's second-biggest market, is expected to overtake America's annual sales of 16–17 million cars, the figure for a normal nonrecession year such as 2007. Russia is overtaking Germany as Europe's biggest market (*Economist*, Nov. 15, 2008: 3). India will take longer to catch up.

What about transportation infrastructure? Since the 1990s China has built an expressway network crisscrossing urban and rural lands that resembles the U.S. Interstate Highway System. The ministry in charge boasts that China's expressway builders achieved in 17 years what the West took 40 to accomplish (*Economist*, Feb. 14, 2008; *New York Times*, Jan. 23, 2009). By 2008 China had built 53,000 kilometers of toll expressways and now aims to add 17,000 kilometers more by 2020. Rural road construction begun in 2006 will increase capacity to 300,000 kilometers by 2010. All this naturally brings a flood of cars, vans, and trucks, accelerates pollution, and produces the same destructive deconcentration of urban population and industry that the United States experienced in the past 100 years. The center of Beijing is a nightmare of congestion, choking fumes, and giant potholes (*Economist*, Nov. 15, 2008: 18). Despite the simultaneous growth of high-speed rail – matching 19th-century developments in the West – China is experiencing an explosion in private car ownership and the use of private cars for both short- and long-distance travel. The heavy-handed approach to land appropriation of a one-party dictatorship speeded up the building of roads, rail, and huge airports and bridges, in the process flattening villages, forcibly resettling untold numbers of residents, and using up productive agricultural land.

India is not far behind in congestion: nearly half the traffic runs on just 2 percent of the roads (*Economist*, Nov. 15, 2008: 4), most of which are rough and bumpy. Two-wheelers add to the crush. Although Asia is home to nearly 80 percent of the world's 315 million motorcycles, China accounts for 100 million of them while India, in second place, has about 45 million (p. 16). Because of traffic jams, cars in India, China, Brazil, and parts of Russia often move slower than walking speed, with motorcycles at daredevil speed snaking through. Russian car makers concentrate on heavy trucks, buses, and light commercial vehicles. Traffic jams in Moscow are legendary (*Wall Street Journal*, Mar. 6, 2009). Until the recent renationalization under Putin in 2005 and the entry of Renault, criminal networks had infiltrated much of the Russian-branded car industry and dealerships. So prices have been high, mass ownership limited, but carbon emissions per vehicle abundant. Of course these trends stalled in the Great Recession of 2007–2009, but they will resume upon recovery.

Tastes in type of vehicles varies among these four. The growing affluent classes in both China and Russia like big SUVs and turn up their noses at small cars, the way Detroit CEOs sneered at Volkswagen, Toyota, Honda, and Hyundai as these and other foreign companies took away their markets. Brazilians, in contrast, are buying smaller cars, especially VWs and Fiats; nearly all new cars can run on sugarcane-based ethanol – flex-fuel cars that accept any blend of ethanol and gasoline (Goldemberg, 2008). India, with the lowest per capita income but a growing middle class, prefers small, cheap cars (most made by a joint venture of Muruti of India and Suzuki of Japan, a small-car specialist, and more recently Hyundai) (*Economist*, Nov. 15, 2008: 8).

Whatever the national variation, the exploding demand for cars in developing countries, let alone continued demand in rich countries, assures major increases in greenhouse gas emissions, unless governments and car producers everywhere quickly modify their transportation systems and apply new technologies to the design of cars and trucks.

The urgency of developing vehicles with very low or zero emissions is plain. There is no mystery about how to achieve this. Multiple measures have already achieved success in one or more countries: a carbon tax is an incentive for car manufacturers to speed up the production of new efficient cars and fuels; investment in R&D has already demonstrated the efficacy of electric cars and all-electric plug-ins; hybrids that have internal combustion engines but are powered partly by batteries that recharge from energy released by the car are already almost 10 percent of the world's fleet (*Financial Times*, July 12, 2008); more efficient batteries using lithium-ion technology are likely to be ready within a few years; and, while sales of smaller efficient cars in the United States slumped in 2009 as the economy and gas prices collapsed, Germany, France, and nine other West European countries were giving buyers of new low-emission cars $1,360 to $4,750 if they scrap a car more than 10 years old – and Renault's subcompact sales boomed. The United States joined the crowd for a couple of months in late 2009. These "cash-for-clunkers" programs are no more than a very short-run economic stimulus, but they likely reduce carbon emissions in the long run. Finally, already far along in research breakthroughs are cellulosic biofuels that can be produced on a grand scale with almost no environmental damage (no conversion of underdeveloped land, minimal erosion and runoff, minimal nitrogen oxide emissions).

In this effort to reinvent cars and fuels, rich democracies must lead. They already have the well-organized environmental lobbies and rising mass awareness necessary to educate voters and pressure politicians for proenvironment policy decisions and consumer acceptance. Equally important, they have the resources for R&D and for production of green vehicles. In a world market they can and do export green cars by the million; such cars have a demonstration effect in developing countries. In other words, we do not have to wait for grand global agreements to be signed and implemented to make global progress with green technology. Each developed nation can do its job. And because science and technology are public, not private, and the vehicle market is global (*Economist*, Nov. 15, 2008: 19–20), developing nations can leapfrog over the old polluting cars and technologies dominant in the rich countries; they do not have to copy the infrastructure errors of the United States. We cannot quickly reverse the rising world demand for cars, but we can quickly change to green cars and fuels, pending payoffs on overdue investments in today's alternative transportation systems, especially high-speed rail, mass transit, and an urban computer-scheduled network of jitneys.

## D. CORN-BASED ETHANOL, "CLEAN COAL," AND OTHER FOLLIES

According to the Energy Information Administration (EIA, 2009), in 2005 coal was the fuel for 27 percent of global primary energy production (oil 37%, natural gas, 23%).[16] In 2006, it was the leading source of world electricity accounting for 41 percent of the total (gas 20%, hydro 17%, nuclear 15%, oil 7%). In the United States, coal was 23 percent of energy consumption and about half of our electricity production. Coal is the largest source of greenhouse gas emissions linked to global warming, contributing around 41 percent of total global $CO_2$ emissions ($CO_2$ accounts for about 80% of greenhouse gas emissions).

Around the world coal-burning power plants are multiplying like rabbits – at the rate of more than one per week (*New York Times*, July 16, 2007). The leading coal burners are the United States, China, Russia, and India. China alone now exceeds the U.S. in coal consumption by a factor of almost two; the coal-fired plants it opens almost every week are each big enough to serve all the households in San Diego (*New York Times*, May 28, 2005). In 2005, China built enough coal-fired power plants to provide electricity to all of Italy (*Wall Street Journal*, Mar. 3, 2006).

In the United States, the economic and political incentives to maintain and even increase the use of coal are enormous: this dirtiest of fuel has an unmatched base of support in Congress from coal-rich states (in descending order of coal reserves: Wyoming, West Virginia, Illinois, North Dakota, Montana, Kentucky, Texas, and Pennsylvania plus Colorado, an above average producer with below average reserves). U.S. senators and representatives from those states are typically reliable supporters of the coal lobby. We can see this in the generous tax breaks and R&D subsidies for coal producers. From 1997 to 2006, cumulative federal R&D expenditures for coal have increased relative to nuclear or, far behind, renewables (Management Information Services, 2008: Exhibit 9, p. 25).

Recently we have heard a great deal about "clean coal." A barrage of institutional ads from the American Coalition for Clean Coal Electricity proclaim that clean coal using coal-to-liquid or coal-to-hydrogen processes is already here or just around the corner. China is investing heavily in coal-to-oil plants. In the United States two senators from coal-producing states, Barack Obama (D-IL) and Jim Bunning (R-KY), introduced a bill to offer loan guarantees and tax incentives for U.S. coal-to-liquid plants. Here are some relevant facts about the mirage of "clean coal."

- The U.S. National Resources Defense Council estimates that the production and use of gasoline, diesel fuel, jet fuel, and other fuels from crude oil release about 27 pounds of carbon dioxide per gallon. The production and use of a gallon of liquid fuel originating in coal is nearly twice that amount, about 50 pounds of $CO_2$ (National Resources Defense Council, 2007). Coal combustion in the United States produces 130 million tons of coal ash every year; the task of regulating more than 600 landfills and impoundments holding this ash is left to the states, which have neither the motive nor resources for anything but lax administration (*New York Times*, editorial, Jan. 23, 2009).
- A second campaign of the coal lobby is to convince top decision makers and Congress that "clean coal" can soon be achieved by a process of capture and sequestration. Even in the stimulus bill of February 2009 Congress allocated about $2.4 billion for this purpose on top of $90 million in the Energy Policy Act of 2005. As Jeffrey Sachs suggests (2008), we must first prove that these new types of carbon-fired plants will reduce costs and achieve reliability. A vast new network of $CO_2$ pipelines must be built after overcoming environmental and property right hurdles. To store the $CO_2$ in coal-plant emissions, the carbon must be separated from other gases such as nitrogen, a costly and energy-intensive process (Peña, 2008: 15). Equally important, a large apparatus for careful monitoring and regulation would be necessary. Finally, the safety of geologic sequestration of $CO_2$ and other greenhouse gases is in doubt while public acceptance of all this is unlikely. This "clean coal" lobby resembles the technocratic boosters of American nuclear power, who also claim cheap and safe outcomes. The only difference is that nuclear power is, in fact, cleaner than any form of coal power and its derivatives.
- A third discussion of "clean coal" accents the possible production and use of hydrogen as a by-product ("coal-to-hydrogen conversion gasifier-related technologies," Management Information Services, 2008: 59). The idea is that hydrogen can be produced by the thermal decomposition of coal to syngas (a mixture of mostly $H_2$, CO, and $CO_2$), which can be reformed to $CO_2$ and $H_2$ by reacting the syngas with water vapor at high temperature; and that hydrogen can substitute for petroleum in a new hydrogen age. Aside from the previous comparison of the near-double cost per gallon of gasoline from coal vs. a gallon from oil, the safe and efficient transportation of hydrogen to a nonexistent infrastructure is a nightmare. This light and leaky gas is difficult, dangerous, and costly to transport to scattered users even if an expensive infrastructure for use developed. Steel pipes as carriers become brittle and burst when hydrogen is pressured into them, and if not under pressure, the hydrogen is no longer economically viable. Using alternative materials would require a new and expensive network of pipes. Further, the idea that fuel cells that rely on the controlled interaction of hydrogen and oxygen can extract electricity to power everything begs the question of where the hydrogen comes from – most likely fossil fuel with the usual $CO_2$ emissions.[17]

Even some boosters of coal-to-liquid plants admit that they are carbon dioxide factories that produce energy on the side (*Wall Street Journal*, Aug. 16, 2002). The minimum implication for public policy: adopt a moratorium on building any more coal-fired power plants until we have proven technology to capture and sequester the $CO_2$ safely and the total costs are lower than those of alternative fuels.

## E. CORN-BASED ETHANOL, NO; OTHER BIOFUELS, YES

If the folly of expanding coal is not enough, we can look at the campaign for corn-based ethanol for a second case. To make a long story short, when the U.S. corn lobby successfully sold the idea, the secondary effects were bad for both the economy and the environment. Corn-based ethanol takes a great deal of energy to produce: energy costs for pesticides and fertilizer to grow the crop; further energy to process it; costs of making and running the farm machinery; erosion and deforestation as by-products; and the need for new infrastructure apart from gasoline pipelines to move this form of ethanol to retailers (Somerville, 2007: R116; Peña, 2008: 3; cf. Pimentel and Patzek, 2005: 65–66). In some regions, where irrigation prevails, it also uses scarce water.[18] That corn producers are heavy users of nitrogen fertilizer leads to the contamination (specifically eutrophication) of waterways, notably the dead zone in the Gulf. (Marine scientists have identified more than 400 such dead zones from the coasts of China to Chesapeake Bay; they periodically or perpetually exhibit oxygen-starved bottom waters. The primary cause is agricultural runoff.)

Most costly for average citizens, the corn diverted to ethanol generates an increase in the price of corn and food based on corn – eggs, meat, poultry, cooking oil, corn syrup, and more. Corn provides the primary animal feed in the United States and Europe and staple foods in Central and South America such as tamales and tortillas. When presidents Carter in 1978, Reagan in 1983–1984, and Bush in 2005–2007 pushed large subsidies for corn ethanol and minimum requirements for ethanol in gasoline, the price of corn futures skyrocketed. When farmers moved to the ethanol solution – with about 100 plants in operation by 2005 – a broad range of food prices rose. Because U.S. corn exports account for nearly two-thirds of the global trade in corn (U.S. Department of Agriculture, 2009), increases in U.S. corn prices are a drag on the budgets of many of the world's households, forcing hundreds of millions, especially urban masses, to buy cheaper junk food, with their long-run effects on health costs. As oil prices declined, the demand for corn-based ethanol also declined. Yet, even in the recession years of 2008–2009 when many ethanol plants shut down, corn prices remained relatively high (*New York Times*, Feb. 12, 2009).[19] In fact, largely due to demand for corn for ethanol, U.S. corn prices in 2007–2008 went up to a record high of $5.12 a bushel; the range before 2007 was $2.00 to 3.25 a bushel (*E & E News*, Jan. 14, 2008).

That corn-based ethanol is a bad idea for energy production does not mean that all biofuels are destructive. A major research and development strategy with early payoffs concentrates on cellulosic ethanol. Production facilities in the United States are currently in development; they are as yet small and scattered. The Energy Biosciences Institute at Berkeley focuses on developing cellulosic biofuels based on dedicated energy crops. The crops chosen offer a net decline in greenhouse gases, are adapted to rain-fed production, create little or no erosion, and do not compete directly with food crops and animal feed – for example, straw and perennial grasses such as switchgrass and Miscanthus, just the opposite of using corn or soybeans to make ethanol. Abandoned land where carbon has already been emitted is abundant; about a billion acres are available worldwide for potential production of cellulosic biofuels that are cheap and solve the problem of emissions. A side benefit of using abandoned and degraded land is that the production of feedstocks for biofuels can build soil fertility and water retention capacity while improving habitat and biodiversity (Peña, 2008: 15).

A sign of accelerated commercial development is the investment in extracting biofuels from plants ($250–$300 million) by the formerly cash-rich energy giant BP PLC. Before its deepwater oil-drilling catastrophe in the Gulf, it had planned to build the world's largest cellulosic biofuels production facility in Florida, using grasses. BP has partnered with a small U.S. firm based in Cambridge, Mass., Verenium, that makes ethanol from sugarcane stalks in Louisiana (*Wall Street Journal*, Feb. 19, 2009: B1). It also planned a major expansion of its joint venture in sugarcane ethanol with Brazil, where the infrastructure and auto fleet are ready to use it (*Wall Street Journal*, Apr. 27, 2009). If BP will be paying for its damage to the ecosystem and economy of the Gulf for years ahead, it may put these plans on hold or abandon them. Other big oil companies, flush with capital and not yet on the congressional investigation frying pan, have also invested modest amounts in biofuels R&D (*Wall Street Journal*, Dec. 30, 2009). The lesson here is not that dyed-in-the-wool oilmen will ever take the lead in alternative energy development. It is instead that the worst greenhouse gas emitters have enormous resources that can be tapped with a well-designed carbon tax. They can be faced with incentives to invest in biofuels and other clean alternatives as they have already begun to do on a small scale.

A strong public commitment and funding comparable to past subsidies for coal and oil and highways, however, is essential for serious progress. The clean energy potential of biofuels from plants is enormous (Somerville, 2007: 118–119; Houghton, Weatherwax, and Ferrell, 2006; Peña, 2008).

Many areas of the globe already face acute water shortages and many popular alternatives to the dominant emitters of greenhouse gases are intensive water users. For instance, the "new unconventional" fossil fuels promoted by the relevant industries – oil sands, natural gas found in coal beds, shale, and tight sands, and carbon capture and storage – as well as nuclear power and food-based ethanol all require water-intensive methods for production. Even hydro-electric power consumes water; more water evaporates from dammed reservoirs than from naturally flowing water systems. Current research on cellulosic biofuels aims to develop processing technologies that are nonaqueous and use less cooling water. If such research on water-efficient cellulosics from rain-fed land pays off, that would be another reason to allocate more resources to this type of biofuel. The pending water wars give urgency to research that reduces the water footprint of alternative energy sources.

A word about the complex role of manure and urban waste in a green energy policy: the technology for capturing biogas (methane and $CO_2$) from manure to produce electricity is quite well developed. It is widely used in Europe to good effect. Beyond the energy recovered, combustion of the biogas in a generator significantly reduces greenhouse gas from manure because $CO_2$ (the product of methane combustion) has about 24-fold less impact than methane. Similarly, the technology to capture biogas from urban waste to produce electricity is mature and is beginning to be used in the United States. In addition to anaerobic digestion of urban waste to produce biogas, scientists are exploring technologies for direct combustion to produce steam for electricity as well as other forms of bioprocessing to fuels or power. On the downside are difficult technical challenges: the chemical complexity of urban waste streams and the need to ensure that toxins in them are contained. If we can remove toxic materials such as heavy metals in some types of batteries and light bulbs already widely used and discourage their further distribution, that would facilitate the constructive use of urban waste.

Finally, as Peña points out (2008: 12), Europe and the United States are more likely than developing areas to produce biomass for energy on land that has already been converted. Their conversion-related emissions occurred in the past. For instance, in the Northern Hemisphere only about a fifth of land remains in forests; in the Southern Hemisphere the figure is 40 percent. This fact reinforces my theme that the rich democracies must lead the fight against global warming, with each country responsible for the life-cycle GHG emissions of the biofuels it uses. Obviously the rich also have the capital to develop and deploy the necessary new technology.

## F. SUMMARY AND INTERPRETATION: THE INTERDEPENDENCE OF POLICIES

Efficiency in the use of energy as a first step is the surest, quickest way to tackle current dependence on oil, coal, gas, and nuclear in both the short run and the long run. If a carbon tax upstream acts as an incentive to make cars, home appliances, homes, and workplaces more efficient, the need for current levels of imported oil, coal-fired plants, and expensive and problematic nuclear plants diminishes.[20] If public incentives and investment in rapid urban transit and intercity railroads are big enough, the need for existing carbon-emitting transportation will diminish. If we rely on wind and solar, they both depend on backup production and storage of energy from other sources when the wind dies down and the sun stops shining. And they both require better access to an electric grid not now designed for them. The antiquated grid of the United States requires major modifications.[21]

If in the next few years when the technology for plug-in electric and hybrid autos and trucks improves and the cost goes down, there is urgent need to improve the sources of the increased demand for electricity now. Plug-ins may provide little gain in emission control if coal-fired plants supply the electricity (Kliesch and Langer, 2006: iii; Samaras and Meisterling, 2008: 3173). A robust low-carbon electricity supply is essential for net gains from new car technologies. Timing is crucial: if we fail to invest the resources to speed up the development of alternatives, fossil fuels, especially coal, will dominate world energy supply into the 22nd century, as Lackner and Sachs predict (2005: 228). If, as Brazil sensibly develops sugarcane-based ethanol to run its cars and reduce greenhouse emissions, it simultaneously destroys valuable forests to make way for cattle breeding or sugarcane cultivation, the gain in clean energy may be limited by deforestation of the Western Amazon.[22] The Brazilian government now has a plan to halt deforestation (Gore testimony at U.S. Senate Foreign Relations Com., Jan. 28, 2009). If Mitsubishi, Nissan, Sumitoma, BMW, Ford, GM, and others roll out electric cars powered by long-lasting lithium-ion batteries or lithium-air batteries as they plan to do within a few years and the demand for this mineral sharply rises, we will face a serious political problem: almost half the world's supply is in Bolivia. One of the least-developed countries in Latin America, Bolivia is led by President Evo Morales. Mr. Morales believes that foreign investors are imperialists and have no role other than client or maybe minority partner; he aspires to make Bolivia the Saudi Arabia of lithium. Still there are untapped supplies of lithium in Chile, Argentina, Tibet, and the United States (*New York Times*, Feb. 3, 2009). Further, if the supply of lithium from all sources is too limited as crucial battery technology develops, alternative technologies are under development: ferrous-ion batteries by BYD, an auto company in China, and zinc-air batteries by Toyota.[23]

In short, the interdependence of public policies and the evidence of acceleration of global warming suggest that each nation must act simultaneously on several fronts so that gains from one policy, one incentive, are not undermined by losses from another. The rich countries of North America and Europe must lead while they try to work with the two coal giants, China and India. International agreements involving scores of countries – rich, poor, and developing alike – may be too politically difficult, too long in coming, and too cumbersome in administration to achieve much. No rich country, least of all the United States, can use the need for world agreements as an excuse for stalling.

Many critics of the essential components of a green energy policy worry that a carbon tax on fossil fuels that increases their cost hits low-income families hardest, at least in the short run. Others suggest that although a green economy might create many jobs in a new solar or wind or rail industry, at the same time it loses many jobs in the shrinking coal-mining and auto industries. Or a green economy that rebuilds the energy infrastructure, including a unified, smart electrical grid and energy-efficient buildings, gives jobs to the already skilled – for example, the building trades, architects, civil and electrical engineers; the least-educated workers remain where they are. (For a detailed account of jobs lost and gained by a shift to green economy see Chapter 6.) Environmental economists argue that these inegalitarian effects can be offset by using carbon tax revenues to cut payroll taxes or fund means-tested benefits to the poor or a lump-sum rebate (Metcalf, 2008; Metcalf et al., 2008: 34–39). Unfortunately, it is difficult enough politically to carry out a green energy strategy without also undermining the main revenues that support Social Security, Medicare, and disability insurance. Far superior is a two-track approach: use all or most revenues from a carbon tax to help fund R&D for innovative green technology; keep the fight against poverty and inequality separate. That means tackling poverty and inequality by the taxing, spending, and policy packages outlined in my cross-national comparison of the welfare state, labor standards, and job security – in the United States such measures would include school reform, especially preschool and K–12, an active labor-market policy, a family policy, national health insurance, wage subsidies, and a restoration of labor's right to organize. These can be adopted in either a green economy or a gray economy. I return to the politics of these policies in Chapters 7 and 8.

The argument that intelligent, timely action on climate change subverts economic performance or increases inequality finds no support in this chapter. The cases of Denmark and Sweden show that economic prowess, equality, and policy packages that sharply reduce both greenhouse gases and dependence on fossil fuels are all compatible.

Underlying all promising energy policy reforms are large and sustained funding for research and development that will hasten breakthrough technologies and for startup subsidies to make a market for green products and processes.[24]

# 3

## What Trade-Offs Are Good and Bad for the Economy?

### Domestic Structures and Policies That Permit Adaptation to Globalization

As we have seen in our discussion of national variations in the welfare state and equality, as well as differences in energy policy and performance, types of political economy shape national responses to common global challenges, such as oil shocks and environmental degradation. These national variations can also provide an answer to the puzzle that corporatist big spenders on average have done better or as well as the fragmented decentralized lean spenders in economic performance; they have also flexibly adapted to external shocks (see Tables 3 and 4). The puzzle is solved by the trade-offs facilitated by both social spending and the national bargaining patterns institutionalized in the more consensual democracies.

Figure 2 shows the causal model I used for regression analysis of economic performance. It singles out one of the three types of bargaining arrangements among major economic and political actors without reference to the five types in Table 1, using numerical scores instead. The inverse of the policies and outcomes in Figure 1 are typical of the confrontational systems of the fragmented and decentralized political economies.

### A. CONSENSUAL VS. CONFRONTATIONAL DEMOCRACIES

The historical sequence of sources of democratic corporatism begins with various forms of proportional representation (PR) – the root cause of the great differences between the 13 countries that adopted this electoral system between 1855 and 1920 and the 6 that had the British Westminster system of "majoritarian" first-past-the-post, winner-take-all elections.[1] With the spread of the franchise came the increasing challenge of labor or socialist and Catholic movements and parties to incumbent Conservative and Liberal parties. Both incumbent powers and challengers had strong motives to adopt PR. Facing the rise of mass-based movements and parties whose increasing electoral success threatened their dominance, the incumbents, anxious about gradual erosion if not extinction, saw PR as a means of ensuring their continued representation in government and as a way to tame the rising militants. In turn, Catholic and left

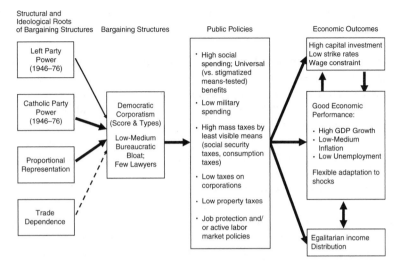

FIGURE 2. Causal model for regression analyses of the major sources of economic performance, 19 rich democracies.

parties, unsure that they would ever reach an electoral majority, also saw PR as their ticket to assured representation. In short, conditions for the PR compromise were ripe. And by 1920 all the countries that now use PR had adopted it.[2]

The PR compromise, in fact, facilitated the rise of parliamentary mass-based left parties (e.g., Socialist, Labor, Social Democratic) and Catholic parties (e.g., Christian Democratic, Social Christian, Christian Socialist). Two explanations of why PR led to a second compromise, the move toward democratic corporatism, are persuasive. First is the effect of PR on styles of governance. Second is the overlapping ideologies anchored in left and Catholic parties that they carried into power.

Students of comparative politics have presented much empirical evidence to show that PR systems have almost all had a benign effect over long periods: they have fostered coalition building and a politics of moderation; and they are a major facilitating stimulus to consensual bargaining among interest groups, parties, and the state (Dahl, 1966; Wilensky, 1981; Bogdanor, 1983: 248–253; Lijphart, 1984, 1990, 1991). In James Madison's words, they have limited "the mischiefs of faction" (1787). The reasons are these: if a strong minority emerges and has no hope of parliamentary representation, it is likely to spend its time purifying its doctrine, finding extraparliamentary means of protest, and training its cadres for militant action (political strikes, street demonstrations, riots). Under PR small minorities stand a good chance of winning representation or, better, becoming a minority party in a governing coalition. This prospect entices them into accommodation to moderate agendas. Instead of pursuing maximal unnegotiable demands, they spend their time bargaining with other parties about policies that might actually be enacted and implemented; they prepare for the moment of real power. Larger parties in decline, for their part, are open to coalition building because PR assures them of a soft landing on the way down. Although they will never win an absolute majority of parliamentary seats, they will be assured of a substantial number and, better, can hope for possible dominance of centrist coalitions. By promoting the inclusion of labor, the Left, and minority groups, by making government more representative of the preferences of the voting public, PR fosters the habit of consensual bargaining conducive to democratic corporatism.

Table 6 is unequivocal about this connection: all the clear cases of democratic corporatism have PR systems; one marginal case (Germany) and two cases of corporatism without labor (France, Japan) have mixed systems; the fragmented, decentralized democracies, with the sole exception of Ireland, do not have PR.

Second, and not so obvious, although left and Catholic doctrines are diverse, political history provides abundant illustration of their functional equivalence, including many episodes of ideological and structural convergence. It is true that Catholic parliamentary groups, drawing on medieval and romantic themes, have often been conservative or reactionary. Nevertheless, the rise of Social Christian and particularly Catholic workers' movements in Belgium, the Netherlands, Germany, Italy, and France pushed European Catholic politicians toward the left. For many decades they have increasingly emphasized support of free labor unions, labor legislation, social security, and an economic order based on industrial self-government and worker participation in management, ownership, and profits, with close collaboration between unions and employer associations. Opportunities for alliances with leftists opened up. For instance, in Germany during the 1920s a Catholic minister of labor, Father Heinrich Brauns, was responsible for vanguard progressive social legislation; the context was intermittent coalition between the Social Democratic Party (SPD) and the Center Party. Similarly, after World War I Belgium saw a variety of coalition governments: Catholic-Liberal-Socialist, Catholic-Liberal, Catholic-Socialist. But through them all, as Fogarty suggests, "the Catholic Party remained the pivot, and a steady stream of political and social reforms came forward" (1957: 299).

What contemporary socialists and Catholics have in common, aside from their desire to attain and maintain power, is a traditional humanistic concern with the lower strata, which has its roots in the early modern era. In the continental Catholic case, we find that Catholic humanists of the 16th century had considerable influence on the approach of urban businessmen and lawyers to their urban crisis and the poor, both "deserving" and "undeserving." Lyon provides one of the many examples of a religious coalition for welfare reform dominated by Catholics. In 1532, the French cleric and humanist Jean de Vauzelles urged the notables of Lyon to introduce sweeping welfare measures including training and education for poor children, the recognition of the right of unemployables to support, and a central treasury administered by laymen (N. Davis, 1968). The contemporary expression of this Christian concern is evident in passages on welfare, poverty, and labor in the "social" Encyclicals of popes Leo XIII, Pius XI, and John XXIII, as well as in the activism of social-minded priests.

TABLE 6. *The Interplay of Left and Catholic Party Power, Proportional Representation, and Trade Dependence as Sources of Corporatism*

| | Political Structures | | | Trade Dependence | | | |
|---|---|---|---|---|---|---|---|
| | Party Power 1920–76 | | | Exports as a Percent of GNP | | | |
| Type of Political Economy | Left | Catholic | Electoral System: PR | 1880–1913 | 1920–29 | 1930–39 | 1950–60 |
| **Left corporatist** | | | | | | | |
| Sweden | H 114 | L 0 | 1.0 | 18.2 (5) | 16.1 (10) | 14.1 (9) | 20.5 (8) |
| Norway | H 73 | L 0 | 1.0 | 17.1 (6) | 16.6 (9) | 14.0 (10) | 20.8 (7) |
| Finland | M 50 | L 0 | 1.0 | – | – | – | 20.0 (9) |
| Israel | H 138 | L 0 | 1.0 | – | – | – | 7.1 (18) |
| Denmark | H 87 | L 0 | 1.0 | 22.0 (3) | 27.2 (4) | 21.8 (3) | 26.8 (4) |
| **Left-Catholic corporatist** | | | | | | | |
| Netherlands | ML 31 | H 79 | 1.0 | 101.7 (1) | 28.5 (3) | 19.2 (4) | 36.2 (1) |
| Belgium | M 42 | H 105 | 1.0 | – | 49.9 (1) | 34.0 (2) | 31.7 (2) |
| Austria | M 39 | H 88 | 1.0 | – | 18.6 (8) | 10.9 (12) | 17.8 (12) |
| **Catholic corporatist** | | | | | | | |
| Italy | L 0 | H 82 | 1.0 | 8.8 (11) | 8.9 (14) | 6.0 (15) | 10.3 (16) |
| West Germany | ML 30 | H 71 | 0.5 | 15.1 (9) | 14.9 (12) | 9.3 (13) | 14.9 (14) |
| **Corporatist without labor** | | | | | | | |
| France | L 7 | LM 7 | 0.5 | – | – | – | 12.3 (15) |
| Japan | L 0 | L 0 | 0.5 | 11.8 (10) | 13.9 (13) | 16.3 (7) | 9.2 (17) |
| Switzerland | L 0 | L 0 | 1.0 | 34.7 (2) | 23.2 (5) | 12.8 (11) | 21.9 (6) |
| **Least corporatist** | | | | | | | |
| United States | H 98 | L 0 | 0.0 | 6.7 (12) | 5.8 (15) | 3.4 (16) | 4.2 (19) |
| United Kingdom | M 47 | L 0 | 0.0 | 15.6 (7) | 15.8 (11) | 8.8 (14) | 18.0 (10) |
| New Zealand | H 60 | L 0 | 0.0 | – | – | 35.2 (1) | 27.1 (3) |
| Australia | ML 35 | L 0 | 0.0 | 21.8 (4) | 19.1 (7) | 16.5 (6) | 16.6 (13) |
| Canada | L 0 | L 0 | 0.0 | 15.1 (9) | 22.4 (6) | 16.2 (8) | 17.9 (11) |
| Ireland | L 0 | L 0 | 1.0 | – | 29.1 (2) | 17.8 (5) | 23.6 (5) |

*Note*: See Appendix for definitions of concepts and measures used in this table.

In short, both Catholic and left parties were sympathetic to the idea of corporatist bargaining arrangements among social partners; in the language of the Lisbon strategy of 2000, they valued social cohesion.

The architects of PR modified it with several devices to discourage very minor parties and splinter movements. But nearly pure PR appears in three exceptional cases – Denmark, Netherlands, and Israel – and all three evidenced political trouble along with Italy, which abandoned its pure form in 1993. Proportional representation is like patent medicine: a proper dose is good for your political health; an overdose can kill you.

It is significant that all of these powerful forces are internal, institutional, and national. Tests of their relative importance show that PR is by far the most important source of corporatism; Catholic power is a close second. Left power is a less important explanation, largely because since World War I left parties are much more frequently thrown out than Catholic parties, and the duration of left power is rarely long. With rare exceptions, left power without PR has little lasting effect on anything. Even if a left party chalks up many years of power (e.g., the Democratic Party in the United States, the Labour Party in New Zealand), in the absence of PR and the coalition politics it fosters and without channels for national bargaining among the social partners, a center-left agenda is hard to enact and even harder to implement. Under those conditions, the risk of policy reversal is substantial when right-wing parties take over; one step forward, one step backward. (For analysis of what it would take to enact a center-left agenda in the United States, see Chapter 8.)

Regarding trade dependence, the results are unequivocal. If we delete the Netherlands and Belgium as extreme cases – the two most dependent on trade for at least a century – export dependence fades as a source of corporatism when any two of the other variables are included. In other words, the hypothesis that the external shock of heavy dependence on fluctuating world markets inspires government, labor, management, and political parties to get their internal act together because they live or die only by agreements on ways to enhance productivity and export prowess finds no support.[3]

That trade dependence had so little effect on national bargaining arrangements suggests strong limits on the impact of globalization, which are discussed at length in Chapter 6.

Once these consensual bargaining arrangements were in place – all by 1950 or so – center-left and center-right coalitions were inevitable. Such accommodative interaction of left power, Catholic power, and corporatism, in turn, produced scores of social, economic, and labor-market policies, some of which facilitated trade-offs favorable to good economic performance (see Figure 2).

To oversimplify, here are the main trade-offs in these more or less centralized bargaining systems.

1. *Labor embraces restraint on nominal wages in return for social security and related programs based on social rights and modest increases in real wages.* The payoff to labor is increases in the "social wage" by universal

categorical benefits. Such benefits and services are a substitute for means-tested benefits like public assistance. The distinction between divisive, highly visible means testing and simple, quiet income testing is important. By "means testing" I mean (1) noncategorical benefits targeted to the poor via a stiff income and/or assets test, (2) applied by welfare administrators with substantial discretion, (3) with a high probability of stigma. "Income testing" is the opposite. It is categorical as a social right with copayments graded by income bracket and, because it is private and invisible, has no stigma. Means testing is characteristic of Britain and other decentralized and fragmented political economies (the United States, Canada, Ireland); democratic corporatist countries, especially those with cumulative left party power, avoid means testing and rely much more on income testing (Wilensky, 2002: 321–332). In fact, they are alternative policy packages that are strongly and negatively correlated.

2. *Employers provide job protection in return for wage restraint, labor peace, and sometimes tax concessions* (e.g., lower taxes on corporations and capital gains). A *high strike rate* – one of the most robust variables explaining poor economic performance – is a proxy for poorly managed industrial relations systems. Strikes are related to other forms of industrial conflict at the workplace: sabotage, slowdowns, output restriction, absenteeism, tardiness, playing dumb, quits, and grievance activity. Both strikes and associated job actions create bottlenecks and other inefficiencies, forestall managerial initiatives, and thereby increase unit costs and reduce economic performance (Flaherty, 1987a, 1987b; Norsworthy and Zabala, 1985: 557; and Hodson, 1995, 1997).

Systematic comparative studies for *job protection* are few but there are numerous case studies of management concessions either coerced by labor movements and government or voluntarily given – ranging from accounts of lifetime employment in large firms in Japan to Western European laws and contracts that enhance job security (e.g., Emerson, 1988; ILO, 1995; OECD, 1997), and several systematic comparisons of "labor rigidities" of Europe vs. the United States and within Europe (Nickell, 1997). What such studies suggest is that job security facilitates the rapid introduction and effectiveness of new technology by reducing labor resistance to change and tapping the know-how of workers; it reduces the costs of turnover and encourages management to invest in on-the-job training (ILO, 1995: 172–173, 180, table 22). Like payroll taxes, job security has no effect on unemployment (Nickell, 1997: 66; Wilensky, 2002, chs. 1 and 18).

Regarding *tax concessions to employers* as a labor or government trade-off to compensate management, the measure is taxes on corporate income, profits, and capital gains. The negative correlations between corporatist scores and corporate taxes as a percentage of total revenue range from -.45 to -.55 from 1955 to 1977 but fade to insignificance thereafter. The effect of such taxes on economic performance is negligible;

if we eliminate Japan from the 19 countries (it had by far the highest reliance on corporate income and profits taxes during the entire period of its excellent economic performance), then we find no relationship between these taxes and economic performance.

3. *Employers provide participatory democracy in the workplace or community in return for labor peace and wage constraint.* A case in point: the German local works councils and national co-determination combined with regional collective bargaining that is coordinated by centralized unions and employer associations setting a broad framework – at least until 1989, when the huge and continuing burden of unification combined with recession and a procyclical monetary policy made Germany the "sick man of Europe." Several countries (e.g., Belgium, Sweden, Denmark, Finland) provide channels for worker and union leader participation in tripartite boards administering parts of the welfare state – medical insurance, unemployment and accident insurance, and pensions (Wilensky, 2002, chs. 2 and 5).

4. *In return for all of the above, the government improves its tax-extraction capacity.* Comparing the tax structures of the 19 rich democracies, I encountered a paradox: the corporatist democracies that fully integrate labor and the left in high policy end up with tax structures that management and center-right parties favor. Thus, both labor and the government tolerate low taxes on either capital gains or profits and avoid property taxes. Previous research (2002: ch. 10) suggests that these tax trade-offs are good for the economy. The government improves public acceptance of taxes on consumption – not irrelevant to reduction of inflation and government deficits. Thus, the combination of high VAT and social-security taxes is a moderately positive contribution to high scores on my economic performance index before 1974 (although it is insignificant after). My findings also suggest that in contrast to taxes on capital gains or profits, property taxes may be a drag on economic performance in all periods. Reliance on property taxes is characteristic of the more fragmented and decentralized democracies.

5. *With the habit of making such trade-offs and faced with strong labor movements, management in the more corporatist democracies tends to join labor in the implementation of a wide range of policies. The result: less intrusive regulation and more effective implementation of laws and executive orders.* Thus, the complaint that Western Europe is hyperregulated and hyperprotected whereas America has an excellent ability to adapt ignores evidence on types of regulation and regulatory styles. The paradox that the most decentralized political economies with the most liberal (free-market) ideologies – for example, the United States – have the most rigid and intrusive regulations can be explained by the weakness of the structure and political power of labor and the absence of channels for collaboration among labor, management, and the state. (I return to regulatory regimes when dealing with the U.S. model in Part II.)

Some students of comparative political economy strongly argue that all this is outmoded, that these advantages of the trade-offs facilitated by democratic corporatism pictured in Figure 2 are dinosaurs from the days before globalization and economic austerity emerged. They suggest that these negotiated economies suffer from bureaucratic rigidity and cannot adapt to changing economic circumstances, that if they are not collapsing, they are giving way to sectoral bargaining by industry or locality, that they face rank-and-file revolts as they fail to deliver benefits for labor, that they require left dominance for their persistence and are therefore unstable, that they bypass and thereby weaken parties and parliamentary democracy, and that globalization sounds their doom.

In my view, these highly institutionalized bargaining arrangements – and the structures of labor, industry, political, and electoral systems and parties that created them – change only gradually and that, while some of them have eroded (Sweden, the Netherlands), others evidence little change (Austria, Norway, Denmark) or have been strengthened (Finland). The name of the game is negotiated adaptation.

The argument that national bargaining arrangements are giving way to sectoral arrangements goes like this: such industries as auto, electronics, steel, chemicals, dairy, and the securities industry develop their own rules, networks, values, and interests – in short, their own system of governance (cf. Hollingsworth, Schmitter, and Streeck, 1994; and Kitschelt, 1991). As economists have noted since Adam Smith, there are, indeed, big differences in economic organization and performance by industrial sector. But whenever comparative analysts have tried to play economic sectors against national patterns of political economy as determinants of outcomes in politics, economies, and welfare, the latter typically win out (evidence and citations reviewed in Wilensky, 2002: 108–109). In other words, national institutional contexts overwhelm sectoral peculiarities. Of course, some sectors within consensual societies are full of conflict and some sectors within decentralized, fragmented, and polarized systems are consensual, but the central tendency, the major contrasts, are national, not sectoral.

The second reason suggested for the sure erosion of consensual bargaining is that corporatist democracies are rigid and bureaucratic and (a related argument) a technocratic threat to democratic accountability. Although corporatist bargaining processes have a technocratic cast, this does not transform political into technical decisions. A prime minister who walks into a room flanked by his or her staff experts to bargain with equally well-staffed management and labor leaders does not forget his or her political base; neither do the bargaining partners. As for bureaucratic rigidities, Chapter 1 has shown that the corporatist democracies respond to external oil and other shocks more flexibly and quickly than do fragmented and decentralized political economies.

Third, it is asserted that because of economic constraints since the early 1970s neither the government nor employers can deliver the continual harvest of benefits (wages, job security, social security, participation in policy decisions in workplace and community) that has sustained consensus and permitted labor leaders to embrace labor peace, wage restraint, and government tax policies and to cooperate on productivity, labor flexibility, and tax breaks for management – the trade-offs already discussed. This inspires rank-and-file protest against the unfavorable bargains their leaders obtain. Thus, it is alleged, worker disaffection is proliferating, and corporatist democracy is fast disappearing. There are three answers to this dire picture: (1) Corporatist democracies provide stronger and more meaningful channels for participation of union members and the general citizenry than the fragmented and decentralized democracies (evidence in Wilensky, 2002: 140–143). Lively participation in broad-based associations provides a prop for continuity; such participation patterns do not fall off because economic constraints appear. (2) The range of economic and noneconomic gains for labor is wide, the kinds of benefits numerous. Often low-cost gains (e.g., expanded participation in managerial decisions, pay for knowledge, flexible schedules) can be substituted for high-cost gains (big increases in wages or pensions).[4] (3) Habits of accommodation among the social partners are of long standing and have survived crises of the past. If we examine the recent developments in the two cases that have evidenced most decline in the strength of bargaining arrangements – Sweden and the Netherlands – we can see that continual adaptation through negotiation is a better concept than collapse or even erosion (pp. 110–116).

The fourth theme in the literature on the demise of corporatism suggests that when the bargaining partners interact with one another and the executive branch of government, they bypass and thus weaken political parties and parliamentary democracy. The mass base for the legitimacy of corporatist democracy therefore erodes. The evidence shows the opposite: corporatism either strengthens political parties or retards their decline (Wilensky, 2002: ch. 11).

The fifth theme is that democratic corporatism requires left dominance and cannot survive the new weakness of left parties since the 1970s. Aside from the fact that in 13 of 15 governments of the European Union (EU) in early 1999 left parties either dominated or were part of center-left governments (Sferza, 1999), a later section of this chapter shows that Catholic party power or alternating Catholic and left-dominated coalitions are stronger predictors of corporatist continuity than left power alone. And the Japanese style of corporatism flourished for decades with little labor-left power.

The final, most strongly argued, theme about threats to the survival of these consensus-making machines is that globalization undermines the economic base for the necessary trade-offs. This is a restatement of the third theme – economic constraints rooted in increased competition subvert the social partners' capacity to accommodate their conflicting interests. Chapter 6 analyzes each of the dimensions of globalization that might undermine labor standards, job security, and the welfare state. The only serious threat, I conclude, comes from the increasing power and ideology of central banks and the internationalization of finance. Adaptation to this threat, like the response to other external shocks, nevertheless varies by the national institutions, politics, and policies in place.

One structural shift that adds strain to corporatist bargaining is the universal increase in the percentage of union members in white-collar unions, especially in public service. It is clear that the interests of government employees at times diverge from the interests of private-sector workers. Public employees, for instance, have an obvious interest in raising taxes to finance expanding government programs; blue-collar workers in manufacturing do not always see it that way. But labor movements, like political parties, have always embraced groups of workers with diverse values and interests – high seniority workers vs. low, skilled vs. unskilled, immigrants vs. natives, minority groups vs. dominant groups, men vs. women, and so on – with fluctuating success in creating solidarity among them. The capacity of labor, management, and government to cope with internal cleavages as well as external shocks varies cross-nationally.

## B. WHICH OF THE SOURCES OF GOOD ECONOMIC PERFORMANCE ARE MOST IMPORTANT?

Tables 3 and 4 have given an overview of the interplay of types of political economy and dichotomies for aggregate level of social spending/GDP and vulnerability to energy shocks, as predictors of economic performance of each country in various periods. This section presents the main conclusions from multivariate analysis, including extensive multiple regression analysis testing those relationships for which we had appropriate data on almost all or all of the 19 countries; these variables appear in Figure 2 in the boxes on public policies and economic outcomes. We used three independent variables at a time in all possible combinations for each period. Here are the results, consistent with all cross-tabulations. First, the proximate causes:

- The most important sources of good economic performance for both the economic performance index and its components are *corporatist bargaining arrangements* (with or without the full integration of labor) and related public policies that foster *low strike rates* (a clue to effective industrial relations systems), *a high rate of gross fixed capital investment* and *wage restraint in shock periods*. The two most consistently robust variables are strike rates and capital investment; either one or the other or both have major effects no matter what is added to the equation. If we ignore history – the causal sequence in Figure 1 – one or the other of these powerful variables consistently predicts more of the variance in the economy than corporatism, leftism, Catholicism, spending or taxing levels or types, or external shocks. The regressions show that capital investment has a positive effect because it increases growth (1965–1974, 1974–1979, and 1980–1984) and lowers unemployment (1965–1974, 1974–1979, and 1985–1989 but not after the second oil shock 1980–1984).[5] And high strike rates have a negative effect because they increase unemployment (1950–1974, 1965–1974, 1974–1979, and 1980–1984) or increase inflation (1974–1979, 1980–1984, and 1985–1989), or both.

- *The crucial importance of labor peace in this analysis is underscored by this finding: of our significant sources of high scores on both the index and its components – strikes, capital investment, corporatism numerical score, Catholic party power, left party power, and social spending – strikes explain more variance in economic performance than all others in almost all equations. Even during the period of recovery in 1985–1989, strikes were consistently more of a drag than capital formation was a help (Wilensky, 2002: 459–461). And as we have seen, labor peace is a product of the trade-offs facilitated by consensual bargaining arrangements.*
- *Social Security spending (SS/GNP) and, to a lesser degree, social security per capita are positive forces for GDP growth 1950–1974 and the general index 1950–1974 but they are neutral after the early 1980s.* If strikes and capital formation are held constant, social spending remains significant in some equations. It is irrelevant to inflation and unemployment. The growth rate of social-security spending, either nominal or real, is not significant if Japan with very high growth in both social spending and its economy is excluded.

    *In no period and for no measure of performance is social-security spending a significant drag,* controlling for leftism, Catholicism, corporatism, capital investment, and strikes, the major sources of economic performance. Where we eliminate both Japan and Switzerland (they have the same unique pattern), social security has no significant effect in any equation, even for 1980–1984. This suggests two roads to good economic performance among the more consensual democracies: corporatism without labor with lean social spending, high capital investment, and low strikes, or corporatism with full inclusion of labor with generous social spending, high capital investment, and, most important, few man-days lost from strikes.

    The literature on the impact of the welfare state confirms this conclusion. In a careful review of the mixed and weak findings of nine studies of the economic impact of social spending on economic performance – most authored by economists – A. B. Atkinson (1995) concludes that none of them shows that the welfare state is a drag on economic growth, employment, or productivity. Similarly, recent research by economist Peter Lindert confirms the point; he shows that from 1980 to 2000 among modern democracies the net impact of social spending on the economy (i.e., GDP/person and growth) is close to zero (Lindert, 2004: vol. 1, ch. 10; vol. 2, chs. 18 and 19).

- *Although total social spending (SS/GNP) is either slightly positive or neutral for economic performance, the structure of spending counts.* The Anglo-American emphasis on stiff and stigmatized *means testing* of benefits and services not only increases tax-welfare backlash and makes it more difficult to finance government but *is a drag on economic performance* because it increases bureaucratic bloat, drains off investment, increases unemployment, and in 1980–1984 was a drag on growth. More important, both case studies and quantitative results show that *public spending on health care and a sensible organization and delivery of health care are positive* for long-run productivity and economic performance, not to mention poverty reduction and reduced inequality (Chapter 4; and Wilensky, 2002: ch. 16).

- Two other components of the welfare state are clearly positive trade-offs for passive policies that emphasize public assistance and unemployment insurance: an *active labor-market policy* (ALMP) and a *family policy*. ALMP includes job creation, apprenticeship training, incentives for on-the-job training and retraining, work-study programs, remedial programs to increase basic literacy and improve work habits, a strong labor-market board to match job seekers and job vacancies for everyone, mobility allowances, relocation assistance and rent supplements tied to mobility for workers trapped in depressed areas and industries, and more (Wilensky, 2002: 706–707 and fig. 2.2 listing 21 types of ALMP). Family policy (ch. 7) includes parental leave, paid and unpaid; child care; before- and after-school leisure centers; family allowances; rent supplements and housing assistance. It is designed to assure the care of children, increase gender equality, and balance parental demands of work and family. Both ALMP and family policy have incidental payoffs. They increase labor-force participation, avoid the feminization of poverty, reduce income inequality and, finally, increase long-run productivity. Sweden has led in both clusters of policies with good economic effects over decades. Chapter 8 suggests that politically these are the two policy clusters most easily transferred from abroad to the United States.

- *Wage restraint*, as a concession by labor, is important in periods of crisis. Although most corporatist democracies had higher wage increases before 1980 than their noncorporatist counterparts, when the shocks of 1974 and 1979–1982 hit, they resisted wage pressures and did better in controlling inflation for the five years after each shock. Regression analysis confirms the findings that restraint of nominal wages strongly reduces inflation in all periods but has no effects on unemployment or GDP growth and no effects on the general index for 1950–1974. In short, their accommodative bargaining gave corporatist democracies more flexibility in coping with external shocks.

- *Taxes*, with one deviant case of Italy, whose spending for long periods exceeded its tax collection, roughly match spending. Big spenders pay their way over the long run, or big taxers spend a lot, or both. From 1965 to 1988, the correlations between the corporatism score and total taxes/GDP range from .60 (1974) to .72 (1980 and 1988). The relationship is especially strong for corporatist democracies with strong left-party power in all periods (e.g., Denmark, Sweden, and Norway are among the top four taxers in all periods; two countries, with both left and Catholic power, the Netherlands and Austria, are among the top seven for all periods).

- *As a percentage of total taxes, the big taxers rely mainly on the least visible and least painful, least unpopular taxes – consumption taxes* (e.g., VAT) and *social-security taxes* (e.g., payroll taxes); as we have seen, they also *avoid heavy taxes on corporate income, profits, or capital gains*, although this relationship faded in the 1980s. Paradoxically, left corporatist regimes even in the 1990s were most friendly to business (Nørregaard and Owens, 1992). Apparently, the trade-offs made when labor is at the high-policy table for many years favor management; in return for payoffs in the "social wage," labor not only constrains wage demands but also supports tax breaks for management. In the absence of a steady labor influence (as in Japan, Australia, New Zealand, Canada, and the United Kingdom), the government turns to business as a source of revenue.

In any case, the main conclusion is that total taxes, like aggregate social spending, have little or no consistent effect on economic performance. But types of taxes, like types of social spending, are often important. *Sales and value-added taxes* remain *significant and positive for economic growth* after controlling for other variables *for 1950–1979*, with *positive impact on the broader index for 1965–1979*. These consumption taxes are consistently negatively related to strikes, whereas they are positively related to capital formation, which may explain why they are good for growth. There are no significant correlations between consumption taxes and inflation or unemployment, however, and no significant correlations with any performance measure in the 1980s.[6]

In short, relative to industrial relations systems and capital formation, the structure of taxes is only moderately or weakly related to economic performance, an effect that almost disappears in the 1980s. If we are concerned only with economic impact, consumption taxes and social security taxes were benign; income taxes, property taxes, and to a much less extent, corporate taxes, were a drag. And the general level of taxes had no effect at all. The tax-cutting obsession of Republican presidents Reagan and Bush and the Republican Congresses of 1994–2006 (and their echoes among conservatives in Europe) and the heated denials of their Democratic opponents that they are "tax-and-spend liberals" – even in the middle of the Great Recession of 2007–2009 – are, to say the least, misplaced.

Whatever their economic effects, the larger significance of these types of taxes is political: property taxes on households are a root cause of tax-welfare backlash movements and parties, which can paralyze a government to the point where it cannot raise necessary revenue for schools, infrastructure, R&D, and budget balancing or meet strong electoral demands for services. Increases in payroll taxes or VAT are similarly political; they are used in the trade-offs in agreements on welfare-state reform among the government, labor, and management. And in the history of tax strategies of consensual democracies, they arrived at an accent on payroll taxes and the VAT because their leaders understood that if they were to pay for the social and labor-market policies they favored, they needed tax balance – as a percent of total revenue, more reliance on the least painful taxes and less on income taxes and property taxes.

The lesson I draw from this history of sustained tax revolts and my interviews (Wilensky, 2002: ch. 10) is that modern voters cannot be mobilized to fight gradual tax increases if the tax take (aggregate revenue of all levels of government) is roughly about a third progressive income taxes, a third consumption taxes, and a third payroll taxes. Such a balanced tax structure may be proportional or even regressive but it raises enough revenue to protect and improve labor standards, job security, and social security, not only for the growing "middle class" but also for the poor. The resulting increase in income equality, security, and dignity reduces the politics of resentment. It also helps voters to realize that "there is no free lunch."

It is a great delusion of center-left Democrats in the United States that the road to equality is through progressive income taxes on individuals and corporations. In fact, politically that strategy severely limits the tax take. If you cannot raise government revenues for nonmilitary uses well beyond the 35 percent of GDP typical of the total counting all levels of American government, you cannot spend it for anything like a center-left agenda.

- *The most fragmented and decentralized democracies have a taste for property taxes.* Of our 19, the 7 top countries in property taxes as a percent of total revenue in all periods from 1965 to 1987 are the United States, the United Kingdom, New Zealand, Australia, Canada, Ireland, and the only corporatist democracy in that Anglo-American club, Denmark. Such taxes appear to be a drag on economic performance, but they are so highly correlated with the rest of our variables that also predict poor performance (Wilensky, 2002: 485–489) that I leave it aside here. Its greatest importance is as a proximate cause of tax revolts. In the years when strong tax-welfare backlash movements and parties emerged (ca. 1965–1975) and subsequently persisted, all the countries so afflicted ranked high in their reliance on property taxes on households – the United States, the United Kingdom, Denmark, and Switzerland.[7]

*What all these findings underscore is that aggregate public spending or social spending or total taxes or "social transfers" obscure the economic and political impact of particular sectors of spending and types of taxes as well as particular social and labor-market policies. Not only do these vary greatly among rich democracies, but some are productive, while others can easily be justified on noneconomic grounds (e.g., guaranteed pensions greatly reduce pretransfer poverty among the aged).*

# 4

## Retrenchment of the Welfare State?

*The Fate of "Cutback Budgeting" in Italy, France, Germany, the United States, the United Kingdom, and New Zealand*

I began by observing that "crisis" talk, however misleading, is universal. But has the action of governments matched the rhetoric of antispending campaigns? What cutbacks have actually occurred in the period of austerity after 1975 or 1980 when economic growth and productivity growth slowed down? With some exceptions, the core programs of the welfare state – pensions, disability insurance, and national health insurance, programs that have generally outpaced GDP growth – have proved most resistant to real cuts in benefits per capita or even in their GDP shares. Most vulnerable to real cuts or at least spending restraint have been education, social assistance, unemployment compensation, and family allowances (but not child care or parental leave).

With few exceptions, there are five main reasons for this pattern of growth and restraint. First, demography, although it is not destiny, does count. Declines in education spending reflect declines in school-age populations. The "young" countries with a school-age bulge cut education expenditures per child while still raising such spending as a share of GDP, but as the school population declined, the GDP share leveled off or declined. The "older" countries spent more on pensions both per capita and in GDP share but at a diminishing rate, eventually leveling off (Lindert, 2004: vol. 1). Aging, as we have seen, also increased health and disability spending, especially as the "old-old" increased their share of the population. Second, after universal coverage is achieved, various measures to control costs or restructure programs have some effect, especially in health care (as in German reforms of the 1980s and early 1990s). Third, programs where abuses are obvious and widespread (sick pay, disability insurance) have evoked substantial government reform efforts with varying success; disability cutbacks have encountered especially fierce resistance (Wilensky, 2002: ch. 15 and table 15.3). Fourth, the rate of economic growth has an automatic effect on these numbers: below-average growth will automatically increase the expenditure ratio (SS/GDP) as the denominator levels off or decreases while social spending continues upward or grows slowly. We see this automatic effect in the current economic downturn. Finally, the interaction of three forces – a very large clientele (all pensioners, all the health insured), strong political organization or influence, and great mass popularity – means that welfare-state leaders have already achieved generosity of benefits; their citizens now have entrenched interests and strong sentiments for maintaining the status quo. Conversely, if clientele is small, organization and influence are weak, and majority sentiment is hostile – as with means-tested benefits targeted to the non-aged, non-disabled poor and to a lesser extent unemployment compensation – real cutbacks are most likely. In a deep recession these cutbacks in cash and services hit the poor and near poor disproportionately, as seen in the U.S. state and federal budget crunch of 2008–2010.

Two patterns in the politics of the welfare state should be noted. First, the welfare state has always been about the aged, who are the heaviest users of such expensive programs as health care, pensions, and disability insurance. But do not assume that this has created some kind of war between the generations, that the aged and "gray power" are running away with the public budget at the expense of the young. The evidence from both cross-national surveys of issue-specific public opinion and failed government efforts to make major cuts in these benefits shows the opposite – strong support for all three programs cuts across generations (Wilensky, 2002: 271–272, 288, n. 8; Taylor-Gooby, 2001; Lynch and Myrskylä, 2009; and Keck and Blome, 2008). In fact the adult children of the elderly are sometimes more enthusiastic about universal pensions than their parents. They know the alternative: without these programs much of the burden of personal support for their retired parents would fall to them at the very time when they are trying to finance their children's college education and parental costs of the young are mounting.

The second pattern concerns the intensity of mass protest against cutback budgeting, whether the reductions are instigated by the Right or the Left. Pro-welfare-state backlash appears wherever the public and its representatives perceive that the incumbent political leaders are serious about retrenchment. This can be seen in the fate of politicians who proposed substantial reforms of pensions and health care, failed, and soon lost their jobs. These examples illustrate:

1. In **Italy**, Prime Minister Romano Prodi's center-left majority coalition of 1998 split over $14.5 billion in proposed spending cuts, specifically the $2.9 billion reduction in pension and health-care programs. Prodi resigned. Renegotiation led to $291 million less in pension cuts, but total spending cuts were reduced to almost one-third of those originally proposed, and in return the left demand for a 35-hour workweek was accepted.

2. In **France** in late 1995, the cuts proposed by the conservative government of Jacques Chirac and Alain Juppé triggered a strike movement that almost shut down the French economy for three weeks. It had a wider base of public sympathy than les grands événements of 1968. It was presented by the government with almost no consultation or participation as a nonnegotiable policy package to save the French welfare state, restore

French competitiveness, and meet the requirements for joining the European Monetary Union. The changes were sudden and radical. Strikers concentrated on protecting pensions, health care, job security, traditional job rights, and working conditions. The government withdrew its proposal to reform public-sector pensions (and was subsequently forced to accept a full-pay pension for truck drivers at age 55) but did not give up its ambition to reform drastically the entire social-security system. In July 1997 Chirac and Juppé were defeated by Lionel Jospin of the center Left. The French rejection of the European Union (EU) constitution in 2005 was partly inspired not only by high unemployment but by Chirac's effort at social cutbacks and the public image of EU policies as imposing an Anglo-American economic model on Europe that would threaten social protections and labor standards ("Unilog for TFI, RTL, and Le Monde," May 29, 2005, Politique&Opinion@ins-sofres.com; *Economist*, June 4, 2005).

The massive weeklong protest strikes of November 2007 were again triggered by "nonnegotiable" reforms announced by President Nicolas Sarkozy. Strikers targeted the government effort to increase years of contributions required for official retirement. Participants ranged from transportation workers to employees at the public gas company and artists at the Paris opera house concerned with their pensions, from judges and court workers to university students protesting other reforms. In contrast to 1995, the government sold the reforms as confined to "special regimes." This inspired broader public support of the government position. In the end the government achieved a largely symbolic victory; the unions ended the strikes amid declining union and popular support. The government and the labor confederations began negotiations to soften the impact on workers, some of which by 2008 were still ongoing. So far agreements covered only limited groups, such as train drivers. Nevertheless, the protests marked the beginning of a substantial decline in Sarkozy's popularity. The decline lasted until he switched his line in November 2008 when he declared that "laissez-faire capitalism is over," railed against the "dictatorship of the market," and called for a new state-subsidized jobs program as well as a cap on executive pay and an end to golden parachutes (*Economist*, Nov. 15, 2008).

3. In mid-1990s **Germany**, Chancellor Kohl proposed to reduce state-subsidized health spa vacations from four weeks every three years to only three weeks every four years and to increase by the equivalent of $0.75 the small copayment per prescription (previously the equivalent of about $1.50–5.00). He also suggested some modest pension reforms. All this might not sound draconian to U.S. ears, but it provoked demonstrations, processions of cars, and brief work stoppages all across Germany; 350,000 protesters poured into Bonn in June 1996 – a postwar record. In the late 1990s through 2003, German governments, both center-right and center-left, continued efforts to reform the welfare state with only modest

results. The Social Democratic Party in 2003 accepted Schröder's "Agenda 2010" aiming to cut nonlabor costs by reducing benefits for the long-term unemployed, liberalizing the pharmaceutical market, increasing copayments by patients, and, again, calling for pension reforms. Once more massive protests greeted the proposals. At first only cuts in unemployment benefits – a move toward a targeted benefit like means-tested social assistance – were adopted. This, for the first time, hit both low-income and middle-income unemployed.

Germany's pension system, however, will soon face a ratio of just over two contributors per elderly beneficiary – far worse than "younger" countries such as the United States (Figure 3). So, despite mass resistance, from 1977 to 2006 it embraced many small but cumulative reforms that add up to a substantial cutback in pensions: the generous earnings replacement rate for a standard pension (for an average earner with a 45-year contribution record) was reduced by 28 percent (Blome, Keck, and Alber, 2009: 342). Party conflict about the welfare state continued in the German election of 2005, a standoff between a free-marketeer and a Social Democrat who defended the German "social market" economy. (For details on recent developments in German social policy, see Alber, 2003.)

4. Although **U.S.** president Ronald Reagan in 8 years and **Great Britain's** prime minister Margaret Thatcher in 12 years both launched verbal assaults on the welfare state, they were unable to make more than a small dent on aggregate social spending (Pierson, 1994), mostly by means testing and tightening eligibility rules for the most vulnerable – the poor. As his first act in this area, Reagan proposed to reduce the minimum guaranteed pension in social security (Wilensky, 2002: 223–224). Immediately, 96 senators voted no and none voted yes. President George W. Bush, with dominance in both the executive and Congress, spent a solid year trying to sell the privatization of social security with no success. Again, in February 2010, learning nothing and sensing President Obama's weakness, the ranking Republican member of the House Budget Committee, Paul Ryan, revived the Bush plan and added a proposal to privatize Medicare.

5. Under successive Labour (1984–1990) and National (conservative, 1990–1999) governments, **New Zealand** engaged in a neoliberal experiment launched with passionate conviction and guided in part by economists in Treasury (American-trained at Chicago, Rochester, or Duke) and partly by Labour finance minister Roger Douglas (known for "Rogernomics") and National minister of finance Ruth Richardson (known for "Ruthanasia").[1] The context before 1984 was a half century of alternating dominance by a center-left Labour Party and a center-right National Party. Standards-of-living were high; politics, pragmatic. The lurch to the radical right was ideological; it was an extremist response to real problems – an export crisis that hit New Zealand especially hard in the mid-1970s and subsequent protectionism and mounting inefficiencies of

industrial policy, especially in agriculture, where big subsidies expanded. In response both the Labour and National parties were determined to try the deregulation thrust of the Reagan and Thatcher experiments in a bold, more rational, and disciplined way. They were inspired by new-right theories of public choice, agency, and property rights. Within the Labour Party, intensive conflict developed, culminating in fist fights at regional conferences: on one side, advocates of a Swedish model, tripartite discussions, and an economic summit to achieve consensus on policy responses to the crisis; on the other side, a sectarian group with a coherent free-market theory and a long list of specific proposals for economic restructuring with cost-benefit analysis attached. The free-marketeers out-maneuvered promoters of the vague idea of consensus among social partners.

Begun by Labour and accelerated by the National Party, the reforms included lowered top income tax rates, a two-bracket flat tax, the targeting of welfare-state benefits via stiff means tests, tax credits for the poor (with low takeup rates), a surtax on pensions, and student fees for higher education. The Labour government abandoned traditional pay-setting and grievance and arbitration procedures (ideology called for full-scale deregulation of the labor market but that would come later). They also cut tariffs, installed a free float of New Zealand currency, privatized quasi-public enterprises, closed unprofitable post offices, and adopted a globally unique central bank statute in 1989 (gave the central bank complete freedom to pursue the single goal of price stability with a specific target of 0–2 percent and a link between the governor's tenure and inflation performance).

The National Party massively defeated Labour in 1990; it then continued the reforms, extended them fully into the labor market, launching a large-scale attack on both unions and the welfare state. Included were a two-step tier system of medical care, heavy targeting of benefits (income and means testing), copayments, and variable prices. The National government also moved toward income testing of pensions but when 80–90 percent of the public polled disapproved, it backed down. Neither party's manifesto mentioned the policies actually adopted, one explanation of the political uproar of 1984–1991.

The effects of these radical policy shifts were devastating for both the economy and the polity. In the absence of the military Keynesianism of Reaganomics, the economic effects of the reforms were disastrous: from 1984 to 1990 unemployment rose from 4 percent to 11 percent, inflation moved up from 12 to 18 percent in 1986, but, with a very tight monetary policy administered by the newly autonomous central bank, inflation came down to 3 percent and with the selling of public assets, the shift in taxes, and cuts in social spending, budgets deficits declined (Stephens, 1993: 46ff.). Bankruptcy rates and welfare dependency soared. Growth rates remained low at under 1 percent a year. This pattern of low or nearly zero inflation, low growth, and high unemployment continued through the early 1990s.[2] Because high interest rates attracted foreign capital and devaluation made exports cheap, however, the trade balance improved. Tax reforms gave Finance Minister Douglas a reputation in financial circles as a bold innovator. The London *Economist* and the economists of OECD praised the new tax structure as "the least distorting in the OECD." What was an efficiency economist's dream, however, was an egalitarian's nightmare. The combination of tax reform and spending cuts sharply increased inequality (Stephens, 1993: 59–61).[3] Labor-market reforms exacerbated inequalities produced by changes in taxing and spending. Union membership plummeted; industry-wide bargaining practically disappeared; firm-level bargaining became the norm. By 1999 New Zealand had become the least rich of our 19 rich democracies measured by per capita GDP in either U.S. dollars or purchasing power parities.

The effects of 10 years of sectarian monetarism combined with Rogernomics (without Ronald Reagan's deficit spending) were also devastating for political legitimacy. The three elections in this period (1984, 1987, and 1990) generated the highest voter volatility of the previous thirty years (Vowles and Aimer, 1993: 14); the flight of Labour voters to two new parties (New Labour and Green) in 1990 brought the Labour government down. In the election campaign the victorious National Party promised cautious pragmatism, decency, honesty, a balanced budget, and a 50 percent cut in unemployment; it said it would make Labour's reforms more fair and efficient. What it delivered were three more years of stubbornly doctrinaire economics. By 1991 the National Party and its leaders were the most unpopular in the history of polling. By 1993, the National Party exceeded the earlier Labour Party collapse in popularity.

The delegitimacy story ends with the voters' vengeance: two referendums (1992 and 1993) on a sweeping change in the electoral system from first-past-the-post to mixed member PR with a 5 percent threshold. The election of 1993 (the last under the old rules) saw four new parties and the further decline of the two major parties. The results of 1993: National won 50 seats with 35 percent of the votes; Labour 45 seats with 34.7 percent of the votes; third parties won 4 seats with an unprecedented 30.3 percent of the votes (a left Alliance, 18.2 percent; a center party, New Zealand First, 8.4 percent; others, 3.4 percent). In November 1994 a new right party, ACT New Zealand, was founded by Roger Douglas and other true believers who created this 10-year experiment in pure theory as the sole guide to policy.

Labour and its junior partner, the social democratic Alliance, took power in the 1999 election with Helen Clark as prime minister; she was an advocate of the Swedish model of political economy. Under this new Labour coalition, many of the policies that decimated both major parties were reversed. The inflation target ceiling was raised to 3 percent, giving the Reserve Bank a little less license to choke off growth by raising interest rates. Public spending on health care as a percentage of GDP rose from low stagnation during 1985–1998 to a steady increase since 1999; such spending per capita increased an average of about 5 percent annually. Market rentals on state housing for low-income families were abolished; rentals were subsidized. Interest on student loans were eliminated for graduates who stayed in New Zealand. Restoring the tattered safety net did not prevent an above-average economic performance for 2000–2007 (see Table 3). Inflation averaged 2.7 percent; real growth per capita 3.4 percent with less fluctuation than the previous decade. Unemployment decreased every year from 2000 to 2007, averaging 4.6 percent, well below the average of other rich democracies. All this with a huge reduction in government debt. The center-left restoration lasted until the worldwide recession brought the defeat of the Labour coalition November 8, 2008.

The New Zealand case is a cautionary tale of economic instability, inequality, and party dealignment brought on by doctrinaire officials and economists in both major parties. It is the longest, most radical test of the combination of cutback budgeting, privatization, deregulation, and their aftermath.

In short, five of these six cases suggest that real cutbacks in benefits since the 1980s are typically small and incremental – trimming around the edges of the welfare state. Health-care reforms are prominent everywhere, but, except for the United States, they do not involve major reductions in universal access to health care. Benefit formulas for pensions are being modified in most countries to account for increased longevity; "normal retirement age" is being raised in many. But nowhere have employment-based pension schemes been redesigned according to the American Concord Coalition recommendation for a tax/transfer needs-based model (Myles and Quadagno, 1996) or the George W. Bush privatization schemes for health care, drug benefits, or pensions. Reform is a slow process that encounters strong public resistance. Small incremental reductions in many programs can add up over time; vast majorities of voters whose income and security are threatened sooner or later rebel. The case of New Zealand is unique: a natural experiment lasting more than 12 years where the cutbacks were bold and sustained, resulting in the delegitimation of the major parties, the creation of four new ones, the destabilization of both economy and polity. It is a lesson for neoliberal ideologues who have convinced themselves that "government is bad; markets are good." That is a simplistic slogan that has today guided the United States into the export of its financial meltdown and the worst worldwide recession since the Great Depression.

## A. SIMILARITIES IN MASS SENTIMENTS ABOUT THE PROPER ROLE OF GOVERNMENT

Cross-national public opinion surveys cast doubt on the idea of large national differences in mass attitudes toward the proper role of government – another reason for forging consensus within ruling parties and interest groups committed to change before any bold reforms are attempted. Scholars and pundits often assert that the citizens of "statist" Europe are "collectivist" while their counterparts in the United States are "individualist." In fact, the citizens of all rich democracies are quite similar in their ambivalence and confusion when confronted with abstract ideological statements about public spending and taxing. More important and even stronger are the similarities in issue-specific public opinion. (The evidence is reviewed in Wilensky, 2002: 369–374, 391–395.)

Two major patterns from this large body of surveys stand out. First, there is nothing uniquely American about mass attitudes toward the proper role of government. Modern voters, including vast majorities in the United States, are ambivalent and contradictory in their values and beliefs. They are simultaneously individualistic and collectivistic, Social Darwinist (every man for himself) and humanistic (pro–welfare state – we're all in the same boat), laissez-faire and statist, meritocratic and populist, believers in both individual liberty and community as well as equality of opportunity and (to a lesser extent) equality of results.

True, if we ask abstract questions such as "Do you think government should see that everyone has a job and a good standard of living?" or "government should let each person get ahead on his own?" the balance of these antinomies will reflect the actual taxing and spending and social policies of the government. Sweden, a big spender, has an edge over Britain in support for affirmative government; Britain, a middle-rank spender, over Canada and the United States, two lean spenders. But the differences are not large and the progovernment intervention preference is a clear majority among all rich democracies.

The great ambivalence of mass publics permits politicians to play it either way. If they are hostile to expansive social and labor policies they can work the tax-welfare backlash; if they are friendly, they can mobilize majority sentiments.

When you read pollsters' claims that Americans have shifted to the Republican agenda or have become "moderate" because they are individualistic and want a less active government or have embraced new values, remember that it is typically media-filtered "information" that is fed back to pollsters as public opinion. My favorite example comes from a focus-group survey on the proper role of government done at the height of the balanced budget debate of 1994–1995. One older citizen on Social Security who was a heavy user of Medicare explained that "I want the government off my back ... I don't want the government messing around with my Medicare" – a formula often repeated by the screaming protesters in the 2009 "town meetings" on health-care reform.

The second pattern of results goes beyond abstract ideology to *issue-specific opinion* about taxes, spending, and particular policies constituting the welfare state. Here there is no confusion and little ambivalence. The structure of public opinion has remained remarkably stable since World War II both in the United States and in affluent democracies with sharply contrasting cultures and politics. Briefly, modern voters everywhere love guaranteed pensions and disability insurance and are only a shade less enamored of national health insurance.

Next most popular and becoming more so are family policies and active labor-market policies (ALMP); both draw majority support. When we go beyond these most expensive and popular policies we find that the mass of citizens in all these countries have serious reservations about passive unemployment compensation and are downright hostile to means-tested public assistance (American "welfare"); they think the benefits too often go to the undeserving. In mass attitudes toward specific programs, Sweden and the United States are brothers (sisters?) under the skin. Again, nowhere do we uncover a mass defection from the core programs of the welfare state. Because the rank order of enthusiasm about specific programs is so similar across these 19 countries, we cannot explain large national differences in the success of tax-welfare backlash movements and parties in a few – the United States, the United Kingdom, Denmark, and Switzerland – by invoking a similar structure of public opinion in all. A uniform and stable structure of opinion does not tell us why sustained tax-welfare backlash appears in only 4 or 5 of our 19 democracies. It is instead types of political economy and their contrasting patterns of politics and public policy that explain national differences.

What about the taxes necessary to finance these social and labor-market policies? As we have seen in our discussion of sources of good economic performances (Chapter 3), my research on tax revolts shows that it is not the *level* of taxes that creates tax-welfare backlash but the *type* of taxes – property taxes on households and income taxes with their visibility and perceived pain. Conversely, consumption taxes (e.g., VAT) and social-security payroll taxes keep things cool; they have never triggered a sustained tax revolt in rich democracies. In the words of an old pop tune, "It ain't what you do, it's the way that you do it."

## B. A REVOLT OF THE "MIDDLE MASS"?

In understanding the political behavior of everyone's favorite category, "the middle class," it is essential to distinguish those in the upper-middle class, college-educated crowd who have good, relatively stable jobs – they are about one-fifth of the labor force – from everyone else. Leaving aside the poor, who may vote Democratic in the United States but are a small minority of the total vote, you have left what used to be called the upper-working class and the lower-middle class. These two have been merging in behavior, values, beliefs, and life styles for more than half a century to form a "middle mass" sharing the same fate.

The middle mass is best measured by level and quality of education, not by the "income" most pollsters use. Survey respondents lie more about income than they do about sex; the refusal rate on this question is higher than any other demographic item in national surveys. Most important, income – whether we are talking about individual income or earnings or hourly wages or household income – fluctuates frequently even in the short run; there is much instability, with frequent income mobility up and down in all rich democracies. Data on education, in contrast, are more reliable, more stable, and above all, predict life chances better than any other measure of "class" or "status." Education is thus the best measure of the middle mass, whose position and orientation are crucial in grasping election results in the four rich democracies where tax-welfare backlash flourished and persisted – the United States, the United Kingdom, Denmark, and Switzerland. (Canada's tax revolts in the past half century tend to be regional and intermittent, concentrated in Alberta and British Columbia.) In the other 15 countries taxing and spending and public policies (e.g., more universalistic and generous welfare states financed with more tax balance) have fostered more solidarity between the middle mass and the poor and less resentment of the upper middle. A contributing factor in this greater cross-class solidarity is electoral systems that encourage stronger parties and greater turnout with more consensual political economies, as we have discussed. So from the mid-1960s until now, we find little evidence of sustained tax-welfare backlash movements and parties in these countries (Wilensky, 2002: ch. 10).

It is no wonder that astute politicians of both parties in the United States have explicitly targeted this middle mass – high school grads or voters with a year or two of apprenticeship or of a vocational school or community college but no baccalaureate. First, their *size*: they are well over half the electorate. Second, most of them feel *squeezed economically* between the rich, including the college-educated crowd, and the poor. They look *up* and see overprivileged folks who, they think, have easy, stable jobs, live well, seem to evade taxes, and send their children to expensive colleges, or worse, to elite state universities at their expense. They look *down* and see a nonworking, non-aged population collecting benefits, including Medicaid, food stamps, and some child care, without paying taxes. In fact, their real income since the mid-1970s, with the exception of six years of Bill Clinton's presidency, has stagnated or deteriorated. These voters are typically restive and resentful.

From Wallace's ordinary folks to Nixon's silent majority, from Reagan's white ethnic Democrats to Clinton's hard-working Americans who pay their taxes and live by the rules, shrewd politicians have had a clear-eyed view of the composition of the middle mass and how their fears and resentments can be mobilized in national elections or calmed down by alternative appeals. The middle mass were 59 percent of the total vote of 1994 when Newt Gingrich Republicans were victorious. Enough Democrats among them defected that year to explain the outcome. These voters are the core of the tax-welfare backlash – antitax, anti–social spending, antibureaucratic movements and parties that achieve electoral success for substantial periods. Think of the time period starting with Reagan through the George W. Bush presidency. In all these cases the tax-welfare backlash is always accompanied by xenophobic appeals – baiting foreigners, welfare queens, minorities. For instance, the white middle mass were the center of support not only for George Wallace but for populist-nativist Pat Buchanan in 1996 and Ku Klux Klan Grand Wizard David Duke, who won a majority of white voters in a Louisiana primary for U.S. Senate. Finally, studies of both the Perot voters in the 1992 and 1996 U.S. presidential elections and the Gingrich Democratic defectors show that they were overwhelmingly non-college-educated white men and women. Voters with modest levels of education typically thought that the economy was getting worse or their personal financial situation had deteriorated.

The popular vote victory – and indeed the Florida victory – of Gore 2000 and the narrow defeat of Kerry reflect a 2004 Republican gain among white high-school and part-college voters who were more than 60 percent of the total vote in 2000 and 56 percent in 2004.[4] Comparing the performance of Gore vs. Bush and Kerry vs. Bush in this strategic majority, there was a shift of about 3 percentage points toward Bush in 2004. The terror, Iraq, and homeland-security brew trumped economic erosion among these voters. The middle mass tends toward intense patriotic fervor, more so than the master's and professional degree holders where Kerry did very well, as he did among the poor (less than high school).

If you add the extremes – high-school dropouts (2.6% of the total 2004 vote) and those graduate and professional degree holders (10.2% of total) – Kerry's big score among the most and least educated was insufficient to offset the defection of middle-mass Democrats.[5] In 2008 Barack Obama and the Democrats brought back enough of the white Reagan Democrats of the middle mass to win a majority, although Obama lost a majority of the total white vote. It was a continuation of the Democratic gains of 2006 when bread-and-butter appeals trumped both the wedge issues of the cultural war – gays, guns, and God – and the real war in Iraq. In neither 2004 nor 2008 did the wedge issues of abortion and gay marriage have a major effect.[6]

In previous publications (e.g., 1976, 1981, and 2002) I describe in detail the successes of tax-welfare backlash movements and parties in the other three countries. In Denmark (a big spender and taxer), the mobilizers of these movements were Mogens Glistrup and the Progress Party. In the United Kingdom (a middle-rank spender and taxer), it was Enoch Powell, Margaret Thatcher, and the Tories. In Switzerland (a lean spender and taxer), it was James Schwarzenbach, who reached his peak with 47 percent of the vote in a 1970 national referendum when he proposed to throw out foreigners to protect the Swiss Way of Life; he claimed that they constituted a staggering burden of social and school services in the national budget. His successors in the 1990s were led by the populist-right charismatic leader of the People's Party, Christoph Blocher of Zurich; he was orchestrating the same themes and mobilizing a succession of disparate right-wing parties. The backlash vote remained steady. Note again that the level of aggregate spending and taxing cannot explain these four cases. It is instead their heavy reliance on the most painfully visible taxes (property taxes on households and income taxes). Further, in all cases except Denmark, they relied heavily on means-tested, targeted benefits and were reluctant to embrace universal, categorical benefits and services for everyone (guaranteed pensions, national health insurance, disability insurance, active labor market policies, family policies) with simple income tests where appropriate. Finally, in all four cases the backlash votes were located in the middle mass.[7]

# 5

# Pensions Converge, U.S. Health Care Remains Unique

That the consensual democracies have the best chance to control costs of the popular social and labor-market policies now in place without sacrificing the principles of social right and universality is highlighted by what they have done in the past and are doing now. If we consider the leading big-cost core programs of the welfare state, pensions and related policies that must be linked to pension reform as well as health care, we see where accommodations between the social partners and political parties are essential. First, consider the problem of pensions and Finland's solution as a model for reform; then the health-care crisis in the United States as a lesson in what not to do.

## A. WHAT IS THE PROBLEM TO BE SOLVED BY PENSION REFORM?

All rich democracies have experienced twin trends that pose a serious issue for policy planners: a century-long decline in the age of exit of men from the labor force; and an increase in healthy older populations. In trying to contain exploding costs of pensions while they cope with an oversupply of healthy displaced older workers who prefer to work at least part time, many governments have tried to devise flexible retirement systems. It is good public policy to transform the healthy aged who want to work into taxpayers, part-time workers, and partial pensioners rather than pressuring them to retire fully. But it is extraordinarily difficult both technically and politically to craft social-security systems that would reverse the long-term slide in the age of exit from work. The first difficulty is the necessity of creating part-time jobs for older workers. A study of 10 of our rich democracies shows that countries that provide part-time work for the elderly have higher overall employment rates (Ebbinghaus, 2006: 102). Several countries, including Germany, the Netherlands, and the United Kingdom, have managed to create an abundance of part-timers among older populations. Ireland, the United States, and Italy are laggards in the creation of such jobs. The second obstacle to reversing the decline of age of exit from the labor force is the prevalence of disabilities of various kinds among the aged. The trick is to find the balance between reductions in benefits for very early retirement and generous partial pensions for continued part-time work for those aged say 60–70 while avoiding pressure on the worn-out workers in the least attractive jobs to postpone retirement. As in the case of the partially disabled, this necessitates adequate income and medical supports; or, if rehabilitation is the focus, a reallocation of funds toward work-oriented rehabilitation and a tight connection to an active labor-market policy.

Both Sweden and Finland, cases of democratic corporatism, have crafted such systems. Both have evidenced a capacity for the necessary policy linkages. For example, from 1990 to 2008 both evidence a growth in part-time jobs for those 60 years old and over as well as their percentage of the total labor force (OECD, 2010). Both countries have accented work-oriented rehabilitation of the disabled.

Finland's recent welfare-state reforms are a model of what corporatist bargaining among the social partners (labor, professions, management, and other relevant and inclusive interest groups interacting with government and political parties) can do to forge consensus on major pension and related programs. It is a lesson in how a consensual democracy, especially if it integrates labor and the Left into high policy, can reform the core programs of the welfare state to cope with issues of both equity and cost.

Here is a broad outline of a major reform of pension and related programs that was adopted by parliament in 2003 after agreement among the "labor-market parties" and after a thorough government assessment of long-run costs and benefits. Most took effect January 1, 2005.[1] The major aims: postpone the average effective retirement age by two to three years; adapt the pension scheme to an increased average life expectancy and other demographic shifts; and achieve unification and simplification of private-sector earnings-related pensions. The new system reforms cover three types of pensions: old age, disability, and part-time. It changes the pension index (so consumer prices weigh 80%, earnings increases 20%). It establishes specific rights to vocational rehabilitation "if illness, handicap, or injury poses a threat to work capacity within about 5 years" and similar rights within the earnings-related pension system, with appeals procedures.

To further enhance flexible retirement and encourage work, changes in both part-time and full pensions are substantial. The part-time pension age is increased from age 56 to 58, with an accrual rate of 1.5 percent of earnings and 0.75 percent of the reduction of earnings because of part-time retirement. Early old-age pensions start at 62. At 63 one can retire at the old-age accrual rate, which begins on earnings after age 18 and climbs in three steps, from 1.5 percent at age 18–52, to 4.5 percent at 63–68 – a strong incentive for continued work. Funding will be increased from 2003 on, but savings from the flexible retirement provisions and later retirement are expected to reduce the growth of pension expenditure as a percentage of wages from 2005 to about 2030 and thereafter to level off. Combined with real cuts made in the 1990s – a product of the same consensual bargaining process among the social partners – the current reforms mean that pension expenditures and premiums will grow much less than they would have without reforms. By 2008 Finland, along with Sweden and Japan, was a standout leader in providing part-time jobs for people 60 years and over; a fifth of the part-timers were elderly (calculated from OECD, 2010). This is an indicator of flexible retirement policies.

A brief cross-national look at the history of public pension policies shows that however they began, the policies tend to converge, which suggests that even the decentralized and fragmented democracies will follow the lead of Finland and other successful reformers.

Whether these countries began with the Anglo-Scandinavian approach of tax-financed universal minimum pensions reflecting an egalitarian ideology (the first were Denmark and Iceland in 1891), or they began with the Continental European approach of compulsory earnings-related pensions reflecting a merito-cratic ideology (the first was Bismarck's Germany in 1889), they ended with universal categorical pensions combining both principles (cf. Overbye, 1994). Further, as these systems matured, coverage expanded, the population aged, and generosity of benefits increased, their cost increased. Political pressure from masses of voters both old and young is the main reason for these trends.

Here is a case where the United States has shown a capacity to act. In 1983 it followed the more consensual democracies. A bipartisan commission on pension reform recommended modest changes, which were adopted by Congress in 1983. The commission included strong Social Security advocates from labor and Congress (such as Lane Kirkland, president of the AFL-CIO, Senator Daniel Patrick Moynihan, and Representative Claude Pepper, a New Deal Democrat from Florida), as well as Robert Ball, a most knowledgeable and articulate commis-sioner of Social Security (1962–1973). Alan Greenspan, representing a Republican ideology and Republican appointees, chaired the commission (chalk up a good deed for the later Fed chairman). The context was a right-wing propaganda campaign using such slogans as "Catch 65," "the young will never see a dime of Social Security," "the system is bankrupt." Neoconservative think tanks produced books "proving" these assertions and put them in the hands of every member of Congress. Note that the composition of the commission included strong advocates of Social Security from the center Left and labor – in contrast to the membership of the budget deficit commission appointed by President Obama in 2010.

What did the commission and Congress do to "save" Social Security? Rather than cutting benefits they raised payroll taxes slightly, taxed benefits for the first time, brought new federal employees into the system to broaden the payroll tax base, and trimmed future costs by slowly phasing in the higher retirement age from 65 to 67 by the year 2027 – sensible steps, which "fixed" the system for 37 years, until 2020 when outgo would begin to exceed income, hardly a revolution. These long-term actuarial estimates of 1983, using the assumption of a medium rate of real GDP growth, were amazingly close to the mark. It turned out that their prediction of the day when revenue would be one dollar short of payout – what the ideologues call "bankrupt" – was only four years different from the current actuarial estimate of the year 2016. Because Congress and President Reagan used up much of the surplus for purposes other than Social

Security, the 1995 trustees' guesstimate of the date when the OASDI trust fund would be fully depleted if we do nothing to change benefits or taxes was 2030, seven years earlier than the current actuarial estimate of 2037 (Social Security Administration, 1995, 2009). When the surplus in the Social Security Trust Fund burgeoned after the modest reforms of 1983, the attack switched; now it was not "bankruptcy," it was the government taking and hoarding your money, which should be returned to you by cutting your backbreaking taxes.

In other words, little incremental steps taken in 1983 overcame the noncrisis in Social Security. We did what the more consensual democracies with much older populations than ours (e.g., Germany, Italy, and Japan) have had to do.

Figure 3 pictures the ratio of workers to retirees in 18 of our 19 rich democracies for 2010 and projections to 2050. It clearly shows that the lean-spending, fragmented, decentralized political economies have much more favorable ratios (five of the six countries on the left) than the consensual democracies (five countries on the right). Thus the countries whose structures make social-security reform more difficult fortunately have more time to do what the United States did in 1983 and will have to do again in the years ahead.

Despite many convergent trends in pension structure, substantial national differences persist. The same sources of national variation in aggregate social spending and equality apply to both public spending on pensions and their average earnings-replacement rate: the corporatist political economies are at the top in generosity, and the fragmented and decentralized political economies are at the bottom.

Table 7 shows that the consensual democracies (top four types of political economy) on average spend more on public pensions as a share of GDP and have much higher gross earnings replacement rates upon retirement than the

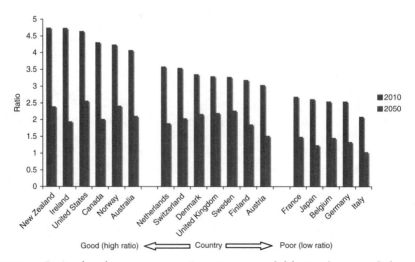

FIGURE 3. Ratio of workers, 15–64, to retirees, 65+, 2010 (*left bar*) and 2050 (*right bar*).
*Source*: UN Population Division, World Population Prospects, 2008; OECD.stat, 2009–2010.

TABLE 7. *Types of Political Economy, Public Pension Spending as Share of GDP 2005, and Gross and Net Pension Generosity 2006*

| | Public Pension as Percent of GDP, 2005[a] | | Gross Earnings Replacement Rate, 2006[b] | | Net Earnings Replacement Rate, 2006[c] | |
|---|---|---|---|---|---|---|
| Left corporatist | | | | | | |
| Sweden | 9.6 | (5) | 49.3 | (9) | 52.6 | (12) |
| Norway | 6.3 | (11) | 55.2 | (7) | 65.3 | (6) |
| Finland | 8.5 | (7) | 56.2 | (6) | 62.4 | (9) |
| Denmark | 7.2 | (9) | 58.1 | (5) | 68.2 | (3) |
| Cell average | 7.9 | | 54.7 | | 62.1 | |
| Left-Catholic corporatist | | | | | | |
| Netherlands | 5.5 | (13) | 88.3 | (1) | 103.2 | (1) |
| Belgium | 7.2 | (8) | 42.0 | (12) | 63.7 | (8) |
| Austria | 12.6 | (1) | 80.1 | (2) | 90.3 | (2) |
| Cell average | 8.4 | | 70.1 | | 85.7 | |
| Catholic corporatist | | | | | | |
| Italy | 11.6 | (2) | 60.4 | (3) | 66.5 | (4) |
| Germany | 11.2 | (3) | 43.0 | (11) | 61.3 | (10) |
| Cell average | 11.4 | | 51.7 | | 63.9 | |
| Corporatist without labor | | | | | | |
| France | 10.9 | (4) | 53.3 | (8) | 65.7 | (5) |
| Japan | 8.6 | (6) | 33.9 | (16) | 38.7 | (18) |
| Switzerland | 6.6 | (10) | 58.6 | (4) | 64.9 | (7) |
| Cell average | 8.7 | | 48.6 | | 56.4 | |
| Least corporatist | | | | | | |
| United States | 5.3 | (14) | 38.7 | (13) | 44.8 | (13) |
| United Kingdom | 6.1 | (12) | 30.8 | (18) | 40.9 | (16) |
| New Zealand | 4.2 | (16) | 38.7 | (13) | 41.1 | (15) |
| Australia | 4.4 | (15) | 33.6 | (17) | 44.2 | (14) |
| Canada | 3.7 | (17) | 44.5 | (10) | 57.9 | (11) |
| Ireland | 2.9 | (18) | 34.2 | (15) | 40.1 | (17) |
| Cell average | 4.4 | | 36.8 | | 44.8 | |

*Note*: Both net and gross replacement rates are based on average earnings adjusted for inflation on publicly funded, defined-contribution pensions, after administrative charges are deducted.

[a] OECD now relabels this as "old-age expenditure," though it is still overwhelmingly pension spending, including disability pensions with other minor added expenditures. Adding "mandatory private spending" does not change these patterns, except for an increase in figure for Switzerland.

[b] Gross pension entitlement divided by gross preretirement earnings for specified years.

[c] Individual cash benefits minus income taxes divided by preretirement earnings minus income taxes and social security contributions paid by both employers and employees.

*Source*: OECD.stat (2009–2010).

fragmented and decentralized democracies at the bottom. A second measure of generous treatment of the elderly is the *net* replacement rate – that is, individual cash benefits minus income taxes divided by preretirement earnings minus income taxes and social-security contributions paid by both employers and employees. Column 3 yields a pattern similar to that of the gross replacement rate in Table 7, column 2:

| | |
|---|---|
| Left corporatist | 62% |
| Left-Catholic corporatist | 86 |
| Catholic corporatist | 64 |
| Corporatist without labor | 56 |
| Least corporatist | 45 |

Plainly, when it comes to government-guaranteed pension spending and generosity, the fragmented, decentralized political economies lag; the consensual political economies with cumulative left party power or powerful and competing left and Catholic parties lead. In fact, the most generous pension benefits appear when there is a competitive escalation of spending between Catholic and left parties. Table 6 also provides a hint that countries with strong Catholic party power (e.g., the Netherlands, Austria, and Italy) accent cash benefits in their welfare states, whereas countries with strong left party power accent both cash and personal social services, such as home care for the elderly, rehabilitation of the disabled, meals-on-wheels (e.g., Sweden, Finland, Belgium, Germany). (For earlier data and observations on services vs. cash, see Wilensky, 2002: 254–260.)

Critics of claims about welfare-state leaders and laggards often argue that tables like this one are misleading because they ignore the generosity of private pensions among the public pension laggards. Typical is a book titled *The Hidden Welfare State* (Howard, 1999; cf. Greve, 1994). The benign effect of private pensions is dubious for two reasons. First, welfare-state leaders also have a private component in their pension systems as well as their health-care systems. However, such "private" components of both systems (Whiteford and Whitehouse, 2006: 84–93) are hard to measure cross-nationally because they consist largely of tax expenditures – tax breaks for the private providers in the form of exemptions, allowances, credits, rate relief, and tax deferrals.[2] Second, and more important, a heavy reliance on private pensions voluntarily given by employers, collectively bargained by unions and management, or bought by individuals from private insurance companies has proved highly unstable. The current crisis of such private pensions in the United States – their squeeze on benefits and coverage, their defaults, their inefficiency, and in some cases their corruption – is entirely due to their subversive impact on public pension spending and generosity, which puts too great a burden on employers and makes private pensions unsustainable. Unions since 1950 have periodically asked employers to join them in political support of expanded Social Security (where there is no "crisis"). Employers have been too shortsighted to shift this burden to government. Recently a vast majority of U.S. employers who have voluntarily provided pensions have been cutting benefits and coverage unilaterally, shifting from "defined benefits" to "defined contributions" where the employee bears all of the risk. In the crash of 2008-on, the value of these private pensions plunged. Finally, some employers abandoned their pension obligations by declaring bankruptcy, which shifts the burden to employees and a government backup fund that has little money left in it.[3]

In the United States private pensions for some years created the cheerful illusion among the stably employed well-off that public pensions were adequate, a myth promoted by right-wing politicians who want to privatize the whole system. The most recent and abortive episode in this recurrent attack was President George W. Bush's yearlong campaign to privatize Social Security. Mass resistance, again, stopped him.

## B. U.S. HEALTH CARE AND REAL HEALTH IN COMPARATIVE PERSPECTIVE

For a great many policies and in system structure and outputs, the United States has plenty of company, principally the United Kingdom, Canada, Australia, New Zealand, Ireland, and sometimes Switzerland. For instance, they share patterns of weak political party strength and fast party erosion in the electorate, vulnerability to the ascendance of mass media in politics and culture, a taste for means testing in welfare-state administration, and high poverty rates.[4] But when it comes to health care the United States is, indeed, unique:

- *No national health insurance.* The United States is deviant in its continued reliance on medical care individually purchased, collectively bargained, or voluntarily provided by employers and in the large number of its people with no insurance coverage (now about 47 million) or clearly inadequate coverage (an accelerating number, surely not less than tens of millions).
- *Big private sector.* The private share of total health-care spending in the United States in 1990 was about three-fifths (accounted for by such commercial vendors as insurance companies, drug companies, medical equipment makers, hospital chains, HMOs, employers, doctors in private practice, etc.). That greatly exceeds the next highest private share – just under a third in Austria, Switzerland, and Australia; and typically less than a quarter elsewhere. Today the United States remains uniquely privatized with a 55 percent private share.
- *A very high ratio of specialists to primary-care physicians (general practitioners [GPs], family doctors, pediatricians), nurses, and midwives.*
- *A uniquely expensive (non)system with a poor cost-benefit ratio.* The total cost of U.S. health care today is over 16 percent of GDP. No other rich democracy comes close to that figure. Yet the United States remains below average on a wide range of health indicators, sometimes at the very bottom among rich democracies.

The American case is a lesson for those medical economists and politicians who advocate privatizing of pensions, medical care, and other welfare-state programs. The odd private-public mix of the United States gives private actors strong incentives to play two games: *cost shifting* and *risk selection*. If the government tries to control the costs of service provided by vendors who serve patients in Medicare (mainly the aged) and Medicaid (means tested for the poor and long-term disabled) or the privately controlled plans, the dominant actors – employers, HMOs, insurance companies, hospital chains – will shift costs to the public sector by restricting coverage and charging patients more. Commercial providers also save money by risk selection; they skim off the younger, healthier patients and dump older, sicker, costlier patients onto the public sector. These games escalate costs while they reduce coverage.

With the cost-cutting, privatizing fervor of the past 25 or so years, we hear such slogans as "Stop throwing government money at the problem," "We need market competition among the providers," "True competition has not yet been tried," "Tell people to take responsibility for their own health, make them cost-conscious so they choose less-costly care." The evidence shows first that the market model of health care borders on the absurd. Second, and most important, it shows that spending per capita through the public sector strongly improves a broad range of health indicators and moves the system toward prevention. (On the public share, see Wilensky, 2002: table 16.3; on recent trends in public shares, see Table 7, and on public per capita spending, see Table 8 in this book.)

The concept of the market applied to health care is taken seriously in the media and public discourse only because medical economists dominate the debate about health-care reform, especially in the United States, the United Kingdom, and New Zealand, three countries with poor health performance. The guiding concepts of these economists include willing buyers and willing sellers contracting for services in a more or less competitive market where the buyer (patient) compares alternative sellers (doctors); is adequately if not fully informed about the nature of the product, its price, and its quality; and makes a rational choice. The seller as he views his competition must provide either higher quality or lower price or both or he will go out of business. The system as a whole will thus tend toward a match between price and quality and a nice equilibrium between demand and supply. Further, under market discipline, as the price-conscious buyer constrains his appetite for service and the seller is constrained to be more efficient, cost containment will be the happy result.

Many medical economists know that when applied to health care, these ideas must be modified; they speak of imperfect competition, managed competition, market failures, and so on. As every observer of the institutions providing care knows, the health-care "market" is wildly different from the market in economic theory. The buyer at the peak of expense may not even be conscious, let alone adequately informed; if conscious, he is anxious, maybe in pain, full of fear and ignorant of the purchases before him. His demand for the service is sometimes urgent, even desperate. Whether the private share of spending is high as in the United States or low as everywhere else, the typical patient is not even spending his own money, and no one in the system can accurately gauge the unit cost. The seller-provider in turn, is a licensed professional monopolist who creates demand by authoritative statements of what the purchaser should want, and the buyer-patient has neither the competence nor the wish to second-guess the monopolist. Is this a market?

It is clear from Table 8 that from 1960 to 2005 all countries except Switzerland moved toward an ever-larger public share of total health-care spending. By 2005 all countries except the United States reached a public share of at least 65 percent

TABLE 8. *Types of Political Economy, Public Share of Total Health-Care Spending, 1960–2005, and Real Health, 2000–2005*

| | Public Share of Total Health-Care Spending (%) | | | | | Govt. Health per Capita[a] | Real Health Index 2005[b] |
|---|---|---|---|---|---|---|---|
| | 1960 | 1980 | 2000 | 2005 | Avg. 00–05 | | |
| Left corporatist | | | | | | | |
| Sweden | 73 | 93 | 85 | 82 | 84 | $2,490 | 11.5 (4) |
| Norway | 78 | 85 | 83 | 84 | 83 | $3,784 | 9.5 (7) |
| Finland | 54 | 79 | 75 | 78 | 76 | $1,764 | 7.0 (12) |
| Denmark | 89 | 88 | 82 | 84 | 83 | $2,254 | 5.5 (15) |
| Average | 73 | 86 | 79 | 79 | 79 | $2,573 | |
| Left-Catholic corporatist | | | | | | | |
| Netherlands | 33 | 69 | 63 | 65 | 64 | $2,093 | 6.5 (14) |
| Belgium | 62 | 83 | 72 | 71 | 72 | $1,972 | 7.0 (12) |
| Austria | 69 | 69 | 76 | 77 | 76 | $2,360 | 9.0 (9) |
| Average | 66[c] | 74 | 70 | 71 | 70 | $2,142 | |
| Catholic corporatist | | | | | | | |
| Italy | 83 | 81 | 73 | 77 | 75 | $1,606 | 11.0 (5) |
| Germany | 66 | 79 | 80 | 77 | 78 | $2,341 | 7.0 (12) |
| Average | 75 | 80 | 76 | 77 | 77 | $1,974 | |
| Corporatist without labor | | | | | | | |
| France | 62 | 80 | 78 | 80 | 79 | $2,340 | 10.0 (6) |
| Japan | 60 | 71 | 81 | 83 | 82 | $2,351 | 13.5 (1) |
| Switzerland | 61 | 68 | 56 | 59 | 58 | $2,682 | 12.5 (2) |
| Average | 61 | 73 | 72 | 74 | 73 | $2,458 | |
| Least corporatist | | | | | | | |
| United States | 23 | 41 | 44 | 45 | 45 | $2,429 | 2.5 (19) |
| United Kingdom | 85 | 89 | 81 | 87 | 84 | $2,043 | 4.5 (17) |
| New Zealand | 81 | 88 | 79 | 77 | 78 | $1,342 | 5.5 (15) |
| Australia | 48 | 63 | 67 | 67 | 67 | $1,646 | 12.0 (3) |
| Canada | 43 | 76 | 70 | 70 | 70 | $1,952 | 9.5 (7) |
| Ireland | 76 | 82 | 74 | 80 | 76 | $2,173 | 4.0 (18) |
| Average | 59 | 73 | 69 | 71 | 70 | $1,931 | |

[a] Average of 2000 and 2005.
[b] See note *a* to Table 9.
[c] Excluding the Netherlands as a deviant case.
*Source*: OECD.stat (2009–2010).

(the United States was at 45%) and all but 3 (of 18) exceeded 70 percent in public share (the three minor exceptions are Switzerland at 59%, the Netherlands at 64%, and Australia at 67%). The lesson: to avoid the fate of the United States and overcome the pathologies of cost shifting and risk selection and the concomitant total cost of over 16 percent of GDP, a country must spend at least something like 65–70 percent of the total through the public sector.

Much of current debate about health-care reform in the United States singles out the alleged inefficiencies – "waste, fraud, and abuse" – of Medicare. Again we have assertions that, to be kind, fail to make the relevant comparisons.

Figure 4 directly compares Medicare and private insurance spending increases for comparable benefits in recent decades (Hacker, 2008: 12). From 1983 to 2006, private plans' spending per enrollee grew much faster than Medicare spending per enrollee (7.6% vs. 5.9% annual average), adding up to a 22 percent difference. The gap is even bigger in recent years – adding up to a full 37 percent edge for Medicare in cost savings. That is even more impressive if we note that Medicare covers all people 65 and over, the population at greatest risk for serious, long-term illnesses. And Medicare cannot engage in risk selection.

One reason for the greater efficacy of Medicare over private insurance for the same service is the extraordinary administrative costs of the private sector, including profits, advertising, sales staff, an apparatus to determine how to limit coverage and avoid sick, older patients and to craft inflated billing – not to mention lobbyists in Washington and elsewhere. All that multiplies paper shuffling (and computer overload) for every actor in the medical-industrial complex (cf. Relman, 2007). Estimates of the total cost of private health-care administration range from 18 to 20 percent of each medical care dollar; some estimates run higher (Wilensky, 2002: 611–614). Public-sector administration is

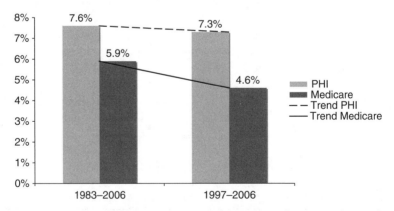

FIGURE 4. Per enrollee average annual percent change in Medicare spending and in private health insurance premiums for common benefits. *Source*: Centers for Medicare & Medicaid Services, Office of the Actuary, National Health Statistics Group, National Health Expenditures, 2008: table 13. Cf. Hacker, 2009.

much lower in Medicare (about 3% overhead) and the Veterans Administration (equally low).

Although the types of political economy that explain so much throughout my analysis do not work as well in predicting health outputs, the scheme does work at the extremes. In the late 1970s, with only two exceptions, leftism, corporatism, public spending per capita, and affluence interact to produce the best health performance among our 19 countries, while least-rich political economies that are also fragmented and decentralized have the poorest health performance.[5] The two exceptions are Japan, with lean spending but excellent performance; and Germany, with big spending and poor performance. Updating that finding to recent years, Table 9 shows four notable exceptions – the United States, Canada, Germany, and Japan. They are explained by additional structures and demographic facts that shape types of spending and the organization of their health-care systems.

Table 9 averages spending in 2000 and 2005 in U.S. currency and the performance index circa 2005. Comparing it with spending data for the late 1970s in all 19 countries (table not included), we first find that per capita spending through the public sector increased at a rate exceeding GDP growth per capita. If we control for inflation, the results show that in 25 years or so public health spending per capita increased on average by a factor of about 2.5, while GDP per capita increased on average by about a factor of 2.[6] Second, there is strong evidence of convergence in health performance and its causes since the late 1970s, with the poorest performers catching up with the top performers and a lesser convergence in spending. By 2005 public education spending became useless as a predictor of good health because of the convergence in universal secondary education and to a lesser extent postsecondary education. Similarly, GDP per capita became ever weaker as a predictor of good health, again as a result of some convergence in affluence among the rich democracies, with the least rich catching up. More important, the threshold of good health has been reached by almost all of the rich democracies, beyond which only the sharp contrasts in lifestyles and the organization and delivery of health care counted. Again, however, government health spending combined with corporatist bargaining structures and affluence still counts at extremes. Of nine countries with relatively good to excellent health performance, circa 2005, seven are consensual democracies; only two (Italy and Australia) are lean public spenders per capita.

Other studies suggest explanations for these two deviant cases among the top performers. Italy has long been known as an odd case with long life expectancy (indeed, disability-adjusted life expectancy) despite relatively low health-care spending and low GDP per capita (e.g., Ngongo et al., 1999; WHO, 2008), and, I would add, some corruption in the delivery of public services. There is consensus that the Mediterranean diet, still dominant in Italy, has an offsetting effect on three components of our index (age-specific life expectancy for men, the same for women, and deaths from circulatory disease) as well as effects on WHO's more numerous measures of health performance. As I found in my study of

TABLE 9. *Interaction of Government Health Spending per Capita (2000 and 2005), Corporatism, and Affluence Fosters Good Health Performance (ca. 2005)*

| | Nine Countries with Good to Excellent Health Performance | | | | Five Countries with Average Health Performance | | | | Five Countries with Poor to Fair Health Performance | | |
| --- | --- | --- | --- | --- | --- | --- | --- | --- | --- | --- | --- |
| | Health Index[a] | Health per Cap.[b] | GDP per Cap.[c] | | Health Index | Health per Cap. | GDP per Cap. | | Health Index | Health per Cap. | GDP per Cap. |
| Big health spenders ($2,340 and over per capita) | | | | | | | | | | | |
| Japan* | 13.5 (1) | $2,351 | $34,112 | Germany** | 7.0 (12) | $2,341 | $28,901 | United States | 2.5 (19) | $2,429 | $38,401 |
| Switzerland* | 12.5 (2) | $2,682 | $43,356 | | | | | | | | |
| Sweden** | 11.5 (4) | $2,490 | $34,154 | | | | | | | | |
| France* | 10.0 (6) | $2,340 | $28,380 | | | | | | | | |
| Norway** | 9.5 (7) | $3,784 | $51,525 | | | | | | | | |
| Austria** | 9.0 (9) | $2,360 | $30,916 | | | | | | | | |
| Cell avg. | 11.0 | $2,668 | $37,074 | | | | | | | | |
| Medium health spenders ($1,764–$2,254) | | | | | | | | | | | |
| Canada | 9.5 (7) | $1,952 | $28,973 | Finland** | 7.0 (12) | $1,764 | $31,171 | Denmark** | 5.5 (15) | $2,254 | $39,358 |
| | | | | Belgium** | 7.0 (12) | $1,972 | $29,579 | United Kingdom | 4.5 (17) | $2,043 | $31,380 |
| | | | | Netherlands** | 6.5 (14) | $2,093 | $32,326 | Ireland | 4.0 (18) | $2,173 | $38,425 |
| | | | | Cell avg. | 6.8 | $1,943 | $31,025 | Cell avg. | 4.7 | $2,157 | $36,388 |
| Lean health spenders ($1,646 and below) | | | | | | | | | | | |
| Australia | 12.0 (3) | $1,646 | $28,146 | Israel | 7.0 (12) | $1,062 | $25,930 | N. Zealand | 5.5 (15) | $1,342 | $20,003 |
| Italy** | 11.0 (5) | $1,606 | $25,448 | | | | | | | | |
| Cell avg. | 11.5 | $1,626 | $26,797 | | | | | | | | |

*Note:* Public spending and affluence each enhances health performance. Corporatism alone has little effect.

[a] Combines infant mortality rate per 1,000 live births, life expectancy at one for females, circulatory disease deaths per 100,000 aged 65–74, and deaths from pregnancy and childbirth complications per 100,000 females aged 25–34 – equally weighted. Dates circa 2005.

[b] Total government health expenditure per capita, average of 2000 and 2005 using U.S. dollar exchange rates. *Source:* OECD.stat (2009–2010)

[c] Average of 2000–2006 GDP per capita in dollars (OECD, 2009–2010). Data for Israel from World Bank (2008).

\* Corporatist without labor. Switzerland perhaps marginal.

\*\* Corporatist. Germany a marginal case.

family policy (2002, ch. 7 and p. 250, n. 17), an additional Italian policy may have a benign effect on pregnancy and childbirth deaths rates: an extraordinarily loose paid maternal leave arrangement. Mothers are required to take off two months before and three months after birth; most working women receive full salaries during leave; and many women routinely claim "risky" pregnancies from day one with the acquiescence of their physicians and thus take off for the entire pregnancy. A high density of doctors may add to this outcome.

The Australian deviation – the years 1981 to 2003 saw marked improvement in both absolute and relative life expectancy despite limited affluence and lean public spending – is easier to understand. As a WHO investigation suggests, there is a strong "healthy migrant" effect. Australia has favored immigrants with high education and socioeconomic status (immigrants are now 23% of its population), a factor that contributes to high scores on national health indices (Page et al., 2007).

Of five countries in Table 9 with poor to fair health performance, only one, Denmark, is corporatist; four are medium to low spenders (Denmark, the United Kingdom, Ireland, New Zealand). For reasons already discussed, the United States moved from below average in 1980 (rank 11) down to poorest performer in 2005 (rank 19).[7] Except for the United States, the exceptional cases of 1980 became less exceptional. German health-care reforms and relative increases in spending paid off in good health performance. Germany moved up from 17th of our 19 countries to 12th on the health index and is now quite high in government spending (with an average $2,341 per capita, it ranked seventh in the average of 2000 and 2005). This public-sector spending on health care may further increase Germany's performance in the years ahead if it continues its reorganization of health-care delivery.

The German reforms of the 1980s and early 1990s underscore the need for the strong bargaining power of government when confronted with powerful actors in the health-care system. Before reforms, Germany ranked very low in the density of nurses and midwives; it rated "poor" in coordination between specialists and primary-care physicians and in "community orientation"; and it evidenced an unusually sharp separation of hospital physicians, most of whom were salaried, and fee-for-service physicians in offices (the effect is to reduce the rate of medically appropriate referrals while increasing unnecessary treatment and costs). There was no effective ceiling on aggregate outlays for fee-for-service, office-based practitioners; per capita administrative costs in the system were second only to U.S. costs.

Most important in the cost escalation of the 1970s was the power of providers and pharmaceutical firms to game the system. Germany has long assured comprehensive near-universal coverage through a complex array of 768 nonprofit *Krankenkassen* (sickness funds based on occupation or region that mediate between the consumer and providers). The federal government administers health insurance for the uninsured poor, supervises private insurance for the affluent who use it, and coordinates a system of negotiations between labor, management, providers, and the *Krankenkassen*. Most of the fee negotiations, however, took place between single sickness funds and doctors organized in regional associations with public-law status. When in the late 1970s I asked the chief negotiator and strategist of the physicians' association whether the *Krankenkassen* functioned as a countervailing power to his organization, he scoffed. He told me that the sickness funds could easily be outmaneuvered by regional KVen (doctors' associations), which were much better equipped with personnel and resources than their bargaining partners. He also observed that competition between different types of sickness funds was not for cost control but for better service ("the region next door has the latest hospital technology, why can't we have the best?"). For the same reasons, physicians' income climbed to new heights. In short, all these characteristics of the German system help to explain its low social efficiency as of 1980.[8]

Reform and cost control came from a combination of budget pressures (mounting when unification required huge budget transfers to the former GDR); an SPD center-left majority in the Bundesrat in 1992 committed to a stronger public presence; strengthening of corporatist bargaining in the health-care sector (e.g., by centralizing the *Krankenkassen*, increasing their coordinating capacity); an increase in the role of salaried physicians; and the breakup of the cozy relationship between physicians and drug firms (e.g., more use of generics). The net effect: a substantial increase in social efficiency; Germany became less deviant in its cost-benefit ratio. It is unclear how Chancellor Merkel's center-right coalition's desire to cut back the budget will play out beyond the small increases in copayments adopted in July 2010. (For further details, see Wilensky, 2002: 617–618, and the citations therein, especially Starfield, Giaimo, Alber, Reinhart, and the Bundesministerium für Gesundheit.)

Since 1980, changes in the other exceptional cases – Japan, Austria, and New Zealand – that made them less exceptional are structural shifts and policy reforms. Japan not only sustained its excellent health performance but became a big spender (fastest birthrate decline and increased longevity resulted in fastest aging of population). Corporatist Austria's improvement can be explained by its persistently excellent economic performance and its increases in government health-care spending; that combination led to a jump in health performance (up from rank 19 to 7). New Zealand, the poster child for free-marketeers, became the poorest country of our 19 and a privatizer of health care. It made four major reforms in the 1990s based on Thatcher's effort in Britain and the American model and driven by various economic theories. Its partial privatization and prohibitive copayments had the usual effects: by 2005 New Zealand stayed well below average in health performance (for details on New Zealand politics and policies see Chapter 4; Wilensky, 2002: 420–424; Gauld, 2003).

In the past hundred years, *the currently rich democracies have converged in the broad outlines of health care.* Except for the United States, they all developed universal and comprehensive coverage for medical care, based on principles of social right and shared risk. They all developed central control of budgets with financing from compulsory individual and employer contributions and/or government revenues. All have permitted the insured to supplement government services with additional care, privately purchased. All, including the United

States, have rationed health care (United States by income, others by medical need). All have experienced a growth in doctor density and the ratio of specialists to primary-care personnel. All evidence a trend toward public funding.

Centralized state funding, by itself, expands access to care and, to some extent, reduces national mortality rates and improves health. In a natural process, state funding eventually leads to increased control over prices and personnel via direct employment, capitation payments, and/or government bargaining with providers. This combination yields better national health performance because it reduces inequalities in access to care by class and region, increases the volume of services available, limits the degree of specialization (and the concomitant duplication and lavish use of expensive high-tech machines and procedures). In general, the assertion of the public interest over the interests of insurance companies, pharmaceutical firms, hospitals, physicians, and other providers results in a gradual reallocation of budgets toward primary care and preventive community care. There is some evidence that centralized control of funding, prices, and personnel under state auspices compared to the alternatives yields greater social efficiency – an improved trade-off between mortality reduction and cost escalation – as well as a better balance between equality of access and levels of health (both improve) and innovation (a mixed effect). The effect on innovation is to speed up the adoption and diffusion of vaccines and effective screening programs while slowing down the use or overuse of expensive high-tech medical practice – basing it on medical need rather than ability to pay.

The American case highlights *the role of the ratio of specialists to primary care physicians, nurses, and midwives as a source of both costs and real health performance*. As the density of physicians everywhere climbed with economic growth, the proportion of all physicians who are specialists also climbed – in recent decades at an accelerating rate. By 1970 the proportion of specialists had risen from a trivial figure at the turn of the century to 34 percent in Britain, 42 percent in France, 56 percent in Sweden, and 77 percent in the United States (Hollingsworth, Hanneman, and Hage, 1992: 14 and table 1). Recent figures show that the specialist share of all doctors in Canada and Germany is a bit less than half, while the United States, despite recent efforts to increase GPs, maintains its heavy specialist lead.

In the absence of state control, a more privatized, commercialized system accelerates the trend toward increasing medical specialization and cost. A high proportion of specialists with little constraint on their high-tech services has several effects: it speeds the diffusion of innovation, especially very expensive technologies; it means more expensive services in hospitals and more staff; it reduces age-sex standardized mortality rates but at ever-increasing cost (Hollingsworth, Hanneman, and Hage, 1992: 30–31). Thus, a high ratio of specialists reduces social efficiency. In fact, both the trend toward doctor density and a rising ratio of specialists boost medical expenditures more than they reduce mortality (p. 151). In other words, there is a diminishing return from increases in this most-expensive, labor-intensive service.

A hint that societies with a medium or medium-high ratio of GPs to specialists have better health performance comes from the four-country study by

Hollingsworth, Hanneman, and Hage (1992). They find that although increases in total number of physicians and the number of specialists both reduce mortality, the sheer number of doctors has a bigger effect than the percentage of specialists. Based on regression analysis the study concludes, "Net of other factors more state control over prices and personnel, interacting with more investment in the number of doctors, has a beta of –0.78 with age-sex-standardized mortality rates; state control over prices and personnel interacting with the level of specialization has a beta of –0.48" (p. 25). They suggest that both types of practitioners have a good effect in all countries, partly because of the marked increase in the past century in the number of visits to doctors. As doctor density increased and access to care widened, doctor-patient interaction increased. The findings on physician density and mortality are consistent with the argument that GPs, compared to specialists, disseminate a broader array of biomedical knowledge throughout society. Specialists may "keep up" better and be a bit more open to scientific evidence and innovation, but they speak to a narrower range of issues and treat only part of the organic whole. Continuity of primary care in which the whole patient can be assessed and managed apparently has a greater effect in reducing population mortality than the uncoordinated care of specialists, however dramatic the latter's impact on the smaller number of intensive-care patients.

If an abundance of GPs, say about 50 percent, can favorably shape health outcomes, what about an abundance of nurses, nurse practitioners, and midwives? Relating our real health index (see note *a* to Table 9) to data on the number of nurses and midwives per 10,000 population for all of our countries but Israel, we see that a high nurse-midwife density is associated with good to excellent health performance (Wilensky, 2002: 592, table 16.2). Of the 7 countries ranked highest in health outputs in Table 9, 5 have the highest density of nurses and midwives. And of the 11 countries ranked average to poor in health performance, only 2 (Australia and the United Kingdom) are high in this staff category.[9]

The very low cost and the lowest specialist share of the United Kingdom suggest caution. It exceeds every other country in its GP to specialist ratio. If it also ranks so high in the nurse ratio, we might infer that the specialist/hospital sector is underfunded and understaffed, as is the whole system. And it was below average in health performance in the late 1970s and remained so in 2000–2005. Perhaps Britain's NHS represents the extreme beyond which the benign effects of GPs and nurses diminish. What is needed, however, is studies of these two broad types of care on a broader range of health indicators and a broader range of countries.

Although data are generally limited to fewer than our 19 countries, my analysis suggests that a balance between specialization and primary care, perhaps 50/50, results in wider diffusion of biomedical knowledge, more continuity of treatment, better diagnosis of "the whole patient," and more time and money for prevention. Further, if primary-care physicians and their assistants serve as guides to specialists and their activities are coordinated, better cost control is likely. Clinics that combine specialists and generalists where they interact freely – and are not hostages to insurance companies, and other managers preoccupied with cost cutting – may be ideal for this balance (cf. Mechanic, 1992: 1723).

Sweden and Norway approximate this picture. So do the few HMOs in the United States that have a decent cost-benefit ratio, rare as they are. Kaiser Northern California, including Oakland, is low-cost, high performance, with very high patient satisfaction. Organized so primary-care physicians act as guides to specialists, referrals are easy – down the hall or across the street. Pay is collective: salaries based on market rates for group practice in the area plus a 5 or 10 percent bonus for performance (patient outcomes and satisfaction); hours are regular (most female physicians choose to work part-time), and the support staff is unionized.

There is some evidence that all of these factors improve a nation's health performance. In contrast, systems with a sharp separation between hospital-based specialists and GPs, such as Britain's and New Zealand's, are below average in real health performance (Table 9). Finally, the case of the United Kingdom suggests that a willingness to pay more than 7 percent of GDP and a specialist ratio higher than 25 percent is necessary for good health performance.

What is true about the effectiveness of environmental policies (Chapter 2) is also true of health care – there is an *interdependence of public policies*. Countries that have reallocated their spending toward family physicians and physician assistants, including public health nurses, and have constrained the overuse of high-cost technology and specialist services, also tend to spend increasing amounts on health-related social policies that reduce the population at risk. They have reduced large inequalities in access and in levels of health. They have invested in public health. They have combined this with programs of subsidized housing, home care for the aged, poverty prevention, and health education in clinics and schools. They have developed family policies accenting prenatal and infant care, parental leave, and child care at every level of child development (Wilensky, 2002: ch. 7). They have crafted policies and programs that reduce teenage pregnancy and drug abuse (ch. 8). They have been effective in cleaning up the air and water (ch. 15). In short, the effectiveness of preventive medicine is greatly increased where it is integrated with broader health-relevant programs for the most vulnerable populations at risk and where cost pressures do not subvert the physician's clinical time and practice.

The United States is deviant in almost all of these measures. Although lifestyle risk factors (e.g., smoking, poor diet, drugs and alcohol abuse, firearms, sexual behavior, and auto accidents) account for about half of premature deaths in the United States in 1990, the United States spends less than an estimated 10 percent of its health-care dollars on disease prevention and helping people to adopt healthy habits (Bodenhorn and Kemper, 1997: iii, 2). That includes all funding for personal preventive health and community health services. Whether in comparative perspective 10 percent is high or low is not known because no good comparable definition or data are available. But there is reason to believe that the preventive percentage is relatively low and, more important, that the money the United States devotes to prevention is less effective than it is in many European countries, especially for younger populations (evidence reviewed in Wilensky, 2002: 593–595).

## C. WHY NO NATIONAL HEALTH INSURANCE IN THE UNITED STATES?

How did the United States make such a mess of its health care? Two explanations are most persuasive and one has little merit. First is the history of public policy choices since World War II; second, and most important, is the fragmented and decentralized structure and operation of the U.S. government. The weak explanation invokes our alleged love of free enterprise and the market, our hatred for government, and a culture of individualism. I have dealt with values and beliefs and the contours of public opinion in Chapter 4 where cross-national public opinion surveys combined with mass resistance to cutbacks in core programs of the welfare state cast doubt on the idea of American cultural exceptionalism. Confronted with abstract ideological questions about the proper role of government, mass publics in all rich democracies show great ambivalence; their sentiments are contradictory and confused. And they display an almost uniform and stable rank order of enthusiasm on issue-specific opinion. Peculiarities of American culture cannot explain our deviant health-care system.

### 1. Historical Legacy as an Explanation

Since World War II, U.S. public policy gave priority to increasing the supply of specialized, technologically intensive health care; widening access took a back seat. Among the measures: the Hospital Construction Act of 1946 and generous public financing of hospital-based care, biomedical research, technological innovation, and the training of specialists. This locked the United States into a payment system – procedure-based, fee-for-service – that discouraged primary care, preventive care, and low-tech solutions (Jacobs, 1995: 144–146). The resulting institutionalization of expensive care made it more difficult to reverse course and embrace universal coverage, quite apart from the political-system barriers to be discussed. In contrast, all other modern democracies began with equality of access as their primary goal, which forced them to concentrate hospital care in fewer places, multiply and disperse primary-care clinics, increase the supply of GPs or family practitioners, and discourage overspecialization. Where they established universal coverage but still centered their care in hospitals, as in Sweden and Germany, their costs did rise beyond the norm (see Table 9), but they were in a position to consolidate the high-tech care and ration it more fairly according to medical need rather than income.

Reinforcing a policy legacy that set the framework for the current health-care mess is a more general and uniquely U.S. legacy of race conflict. An unanticipated effect of the civil rights movement has been to block the expansion of social rights, especially since the 1960s. Although President Johnson fought vigorously for Medicare and Medicaid, he fought even harder for civil rights, a turning point in big policy. Subsequently the political time and energy devoted to the civil rights agenda and related court cases focused on blacks and other minorities no doubt diverted efforts that otherwise could have gone to the achievement of universal social rights such as national health insurance covering everyone. Although several other rich democracies with strong social cleavages (the Netherlands, Belgium) have crafted some form of affirmative action for minorities, they had already put in place more integrative social policies and bargaining structures. The United States is unique in degree if not kind in its political concentration on minority rights. This, of course, was a major source of the southern ascendance of a Republican Party hostile to social rights, as well as the revolt of the white middle mass (see analysis of the politics of the middle mass in Chapter 4 and Wilensky, 2008).

## 2. Electoral System, Structure, and Operation of Government

This is the most powerful explanation for past failures to achieve national health insurance. It is a reminder of what you learned in Political Science 101. It is worth repeating because it is basic to any understanding of the U.S. lag in many social, labor, and environmental policies. The uniquely extreme commercialization of the medical-industrial complex with its high administrative costs, a private sector that greatly exceeds that of every other country, a chaos of private and public regulation, a very high ratio of specialists to primary-care physicians, a shortage of nurses, and much higher use of expensive technologies account for the poor cost-benefit ratio; they also make change difficult. The most important political barrier to the adoption of national health insurance is the dominance of the insurance companies. All other countries have contained their power and confined their reach.

In view of these structural barriers, it is understandable that the center Left and even parts of the center Right who favor national health insurance have shied away from it. Reform efforts from Teddy Roosevelt through Truman to Clinton have failed. FDR's two-to-one to four-to-one margin in the U.S. Senate when he signed New Deal social legislation did not bring national health insurance; and Johnson, with his big margin, had to settle for Medicare for the aged and Medicaid for the poor and long-term disabled.

The political barriers that account for these failures can best be understood if we compare Canada and the United States. They are similar in so many ways, yet Canada was able to achieve national health insurance at less cost and better outcomes, while the United States remained odd man out. First, the similarities: both countries share origins in the British Empire but lack a feudal past. Both have a decentralized federalism with continual battles over "states (provincial) rights," alternating major party control of government, a "majoritarian" electoral system with the rule of first-past-the-post winner take all, and fairly rapid erosion of political parties in the electorate. Both are well below average in their social spending. There is even a parallel in the regionalism of the two countries: from President Johnson on, federal largesse has flowed disproportionately to the South and Southwest just as federal funds in Canada went disproportionately to Quebec (militants derisively call this "fedéralisme de portefeuille" as they win attention and cash by threatening to secede). Finally, and most important, before Canada adopted comprehensive reform in the early 1970s, the medical systems of the two countries were much alike and their health-care spending as a percentage of GDP was nearly the same (about 7.5%); both countries paid physicians by fee-for-service, and physicians' training and outlook were alike (Kudrle and Marmor, 1981: 104). Even the political coalitions strongly opposed to national health insurance were similar.

Despite these notable similarities, several small structural differences in this one policy area added up to a near-insurmountable obstacle for U.S. efforts to achieve national health insurance. My comparison of the two countries points to five structural differences.

- *More paralyzing federalism.* There are 50 U.S. states vs. 10 Canadian provinces. Beyond the higher number of units, there is no greater division of powers, no weaker central government, no more fragmented and decentralized federalism than that of the United States The dogma of local self-government is enshrined in its constitution and laws; a federal system divides powers among central government and 50 sovereign states, which in turn, divide powers among thousands of counties, townships, municipalities, and other local units. To survive and deal with real problems that don't fit these arbitrary boundaries, the modern metropolis is therefore forced to create a staggering number of special district governments – school districts, water districts, fire districts, sanitation districts, park and port districts, rapid transit authorities – each concentrating on a limited area-wide task; each competing for budget, tax base, or subsidy; all adding to the maze of overlapping and duplicating units. It is free enterprise in government – with every municipality, every district, every state for itself. If there is a constitutional explanation of why the United States finds it so difficult to come to grips with urban problems or to develop national social, labor, and industrial policies, it is here, in the tyranny of the locality, made possible by an extreme federalism and the separation of powers (Wilensky, 1965: xviii–xix).
- *Weaker demonstration effects.* You can have progressive legislation in Minnesota, Wisconsin, or New York, including health-care reform – and nothing will happen nationally. In Canada, if a progressive province such as Saskatchewan or British Columbia lights the way, their demonstration effects can spread. This occurred not only with health care but also with the late 1990s' reform of the pension system, when 11 provincial governors gathered with the prime minister and followed the model of Quebec.
- *An electoral system more unfavorable to a left third party.* In Canada the New Democratic Party (NDP) and parties in Quebec, believers in an active affirmative government, hold many seats and can dominate in important provinces, moving the whole political spectrum a little to the left. Electoral laws in the United States block such parties.
- *Unique rules of the U.S. Senate – the tyranny of the minority.* First is the use and abuse of the filibuster, used by Republicans under Clinton more than in the

entire history of the country. Since the days when Strom Thurmond talked on the Senate floor for 24 hours to stop a civil rights bill, the frequency of filibusters has soared. Barbara Sinclair (2008a) shows that there was an average of only one filibuster per Congress during the 1950s; that figure grew geometrically reaching a peak of 52 filibusters in 2007–2008 (the 110th Congress). Also prominent is the privilege of a single senator to delay or kill an appointment or a bill by putting a hold on it. (For a longer list, see Mann and Ornstein, 2006.) Including all of what Sinclair labels "extended-debate-related problems" – such as procedural abuses, filibusters, threats to filibuster, and holds – only 8 percent of major legislation in the 1960s was involved; by 2007–2008 that formula for paralysis reached 70 percent. Now, with the election of Obama and a Democratic majority, the mere threat of a filibuster is enough to kill such measures as health-care reform, energy policy, labor policy, and the like.

Of course rural and small-town overrepresentation embedded in the Constitution explains much. A dramatic example of such unrepresentative government is the role of the Senate Finance Committee headed by Max Baucus (D-MT) in undermining the House effort to include a robust public option in the health-care reform of 2009. The six states of the "gang of six," the chief negotiators in charge of writing a bipartisan bill, represent a whopping 2.8 percent of the American population (Montana, Iowa, New Mexico, Wyoming, North Dakota, Maine). It is these highly unrepresentative senators, three Democrats, three Republicans, to whom President Obama deferred in both timing and substance in an obsessive effort to achieve bipartisan consensus. Given the political complexion of the current Republican Party and of the "gang of six," the political energy spent cultivating them was wasted; the strategy was doomed from the outset. An extreme federalism interacting with a flawed presidential strategy was fatal. More of this in Chapter 8.

• *Weaker party discipline*. Entrepreneurial senators can go their own way. Even with a recent increase in party discipline among congressional Democrats (Republicans have long marched in lockstep), there are numerous deviations from the Democratic party line.

These are modest differences between Canada and the United States that make a difference. Added up, they explain why we failed to achieve national health insurance, whereas Canada, starting from the same place, similar in so many ways, ended up with national health insurance and good health performance (see Tables 7 and 9). Chapter 8 suggests political requisites and strategies to overcome American exceptionalism in this area and, more broadly, to restore some aspects of deliberative democracy.

# 6

# The Impact of "Globalization"

## An Overview

In recent decades, one group of social scientists has argued that the nation-state is eroding in its political capability and analytical utility. They include Immanuel Wallerstein in his analysis of the relations of core, semiperiphery, and periphery in the modern "world system" (1974); Peter Evans in his early treatment of "dependent development" in Latin America (1979); and such students of international relations as Robert Keohane and Joseph Nye (1971 and 1977; cf. Keohane and Nye, 2000) and Peter Gourevitch (1986), who emphasize the increasing power of transnational and international actors (multinational corporations, international organizations) and the global forces of technology, communication, and trade. Globalization theorists who have more recently articulated these themes include Susan Strange (1996), Philip Cerny (1994), Peter Evans (1997), and Louis Pauly (1997). Another similar argument is that the rise of supranational political arrangements such as the EU is eroding the legitimacy of the nation-state (Keating and Hooghe, 2005; McCormick, 2007). These scholars vary in their depiction of the specific sources, degree, and speed of global threats to state autonomy. But when they analyze national differences in public policy, they all argue that a nation's position in the world economy determines its institutions and policies more than anything else, or at least is becoming a prime determinant.[1]

A second group of scholars, which includes myself (1975, 1976, 1981, 1983, 1987, 2002, 2006), Peter Katzenstein (1985), Peter Flora (1986; Flora and Heidenheimer, 1981), David Cameron (1982, 1984), Hugh Heclo (1974), Gosta Esping-Anderson (1985), Walter Korpi (1978), Paul Pierson (2001), Iverson and Cusack (2000), Hemerijck and Ferrera (2004), Brady, Beckfield, and Seeleib-Kaiser (2005), Jonah Levy (2006), Brady, Beckfield, and Zhao (2007), and most students of the welfare state, are much more impressed with the importance of national differences in social, political, and economic organization as sources of variations in public policy and system performance.

In all the talk about the fiscal crisis of the state or the crisis of the welfare state, we often attribute changes in national policies and patterns of behavior to globalization, international competition, or external shocks rather than to these internal structural differences. There are two things wrong with this. First, it ignores the previous history of diverse national responses to cross-national capital and labor flows and external shocks. Second, it underplays evidence of the internal causes of labor policies and welfare-state development and their economic effects.

As I have shown, the external pressures that are labeled "globalization" have little or no effect in explaining social policies or system outputs – such nontrivial outcomes as economic performance, political legitimacy, equality, poverty reduction, and real health. What counts are national differences in political, economic, demographic, and social structures. Although these structures are converging with continuing industrialization, the national differences remain large.

This is demonstrated in four parts of my analysis where one might expect external forces to have some influence: findings regarding (1) the causes of types of bargaining arrangements – especially democratic corporatism vs. others (in Chapter 3); (2) the effects of the welfare state on economic performance (Chapters 1 and 3); (3) the effects of the three oil shocks in 1974, 1979, and 2002 and sudden shifts in the terms of trade on subsequent economic performance (Chapter 1 and Wilensky, 2002: ch. 12); and (4) national variations in energy policies and performance (Chapter 2). In each area, the domestic structures overwhelm the external pressures and shocks as sources of national policies and performance.

This is not to deny the recent effects of financial deregulation and the speculative and even corrupt innovations in financial instruments, effects that spread from the United States to the world. Plainly, however, all external pressures and shocks are filtered through and greatly modified by domestic structures. But maybe increased global competition will have a stronger impact on the welfare state and labor-market policies in the future, whatever its limited impact in the past. Many politicians and scholars believe that increased immigration, the spread of multinational corporations (MNCs), the deregulation of labor markets, the outsourcing of jobs, and the globalization of finance, especially the increased autonomy of central banks, will undermine all the national differences that make a big difference in human welfare. A capsule summary of my findings about their impact may help.

## A. THE IMPACT OF CAPITAL FLOWS

Neither capital flows nor labor migration is new. It is not even clear what the trend is. We must remember that all the great empires since the 16th century were built on the flow of capital from creditor nations to debtors.[2] It appears that since the late 19th century net foreign lending of creditor nations as a percentage of GNP declined to a low in the 1950s and then rose again in recent decades (Edelstein, 1982: 3; calculations from OECD, 1974 and 1992 National Accounts). It does not yet quite match the earlier rate. But if we go back more than a century, sovereign debt as a proportion of creditor-country GNP shows a steady decline since the early 1800s (Eichengreen and Lindert, 1989: 2–3).[3] In short, compared to the mid-20th century, capital has become somewhat more mobile; compared to previous

50-year periods, capital has become less mobile. The period just preceding the financial crisis of 2008–2009 saw a spike upward in international capital flows, especially the wide use of financial instruments such as derivatives – interest rate swaps and options, currency swaps, and equity derivatives. These esoteric instruments increased fivefold from 2002 to 2008, reaching a "value" of $684 trillion before the crash. That is more than 10 times the total GDP of the entire world. There was a short dip during the crash but by June 2009 derivative "values" were back above December 2007 levels, not yet reaching the previous peak but trending up (Bank of International Settlements, 2009).

Whatever the trend in capital flows, the assertion that we now live in a new world with a single capital market in which funds flow freely to the investments with the highest rate of return is simply wrong. As Martin Feldstein observes in an analysis of global savings and investment, "The patient money that will support sustained cross-border capital flows is surprisingly scarce. ... Only 10 percent of the value of the assets in the 500 largest institutional portfolios in the world is invested in foreign securities" (*Economist*, June 24, 1995: 72–73). Or if we focus on all recent U.S. investors, only about 12 percent of their portfolios is in foreign equities, far below the percentage that would be invested on the basis of the capitalization of markets in the rest of the world (Ahearne, Griever, and Warnock, 2004). In other words, even today there is a strong home-country bias among both managers of big money and the average investor, a bias globalization has done little to erase.

There is a similar home-country or more precisely a "home region" bias in international trade – an almost exponential decline in trade activity the greater the distance between the trading partners (Thompson, 2006: 14, table 2; Held and McGrew, 2007: 80, fig. 5.5, and 100, table 5.4). In fact, after about 1,000 kilometers (631 miles) from the home base, there is a sharp drop-off in trade. Trade patterns, like financial flows, are global only in small measure.

## B. CONVERGENCE IN IMMIGRATION, DIFFERENCES IN POLICIES AND POLITICS

Like the trend of capital flows, labor may or may not be more mobile than in the past. For the European countries where data are available, migration rates (immigration plus emigration as a percentage of the total population) were at about the same levels in the early 1980s as they were at the turn of the century.

For the United States, Canada, and New Zealand – countries of popular destination – there was less immigration in the 1980s than there was before World War I. Immigration as a percentage of population plainly dropped sharply from the early 1900s to 1988 in all three countries. Although in recent years mass migrations have again picked up they do not yet match the historical patterns.[4]

As Philip Martin suggests, industrial democracies are not being overrun by a tidal wave of immigrants. In the mid-1980s there were only about 40 million of them in all the industrial countries: 15 to 20 million in North America, 15 to 20 million in Western Europe, and 2 to 3 million in industrial Asian countries

(P. Martin, 1992: 11–12; cf. P. Martin, Abella, and Kuptsch, 2006; and UN, 2002). "International migration remains an extraordinary event despite the evolution of demand, supply, and network factors that encourage migration" (P. Martin, 1993: 6). The United Nations projects that the number of worldwide migrants will reach 214 million in 2010. Compared to the 155 million of the 1990s, that sounds like a big burst, but it is up only slightly as a share of total population from a steady 2.9 percent in 1995–2005 to 3.1 percent in 2010 (UN, 2009: 75). The main reason is that return flows almost canceled out new outflows over that period. Substantial numbers of immigrants throughout modern history return to their homelands.

Where do the migrants land? A third of the world's migrants move from developing countries to industrial countries, as from Mexico to the United States; almost a third move from one developing country to another, as from Indonesia to Malaysia; almost 30 percent move from one rich country to another, as from Canada to the United States; and about 7 percent move from an industrial country to a developing country, as with Japanese expatriates in Thailand (*Migration News*, Oct. 2009).

The percentage of refugees as a share of international migrants has been fluctuating around a slow downward trend. From 1990 to 2005 that figure dropped from 11.2 percent of the total to 7.1 percent (UN, 2006: 74), but it has recently moved up. Between 1990 and 2010 the number of refugees changed little, except for a one-year dip in 2005, and in the past few years the refugee share of total migrants crept up. In Europe the migrant percentage actually increased between 1990 and 2005 – largely due to a post-Soviet bump 1990–2000 – and faded thereafter.

The main source of refugee flow is the combination of deep poverty and repressive regimes: almost all of the most serious refugee-generating countries fall below $400 per capita GNP and are ruled by military governments – for example, Vietnam, North Korea, Haiti, Uganda, Ethiopia, Chad, Mali, Zaire, Laos, Afghanistan under the Taliban, Burundi, Rwanda, and Sudan. Since the early 1980s, the "Third World" share of the world's refugees (both sending and receiving countries) is about 80 to 90 percent (Hakovirta, 1993: 37, 40–44). Most of the world decline in the share of refugees in migrant streams from 1990 to 2010 can be attributed to some falloff in the less developed countries.

Returning to total migration, in the late 1990s there began a decade-long resurgence of intra-European migration, especially from Eastern Europe to countries with explosive growth such as Ireland and Spain. However, the Great Recession of 2007–2009 brought an explosion of unemployment in the same countries, triggering a backflow of migrants. In one year, 2008–2009, an estimated 50,000 immigrants to Ireland returned home, mostly to Eastern Europe. In Bucharest, Romania, construction workers from China were camped out at their embassy trying to get out (*New York Times*, Apr. 25, 2009). Subsidies to go home were common. Spain was paying substantial sums to unemployed immigrants from Romania and South America (mostly from Brazil) if they agreed to leave and not return for at least three years. The average payout was $18,500 (*Wall Street Journal*, Apr. 28, 2009). The Czech Republic was giving each foreigner who had lost his job and wanted to go home about $660 plus a one-way plane ticket. All these comings and goings match the recent boom-and-bust economic patterns and are likely to subside when the worldwide recession recedes and the labor market slowly returns to something like normal.

Of course, if we do nothing about climate change, the long-term trend will reverse. We will see an enormous flow of climate refugees (Chapter 2). The current lack of a tidal wave of immigrants from poor to rich countries will turn into a tsunami of refugees from coastal and southern regions to high-ground regions and countries.

Perhaps an increase of net migration to the successful political economies of Europe will make them look a bit more like Canada, the United States, and Australia in their cultural and social diversity and minority group conflict. But it is not clear that this will mean a dualism in jobs, wages, and living standards as radical as the dualism of North America and Australia, countries that have developed a large "underclass." Those latter countries have been among the leading job creators from 1968 through the 1980s while France, West Germany, Austria, and the United Kingdom were below the median in job creation. The top job creators, as I have shown (Wilensky, 2002: ch. 13) were responding to demographic changes (high net migration rates and high rates of 15–24-year-olds entering the labor force) and changes in social structure (the combination of high and accelerating rates of female labor-force participation, high rates of family breakup with no family policy to cushion the shocks, and the feminization of poverty). The jobs they created were mainly low-paid, low-skill service jobs using migrants, young people, and divorced women pressed to the wall, many of them part-time or temporary workers looking for full-time work. The net outcome over long periods has been high job turnover, lowered investment in training, deterioration in real wages, and an increase in unproductive welfare spending – all of which puts them in competition with the newly industrializing countries, for example, South Korea and Taiwan, themselves moving in the opposite direction toward high wages and high-value-added products. There is no reason that Germany, Japan, Belgium, Austria, the Netherlands, and the Scandinavian countries would now want to go down that road – that is, no reason other than politicians in thrall to neoliberal economists whose pyrotechnical models boil down to "government bad, market good."

Some of these nations are able to regulate immigration from outside the EC a bit better than the North Americans can. For instance, Switzerland has long practice in controlling its borders; Germany levies stiff fines and penalties on employers who hire illegal workers and enforces these regulations, more or less, by identity cards and inspectors visiting work sites (e.g., building construction). Historically, both countries were able to incorporate immigrant labor into the secondary sector: a few years after foreign workers were stabilized, 73 percent of West German immigrants (1975) and 67 percent of immigrants to Switzerland (1972) were in manufacturing and related jobs, not in agriculture, construction, and service (Sassen, 1988: 44–45). The Mediterranean countries – Italy, France – as well as the United States may have a harder time regulating and integrating foreign labor because of long-unfenced coastlines and easier access.

Aside from variation in border control, national differences in educational and integration policies matter in reducing conflict. The United States had great success in integrating earlier immigrant groups during the big waves of immigration before World War I. Among the policies that helped was a strong commitment to host language learning for both adults and their children, with only a secondary focus on promoting the heritage culture and language. In an odd switch of policies, it is now the rich democracies of Europe that accent host language training whereas the United States has turned to an accent on race consciousness, identity, and civil rights, neglecting education in host language and culture and the idea of integration (Bloemraad, Korteweb, and Yurdakul, 2008: 8.17; OECD, 2008b).[5] This is one reason why almost half of all immigrant workers in the United States are classified by the U.S. Census as "limited English proficient" (*American Community Survey*, 2005):

Whatever these differences, liberal democracies evidence convergent trends in immigration experience (cf. G. P. Freeman, 1994: 17–30; Collinson, 1993: 57–59; Hollifield, 1992: 32–33, 84–85, 204–213; Martin et al., 2006):

- Increasing effort and capacity to regulate migration flows, especially absolute numbers.
- The increased moral resonance of family unification as a major criterion for admission, accounting for an increasing percentage of total immigration and decreasing state control of the social characteristics (education, skills) of the immigrants.
- An hourglass shape of the education and skills of the recent immigration population. Although there are some national differences here, the central tendency is toward some overrepresentation of college graduates and a very big overrepresentation of the least educated and least skilled. Philip Martin (1992: 14) estimates that American immigrants are 30 percent highly skilled, 20 percent in the middle, and 50 percent unskilled.
- The transformation of temporary work programs into permanent immigration. (Like The Man Who Came to Dinner and stayed for several months, the guest workers of Europe increasingly settled down in the host countries for long periods, even their whole working lives.) Movements for expanding immigrant rights were a natural outcome.
- The uneven spread of migrants in Western Europe 1950–93.[6] The explanation is variation in the demand for and recruitment of "temporary" labor and in the openness to the rising tide of political refugees, East to West and increasingly South to North, an openness that has gradually diminished in the past two decades.
- As legal entry routes are restricted in response to xenophobic political pressure, illegal entrants and visa overstayers have increased, although, as we have seen, nations vary in their capacity to police their borders and control illegal immigration.

Openness to refugees also varies, although recent steps toward EU standardization is reducing national variation on the Continent. In 1992 Germany took in two-thirds of the 572,000 asylum seekers entering Europe as it struggled to get other countries to share the burden. On July 1, 1993, it changed its open asylum policy to accept refugees only from regimes that were persecuting them. That made it difficult for persons who passed through "presumably safe countries" – including Romania, Bulgaria, Gambia, Ghana, and Poland – to apply for asylum. Germany worked out arrangements with each adjacent country to help police its borders, giving money for that purpose to Poland and Czechoslovakia (the Czech Republic and Slovakia as of January 1, 1993). All this sharply cut the number of applicants. The German Bundestag later approved an expansion of the number and power of the border police and raised penalties on illegal alien smugglers. Again, it is far from impossible to regulate immigration (*Migration News*, Aug. 1994). Of course, it is a beggar-thy-neighbor policy – one country's successful border control is often another country's headache, a powerful reason for international agreements on burden sharing. The European Union, as it enlarged eastward, has moved in this direction, increasing the use of cross-border police, common support for external border guards, and judicial cooperation (Plender, 2008).

Because unskilled jobs are a declining portion of the labor force in all these countries, however, they all confront a choice between burgeoning welfare costs for their least-educated new immigrants, women heading broken homes, and young people, on the one hand, or the more productivity-enhancing strategies they have already pursued, on the other. The Scandinavian model (e.g., Sweden, Finland, Norway, Denmark) and the Japanese model of corporatism without labor (e.g., cultivate worker loyalty and labor peace, invest heavily in human and physical resources, maintain high rates of capital investment) or the North American model (maintain confrontational labor relations and adapt the technical and social organization of work to a large, cheap labor supply) – these are the real choices. Happily the demographics of the next few years are favorable in many countries: the lower rate of entry of native young people will create labor shortages that immigrants, if trained, can fill. That window of opportunity in the United States, however, has almost closed because the bulge in secondary school (the "baby boom echo") has reached college and/or the labor market. Because the marked acceleration of American retirees will not take hold until about 2020, American reliance on immigrant labor will be about 10 or 15 years behind Europe's: from about 2005 to 2020 we can expect increased tension between natives and immigrants in the United States – even beyond what we already see in California, Texas, New Mexico, Arizona, and Florida.

The economic impact of immigration, considering all costs and benefits over the long run, is very likely positive. This reality, however, is not what plays out in politics, where immigrants are used as scapegoats for a wide range of troubles. Complicating any assessment, the real economic effects vary over time and place.

Studies of the United States using data from before 1980 (Borjas, 1990: ch. 5; Abowd and Freeman, 1991a; Muller, 1993) show that "immigrants have been absorbed into the American labor market with little adverse effect on natives" (Abowd and Freeman 1991b: 22). In fact, in areas of greatest immigrant concentration – for example, Miami, Los Angeles, New York, San Francisco – employment of natives increased with rising immigration, except for New York (p. 24). The reasons: immigrants purchase goods and services where they work, thereby raising demand for labor; immigrant skills complement the skills of many native workers, raising demand for them; even with their concentration in gateway cities, if immigrants had not taken the low-skilled jobs there, similarly young, uneducated Americans would have filled the gap via migration from other areas (pp. 22–24); and natives attenuate the negative earnings effects of recent immigration by moving to other localities (Borjas and Freeman, 1992: 11) while at least 20 to 30 percent of the foreign-born in the United States, probably the least self-supporting, return to their birthplace or migrate elsewhere within a decade or two, thereby relieving pressure on the labor market (Borjas, 1992: 18).

But as the percentage of uneducated, unskilled immigrant labor rose after 1980 when the U.S. job market for the least educated was deteriorating, studies of subsequent years concluded that immigration was depressing the earnings of natives, especially the relative earnings of high-school dropouts, including young blacks and earlier-arriving Hispanics (Borjas, Freeman, and Katz, 1992: 238–242; Wilensky, 1992b and 2002: ch. 13). An oversupply of cheap immigrant labor was competing with an oversupply of cheap native labor.

Are immigrants a disproportionate burden on the welfare state? This myth was given credence by Donald Huddle's flawed research (1993) claiming that the 19.3 million immigrants entering the United States from 1970 to 1992 were in 1992 a net burden on native taxpayers of $42.5 billion, projected at $67 billion a year in 1993–2002. (Subsequent political campaigns repeated such claims.) On the contrary, immigrants – even those arriving since 1980 – are probably being ripped off by American taxpayers. The reasons: first, they are overwhelmingly young workers who pay Social Security and Medicare taxes (not the native aged who use most of the expensive pension, disability, and health-care services). And their fertility rates are on average as low as the comparable young natives (no disproportionate use of schools). The very youth of the immigrant population is a boon for the United States; the immigrants will help pay for the baby boomers' retirement and medical care, partially offsetting the looming mismatch of pensioners and workers. Second, they pay state sales taxes, local property taxes, and gasoline taxes; their employers pay unemployment insurance and worker's compensation taxes. Third, if they are legal, their use of social welfare benefits in earlier decades was less than that of natives. Although such use is now slightly above the natives' (because of higher unemployment rates of the young and because the aged among them use means-tested SSI), these are the smallest parts of welfare-state burdens and have deteriorated in real value.[7] Finally, if they are illegals, they are by law denied almost all welfare benefits and are afraid to use any services for fear of being deported.

All this leaves aside the long-run assimilation of immigrants and the economic recovery since 1992 as well as the contribution of their work to GNP. Thus cross-sectional estimates (e.g., 1990–1992) capture neither business-cycle variations nor variations over the life cycle that show more long-run payoff and less cost. Today's cross-sectional picture overrepresents new arrivals who earn less and use more state services; later, like their predecessors, they earn more, pay more taxes, and use fewer public services. Even those initially in an enclave economy (e.g., Asian immigrants in ethnic neighborhoods in Los Angeles whose job histories were analyzed in the early 1990s) typically transcend the ethnic economy and enter the mainstream metropolitan economy as they gain local work experience and increase their human capital (Nee, Sanders, and Sernau, 1994). As Fix and Passel (1994) show in their careful review of studies emphasizing the immigrant burden, all of them understate the revenue stream from immigrants and overstate the cost to government.[8]

Again, national experiences differ depending on institutions and policies. In Germany, for instance, although foreigners are increasingly overrepresented among the recipients of social assistance (which is only 5 percent of the Federal Republic's social expenditures), the aggregate impact of foreigners on the entire German system of taxes and transfers is positive – for example, a fiscal gain of about DM14 billion in 1991 (a 1992 study by Barabas et al. from a leading economic research institute cited by Alber, 1994: 5). A similar finding of net gain is reported from studies of France (Hollifield, 1992: 85–86). Regarding the labor market, both Australia and Germany evidence much less negative earnings impact than the United States because their occupational wage differentials are smaller than those of the United States and their unionization rates are much higher. Germany also invests more in training, job creation, and job placement. A study of migrants to Britain from 1983 to 2008 showed an initial pay gap with native-born of more than 30 percent for men and 15 percent for women that took only 20 years to disappear for men and a very short 4–6 years for women (Dickens and McKnight, 2008). And Australia from the 1970s through the early 1980s used education and skills as criteria for admission so the differences between natives and immigrants did not grow so much (Abowd and Freeman, 1991b: 23). On the other hand, countries that match Sweden's generosity in social programs for immigrants may find that the economic costs exceed the benefits even in the long run.

Whatever the European and Asian political economies do about the welfare state, the labor market, and social policies, and whatever the real economic effects of immigration, I suspect that they will all experience a moderate increase in ethnic-racial-religious conflict, hardly unknown in the past, only this time without major war.

Insofar as rich democracies converge in the number of immigrants as a fraction of the labor force, they are likely to experience cycles of nativist, xenophobic protest, some of it parliamentary, some violent, as in the history of the older immigrant nations, the United States, Australia, and Canada. The cycles of protest are driven by the convergence of economic downturns (unemployment, downward mobility, declines in income), immigrant population numbers and concentration, and the social distance between immigrants and natives.[9] How anti-immigrant sentiments are channeled, however, is another matter. National and local mobilizing structures – political parties, legislatures, prime ministers, interest groups – can either legitimize or oppose xenophobic expression, exploit mass fears and prejudices in a search for scapegoats, or try to contain them.

We can see the interaction of strong economic deprivation, much immigrant concentration, great social distance, and nativist political mobilization at work in the United States and Germany in the early 1990s. In the Los Angeles riots of 1992 much of the violence of blacks was targeted at Koreans and Chinese; the locations were areas of high unemployment of young males. In the 1994 election in California and in most closely contested congressional districts in many states the Republicans used the problems of crime, welfare mothers, and illegal Mexican or Caribbean immigrants as negative symbols in a successful campaign to direct a frenzy of anger at their Democratic opponents. Media "talk shows" poured oil on that fire. White men of the middle mass (high school or part-college educated) from the West and South who said their family's economic situation had worsened in the last four years were especially attracted to those appeals (based on exit polls, *New York Times*, Nov. 13, 1994; see Chapter 4 on the revolt of the middle mass). The intense congressional debate over reform of immigrant laws in 2006 reflected the same political lineup.

That increased minority-group numbers and concentration can produce intensified resistance from native populations is evident from an earlier time in U.S. history. Lieberson (1980: 284–291) shows that in the early 20th century, major increases in both the residential segregation of blacks and their percentage of the population brought on an escalation of violent protest by whites, most of them earlier-arriving immigrants who felt threatened by black encroachment.

Anti-immigrant violence and voting in Germany has similar roots. Since 1961 the percentage of foreigners in the German population rose from 1.2 percent to more than 8 percent (Alber, 1994: 5) – about the same as the 8.7 percent of the United States in 1994. As Alber shows (graph 7 and table 1), bursts of nativist violence (acts per 1,000 asylum seekers) occurred in 1983–1984, a time of accelerating unemployment, and 1991–1993 (combining recession, the economic strain of reunification, and rising immigration). He reports an average of nearly six violent acts per 1,000 asylum seekers every day, including several arson fires during 1991–1993. Regarding social distance, although Germany's proportion of resident foreigners was not as large as Belgium's, its percentage of immigrants from non-European countries (6%) put it first among countries of the European Union. Regarding mobilization, in the 1990 election male East German voters below the age of 25, whose unemployment was greatest, gave the extreme right nativist Republican Party its best election result of 7 percent (p. 8). The party broke through first in Bremen, a port city with a declining industrial center, a high rate of unemployment, and a heavy concentration of Turks, Poles, and other immigrants. The combination of youth unemployment and social distance is also captured in Solingen, where the killers of a Turkish girl in May 1993 were members of a youth gang who had been kicked out of a Turkish restaurant (p. 11); five other Turkish females, long-term residents, were killed in a single gruesome arson fire in the same city that month.

That public policies toward immigration shape the intensity of anti-immigrant violence and voting is suggested by a comparison of two countries with substantial recent immigration, generous social policies, and low rates of poverty and inequality, but contrasting immigration policies: Germany, where the principle of *jus sanguinis* was dominant and nationality was conferred mainly by blood ties (until the center-left reform of 2000), and Sweden, where the principle of *jus soli* is dominant and nationality is conferred mainly by place of birth. In 1992 Germany accepted 5.3 times as many asylum seekers as Sweden but experienced 29 times as many acts of antiforeign arson or bombing attacks (Alber, 1994: 3). In a rough comparison of nativist violence in the early 1990s in five European countries (France, Britain, Switzerland, Sweden, and Germany), Alber suggests that, although Britain, Switzerland, Sweden, and Germany all experienced an increase in violent incidents, the number and intensity of anti-foreign violence are highest in Germany (p. 3). An explanation of Sweden's much lower rate of violence is its policy of assimilating immigrants by aggressive education, training, and integrative social programs and by giving immigrants the right to vote and run for office in community and regional elections after three years of residence. Sweden is also first among 12 European countries in its naturalization rate.[10]

Comparing Germany and France yields a hint of an inverse relationship between anti-immigration voting and anti-immigrant violence.[11] It also validates the idea that integration policies reduce the rate of violence even where perceived economic deprivation and social distance are similar.

First, the similarities. The supporters of anti-immigrant, populist-right groups and parties in both countries are concentrated in areas of exceptional immigrant concentration and economic instability or at least perceived instability. These groups draw support from both the losers and winners of structural readjustment. It is not only economic deterioration that provokes protest; any major economic change, up or down, heightens the sense of insecurity. For instance, among the German winners are Baden-Württemberg and Bavaria; among the French winners are Paris and the Ile-de France and Alsace. German losers include Schleswig-Holstein and Bremen; French losers include Marseille and Bouche du Rhône. All of these areas are either strongholds of protest voting or evidence above-average support for anti-immigrant politicians.

The core supporters of Le Pen in France and the Republikaner in Germany are not especially marginal. They are citizens of the middle mass (lower white collar, upper working class, self-employed). In both countries, most are males with vocational training or high school but no higher education. Whether they are employed or not, they have a strong sense of insecurity – economic and physical – that is much more intense and widespread than among voters for other more established parties. They rank insecurity, law and order, and crime at the top of their concerns. Even the lawless skinheads in Germany identify their biggest worry as *Zukunftssicherheit* or "future security." Responding to political demagogues, they blame their job insecurities and other troubles on immigrants.

In both countries the targets of protest voters and violent gangs are distant in language and appearance; they are typically Islamic – for example, "guest worker" Turks and Balkan refugees in Germany, and Arabs from North Africa and the sub-Sahara in France. In both countries ethnic segregation in substandard housing and poor neighborhoods is common. Both include immigrants in universal welfare-state benefits, whose alleged drain on the taxpayer-citizen is a centerpiece of political propaganda (Wilensky, 2002: ch. 10). All this should sound familiar to television viewers in the United States who were exposed to saturation advertising on crime, immigrants, and welfare during the poisonous congressional campaign of 1994 and again in the 2006 election.

With all these French-German similarities, it is striking that Germany has much more anti-immigrant violence than France, whereas France has much higher populist right anti-immigrant voting than Germany. For instance, per capita acts of extreme right xenophobic violence in Germany after 1990 were at least 2.5 times higher than in France. But electoral support shows the reverse pattern: Le Pen's Front National (FN) received between 26 and 28 percent of the vote in 1988 presidential elections in areas of high immigrant concentration in Southwest France – Marseille, Toulon, and Nice (Frears, 1991: 116); in February 1997, the Front National won its first absolute majority of the vote in a municipal election in the Marseille suburb of Vitrolles. And in 2002 Le Pen finished second in the first round of the presidential election with just under 17 percent of the total vote, concentrated in the middle mass (Cayrol, 2002).[12] In contrast, from 1973 to 1989 German support for similar extreme right-wing parties at its peak in the 1989 Euro-elections was only 7.1 percent (excluding Bavaria and Baden-Württemberg, the other *Länder* ranged between 4 and 6 percent of the vote going to the Republikaner Party [REP]). At its peak in national elections since unification, that vote was less than 5 percent. In fact, in the 1994 national election Republikaner got only 1.9 percent of the vote. Although the REP as the leading far right party has been replaced by the National Democratic Party, the latter performs at the same fading low level. In the 2005 Bundestag elections, the NDP received only 1.8 percent of the constituency votes and only 1.6 percent of the party list votes.[13]

Contrasts in public policy and politics as well as rates of immigration provide a reasonable explanation. The German policy of ethnic exclusion based on descent and combined with wide open access to refugees up to 1993 (perhaps driven by historical guilt) makes the cultural and social integration of minorities difficult, no matter how long they stay (some of the Turks are third-generation workers).[14] Sheer numbers add to nativist resentment and violence.[15] In contrast, French policy, though not as assimilative as that of the United States or Canada, is inclusive (Esman, 1992: 3–4, 36, 39). French official administrative classifications from the first have been socioprofessional or "national"; from the Third Republic on, the French forbade all census questions about ethnic, religious, and linguistic origins. The French version of the melting pot myth is that the fusion of peoples came to an end with the Revolution and no redefinition of "French" can come from subsequent waves of immigration (Noiriel, 1992: 72–73; Brubaker, 1992: 104–110). French universalism has had a paradoxical result: it exaggerates the social distance between nation-conscious Frenchmen and foreigners; at the same time it shapes the law of immigration in more liberal directions. Encouragement of assimilation may reduce violence but still permit political expression of nativist sentiments. As an added explanation of Le Pen's strength, France ran a much higher rate of unemployment than Germany for many years. Vitrolles, where Le Pen's party reached its first majority, had not only a large concentration of North African immigrants but also an abundance of alienated French workers hard hit by 19 percent unemployment (*New York Times*, Feb. 10, 1997).

A final piece of this puzzle is the role of electoral laws as they shape protest voting. Both France and Germany have mixed proportional-plurality electoral systems with two-stage voting (Wilensky, 2002: ch. 2). But the two ballots in the French case are cast a week or two apart; only the second is decisive. The two ballots of the Germans – one for the candidate, one for the party – are simultaneous and both ballots shape the final political composition of the government. French voters can therefore indulge their xenophobic sentiments in a first-ballot protest against the political establishment with little consequence in most cases; German voters are denied any second thoughts. In short, the German combination of much higher numbers of socially distant strangers, an exclusionary naturalization policy, and an electoral system that discourages pure protest voting (and incidentally makes neo-Nazi parties illegal) encourages violence; the French combination of lower numbers of immigrants, universalistic ideology and assimilative policies, and greater unemployment but electoral laws and traditions favorable to protest voting minimizes violence and provides xenophobic movements with an abundance of voters. Recently, as numbers of socially distant Muslims in France increased, however, and integration policies faltered, violence in France climbed toward the German rate.

In sum, migration from areas of economic despair and repression to areas of opportunity and hope is as old as poverty and persecution. Such mass migration is new in neither its rate nor its consequences. Rich democracies are now converging in their cultural and social diversity and in their conflict focused on immigration. They differ, however, in their openness to political and economic refugees, their policies toward immigrant integration, and the intensity of anti-immigrant mobilization. Anti-immigrant sentiments are most intense where the number and concentration of immigrants are heavy, the social distance between natives and strangers (in education, religion, language, ethnicity, and race) is great, and the economic instability of industrial readjustment is most widely experienced. Most important, industrial democracies differ in their ways of channeling mass prejudices and populist-right movements. A country that makes a serious effort to minimize illegal immigration, and to assimilate immigrants via inclusionary naturalization policies, job creation, training and placement, and language and citizenship education will minimize nativist violence. It may ultimately reduce the electoral appeal of political demagogues who intensify mass fears and hatreds to achieve power.

Finally, I doubt that European democracies and Japan, as they experience increased immigration, must necessarily produce an alienated underclass, the target of a middle-mass revolt, American style. Only if they abandon the public policies that encouraged labor peace and kept their poverty rates low – family policies, an active labor-market policy, an accommodative framework for industrial relations, a universalistic welfare state – will they drift into the Anglo-American pattern. Some may choose that road; but the choice is there.

The main point is that most mass migrations are an endemic feature of industrialism, nothing new in either degree or kind. It is unlikely that the rate of change since 1960 is greater than the rate for previous 50-year periods. Similarly, external shocks – wars, energy price fluctuations, and quick changes in trade patterns (like the deterioration of world trade in the Great Recession of 2007–2009) – are not new. Neither are the concomitant dislocations of employment. Industrialization for two centuries has meant the continual dilution and obsolescence of old skills and occupations and creation of new ones (Wilensky and Lebeaux, 1958: 59–65, 90–94).

There is no tidal wave of immigrants to the affluent democracies. In relation to world population, international migration is a rare event. In general, the negative economic effects of increased migration are exaggerated, and the political effects can be contained. Only if we do nothing to arrest global warming will we create mass migration of climate refugees that can overwhelm the capacity of receiving nations to absorb them.

As they argue that globalization undermines national institutions and policies, many scholars go beyond international capital flows and migration to four other supposedly eroding forces: the deregulation of the labor market, the growth of multinational corporations, the outsourcing of jobs, and the internationalization of finance, including the autonomy of central banks. The next four sections discuss these trends.

## C. DEREGULATION OF THE LABOR MARKET?

The 1980s saw accelerated rhetoric regarding the evils of job protection in law and collective bargaining contracts; there was even some shift in public policy. A number of countries, including the United Kingdom, Germany, France, Italy, and Spain, relaxed legal restrictions on layoffs and dismissals and widened existing loopholes in established systems of job protection. For instance, they encouraged fixed-term vs. permanent contracts or reduced barriers to hiring temporary labor (OECD, 1989; Auer and Büchtemann, 1989). The aim: reduce institutional rigidities, increase the efficiency of labor markets, and decrease labor costs and thereby increase employment and speed up innovation and industrial readjustment – all the goodies in the promised land of the free-marketeers.

If we examine employer behavior and recent research comparing the effects of "rigid" vs. "flexible" labor market policies, however, we see a different picture. The evidence shows that job and earnings protection have positive effects on productivity and are not a drag on employment. First consider a thorough study of political rhetoric and industrial practice in Germany. Then we can turn to the comparative research. Germany is a good case for demonstrating the radical disjunction between ideology and behavior. Some good evidence suggests that most industrial managers themselves do not want what orthodox economists and center-right politicians say they want – deregulation of the labor market – and for good reasons. Germany has long had an elaborate system of job protection, a model followed by other countries in the 1960s and early 1970s, and in 1985 was the European leader in job stability; in continuous job-tenure rates, Germany was second only to Japan (Büchtemann, 1991: 10). "In 1985 almost two-thirds of all workers in Germany had been continuously employed in their current job for more than five years (U.S.: 45%; France: 58%; U.K.: 52%)," most of them for more than 10 years (Büchtemann and Meager, 1991: 10).[16] To the tune of the ideological music of the 1980s, Germany passed a new Employment Promotion Act (EPA) in 1985. Among other legal changes, it relaxed job protection rules for new enterprises, extended maximum periods for the use of temporary workers hired from agencies, and, most important, made it easy for employers to hire workers on fixed-term contracts and fire them at the end without "just cause" or consultation. The law was pushed mainly by the Free Democrats (FDP), the free-marketeer wing of Chancellor Kohl's coalition government and later a stronger component of Chancellor Merkel's center-right coalition after the election of September 2009.

In a careful evaluation of the employment impact of the law, based on a review of subsequent studies, including a representative sample survey of 2,392 establishments, using ingenious measures of changes in hiring-and-firing practices that could be attributed to the law, as well as in-depth case studies of the motives of employers who did and did not use the new law, Büchtemann (1989 and 1991) found that the employment effects of the EPA were negligible; employers were overwhelmingly uninterested in using the law. Here are the relevant findings:

- Despite strong job protection, the annual labor turnover and job separation rates of Germany both *before* and *after* the EPA of 1985 are quite high (more than one in four) (Büchtemann, 1991: 10).
- In the two years after the law, worker turnover was highly concentrated in small and medium-sized firms in construction, food processing, and low- to medium-skill personal services (hotel and catering, transportation, body care, and cleaning). One-half of all terminations and new hires were accounted for by only 19 percent of all firms. These are firms with low-skill, high-labor costs as a fraction of total costs, and big fluctuations in demand. Their massive labor turnover, however, does not reflect superior adjustment efficiency. Both before and after the law these high-turnover firms pursued this "hiring-and-firing" strategy (Büchtemann, 1991: 11–15).

- Before and after the law, dismissals have played only a minor role in total turnover; German employers tend to avoid layoffs as long as possible by such methods as attrition, adjusting hours, and early retirement schemes. Most turnover is from voluntary quits, expired apprenticeship contracts, or early retirements. In downturns, employers hoard labor to avoid high search, recruitment, and training costs on the upswing.

- Before the EPA, a comprehensive study of dismissals in private industry in the late 1970s found that neither unions and works councils nor job protection laws strongly impede employers from firing workers they wanted to fire. That is why 85 percent of personnel managers interviewed at the time said that their firms had been able to fire and lay off close to all the workers they wanted to without any major financial and/or legal difficulty. Personnel managers in the post EPA period reported the same judgment: employment protection legislation both before and after the reforms was no major obstacle to dismissals and necessary work force reductions.[17]

- Actual use of the options offered to employers by the EPA for temporary hires was confined to a small minority (4%) of all private-sector firms and to a tiny number of cases (2% of all new hires) (Büchtemann, 1991: 22). Only 0.6 percent of all firms in the private sector used the new fixed-term contracts created by the EPA in order to adjust their work forces more flexibly to external demand.

- Far from expanding employment, deregulation had negligible net effects. If anything, it had slightly negative effects. It increased the layoff risks for fixed-contract workers in a downturn but increased hiring only slightly in expanding firms (Büchtemann, 1991: 24).

Most damaging for the advocates of labor-market deregulation, the German employers in the most dynamic sectors, the expanding engineering and higher-skill service industries – the drivers of the economic machine that conquered world markets – said that they do not take advantage of the law because they do not want to incur the costs of a "hire-and-fire" strategy: transactional costs and productivity losses, training costs, loss of loyal workers motivated by job security and good wages and benefits. German employers, unlike the ideologues who inspire the laws, know that investment in human capital pays off in the superior long-run productivity and flexibility of a stable work force. For the same reasons, Japanese employers in the most productive sectors – even during the crisis years of 1992–2002 – show the same reluctance to abandon long-standing stable relations with their employees and workplace unions (Vogel, 2006: 56–58).[18]

Even in 2009 during the Great Recession when Germany's export market was fading, German job-protection programs were avoiding massive layoffs. The government's "short shift" program was subsidizing the wages of more than 2 million workers. This allows firms to cut working hours and receive partial government compensation. Workers suffer pay cuts but keep their jobs while the labor office makes up some of the shortfall in wages. Under discussion in April 2009 was an extension of this program from 18 months to two years and a reform and expansion of the long-standing active labor-market program (ALMP), accenting training and retraining to keep unemployed workers' skills up-to-date until rehiring can take place (*Wall Street Journal*, Apr. 21, 2009; *New York Times*, Mar. 3, 2009). Similarly, from 1995 to 2004 German employers' investment in training and skill development of their employees remained steady (Croucher and Brookes, 2009). In 2009 they were keeping workers on payroll or, with government subsidies, in retraining (*New York Times*, Mar. 27, 2009).[19] Of course, none of this could prevent an increase in unemployment in a deep worldwide recession, but these programs moderated both the suffering of families and the rate of decline in jobs.

In short, whatever the political rhetoric of deregulation and the free market, German employers in the late 1980s and even in the current crisis, like their Japanese counterparts to this day, were pursuing labor policies similar to those that brought them success since 1960 (Turner, 1998; Vogel, 2006).

Going beyond the case studies of Germany and Japan, systematic cross-national research confirms the negative economic effects of labor-market deregulation and the positive effects of job and wage protection, again contradicting free-market theology. For instance, the German findings are consistent with older industrial relations research and with economic theories of "efficient wages": firms may pay a premium over market-clearing wages because they want to retain worker loyalty and encourage hard work (Weiss, 1990; and Akerlof and Yellen, 1986). Many opponents of job protection by government and by high-performance firms argue that, while this may be good for a minority of workers, it is bad for job creation in the economy as a whole. Cross-national evidence reviewed in an ILO report on the creation of stable long-term jobs, however, shows that labor-market regulations (including rules on hiring and firing, levels of unemployment benefits) are not responsible for a nation's unemployment, job insecurity, or poor job creation. The trouble lies in the combination of technological change, weakened unions, poor industrial relations, and reduced demand with slow economic growth (ILO, 1995: 155–157), as well as demographic shifts (see Wilensky, 2002: ch. 13 on job creation).

More recent cross-national research provides strong confirmation of this: Storm and Naastepad (2009) compare 20 rich democracies in the OECD (all of mine minus Ireland as an outlier and Israel and including not-quite-so-rich Portugal and Spain) for the period 1984–2004. They devised extensive measures of labor-market regulation and deregulation and of industrial relations systems paralleling the classification in Table 1 (highly regulated and coordinated vs. unregulated, "liberal," free-market systems). They find that labor productivity growth is higher in countries with relatively regulated ("rigid") labor markets and corporatist bargaining arrangements (their phrase is "highly coordinated industrial relations systems"). These high-productivity countries are also most egalitarian in earnings, have strong unions, and strong job protection rooted in law and collective bargaining. Further, this study confirms the repeated finding that such job protection, high wages, and equality have little or no effect on unemployment (Baccaro and Rei, 2005; Baker et al., 2005; Howell et al., 2007; and Tables 1, 2, and 3). The explanation is that "because labor market regulation simultaneously raises wage claims *as well as productivity growth* ... its impact on production costs, inflation, and, ultimately, unemployment, is likely to be small and even insignificant" (Storm and Naastepad, 2009: 649.)

For an overview of leaders and laggards among the rich democracies in their provision of job security for their workers, we used OECD data and averaged an index of "strictness of employment protection" for 18 countries for every year from 2000 through 2008 and fitted them to my types of political economy (OECD, 2010). The high scorers on this index have strong protection for full-time and part-time workers, and they avoid permanent mass layoffs. Here are the median scores for the five types (means yield the same rank order):

| | |
|---|---|
| Left corporatist | 2.11 |
| Left-Catholic corporatist | 2.09 |
| Catholic corporatist | 2.04 |
| Corporatist without labor | 1.43 |
| Fragmented and decentralized | 0.90 |

We see the usual pattern: the well-being of people measured by the widely shared value of job security moves from top to bottom with the greatest contrast between the top three and the bottom two, as they do in most of the tables in this book. A second measure concentrates only on national bargaining arrangements; it provides further confirmation: the top nine in job security are consensual democracies (only France keeps labor at a distance), whereas eight of the bottom nine, the lowest in job security, are fragmented and decentralized political economies (Denmark, the exception, scores medium).

Finally, in assessing the idea that globalization subverts job security and job security subverts productivity, it is important to distinguish among types of industries. Until the financial meltdown of the Great Recession, in the high-wage export sectors of Japan, Germany, and several smaller European democracies, job security has been high partly because labor costs as a percentage of total costs are low (as in pharmaceuticals, chemicals, main-frame computers, or oil refining), or because productivity in export sectors is high and exports are growing, or because worldwide investments have long been the core of profits (insurance and banking, until the financial meltdown of 2008). It is the nonexport service industries and trades that evidence most fluctuation in employment and minimum job security. These "domestic" sectors are much less affected by globalization; they continue to fluctuate according to business cycles and local markets. The export sectors, however, remain much the same as they were before all the talk about globalization: they were and are dominated by productive, high-wage firms with continued growth. It is hard to see how migration and capital flows will change this established pattern very much – except in the biggest crisis since the Great Depression.[20]

If there is convergence in the programs and expenditures that constitute the welfare state and job protection, it is not the convergence downward imposed by greater ease of mobility of labor and capital across national boundaries. It is instead the convergence rooted in continuing industrialization and the trends all rich democracies share: the continued aging of the population, now accelerating in Japan and North America, the upgrading of skills and job demands, and the convergent rise in female labor-force participation. These common trends will most affect family policy, active labor-market policy, and pension expenditures, all of which I believe will become more, not less, alike.

In sum, whether job protection and labor standards are threatened by the international mobility of labor and capital or by countries with very low labor costs depends on the institutions and policies in place. Calls for the deregulation of labor markets and complaints about the role of unions and center-left parties that bargain for job security are largely ideological, part of a free-marketeer mantra that government regulation and union protection for employees undermine the free job choice of workers, constrain the entrepreneurial spirit of industrial managers, and harm their competitiveness in world markets. Like all sectarian ideology, these claims are impervious to empirical evidence. In fact, we have seen a sharp disjunction between such ideological assertions and the actual behavior and preferences of employers in the most successful sectors of industry over long periods.

This section has shown that job security and low labor turnover combined with worker participation in workplace and community greatly enhance enterprise productivity and flexibility. Such findings are reinforced by the discussion of trade-offs in consensual democracies (Chapter 3) and by Tables 1, 2, and 3 where I show that the big-spending corporatist democracies that fully include labor and center-left parties in high policy had an edge in both productivity and the flexible adaptation to external shocks for more than half a century.

The threat of the great economic shifts of recent decades is not to countries with efficient managers and relatively high wages, job security, workplace safety, strong unions, and low strike rates. The threat is instead to countries and industries that rely heavily on the least-skilled, least-educated, least-trained workers, who in any case are a declining breed, with or without globalization. And modern democracies that attend to education, training, job creation, labor standards, and poverty prevention can reduce the pain of their transition to other, often better jobs.

## D. WHAT JOBS CAN BE OUTSOURCED WITH WHAT EFFECTS?

If the deregulation of the labor market varies so much among 19 rich democracies, won't the "new industrial revolution" or "postindustrial society" engulf all countries in an orgy of "outsourcing" or "offshoring" of jobs? In the U.S. 1992 presidential campaign Ross Perot warned of "a giant sucking sound of jobs going to Mexico," a resonant slogan that, despite the fact of the opposite net reverse flow to the United States, helped him achieve 23.5 percent of the popular vote. He scored especially big among white non-college-educated workers who felt an economic squeeze. Plainly, the politics of outsourcing can be potent; it simultaneously taps resentment of foreigners, immigrants, racial minorities, and job insecurity.

Outsourcing, used interchangeably with offshoring, is a slippery concept. Both researchers and media pundits have often confused outsourcing with subcontracting, downsizing, downgrading, restructuring, deregulation of the labor market, deindustrialization, rising unemployment, recessions, or job loss in general. These are all painful but they are not outsourcing. When Detroit lost auto-market share to European and Japanese imports with a massive loss of jobs, it was not outsourcing; if, like Toyota and Honda locating plants in the United States ("insourcing"), the big three had shut down Detroit while relocating in Mexico, Japan, or Europe, that would be outsourcing. When the Silicon Valley bubble burst in 2000–2001, the loss of jobs and markets was not outsourcing; but when the U.S. semiconductor assembly industry moved abroad to reduce costs – today more than 90 percent of U.S. chip assembly is done in Asia – that is offshoring. When a company subcontracts such jobs as janitorial or maintenance or payroll accounting to a domestic service company, it is not outsourcing, but when it shifts its payroll operations to Asia, it is. When the telecom industry sheds excess labor and cuts employees pay in a recession, it is not outsourcing, but if it sends telephone call-center jobs to India, it is outsourcing.

If we are to grasp what, if anything, is new about it and estimate its size and composition, if we are to judge the "offshorability" of 140 million people at work in the United States in 2009 or its net effects on job security and equality, let alone its size and effects in 19 countries, we must define it more precisely. Even then, data deficiencies will make any conclusions speculative.

## 1. Definition and Numbers

Outsourcing is the relocation of jobs and production to a foreign country. We cannot say with confidence how many or what kinds of jobs have been or might be outsourced. The most speculative are estimates of the offshorability of jobs – projections for 5 or 10 or 20 years ahead. As Alan Blinder notes (2009), they range from 11 to 38 percent of total U.S. jobs. For instance, Bardhan and Kroll (2003) predict that "up to 14 million Americans," including workers in office and administrative support, financial analysts, data entry keyers, medical transcriptionists, paralegals, and computer and math professionals, are in occupations where jobs or wages are "at risk." That is only about 10 percent of today's employed. Forrester, an information technology firm, expects offshoring of U.S. jobs in the "service sector" to total 3.3 million by 2015 (CRS Report RL32292, 2007). That is only 2.4 percent of total employment in 2010 but, if we assume some job growth, by 2015 it will be less. Jensen and Kletzer (2006), however, using a geographical Gini concentration measure by industrial category and another by occupation, conclude that 39 percent of U.S. workers are in "tradable" and therefore "potentially" offshorable occupations.

Studies of actual outsourcing in the recent past also show a wide range of estimates. Using an indirect indicator – the share of foreign-sourced goods in total manufactured inputs – Burke, Epstein, and Choi (2004, table 1) conclude that outsourcing rose from 12.7 to 22.1 percent in the manufacturing sector as a whole between 1987 and 2002. Greenwald and Kahn (2009: 69–70), using Bureau of Economic Affairs data, find that from 1981 to 1991, 85 percent of the job loss in U.S. manufacturing was from productivity increases (fewer workers producing more goods); only 15 percent could in any way be attributed to overseas outsourcing. However, by 2000–2006 the percentage attributable to outsourcing had climbed to 35 percent. A broader Berkeley study (Bardhan and Kroll, 2003, table 4) is cautious. It classifies the 770 detailed occupations in the BLS Occupational Employment Statistics; it includes only "those occupations where at least some outsourcing has already taken place or is being planned, according to business literature" (p. 6). These researchers estimate that in 2001 the "outer limit" of U.S. employment in occupations at risk to outsourcing numbered 14 million or about 11 percent of all occupations. Autor, Levy, and Murnane (2003) and Levy and Murnane (2004), however, using the same BLS detailed occupational data plus the Dictionary of Occupational Titles (now O*Net) estimate that in the next 10 years (2004–2014) there will be a continued decline in demand for "moderately skilled and less skilled labor" – the jobs "most substitutable" by computer. From their study we can only infer what substitutability by computer means for offshoring – that routine jobs at every level are vulnerable but that the offsetting demand for expanding nonroutine, analytic, and interactive jobs are complemented and reinforced by computers, so the net effect would be a decline in offshoring. Alan Blinder (2006: 120–122), in contrast to Bardhan and Kroll, using more inclusive occupational categories, comes up with a much higher ballpark figure of 28 million to 42 million jobs but warns that not all vulnerable jobs will actually migrate out (Blinder, 2009). In another analysis (2009), Blinder and Krueger based their conclusions on a sample survey by telephone of U.S. workers with coders rating each self-reported job; they estimate that about "25% of U.S. jobs are offshorable." Obviously no consensus among serious researchers is possible with such a range of concepts, measures, samples, and time spans.

A final complication in calculating the current amount or future trajectory of outsourcing is this: what is outsourcing to one country is insourcing to another. Foreign-owned companies in the United States employ more than 5.3 million working people, about 3.5 percent of the work force, spread across 50 states in sectors ranging from manufacturing to retailing to publishing. If outsourcing of jobs moves, say, 10 percent of total jobs overseas but 3.5 percent of that total are added by foreign firms in the United States, the net loss is only 6.5 percent of the work force. In some sectors the net effect is a gain for the home team. In a 2005 study, Catherine Mann (*New York Times*, Aug. 13, 2006) found that from 1999 to 2003 the United States lost 125,000 programming jobs but added 425,000 jobs for better-paid, higher-skilled software engineers and analysts (cf. Brown and Linden, 2009).

## 2. Heterogeneity of "Manufacturing" and "Services": Is Modern Society "Postindustrial"?

Regarding the causes of offshoring, whatever its incidence, we can learn something by a brief look at the past. Comparative studies of the impact of early and later industrialization on the number and composition of occupations over long periods shows first that rising national affluence, by increasing consumer incomes, is the major cause of the rapid increase in the percentage of the labor force in manufacturing during early industrialization. Second, past some threshold of modernization, where roughly three-quarters of the modern labor force is no longer in agriculture (because of extraordinary increases in agricultural productivity) and about 40 or 50 percent of adult women are at work in non-domestic settings, the proportion of jobs in manufacturing declines, while the "service sector" expands (Clark, 1940; Wilensky and Lebeaux, 1958: chs. 1–4; and Wilensky, 2002: ch. 1). To say that "service occupations" in the new "service economy" grew to 80 or 85 percent of the labor force, however, is not to say much of interest to students of modern work. And to use such categories for an estimate of net offshoring is to say even less.

Consider these complexities in classifying the huge variety of occupations. All the studies of outsourcing are plagued by catchall categories – "services" vs. "goods" or even "professional services." This is evident in historical data on contradictory trends in diverse types of service occupations and industries and the similar variety in manufacturing occupations and industries. The broad occupational trends are well known: a drastic decline in farm people (only 2% of the U.S. labor force now works on farms); a steady increase of white-collar and professional and administrative employees; very fast growth in the newer professions and a host of semiprofessional, semitechnical occupations; growth in the proportion of "non-farm proprietors, managers, and officials," especially since 1940; a small decline in the "working class" from 1910 to 1988, accelerating since then but within it a sharp drop in laborers and the semiskilled, some growth in low-paid service workers, and stability in the percentage of skilled craftsmen, repairmen, and foremen. The net effect has been a general upgrading of the whole population, reflecting both the average skill and educational level required. All these trends were evident from 1910 (the earliest date for good data comparability) to 1950 (Wilensky and Lebeaux, 1958: 90–94); they cannot be called either new or postindustrial. They are merely occupational changes induced by continuing industrialization.

If we like such phrases as the 'High-Tech Society" or the "Information Age" or "Postindustrialism," we must not go overboard. Much is made of the explosive growth of the half-dozen Silicon Valleys in the United States in recent decades,[21] and we often think of their computer scientists and engineers as the symbol of the New Age. They, of course, compose a tiny fraction of all 130 million of those at work or seeking work in the late 1990s. If instead we focus on very large occupations and their growth, a different picture emerges. Consider the 10 largest detailed job categories in 1983 that also grew substantially from 1983 to 1997. They are, in descending order of employment in 1983, sales supervisors and proprietors; truck drivers; janitors and cleaners; cashiers; cooks; sales representatives (commodities except retail);[22] registered nurses; elementary school teachers; nursing aides, orderlies, and attendants; and carpenters. Waiters and waitresses would make the top-10 list (about 1.4 million) but grew only 1 percent. Each of the 10 began the period with more than about 1.2 million employed. Not one is "high tech." Together these 10 categories added 6.49 million jobs in 1983–1997 and employed 23,723,000 people by 1997. Or take another cut at reality: of the 16 fastest-growing occupations for the same period, only 1 – computer systems analysts and scientists – was unambiguously high tech (960,000 jobs added). More ambiguously we might add "management analyst" (255,000 added), and even "securities and financial services sales" (217,000 added). These three added only 1,432,000 jobs over the 14 years, bringing their total 1997 employment to a mere 2,054,000, 1.59 percent of the total employed (my calculations from U.S. Department of Labor, Jan. 1998, table 11; Jan. 1984, table 22). In short, statistically speaking, modern society remains "low tech" or "no tech" in the experience of vast majorities, whatever the privileged position and power of highly trained elites.[23] (Wilensky, 2002: 58.)

What about a postindustrial shift in the types of industries in which modern populations work? Are these trends recent? At some threshold of development are they universal?

Data available on the percentage distribution of employment for seven rich democracies from 1920 to 1992 (Wilensky, 2002: table 4.1) cast doubt on the postindustrial thesis. I concentrate on three categories that have shown substantial trends or notable national differences and are most relevant to the theory of postindustrialism: "transformative industries," "producer services," and "social services."

1.  *Transformative* (almost all of this is manufacturing). It includes machinery, construction, food, textiles, metals, chemicals, and miscellaneous manufacturing and utilities. The pattern is a rise in percentage employed in these manufacturing industries from 1920 to 1970 in Japan, Germany, France, and Italy, and stability in Anglo-Saxon countries (the United Kingdom, United States, Canada). (Was this the coming of postindustrial society?) Then, after 1970, there was stability in Japan, and a decline in the rest, ranging from small declines in Germany (47% to 40%) and Canada (27% to 22%) to large declines in the United Kingdom (47% to 27%) and Italy (44% to 30%). What is significant is that the end point (ca. 1990) for Canada, France, and Germany is about where they began in 1920, while Japan and Italy *increased* the manufacturing share of employment. Only the United Kingdom and the United States evidence a decline.

Can increases in manufacturing jobs or a 1990s return to the manufacturing share of 1920 for five of these seven advanced industrial societies over 60 years be called "postindustrial"? It is true that those jobs have recently continued to decline in all our rich democracies, but what has taken their place?

2. *Producer Services.* Manufacturing vs. services is a false dichotomy. Throughout the history of industrialization, the two have been inextricably meshed. "Producer services" includes insurance, banking, real estate, legal services, accounting, engineering, and miscellaneous business services. Very few of these occupations are new to the post–World War II period, let alone to the 20th century. They were essential to 19th-century industrialization and accelerated along with manufacturing. Lloyds of London did not spring forth in some postindustrial era. Its members were covering risks of trade and manufacturing as early as 1734. And the Philadelphia gentlemen, educated as scientists and engineers, who gathered in the railroad shops of Pennsylvania as design consultants in close collaboration with skilled machinists and craftsmen to forge the new steam locomotives of the 1830s, were hardly "postindustrial" (Green, 1972).

For as long as we can find data, manufacturing and producer services grew together, the latter faster than manufacturing, as specialized services grew to serve the needs of increasingly complex organizations, sometimes located in the same firms as with house counsel, house publicists, or accountants. Similarly, where technology is truly new, the old ambiguity of the distinction between material goods and intangible services remains. Castells and Aoyama (1994: 8) note this ambiguity for computer software, genetic-engineering-based agriculture, and many other modern products; they ask, "Is a software programme sold as a disk a 'good' but, if sold on-line does it become a 'service'?" (cf. Singelmann, 1978).

3. *Social Services.* There is nothing new or uniformly "postindustrial" about the growth of social-services employment. As I show in our 19-country analysis in Chapters 1 and 4, the welfare state, which generates such employment, is more than a century old; it accelerated after World War II; and its rate of growth slowed since the mid-1970s or early 1980s. However, both its efficiency and program emphasis, and hence public employment, vary across nations and time because of national differences in affluence, left power, types of political economy, minority-group cleavages, and rates of mobility. There is nothing in this picture of substantial variation among rich democracies to suggest a postindustrial trend; merely a continued universal growth of the welfare state. The remaining national variations in spending, finance, and program emphasis are rooted in politics as well as the level and timing of economic development and its demographic correlates.

I have excluded three categories: "extractive" industries, "distributive services," and "personal services." They either show no trend or are irrelevant to the concept "postindustrial." *Extractive industries*, or what Colin Clark called "primary," include agriculture and mining. These industries, with remarkable increases in efficiency, everywhere decline in employment as they increase in output (Wilensky and Lebeaux, 1958: 93–94). By 1992 in the seven countries, employment in all extractive industries had plunged; it ranged from the United Kingdom's 3.3 percent to Italy's very high 9.5 percent. It is a universal, long-term trend of all rich countries, a product of continuing industrialization. *Distributive services* includes transportation, communication, and wholesale and retail trade; with small variations, they account for a more or less stable percentage of employment from 1920 to 1992, ranging from a fifth to a quarter of all employment, again belying assertions about a postindustrial pattern. Finally, I have excluded *personal services*. It includes domestic service, hotels, eating and drinking places, repair, laundry, barber and beauty, entertainment, and miscellaneous personal services. There is no pattern in either trend or cross-national comparisons. For instance, from about 1920 to 1992, "personal services" as a percentage of employment roughly doubled in Canada, France, and Japan; increased somewhat in the United States; but was stable or dropped in Germany, Italy, and the United Kingdom. What can be said with certainty about this heterogeneous category is that domestic servants steadily decrease with industrialization; as mass standards of living climb, fewer people are willing to serve the persons or households of others. With mechanization, laundry services show a similar decline. These declines are offset by stability in the percentage employed in hotels, repair services, entertainment, and barber and beauty shops (beauty salons become innovative and mechanized and grow, whereas barbershops stagnate and decline). The most important offset is the sharp climb of jobs in eating and drinking places – if we can take the U.S. experience as typical (Castells, 1984: 58, table 13).

A major problem with the idea of postindustrialism or the "High-Tech Society" is the great heterogeneity of "services" – heterogeneity in income, status, power, freedom on the job, skill levels, and related political orientation and life styles. Services also vary in their outsourceability. If the purpose of this theory is to connect changes in occupational and industrial structures with shifts in culture, politics, the nature of work experience, offshoring, or anything important, "the service economy" is both vague and hopelessly heterogeneous. For instance, "retail services" include the big-ticket salesperson in a posh department store and the entrepreneur of the hot dog stand; the manager of a large auto-repair shop and the owner of a mom-and-pop grocery store; the maitre d' at New York's Chanterelle and the hamburger flipper at McDonald's. "Services" embrace a computer scientist and an urban dog walker; the full-time, stably employed office supervisor in the headquarters of a drugstore chain and a part-time temporary worker at the check-out counter in the supermarket whose wages place her among the working poor; a high-tech consultant in a firm selling software for financial managers and a no-tech salesperson in a local dress shop; a corporate lawyer in a firm with 200 partners and associates (if in marine law, patent law, some types of corporate law, offshorable) and a solo lawyer with an ethnic clientele (almost never offshorable). In practically every routine of life that is important to people – the nature of their work and use of their skills, their income, status, security, and opportunities for upward mobility, their family life and leisure style – these pairs are in different worlds.

In short, if all the occupational and industrial shifts now labeled "postindustrial" amount to is a continuation of more than a century's rise in the level of education, an increase in the skill, discipline, and perhaps knowledge of the average worker, and the increased employment of experts, then we should talk about those long-term trends and not impose an elaborate superstructure of dubious claims about the revolutionary character of these gradual shifts. Fortunately, the most thorough analyses of the kinds of industries and occupations most and least vulnerable to offshoring do just that.

### 3. What Kinds of Jobs Can Be Offshored?

There is some agreement among students of labor markets who use detailed occupational and industrial data on the most and least vulnerable jobs. Here are a few safe conclusions from U.S. studies:

1. "White-collar" jobs have joined "blue-collar" jobs as vulnerable to outsourcing, maybe more so. It is not just textile manufacturing jobs going to cheap labor in Asia but routine customer service and computer programming to India. Stock-market research for financial firms and medical transcription services are also vulnerable. In general, the information technology sector – especially business process software – has since 1987 been moving to India, the Philippines, Malaysia, China, Russia, Israel, and Ireland. Domestic growth and insourcing offset many of these shifts. Moreover, much of outsourcing is simply a response to labor shortages in times of tight labor markets.

2. The content of occupations most and least vulnerable to outsourcing is well summarized by Bardhan and Kroll (2003: table 4) and in other work by Kletzer (2007), Blinder (2006), and Levy and Murnane (2004). There is general agreement with the following picture of job content among these and other scholars who have analyzed detailed classifications of occupations and industries.

*The specific content of jobs vulnerable to outsourcing includes:*

No requirement for face-to-face customer servicing.

High information content that can easily be delivered electronically. Well-defined tasks that can be accomplished by following explicit rules and are therefore programmable.

High wage differential with similar occupations abroad. But as Brown and Linden note (2009), it is easy to exaggerate the comparability of, say, "engineers" across such countries as the United States or Japan vs. India, Russia, and China.

Work process is telecommutable and Internet enabled (e.g., telemarketers, switchboard operators, computer operators, data-entry keyers, word processors and typists, office machine operators, medical transcriptionists).

Low set-up barriers – least requirements for resources, space, and equipment (e.g., telemarketing, word processing).

"Impersonal services" with low social networking requirements – the opposite of teachers, therapists, coaches, most salespeople, lawyers, and primary-care physicians.

Manufacturing and service jobs located in metropolitan areas. Urban centers have a higher proportion of jobs at risk than nonmetropolitan centers. Hi-tech markets such as San Jose, San Francisco, and Boston are at high risk of outsourcing; their jobs more often fit the list above.

*The specific content of jobs likely to be retained, with minimal outsourcing, includes:*

Geographically dispersed jobs. Jobs in local labor and product markets (e.g., workers in building trades, restaurants, day-care centers, barber and manicurist shops, intracity trucking, most retail stores).

Government jobs – local, state, national – even if they fit the vulnerability list. Politics will keep them home.

Nonroutine, non-rule-based jobs that cannot be programmed – that is, complex problem-solving or communications work. (Today the three top design-only semiconductor companies are based in the United States. It is the routine production of commodity memory chips that has been outsourced.)

Jobs that require face-to-face contacts – "personal" relationships (e.g., negotiation and management skills, assisting or caring for others). Expert-heavy work.

Jobs that require high to medium levels of literacy and numeracy. Analytic tasks.

Although I have shown that the 10 largest and fastest-growing occupations in the United States are low-tech or no-tech, two characteristics of these jobs stand out. First, they typically fit three of the criteria for low risk of outsourcing (local labor and product markets and/or government jobs and/or face-to-face contacts). Second, they still find themselves facing rising demands. As many students of work have observed (Wilensky, 1967; Levy and Murnane, 2004), a modern labor force – from semiskilled work on an automated assembly line to the physicians, nurses, and semitechnical, semiprofessional folks in the large medical-industrial complex to the vast number of occupations and professions in the educational complex – now require an accent on mental clarity and alertness, discipline, reliability, and adaptability, the capacity to learn new tasks quickly, what employers mean when they say "good work habits." Such jobs and occupations cannot easily be outsourced. Further discussion appears in Chapters 7 and 8.

## 4. Causes of Outsourcing vs. Causes of All Occupational Change

Whatever the changing occupational structure, the net effect of continuing industrialization in both the 19th and 20th centuries (the increasing use of high-energy technology and inanimate sources of power, the continuing rise in productivity) has been an increase in the size of the labor force, not a contraction. Again, the process continues to make some skills obsolete and dilutes others (when complex operations handled by one skilled craftsman are torn apart and assigned to several less-skilled workers), while accelerating the creation of new jobs and occupations. Despite recurrent predictions of permanent mass unemployment, from 1910 to 1998 the American labor force – all those at work or seeking work – grew from 36 million to 130 million (Wilensky, 2002: 40–42) to 154 million now. Even with two "jobless recoveries" in 2002–2003 and 2009–2010, the percentage of the population 16 years of age and older who are employed continued to increase (57% in 1948 to 59% in 2009; BLS, 2010a).

What about globalization and outsourcing as causes of these occupational and industrial trends, especially in recent decades? A rare cross-national study of "deindustrialization" in the "information age" showed that the driving force of occupational changes had little to do with globalization. Moreover, other studies suggest that outsourcing thus far has been a small portion of the explanation. Systematically comparing 18 rich democracies, Kollmeyer (2009) found that from 1970 to 2003 expanding links between rich and developing countries, especially those in the Southern Hemisphere, had only a slight effect on the contraction of manufacturing and the expansion of services. Further, "capital flight" (foreign direct investment) had no independent effect at all. The force that explains almost all of this outcome is sheer levels of consumer affluence at higher levels of national economic development. As William Baumol et al. (1989) observed and many others have confirmed, productivity growth has been much greater in manufacturing than in services. So surviving "goods" producers can increase output with fewer and fewer workers and no sacrifice of quality, whereas most service jobs – for example, teachers, psychotherapists, counselors, primary-care physicians, lawyers, musicians, artists – do not lend themselves to such productivity bursts. As most consumers gained in family income, they were willing to pay more for services. These findings underline the domestic causes of big occupational shifts and the personal and community dislocations they impose.

## 5. Effects of Outsourcing

There is some agreement here. Although the net effect of outsourcing has so far been small, it is likely to increase, most of it from one rich country to another. By how much and whether insourcing will offset outsourcing remain speculative. As developing countries such as China, India, and Brazil increase the quality of their infrastructures, including the education and training of their populations, they may become more a target of outsourcing than they are now. But that may occur only in the long run.

Effects on "skill" levels are to reinforce and perhaps accelerate long-standing trends, the upgrading of Everyman and Everywoman described earlier. At the same time a continued decline in relative wages of the least educated is very likely. These workers have a harder time finding jobs than their more educated compatriots; when they lose their jobs they remain unemployed longer, and if and when they are reemployed, they suffer a larger loss of earnings and job status compared to their predisplacement position (Rodrik, 1997: 23 and the citations therein). This applies to "middle-class" occupations as well. For instance, Alan Krueger (1993) finds that workers who use computers have about a 15 percent wage bonus (cf. Mann, 2005). The digital divide grows. Not only does it persist in wage advantage, but old socioeconomic status (SES) differences in political participation remain much the same as they were before. The claim that the Internet provides a new mass channel for meaningful social and political participation is baseless; it has not overcome any of the deficits suffered by the least privileged (Schlozman, Verba, and Brady, 2010; and Wilensky, 2002: 174–175).

If union workers are directly affected by offshoring to areas of comparable jobs with cheaper labor, their bargaining power erodes. This was evident in U.S. metal manufacturing, textiles and clothing, machinery, lumber and paper, and aerospace. Drastic union decline in the auto industry and its suppliers, though not mainly due to offshoring, illustrates a larger point: wherever labor is substitutable, both wages and the bargaining power of individual workers and unions deteriorate. The main sources of union decline in the United States, however, have been domestic – employer antiunion action reinforced by a negative legal and political climate plus the failure of labor unions to devote enough resources to organizing (see Chapter 7). Richard Freeman (1997) estimates that about one-fifth of the rise in U.S. wage inequality can be attributed to the decline in unionization.

There may be mitigation of the effect of outsourcing on union density and power in the future. When manufacturing suffered employment declines from the combination of loss of markets, increased productivity, and some outsourcing, unions were undermined. Today among many nonmanufacturing industries and occupations, as we have seen, there is less loss of markets and surely less potential for large increases in productivity, so the impact of outsourcing on labor's bargaining power should diminish.

Obviously the effects of outsourcing on employment, once confined largely to manufacturing, now appears in a growing segment of the rest of the economy among the more educated. As always, however, it depends on what occupational or industrial niche the educated find themselves; their location will determine whether they experience decline, growth, or stability in demand for their services and advice. Regarding the effects on societal levels of unemployment and job creation, if past is prologue, there is little danger of mass unemployment from outsourcing. Again, the main burden of job changes, whether from outsourcing or not, typically falls upon the least educated. When educated workers are displaced, they adjust more quickly to new jobs than those without college degrees – an added source of inequality in lifetime earnings.

In general, outsourcing trends reinforce economic inequality in the workplace and society, with national variations rooted in fiscal and monetary policies and social and labor-market policies. National responses to the plight of losers from all these job shifts continue to divide the United States, the epitome of a country on the Low Road, from the more consensual rich democracies of Continental Europe on the High Road.

### 6. A Postscript on Job Creation and Poverty Reduction from a Green Economy

Clean energy enthusiasts have claimed that tackling the urgent problem of greenhouse gas (GHG) emissions will create a new, large, growing green economy with good-paying jobs that cannot be outsourced (Pollin et al., 2008; Huh and Grange, 2009; Roberts, 2008). A few have even claimed that a green economy can greatly reduce poverty in urban ghettos; the most visible of these activists is former Obama aide, Van Jones.

Although Chapter 2 has shown that rich democracies that have markedly reduced GHG emissions such as Denmark and Sweden have also led in economic performance, the excessive claims about clean energy policies do more harm to the cause than good. For instance, even the limited data available on the size and occupational composition of a green economy suggest that clean energy job creation will continue to disadvantage the least educated. The notion that effective environmental action will wipe out poverty is a fairy tale.

Without detailed discussion, here are a few of the most useful findings about green jobs now in being or likely to result from serious investment.

1. *A working definition of a clean energy economy.* It generates jobs, businesses, and investments, while it expands clean energy production, increases energy efficiency, reduces greenhouse gas emissions, waste, and pollution, and conserves water and other natural resources (Huh and Grange, 2009: 25). A typical list of energy and renewable strategies (Pollin et al., 2008: 2) includes: retrofit buildings to improve energy efficiency; expand mass transit and freight rails; construct a smart electrical grid; use wind power; use solar power; develop next-generation biofuels.

2. *How many green jobs?* Using both detailed information on individual companies and the National Establishment Time Series (NETS) database of U.S. public and private establishments, the Pew Charitable Trusts study of the growth of clean-energy jobs from 1998 to 2007 concludes that more than 68,200 businesses across all 50 states and the District of Columbia accounted for 770,000 jobs that fit the "clean energy" definition. That is only one-half of 1 percent of all U.S. jobs at the end of 2007. And green job growth over nine years was 9.1 percent, little more than 64,000 jobs (calculated from BLS, 2010a). For context and caution, retail trade created 822,900 jobs during that period, most of them low-paid with minimal benefits – about 13 times as many as green jobs. Unfortunately for

these numerous workers in retail trade, the Great Recession hit them hardest; their employment dropped to 1998 levels. It is uncertain how many will be rehired on the upswing. In any case, they remain many times the number of green workers.

3. *More important are the net job creation and destruction of a green economy.* Job losses from 1998 to 2007 in transportation equipment (82% of which are motor vehicles and parts), mining (coal, oil, gas), and gasoline stations add up to 274,800 "dirty" jobs lost. Compare the 64,000 clean jobs gained.[24] This is not to deny that huge government subsidies to coal, oil, gas, and nuclear, if shifted to a green economy with similar funding predictability and stability, would create far more jobs than jobs lost.[25] It simply underlines the need to treat those workers who lose jobs in a change from a gray or black economy to a green economy decently and craft policies that counter their pain (see Chapters 7 and 8). The oil and natural gas industries alone directly employ 2.1 million Americans, including gas station workers (PriceWaterhouseCoopers, 2009).

4. *What kind of jobs does a green economy create?* Some students interpret the Pew research as showing benefits to Americans cutting across the economic and educational spectrum (Huh and Grange, 2009: 27). But if we examine the categories, we see that few of these jobs, as always, go to the least educated; the overwhelming majority go to highly skilled blue-collar workers, scientists, and professionals. Pollin et al. (2008: 6) list 63 "representative" green occupations and jobs to be created by investing $100 billion over two years in a low-carbon economy. By the most generous definition of "unskilled" or "semiskilled," only 7 of the 63 qualify – for example, welders, assemblers, laborers, installation helpers, machine operators. The rest range from skilled building construction crafts (electricians, carpenters, sheet metal workers) up through the most in demand (managers, supervisors, building inspectors, architects, civil, electrical, environmental and chemical engineers, chemists, and other scientists). It is certainly good that skilled building trades workers who have been hardest hit by the housing collapse might be reemployed with enough investment in a green economy. But few of them are at the bottom of the educational ladder. It is also definitely good that the likely jobs from green investments are overwhelmingly local and national – not easily outsourced. As we have seen in Chapter 2, the quickest and most efficient way to reduce our carbon footprint is to make our workplaces and homes more energy efficient. The problem is how politically the United States can produce the funding to match elite rhetoric about green jobs.

I infer from these limited data on job creation and destruction in a green economy that environmentalists should avoid shaky claims that doing the right things about climate change will solve the problem of unemployment if not poverty; they should concentrate on the theme that rising greenhouse gas emissions will destroy civilization as we know it and sooner than scientists used to think (see Chapter 2), while creating good jobs that cannot be outsourced.

## E. THE IMPACT OF MULTINATIONAL CORPORATIONS

There is no doubt that multinational corporations (MNCs), using economies of scale and scope, have dispersed all their activities across the globe, accelerating the flow of goods, services, investment, technology, and people. They are increasingly important in employment, sales, and investment, especially in the already rich countries.[26] It is not obvious, however, that the MNCs have negative effects on unions, industrial relations, earnings, income distribution, economic performance, and political legitimacy of nations, or that they subvert national cultures, social structures, or politics – the subject of *Rich Democracies* (Wilensky, 2002). In fact, some recent research suggests that the MNCs typically adapt to national patterns; they are not aggressive change agents. The evidence comes from studies of the behavior of foreign firms in the United States and Europe, especially Germany, and from analysis of the growing importance of various forms of interfirm networking, overwhelmingly driven by large multinational firms.

As Abowd and Freeman show (1991b: 2, 22–23), foreign-owned firms in the United States employ only 3 percent of American workers. In 2007 it was only 4.4 percent of the private-sector labor force (Bureau of Economic Analysis, 2009). European firms make up the bulk of direct foreign enterprises in the United States; they use more highly educated labor, use more R&D personnel, and, compared to domestic producers, are more concentrated in traded goods sectors (exports). Despite popular complaints about their subversive effect on labor standards, the wages of production workers in fact are higher in foreign-owned firms and the rate of unionization is the same as those in domestic-owned companies.

That the MNCs adapt to local and national laws and customs rather than changing them is shown by a detailed study of 34 Japanese production systems in the United States and Canada from 1989 to 1994, which also compared eight U.S.-owned and Korean-owned plants in the United States and seven Japanese-owned plants in Mexico. Plants from four industries were included: auto assembly, auto parts, consumer electronics, and semiconductors. The case studies were supplemented by a questionnaire sent to 450 manufacturing companies fully or partly owned by Japanese in North America (with a response rate of only one in five) (Abo, 1994). The conclusion: Japanese transplants did not significantly change the industrial landscape of the countries in which they operate. In the United States, for example, they either adapted to existing practices (unions, wage structures) or brought in from Japan those people and machines essential to production that they could not find in the United States (trainers, managers, equipment, high-quality suppliers). Japanese firms adopted the American wage system with its big differentials; they embraced American job classification schemes and promotion criteria (compensation based on job grades rather than seniority and merit and very little mobility between blue-collar and white-collar jobs). If unions already existed (about one in five cases), they included unions; where workers were not organized, they followed American managerial practices (no union) (Abo, 1994: ch. 4). If the industry practice was easy firing and hiring as with the least-skilled workers in electronics, Japanese transplants conformed; if the industry required high skill, they kept to the Japanese practice of low turnover. They did emphasize training and teamwork more than their American counterparts: two-thirds sent Japanese trainers to the United States for training sessions followed by on-the-job training; most sent either engineers or workers or both to Japan for study. And where they felt American parts suppliers and equipment were inferior, either they procured them from Japanese parts plants (highly sophisticated parts) or Japanese plants in Southeast Asia or Mexico (less sophisticated parts) or they established local suppliers in the United States to avoid friction with local managers (pp. 78–79; Encarnation, 1993: 21). Similar conclusions were reached in an intensive study of 8 of the 11 Japanese auto assembly transplants in the U.S. (Pil and MacDuffie, 1996) and a broader survey of industrial relations in foreign-owned subsidiaries in Europe (Schulten, 1996: 306–307; cf. Hyman, 1994).

There is nothing here to support the idea that the transplants are subverting labor standards or collective bargaining. Indeed, the net effect may be a slight upgrading of training and labor-management relations. What the Japanese leave at home is their more organized enterprise unions, their flat hierarchies, and their more egalitarian wage and income distribution. They are not bringing Japan to the United States. When the aftershocks of the Great Recession of 2007–2009 are over, we can expect these patterns to continue.

The necessary adaptation of MNCs to national customs and laws is also evident in Germany. Foreign firms get the German benefits of long-term financing, technology, information sharing, and the apprenticeship system only if they adopt German employment practices – pay high wages to highly skilled workers, observe rules for on-the-job security, safety, and worker participation (cf. Harrison, 1994: 213–214, 165; Lincoln, Kerbo, and Wittenhagan, 1995: 433ff.).[27] Perhaps this explains why when Germans bought an Opel (made by GM in German plants until GM sold control in 2009), they did not think of it as an "American" car.[28]

The same picture emerges if we examine U.S. foreign investments by industry and world region. The complaint that U.S. MNCs are merely escaping high union wages and benefits in the United States by moving to places with very low labor costs – America's average compensation for production workers is five times higher than Taiwan's, nine times higher than Brazil's – has no empirical foundation. A study of 32 manufacturing industries in 10 geographical regions found that U.S. foreign investments were "no more likely to originate in heavily unionized industries than in lightly unionized ones," a finding that holds even in developing countries where corporate flight from union strongholds should be most apparent (Karier, 1995: 117). This study confirms what many others have concluded: American MNCs, like the foreign transplants in the United States, are involved in foreign production mainly to avoid trade barriers; to use their concentrated capital in areas with infrastructure advantages (transportation, communication, and housing and other urban amenities),[29] worker quality (including education, training and development of executives, technicians, and workers), and access to universities and research laboratories and their R&D advantages; and to seek new lucrative markets close to home. The search for low wages or non-union localities, if not completely absent, is low on their list. If labor costs were at the center of corporate location decisions, the rich democracies would have emptied out long ago. Finally, there is evidence that MNCs, compared to national industries in local labor and product markets, pay better wages and benefits (cf. Woodward and Glickman, 1991; Wasylenko and McGuire, 1985; Davidson, 1980; Ajami and Ricks, 1981; Dunning, 1977, 1988; Abowd and Freeman, 1991a; Cooke and Noble, 1998; Drezner, 2001; Flanagan, 2006, ch. 6).[30]

Reinforcing and reflecting the MNCs' bias toward national cultures and policies are two trends in the concentration of corporate investment from 1970 to 1992. First, capital flows became increasingly concentrated on the richest parts of the world; direct foreign investment in developing countries was only about 25 percent in the 1970s; it is now below 20 percent. Modern countries are less risky than the rest.[31] Second, the MNCs, except for oil companies and similar natural resource firms, are not typically global, they are regional: European firms invest mainly inside Western Europe; American firms in the United States, Canada, Mexico, and South America; Japanese firms principally in Japan, South Korea, greater China, and Southeast Asia. In short, MNCs take the line of least resistance, moving along geographical and cultural lines – areas close to customers, where recruiting and managing is easiest, and where familiarity with national customs is greatest (*Economist*, Mar. 27, 1993: 12; Davidson, 1980; Hirst and Thompson, 1996: 58ff.).

It is possible that one characteristic of big MNCs – their effort to orchestrate various forms of interfirm networking or partnering – will increase the death rate of small to medium-sized firms dependent on them and thereby increase job insecurity and earnings inequality. Bennett Harrison (1994) argues that the suppliers and decentralized producers who face powerful MNCs that centralize finance, control, and distribution will promote the growth of a contingent work force. All networked firms rely on a core labor force of high-paid, highly trained, secure workers in whom the firm heavily invests and a large number of contingent workers employed by small subcontractors as needed and replaced at will. Outsourcing and downsizing are the watchwords. "Lean and mean" is the slogan. The core remains small, the periphery grows, subcontracting spreads. The subcontractors are played against one another by the MNC. This "dark side" of "alliance capitalism," Harrison argues, means wage stagnation and rising earnings inequality – most obvious in microelectronics and computers, but spreading to other industries where MNCs are prominent.

I am not convinced that these trends originated with MNCs or that the MNCs greatly accelerate them; they have been long evident in the United States and the

United Kingdom. First, the contingent labor force of temporary and part-time workers is more prominent among non-MNCs in domestic sectors – the service industries such as retail trade, hotels and restaurants, and the building trades – than in the export sectors. Second, subcontracting and downsizing have a long history, preceding the rise of MNCs as in the old days of the "putting out" system – sweatshops in the needle trades turning out clothing and textiles – a system still alive in American central cities. Third, Japan and Germany had such networks for many decades without much increase in earnings inequality or job instability. Japan, in particular, has long had a dual labor force of core workers (about one-fourth to one-third of the economy) and layers of dependent firms that do not provide its famed lifetime employment. As we have seen, much depends on the countervailing power and policies of governments, parties, and unions as they shape managerial behavior.

Much is attributed to MNCs that is simply due to variations in corporate size and patterns of public policy, including regulatory regimes. It is true that the market power of the world's largest retailer, Wal-Mart, with its ability to squeeze its suppliers and employees and its antiunion policies, provides little job security and low wages and benefits (Stiglitz, 2006b: 192). But other large firms like its competitor, Costco, though not as huge as Wal-Mart, pursue the opposite strategy with just as much efficiency (Cascio, 2006). It is the weakness of constraining public policies discussed in this book – social, labor, and regulatory – that gives such large firms the power to choose between the low road and the high road.

Observers of transnational corporations contend that even though on average they adapt to national laws and customs, their immense resources and strategic alliances permit them to shift operations across national boundaries in a continual search for new markets and friendly environments. The global network model is therefore a threat to corporatist bargaining and more generally to the national institutions through which labor has demanded job security, good earnings, and participation in both business and government policies. Consistent with this idea is the fact that some MNCs in recent years have relocated production at the site of the most "flexible" labor and the union response – international labor collaboration – has been weak. For instance, Hoover, the vacuum cleaner company owned by Maytag, eliminated 600 jobs in Dijon while adding 400 at its plant near Glasgow, partly because the engineering union in Scotland offered it more concessions than the French unions would give (Turner, 1993b: 7–8). Such whipsawing provides a strong incentive to unions to collaborate across national boundaries. But strong incentives are not enough, and the prospects for European-wide collective bargaining, like the promise of an effective European social charter, are, to say the least, uncertain.

Embryonic structures for European-wide collective bargaining already exist – the European Trade Union Confederation (ETUC) with its staff of 45, many sectoral European industry committees, a few European Works Councils at large MNCs, and many informal networks of union leaders, as well as their employer counterparts, the European Confederation of Employer Associations for private industry (UNICE) and the parallel confederation of employers in the public sector (CEEP) (Turner, 1993b; 1996). Of course, several of the member confederations (including the German DGB and the British TUC) do not themselves possess bargaining power; they have no mandate to negotiate substantive agreements on most issues. And the employer federations are in Brussels to prevent the passage of any binding laws or directives that would restrict employer discretion. Further, the variations in structure, interest, and ideology among these national labor movements and employer associations are substantial (Streeck, 1991; Timmersfeld, 1992; Lange, 1992; Turner, 1993a, 1993b; Martin and Ross, 2000). These are powerful barriers to cross-national collective bargaining. Exacerbating the situation is the extraordinary cost of German reunification: inflationary pressures meant high interest rates (at least in the early years and in 2007–2008) and unemployment, but German union leaders, who are at the center of ETUC and other cross-national networks, were preoccupied with the incorporation of East German workers and the subsequent decline in their membership. They continue to be diverted from the tasks of European integration.

For all these reasons, the protracted union campaign for EC-wide collective bargaining and worker participation rights has been largely unsuccessful. The exceptions – glimmers of possible progress – are instructive in assessing the role of MNCs. So far, union progress has been confined to a few French- and German-based multinational corporations. They have agreed to a limited arrangement for cross-national consultation and information sharing, not negotiation (Turner 1993a: 61–63; 1996), but it is a union foot in the door. Another foot in the door is the coordinating role of the European Federation of Building and Woodworkers (EFBWW), closest to becoming a European-wide labor union. It has a long history of "sectoral social dialogue" with its employer counterparts, for example, the European Construction Industry Confederation. It has achieved agreements on health and safety and training and, though it has little hope of establishing international contracts setting wages and labor standards, it is becoming increasingly important as a means by which unions can coordinate disparate strategies in relation to MNCs.[32] In other words, if there is any relaxation of employer resistance to multinational works councils and community-wide collective bargaining, it is found among MNCs in particular industry sectors (e.g., VW in auto, EFBWW in construction), not in the European Community (cf. Schulten, 1996). This is not a case for arguing the negative impact of MNCs on labor.

The picture is one of strong union motives for cross-national collaboration meeting equally strong institutional barriers. The outcome is unclear. With the shift from unanimity voting to qualified (weighted) majority voting, the European Community in 1994 adopted a new directive on European Works Councils mainly devoted to information sharing, so long vetoed by the British and opposed by employers. The EU mandate applies to all firms with 1,000 or more employees doing business in two or more countries (about 1,200–1,300 companies). This may be a precursor for more significant rights of consultation and power sharing. Progress in multinational bargaining, however, is most likely to be made at the MNC level. This is where some works councils were earlier established by the European Metalworkers Federation using funds provided by the European Commission (Turner, 1993b: 27) and where most of the cross-national labor-leader contacts and activist networks are growing (Martin and Ross, 2000: 20).

In sum, the argument that multinational corporations undermine labor standards and collective bargaining finds no support when we compare nationals with multinationals and trace recent trends in the MNC's investment targets, ready adaptation to national laws and practices, and policies on wages, union recognition, and consultation.

### F. THE REAL CULPRIT: THE INTERNATIONALIZATION OF FINANCE AND THE POWER OF STRONG CENTRAL BANKS

If the emergence of multinational corporations, the flow of migrants across national boundaries, and even the international flow of capital are only a moderate to small influence on consensual bargaining, domestic politics, and public policies, perhaps another global trend will be a stronger threat – the internationalization of finance and the spread of independent central banks as their autonomy and power increased.

My theme is that in the past quarter century these developments, with some national variation, have undermined the capacity of modern democracies to shape their economic destinies. The increasing independence of central banks and the ideology of their managers do, indeed, threaten collaborative relations among labor, industry, and the state and make the flexible use of fiscal policy (taxing and spending) more difficult. A related trend is the internationalization of finance and the effects of the deregulation fervor of the United States – ideology and practice spreading to many countries. Similarly the ideology and practice of the Bundesbank spread from Germany to the EU through the rise of the European Central Bank. We can begin with the changing role of central banks, then move to the internationalization of finance and its role in the credit crisis and Great Recession of 2007–2009.

### 1. Central Bank Autonomy and Ideology

Recent cross-national research on financial markets and central banks suggests that, although there is still some variation among nations, there is a general trend toward the increased power of central banks. As Sylvia Maxfield (1997) and Alesina and Summers (1993: 153) show, central banks with strong formal-legal and informal independence, Bundesbank style, are spreading among both developed and developing countries. Where once the German Bundesbank and the American Federal Reserve Bank were the standard cases of powerful central banks, in the five years from 1989 to 1993 at least 27 countries, most of them in Europe and Latin America, created or increased the independence of central banks (including Japan, New Zealand, Italy, France, and Belgium) (Maxfield, 1997: table 4.1). And the Maastricht Treaty stipulated that by 1997 the central banks of all participating member states must be independent. Finally, in 1999 a European Central Bank modeled on the Bundesbank formally took over responsibility for European monetary policy.

If we can locate the sources of the national differences in the independence of central banks, we can better understand the recent general trend toward increased autonomy. From research we can infer that four structural differences among developed or developing nations explain national differences: (1) the size and internationalization of credit markets; (2) the relation of industry to government, especially the degree to which industry relies on government for credit; (3) the presence or absence of a corporatist bargaining structure that permits either labor and the left or industry or both to shape economic policy; and (4) the role of key currencies when countries increase their trade dependence. Let us first briefly examine each of these interacting forces. Then we can look at the rank order of our rich democracies in central bank autonomy (before 1990 when there was much national variation), assess whether central bankers know what they are doing, and gauge the economic and political consequences if their power continues to increase.

Strong, autonomous central banks emerge where the size and internationalization of financial markets (especially robust bond markets), and the perception of the need for capital these markets create, induce politicians to cede authority to central banks (Maxfield, 1997: 4, 35–49; Cukierman, 1992: 449–450). There is likely an added reason for leftist governments to move toward central bank autonomy (CBA): more than conservative governments, they need to demonstrate credibly that they are willing to work with international investors (Hicks, 2006). Financial communities want price stability, stable currencies, guaranteed bank transactions, and restriction of "excess" competition among private banks. If they get into trouble, bankers and investors want central banks that will bail them out, as in the October crash of 1987 when Federal Reserve Chairman Greenspan ran the Fed's printing press overtime or when his predecessor, Paul Volker, earlier bailed out Continental Illinois, or when a systemic credit crisis like the meltdown that began at the end of 2007 occurs. Almost all the time, however, the financial community believes that restrictive monetary policies serve its interests (Maxfield, 1997: 22) and that central banks independent of elected officials can administer the necessary strong medicine, that is, vigorous anti-inflation measures. Among developing countries, where hyperinflation has often emerged, the same beliefs, institutionalized in such creditor agencies as the IMF, the World Bank, and money-center banks, have even more force. The fear of creating an excuse for foreign intervention or the need to establish or reestablish international credit worthiness inspires government reform of public finance and a move toward strong central banking (Mexico and Thailand in the late 19th century and early 20th). More recently, the growth of international financial markets, as well as the incentives for cross-national capital mobility it creates, has again forced the leaders of newly industrializing countries (NICs) to cede more authority to central banks because they think such a move helps to attract or reassure creditors and investors (Maxfield, 1997: ch. 3). In the rare case where a developed country experiences hyperinflation and successfully stabilizes its currency (Israel in the late 1970s, Germany after the 1920s), it too will cede more authority to its central bank. Cukierman (1992: 455) suggests that the crisis of hyperinflation makes competing interest groups aware of their shared interest in preventing chaos.

If, in contrast, financial markets and private banks are weak and industrialists must rely on government credit, industry and government alike will have a stake in the subordination of central banks to government mandates. If, in addition, industry and government have achieved a corporatist compromise – without labor (Japan, France) or a collaboration with labor (Austria, Sweden, Norway, Belgium) – the countervailing power to the financial community will be enhanced. Finally, state-led industrialization as it interacts with trade dependence limits the power of central banks. If initially a government, motivated by its own financial needs, collaborates with credit-hungry exporters and industrialists to set up a central bank, that bank will be weak (e.g., South Korea and Brazil) and may remain so for generations. The enthusiasm for tight monetary policies will be minimal (Maxfield, 1997).

Reinforcing this tendency is export dependence in the early stages of industrialization. Where a large portion of state revenue comes from international trade, fluctuations in export earnings will provide an incentive for the state to create suppliant central banking institutions that finance industrial and growth policies of government. Cases that fit include Japan and Korea in recent decades and New Zealand, Belgium, the Netherlands, and Denmark in an earlier period, 1880–1934. (On trade dependence, see Table 6.) Again, a more accommodative, flexible monetary policy is likely to be institutionalized and to persist. Some of these banks virtually print money on government demand. Contrasting cases are Germany and the United States: after World War II they have both been below average in trade dependence and for decades remained at the top in bank autonomy and monetary conservatism.

In sum, where industry relies on government for credit and stock and bond markets are small, where labor or industry or both act as countervailing powers in the context of increasing trade dependence, central banks remain weak; their autonomy is limited. Where credit markets are large and internationalized and key currencies (the U.S. dollar, the Japanese yen, the German mark) dominate, and where the countervailing power of industry and labor is weak or absent, central banks acquire increasing power. Data tend to support both this picture of national differences and the idea that some convergence is taking place.

To test the idea that the increasing power of central banks undermines the welfare state, labor standards, and job security as well as the economic progress necessary for their expansion, I used various measures of central bank autonomy (CBA) from the mid-1950s to 1989 and related the national variations among our 19 rich democracies to economic performance. Although it is very difficult to measure the autonomy of central banks cross-nationally, several students of the political economy of banking have produced estimates of reasonable quality. Their rankings of our rich democracies tend to agree. (Wilensky, 2002: table 17.4, not shown here, summarizes their findings and appendix H discusses the measures.) *Again it was necessary to cut off analysis after 1989 because so many countries had insulated central banks from "outside" political and economic influence by the 1990s that national differences in autonomy became minimal.* Here is a brief summary of my findings.

There is no clear pattern of relationship between type of political economy and central bank autonomy for the postwar period 1955–1988. The least-corporatist countries appear at every level of central bank autonomy (the United States high; the United Kingdom and Canada medium; New Zealand and Australia low) as do the more negotiated economies (Germany and Switzerland high; Italy, France, and Japan low). However, there is a tendency for corporatist countries that also have strong left parties to cluster in the medium autonomy category (Austria, Netherlands, Denmark, Sweden, Norway, Belgium). That may reflect the countervailing power of labor movements and left parties that participate in high policy. In these countries tight money that restricts growth and employment are not popular. The idea that all groups gain from growth and job expansion takes hold; central banks are constrained.

In the cases of France (medium central bank autonomy) and Japan (weak autonomy), the constraints on bank autonomy come not from labor and left power but from centralized governments and key ministries. Japanese elites – at least during their period of greatest economic success (up until 1992) – have clearly been less enthralled by an ideology of monetarism and perhaps a bit less obsessed with the dangers of even moderate inflation than has the Federal Reserve Board in the United States. The tight connections between industry and government and industry and finance are celebrated in every description of Japanese economic prowess (see, e.g., Wilensky, 2002: chs. 1, 2, 12; C. Johnson, 1982; Dore, 1986; Zysman, 1983). The recent increase in the independence of the Bank of Japan was quite modest and, until 1998, informal (Maxfield, 1997: 20; Deane and Pringle, 1994: 259). Japanese industrialists, like MITI (now METI, the Ministry of Economy, Trade, and Industry) and the Finance Ministry, are seldom interested in a contractionary economy; they like a monetary policy that accommodates the expansion of markets, prices, profits, and credit.[33] Thus, when industry-finance relations are cooperative and close, industry can counteract the central bankers' phobia about inflation. At the extreme, bankers and industrialists see themselves as part of the same industrial group; credit relations focus on bank financing of industry. As one indicator of this relationship, Epstein (1992: 14) notes that in 1970–1984 Japan, like France, Germany, and Italy, had a large share of nonfinancial assets held by banks, a pattern he calls "enterprise finance," whereas the United Kingdom, United States, and Canada did not, a pattern of "speculative finance."

In contrast, where financial systems have large stock and bond markets dominated by large private banks and other large investors oriented toward global exchange, industry and finance, as Thorstein Veblen (1921) foresaw, are in conflict over monetary policy. For instance, in September 1994, after the U.S. Fed had raised interest rates five times, the National Association of Manufacturers reported that its members were deeply anxious and suggested that the Fed constrain its enthusiasm and stop killing the recovery. Credit relations in these systems tend to be more speculative, unstable, and short-term. Add to restrictive Fed policies the foolish deregulation of investment banks and you will see an explosion of U.S.-originated subprime lending and esoteric derivatives. These devices led to the 2007–2008 housing and financial meltdown, the epitome of casino capitalism.

Previous to 1990, there remain the anomalies of Germany and Switzerland, the two highest scorers on bank autonomy. Although I have scored them as only marginally corporatist (see Wilensky, 2002: ch. 2), it is clear that both countries evidence substantial institutional offsets to the ideology and power of their independent central banks at least during some of the period preceding the establishment of the European Central Bank. In Germany, the major counter-influence is left and labor strength; in Switzerland, it is more the tight connection between industry and finance than it is labor-left politics. The Swiss central bank, which began operations in 1907, by a 1978 revised law aims at "a balanced positive growth, especially ... protection against and prevention of unemployment and inflation" (Schweizerische Nationalbank, 1993: 26–27). Although it is more autonomous than the Bank of Japan (before Japan increased its autonomy in 1998), it fits the Japanese pattern of enterprise finance. Swiss bankers not only work closely together in and around the central bank but also work in intimate association with industrialists and entrepreneurs. In his analysis of the Swiss international multifunction bank, W. Blackman (1989: 241ff.) notes that Swiss bankers early on adopted the slogan, "It was not industry which was short of capital but capital which was short of industry." Bankers often serve as board members of the corporations in which they invest; their interest in industrial growth balances their interest in fighting inflation. In Germany, too, banks and industry have long had a close relationship, although this has diminished since Shonfield's (1965) account of that interplay (Soskice and Schettkat, 1993: 106–108).

The German labor movement for decades remained a major countervailing force to the Bundesbank. Although the German labor federation, the DGB (Deutscher Gewerkschaftsbund), has little control over its eight member unions, there is much coordination of union policies because of the dominance of IG Metall and quite strong employer associations. As Carlin and Soskice (1990) have shown in a study of 17 of our countries from 1965 to 1985, Germany therefore ranks above average in coordinated wage bargaining despite its low degree of centralization. Thus, the postwar record of low inflation with only medium unemployment is a product not only of the Bundesbank's autonomy but of a labor movement that has traded off wage restraint and industrial peace for social benefits and worker participation (see the detailed analysis in Wilensky, 2002: ch. 12; Soskice and Schettkat, 1993). The consensual bargaining between labor, government, and industry eases the Bundesbank's task of controlling inflation without greatly reducing employment (Wilensky, 2002: 38–39 and Chapter 3 on wage restraint; cf. Hall, 1994). The ascendance of the European Central Bank, however, changed all that.

Adding to Bundesbank accountability and intermittent moderation before 2000 is the presence of six prominent, independent economic research institutes whose concerns transcend inflation and whose orientations differ.[34] They present their economic forecasts every spring and fall. The institute in Berlin is viewed as more "left" than the others, but together they constitute another countervailing source of data and interpretation. Even so, the power of the Bundesbank occasionally overwhelms the opposing interests. For instance, when the huge costs of reunification mounted after 1989, and especially in 1992, the Bundesbank insisted on maintaining high interest rates, refusing to accommodate the demands of either the German government or its opposition and driving unemployment up to 8.2 percent in 1993 (9.7 percent by the first quarter of 1994), forcing its European neighbors into devaluation and/or recession.[35] Modeled on the Bundesbank, the European Central Bank currently follows similar procyclical policies. Beyond these national differences is a second message from this analysis (Wilensky, 2002: table 17.4, col. 3): rich democracies have converged toward more central bank independence, often because of what they think is the success of the Bundesbank and always because of the weight of the German economy in determining exchange rates. From 1990 to 1993 at least six of the countries that are ranked low or medium in central bank autonomy in my study increased the independence of their central banks. And in Britain, already medium in bank autonomy, the victorious Labour government of May 1997, in a surprise first step, gave the Bank of England "operational independence" – the right to set interest rates, formerly in the hands of the Treasury. Even in Japan, where key ministries have dominated economic policy, the Bank of Japan achieved official independence in 1998. However, its complex informal relations with the top officials of the Ministry of Finance, METI, and other powerful agencies persist.

In most rich democracies, it is a shift in power to increasingly insulated bankers and economists, technocrats hostile to the welfare state and the taxes to finance it, enthralled by an ideology of monetarism, obsessed with the dangers of even moderate inflation, ignoring cross-national evidence that there is little link between such inflation and economic growth. In essence, a small elite of central bankers acts as agents for big international investors with, at best, only incidental concern with unemployment or even steady growth.

The evidence that they know what they are doing is, to say the least, slim. A major study of the effects of the monetary policy of the Federal Reserve Board (FRB) on economic performance in the postwar period 1947–1990 (Romer and Romer, 1989; 1994) shows that in the six episodes when the FRB attempted to contract the economy to fight what it said was "excessive" inflation (October 1947, September 1955, December 1968, April 1974, August 1978, and October 1979) it precipitated and then prolonged and deepened recessions (beyond what would have occurred for other reasons), although it also prolonged recoveries. Updating that study to 1950–1990 and concentrating on the effects of the Fed on the pace of recovery (from the depths it often caused), the Romers conclude that Fed policy "has made recessions more severe, and recoveries more rapid, than they otherwise would have been" (Romer and Romer, 1994: 51). For instance, without Fed action, the 1953, 1960, and 1969 recessions would not have occurred at all, and the output declines in the 1973 and 1981 recessions would have been half as deep as they were. Monetary policy "helped to both start and stop postwar recessions" (p. 52). In other words, the Fed's penchant for tight money when growth rears its ugly head triggers and deepens recessions, but when the governors decide to loosen up, their reductions in interest rates are crucial to recovery. The Romers also find that Fed policy, whether contractionary or expansionary, has long-lasting effects. Fiscal policies – both automatic changes in taxes and spending and discretionary changes – also aid recovery, but their effects are not as strong as the effects of monetary policy.[36]

What we can infer from this careful study, which adds the Federal Reserve Board's contemporaneous records to its quantitative narrative, is that the U.S. central bank, in its zeal to fight inflation and its limited concern for unemployment, has destabilized the American economy, creating more and bigger booms and busts. Because its mission in the words of the Federal Reserve Reform Act of 1977 is "to promote the goals of maximum employment, stable prices, and moderate long-term interest rates," and because Fed chairmen often announce that the governors aim at "stable prices and sustainable growth," we can conclude that either they lack the knowledge to carry out their mission or, as the Romers seem to imply, they deliberately create recessions to avoid inflation, whatever the social costs. I prefer the hypothesis that they are guided by a combination of ignorance and ideology. For many years the Fed believed that manipulation of its measures of the money supply (M1, M2, M3) would bring low (or even zero) inflation with steady growth; then in the early 1990s, as evidence mounted that these were poor measures and/or that the underlying theory was weak, the Fed shifted its attention to commodity prices as harbingers of inflation and justified its preemptive strikes (interest rate hikes, tighter money) on those grounds (Greenspan in testimony and answers to questions before congressional committees in July 1994). To many observers and investors, the game was not to assess the real economy but to assess what the prevailing ideology of the Fed would make it do and when, an even more difficult task. Don't worry about your country's economy; worry about what the Fed thinks about the economy. So investors dump bonds and buy commodities in anticipation of hard-line preemptive action by the Fed. Then the Fed interprets the bond traders' fear of the Fed as a sign of an inflation threat. It is a model of the self-fulfilling prophecy.[37]

My skeptical observations about the limits of Federal Reserve Board knowledge are reinforced by cross-national research on the relationship between central bank autonomy and economic growth, unemployment, and inflation. Regarding growth, where researchers have controlled for initial GDP, they find

TABLE 10. *Central Bank Autonomy (CBA) and Economic Performance by Periods, 1965–1989*

| Autonomy | CBA Average Score by Group[a] | Average Score for Economic Performance Index[b] | | | |
|---|---|---|---|---|---|
| | | 1965–74 | 1974–79 | 1980–84 | 1985–89 |
| High | 3.8 | 3.0 | 3.7 | 4.3 | 4.3 |
| Medium-High | 2.5 | 2.3 | 2.5 | 1.5 | 2.3 |
| Medium | 2.0 | 3.6 | 3.3 | 3.1 | 3.0 |
| Low and Low-Medium | 1.4 | 3.0 | 3.0 | 3.7 | 3.0 |

[a] Average score for legal autonomy using comparable metrics from Bade and Parkin, 1987, as extended by Alesina, 1988, and the sum of political and economic independence computed by Grilli, Masciandaro, and Tabellini, 1991. Austria is ranked medium by Burdekin and Willet, 1991. See Wilensky, 2002: 660–661 and appendix H, which compares these scores and rankings with Cukierman's (1992) survey data for validation. Researchers differ greatly in ranking CBA for Japan (see Wilensky, 2002: table 17.4, note e). In my judgment, it ranks low for this period.
[b] The economic performance index equally weights unemployment, real GDP growth per capita, and inflation. See Chapter 1 and notes to Tables 3 and 4.

that CBA has a positive effect on growth in the NICs but no effect in the rich countries I am discussing (e.g., Alesina and Summers, 1993: 151; Cukierman et al., 1993: 110–112, 136; Grilli, Masciandaro, and Tabellini, 1991).

Using the economic performance index of Chapter I (equally weighting low inflation, good growth, and low unemployment) for four postwar periods and averaging those scores for four degrees of central bank autonomy (CBA high, medium-high, medium, and low) among the 18 rich democracies in Table 10, we can see that central bank autonomy is unrelated to economic performance.

In 1965–1974 the three countries with the strongest CBA tied the three countries with the weakest CBA, and the best performers were those with only moderate bank autonomy. In all periods after the first oil shock, the top economic performers were countries with the strongest banks (Germany and Switzerland taking the lead), but the worst economic performers were the countries with medium-high CBA (Canada, the Netherlands, and Denmark), whereas the close second in performance 1974–1979 was the medium CBA and the close second in 1980–1984 was the low CBA. (For details on economic performance, see Chapters 1 and 3; Wilensky, 2002: ch. 12 and appendix G.)

Decomposing the economic performance index and correlating each of its three components with central bank autonomy among the same 18 rich democracies, again we find only weak relationships. What other researchers who include less-than-rich countries in their studies conclude – CBA dampens inflation – is evident for our countries, too. But the correlations are strong only for 1974–1979 ($r = -.60$). For other periods, CBA has only a marginal or moderate negative correlation with inflation: $r = -.42$ (n.s.) for 1965–1974; $-.40$ ($p = .10$) for 1980–1984; $-.47$ ($p = .05$) for 1985–1989. More important, if we exclude Japan as an outlier during this period (low bank autonomy, very high growth),

CBA has a negative or no effect on real GDP growth per capita (–.11, –.09, –.42, and –.29) and no effect on unemployment. Of course, these averages obscure the more interesting results at the extremes uncovered in Table 10 and the much more important institutional sources of economic performance discussed previously. The averages for growth and unemployment also obscure the destabilizing effects of some powerful central banks as they initiate and exacerbate slumps and accelerate recoveries (net average effect may be zero). If the more independent central bankers knew what they were doing, we would surely get stronger results on inflation and some positive results on growth.[38]

That several of the countries whose central banks had limited autonomy before 1990 (Japan, Austria, Norway, or Belgium, 1965–1974, 1985–1989) outperformed countries with more independent central banks (Canada, the Netherlands, Denmark, or the United States before 1980) should give pause to those who adopted the "Bundesbank model" for the European Central Bank without the German labor, management, state, political, education and training, and other institutions that made it work. Unfortunately, the European Union has neither the offsetting institutions to constrain such a bank's behavior nor the European-wide welfare state and job creation antidotes to its strong deflationary medicine. Supporting these observations about the spreading effects of the ideology and rising power of central bankers is the finding that the worldwide variation in national interest rates has declined over the past 40 years (Held and McGrew, 2007: 86, fig. 5.9).

I do not deny the need for a relatively stable currency, the avoidance of huge price fluctuations, and a "lender of last resort" to supply emergency cash reserves to faltering banks or other action to avoid financial panics.[39] The trouble comes with the radical shift in power away from elected politicians to a group of bankers, shadow bankers, and economists with a highly specialized ideology who are only remotely accountable. The ideology in most cases goes beyond monetarism to Reaganomics: deregulate, privatize, reduce taxes (especially on upper-income groups and corporations), cut social spending – these are the cure-alls typically advocated by many authoritative central bankers.[40] Like the doctors of the 18th century who bled their patients to cure them, some central bankers also regard recessions as a necessary purge to restore labor discipline as well as confidence in the currency. (Michael Kreile [1978: 209] cites former Bundesbank president Emminger to this effect.) And if the political class does not shape up, these ideologues, given enough autonomy, can administer shocks that will threaten politicians' survival.

The current Fed chairman and former Princeton professor, Ben Bernanke, is the exception that proves the rule. When Bernanke, an expert on the causes of the Great Depression and a student of the Japanese deflation of the 1990s, became Fed chairman and cut interest rates and injected huge sums of money into the economy by buying mortgage and Treasury securities, while the European Central Bank held fast to high rates and stalled on stimulus, he was attacked by ideologues whose indifference to labor and product market deterioration was obvious. In any case, the succession of Bernanke could not reverse the cumulative effects of foolish deregulation of financial institutions in the United States, precipitating a worldwide recession.

As I have shown in Chapter 1, this ideology is contradicted by empirical evidence on variation in the economic performance of rich democracies from 1950 to 2005. Sheer level of taxes and social spending has no consistent effect on economic performance; before 1974 the impact of aggregate social spending was actually positive as a trade-off for labor peace and tax concessions to industry; it fades after 1973 and is neutral after 1979 (Wilensky, 2002: 79ff., tables 2 and 3). Indeed, some components of the welfare state continue to be productivity-enhancing – for example, health-care access, occupational health and safety, active labor-market policy (chs. 2, 12, 15, 16, and 18). Tax structures have a modest effect: consumption taxes, because they are negatively related to strikes and positively related to capital formation, foster economic growth; social-security payroll taxes (used to finance health care, pensions, etc.) actually restrain inflation in normal times; they rarely lower growth (only in the brief period of multiple shocks, 1980–1984). Property taxes, however, may be a drag on the economy (pp. 37–44). Intrusive regulations in a context of combat between labor, management, and the government are indeed a drag on the economy. But it is the least corporatist countries with the most free-enterprise ideology that evidence ineffective intrusive regulatory styles (as in the controls over medical professionals introduced by President Reagan and Prime Minister Thatcher); corporatist democracies, in contrast, arrive at consensual rules that can be better implemented (Chapter 7).

There are already enough elected politicians who ignore such evidence and pin economic troubles on the welfare state, high taxes, and government regulations. Why enhance the power of ideologues in central banks who share their views and cannot be removed when the limits of their revelations become apparent?

Even if the effects of central bank independence and ideology on employment and growth were not on balance negative, their effects on political legitimacy would be worrisome. The extreme case of New Zealand may be a sign of things to come; it recently concocted a brew of radical and sudden shifts in fiscal, monetary, and social policies and simultaneously created the most powerful independent central bank in the world. Within 10 years this combination of sectarian economics, indiscriminate deregulation, means testing, cuts in social spending, shifts in tax burdens to the middle and bottom, and union bashing brought about the near-collapse of the major political parties, the emergence of several radical parties of the right and left, a drastic decline in public confidence in all institutions, and a massive popular revolt. It culminated in a referendum marking the first and only postwar shift among rich democracies away from a simple plurality electoral system to a mixed member proportional representation system. Ironically, that seems to have produced the very center-left coalition that the right-wing sectarians wiped out. The full story of New Zealand's neoliberal experiment appears in Chapter 4. A similar case, the Bush deregulation, privatization, and cuts in social, labor, and environmental budgets, had similar results in the United States: a popular revolt in the elections of 2006 and 2008.

In short, strong central bank independence without at least the medium-strong corporatist institutions of Germany and Switzerland can destabilize both the economy and the political system and increase the potential for polarized politics.

Reinforcing this trend is not any unprecedented flow of capital and labor across national boundaries but the flow of peculiarly American model-building, pyrotechnical economists, theorists of unmodified free markets, sectarian in style, less knowledgeable about political and economic institutions than their predecessors. Some of them, marketing a blend of Reaganomics and monetarist ideology, have penetrated finance ministries and financial communities, on the way converting journalists who cover economic issues. This recent tendency was apparent in the 1990s in New Zealand, France, and for a brief moment (1989–1994) even in Sweden.

Large national differences in bargaining structures and public policies remain; they are associated with differences in central bank autonomy and behavior. That is the main story. Yet increasing trade dependence, though it so far has little effect on national institutions, policies, and politics, may foster convergence in monetary policies when it is combined with the growth of international financial markets. Insofar as center-left political pressure and labor movements in Japan, Germany, and the United States decline, insofar as the relations between industry and finance weaken, the central banks in these three countries will become still more independent, as will the Central Bank of Europe. As trade dependence increases among all our rich democracies, these banks – whose comparative advantage will increasingly rest on maintaining a stable value for their key currencies – will become even more preoccupied with fighting domestic inflation and less concerned with either domestic or world economic growth and oblivious to unemployment. The rest of the democracies – increasingly dependent on trade and international financial markets with their central banks forced to follow the lead of the big three and the ECB – will be constrained in their economic policies. The option of moderate global reflation and growth to resolve the conflict between central bank restrictive monetary policies and pro-employment, progrowth fiscal policies will be foreclosed. The flexibility and benign effects of taxing and spending would be reduced. Remember that Bretton Woods, aiming to support expansionary national macroeconomic policies, explicitly limited the role of central banks. The reverse is now occurring – a convergence in the independence of central banks with a bias toward restrictive monetary policies. Speculative international financial markets dominated by ideologically driven private bankers and managers of financial enterprises oriented toward like-minded central bankers could threaten the state-labor-industry collaboration that has been so productive since World War II.

In other words, if there is any one force that can in the long run undermine the capacity of modern democracies to shape their economic destinies and, more specifically, the policies adopted by consensual democracies, the spread of autonomous central banks linked to the internationalization of finance is it. We do not know whether similar research on central bank behavior in other modern democracies would conclude as the Romers do that central bank autonomy triggers and deepens recessions.

Even here, however, even with the rise of central bank autonomy and the export of American-trained doctrinaire economists, national differences in the strength of countervailing powers are substantial: a Bundesbank in the German sociopolitical context or a European Central Bank in an EU context is not the same as a Federal Reserve Board in the American context, let alone a bank in a Japanese or Swedish context.

## 2. Financial Deregulation and the Crisis of 2007–2010 in Comparative Perspective: Origins, Sequence, Policies, and Effects

Today's big private banks are "global in life but national in death." Mervyn King, the governor of the Bank of England (2009)

When the capital development of a country becomes a by-product of the activities of a casino, the job is likely to be ill done. John Maynard Keynes (1936)

The most thorough comparative historical analysis of economic crises is *This Time Is Different* by Carmen Reinhart and Kenneth Rogoff (2009). They analyze such crises over eight centuries and as many as 59 nations. They observe three different types of financial turmoil: *sovereign debt crises* (investors lose faith in a government's willingness or ability to meet its financial obligations, as occurred in the case of Greece in May 2010 and Argentina 2001–2003); *inflationary crises* (governments print money to pay their bills or inflate away the real value of their debts as in the case of Germany's hyperinflation of 1923); and, the most devastating, *banking crises*, which are correlated with corporate defaults. Banking crises overlap and intensify sovereign debt crises and inflationary crises. For instance, financial speculation promoted by bankers aiming at large, quick returns drives economic crises; that typically fosters a sharp rise in housing and stock market prices, where possible a devaluation of currency relative to others, and perhaps a deflationary spiral as the bubbles burst, credit freezes, and capital investment erodes (e.g., Japan in the 1990s).[41] Worse, in our time banking crises spread more easily and quickly from large economies to other nations and regions to create worldwide recessions and depressions.

*Recessions vs. Depressions*

As we have seen in the record of central bank performance, almost all postwar recessions in the United States have been triggered by central bank monetary policies – tight money and interest rate increases. Typically they have been short and confined to one or two nations or one region. Depressions, in contrast, are the result of bursting asset and credit bubbles, a contraction in credit, and a decline in the general price level (*Economist*, Dec. 30, 2008). Further, they start in a nation that has a large share of world GDP.

Thus, in its causes, severity, and swift spread around the globe, the Great Recession of 2007–2009 resembles the Great Depression of 1929–1933 more than it fits all of the plain-vanilla recessions of 1945 to today (Reinhart and Rogoff, 2009: ch. 16; Stiglitz, 2010a; Eichengreen and O'Rourke, 2010).[42] And, like the Great Depression, it was "Made in America." A few U.S. indicators of severity tell the story:

- *The evaporation of wealth* is unmatched since 1929–1933. For instance, $7.9 trillion was lost in home equity from January 2007 to April 2009, down 60 percent (Federal Reserve System, 2010: table B100). Added trillions were lost in the crash of securities held in private pension funds and retirement plans. These were far more widespread than they were in the Great Depression.
- Although the official *unemployment* peak of 10.8 percent during the worst oil shock and multiple crises of 1981–1982 (Chapter 3 and Table 3) was not quite reached in 2007–2009, *recent job losses are deeper*. The reasons: the Great Recession started with a lower unemployment rate than that of the 1981–1982 slump so the decline is steeper, a 4.7 percent decline (6.7 million fewer Americans working June 2009 than December 2007) vs. a 3.1 percent decline in 1981–1982. The total job loss from the start of the Great Recession to April 2010 was 8 million; in the 2010 "recovery," only 500,000 of these jobs were regained. Because of the growth of population aged 16–65 from first quarter 2000 to first quarter 2010, the United States must create about 175,000 jobs *per month* just to stay even (my calculations from BLS, 2010a). Moreover, the official count of the unemployed underestimates the real rate. If we count part-timers who want to work full time and discouraged workers who have ceased a futile job search, the rate is near double the official rate (for details, see Chapter 7). Another way to understand the depth and breadth of insecurity in the Great Recession and its aftermath is to note a combination of events: in May 2009 more than half of the U.S. labor force experienced two or more of official unemployment, or a pay cut, or forcibly reduced hours (*Wall Street Journal*, June 20, 2010).
- *Costly long-term unemployment reached a record* unmatched since the BLS started measuring it in 1948. In April 2010 almost half (46%) of the unemployed had been jobless for six months or more.
- *Industrial production fell* 16 percent, far more than any postwar recession. Ditto the *plunge in payrolls*.
- The *collapse of the housing market from 2006 on* brought its own form of misery – *mortgage delinquencies and foreclosures*. Mortgage delinquency rates continued to increase, by the first quarter of 2010 reaching more than 10 percent of all loans outstanding. Counting all homeowners in trouble – from those who have missed one payment to those awaiting eviction – the total reached about one in seven of the 52 million households with home mortgages. Starting with bankers and brokers who peddled toxic subprime mortgages, the crisis of defaults spread to prime borrowers suffering unemployment and/or loss of income and savings, including private pensions. New foreclosures in the first quarter of 2010 that were conservative prime fixed-rate loans had climbed to 37 percent. Meanwhile the construction bubble

burst. From the April 2005 peak to April 2009 new housing permits had plunged to about one-quarter of the peak (U.S. Census Bureau, 2010). In April 2010 housing starts were still only 29 percent of starts at the top of the bubble. The collapse of commercial real estate loans added to a depression in the construction industry.

- *Bank failure rates reached a new postwar high.* In 2009 alone, 135 banks, most of them small or midsized, failed. The number of failures in 2010 is expected to exceed that number, and 775 more were listed by the FDIC as "problem institutions" (FDIC, 2010).
- *Personal bankruptcy rates soared*; they hit 1.41 million in 2009, up 32 percent from 2008. And they were not confined to low-income filers; they included a rising percentage of people with high education and income (*Wall Street Journal*, Jan. 5, 2010). The trend continued in early 2010, embracing families at every level of the "class" structure.
- *Going beyond the United States, the meltdown of world financial markets –* the sharp increase of volatility in stock prices and exchange rates, the rapid decline of export markets – *was at least as bad as the collapse in the Great Depression.* In fact if we compare several economic indicators for the early 1930s and the first 18 months of the Great Recession, we see that the recent data closely track the 1930s rate of fall in world industrial production, trade volume, stock market prices, and industrial output (in rate of decline of output, Italy and France did worse than the 1930s, United States and Canada about the same) (Eichengreen and O'Rourke, 2010).

Why did we not sink into a second Great Depression? The saving grace this time around is a combination of the welfare state, which automatically cushions the shock of economic downswings among all rich democracies (Chapter 1), anti-cyclical deficit spending, and a near-zero interest-rate policy of the Fed. However modest and delayed the Obama stimulus package of 2009–2010, it did help avoid a deep depression. In contrast, during the 43-month depression of 1929–1933 the United States slashed spending in a failed effort to balance the budget. It also raised interest rates to preserve the gold standard. Italy, because it engaged in military Keynesian deficit spending as it invaded Ethiopia, came out of the Depression early with a quick return to full employment. Ignoring Keynes's advice, FDR, who had restored growth and cut unemployment in half with the social spending and increased wages of his New Deal, reverted to the old-time religion in 1937; he moved to balance the budget, triggering a new recession. (As a candidate in 1932, Roosevelt had made a little-publicized speech in Pittsburgh promising a balanced budget.) The economic crisis did not fully end until the big spending of World War II.

During the Great Recession, deficit hawks in Congress and the White House screamed that the Debt Devil would ruin the country for generations to come; their revelation was echoed and amplified in the mass media until it became a bipartisan mantra. As Table 1 and my discussion in Chapter 1 suggest, among rich democracies government spending had little to do with the size of the debt (that depends on what else governments do). Further, deep national debt is much less dangerous for rich democracies than for developing and poor countries. This is illustrated by scores of debt-driven crises among nonrich countries of Latin America, Asia, and Africa, as well as the current plight of the Eurozone's less-rich countries, Greece, Portugal, and Spain.[43] Rich Japan, however, has run a big debt for two decades – often more than 100 percent of GDP – without impairing its capacity to borrow long-term at very low rates. The United Kingdom's debt exceeded its GDP from World War I to the 1950s while its credit remained good (Reinhart and Rogoff, 2009).

As Chapters 1 and 3 show, the rich democracies have more options than the poor in handling debt. They can more easily raise and collect taxes in the upswing; they can choose to spend productively, investing in human and physical infrastructures; they can choose sensible tax structures that do not provoke sustained tax revolts. Their riches provide more margin for error. In the Introduction I mentioned that the U.S. GDP, even in 2009 in the middle of the great contraction, was $14.3 trillion; at that level, a growth rate of only 3 percent brings in an extra $429 billion a year. Finally, their governments are relatively stable and can choose to regulate the financial sector to prevent large-scale speculation, corruption, and similar pathologies. This is not to deny that there is a downside to large sustained national debt. Interest on debt cannot be spent on more productive goals such as education, the environment, R&D, child care, an active labor-market policy, wage subsidies, poverty reduction, federal aid to hard-pressed states, and more.[44] Again, the main point is that an ideological obsession with debt and balanced budgets with no attention to the productive or countercyclical uses of government spending, regulation, and policies for economic growth is, to say the least, misplaced. If in 2010–2011 the deficit police can prevent the further fiscal stimulus needed to restore jobs with moderate growth or if they persuade the Fed to raise interest rates prematurely, the United States could sink into the really dangerous trap – a deflationary meltdown that matches Japan's lost decade.

### Causes and Sequence of Global Financial Crises

The major causes are difficult to unscramble sequentially; they interact and they do not all apply to each economic crisis. However, we can make a tentative judgment about how the United States led the world into its current mess.[45] The current sequence fits the global financial crises analyzed by Reinhart and Rogoff (2009: 240–273 and the citations therein). They include the crises of 1825–1826 centered in the United States and the United Kingdom and spreading to Europe and Latin America; the panic of 1907 centered in the United States and spreading to Europe, Asia, and Latin America; the Great Depression of 1929–1933 centered in the United States and France, spreading to all regions; and the global contraction of 2008–2009 again starting in the United States and spreading to all regions. In all these cases the big-economy crisis fueled extremely rapid cross-border contagion.

The root cause of worldwide financial crises is financial deregulation ("liberalization"). In the United States it was a cascade of measures to free financial institutions from government oversight by a combination of changes in law, executive orders, and the appointment of officials to head regulatory agencies who did not believe in regulation or took their lead from the industries they were supposed to regulate. The most important of the several measures was the 1999 repeal of the Glass-Steagall Act of 1933. That act, part of the Banking Act of 1933, separated investment banks from commercial banks. It prohibited investment banks from acting as regular depositor banks. It tightly regulated banks that receive deposits, pay interest on those deposits, and make loans to individuals and businesses. The Banking Act also created the Federal Deposit Insurance Corporation (FDIC), which insured depositors against possible bank failure. And the Security and Exchange Act of 1934 establishing the SEC brought some order to the exchanges; it reduced assorted frauds, scams, and abuses.

The banking reforms of the New Deal fostered six decades of relative stability in the financial system. (There are other cycles of deregulation and reregulation including the Savings and Loan crisis of the 1980s, but they do not come close to today's meltdown.) Until the deregulation fever of 1999–2009, these New Deal reforms did what they aimed to do: facilitate transactions between depositors and the sellers of goods and services, while managing risk and making long-term loans to individuals and businesses. In other words, the regulatory regime gave us banks that performed the traditional function of promoting sustainable economic expansion in communities and the nation.

Repealing Glass-Steagall freed investment banks and mortgage companies from government regulation and constituted a powerful incentive for their expansion in size and power. It allowed investment banks to absorb commercial banks and insurance companies. They are now called "shadow banks" – institutions such as Citicorp, Lehman Brothers, AIG, and Goldman Sachs that do not accept deposits and so are not covered by routine banking regulations (cf. Krugman, 2009: ch. 8). They have followed the lure of easy short-run profits from transaction costs. Unregulated mortgage companies (some are subsidiaries of shadow banks) hustled teaser mortgages with little or no down payment, but high fees, variable interest rates, payments that could spike sharply up – all in small print, with no protection against loss of home values or jobs. These toxic mortgages, most of them subprime, have earned the label predatory lending.[46] Similarly unregulated credit-card companies reaped a harvest of high fees by promoting household debt among millions of borrowers who could not sustain the payments. Together mortgage companies and credit-card companies reinforced the housing bubble.

Then comes the next act in this deregulation drama: the shadow banks bought and repackaged the mortgages, sold them as securities, charging sizable fees. The big buyers of these securitized mortgages – for example, state and private pension funds with investments in the trillions – had no idea of the credit worthiness of the hundreds of home owners and commercial real-estate builders in each package. Why did they buy? Enter the rating agencies, principally

Standard and Poor's, Moody's, and Fitch. Pension funds such as the biggest in the country, the California Public Employees Retirement System (CalPERS), typically have a fiduciary responsibility to purchase only AAA-rated securities. The rating agencies gladly bestowed AAA ratings on a huge number of the toxic financial products, hundreds of billions worth. From 2004 to 2007 rating agencies made hundreds of millions of dollars rating thousands of opaque deals in residential mortgage-backed securities and collateralized debt obligations. The raters were being paid by the institutions selling the products they were rating.

There was certainly competition among the big three raters – a race to see which one of them could give the easiest, highest ratings. The shadow banks could direct their business to whichever agency would give the AAA rating, sometimes applying quiet pressure. Just to make sure of the cooperative spirit of the raters, they hired a few at munificent pay packages, a demonstration to the agency employees of a possible career enhancement if they played ball and, incidentally, to learn more about the financial models used by the raters. By April 2010, in the context of media exposés and congressional investigations, 93 percent of the AAA subprime mortgage-backed securities issued in 2006 had to be downgraded to junk status. In short, the rating agencies were engaged in a colossal conflict of interest.

The enormously profitable, risky, and destructive character of the devices employed by the shadow banks are as complicated as the bankers' fees are large. They are typically derivatives whose value is linked to or derived from some underlying asset such as a stock, bond, commodity, currency, or a package of mortgages. In the deregulated years since 1999, the Wizards of Wall Street piled derivatives on top of derivatives. They also adopted a strategy of accelerating leverage; their debt obligations persistently increased in relation to their assets, an unsustainable path. When the banks finally faced failure, they turned to the government for rescue; they received lavish corporate welfare (see Chapter 7).

The specific speculative devices they used multiplied bankers' transaction fees like rabbits. Consider the most prominent:

- *Collateralized debt obligations* (CDOs). These are securitized products that bundle often-toxic home loans or other risky assets and provide fixed income streams to purchasers of the derivative security (the CDO). This type of derivative may be the biggest money loser in Wall Street history. Their content is often opaque, the payoff to the buyer when bubbles burst, history shows, unlikely. Before the meltdown, Wall Street firms issued a total of $1.08 trillion in CDOs between 2005 and 2007 (*Wall Street Journal*, May 13, 2010).
- *Credit default swaps* (CDSs). These are like credit insurance where the owner of the security or other asset pays the seller, for example, the shadow bank, for a return payment if the financial product defaults or fails. Even more complicated is that the bank can pile a CDO on a CDS, with the "insurance" contract as the underlying asset for the CDO. The reason banks shun the label insurance is to evade the requirement that regular insurance companies set aside reserves to cover their risks. Calling them "swaps" meant that

traders in CDSs could make whatever speculative decisions they wished without government oversight.

- *Total return swaps* (TRSs). Banks use this type of derivative to provide hedge funds with low-cost financing. The hedge funds in turn use the swaps to purchase leveraged loans or other assets from the bank, pledging the purchased assets as collateral for the loan. Hedge funds are another source of mounting transaction fees on Wall Street. They invented the formula of "2 and 20." Hedge fund managers collect 2 percent of assets they manage plus 20 percent of profits they gain, a very quick way to become a billionaire – or go bankrupt. By mid-2010 they had amassed roughly $2 trillion in assets and when they fail – well, when Long-Term Capital Management collapsed in 1998, it lost almost $6 billion (*Wall Street Journal*, June 12–13, 2010).

At times, the shadow banks were on both sides of a trade in derivatives. They put together a package of toxic items designed to fail, collect fat fees from a favored hedge-fund client who bets on the failure, promote their sale without disclosing their toxicity to another client who is betting on success, again collecting transaction fees. And then, to top it off, the investment bank bets on the CDS's failure for its own account, again reaping the profits when the price collapses.

Long after the taxpayer bailouts of Wall Street, major U.S. banks and nonbanks were back doing the same things that created the crash: financial engineering of exotic derivatives for quick profits, a renewed appetite for risk, with executives awarding themselves obscene bonuses and pay packages, even in the face of failure (Enrich and Paletta, 2009). They now cobble together mortgage-backed or other securities and repackage them into mini-CDOs to make them look more credible to investors. By April 1, 2009, the "value" of credit derivatives outstanding in the U.S. banking system stood at $14.6 trillion, according to the Office of the Controller of the Currency, triple the level of 1996. Chapter 8 discusses the U.S. government policy response, which can be described as TLC (tender loving care) accompanied by populist rhetoric trashing Wall Street plus a rare court action. In April 2010 the SEC sued Goldman Sachs in a federal court for allegedly misleading clients and knowingly faking them out with a CDO derivative (Pulliam et al., 2010).[47]

All these quick, easy profits fueled the growth of the main players so that by 2007 only five very large shadow banks dominated the derivatives market. They include Citigroup, Bank of America, Goldman Sachs, Morgan Stanley, and the financial institutions they have acquired (Merrill Lynch is now part of Bank of America; Countrywide, the largest mortgage lender of the housing boom, also became a unit of Bank of America). Deregulation had given them an incentive to ever-greater risk, ever-shorter time horizons, and ever-more esoteric financial instruments – and consequently shadow-bank expansion. When all these speculative transactions inevitably collapsed, the shadow banks had grown so large that the government saw them as "too big to fail" and there followed, at breakneck speed, the Wall Street bailout package publicized as $700 billion. Later analysis shows actual outlays to "banks" (including the AIG bailout of $183 billion) were less. But few analysts argue that the Troubled Asset Relief Program (TARP) and related costs were small. (The Appendix discusses bailout accounting.)

This concentration of power in a few unregulated shadow banks accelerated the rapid spread of the meltdown not only in the United States but abroad. Because the United States is a major importer of global goods and services – it has run a poor balance of trade every year since 1976 – its economic crisis is central as a source of deep worldwide recessions. Equally important is the increasing internationalization of finance, so that a credit collapse in a large shadow bank in the United States or United Kingdom has a direct effect on many regions. Citigroup, for instance, has a presence in about 100 countries. And at mid-2010 foreign banks and financial institutions held about $2.6 trillion, a mountain of bad loans to Greece, Spain, and Portugal. Among the main creditors were France, Germany, Britain, the Netherlands, Italy, and the United States.

Although lax and even predatory lending practices and excessive borrowing by households contributed to the U.S. meltdown, a few big, powerful banks and shadow banks were at the epicenter of the crisis that brought the economy down.

In sum, the sequence looks like this:

Financial deregulation $\longrightarrow$ Banks and shadow banks adopt easy lending practices and escalate their most profitable speculations $\longrightarrow$ Housing bubble, stock-market bubble, boosted by low interest rates $\longrightarrow$ Bubbles burst $\longrightarrow$ Banking crisis begins; many banks fail $\longrightarrow$ Currencies in both initiating nation and abroad fluctuate abruptly $\longrightarrow$ Banking crisis peaks and credit dries up $\longrightarrow$ Recession or depression deepens and spreads $\longrightarrow$ Using taxpayers' money, government bails out big troubled banks, insurance companies, brokers, hedge funds, and some large manufacturing firms.

As deregulation proceeded, a parallel development made things worse – the erosion of household income. From 2000 to 2008, real median household income in the United States declined about 4 percent, thereby restricting consumption or making consumption based only on debt unsustainable. Similarly, in the first quarter of 2010 paychecks from the private sector shrank to their smallest share of personal income in the postwar period, 41.8 percent, down from 44.6 percent when the Great Recession began (Bureau of Economic Analysis, 2010).

Paraphrasing two Nobel Prize–winning economists, Paul Krugman and Joseph Stiglitz, the right question is this: How could the consumption boom of the 1990s, propped up by household debt and a housing bubble, both driven by deregulation and low interest rates accompanied by a near zero savings rate (only the very affluent and the rich were saving), combined with the shadow bankers' invention of occult derivatives, laced with a heavy dose of corruption – how could all this be sustained?

One last nail in the meltdown coffin is the collapse of international trade. Thus, in both the Great Depression and the Great Recession there was little or no export market to cushion the shock. When the multiple bubbles burst and the banking crisis spread in the United States, the meltdown quickly spread across borders, ultimately engulfing the world. That deepened and prolonged the slump in the successful export industries and nations of Europe, Asia, South America, and Africa.

A word about "too big to fail." Much discussion centers on the idea that a few large worldwide financial institutions are so critical to U.S. prosperity and the world economy that the government must bail them out when they are in trouble, whatever the cost. I suggest two arguments that should receive more attention – beyond the debate about whether too big to fail makes them too big to exist. First, these financial giants not only are too big to fail but, given their complexity and their unregulated speculative bets, are "sure to fail." Second, whereas their economic centrality is clear to everyone (though there is little consensus about what public policies would minimize their damage), there is too little attention to what their size and resources mean for the concentration of power in their host country.

### *"Sure to Fail"*

The structure and operation of today's computerized financial sector make failure inevitable and meltdowns quick and widespread. As I showed in *Organizational Intelligence* (1967) and Charles Perrow showed in his *Normal Accidents* (1984), large, complex, complicated and highly interconnected systems are sure to suffer occasional unpredictable breakdowns. We see this in systems designed for redundant safety backups such as aircraft carriers, nuclear power plants, oil shipping and drilling (see Chapter 2), and, of course, big financial firms. The inevitable errors and accidents are speeded up by computerization; a failure in one part of a tightly interconnected system can ricochet swiftly throughout the system. The GIGO principle holds (garbage in, garbage out), but the consequences can be catastrophic when poorly regulated shadow banks speculate in esoteric derivatives neither they nor anyone else understands.[48]

Contributing to this confusion is a new breed of young mathematicians and computer scientists hired by the largest financial firms to model their various markets. Known as "quants," they devised fine-tuned formulas based on computer algorithms to guide bets on which of the innovative financial instruments would rise in price and how much, and when to hedge their bets, estimating risk-adjusted rewards. Ignorant of economic history, surprised that housing bubbles, credit bubbles, commodity bubbles, currency bubbles, and stock-market bubbles always burst, their bets on the future were no better than the predictions of the folks who participated in the tulip mania of 1636–1637 in Holland (MacKay, 1841). Happy panics on the way up, unhappy panics on the way down, or vice versa if the client was going short, but the net effect seems clear: the quants' computer models speed up the volatility characteristic of economic crises. These math whizzes were joined by middle-level executives whose bosses pressed them for quick results. In a situation of great ambiguity with lavish bonuses on the line, they looked to the quants for answers. Top executives were pleased with the results – so long as the profits rolled in.

When the crash came, the top American financial executives who brought the world economy down, when they were not blaming one another or overregulation by the government for their mistakes or malfeasance, argued, "How could anyone have foreseen the meltdown?" In fact, many economists and other analysts gave long advance warning of unsustainable multiple bubbles. Joseph Stiglitz (2010a: 18) lists six notables, including himself, whose warnings were clear and timely. We can forgive any bias in that list – they are all Keynesian – but it does belie the idea that everyone is as clueless as the self-aggrandizing financial magicians whose free-market theology blinded them to the lessons of history.

## The Power of the Financial Lobby

Beyond their vulnerability to periodic meltdowns, large financial enterprises are now so large and so rich that they constitute an unprecedented concentration of power in the politics and policies of the United States. In scope and depth, they matched the power of oligarchs of the Robber Baron Era and far exceeded them in subtlety and negative consequences. It is no mystery that the concentration of economic power generally leads to substantial political power. The research problem is to trace the types of economic institutions that have most and least power, the channels through which economic actors exercise power, the strength of the countervailing forces – politicians, political parties, public agencies, interest groups, and social movements – and their interaction. All chapters of this book attempt to do that by linking national variations in the structure and interplay of these groups to variations in the well-being of people. Here is a brief account of how the dominant actors in the American financial sector were able to amass increasing political power through boom and bust, swiftly obtain big bailouts, and block serious regulation of their irresponsible behavior, even in the face of intense popular anger and politicians' increasing knowledge of their role in the meltdown.

I begin with an oligarchy dominated largely by five firms. Ranked by assets, the five top surviving "banks" in June 2009 were Bank of America ($2.25 trillion), J. P. Morgan Chase ($2.02 trillion), Citicorp ($1.85 trillion), Wells Fargo ($1.28 trillion), and Goldman Sachs ($890 billion). Add to their size the financial institutions they have acquired: Merrill Lynch, Bear Sterns, Washington Mutual, and Countrywide. The government allowed another big firm, Lehman Brothers Holdings, to collapse in September 2008. When it filed for bankruptcy, Lehman had 1.2 million derivatives transactions outstanding with a theoretical value of $39 trillion with 6,500 trading partners (including many municipalities, counties, schools, and nonprofit institutions). Observing the swiftly spreading shock waves spreading out from Lehman's demise, the Fed and both the Bush and Obama administrations vowed never again to allow a large bank or shadow bank to fail if it constitutes a systemic risk. In the new world of no regulation (Bush) or "nudge" regulation (Obama), profits are private but losses are socialized. In September 2008 taxpayers kicked in hundreds of billions, the mother of all bailouts (for bailout accounting, see Appendix). In the absence of strong constraining legislation and regulation, all the big actors now have incentive to take greater risks than they had before; they and their trading partners assume a government rescue if their speculations fail.

We have seen that after receiving bailout billions, the big financial firms engaged in more of the same and even invented still more esoteric instruments for short-run profit. They have elaborated such derivatives as credit default swaps, total return swaps, or collateralized debt obligations. Now they have crafted new devices to outsmart other traders such as high-frequency trading (placing your order a split-second faster than anyone else thereby gaining an advantage) – the epitome of "short-run" profits. As of this writing no reregulation bill from Congress or the White House effectively reins in this behavior.[49]

The power of the Wall Street lobby is palpable. First, as Paul Krugman indicates, high finance – securities and commodities trading, not ordinary old-fashioned banking – has increased its share of GDP by a factor of six since 1980 (*New York Times*, Aug. 3, 2009). Second, additional clues to the size and influence of Wall Street's political action are expenditures on lobbying and political campaigns. According to the Center for Responsible Politics, in the period 1998–2010 the finance/credit, insurance, and real estate complex was the largest lobby in the United States, at $4.05 billion, topping even the medical lobby, discussed in Chapter 5 ($3.98 billion). In 2009 alone, while the economic crisis deepened, the combined securities and investment, commercial banks, finance/credit enterprises, plus a small "Miscellaneous Finance," spent about $211 million on lobbying (excluding the quite low lobbying cost of community credit unions and savings & loans) (CRP, 2009.)

Campaign contributions in 2008 were equally lavish: $158.1 million from securities and investment firms, $37.6 from commercial banks, $7.7 million from finance/credit firms, making a total for the 2008 election of $203.4 million. As usual, the campaign money was bipartisan and continued to escalate over time. For 2008 the Democrats, in ascendance, had a slight edge in gaining Wall Street contributions. When the Republicans dominate congressional committee chairmanships and are in ascendance, they collect more than the Democrats; Wall Street views Republicans as more reliable fighters against financial regulation. In other words, all corporate PACs put together give much more to Republican candidates; but Wall Street is more even handed.

More direct evidence of the financial lobby's influence is the development of a U.S. Treasury/Wall Street Axis. For 6 of 13 years (1996–2008) the secretary of Treasury was a Goldman Sachs alumnus (Zingales, 2008). Robert Rubin went from Goldman Sachs to Clinton's Treasury and back to Citigroup. Henry Paulson went from Goldman Sachs to Bush's Treasury. As Zingales notes in a *Financial Times* column, Paulson "was among the five major investment banking chief executives who persuaded the Securities and Exchange Commission not to extend prudential reserve requirements to their companies" (2008). He led Goldman Sachs to new heights of leverage.[50] As secretary, Paulson also proposed a $700 billion bailout for Wall Street with no strings attached on either the government giver or the corporate receiver. But the uproar of protest that greeted this lavish gift forced a temporary withdrawal. It fell to the new secretary, Timothy Geithner, to recraft the gift – a $700 billion bailout, the Troubled Assets Relief Program (TARP), with some very limited public control. He moved from head of the New York Federal Reserve (the most clubby bankers' circle with the most indulgent regulators) to the Obama administration. Geithner had been a deputy to Robert Rubin and Larry Sommers, prominent architects of the deregulation movement under Bill Clinton. Bush's choice of Fed chairman, Ben Bernanke, was carried over by Obama. The new chairman inherited a bubble created by his predecessor, Chairman Greenspan, and let the bubble continue.[51] Finally, coordinating the Obama economic team was Rubin's former deputy, Larry Sommers, "who proclaimed that one of his great achievements as Secretary of Treasury in 1999–2001 was ensuring that explosive derivatives would remain unregulated" (Stiglitz, 2010: 46).

The coziness between Treasury and Wall Street was thus continued through administrations of different political parties, administrative styles, and campaign rhetoric from Clinton to Bush to Obama. (For an account of probank policies and budgets before and during the meltdown and an estimate that the magnitude of the guarantees and bailouts under Bush and Obama approached $12 trillion [80% of U.S. GDP], see Stiglitz, 2010a: 45–51, 110, and chs. 4 and 5. Even if we subtract unknown numbers of billions that will not be claimed or will be paid back, the financial sector has walked away with a humongous sum with hardly a slap on the wrist.)[52]

The strategy of the financial-sector lobby was shaped by its access to these friends in high places. As Stiglitz observes, when people in the White House or Congress give speeches attacking their interests, Wall Street elites make what may be a correct assumption: "Let the advocates for real change . . . talk and talk; the crisis will be over before an agreement is reached – and with the end of the crisis the momentum for reform will disappear" (Stiglitz, 2010a: 44–45).

Of course, a shared outlook rooted in similar work histories and social networks helps to explain the success of Wall Street elites in preventing government restrictions they oppose and gaining tax breaks and corporate welfare they like. In the past half century there has been a striking shift in the ideological themes sounded by corporate interests and their political contacts. The propaganda shift parallels the occupational and industrial shift from manufacturing to financial services, most extreme in the United States. This is captured in the bold comment of Charles E. Wilson, Eisenhower's secretary of defense, recruited from his job as CEO of General Motors: "What's good for GM is good for the country." Today, the Obama economics team, some of whom came from finance, are more subtle than GM's man in Washington; they avoid the up-front celebration of laissez-faire but simply act as though they believe "What is good for Wall Street is good for the country." That takes its form not only in the too-big-to-fail-let's-bail-them-out ideology but also in the defense of self-correcting markets in finance. When confronted with the assertion that government regulations of finance are necessary to prevent a repetition of economic catastrophes, top Wall Street executives respond that government regulations would stifle the innovations that drive productivity and economic growth, create jobs, and keep America competitive. The Obama economics team adopted a similar stance: "let's-be-light-on-regulation" – only market-conforming rules will maintain a vibrant trading environment in Wall Street.

Not all innovations, however, are born the same. Nor are all bubbles the same. Think of the innovations of Silicon Valley, the semiconductors and other inventions that led to the Dot.com bubble and its burst in 2000–2001. Then compare the impact of the financial innovations that drove the bubbles of finance, whose collapse was a key to the world recession of 2007–2009 and on. The former is Schumpeterian "creative destruction," leaving in its wake real products and services like the computer that have long-term positive effects on the United States and even the world economy. In contrast, the Wall Street innovations we have discussed are, in the immortal words of insider Warren Buffett, "financial weapons of mass destruction"; they have no redeeming social and economic value.

Of course, hedging strategies that insulate investors against big market swings in securities, currencies, and commodities serve a useful function in financial markets. It is when the Wizards of Wall Street abandon their traditional roles that we should sound the alarm. Instead of managing risks, allocating capital, and encouraging savings while keeping transaction costs low, they piled derivatives on derivatives, each less transparent than the last, increased risks and debt by leveraging bets, and drove bubbles to their bursting point, all the while collecting enormous fees. Joseph Stiglitz reports a startling figure: "At their peak in 2007, the bloated financial markets absorbed 41 percent of profits in the corporate sector" (2010a: 7). A not-so-incidental social cost is the drain of bright college graduates away from more productive occupations.

Despite the wreckage they caused – the loss of jobs, homes, pensions and health care, the downward pressure on wages, the consequent suffering of families and communities, the increase in poverty and personal and business bankruptcies, the collapse of state budgets, the more rapid erosion of schools and universities – despite all that, financial elites were treated with tender loving care throughout the Great Recession by their colleagues and the political establishment. At the end of 2008, Wall Street paid out $18 billion in year-end bonuses to its New York City employees alone, after the government handed over $243 billion in emergency assistance to the financial sector (Johnson, 2009: 7). The 2009 pay packages on Wall Street were the best ever. For instance, the top 25 hedge fund managers earned a total of $25.3 billion – an average in total compensation of $1 billion each. The lowest-paid manager pocketed only $350 million in 2009. Or look at the Federal Reserve Board's emergency loans to banks. By April 2010 banks were borrowing billions from the Fed at a cost of about half a percentage point. They then lent this money back to the U.S. Treasury at yields of about 3 percent or higher a moment later. Not only is this perhaps the easiest and most profitable low-risk trade ever invented, it is an outright and ongoing gift from American taxpayers to Wall Street (Cohan, 2010).

The power of the financial lobby is also revealed by comparing the Obama administration's auto industry bailout and the Wall Street bailout. Obviously, a double standard favoring the more powerful Wall Street lobby prevailed. We have seen that for the financial firms action was quick, enormous sums were produced, few strings were attached, there was no interference with the CEOs' custom of feathering their own nests, and the whole process lacked transparency. In contrast, when it became clear that GM and Chrysler were headed for bankruptcy, the government response was delay after delay, modest sums were doled out over time with strong restriction on their use, labor was pressured to make further sacrifices in wage and benefit standards – all in a transparent process run by a government-appointed czar who eased out failed executives and speeded up an orderly bankruptcy. Even the traditional power of the highway-auto-transportation lobby (Chapter 2) could not match the Titans of Finance.

Revolving doors are not new in Washington, but the consequences are now much greater than they have been since World War II: the accelerating concentration of financial power with concomitant economic and social damage. The coziness goes beyond the Treasury–Wall Street Axis. Whether through deregulation by legislation or executive order, or by choosing agency directors hostile to the regulatory mission of their agencies, the end product was the same: unrestrained capitalism flourished until it unraveled in 2007–2009 and is set for more of the same. (For examples of the revolving door and agency capture, see Chapter 7, sec 12.)

Considering all these developments in credit derivatives, securitization, and similar devices, the increasing number of esoteric and opaque trades, and the easy interaction between top people in Wall Street and top people in Washington, D.C., I am tempted to use the popular label "casino capitalism" – if it were not an insult to Las Vegas. That the gambling tables are stacked in favor of the House is well known to the gambler, who can even calculate the odds against her; the rules of the game are also well known. Contrast the financial casino on Wall Street; the investor has little or no information about the underlying assets of the derivatives on which she is betting; the House often operates on the principle, Heads or tails, I win; heads or tails, you lose. The whole process in Vegas is visible, even state regulated; the process on Wall Street is murky, often corrupt.

## G. SUMMARY AND INTERPRETATION

The nation-state may no longer be a viable unit of security; collective security and regional alliances are necessary; the UN may occasionally contribute something. Modern economies are no longer independent, if they ever were; economies are becoming more open. Problems of the environment, of human rights, and of terrorism transcend national boundaries, as do the solutions to such problems. Yet the nation-state remains the center of political action, social solidarity, and personal identity. Indeed, in recent decades globalization has proceeded in tandem with the proliferation of nation-states. It is a paradox: the more globalization, the more national fragmentation.

This chapter has shown that neither the flow of capital and labor across national boundaries nor the increasing prominence of multinational corporations and the modest outsourcing of jobs are major threats to the social and labor-market policies of rich democracies. Because social spending has both positive and negative effects on productivity, and net effects since 1974 are nil, the welfare state is not the culprit that explains the lagging economic performance of some nations. Because national responses to similar external shocks are so varied, we must look to national institutions – to variations in political, economic, and social organization – for an explanation.

Even in tackling the world problem of climate change, as Chapter 2 has shown, national action is the place to begin. Enforceable international agreements are a long way off while the tipping point for the emission of greenhouse gases, the point of no return, is by conservative estimates only 40 to 60 years ahead. We cannot wait for 20 or 50 of the 193 nations at Copenhagen December 2009 to sign a protocol that will be honored in the breach. Several models of national environmental action now show the way, among them Denmark, Sweden, and (in low emission autos) Brazil.

Are job protection and labor standards threatened by the international mobility of labor and capital or by countries with very low labor costs? Again, the answer depends on the institutions and policies in place. Job security and low labor turnover combined with worker participation in workplace and community greatly enhance enterprise productivity and flexibility. In contrast are countries and industries producing many low value-added products whose workers are hired and fired frequently, have low job security, little union voice, declining real wages, and increasing poverty rates (to these costs the United States adds the costs of adversarial legalism [Kagan, 2003] – litigation about safety, labor standards, unfair labor practices, etc.). Such countries and industries are no major threat to countries and industries with more collaborative industrial relations and efficient employers. The threat of the great economic shifts of recent decades is to the least-skilled, least-educated, least-trained workers, who in any case are a declining breed, with or without globalization. And modern democracies that attend to education, training, job creation, labor standards, and poverty-prevention can reduce the pain of their transition to other, often better jobs.

Analysis of the very limited data on "outsourcing" (or "offshoring") remains speculative. Plagued not only by the complexities of occupational and industrial classifications in one country, let alone 19, studies of outsourcing also suffer more than usual from contrasting concepts, measures, databases, and time periods. So any conclusions about the amount, kinds, causes, and effects of outsourcing are tentative. A few generalizations are likely to be true: outsourcing, now only a small portion of job loss, is likely to increase somewhat, counterbalanced partly by "insourcing" (the location of jobs and workplaces *from* abroad). Outsourcing is not a source of mass unemployment. Continuing industrialization and technological change has for a couple of centuries brought obsolescence of many jobs, dilution of the skills of others, and an accelerated creation of new jobs such that total employment continues to grow. "Deindustrialization" – the decline of "manufacturing" and the increase of "services" (gross categories of limited use) – has little to do with outsourcing. The effects of outsourcing are similar to the effects of continuing technological change, an upgrading of most of the labor force. What was once a threat to many manufacturing jobs is now hitting white-collar service jobs, even some educated workers, specified in this chapter. But the main losers, as before, continue to be the least-educated, least-trained, least-disciplined, and least-adaptable workers. Large investments in a green economy, clearly justified by environmental threats to civilization as we know it (Chapter 2), will not help many of these losers. Indeed it creates expanded job and career opportunities for the more skilled and professional people – many of them in local and state labor and product markets and therefore not vulnerable to offshoring.

Migration from areas of economic despair and repression to areas of opportunity and hope is as old as poverty and persecution. Current rates of immigration into rich democracies have not even reached the level of a century ago. In recent decades, industrial societies have been converging in the ratio of foreigners to natives and hence in their social diversity and in their conflict about immigration. What is most striking is a radical disjunction between the economic and employment effects of immigrants, which on balance are positive, and the political effects, which vary from mild animosity to intense nativist voting and violence. Intensity of such protest varies with the number and concentration of immigrants, the degree of mass insecurity, and the social distance between immigrant groups and natives. Most important is the political structure that mobilizes or dampens these common xenophobic sentiments. If political elites adopt liberal naturalization policies, if they combine efforts at border control with programs for cultural and economic integration, they can reduce the electoral appeal of anti-immigrant demagogues who inflame mass fears and hatreds. Comparison of Sweden, Germany, and France affirms the importance of such policies.

What about the impact of multinational corporations and "alliance capitalism"? Analysis suggests that if a country or industry has high labor standards and accommodative labor relations, the MNC adopts the high road; if a country or industry has low labor standards and confrontational labor relations, the MNC tends toward the low road. Multinationals are anything but aggressive change agents. Regarding their decisions to relocate plants from rich democracies to the NICs or poor countries, such moves are infrequent, except for industries with low-skill and low-value-added products that are labor intensive. Studies of location decisions of both MNCs and national corporations both within nations and among nations generally show that they are determined less by labor costs than by infrastructure (transportation, communication, housing, and other urban amenities), worker quality (including education, training and development of executives, technicians, and workers), access to universities and research laboratories, and access to markets.[53] That is why despite their increasing interest in new markets in Asia and Latin America, the multinationals' capital investments are still overwhelmingly targeted to rich, stable democracies. If labor costs were at the center of corporate location decisions, the rich democracies would have emptied out long ago. Finally, MNCs compensate their workers better relative to domestic firms.

How about the impact of such international organizations such as the EU? Do they not shape the domestic policies of member nations? It is true that where the European Commission (Economic and Financial Affairs Directorate) issued the 3 percent rule for deficit ceilings and similar rules, presidents and prime ministers already inclined to reduce spending on the core programs of the welfare state used such rules as further rationales for cutback budgeting. But these measures meet strong resistance and typically result in electoral defeat (Chapter 4). Serious reform works only when domestic institutions create channels for bargaining among political parties and the social partners. Much has been made of the shift from the EU rule of unanimity to a qualified majority rule (Felsenthal and Machover, 2008). Whatever its effect on minor matters – product standards, consumer safety, antitrust regulations that can stall mergers but seldom stop them (only two stopped in the past five years), encouraging union consultation but not collective bargaining – the record suggests that on major issues the EU still operates on the unanimity principle. In practice, unanimity still applies to such issues as the welfare state, coordination of social-security systems, internal or external security, judicial or police matters, currency, financial regulation, and taxation (Heisenberg, 2005; Matilla and Lane, 2001).

Perhaps one recent trend does undermine the capacity of modern democracies to shape their economic destinies: unregulated internationalization of finance and the increasing independence of central banks, a clear threat to collaborative relations among labor, industry, and the state and to the flexible use of fiscal policy (taxes and spending). Reinforcing this trend is the flow of recently ascendant American economic doctrines across national boundaries – a blend of 19th-century liberalism (unmodified free markets, private property, minimum government), Reaganomics, and monetarist ideology. This was the ideological base for the deregulation of the financial sector at the root of the meltdown and the Great Recession.

Even here, however, even with the rise of central bank autonomy and the export of American-trained doctrinaire economists, national differences in the strength of countervailing powers, while diminishing, are still substantial. More important, the free-marketeer ideologues who inspired many of the measures at the root of the financial meltdown of 2007–2009 have been discredited – at least for now, until collective memory fades and once again deregulation supplants reregulation.

The nation-state remains the ultimate object of allegiance; national institutions and policies continue to make a big difference for real welfare.

# PART II

# MOVING THE UNITED STATES OFF THE LOW ROAD

*Lessons from Abroad*

# 7

## Low Road vs. High Road

### American Exceptionalism?

> It was the best of times, it was the worst of times. . . . It was the spring of hope, it was
> the winter of despair; we had everything before us, we had nothing before us.
>
> Charles Dickens (1859)

By the mid-1960s all of our 19 rich democracies had achieved a level of affluence
that put them in the top one-sixth of the world's countries in per capita GNP and
have since become richer still. All are market-oriented, stable democracies. All
evidence a level of liberty unprecedented in world history. What I have shown so
far is that some countries within each type of political economy in some lengthy
periods have done quite well in economic performance for the last half century
even though their policy mixes have had drastically different costs and gains in
the well-being of their people. One way to put the findings above into bold relief
is to outline contrasting paths to economic success, comparing extremes – the
strongest corporatist democracies vs. the United States, a model that appeals to
many economists who, before the economic collapse of 2008–2009, promoted
U.S. policies as the answer to the problems of the EU or Japan. I shall call the
contrasts the "high road" and the "low road."

Figure 5 shows the policy mixes and the resulting well-being we see on the
high road. What I have not already covered is elaborated in my earlier book
(2002), which demonstrates the connections pictured in that figure.

Now let us focus on the United States as emblematic of the low road. Again, the
American model is roughly matched by another 6 of the 19 rich democracies.[1]
Although these countries did worse or about the same as more consensual democracies in their economic performance for more than a quarter century, when the
low-road strategy in the United States was fully developed in the early 1980s, the
subsequent 20 years produced very good economic indicators in some periods,
putting it above the average EU-15. For example, during Clinton's best years, 1995–
2001, U.S. real growth in GDP averaged 3.6 percent per year. The figure for the EU
was 2.1 percent. U.S. unemployment fell below 5 percent; EU unemployment rose
above 10 percent (Ferguson, 2003). (Although Clinton's eight years were unusual

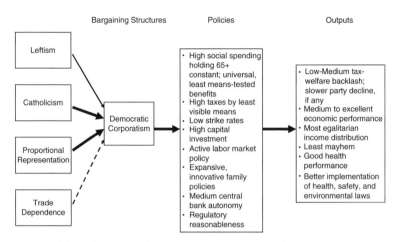

FIGURE 5. Model explaining performance, noneconomic and economic, among 19 rich democracies.

in both policy and performance, the low road had been fully followed throughout the 1980s and continued to be after 2000 at least until 2009.)

In the worldwide recession of 2007–2009, started by the financial meltdown in the United States, Western Europe briefly outpaced the U.S.; it fell into recession later. The United States began to recover earlier than rich democracies of Europe. In an odd reversal, the Americans used massive stimulus, and the Fed maintained near-zero interest rates, whereas the ECB continued to fight the inflation phantom with tight monetary policies, thereby delaying Western Europe's recovery, ultimately putting the newer members of the Euro zone at risk of sovereign default.

Or consider a measure of living standards that controls for population growth. From 1980 to 2009, per capita real growth in the United States rose 1.95 percent a year, while that growth in the EU-15 countries – 9 of which are rich democracies with consensual bargaining arrangements on the high road – averaged about the same, 1.83 percent a year.

If we ignore the fact that the financial meltdown in the United States initiated the deep worldwide recession, economic performance on the high and low roads in the Great Recession of 2007–2009 and so far in the recovery is roughly a draw. The rich democracies of Western Europe fell into recession later than the U.S. (score one for the high road). The United States began its anemic recovery earlier, however, using massive Wall Street bailouts and Keynesian fiscal and monetary stimulus, while Germany and the tight-fisted ECB, inspired by a misplaced fear of inflation and debt, kept interest rates high and fiscal stimulus minimal (score one for the low road, with the caveat that for some months the United States turned to a pale imitation of the high road). By June 2010 unemployment in the nine rich democracies on continental Europe with corporatist bargaining arrangements had fallen to 7.3 percent, whereas the United

States was still near 10 percent – score one-third of a point for the high road (Eurostat, 2010). Score for the game: about even.

## A. THIRTEEN POTHOLES ON THE LOW ROAD

The advocates of a low-road strategy call it "flexibility" and "deregulation of labor markets." Its critics call it a "labor crunch" strategy. There are 13 inter-related dimensions of the American version we can summarize briefly. Only 5 are so extreme that we can say they are unique to the United States: the lack of national health insurance (item 9), the greatest concentration of wealth, the most poverty and inequality (item 3), family breakup without family policies to cushion the shock (item 9) and related mayhem (item 10); and very high military spending (item 11). They are all interdependent.

### 1. Decreasing Power of Labor Unions

Since 1970 union decline has been fastest and greatest in New Zealand, Australia, the United Kingdom, the United States, France, and Japan. At the same time, union density in a few countries has increased (as in Belgium and the Scandinavian countries), while density stabilized or declined only slightly in others (Visser, 2006, table 2). The rapid, large declines can be explained by a combination of a hostile legal-political climate, militant employer opposition, and union failures to invest resources in organizing characteristic of the Anglo-American democracies and the two cases of corporatism without labor (Wilensky, 2002: 696–698).

Students of industrial relations have shown that a substantial portion if not most of the decline in U.S. union density in recent decades is explained by rising management antiunion militancy reinforced by state laws hostile to unions and collective bargaining and the promanagement bias of the White House in the 1970s, 1980s, and 2000s. A full range of union-busting devices, legal and illegal, came into play. Law firms devoted to a "union-free environment" devised sequences of actions to defeat union organizing. Some are legal under "free speech" doctrines: order supervisors to tell their immediate subordinates about the dangers of unionism and strikes, accuse union leaders of corruption, deny union organizers access to the workplace, and challenge the "election district" and in other ways prolong the election campaign. Some are illegal: threaten to move the plant or cut wages and benefits if the union wins, fire union activists, and threaten reprisals for workers who vote union.[2] Finally, if after a several-month campaign of intimidation, workers vote for a union, employers increasingly refuse to agree to a first contract; they stall and stonewall. This rising employer militancy and the hostile political-legal climate that gave it expression are not the only forces accounting for American labor's decline. Equally important is the failure of labor to devote resources of money and personnel to the tasks of organizing. Counterintuitively, the studies suggest that changes in the occupational and industrial composition of the labor force, in the increase of women and minorities at work, in regional population shifts, and even in business cycles are of minor significance relative to the growth in management opposition, the bias of public policy, and the weak organizing effort of unions (e.g., Freeman and Medoff, 1984: 221–245; Dickens and Leonard, 1985; Rogers, 1990). In comparative perspective, a similar and familiar message is that since 1970 corporatist democracies with centralized labor movements (except for Austria and the Netherlands) have experienced growth or little or no decline in union density, especially if they administer unemployment benefits. In contrast, fragmented and decentralized democracies (except for Ireland) and countries whose corporatist bargaining excludes labor (except for Switzerland) have labor movements in decline (Blanchflower and Freeman, 1992: table 1; Western, 1993, 1995: table 1; Visser, 1992).

Congressional voting on labor-law reform from 1965 to 2007 shows four bills to correct one or more of these abuses. They all passed in the House and died in the Senate (Dark, 2009). The fight for the Employee Free Choice Act after the Democratic victory of 2008 fared no better. What political conditions would be necessary for a reversal are discussed in Chapter 8.

## 2. Relatively High Man-Days Lost in Strikes; Generally Confrontational Labor Relations at the Workplace and Beyond

Although strike rates have been converging downward among our 19 countries, corporatist democracies remain relatively low. If it is every union, every employer for himself, if the legal and political climate is hostile to unions, strikes will be one of many expressions of labor protest. In contrast, coordinated bargaining shifts industrial conflict to the political arena where more centralized accommodations can be reached. The exceptions to this rule are three democracies with a strong legacy of Communist Party domination of labor federations – Italy, France, and Finland. They maintained higher strike rates than others long after the collapse of the Soviet Union.

## 3. Low and Stagnant Wages in the Bottom Half to Two-Thirds of the Income Distribution, High Rates of Poverty, Greater Concentration of Wealth, and Inequality in Household Income

Before the Great Recession, the real median wage in the United States was lower than it was before the oil shock of the early 1970s.[3] Both low median wages and high poverty rates put the United States at or near the bottom among rich democracies; they were both worse in 2005 than in 1969 (Freeman, 2007; cf. Levy and Murnane, 1992). Regarding income, before the financial meltdown the top 1 percent of families by income accounted for nearly a quarter of U.S. income – their largest share since the late 1920s (Piketty and Saez, 2003). Pay packages have grown so fast at the high end that the top 1 percent of taxpayers have taken home 94 percent of the growth in total income since 1973 (Kreuger, 2002). Executive pay rose to astronomical levels, continuing to rise even in the depth of the recession and even in corporations badly managed – no doubt a "free market" reward for abject failure. In 2009, for instance, S&P 500 CEOs averaged $10.5 million in pay – 344 times the pay of typical American workers.[4] For an obscene example, the top 50 hedge and private equity fund managers averaged $588 million each, topping 19,000 times the median worker's pay (Stiglitz, 2010a: 350, n. 17).

Meanwhile, from 2000 to 2008 real median household income in the United States decreased by almost 4 percent (Stiglitz, 2010a: 302, n. 2). Or, if we look at family incomes for the past half century, the real income of the top .01 percent of Americans soared sevenfold between 1980 (Reaganomics) and 2007. In the same period the real income of the median family rose only 22 percent, less than a third of its growth over the previous 27 years (1952–1979) (Krugman, *New York Times*, Aug. 24, 2009). In short, recent decades have given new meaning to the phrase, "The rich are getting richer." There would have been no income growth at all for the majority if it were not for the intensification of labor – the big increase in double- or triple-earner households, the increase in overtime hours, the continued, probably steady rate of moonlighting (Wilensky, 1961; 1963) – and President Clinton's best six years (see Chapter 1).

The usual gradation by education holds for earnings: the average annual median weekly earnings of full-time wage and salary workers for 2008 has a similar gradient: doctoral degree, $1,555; professional degree, $1,228; bachelor's degree, $978; some college, no degree, $645; high-school graduate, $591; less than high school, $426 (BLS, 2010a).

The U.S. version of the low road brings not only rising inequality of income and pay but also a striking increase in the concentration of wealth. Edward Wolff (1996) in a study of long-term trends in such concentration from 1922 to 1989 found a modest diffusion of wealth before 1970 (largely from the expansion of home ownership and pensions) that was sharply reversed in the United States since then. Updating his earlier study, Wolff (2010) finds that wealth inequality continued to climb from 1989 to 2007. The share of wealth held by the top 5 percent of households increased from 58.9 percent in 1989 to 61.8 percent in 2007, and the share of the top quintile rose from 83.5 to 85 percent. At the very top there was a virtual explosion of the rich, whether we use assets of $1 or $5 or $10 million or more in wealth. Just from 1989 to 2001 the number of "deca millionaires" ($10 or more million in wealth) grew more than fivefold. Much of this came from the surge in stock prices.

Media pundits and Wall Street boosters make much of the diffusion of wealth to the masses, claiming for instance that half of our households own securities. But in 2007 the middle three wealth quintiles (60% of households) directly or indirectly (e.g., in pension funds) held only 7 percent of their total assets in stocks. Or, if you prefer a boom period, in 1995 the bottom 90 percent of households, by wealth class, held only 11.6 percent of stocks and mutual funds (Mishel, Bernstein, and Schmitt, 1999: table 5.4). In 1998 more than half of all households owned no stock whatever, directly or indirectly; only 36 percent of all households had more than $5,000 worth of stock (Wolff, 2001).

The lion's share of wealth held by vast majorities, as before, was in owner-occupied homes (65% of their assets). Housing inflation, however, was accompanied by exploding debt. In fact, in 2007 the middle three-fifths, the middle "class," had a debt-to-equity ratio of 61 percent and a debt-to-income ratio of 157 percent – both much higher than those of the top quintile and climbing, what Wolff calls "the squeeze before the storm." So when the crash came, as we have seen, there was enormous wealth destruction all the way down the wealth ladder, wiping out assets of vast majorities who could cope with it least.

If we move from the very top to the very bottom, the low-road strategy always increases poverty rates. During the past 30 or 40 years, as poverty rates rose, a burgeoning industry of poverty researchers among academics, think-tank advocates, and congressional staffers has developed in the United States. A few safe generalizations based on the more systematic research follow (Wilensky, 1965: xxx–xxxvii; 1978; 2002: 14–33, table 8.4, table 14.4, and 620–633 review much of the evidence).

- *Poverty Level.* Among 18 of our 19 rich democracies (without Israel) for which we have recent data on household poverty rates after taxes and transfers (50% or below of median income), the United States tops them all. The usual rank order by type of political economy is evident (OECD, 2010):

| Type of Political Economy | Mid-1990s | Mid-2000s |
| --- | --- | --- |
| Left corporatist | 5.1 | 6.2 |
| Left-Catholic corporatist | 8.2 | 7.7 |
| Corporatist without labor | 10.6 | 10.2 |
| Catholic corporatist | 11.3 | 11.2 |
| Least corporatist | 11.3 | 12.6 |

Table 2 in Chapter 1 specifies the countries in each type of political economy (Switzerland is missing for mid-1990s data).

Among the fragmented and decentralized political economies – the worst performers whose average is 12.6 percent in mid-2000s poverty – the United States again is in a class of its own: it scores 17.1 percent. That is well over three times the poverty rate of the most egalitarian democracies, "left corporatist" Sweden and Denmark.[5]

- *U.S. Poverty Trend 1960s to Now.* Poverty declined during President Johnson's "War on Poverty" and increased after the oil shock of 1973–1974, never to return to the lower rate of the 1960s (Cancian and Danzinger, 2009). A sharp acceleration occurred during the lost decade of 2000–2009.

- *Volatility of Income.* With some national variation, family income has long been quite volatile – unstable for majorities in all rich democracies. Put another way, income mobility up and down is a common feature of continuing industrialization (Wilensky, 2002: 40–51, 243–244, 526–528). But in the United States in the past three decades, big drops in income became more frequent (Hacker and Jacobs, 2008: 5). Thus the poverty population expands with each new recession. "The chance of at least one 50% drop in family income over a five-year period from about 15% in the early 1970s to about 23% in recent years" (p. 8). This, in the face of deterioration in major parts of the American welfare state – e.g., health care and pensions – which elsewhere help to prevent a descent into poverty.

- *Heterogeneity of the Poor.* The poor vary greatly in their depth of poverty, their social-economic backgrounds, ethnic-racial-religious and linguistic characteristics and origins, and location. Some live on welfare checks, some on pensions; some are unemployed, others not; some are sick, others well; some are refugees from rural poverty, others are veterans of urban slums; some are migratory workers following the seasons and the crops; others are fixed in low-paid jobs as janitors and housemaids. When you hear of "the poor" or the "lower class," it helps to know whether they are the working poor or the nonworking poor, the welfare poor, the aged poor, or the single-parent poor; whether they are Appalachian poor whites, the suburban poor of any color, or upwardly mobile Asian entrepreneurs; and whether they are militant young blacks of gangs in the ghetto or apathetic old men on skid row.

The rate and trend, the increasing volatility of income, the heterogeneity of the poor – all suggest that the most effective strategy for poverty reduction that will work in the long run, leaving aside anticyclical fiscal and monetary policies, is to follow the lead of rich democracies that have reduced poverty rates to quite low levels. They achieved this not by targeting one or another segment of the poor with an apparatus of means testing but through more universalistic policies that mobilize majority support. (Chapter 8 suggests how the United States can get off the low road, what policies are necessary, what political coalitions and reforms are possible.)

We have seen in Chapters 1 and 5 that the United States ranks high or highest among rich democracies in various measures of inequality, that the least educated have long borne the brunt of technological and organizational disruptions rooted in continuing industrialization and high inequality. There are numerous explanations for the stagnation or decline in wages and household income, as well as the increase in poverty and the concentration of wealth. First, consider the causes of wage dispersion. They include deunionization, the decline in K–12 performance and the more recent deterioration of higher education, and occupational shifts that require an upgrading of skills. Aside from the decline in the bargaining power of labor, the most persuasive explanations for increased dispersion of wages in the economy and workplace are complementary: the increasing mismatch of job "skills" (education and training) and job requirements; and the increasing lifetime earnings return from college education, especially among those with graduate or professional degrees. There is an acceleration of the long-term trend toward the economic payoff for the highest educated workers. At the same time there are cascading displacements in the rest of the distribution, at least for men (Pryor and Schaffer, 1999). As I have shown in my critique of postindustrialism (Chapter 6 and 2002, ch. 4), the number of jobs in very large occupations that are non-tech or low-tech (janitors and cleaners, cashiers, cooks, nursing aides and orderlies, sales clerks) has been growing along with the most skilled of Silicon Valley. Only about a fifth to a quarter of the labor force is in occupations that benefit from or require a B.A. or above. Thus, only the most skilled and better educated have actually experienced increases in real wages from the early 1970s until 2000. Not all of the more or less well educated end up in the top fifth of the wage distribution. Some of them find themselves competing for jobs beneath their level of education. That creates a cascading effect all the way down the jobs ladder, pressing down on the median wage.

In short, this dimension of the trend toward inequality, the growing dispersion of wages and salaries, is no doubt partly rooted in a skills mismatch; the upgrading of jobs in particular places and industries outpaces the upgrading of people to fill them. At the extreme of neglect of schools and universities, as in the United States, this mismatch increases as a relative cause of inequality. Whatever the contribution of the mismatch, however, we must add to the mix what Pryor and Schaffer (1999) call a "cascading displacement effect."

Low-road wage pressures from antilabor laws and politicians, fiscal and monetary policies, and other official sources are made worse in the United States by widespread illegal cheating on minimum wages and overtime pay. A study of 4,387 workers in low-wage industries in Chicago, Los Angeles, and New York in 2008 found that 26 percent had been paid less than the minimum wage the week before the survey and 76 percent of those who had worked overtime were not paid their proper wage. Violations of minimum wage laws were most frequent in large occupations – in apparel and textile manufacturing (43% of all workers paid below), personal and repair services (42%), and private households (42%) (Bernhardt et al., 2009).[6]

So far I have concentrated on men because they are the most vulnerable to the causes of wage dispersion. What about women workers? True, the United States, like other countries, has steadily increased women's urban labor-force participation. On the low road, this adds to the supply of cheap labor (see sec. 13 on job creation), often displacing older, high-seniority men. Further, women are still concentrated in service jobs, both high and low paid, and are disproportionately in low-paid part-time jobs. Nevertheless, they have steadily closed the gender gap in pay not only among rich democracies that have strong unions and left parties but even in the United States and other low-wage countries (e.g., the United Kingdom).

The puzzle – how can the gender gap close while low-wage workers are sinking –can be solved by noting three clear changes: (1) the improvement in women workers' relative qualifications (education, experience, commitment to work); (2) declining discrimination; and (3) the larger negative effect of deunionization on male than female workers (women actually increased as a proportion of union members) (Blau and Kahn, 1997). These gender-specific trends occur within a larger trend toward wage and income inequality. As Table 2 shows, despite improvements in gender equality, the United States remains at the bottom in cross-national comparisons of income equality. For instance, a study of earnings differentials in 10 rich democracies (Blau and Kahn, 1996) shows that the United States has both the greatest concentration of very low wages at the bottom compared with the middle and the greatest rewards to "skill" (i.e., education). Two more recent comparative studies (Applebaum, Bernhardt, and Murnane, 2003; Gautié and Schmitt, 2010) show the same pattern: the United States remains a champion of low-wage work, sometimes joined by the United Kingdom at the very bottom. The extremes of high and low wages hold (e.g., Sweden and other Nordic countries vs. the United States and the United Kingdom) no matter what controls, such as measures of productivity, are applied (Wilensky, 2002: 28–31, 77, n. 30; Gottschalk and Smeeding, 1997a: 636–637, 660ff.).

The most powerful explanation of these country rankings is that the most egalitarian countries have national bargaining structures that result in wage compression and more income equality affecting both men and women. In other words, although postwar increases in gender equality in the United States are partly due to the rise of female labor-force participation and women's relative qualifications common to all countries, when we compare nations, we must look to types of political economy to explain the remaining U.S. lag in gender equality as well as its top rank in income inequality and poverty.

Part-time jobs are a handicap for promotion in job ladders. Are women in those jobs because of discrimination and labor crunch strategies? Or is this a matter of choice? Can the 40 to 50 percent part-timers among all women workers in Sweden and Norway be pinned on gender inequality? Not likely. The extraordinary set of expensive public policies that have prevailed in these countries, pioneered by Sweden for eight decades, helped to close the pay gap while they broadened women's choice of hours and schedules of work. Such policies as government-subsidized child care, paid parental leave, and an active labor-market policy brought choice to the forefront and pushed coercion to the rear.[7] The reverse is true on the low road of the United States where the economic survival of the typical household depends on women working, whether they want to or not. In Sweden and other countries that have a strong family policy and enforce minimum labor standards, women are choosing a different balance between paid work and childrearing and other domestic management work.

An ironic outcome of the reduction of gender inequality on the low road is that it reinforces inequality across families. A study of married couples from 1967 to 2005 concludes that about 25–30 percent of the growing earnings inequality in the United States can be attributed to the many ways husbands and wives have become more equal (Schwartz, 2010). Spouses have become more alike in education and income so more marriages now consist of two high- or two low-earning partners, increasing the distance between the most and least well-off families. Single parents in the United States, of course, fare the worst (see sec. 9 on family policy).

One last observation about rising wage inequality concerns its effect on the depth and cost of recessions. In the business cycle, low and stagnant wages foster household debt, reinforcing credit bubbles on the way up; when the crash comes, workers displaced are more numerous and lack resources. Coming out of recession as in 2010–2011, they encountered great barriers in attempts to recover. Low-wage workers in the United States faced a toxic combination of exploding health-care costs and rising mortgage payments and fees, while housing values collapsed and jobs disappeared. To cope, these workers ran up piles of household debt. The natural outcome was a proliferation of home foreclosures and personal bankruptcy. The consequent reduction of consumption prolonged the recession and slowed the recovery. Even in a period of prosperity as the United States recovered from the recession of 1990–1991, the Labor Department reported that only 70 percent of workers displaced from 1993 to 1995 found new jobs by February 1996 (BLS, 1996). Of those reemployed, 204,000 found only part-time jobs, and 926,000 found jobs paying less than their previous earnings. Add 1.3 million who did not find jobs at all. In short, in the brisk recovery of the mid-1990s about two-thirds of the displaced either could not find jobs, found only part-time jobs, or found jobs paying below previous earnings. The recovery from the much worse near-Depression labor-market of 2007–2010 displays the same pattern on a larger scale.[8]

Problems of moving people out of poverty through work are complicated by a low-wage structure. Thus, the working poor are a large part of the poverty population in the United States; in 2008, 61 percent of poverty families had at least one worker. Even more incredibly, about 13 percent of poverty families had two or more members at work (U.S. Census Bureau, 2009). Most important politically, voting studies show that the middle mass of high-school graduates and part-college people – a majority of the electorate – feel squeezed economically (Chapter 4; Wilensky, 2002: 46–47, 372ff., 679–680; 2008). In fact, the past seven years have seen very little wage growth for the bottom 80 percent of the U.S labor force, despite continued productivity increases.

## 4. Intensive Use of Low-Skilled Workers and the Least-Educated Workers in Large, Rapidly Growing Sectors (e.g., Retail Trades)

One of the great structural uniformities of modern societies, established in sociological studies of stratification, is the rank order of status or prestige of occupations across decades and nations. This is reflected in the structure of pay. A wide-ranging, thorough study of pay differentials concludes:

With the partial exception of the lower white-collar occupations, and the notable exception of the Kibbutzim, in every society and period we have surveyed we have found that the grades of work requiring more education, experience, and skill, and carrying more responsibility, have been the more highly paid. This has been found to be so even in Mao's China and Castro's Cuba. It shows that the inequality of pay arises from factors common to societies of very various economic, political, and social complexions. (Phelps-Brown, 1979: 65)

But, as we have just seen, our 19 rich democracies vary hugely in the size of the low-wage labor force, its pay, its distance from the middle and the top, and the trends in pay differentials, all differences explained by the low-road strategy (all the items on this list).

Adding to the expansion of the low-status, low-pay work force is a *rapid growth of the contingent labor supply* (part-time, temporary, or subcontracted workers), a general trend in all rich democracies that is most developed on the low road. Part-timers ranged between 16.2 and 16.8 percent of the labor force from 2000 to 2008 and reached a peak of 17.7 percent in 2009 through May 2010 (seasonally adjusted figures, BLS, 2010a).

Regarding temporary workers, in previous recessions, as demand rose, American employers moved quickly – in two or three months – away from "temps" to more or less permanent workers. In 2009 to mid-2010 employers have stuck with temps and other casual labor or they have extended a part-timer's hours or brought in free lancers (*Wall Street Journal*, Dec. 21, 2009). That may swell the official job creation rate, but it also expands the ranks of insecure, low-wage workers without benefits.

A related trend is the *rise of unconventional schedules* (nonstandard days of work and hours of work) with negative effects on family life and health (Presser, 2003). By 1997 a whopping 45 percent of the U.S. labor force were on non-standard schedules.

## 5. Long Hours of Work

Annual hours in all rich democracies declined steadily from the late 19th century to about 1960. Then a hint of divergence appears when, of 11 countries for which we had OECD data for 1960–1994 for manufacturing, all but the United States and Canada continued substantial declines in annual hours.[9] The average drop in annual hours for the four hardest working countries is 16.3 percent; the average drop for the leisured five is 21.5 percent (Germany dropped 27%). In other words, the leisure-rich countries are becoming richer; the leisure-poor countries are becoming relatively poorer.

More recent data for 18 of our countries (absent Israel) shows that in 2006 the type of political economy explains nearly all of the variation. Of the top 11 countries in average annual hours, 8 are fragmented and decentralized political economies – United States (1,797 hours), New Zealand (1,787), Canada (1,738), Australia (1,723), the United Kingdom (1,669), and Ireland (1,640) – or they are corporatist without labor, Japan (1,784) and Switzerland (1,657). Italy (1,814 hours) is the only clear exception; Finland and Austria are near the median for the 18 rich democracies. In contrast, 6 of the bottom 7 in hours of work, the leisure rich, are all democratic corporatist: Sweden (1,576), Denmark (1,574), Belgium (1,571), Germany (1,433), Norway (1,408), and the Netherlands (1,391). The one exception is France, a case of corporatism without labor that dropped from long hours in 1994 to short hours in 2008 (OECD, 2009).

The best explanation for these differences in labor-market policies is the power of labor unions and left parties to trade lower hours and other benefits for industrial peace, wage restraint, and proemployer tax benefits through corporatist bargaining arrangements (Chapter 3). Many scholars argue that longer-hours countries have an economic advantage, and at some extreme – United States (1,797) and Japan (1,784) vs. Germany (1,433) and the Netherlands (1,391) – that may be true. The more you work, the more widgets you produce. The puzzle, however, is how have the leisure-rich folks done so well for so long despite their short hours. Could it be that they are working smarter, and this is another trade-off?

## 6. A Widening Spread between High-Wage, High-Skilled Workers and the Least Educated

This trend, the downward pressure on medium and low wages, is the result of four other trends: deunionization; the absence of an active labor-market policy; lack of a family policy to cushion the shock of family breakup and help all working parents to cope better with demands of work and family and ensure the care and cognitive development of children; and, finally, the neglect of K–12 schooling. Despite recent expansion of higher education in other rich democracies and sharp recession cutbacks in university budgets, the United States remains among the most outstanding in the excellence, diversity, and expanded opportunity of its higher education. But it has virtually abandoned academic standards in all but upper-middle-class primary and secondary schools. This adds to the supply of least-educated, low-paid labor. Employers adapt accordingly (see sec. 13 on job creation).

## 7. Decreasing Job Security for Most of the Labor Force

Unemployment and underemployment remain high and increase among the least educated, the elderly, and the young (sec. 3). In discussion of inequality and poverty, I have already covered the decline in the growth rate of real household income since 1980, the increase in poverty rates, and the extraordinary explosion in the wealth of the very rich. In recent decades the increasing volatility of family income and the stagnation or decline of wages add to the insecurity of a majority of working Americans.

Insecurity is intensified by unemployment, both short term and long term. The problem here is that official unemployment has been understated since data have been collected, so comparison with other rich democracies is shaky. The U.S. Bureau of Labor Statistics (BLS), however, has since 1994 added measures of underemployment and long-term unemployment and has recently made estimates that go back to 1970. Thus, we can now safely say something about the depth of insecurity and misery that accompanies both.

Consider the official unemployment rate by education from October 2007, before the Great Recession, to October 2009, the depth of recession. Starting at

4.7 percent it climbed to 10.0 percent (BLS, 2010a). The job growth needed to recoup the eight million jobs lost by 2010 would be about 400,000 per month, no cause for optimism. As always, the most educated (according to the BLS Current Population Survey, 2009) come out much better than the least educated.

| | Oct. 2007 | Oct. 2009 | % Point Increase 2007–2009 |
|---|---|---|---|
| Less than high school | 7.3% | 15.5% | 8.2 |
| High school | 4.7 | 11.2 | 6.5 |
| Some college or associate degree | 3.5 | 9.0 | 5.5 |
| College degree and above | 2.1 | 4.7 | 2.6 |

The average annual median weekly earnings of full-time wage and salary workers for 2008 has a similar gradient: doctoral degree, $1,555; professional degree, $1,228; bachelor's degree, $978; some college, no degree, $645; high-school graduate, $591; less than high school, $426 (BLS, 2010a). The unemployment rate in 2008 for workers at least 25 years of age with doctoral, professional, or master's degrees was 2.4 percent or below. "Some college" or high-school graduates ranged from 5.1 to 5.7 percent; those with less than high school, 9.0 percent.

Official unemployment by age shows that at both ends the young and elderly experience most unemployment. The number of officially unemployed workers aged 55–64 nearly tripled since the Great Recession began. For comparison, the official rate of jobless workers of all ages roughly doubled. Most of these "young-aged" are less educated, earn low income, and are less likely to have investments or other savings (*Wall Street Journal*, Dec. 8, 2009). In short, they are more dependent on the lean benefits and services of the American welfare state and suffer more when access to government help is reduced; many are forced into early impoverished retirement before they are eligible for either Social Security or Medicare (see Chapter 5). In previous research I found that contrary to the stereotype of gray-power lobbies running away with the public purse, the aged and near-aged are the only minority group in the United States that has suffered increased job discrimination since World War II (Wilensky, 2002: ch. 1 and 31–33).

Similarly, unemployment of young people during the anemic recovery of 2010 climbed to new highs. In March 2010 the national unemployment rate of workers aged 16–29 was 15.2 percent, the highest rate since 1948 (BLS reported in the *Wall Street Journal*, April 5, 2010). Taking a younger slice, the rate for workers aged 16–24 is higher; it reached a peak of 18.5 percent (BLS, 2010a), seasonally adjusted, for March 2010.

The worst of what we can call a jobless recovery is the unprecedented rate of long-term unemployed. In May 2010 almost half (46%) of the unemployed had been out of work for six months or more – up from an average of 18 percent in 2007 and 19 percent in 2008 (BLS, 2010a). That is the highest rate since records began in 1948, and it is worse than it was during the deep slide of 1981–1982 when only 26 percent of the jobless were long term.

The usual gradation by education appears for the long-term unemployed. In June 2010, 58 percent of workers out six months or more were either high-school grads or those with some college but no degree. They compose the middle mass – a strategic majority of the electorate discussed in Chapter 4. In contrast, only 18.7 percent of the long-term unemployed were college grads, whose prospects for reemployment were much better than the rest.

Whether unemployment is structural or cyclical, the effects of long-term unemployment are typically devastating and long lasting. As studies since Paul Lazarsfeld's account of the effects of such unemployment in Marienthal, Austria, in the early 1930s have repeatedly shown, long-term unemployment leaves a permanent mark on the workers and families who suffer it: loss of dignity, collapse of morale, mental and physical illness, family breakup, loss of skills, and decline in civic attachment (Wilensky, 2002: 432, 510–511). These effects and the associated public costs – foregone productivity gains, increased spending for health care, disability, and income maintenance – will be with us for many years, if not decades.

So far we have been using official unemployment rates. Now look at the October 2009 national underemployment or the "hidden" rate. The official seasonally adjusted rate at that depth of recession was 10.1 percent.[10] To that, we can add the hidden unemployment involving those working part-time who want to work full-time, 5.9 percent; and those marginally attached to the work force, 1.4 percent.

The trio of measures – official unemployment plus part-timers wanting full-time plus marginally attached workers (discouraged workers who have searched for a year and have given up or who cannot work for reasons including ill health but want to work anyway) – adds up to 17.4 percent, counting both official and hidden unemployment. (If we exclude discouraged workers with ill health the rate is still 16.5%.) That official-plus-hidden figure was much higher among states hardest hit by the economic crisis – Nevada, Oregon, Rhode Island, Michigan, Ohio, South Carolina, and California. The picture is consistent with the near-depression chaos in the labor market in the first half of 2010 (most pundits and White House officials called it a modest recovery): there were five job seekers for every job opening (BLS, 2010b). Violent crime and the highest incarceration rate (sec. 10) suggest a fourth source of hidden unemployment, estimated at 1.9 percent for the prosperous year of 1995. If added that would bring total unemployment and underemployment to more than 19 percent.

Does the United States outpace other rich democracies in its high rate of hidden employment? Unfortunately there are no good cross-national data comparable to the BLS's careful effort to estimate discouraged workers and involuntary part-timers. Labor economists, however, have for decades established that the longer unemployment lasts, the more of the official unemployed drop out of the official labor force, answering no to both survey questions: Are you at work, or have you sought work in the last four weeks? So it is important to arrive at a good concept and measure of this discouraged worker component of unemployment for more reliable cross-national comparisons than now available. If we wish to grasp the real experience of people at work or seeking work or giving up, we must go beyond the official measure of unemployment. All comparisons, however, are not lost. My analysis of the deregulation of the labor market in Chapter 6 uses adequate cross-national data on protective legislation and the enforcement of labor standards. It concludes that the more consensual democracies minimize job insecurity, whereas the United States and other fragmented and decentralized countries clearly have the most job insecurity.

Private corporations play their part in mounting job insecurity. Typical executives in the United States, confronted with a downturn in their industry or the national economy, adopt the quickest, easiest way to protect profits; they downsize the payroll. Downsizing on the low road often becomes "dumbsizing" – hasty across-the-board cuts that incur new costs and may require more expensive outsourcing. This strategy demoralizes remaining employees, strains relations with suppliers and customers, and disrupts established relationships. Moreover, depending on how many and which workers, midlevel executives, and experts it eliminates, it may result in lost organizational memory, essential for sensible decisions.

Regarding outsourcing, often this involves subcontracting to firms with low wages and high turnover, little or no training, pressed to cut corners. The higher accident rates of subcontracted workers (vs. stable, direct hires) has been evident for some time, especially in construction, maintenance, and repair. For instance a detailed study of the petrochemical industry in the United States (Kochan et al., 1994), where safety mishaps can be catastrophic, showed that subcontractors using temporary workers increased greatly in the 1970s; by the late 1980s they accounted for 32 percent of the normal hours worked in an average plant. The subcontractors were typically non-union; their workers were lower paid, less educated, less trained, and less experienced than their regular counterparts in the contracting firm and had a much higher accident rate. One reason for the contrast in accident rates is that the host employer typically accepts no responsibility for the training and supervision of the contract workers, and the subcontractors are indifferent to training. Equally important, experienced regular workers in the host plant are loath to share their know-how with temporary workers who threaten their jobs and wage standards. By their fixation on short-run savings in wage and training costs, petrochemical executives were incurring long-run costs in injuries, accidents, explosions, and shutdowns and concomitant lawyer costs, only some of which they could dump on the public. If this story sounds familiar and BP's contractors for deepwater drilling, Transocean and Halliburton, come to mind, the Gulf's most disastrous oil spill fits quite well. As do many an explosion at oil refineries.

In short, corporations on the low road pursue a labor-crunch strategy, downsizing payroll and subcontracting to cut costs in the short run, thereby increasing the danger of costly accidents, some of them catastrophic.[11]

As I have emphasized throughout this book, this picture of intensive, wide-spread, and growing insecurity on the low road is most important politically for any center-left coalition in the United States that hopes to do anything about it. When insecurity spreads, the chance for demagogues to use divisive appeals mounts. The politics of resentment escalates, even as the urgency of bold action to reverse course becomes obvious. (See Chapter 8.)

## 8. Meager Investment in the Infrastructure

### *Low and Unstable Investment in Physical Capital*

A major cost of the ascendance of the free-marketeers and the short time perspectives of both public and private sectors is the erosion of the physical infrastructure – the systems of transportation, communication, energy production and transmission (including the electric grid), and the application of information technology to public purposes. Even when the economic crisis of 2007–2010 presented an opportunity, the U.S. response was, understandably, to correct the mistakes of the past with bailouts of banks, countercyclical spending, and tax cuts. But in view of decades of neglect of the American infrastructure and the increase of population that must be served, there is no alternative to large sustained investment, public and private, in these long-term boosts to economic growth and a sustainable planet. Unless, that is, we accept long-term, accelerating erosion of our standard of living.

Here is a summary of the American Society of Civil Engineers study (ASCE, 2009) of the severity of the situation in 2008, a report that concludes the infrastructure is close to "failing" and deserves a grade of D. Nearly 30 percent of the nation's 590,750 bridges are "structurally deficient or functionally obsolete" and "it will take $9.4 billion a year for 20 years to eliminate all bridge deficiencies." "The number of unsafe dams has risen by 33% to more than 3,500." Public transit facilities – buses, subways, and commuter trains – remain underfunded, even as demand for them has "increased faster than any other mode of transportation." Current funding for safe drinking water amounts to "less than 10% of the national requirement," while "aging wastewater management systems discharge billions of gallons of untreated sewage into U.S. surface waters each year." Current government investment in these vital systems is typically below the level simply to maintain them in their current poor state. The ASCE estimates that it will take more than a quarter of trillion dollars just to bring U.S. public school buildings up to "good" condition. Yet it is estimated that federal spending on infrastructure (inflation-adjusted) was actually lower in 2008 than it was in 2001 (Ehrlich and Rohatyn, 2008). Finally, investments in energy R&D by U.S. companies fell by 50 percent from 1991 to 2003 (Kammen and Nemet, 2005). Similarly, annual federal spending for all energy R&D in 2006 was less than half of what it was in 1994 (*New York Times*, Oct. 30, 2006). My speculation about feasible steps to reverse this deterioration, including a tax structure to finance it, appears in Chapter 8.

## Low and Unstable Investment in Human Capital

Economists define human capital as the skills and knowledge embodied in the labor force. Other social scientists include social and cultural as well as cognitive development. We can start with America's unique lead in education and its extraordinary reversal in recent decades.

The historical origins of the U.S. lead in schooling are well known. In the timing and sequence of educational expansion, the United States was a pioneer. In the 19th century, universal primary education for basic literacy and good citizenship was a demand of employers interested in a disciplined labor supply, Protestant sects and churches concerned that children be able to read the Bible, a labor movement interested in contradictory ideals of equality of opportunity and absolute equality, and a state concerned about political integration and social control. None of these concerns were unique to the United States: employers everywhere increasingly required literate employees, Protestant churches in Europe led in the desire for Bible-reading children, and left-labor movements were, in fact, stronger in Europe than they were in the U.S. But the United States was an early industrializer, and employer needs for a literate labor supply were early and urgent while problems of social-political integration in the context of a highly decentralized federal system and the absence of either a feudal past or a state church were more intense. In fact, the founding fathers were keenly aware that they had to overcome the fragmentation and paralysis of the Articles of Confederation. Although they feared both a strong central authority and the tyranny of the majority and therefore set up a complex system of checks and balances in the Constitution, they also were alert to the dangers of social disintegration and the tendency of the states to fly apart. They explicitly advocated public education to create citizens with a national identity who would hold American society together and to foster the informed electorate they believed essential for democracy. Education to this day, at least in political rhetoric, is an American secular theology.

As economic development accelerated in the late 19th and 20th centuries, the spread of universal compulsory schooling and the rise of mass higher education proceeded. The United States led in both developments. Educational expansion is a convergent tendency in all rich democracies, but the other 18 countries followed our lead.[12]

The U.S lead in mass higher education is seen in enrollment ratios and per capita expenditures as early as 1965–1971 when about a third of 20–24-year-olds were in postsecondary education. California by then had about two-thirds to three-quarters of high school grads going on to some form of postsecondary education. If we confine ourselves to California public school graduates who went on to any California public college or university, we get a figure for 1986–1987 of just over half (California Postsecondary Education Commission, 2010). Whichever figure we use, California's three-tier system was a great achievement in equality of opportunity.

For more than a century, education has been the main channel for upward mobility in occupation, income, and social status. Although the mobility function of mass higher education is clearest in the United States, in recent decades it has become prevalent in all rich democracies. In the late 19th century and well into the 20th century, established elites in the United States (native-born whites) could rely on family origin and related advantages for access to white-collar jobs, but less-favored groups – the foreign born, racial and ethnic minorities – got access to such positions only by achievement through secondary schools. A century later, as we know, the same educational road is traveled by the least privileged young people, including blacks and other minorities. Where it once took a high school diploma, it now takes a college degree or graduate degree for such minorities to secure entry to upper-level occupations, affirming the essentially meritocratic character of modern higher education for most of the population.

The ambivalent mass demand for some combination of absolute equality and equality of opportunity – which often takes the form of demands for affirmative action or quotas for those groups presumed to be deprived – has had little effect on the essential character of higher education. Colleges and universities remain meritocratic, very much attuned to the demands of the economy, and quite vocational in emphasis. Why this has its downside, the erosion of liberal arts education, is discussed in Chapter 8. Education for alert citizenship and critical thought, for making moral judgments, for the pursuit of wisdom, for the enhancement of capacities of appreciation and performance in the arts, for broader understanding of the individual in society – all tend to take second place. The United States established a long-term lead in postsecondary enrollment ratios, but all rich democracies now share the three trends toward specialization, universality in higher education, and institutional stratification.

As rich countries become richer and mass higher education spreads, however, quality variations within the same level of education become increasingly important. For mass education necessitates a huge diversity of schools, colleges, universities, and vocational training institutes to accommodate a great variety of people and meet the intensified demand for skilled labor. The resulting specialization and institutional stratification of modern educational systems means that the higher quality, resource-rich schools and colleges recruit and graduate people whose abilities, motivation, and information give them a competitive advantage over people with identical formal levels of education. Plainly, there is a head of the academic procession and a tail. Berkeley is not Contra Costa College, Harvard is not Bunker Hill Community College, and the University of Michigan is not Central Michigan. This growth in quality variation helps to explain why the basic relations of social origin (i.e., education of parents), school completion, and occupational fate did not change much in most of our rich democracies during the 20th century, despite expanded educational opportunities for vast majorities. Nevertheless, the channels for mobility through education are now so many and so varied that something like three-quarters of high-school graduates can find a niche in the system.

Now the bad news. Despite its early lead in schooling, despite its unique achievement in the diversity, openness, and excellence of its higher educational institutions, the United States has been extraordinary in its neglect of preschool and K–12 schooling, evident in a poor performance compared to both other countries and its own past. American exceptionalism on the way up; American exceptionalism on the way down. Today even the lead in higher education is fading.

Since the late 1960s the rapid erosion of K–12 schooling has been obvious. Our investment of resources in education has slowed dramatically whether we look at per pupil expenditure or share of GDP devoted to the cause, that is, national effort. Between 1970 and 2005, only about two-thirds to three-quarters of American teenagers (and just half of all black, Latino, and Native American teens) graduated with a diploma four years after they entered high school. (About 10% of the total later complete a high-school equivalency.) Worse, the Program for International Assessment, reporting on the reading and math skills of 15-year-olds, found that in 2005 the United States ranked 24th out of 29 nations surveyed in both math literacy and problem-solving ability. Of 2.1 million high-school graduates (40% of total graduates) who took the ACT, a test of college readiness, only 51 percent achieved the rather easy benchmark for reading, 41 percent in math, 26 percent in science. High-school curricula and standards were one cause among many: only 56 percent of that year's graduates who took the test had completed the core curriculum for college-bound students – four years of English and three years each of social studies, science, and math at the level of algebra or higher. That low percentage of preparation has been falling for some time. (For further evidence of the decline in school performance, see Goldin and Katz, 2008: 324–350.)

The roots of rapid decline in K–12 compared to other rich democracies could take a book, but a few important causes can be listed, where a research consensus prevails. The first invokes demographic data, a terribly unromantic account of the student uprising of the 1960s.

- *The postwar baby boom as it moved through schools and colleges overloaded both.* What was happening in all the rich countries having enough freedom of association to permit organized protest was a convergence of several powerful forces peaking in the 1960s: (1) Mass education expanded apace, especially at the postsecondary level (a bit earlier and more vigorously in the United States but quickly followed by other modern societies). (2) The expansion of education was a response to the postwar baby-boom cohort born 1946–1960 and to the rising demand of their parents for more educational opportunity. Schools and then colleges became overloaded. American society was like the proverbial python that swallowed a pig and suffered indigestion. (3) Unusually swift economic growth in 1950–1965 enhanced mass appetites for a better life at the same time that social-political movements for minority rights gave urgency to the thrust for equality, for expanded opportunity. But, more important, just before the outbursts of the mid-1960s, college opportunities expanded at a rate much faster than opportunities for good jobs that could accommodate the baby-boom cohort, especially ethnic minorities among them, leaving many of the most ambitious and energetic with a sense of betrayal, ready to scream "discrimination" or "false promises."

- The demonstration effect of U.S. student protests amplified by television may have reinforced these convergent structural shifts among other rich democracies, although the United States was again in the lead with the largest baby boom, hence the heaviest overload of college-age boomers. It is an irony that the outstanding American achievement in equality of educational opportunity should lead to the greatest strain on its schools and colleges and trigger their slow decline.

- *The United States lacks universal access to preschool education and day-care facilities.* There is consensus among scholars that the years from o to 5, if not critical to the cognitive and social development of children, are of paramount importance. There is evidence that the day-care centers and child-care facilities that operate in the United States, whether public or private, range from inadequate to abusive. Expensive ones in the most affluent areas are exceptions. The most thorough study of cost, quality, and child outcomes based on 400 randomly chosen child-care centers in California, Colorado, Connecticut, and North Carolina found that 40 percent of infants and toddlers were in conditions that threaten their health and safety and discourage learning; only 14 percent of centers – the well-funded centers with stable, well-educated, well-paid staff – offer high-quality care, including safe surroundings, adult warmth and support, and learning opportunities (*Wall Street Journal*, Feb. 6, 1995; cf. similar conclusions in Scarr, 1996). In the United States, only 49.8 percent of three- and four-year-olds were enrolled in preprimary education in 2007. In 14 of the other 18 rich democracies for which data are available, the average was 77.3 percent, a gap of 27.5 percent.[13] In Europe, enrollment in preschool establishments is typically part of broader family policies.

- *The swift erosion of U.S. primary and secondary schools is rooted first in the extraordinary decentralization* of the system, the tyranny of locality; second, the grip of schools of education on *teacher training and certification;* and, finally, *inadequate and erratic funding.* We have discussed our radical federalism in Chapter 5 on "why no health insurance in the United States?" It has similar effects on the school system. The United States has about 13,500 independent school districts, each making its own decisions on organization, budget, curriculum content, standards, and assessment, all under the pressure of the loudest, most parochial religious and political interest groups. Federal support comes in the form of endless speeches about the crisis of American education and recurrent commissions to sound the alarm. But federal funding for K–12, when President Clinton increased its share, reached the munificent level of 6.6 percent of total costs, less than it was during President Johnson's Great Society. Much of the talk is driven by intellectual fashions focused on private vs. public schools, vouchers, and, under President Obama, charter schools.

A major source of the decline of K–12 is the main method of funding, property taxes on households – the most painfully visible, most unpopular tax ever invented, one with a long history of triggering sustained tax revolts (Chapter 4; Wilensky, 2002: ch. 10).

With the decentralized political structure and meager federal funding of the system, it is hard to see how a national curriculum or meaningful national standards could be imposed, although any step in that direction would be worth the fight required.

In the critical matter of teacher education and training, with rare exceptions the dominance of schools of education diverts attention from academic content to dubious lists of methods of teaching and stages of child development as well as aimless statistics while it turns off bright students who would otherwise enter teaching.[14] Suggestions about how to bypass such content and upgrade teacher education and professionalism as well as the role of testing are in Chapter 8.

Bad news continues, if more recent, when we consider changes in higher education. How far we have fallen from our early lead can be seen in an OECD study of higher education in 14 of our 19 rich democracies. From about 1995 to 2005 the average postsecondary enrollment rate for those aged 18–24 was stuck at between 35 and 38 percent. In contrast, many other rich democracies have reached 50 percent among this age group, and several score higher than that; the United States slipped from first among developed countries to 14th. Or take graduation rates. In 2004 the percentage of higher-education graduates at the typical age of graduation for each country put the United States at 16th, behind Australia, New Zealand, Finland, Denmark, the Netherlands, Italy, Norway, the United Kingdom, Sweden, Japan, and Israel, plus a few developing countries (OECD, 2004). Most striking is a study of schooling for two cohorts in 2002 – one aged 25–34, the other aged 45–54 – in 12 rich democracies plus South Africa and Spain. It found that the United States was the only country that failed to increase its share of adults with postsecondary degrees.[15] The older cohort from our better days ranked second; the younger cohort from the recent decline ranked fifth (Smeeding, 2009: 3–4).

A final feature of the recent move away from its early excellence in higher education – both cause and effect of its decline – is the spread in colleges and universities of a labor strategy resembling that of the more backward businesses in the United States. For instance, contingent labor has become the rule in much of higher education. In 2003 the U.S. Department of Education conducted a national survey of postsecondary instructional faculty. Respondents numbered 26,108, representing 1.2 million university employees in institutions offering an associate or higher degree. About 44 percent of respondents reported that their institutions considered them part-timers. Today, hardly a major university is without itinerant English professors or instructors who teach remedial writing and reading, moving from place to place, a large migrant academic proletariat. (Of course, the small, diminishing number of highly selective colleges and universities stand aside from all this.) This trend underscores a problem confronted by curriculum planners in major universities that attempt to expand equality of opportunity. A country cannot dumb down its K–12 and neglect preschooling without putting downward pressure on the requirements and standards of higher education. The Great Recession and its special burden on state budgets accelerated all these unhappy trends in American educational performance.

Beyond education, the United States evidences a second major neglect of human capital, an area where it was a laggard from the first. Like other fragmented and decentralized political economies, the United States emphasized passive labor-market policies with lean funding, whereas the more consensual democracies accented active labor-market policies (ALMP) as well as unemployment compensation and other cash benefits, with more generous funding (see sec. 9 on the U.S. approach to labor-market policies).

In Chapter 8, I suggest a political coalition and agenda that could move the country toward better educational performance at every level, a more active labor-market policy, maintenance of our lead in many areas of science and technology and restoration of our lead in others, as well as a tax structure that would permit serious investment in both physical and human capital.

## 9. A Welfare State That Is Below Average in Spending (GNP Share) and, with the Exception of Public Pensions and Medicare, Is Inefficient and Ineffective

Chapters 1 and 5 and other sections of this book cover the ground in detail. So this can be brief. The basic idea of the welfare state, a convergent trend in all rich democracies, is government-protected minimum standards of income, nutrition, health and safety, housing, and education assured to every citizen as a social right, not as charity. On the low road, and especially in the United States' reluctant welfare state, some aspects of social and labor-market policy are unique to the United States or simply so extreme in degree that they are exceptional; others we share with Britain and Britain abroad (and sometimes with Switzerland).

### No National Health Insurance

The United States is the only rich democracy without national health insurance. As we have seen in Chapter 5, its health-care (non)system spends more than 16 percent of GDP and yields a below-average national health performance. It is unique in its continued reliance on medical care individually purchased, collectively bargained, or voluntarily provided by an employer and in the large number of its people with no or inadequate insurance coverage; a large private commercial sector; and, by some measures of population health, a position of 19th among the 19 rich democracies. Even after a year's Democratic Party control of the presidency and the Congress, the United States was still unable to assert public bargaining power over the medical-industrial complex and thereby move toward national health insurance.

One significant trade-off on the low road remains: the national differences in reliance on *means-tested public assistance* vs. reliance on universal, categorical social rights still prevail. For understanding national differences in poverty reduction and the politics of the welfare state, I have found a distinction between complex, most-visible "means tests" and simple, least-visible income tests most useful. Means testing refers to noncategorical benefits (1) targeted to the poor via a stiff income and/or assets test; (2) applied by welfare administrators with substantial discretion; and (3) administered with a high probability of stigma. "Income testing" is the opposite. It is categorical as a social right with copayments graded by income bracket and, because it is private and invisible, has no stigma. An example of means testing is U.S. "welfare," a pejorative term uniquely American that refers to public assistance and related programs carefully targeted to the poor but is widened in political debate to condemn the entire welfare state. An example of income testing is the highly successful earned-income tax credit for the working poor in the United States.[16] Other examples include the many programs of the universalistic welfare states in the more consensual democracies, such as access to child care with a simple, private declaration of income at the point of service to assure the right to service with an income-graded copayment.

In its large, intrusive apparatus of investigation and surveillance of the non-working poor who receive *means-tested* benefits, the United States shares its approach with Britain and Britain abroad. But the United States tops them all in its reliance on means testing, with the United Kingdom and Canada a close second or third (Wilensky, 2002: table 8.3). Modern debates about the causes of poverty – personal moral failure or lack of opportunity – are as old as the English Poor Laws of the 16th century. The welfare reform bill of 1996 ("Temporary Assistance for Needy Families") is merely one more episode in a long cycle of crackdowns on the poor followed by reforms to ease up a bit. Even the harshest of them all, the British Poor Law of 1834, was quickly followed by strong criticism. The critics noted that it did not distinguish between the nonworking poor who receive poor relief and the more-deserving poor who did not; or that it undermined incentives to obey the work ethic; or that it lumped together the worthy and unworthy in a miserable poorhouse, where criminals, alcoholics, women, mothers, children, infants, the aged, and the sick were jammed together and where brutality and corruption were common. Serving later as Conservative prime minister (1874–1880), Benjamin Disraeli complained that the Poor Law Reform Bill of 1834 made it "a crime to be poor" – an idea echoed by today's liberals who are repelled by the "conservative" urge to punish the poor for their poverty. The principles of Elizabethan poor law – direct aid for the unemployed, work (or the workhouse or alms house, or prison) for the able bodied, and local administration that would keep welfare benefits below the lowest wage and thus provide incentives to work – persist to this day in the United States (Handler, 1995: 12ff.).

Economists, like many Democratic politicians who want to rein in public spending and yet reduce poverty, love means testing as efficient targeting to the needy. They appear to be oblivious or indifferent to its political costs. For the center Left it is a sure way to lose middle-mass votes (Chapter 4), increase the politics of resentment, and keep funding meager. In fact, the countries that rely heavily on means testing are the countries with high rates of poverty (United States, United Kingdom, Canada, Ireland).[17]

The policy choice to use stiff means tests to target the poor instead of income testing for everyone is a drag on economic performance. As I have shown in a multivariate analysis of 19 countries (2002: 455–456), a heavy reliance on means testing as a percentage of GDP creates bureaucratic bloat and reduces capital investment, which in turn, slows growth and increases unemployment. But its main significance is political; it is a weapon to divide and defeat center-left coalitions.

### Deteriorating Private Pensions and Individual Savings Accounts

Chapter 5 has shown a marked erosion in the percentage of the elderly covered by private pensions and the size and stability of their benefits. Part of this story is changes in the benefit structure. Over the past three decades, U.S. private-sector employers, if they have not abandoned pension benefits entirely, have shifted from the traditional defined benefit (DB) pensions to defined contribution (DC) retirement savings accounts such as 401(k) plans. By 2005 about three-quarters of these employees who had any plan were on DC plans (calculated from U.S. Department of Labor, 2009: table 1A). Not only are these DC plans little more than a high-stakes crap shoot; they are about twice as costly as DB plans in providing a given level of retirement (Almeida and Boivie, 2009: 9). Right-wing politicians who favor privatization of Social Security and Medicare have recently advocated that this DC poison should be drunk by the public employees, who they claim are overpaid. Aside from this big U.S. shift, the only other rich democracies that have in various ways introduced a smallish DC component in their pension systems are Australia and Sweden (Whiteford and Whitehouse, 2006: 181–183 and table 4).

### Passive Labor-Market Policy vs. Active Labor-Market Policy

The U.S. approach to *labor-market policies* is passive: for the disabled, little rehabilitation; for the unemployed, limited cash but no serious investment in training or the dozen other active policies that improve the efficiency of the labor market and the quality of labor. By *active labor-market policy* (ALMP) I mean direct government action to shape the *demand* for labor by maintaining or creating jobs; to increase the *supply and quality* of labor via training and rehabilitation; and to encourage labor *mobility* via placement, counseling, and mobility incentives. (Wilensky, 1985 and 1992a, discusses 21 types of policies included by researchers as ALMP, of which 4 are government policies to decrease the labor supply and arguably should not be seen as active measures – e.g., shortening the workweek, lowering the age of retirement, reducing immigration, raising the age of compulsory schooling.)

ALMP is counterposed to such passive policies as unemployment insurance and public (social) assistance. Excluded by most experts are policies that aim merely to redistribute existing work rather than increase it, such as affirmative action or coercion and bribes to remove older workers or immigrants from the labor market. Always excluded are measures that may affect the labor market indirectly: fiscal and monetary policy, regulation, or deregulation.

In earlier research, I found a hint of a trade-off between active and passive policies for a few countries that varied greatly in their labor policies in the mid- to late 1970s. For instance, as a percentage of GNP, Sweden was spending roughly four or five times as much on active labor-market programs as it was on unemployment insurance; the ratio was about 2:1 for Norway. In contrast, Canada and the United Kingdom reversed the ratio: Canada about 2.5:1 and the United Kingdom about 1.2:1 in favor of unemployment insurance (based on Johannesson and Schmid, 1980: 401; OECD, 1978: 118–119). By 2000–2006, however, that correlation had become strongly positive. The leaders in ALMP became more generous in unemployment compensation and other passive measures while increasing their spending on such ALMP measures as training, job creation, and wage subsidies.

Some economists and politicians argue that government spending on all kinds of labor-market policies provides disincentives to work, creates unemployment, and reduces labor-force participation, as people laze about on lavish benefits or in useless training programs. Data estimating program spending in 18 of our rich democracies over a recent seven-year period, 2000–2006, covering both recession and growth contradict this notion. The correlation between active measures and unemployment is near zero (0.07). The correlation between unemployment and spending on active labor-market policies as a percentage of total labor-market spending is a weak negative (-0.32). That mildly suggests that either increased unemployment leads to more passive expenditures like unemployment compensation or increased attention to ALMP lowers unemployment rates.

Again we find that the countries on the low road are laggards in resources devoted to an active labor-market policy. Here are average public spending on ALMP/GDP 2000–2006 for these 18 rich democracies by type of political economy (OECD, 2009):

| Type of Political Economy | Avg. Public ALMP Spending/GDP (2000–2006) |
| --- | --- |
| Left-corporatist | 1.19 |
| Left-Catholic corporatist | 1.07 |
| Catholic corporatist | 0.83 |
| Corporatist without labor | 0.66 |
| Least corporatist | 0.40 |

The types of political economy, as usual, predict the extremes very well. The top five in funding active labor-market programs (Denmark, Sweden, the Netherlands, Belgium, and Germany) are all either consensual democracies with strong cumulative left party power or corporatist democracies with strong and competing left and Catholic power. In contrast, the bottom five in descending order (New Zealand, Australia, Canada, the United Kingdom, and the

United States) make little effort to fund ALMP. The United States ranks last at 0.15 percent of GDP, less than it was in the mid-1980s. With the United Kingdom, it is also at the bottom of our rich democracies in passive expenditure (e.g., generosity in coverage and size of unemployment cash benefits).[18]

The only remaining hint of a trade-off between spending on passive and active measures appears in only two countries among the 18, Sweden and Norway. The overall correlation, however, is strongly positive ($r = .81$). It is likely that all countries as they got richer could be more generous with both unemployment compensation and ALMP. In short, the welfare-state leaders retain their lead on almost all programs whereas the laggards, as we have seen, lag in both active and passive measures.

### Family Breakup without Family Policies to Cushion the Shock

The story of changes in family structures, functions, and lifestyles, as well as government responses to those changes, is the story of common outcomes in the problems to be solved but divergent response in social policies.

Convergence is driven by the demographic and organizational accompaniments of continuing industrialization – especially educational and occupational shifts that expand opportunity for intergenerational and worklife mobility in nonagricultural and nondomestic settings, thereby increasing mass aspirations. As a result of these shifts in social structure, in the past 100 years or so the currently rich modern countries, whatever their political systems or cultural traditions, have experienced very similar and accelerating trends in family life: increased participation by women in the nonagricultural labor force, declining fertility and an expanding percentage of the aged, reduced family and household size, an increasingly widespread push for gender equality, and rising divorce rates. Although these trends have not eliminated the independent nuclear family as the center of daily life, they have increased its instability and in recent decades increased the population of lone parents and the threat of child poverty.

In timing and policy packages, governments have diverged in their responses to the social problems posed by structural change. My empirical analysis of family policies and politics among our rich democracies explains the differences: countries with strong mass-based Catholic or left parties move toward corporatist patterns of interest-group bargaining that produce expansive and innovative family policies, with somewhat different policy mixes, depending on types of corporatism and the relative strength of Catholicism and leftism. More fragmented and decentralized political economies are slower to develop family policies, as we can see from striking contrasts in the politics and policies of extreme cases, Sweden and the United States.

Types of political economy display the usual rank order, in this case, ranking of investment in family policies, specifically public access to government subsidized child-care centers, preschool education, before- and after-school programs; the amount and duration of paid and unpaid maternity and parental leave, and flexible retirement (see Chapter 5). To get at these national differences, I devised an index of innovative and expansive family policies; it ranges from a high of 11 to a low of 1.[19] At the top of investment in such policies (scoring 11 to 9) are left corporatist democracies (Sweden, Norway, and Finland, with Denmark a marginal case at 8), Catholic-left corporatist Belgium, and corporatist without labor France. Scoring medium (7 to 4) are Catholic-left or Catholic corporatist Germany, Austria, Italy, Netherlands, with the United Kingdom a marginal case. At the very bottom (scoring 3 to 1) are Japan and Switzerland (corporatist without labor) and the United States, Canada, New Zealand, Australia, and Ireland – fragmented and decentralized political economies on the low road.

The trade-off between investment in universal access to family benefits and services vs. heavy reliance on means-tested public assistance (American-style "welfare") is plain. Laggards on family policy are leaders in targeting the poor with stiff means-tested programs. There is a strong negative correlation between the two.

The effects of an accent on family policy are also clear and certainly not trivial: it reduces family poverty, increases labor-force participation by women, and thereby increases gender equality. Most important, it permits working parents to balance work and family demands and assure the care of children. All of the above have the incidental effect of reducing delinquency and crime among the young. In general, family-policy leaders take better care of their children.[20]

Although contrasting political and economic structures explain current differences in family policies, there is much evidence to suggest some convergence even here, where moral-social agendas (abortion, gay rights, family planning, sex education) are most passionately pursued. Continuing industrialization means continued increases in both women at work and the aged, more family breakup, and stronger demands for gender equality. In some measure these universal forces may overcome the forces for divergence. Perhaps recent legislation and continuing family-policy debates in the United States are clues to the direction of change. Similarly, the rapid aging of Japan's population has in the past 20 or so years moved both government and employers toward much more flexibility in retirement rules. In fact, swift changes of recent years in aging, fertility, and women's work in both Japan and the United States have already changed the politics of gender equality, aging, and child care and triggered more serious policy debates in those two most deviant countries. As I suggest in the next chapter, family policy is a feasible area for political action and reform in the United States.

### 10. Violent Crime and the Highest Incarceration Rate among 19 Rich Democracies (High Murder Rates and Correlated Violent Crime)

The United States is in a class of its own on two measures of internal violence – murder rates and incarceration rates (prisons are crowded and violent places with little effort at rehabilitation). Since the early 1970s the prison industry has been rising and violent crime has been on an upward swing with some fluctuation and in recent years declined. This decline in violence rates did not reverse the escalation in the public fear of crime and the crackdown response of politicians and courts, nor did it change our top rate compared to other modern democracies.

The national murder rate per 1,000 from 1980 to 2008 remained high and essentially constant – that is, the rate of 2008 was like the rate of 1980. The recorded violent crime rate – including murder and nonnegligent manslaughter, rape and sexual assault, robbery, and aggravated assault – remained very high at about 46 to 53 from 1980 to 1995, then began a slide downward to a low average of 27 in 2004–2008, still high by international comparisons. According to a 2008 study by the Pew Center on the States, in the past 25 years the prison population of the United States has nearly quadrupled while the nation's population has grown by less than a third. One in 100 adults is now behind bars. The effects on children are devastating. Christopher Wildeman (2009) found that 1 in 25 white children born in 1990 had a parent imprisoned; a full 1 in 4 black children born the same year had a parent imprisoned. If we restrict analysis to children of black parents who were high-school dropouts, we find that just over half of those children experienced childhood with an imprisoned father.

American exceptionalism in this area, its high rate of violent crime, cannot be explained by a permissive culture that is soft on crime; by minority group cleavages or the legacy of slavery; by a flood of immigrants; or by a southern subculture of violence and guns. Whether we compare our 19 rich democracies or look at the United States' own past or consider variations in violent crime by states, none of these theories helps.

After demonstrating the limitations of alternative explanations (2002: ch. 14), I show that, across time and geographical areas and under modern conditions, the combination of poverty and inequality (i.e., great absolute and/or relative economic deprivation) and family breakup without a family policy in the context of crowded urban living conditions powerfully and consistently explain homicide rates and related crimes of violence. This holds even if we eliminate the United States, which is extreme in its mayhem and murder. No one of these works alone; all interact to explain the variance across countries or even across states within the U.S. A broader measure of mayhem evidences the same causes.

Here are a few conclusions about two of the most popular explanations – that more crackdowns and policing deter crime and a racial subculture causes violent crime.

- For four decades the United States has had increasingly tough laws on crime and drug use; its incarceration rate, already high, became the highest among rich countries and is now the highest in the world. These crackdowns not only failed to reverse the trends but likely contributed to their rise.
- The prison boom coincided with a rise in violent crime. Wars on drugs – interdiction of supplies (with minimal effort to cut demand), arrests of dealers, and even minor users – were accompanied by an increase in drug-related crime and a decreasing rate of apprehension of murderers. Judges' discretion

in sentencing was replaced by long fixed sentences for violent criminals and nonviolent drug offenders alike. Arrests for drug sales and more often for drug use are still rising; in 2006 the FBI reported that 4 in 10 of all drug arrests were for marijuana possession.

- Incarceration, now nearly eight times its historical average and at a cost of $70 billion per year, has reached the point of no return in reducing crime. There is consensus among hawks and doves, scholars on left, right, and center, that the possibility of improved public safety through increased imprisonment has been exhausted (Western and Pettit, 2010: 17). In view of the extraordinary cost of incarceration – $700 billion over 10 years at current levels – measures to improve schooling, a family policy, and an active labor-market policy would yield a better cost-benefit ratio in reducing delinquency, crime, and poverty.

- Increasing resources for traditional policing (until the Great Recession forced states and cities to cut police forces) had little effect, although it is likely that increasing resources devoted to community-oriented policing if combined with an attack on the root causes of violent crime would have some effect. Of course, we cannot know what the violent crime rate would have been if no crime crackdowns occurred. But the advocates of crackdown must accept a burden of proof that they have not yet met.[21]

From 1992 through 2000, there was a substantial decline in the homicide rate as well as rates of other serious crimes in the nation as a whole with several of the previously most violent big American cities leading the decline (e.g., from New York City's best record along with San Diego, San Francisco, Dallas, and Houston to the worst five, least-declining Baltimore, Philadelphia, Columbus, Detroit, and Phoenix) (Zimring, 2006: 5–12, table 1.3). Research to gauge the importance of community policing relative to the structural shifts discussed earlier has not yet been done. Those years did see a shift in numbers and missions of police. In New York City, for instance, more officers patrolled the streets, more undercover agents bought drugs and guns and collected intelligence on gangs; there was more cooperation among city, state, and federal law enforcement agencies, more arrests for minor "quality-of-life crimes" – which provides search warrants and the seizure of guns and arrests for gun possession. Simultaneously, however, during the early and mid-1990s the percentage of violence-prone 15- to 24-year-olds was declining in both New York City and the country, unemployment rates were dropping, job creation accelerating, and even poverty and inequality were declining for a few years. In short, the crackdown aspects may have played a role, especially because community policing did advance a little, but our old powerful variables – reductions in poverty, inequality, unemployment, and number of youths; and improved job opportunities – were also evident. Because cities vary greatly in their recorded crime rates, both violent and nonviolent, unscrambling the causes will require a multivariate analysis of both policing and the causes I have found for nations and states (e.g., from 2009 to 2010, why did crime drop in New York and Los Angeles while it increased in Denver?).

A minor contribution to the decline in homicide rates came from trauma center improvements in the 1990s, which have continued in the 2000s. Such centers remove potential murder victims from the statistics; they appear as injuries, thereby lowering the official homicide rate. Some observers of the drug trade suggest a final structural shift in the 1990s that may have lowered murder rates in some urban centers: older drug kingpins, the big businessmen of the trade, have consolidated their power and suppressed the random violence of teenage gangs competing for status and territory so common in the 1980s; ironically, this more-efficient criminal organization for drug distribution reduces street warfare and hence violent crime rates (Skolnick, 1997).

• Finally, as always, localized police crackdowns often shift the locus of violence. Because of the New York City gun-control campaign, gun traffickers have moved to the Carolinas and Florida. For the country as a whole, the homicide rate remains high by international standards and higher by about 15–20 percent than it was in the early 1960s (Zimring, 2006: fig. 1.1). As we have seen, the advances in jobs and reduction in unemployment in 1995–2000 as well as a few years of decline in poverty and inequality no doubt account for most of the decline in the broader violent crime rates. The national crime rate remains high as does the crackdown mentality, a sustained drumbeat of "law 'n order."

If we add these statistical studies of abstract murder rates to ethnographic studies of violence found in urban ghettos, we can confirm that the cause is not a subculture of violence. Instead it is the interaction of poverty and inequality with family breakup (as a symbol of weak social networks), the lack of parental and school supervision, and the absence of conventional job opportunities and job networks, especially for black teenagers and young adults.[22]

Cross-national data can shed further light on the question of American exceptionalism and the theory of a racial subculture of violence. It is true that the American homicide rate in 1988 (18 per 100,000 population) was 3 to 15 times that of all other rich democracies, but if we eliminate the United States as an extreme case and examine the other 18 countries ranging from medium-high rates (5.7–3.8) to low (1.8–1.3), none of the other high scorers in violence had our history of slavery. And until recently countries with above-average homicide rates (Finland, Canada, Italy, Australia, Belgium) have had no substantial racial minorities. Moreover, if we consider the intensity of minority-group cleavages based on religion, ethnicity, and language as well as race, three countries with strong social cleavages – Switzerland, Israel, and the United Kingdom – have low homicide rates.

The strongest explanation of national differences among our 19 democracies remains. The United States scores very high on concentration of wealth, increasing poverty and inequality, and family breakup without a family policy to cushion the shock. The interaction of all three in a dense urban context – plus tough talk, tough laws, and tough administration of the criminal justice system – results in by far the highest incarceration rate among 19 rich democracies. Incidentally, this is a fourth source of underestimated figures for unemployment other than the officially unemployed, part-timers who want full-time work, and discouraged workers – namely, imprisonment. Western and Beckett (1999) show that America's high incarceration rate combined with a high recidivism rate lowers the conventional unemployment rate by hiding joblessness. Using their careful measures for 1995 for 14 of our rich democracies, U.S. unemployment would increase by 1.9 percent while European unemployment would rise only infinitesimally if all these countries included prison inmates in the jobless figures. They argue that long prison terms (now the standard in the United States) for both violent and nonviolent offenders, escalating prison violence, and overcrowdedness reduce the long-term employability of inmates. Thus, the United States will have to continue to advance its incarceration rate if it is to sustain its two-percentage-point advantage (economic policies equal) – a bizarre road to good labor-market performance.

## 11. Very High Military Spending, Which Subverts Both Social Spending and Civilian R&D

Although the destruction and total mobilization of World War II brought an ideology of shared sacrifice, the spread of social rights and benefits, and the reduction of unemployment, the Cold War and small wars of 1951–1973 undermined both the welfare state and economic progress. This was especially true of the welfare-state laggards or middling spenders that launched a military effort of well beyond 6 or 7 percent of their GNP in the early 1950s – United States, the United Kingdom, and Canada, countries located at or near the center of pacts and alliances. The effect was to retard both social spending and GDP growth and to increase unemployment in subsequent years (Wilensky, 1975: 78, 84). Similar results are evident in the lagging social spending of Israel and the United States in 2005, the two heaviest military spenders: Israel ranks 18th in social spending/GDP (16.4%) but 2nd to Sweden in total government spending/GDP (49.1%); the United States lags in social spending (15.9%, last among 19 rich democracies as shown in Table 1) but is 2nd to Israel in military spending.

### *The Economic Explanation*

A heavy military burden diverts skilled workers and managers and scarce funds away from more productive investment and employment and thereby slows down economic growth and worsens unemployment. Budget deficits in the absence of productive uses of the borrowed money may be an additional but modest drag (Wilensky, 1975: 74–85).

Two findings emerge from our multivariate analysis. First, in regressions including corporatism, leftism, Catholicism, and military spending as independent variables, *the military effort (military spending/GNP) from 1960 to 1986 is consistently and strongly a drag on capital investment*. This relationship remains strong even when Israel and the United States and Japan are removed from the equation as extreme cases. Second, that advantage in investment enjoyed by countries with a small military burden gives them a clear edge in economic performance, notably by increasing growth. The military impact is entirely rooted in the negative correlation with economic growth. Using time series and comparing the multiplier effects of military and nonmilitary government spending, research on the United States also provides strong evidence that military spending has an indirect, delayed impact: by reducing investment, it is a drag on economic growth (Mintz and Huang, 1991; Ward and Davis, 1992) – consistent with our 19-country analysis. These findings apply to Bush's escalating military spending and his war in Iraq as well; they may be one factor in U.S. anemic recovery 2001–2003 and the subsequent slowdown in productivity growth.

### Erosion of the U.S. Lead in Science and R&D

A second finding concerns *science and R&D*. On the basis of a review of literature and my limited six-country analysis (2002: 462–465), we can say that despite some positive technological spinoffs from military R&D (radar, jet engines), military R&D is much less productive than civilian R&D, and the United States, which leads in military, has fallen behind in the latter. This reflects another trade-off – a long-run cost of adopting the role of the world's only superpower.

Accelerating the U.S. slide in civilian R&D is a recent rise in Christian-right power within the Republican Party. (Evangelicals are now more than one-third of the Republican presidential vote.) "Wedge issues" (abortion, gay marriage, "creationism") intensified the antiscientific bias of the Bush administration. One result: the American lead in biotech research, a most promising area, has been diminished because of restrictions on stem-cell research. More important for the long run is the erosion of serious teaching of science in American secondary schools in recent decades. Eight years of the most antiscience administration in the past century and the longer ascendance of the Christian Right in the Republican Party exacerbated the effects of the neglect of K–12.

A recent national survey of public school teachers who taught a high-school level biology course in the 2006–2007 academic year (Berkman, Pacheco, and Plutzer, 2008) reflects these political shifts in their teaching of evolution. Three-fifths devoted only between 3 and 15 hours to general evolutionary processes (including human evolution) all year. Another 17 percent did not cover human evolution at all. In fact, of the one in four teachers who devoted time to creationism, nearly half agreed or strongly agreed that they teach creationism as a "valid scientific alternative to Darwinian explanations for the origin of species." Nearly the same number agreed or strongly agreed that, when they teach creationism or intelligent design, they emphasize that "many reputable scientists view these as valid alternatives to Darwinian Theory." It is not surprising that the survey analysts found that variations in the embrace of pseudoscience depend on the teachers' lack of college-level exposure to science classes and their personal beliefs about evolution. Finally, it is no wonder that in other national polls about half of the public believes in the "young earth" creationist doctrine – that humans were created by God in their present form at one time in the past 10,000 years. The spirit of the Tennessee court conviction of Scopes is alive and well, far beyond Tennessee.

## 12. Intrusive Regulation or Weak Regulation: Cycles of Deregulation and Reregulation

Students of regulatory regimes who have compared rich democracies have concluded that the United States and, in some areas, other countries in the Anglo-American club tend to move between extremes – confrontational and intrusive regulations followed by deregulation with a light touch and back again. Deregulation is guided by free-market ideology, agency capture, and industry gaming, as we have seen in the U.S. approach to climate change in Chapter 2 and financial deregulation in Chapter 6.

My earlier analysis of the environment (2002: ch. 15), violence (ch. 14), and health care (ch.16) shows how national regulatory regimes differ as they confront similar risks – health and safety, nuclear energy, smoking, and air pollution. Both public policies and performance vary markedly by type of political economy. As the EU attempts to write rules in these areas, it might look at these contrasting records of the past half century. For instance, consider health care in the United States. In spending, it is 55 percent private and 45 percent public. The larger the private share, the more decentralized and diffuse the financing, and consequently the greater the administrative cost and waste (Chapter 5; 2002: 629) and the more corruption (pp. 613–614). It was the antiregulation Reagan and first Bush administrations that adopted the most intrusive regulations of hospital and physician payments such as rate-setting, prospective payment plans based on diagnostic-related groups, and resource-based value scales (ch. 16, especially 597ff.). The net effect was to increase administrative complexity and costs; enrage physicians; and shift costs to private insurers, who then raised premiums and gave employers and providers strong incentives to reduce coverage and services, shifting costs back to government. Even with all that, as Chapter 5 shows, the public programs remain much cheaper than the private.

Similarly, consider the policies of Prime Minister Thatcher, a dedicated deregulator-privatizer. The trend she completed in the name of free and fair competition was more thorough and comprehensive, more juridical and codified, more bureaucratic, more confrontational, and less consensual than anything Britain had seen before. To cope with the process and consequences, the Thatcher government had to create 11 major new independent regulatory agencies (her successor, John Major, added one), some of them sharing power with the ministries. "Liberalization" required a proliferation of rules and a boom in lawyers and accountants to keep track of it at all. The government, of course, had to set the rules governing market competition but also to cultivate new entrants, prevent or respond to financial scandals that frighten politicians, raise revenue (but, God forbid, not taxes), and even to protect workers and consumers when they screamed too loudly about the dangers of free-swinging competition to quality, safety, health, employment, and job security (Vogel, 1996: chs. 5 and 10 – a book titled *Freer Markets, More Rules*). In short, in regulatory reform of both industry and the welfare state, what actually happens is contrasting mixes of *re*regulation and liberalization shaped by national institutions.

The road to effectiveness has three barriers: *confrontation* and *free-market fundamentalism* in making the laws (as in congressional debate regarding a possible price on carbon emissions), *agency capture* (foxes guarding the chicken coop), and *industry gaming* (as in GGE cap and trade), a trio that undermines any attempt at regulation. We have seen how the deregulation bonanza of 1999–2009 turned shadow banks into complex and opaque centers of short-term speculation.

The structure and interaction of the regulatory agencies also helps to explain their relative effectiveness. Where there are too many specialized agencies, the regulated parties – bankers, brokers, insurance company executives – can quietly shop for the easiest regulatory agency while they stridently attack the regulations and game the system. This often provides opportunities for corruption. Discussion in Chapter 6 provides many examples; one is the financial sector's rating agencies such as Standard and Poor before the economic meltdown. Pension funds and other big investors cannot buy securities (bonds, other) rated less than AAA. Credit rating agencies got paid only if the security they rate was sold. And their pay or fee was often a percentage of the rated security's sale price. It is a conflict of interest of gigantic proportion. Like health-care corruption – hospitals and other providers padding bills, charging for ghost patients, or cozy and profitable relations between doctors and drug firms – it is plain vanilla corruption.

Regarding effectiveness of regulations, the more consensual democracies have a clear advantage in implementing laws and executive orders. If industry, labor, and the professions are involved in making and executing the laws, no party fights to the death to subvert them, exaggerate their negative effects, or evade them, as they routinely do in the more confrontational American system. Such evasion is evident in the barriers to implementation of environmental rules of EPA or the occupational health and safety regulations of OSHA or, most dramatically, the combination of capture, corruption, and evasion in the Minerals Management Service oversight of deepwater oil drilling.

More fateful was the ineffectiveness of many agencies devoted to regulation of financial institutions. Here it was a case of capture of the agencies either by the industries to be regulated or by top administrators of neoliberal persuasion or both. They presided over what may be the greatest regulatory failure in modern history. Reinforcing the light regulatory touch is the highly specialized missions of uncoordinated agencies – nine separate regulatory agencies, from the Securities and Exchange Commission (SEC) to the Commodities Futures Trading Commission (CFTC) and the Financial Industry Regulatory Authority (FINRA). FINRA is essentially a corporation paid by the financial firms it is supposed to control. For the chair of SEC, President George W. Bush had appointed Christopher Cox, a loyal Republican representative from California; Cox subsequently ignored numerous warnings about the biggest Ponzi scheme in American history, the Bernard Madoff fraud. For Cox's replacement President Obama appointed Mary Shapiro, a Democrat. Shapiro previously headed FINRA when the agency steadily decreased the fines and sanctions it levied against Wall Street firms during the four years leading to the financial meltdown. She was involved in several examinations of the brokerage business of Mr. Madoff. FINRA concluded in 2007 that his firm had committed only minor technical violations (*Wall Street Journal*, Jan. 15, 2009). Similarly, the little-noticed Office of the Comptroller of the Currency (OCC) operates a consumer service center that processes thousands of complaints each year about the nation's banks. President Bush appointed Controller John C. Dugan in 2005 and he was still there, presumably protecting consumers from abusive bank practices, in 2010. Dugan, an ally of Treasury Secretary Geithner, was for 12 years a lobbyist for the banking industry. That might explain why, as a major regulator of big national banks such as Citigroup and Bank of America, he fought efforts by state attorneys general (e.g., in West Virginia, New York, and several New England states) to stop banks from credit-card abuses, gift-card fees, and predatory lending. He encouraged the banks facing court suits to apply for a national charter with OCC, which he gladly approved, notifying the attorneys general that they no longer had jurisdiction – now in the hands of Mr. Dugan (*New York Times*, Mar. 28, 2010).

## 13. Good Job Creation until the Decade of 2000–2009

This low-road achievement requires separate analysis because job creation is unrelated to my economic performance index or its components. In fact, the great job-creation machines are sometimes the great unemployment machines. In 2002 (ch. 13), I found that the consistent big job creators among 18 countries, 1968–1987, are Canada, Australia, the United States, and Norway. New Zealand makes it to the top in 1968–1979, but not in the 1980s. The four countries consistently below the median are France, West Germany, Austria, and Great Britain. This list resembles an inverse of our usual variation by types of political economy.

In explaining such differences I made two assumptions. First, discussion of job creation in the United States vs. Europe before 2000 overemphasized demand policies and (presumably European) barriers to labor mobility. If job creation is a product of demand policies and is an end in itself, policy analysts should be concentrating their attention on an appropriate mix of fiscal and monetary policies. But if job creation before 2000 was little affected by economic policy and came at too high a cost (earnings deterioration, low investment in training, low-quality products and services, declines in union voice and worker participation, anemic long-term productivity gains, and a concomitant stagnation in national standards of living), then a very different strategy for reshaping the supply and quality of labor is appropriate – an active labor market policy, an education policy (Wilensky, 2002: ch. 12), a family policy, and labor-law reform

(Chapter 8; Wilensky, 2002: ch. 18). Of course, it is likely that both economic and labor-market policies contribute to job creation; it is a matter of emphasis.

Second, I assumed that, in every country where there is an expanding labor supply, it is possible that countercyclical demand policies help to turn the supply into jobs. Data on precise policy mixes for the 19 rich democracies over time are skimpy, however. Yet it is very likely that when they are compared, their fiscal and monetary policies will not vary nearly as much as their employment growth rates. Similar economic policies cannot explain large differences in job creation. In fact, it is variation in the growth and social composition of the labor supply that accounts for national differences in job creation, at least up to 2000–2009, the lost decade when U.S. fiscal, monetary, and labor policies brought a net gain in jobs of zero. And, of course, in the Great Recession of 2007–2009 large stimulus measures were necessary everywhere.

Here is the bare outline of the results of my regression analysis by relevant period of the job-creation record of these 18 rich democracies in the past (Israel missing). The most powerful structural sources of job creation are demographic and social structural: the age structure of the population; net migration (roughly immigrants minus emigrants); family breakup (e.g., divorce rates) in the absence of a family policy; and the rate of increase in women's labor-force participation. A country that has a large fraction of people aged 65 and older will not need to create as many jobs as the "young" countries. The top job creators have a low percentage of the aged. A supply of cheap labor comes from young people, many immigrants (most of whom are also young), a rapid rate of increase in the female labor supply, and impoverished women heading broken homes. Top job creators score high on all of these sources of low-cost labor. In many industries employers confronted with an abundance of young, cheap labor will organize work to facilitate their use. Conversely, if a country has an abundance of older retired adults and mature high-seniority workers, and a shortage of cheap labor because of a family policy that makes divorced women less desperate, a low rate of increase of women workers of any age, and few low-skilled immigrants, it will not create so many jobs and might even move toward high value-added products.

In short, most of the sources of job creation – changes in family structure, age structure, and immigration – are beyond the reach of economic policy, except those policies that would directly discourage low-wage work, such as a strongly enforced high minimum wage and a Berlin Wall for every border.[23] A reminder: growth and reduced unemployment, because they are unrelated to job creation, do respond to fiscal and monetary stimulus.

## B. FINAL MESSAGE

The final message of this chapter is that the gains and costs of a low-road strategy are very different from the gains and costs of a high-road strategy. Either one can at various times and places result in good economic performance. The sharp contrasts appear in social and political performance. The choice is a matter of one's values.

# 8

## Policy Implications for the United States

### *How to Get Off the Low Road*

#### A. RECAPITULATION: WHERE WE HAVE BEEN

Since the early 1970s the Anglo-American democracies have increasingly chosen the low road to economic growth and job creation: low and stagnant or declining wages; intensive use of low-skilled, least-educated workers in large, expanding sectors (e.g., retail trades); a widening spread between high-wage, high-skill workers and the least educated; emphasizing low-value-added products and services for much of the economy while upgrading processes and products in the most sophisticated sectors that employ a minority of the work force; meager investment in both physical and human capital; increasing reliance on subcontracting, a system of low-wage, no-benefit workers concentrated in small firms, themselves highly unstable, who are pressed to cheat on payroll and other taxes and evade minimum wage and safety laws; the rapid spread of contingent labor and unconventional schedules; decreasing job security for most of the work force; greater concentration of wealth; increasing poverty and inequality, and associated mayhem.

The corporatist democracies of Continental Europe and Japan followed various versions of the high road: greater participation of unions in workplace and community and in national policy making; relatively high wages, greater job security; labor and social policies that retard the growth of the contingent economy; heavy investment in human capital; more stable relations between large corporations and their subcontracted suppliers and salespeople; high productivity (working smarter, fewer hours); a lesser spread between high- and low-wage workers; much lower poverty and inequality; and a concentration on high-value-added products and processes, with R&D that accents the D. And they avoid the worst pathologies of poverty. Just as the increasing autonomy of central bankers obsessed with inflation, suspicious of growth, and unconcerned about unemployment did nothing to lower the high unemployment rates of the 1990s in Europe (Chapter 6), the high-wage short-hours strategy at its extreme may also play its part in the 1990s' rise in unemployment in some of the corporatist democracies.

After considering what we share with five other English-speaking countries, is there anything that we can call truly exceptional about the United States? If we are willing to see the U.S. as an extreme case within the fragmented and decentralized fraternity and call that exceptional, Chapter 7 covered five such areas: the lack of national health insurance, the greater concentration of wealth, increasing poverty and inequality, family breakup without family policies to cushion the shock, and the highest military spending. All of those peculiarities interact to give the United States unparalleled rates of violent crime and imprisonment. This chapter adds another five patterns of behavior that are so different in degree that they are differences in kind. These interact in destructive ways in politics and policy: the dealignment of parties-in-the-electorate (if not in government); the swift rise of the commercial media in politics and culture; the near-paralysis of government, especially the increasing abuse of arcane Senate rules that thwart the will of even substantial majorities; the criminalization of politics (searching the financial records and private lives of political opponents or nominees to government positions, some far from top positions, not merely for signs of poor judgment or wrongdoing but for opportunities to accuse them of criminal behavior); and finally the heavy weight of lawyers and judges in shaping public policy.

## 1. Restoring Deliberative and Representative vs. the Plebiscitary Aspects of Democracy

The most disturbing developments in American politics are shared by other democracies with fragmented and decentralized political economies, but America has carried them to an extreme. It has become most vulnerable to mass society tendencies – a decline in the strength of broad-based, integrative political parties, churches, labor unions, and community-wide neighborhood associations and the vitality of participation in them. That creates a vacuum of power into which the mass media in symbiotic relationship to the more parochial interest groups, fringe groups, and sectarian religious groups pour. Our unusual and increasing density of lawyers and judges is the consequence, not the cause of these developments. Lacking the consensus-making machinery of the corporatist democracies, unable to find other channels for conflict resolution, we overload our courts and multiply lawsuits in a pattern of adversarial legalism. (A detailed account of these trends with cross-national comparisons is in Wilensky, 2002: ch. 3. Cf. Dahl, 1994.)

That the deliberative and representative aspects of American democracy in its legislatures and the electorate have declined is most dramatically visible in California, which has embarked on a radical experiment with direct democracy since the 1970s. When scholars label this "plebiscitary democracy" they do not refer to a village of a few hundred citizens in the New England of the distant past, where it could more or less work, but to a polity of 37 million people where it is totally misplaced.

## 2. Direct Democracy, Election Frequency, Voter Fatigue, and Voter Turnout

California is a case, echoed in much of the rest of the American polity, where advocates of clean government, the populist Right, and the populist Left combined to paralyze government in the name of rule by the people. In states that allow the initiative, the number of initiatives on each ballot started to increase in the late 1970s. In vanguard California, initiatives exploded in the 1980s, reaching a peak of 28 or 29 in 1988 and 1990, then slacked off to a still high of about 15 per ballot in the early 1990s and back up to a combined total of 27 in the March and November elections of 1996. The high level of referenda and initiatives continued in 2000–2010, with an average of 19 ballot initiatives in national election years. Although California is the champion in the use of this direct democracy device, other high-use states (Oregon, Washington) have also accelerated their use of the initiative, whereas states that have rarely used it in the past (South Dakota, Utah) are more recently voting on such measures more often (Magleby, 1994: 232). Beyond the rise of statewide initiatives are proliferating municipal and county initiatives.

The spirit of direct or populist democracy is also evident in the U.S. lead in the sheer number of elections – one result of its extreme decentralized federalism. Ballots are as abundant as berries. Ivor Crewe (1981: 232) describes this American peculiarity:

No country can approach the United States in the frequency and variety of elections and thus the amount of electoral participation to which its citizens have a right. No other country elects its lower house as often as every two years, or its president as frequently as every four years. No other country popularly elects its state governors and town mayors; no other has as wide a variety of nonrepresentative offices (judges, sheriffs, attorneys general, city treasurers, and so on) subject to election.

In addition, U.S. voters choose thousands of officials of school districts, water districts, tax districts, transportation districts, sanitation districts, and more. In referenda and initiatives in the United States a single ballot typically includes multiple and disparate issues.

Does direct democracy create new channels for participation by the people? California is the scene of an entire industry devoted to qualifying initiatives on the ballot and selling them. Interest groups hire firms of specialized consultants who pay signature collectors $1.00 to several dollars a signature to reach the qualifying number. Advertising budgets on many issues are huge; the money is both raised and spent mainly in mass media buys and computerized mailing blitzes. Voters rely heavily on political ads to make up their minds on initiatives; they display great volatility in their vote intentions (Magleby, 1994: 249), which suggests both confusion and vulnerability to manipulation. That money talks is demonstrated by the pattern of winning and losing initiatives. Three careful studies converge in the conclusion that there is at least a modest impact of big one-sided spending in passing initiatives and an overwhelming impact of big one-sided spending in defeating initiatives (Owens and Wade, 1986; Magleby,

1994; Banducci, 1998).[1] The ballots themselves and the explanatory material accompanying the ballot require a high level of reading comprehension (one California study claimed that a graduate degree was necessary). The legislature increasingly abdicates its deliberative role and turns over all manner of issues to "the people" in referenda. In fact, since 1978 when it passed Proposition 13, California has been on what Peter Schrag calls "a plebiscitary rampage ... a continuous cycle of reform and political frustration, with initiative after initiative imposing state and local tax limitations, spending limits, term limits, a formula for school spending, three strikes [lifetime imprisonment for third-time offenders, a kind of pension for older criminals way past their prime], and prohibiting public education and other services for illegal immigrants" (1996: 28; 1999; cf. Citrin and Martin, 2009).

Students of California government agree that the net effects have been largely unintended: a shift in power from local government to a state government paralyzed by uncoordinated restrictions on its taxing and spending powers and its staffing; lengthy gridlock on annual state budgets (California is the only state that requires a two-thirds majority for passage of a budget, another triumph of the initiative); growing inequities in property taxes; excessive dependence on bond issues; an increasing difficulty for voters to comprehend the system and hold anyone accountable for the deterioration of services and the physical infrastructure; and a rise of populist demagoguery of every kind. Despite the obvious attractions of direct democracy, where it is most fully developed its practical results are frequent elections, voter disaffection and confusion, voter fatigue, and, finally, low and declining turnout, and party decline. Unless there are strong countervailing sources of consensus as there are in Switzerland, direct democracy also produces government paralysis.[2]

Thus, California has become the clearest case of the destruction of representative and deliberative government. Once a leader in education, in the quality of its civil service, in the efficiency and staffing of its legislature, it now ranks below average or toward the bottom of these indicators. "The People" have stripped their government of its main functions – taxing, spending, making and implementing public policies, public regulation of private interests.

I dwell on California as a way to highlight the dangers of ersatz democracy in the name of the people's right to know or the people's participation in government. The interaction of the domination of the media, money, and the narrowest of interest groups has undermined representative democracy and meaningful citizen participation. Must the obvious be said? The main functions of government in a modern democracy can be carried out only with elected officials in deliberations of committees, testimony from groups affected by laws and executive orders, along with indispensable expert testimony from inside and outside government.

A word about the popular notion that the new information technology has provided new channels for social and political participation and even party revitalization. If we take the Internet as the epitome of the new possibilities, not much is known about who participates in what chat rooms, message boards, or newsgroups on the Internet with what effect on politics or culture. The hope of the revitalization of "community" and civic engagement, however, appears to be an illusion. There is the nontrivial matter of the unequal distribution of income, motivation, and the quality of education necessary to use the new technology, a barrier to mass use that is likely to persist for a long time.

That the digital divide is not only long-standing but remains steady is shown by analysis of an August 2008 national survey (Schlozman et al., 2010). Even when only the subset of the population with Internet access is examined, such acts as "contributing to candidates, contacting officials, signing a political petition, or communicating with political groups are as stratified socio-economically when done on the Web as when done offline" (p. 487). As for age and politics, the young may be Web savvy but, as always, they are not nearly as politically active as the rest of the age grades.

But suppose everyone goes down the Information Highway. If the Internet users can narrowly tailor the information they receive and confine their cyber-space "conversations" only to those who share their interests and beliefs, it is hard to see how they can connect with the larger community and society. An already fragmented and decentralized political economy can with Internet use become still more balkanized. Further, if the issue is overcoming tendencies toward political polarization, it is unlikely that a medium without even the porous gatekeepers of print and broadcast media can restore civility in political discourse or promote accommodation of clashing interests and values. As David Shaw (1997) suggests, the Internet provides worldwide access to fringe groups who otherwise would reach only tiny audiences or be constrained in their invective; such groups can now make a larger public still more vulnerable to rumor, nonsense, and scandal mongering.

Or if the problem is party decline, none of this would seem to reverse that trend. In fact, a study of U.S. Senate campaigning on the Web suggests that it will further strengthen the already well-developed trend toward individualized campaigns. The party affiliation of candidates is seldom mentioned on their Web sites and sometimes is not mentioned at all. Candidate "issue platforms" are highly individualized (Klotz, 1997). Although there may be some gain in a more positive spin and a more equal playing field than that provided by media ads, the likely net effect is a further erosion of political parties. This is another reminder that we cannot rely on any technological fix for the revitalization of political participation and deliberative democracy.

## B. CAN THE TWO MAJOR PARTIES BE REVITALIZED FOR GOVERNING?

Should any political party attempt to abolish social security, unemployment insurance, and eliminate labor laws and farm programs, you would not hear of that party again in our political history. There is a tiny splinter group, of course, that believes you can do these things. ... Their number is negligible and they are stupid. Dwight D. Eisenhower (letters, 1954)

The Republican Party has been in ascendance since Goldwater's invention and Reagan's implementation of the southern strategy. Add the grass-roots Christian Right takeover of much of the local Republican machinery not only in the South but in large parts of the Midwest and Mountain states, and you can understand why polarization is almost entirely a Republican success in moving the political spectrum to the right (cf. Hacker and Pierson, 2005).[3] That one-sided redefinition of "conservative" applies not so much to the social-moral issues as to the free-market, private-property, minimum-government agenda. We can see this in the rise of Blue Dog Democrats and the defensive posture of the rest of the Democrats as they echo some of the slogans of the radical Right about tax cuts, deficit and debt threats, and reining in runaway "entitlements." What used to be a mainstream Democratic agenda is now the "left," "conservative" is now called "moderate," and "radical Right" or the "hard Right" has metamorphosed into "conservative" – a vast confusion of language, having little to do with the political spectrum or the policies composing it. Since when has Social Security or unemployment compensation or the minimum wage become left or radical?

In this situation, it is difficult to see any "moderation" taking hold in the Republican Party. Moderate Republicans in Congress have retired early in frustration or exhaustion, been defeated in primaries or in reelection races, or refused to run. Using the definition of conservative to liberal on the seven-point scale of the National Election Study, Alan Abramowitz (2010: table 1) found that "moderates" in the Republican Party numbered 41 in the 91st 1969–1970 Senate; there were only 5 left in the 2009–2010 111th Senate, while strong liberals and conservatives more than doubled – from 22 to 49. Meanwhile, the electorate was increasingly volatile in its party attachments. For instance, party loyalty and voting the straight party ticket in U.S. Senate elections declined sharply from the 1950s to the 1970s, then climbed sharply from the 1980s to 2009 (ibid., fig. 4). The popular label for this recent trend both in the electorate and in government is "polarization."[4] I prefer another label, "party discipline." Democracy cannot flourish without political parties competing for power, each representing real differences in values and interests. The problem to be solved is not polarization of either parties-in-government or parties-in-the-electorate, but the decline in the representativeness of both parties so their shift to the right has become increasingly at odds with voter preferences, and their governance increasingly paralyzed or ineffective. It is *that* trend that accounts for the failure to confront the problems that beset the United States (Chapter 7) and the consequent mass disaffection.

## C. POLICY AND POLITICS

### 1. The Idea of Policy Paralysis

All rich democracies must cope with similar social and economic problems. Many students of American politics suggest that the United States is paralyzed in dealing effectively with those problems. They often list their favorite policies and call it paralysis when these are not enacted. A more precise definition is needed. Clearly where (1) a substantial majority of both masses and elites – political, cultural, and some economic – favor a policy or program, and (2) other countries have acted successfully, and (3) there is no action in the United States for long periods, say 25 to 50 years, we can call it paralysis. Examples that approximate this idea include national health insurance, effective gun control (domestic disarmament), family policy (including child care and long-term care for the frail elderly), serious investment in wide access to preschools of acceptable quality and in raising standards for K–12, and policies to reduce violence in the media and to increase party and candidate access to the media in election campaigns.

This disjunction between public policy and public opinion as well as elite inclinations is evident in my discussions on the welfare state, tax-welfare backlash, and pensions and health care in Chapters 1, 4, and 5 (cf. Fiorina, 2009; Fiorina and Levendusky, 2006). I believe that there is an agenda around which a political coalition could be built to reduce paralysis. But to identify it we must first cut through the abuse of language reflected in media diffusion of slogans about "moderation" or "centrist politics." Then we must ask, What potential progressive coalition could be created and persist long enough to break deadlocks on these issues, where in the political spectrum does it lie, and what election reforms and results are required?

## 2. The Myth of Moderation, the Independent Voter, and the Rightward Shift: Why Old Issues Are Good Issues

In the mandate mongering that follows every election, the media pundits of the 1990s told us that the victories of the Republican Right (e.g., in 1994) signified the electorate's dislike of "big government" and that the elections of Bill Clinton, Tony Blair, and Barack Obama were the triumph of centrist politics, by which they meant "fiscal responsibility," "balanced budgets," and "control over entitlements," as well as the neutralization of right-wing claims that Democrats in the United States and Labourites in the United Kingdom were soft on crime and welfare cheats. These claims have been echoed in the 2000s. Joined by many academics, the pundits now see a major shift toward the "vital center" (what Europeans call the Third Way and what left critics call the "dead center"). According to this vision of voters' motives, the Clinton-Blair victories, and now the Obama victory were possible because "New Democrats" and "New Labour" appealed to moderate, affluent voters searching for financially prudent government that would be more market friendly.

There is some truth to the claim that many voters were attracted to the left articulation of values of work and family security; this tapped into widely shared sentiments (including the idea that government must ensure public safety) – sentiments that are long-standing and more universal than "moderate." But this vision of centrism misses both the social composition of the center-left vote and the themes that, in fact, appealed to Clinton-Blair voters. In both countries, victory was based on the return of the middle mass – the Reagan Democrats, the Tory lower-middle and working-class voters – and the candidates' pledges about jobs, education, medical care, and tax fairness. These are rather old populist-left concerns. The only pollster who served both Clinton and Blair, Stanley Greenberg (1997), is adamant that the main reason voters gave for voting for Clinton in 1996 was his defense of Medicare, Social Security, and expansion of educational opportunity. In 1992 it was Clinton's pledge to create eight million jobs, expand public investment, and guarantee health-insurance coverage for everyone. Equally important he promised to raise taxes on the wealthy, move people from welfare to work, and get tough on crime. Similarly, the Blair voters in 1997 wanted "a government that would slow privatization and diminish inequality" (p. 44), while it saved the National Health Service (Blair promised to increase NHS spending each year, to cut the waiting list, to increase the number of nurses, and to abolish Thatcher's "internal market" for health care). British voters also responded to Labour's pledge to increase the percentage of GDP going to education, shift state subsidies from private to public schools, institute a minimum wage, stop the privatization of pensions, sign the European Social Charter, and tax excess profits of utilities to finance 250,000 government-created jobs for the long-term unemployed. In the 1990s, Greenberg concludes, "both countries voted for reformed center-left parties that would fight the extension of Reaganism and Thatcherism and that would strive to make government work for ordinary citizens" (p. 44). Data in Chapters 4 and 5 on welfare-state retrenchment and backlash show that issue-specific mass opinion everywhere continues overwhelmingly to favor the core programs of the welfare state. And, when pollsters offer questions that connect program support with willingness to raise taxes to pay for favored programs, the support remains strong – in the United Kingdom, steadily increasing in the sixteen years leading up to Blair's huge victory (Wilensky, 2002: table 10.1). More significant is the fierce mass resistance to government efforts to cut universalistic social programs in all countries, evident throughout this book.

In short, nothing in the voting and opinion record of the 1990s and 2000s in these two presumably most free-marketeer democracies shows a shift toward the centrist politics of media invention, let alone a shift to the right. The 2010 ascendance of Tories matches the rise of Thatcher; in both cases a substantial majority of voters voted against the Conservative Party, and minority-party government was a product of the Westminster electoral system of first-past-the-post, winner-take-all (Chapter 3).

Related to the myth of the rightward shift is the Myth of the "Independent" Voter. For many elections the Gallup Poll has asserted that upward of 30 percent, even 40 percent of Americans are self-described "independents." Ray Wolfinger and his colleagues, however, show that real independent voters remain roughly stable at 1 in 12 or 1 in 10 voters since 1950. If we measure independence not by self-identification in one question ("I think of myself not as a Democrat or Republican but as an independent") but follow up with "Do you think of yourself as closer to the Republican or Democratic Party?" we find that about two-thirds of the respondents who initially called themselves "independent" say they are closer to one or another party and overwhelmingly vote that way. This percentage remained roughly stable for half a century. For recent elections (1980–2010) and the same conclusion for both California, supposedly the epitome of the rise of the independent voter, and for the nation, see Lascher and Korey (2011); they also confirm the recurrent finding that the pure independents, 1 in 10 of the electorate, are most ignorant about politics and are least likely to vote.[5]

In the sense that large majorities of voters reject extremes of the sectarian Right and Left, "centrist" politics is here to stay. But beyond that vague idea is a host of mass preferences, voting patterns, and party appeals that point to a left-of-center majority in the United States, as elsewhere. That these lessons of the 1990s hold for 2002–2008 is clear from this entire book.

This leads me to Table 11 as my reason for spending the rest of this chapter on the question of the revitalization of the Democratic Party and the prospects for a center-left agenda. In my judgment, for 10 or 20 years ahead the hope of a resurgence of moderates in the Republican Party resembling those of the 1950s, 1960s, and early 1970s – the Nelson Rockefellers, the Everett Dirksens, the Howard Bakers, the William Brocks, the Charles Percys, the Bob Doles, and the Mark Hatfields – is a fantasy. To buy the theme of moderate resurgence, you have to believe that the Christian Right and the Palin-type celebrity demagogues share so little with the more educated and well-off business and professional political activists that a final split is imminent and that in an all-out fight the moderates would take over the Republican Party. You would also have to believe that ascendant moderates would abandon wedge issues that have been so impor-tant in close Republican victories since Reagan that they would give up the antitax, antispend, antibureaucratic rhetoric that, when combined with racial and nativist appeals, has brought them so many white middle-mass defectors from the Democrats (Chapter 4). Shall we say possible but highly improbable?

Table 11 shows several measures of the economic and noneconomic well-being of the population under Democratic vs. Republican presidents from Truman through George W. Bush. The conclusion is inescapable: on average and for well over half a century, Democratic rule has been better, in some areas far better, than Republican rule. Specifically, and including findings from other studies of party differences, here are the highlights (The period lengths are not arbitrary; they are limited only by data availability):

- For 1947–2005, compared to Republicans, *family income growth* under Democratic administrations was six times as large for the lowest fifth of the income distribution (poor or near poor). For the middle two-fifths differences are three times larger, and for the 60th percentile (the near-upper-middle income bracket) more than twice as large. Finally, income growth for upper-middle income families (80th percentile) is 70 percent larger. Even income growth among the rich (95th percentile) is 12 percent larger under Democratic admin-istrations (Bartels, 2008: 32, table 2.1). As always, the super rich, the top 1

TABLE 11. *Differences in Economic, Social, and Political Performance under Democrats and Republicans, 1946–2010*

| Indicators | Years | | Democratic President (total n = 28) | Republican President (total n = 36) |
|---|---|---|---|---|
| Economic | 1946–2009 | DJIA average growth | 8.8% | 6.8% |
| | 1946–2009 | Federal deficit as % of GDP | 1.2% | 2.2% |
| | 1948–2009 | Unemployment | 5.3% | 5.9% |
| | 1946–2009 | Real annual GDP growth | 3.3% | 2.8% |
| | 1946–2009 | Inflation | 4.4% | 3.7% |
| | 1960–2009 | Average annual balance of payments/ exports, % | −6.2% | −21.9% |
| Social | 1959–2008 | Family poverty rate average annual change | −0.5% | 0.1% |
| | 1947–2008 | Family income inequality (top 20%/ bottom 20%) | 9.1 | 9.2 |
| | 1960–2008 | Violent crimes/1,000 pop. | 4.4 | 5.1 |
| | | Income growth by percentile | | |
| | 1948–2005 | 20th percentile | 2.7 | 0.4 |
| | 1948–2005 | 60th percentile | 2.5 | 1.1 |
| | 1948–2005 | 95th percentile | 2.1 | 1.9 |
| | 1979–2005 | Average 10-year change in real minimum wage | −$0.30 | −$1.30 |
| | 1979–2005 | Unionization average annual change | −0.4% | −0.5% |
| Political | 1969–2010 | Senate filibusters | Democratic minority: Hold steady | Republican minority: Big steps up |
| | 1991–2010 | Average earmarks ("pork") per fiscal year, $billions | Democratic Congress: 10.4 | Republican Congress: 18.6 |

*Note*: For sources, definitions, and statistical significance, see Appendix.

percent or .01 percent as Chapter 7 suggests, do extremely well no matter who is in power.

• *Post-tax household real income growth* for a more recent period, 1980–2003, presents a similar picture of superior Democratic performance. Larry Bartels (2008: 56–57 and table 2.4) finds that households at every income level did about equally well under Carter and Clinton – growth rates between 1.4 and

1.6 percent. In contrast, Republican administrations brought weaker growth in the upper half of the income distribution and no growth at all for the bottom half. Or if we consider a slightly different measure and add a few years, we find the same: the average annual growth of *post-transfer* and post-tax income for the bottom two-thirds or so of households, 1979–2005, clearly fared better under Democrats than Republicans (Kenworthy, 2010: 104).

- In both pretax and after-tax household income growth, the *major gains or losses occurred in the second year of each presidential cycle*, the product of policies adopted during the first year's "honeymoon" period just after each election or reelection (Bartels, 2008: 52–53, table 2.6).
- *Macroeconomic performance in both Table 11 and Bartels's detailed analysis (2008)* shows that for the entire postwar period Democrats, compared to Republicans, did better for the stock market, kept federal deficits lower, unemployment lower, real GDP growth higher, and the balance of payments closer to even (adjusting for size in total trade). The only economic indicator on which Republicans performed better was a slight edge in controlling inflation (3.7% vs. Democrats' 4.4%).

  Using a long period that is a few years shorter than our Table 11, Bartels found that from 1948 to 2005 under Republican rule unemployment was higher, growth was lower, and inflation almost the same (pp. 48–49). Specifically, unemployment over the whole period has been almost 30 percent higher under Republican presidents while the average rate of real per capita GNP growth was more than 40 percent lower. Republican inflation hawks cannot claim to outperform the Democrats; the average inflation rate has been virtually identical, although some statistical techniques that Bartels applies show a very small Republican edge in controlling inflation. Most important, Bartels presents strong evidence (table 2.5) that these partisan differences in unemployment and growth remain robust even after taking account of differences in specific economic circumstances and general historical trends such as oil prices and labor-force participation. It is partisan differences in economic, social, and labor policies that count.

- *Republican deficit hawks talk a good game but fail the test of performance.* In power, they run up federal deficits much more than Democrats (Table 11).
- *Partisan differences in the fate of the poor and near-poor.* Table 11 shows that *Democrats do much better in reducing the official poverty rate.* From 1959 to 2008 under Democratic presidents family poverty went down an average of half a percentage point per year; under Republicans poverty climbed 0.1 percent per year. Specifically, if we exclude the first year of presidential tenure to give changes in policy a chance to take effect, the best performance goes to Johnson (–1.3% a year reduction in poverty) and Clinton (–0.5% reduction); the worst goes to G. H. W. Bush (0.5% increase in poverty) and G. W. Bush (0.2% increase). Nixon was the only Republican who reduced poverty slightly (–0.2%). Carter was the only Democrat who presided over increased poverty (0.2% per year), largely because of the worst oil shock of the postwar period (see Chapter 1, Table 3).

Similarly Bartels's analysis of annual real post-tax income growth for households at the 20th percentile of income distribution (poor and near poor) for the shorter period 1981–2003 is consistent with Table 11. He measured partisan control from one year following inauguration (leaving time for policy to take effect) to one year following a subsequent inauguration (what a president's performance leaves to the successor). Bartels also held constant economic events that are beyond presidential control in the short run (oil shocks, labor force participation). The result: Democratic presidents bring higher average income growth across the board and substantially higher growth for the poor and people of modest means (2008: table 2.8).

- *Other social indicators* in Table 11 show an edge for the Democrats in controlling violent crime and preserving a real minimum wage. Violent crimes per 1,000 population for 1960–2008 are higher under Republican presidents (5.1) than Democratic presidents (4.4). This finding is consistent with Chapter 7's account of the causes of homicide rates, poverty, and inequality among them, where Democrats do better in reducing both.

  Related to the plight of the working poor are partisan differences in the minimum wage. Although the inflation-adjusted value of the minimum wage has plunged since its peak in 1968, Democratic rule has slowed the decline to a small 10-year average of -$0.30, whereas the same figure under Republican presidents was near four times that loss, -$1.10. And this leaves aside the question of possible differences in the enforcement of minimum wage laws (see Chapter 7). Although union decline has been steady across both Republican and Democratic administrations, it has declined more slowly under Democratic presidents than under Republicans.

- *Political indicators* in Table 11 affirm the Republican penchant for paralysis of government and the Democratic desire to govern. There are very strong differences in the recent history of Senate filibusters use and in related rules for paralysis. From 1987 to 2010 the record shows sharp upswings in Republican use of filibusters when Democrats control the Senate. When Democrats are in the minority they adopt the new level but do not step it up. That pattern of Republican minorities notching it up briskly and Democratic minorities leveling off is consistent. The record was reached in 2007–2008 when with Democrats in control Republicans used what Sinclair calls "extended debate-related problems" – procedural abuses, filibusters, threats to filibuster, and holds – on 70 percent of major legislation. There were more filibusters by Republicans in the Clinton years than in the entire history of the Senate. Yes, it is used by both parties – one reason it is hard to get rid of. But it is used more sparingly by the party that believes in government and governing than it is by the party that hates government and would like to cut it down to where is was before the New Deal.

- Earmarks ("pork") are a very small portion of federal budgets and in most cases are perfectly reasonable investments in education, culture, or the physical infrastructure. But because the Republicans use them as bludgeons against Democrats, Table 11 includes them. It shows that Republican-controlled

Congresses have averaged nearly twice as many billions of dollars in "pork" as Democratic-controlled Congresses.

In sum, in absolute numbers, the score in Table 11 favors Democrats 14 to 1. Using a *t*-test for differences in means, the Democrats win 8 to 0. Democrats outperformed their Republican counterparts with statistically significant differences for federal deficits, unemployment, balance of payments, reduction of family poverty, income growth for the 20th and 60th percentiles, reduction of violent crimes, and controlling pork spending. For no indicator did the Republicans outclass the Democrats in this test of significance.

Plainly, in view of decades of poor performance of the Republican Party and the decimation of any possible center-right coalition, the United States cannot rely on a revival of moderate Republicans to achieve the most widely shared goals of a center-left agenda. Instead, I turn to the question of the revitalization of the Democratic Party and a coalition that could begin to get the country off the low road.

## D. THE SOCIAL COMPOSITION OF A WINNING CENTER-LEFT COALITION, PAST AND PRESENT

The social and economic composition of the 2006 victorious Democratic vote compared to the 2002 vote reads like the coalition put together by Lyndon Johnson in the tradition of FDR.[6] (The 2008 election was about the same, with the much celebrated turnout of the young and notable differences among white defectors.)[7]

- *The labor vote* (union member or member in household were about a quarter of the total 1996 vote): 72 percent of members with another member in the household voted Democratic; 68 percent of union members and 58 percent of nonmembers with someone else who was a union member voted Democratic. Union households scored an 18 percent point edge over non-union households. As one of the last practitioners of retail politics, labor remains the pragmatic core of the center-left coalition. Even with its declining membership base, the American labor movement in many recent elections has offset the decline in Democratic Party loyalty by its vigorous field work, doing the job political machines once did; the labor vote, a crucial part of FDR's coalition, is still alive. To say that union members are only 16 million (not a trivial figure in itself) is not only to overlook this recent record of voter education and mobilization but to ignore the network effect. Union members have families; union contracts cover another million and a half nonmembers; union leaders are coalition players. Union political influence is not only stable, organized, and concentrated in strategic states; it goes beyond the number of members.

  This performance was repeated in 2008: Obama beat McCain by 18 percentage points among white males who belonged to unions while losing among white, male, non-union members by 16 points.

- *The middle mass* (see Chapter 5). About 52 percent of the 2006 total vote, high-school graduates and part-college voters, gave Democrats 59 to 40 percent for Republicans, a 9 percent point gain over 2002. This part of the old coalition returns to Democrats when they accent jobs and job security, the protection of the universalistic welfare state (national health insurance, guaranteed pensions, disability insurance), crime control, tax fairness, education, and family policies. These issues can offset racist and nativist appeals, as they did in 2006. The media labeled this "left" or "economic populism," but it is no more than a traditional Democratic agenda reflecting majority preferences. Because union membership is concentrated among these voters, their bread-and-butter appeals effectively offset divisive wedge issues, including race.[8]

  Incidentally, in 2006 college graduates split about 50–50 (an 8% gain for Democrats) and, as usual, holders of professional and graduate degrees gave Democrats a large lead – 59 to 40 percent, an 11 percentage point gain over 2002. In the 2008 primaries and especially low-turnout caucuses, Obama did very well among the highly educated. But the main message from 2006 is the return of defecting Democrats in the more numerous middle mass. And the main message of the 2008 election is that enough whites among them defected again to make the election closer than it should have been (Lewis-Beck, Tien, and Nadeau, 2010). He won 43 percent of the white votes, less than any other victorious Democratic president.

- *Women, including single women and single mothers.* Everywhere women, who are a now a majority of the electorate, are attracted to center-left parties that support family policies, educational reform, expanded health care, active labor-market policies, and environmental protection, and avoid government intrusion into their private decisions about birth and abortion. The development of the gender gap and the image of homogeneous affluent suburbs account for the myth of moderation as applied to women. "Soccer moms" are a small minority of women voters; suburbs or exurbs come in many shapes at every level of education and income. There have long been black suburbs, ethnic suburbs, young singles suburbs, married-with-children suburbs, working-class suburbs, upper-middle affluent suburbs, retirement suburbs – the label obscures everything important in politics. It is nonaffluent women trying to balance work and family who respond most to progressive politics – wherever they live. White women, many of whom defected from the Democrats in 2004 (fear of terrorism was one reason), voted Democratic 56 percent in 2006; white males voted Republican 53 percent, although both men and women gave Democrats substantial gains over 2002. Single men and women, *a third of the total vote in 2006*, broke 3 to 2 for Democrats and Democrats ignore such issues at their peril.

- *Public-sector employees* who, for obvious reasons, favor an activist government. Women and minorities are prominent among them.

- *Sophisticated business leaders*, especially those in export industries or high-tech firms who strongly support government-imposed education standards, government support for research and development and infrastructure investment, and who often favor family policies and active labor-market policies. Many would be glad to have the government take over the burden of financing health care. While not numerous, they help to neutralize strident business opposition to center-left causes. More generally, graduate-degree holders disproportionately vote center-left.

- *Racial-ethnic-linguistic-religious minorities and immigrants.* In 2006, 9 in 10 self-identified blacks and Jews, 7 in 10 Hispanics/Latinos, and more than 6 in 10 Asians voted Democratic; in 2008 they gave Democrats similar leads. All except blacks represented substantial gains since 2002. In congressional races where Republicans ran on illegal immigration, they failed. Among the notable defeats of migrant-bashing Republican incumbents in 2006 were J. D. Hayworth (white suburb of Phoenix) and Randy Graf (southern Arizona district where Minutemen patrol the desert). Hispanics are the fastest growing part of the electorate in Arizona, Nevada, Colorado, New Mexico, Texas, and California. In the primary/caucus season Obama won only one of the six – Colorado. The same undertow of race was evident in the Latino rejection of Obama. In these states Hilary Clinton was able to sound populist economic themes convincingly, but they returned in November.

Regarding religion, although Democrats in 2006 piled up big margins among voters who are least-active attenders at religious services (those who say "never," 67% Democratic; a few times a year, 60%; a few times a month, 58%), they also made inroads among the most observant and held their own among Catholics (55% voted Democratic, same as 2002). And, most remarkably, they got almost a third of the "white Evangelical/born-again Christian" voters (in these exit polls, they were a quarter of the total vote, about the same as the labor vote). More detailed examination of the successful congressional challengers once again suggests that for a growing minority of Evangelicals, economic populism and Republican corruption helped to overcome Republican wedge issues so popular among the Christian right.

Obama can easily get the usual 9 in 10 of black voters in 2012. Much more important, he must hold the white middle-majority voters who returned to the Democrats in 2006 and defected in substantial numbers in 2008, while he mobilizes Latino voters and offsets Republican immigrant bashing and underground race baiting. But he cannot do this with soaring rhetoric about bringing people together while he attacks "Washington," reinforcing Republican ideas that government is the problem. Nor can he succeed if he ignores or obscures the winning center-left issues.

There is plenty of evidence in surveys of voting behavior and political orientation that the six groupings constitute a large majority of voters and respond to a center-left agenda. They constitute a stable Democratic winning coalition if Democrats, when in power, act on issues that hold them.

As Chapter 4 shows, the past 50 years of national/attitude surveys among our rich democracies, coupled with the defeat of politicians who appear to be serious about cutting back or reforming the core programs of the welfare state, contradict the idea that we are in a new society with new values and the Democrats must radically change to win again. There is more continuity than meets the eye. The southern ascendancy of the Republican radical Right may be only as old as Goldwater/Reagan, but the issues that remain important to modern voters are as old as the New Deal. Even today's successful environmental movements had their counterparts in the time of Teddy Roosevelt, Gifford Pinchot, and John Muir.

Findings about the basic difference between abstract ideology and issue-specific opinion in surveys reviewed both in the United States and abroad show that, when confronted with abstract survey questions, vast majorities of voters in the United States are ambivalent and contradictory in their values and beliefs about the proper role of government. Despite this ambivalence, surveys consistently show that a majority of voters have progovernment intervention, pro-welfare-state sentiments.

The second pattern of results goes beyond abstract ideology to *issue-specific opinion* about taxes, spending, and particular policies constituting the welfare state. Here there is no confusion and little ambivalence. The structure of public opinion has remained remarkably stable since World War II both in the United States and in affluent democracies with sharply contrasting cultures and politics. The rank order of enthusiasm is steady: wild about government-guaranteed pensions, disability insurance, and related programs; almost as overwhelmingly supportive of national health insurance; a majority increasingly enthusiastic about family policies, including parental leave, publicly subsidized child care, before- and after-school leisure centers, and preschool education. Active labor market policies (Chapter 7) draw majority support. Go beyond these most expensive and popular policies and you encounter serious reservations about passive unemployment compensation and downright hostility to means-tested public assistance (American "welfare").

Everyone knows the results of just a little probing in focus groups: "I want the government off my back; I don't want the government messing around with my Medicare." Again, do not conflate ideological slogans learned from last night's "news" broadcast with serious issue-specific opinions. When you read pollsters' claims that Americans have shifted to the Republican agenda or have become "moderate" because they are individualistic and want a less active government, remember that it is typically media-filtered "information" that is fed back to pollsters as public opinion.

When before elections and in exit polls pollsters spend enough time and ask specific questions to at least an approximation to probability samples, they uncover the same pattern – the resonance of center-left issues. In 2006: "In your vote for the U.S. House how important was [issue]?" [Extremely, very, somewhat, not at all important], bread-and-butter issues in 2006 rose to the top along with Iraq and they were more unequivocally helpful to the Democrats than Iraq. Accenting the economy, jobs, and health care were critical to Democratic success.

More important, Senate campaigns of Democratic winners were effective not only in their attacks on Bush's Middle East catastrophe but were heavy with aggressive articulation of left-of-center themes: protect Social Security and

Medicare, move toward universal health coverage, increase the minimum wage, restore the right to organize. They treated increasing inequality and our high rate of poverty as moral scandals. Combat veteran Jim Webb (Virginia) ran on these issues, going far beyond his attack on Bush's war. In case anyone missed his passionate convictions about economic fairness and social justice, he wrote an op-ed piece in the *Wall Street Journal* just after his victory repeating his theme that the rich are getting richer while the well-being of the middle erodes and poverty increases. Organic farmer/environmentalist John Tester (Montana), who got into politics opposing the deregulation and privatization of electric utilities, as well as Sherrod Brown (Ohio) and Bob Casey (Pennsylvania), sounded the same alarms. These candidates were typical of Democratic winners in both Senate and House races in every region. Almost all played down wedge issues of abortion and gay marriage in favor of unifying themes, the old Democratic Party agenda.[9]

The lessons from recent elections and survey analysis is that where Democrats spend their energies and money on bread-and-butter issues, where they avoid burning themselves out fighting the culture war and quit searching for a middle mushy ground to accommodate current Republican leadership ("bipartisanship"), they win. Meanwhile, Democrats can try three short sound bites that resonate with the center-left majority coalition and can turn a squeaker into a rout: "Medicare for Everyone," "Work Should Pay," and "Make College Education Affordable." In elections ahead, spell them out credibly and repeat them several times a day.

## E. POLICY IMPLICATIONS: A CENTER-LEFT AGENDA

It is highly unlikely that the United States will in the near future cut new channels for centralized bargaining that facilitate the adoption and implementation of public policies widely supported by mass publics and most elites. It lacks the structural and ideological sources of corporatism discussed in this book. The United States is not about to adopt a modified form of proportional representation, create mass-based Catholic or left political parties, or launch a serious left challenge to the two major parties, abandon its decentralized federalism, or transform its numerous, narrowly focused interest groups – labor, industry, commerce, and professions – into a more coherent, inclusive, and centralized system of representation. In the absence of such consensus-making machinery, what shifts in structure are possible? What public policies can realistically be adopted under what political conditions? How can political deadlock be reduced?

There are some modifications of law and structure that might reduce the disjunction between stable popular demands and policy responses. Three of these would require major shifts in the political landscape: national health insurance, labor law reform, and improvements in the representative and deliberative aspects of American democracy. Such policy changes would require a rejuvenated Democratic Party, maybe a little revival of "moderate" Republicans in Congress (most likely through a rebellion against Christian Right dominance), a substantial Democratic majority in the Senate – perhaps not the two-to-one margin President Johnson had when Medicare and Medicaid became law but something like the margin of the 2009–2010 Senate – and a strong activist president with a substantial popular majority of the same party[10] who is committed to a center-left agenda and most important, is passionate about three or four policies that can move America off the low road.

## 1. The Need for White House Leadership

I once thought that presidential character structure, personality, and leadership style were not nearly as crucial for governing as the party coalitions that elected the president, the interests represented in Congress and the White House, and changes in the distribution of power in society and polity – a major theme of this book. But I am now a convert to weighing leadership a bit more heavily. By leadership I do not mean emotional vs. cool, or empathic vs. distant (Clinton vs. Obama); I mean strong vs. weak, agenda setting vs. drift, courage and commitment when facing opposition.

Although it is too early to assess the outcomes of President Obama's leadership, here is some speculation based partly on an article I published during the primary campaign (July 15, 2008). When historians go to work on the first year or two of this administration, they are likely to conclude that the outcome can be partially explained by a flawed strategy of the White House interacting with obstacles in government structure. The components of that strategy include a mistaken notion expressed in the campaign and repeatedly acted upon in 2009–2010 that cultivating Republicans to create a bipartisan coalition for change was the first priority. It was a sustained exercise in futility. The second component was to embrace the myth of moderation and the related myths of the independent voter and a swing to the right among the electorate (see Chapters 4 and 8). Believing these three myths ensured a conservative approach that would avoid major confrontation with the most powerful lobbies in Washington: the medical-industrial complex, Wall Street and the financial lobby, and the fossil fuels lobbies. The third component was that Obama's governing was not much different from Obama's winning election campaign – convey a unifying theme, making sometimes-eloquent speeches devoid of clear and consistent commitment to issues or party. The consequence of this belief was a passive style of leadership where the president remains aloof from the down-and-dirty job of forging congressional majorities for a legislative agenda and instead says, "You guys (gals) do it" – meaning 100 senators and 435 members of the House – while his verbal output reflects ambiguity about where he stands. The fourth was a misreading of polls and political consultants' instant analysis that has plagued isolated White House culture for many years but which seems to have dominated the daily tactics of this administration more than others.

A reading of the domestic policy record of more successful modern presidents such as Teddy Roosevelt, FDR, Johnson, even Reagan, Kennedy, and Clinton, suggests instead the need to stand for something, lead on issues, use the bully pulpit, fight hard, cajole, persuade, manipulate and threaten allies and potential allies – or forfeit all chance of success. A thorough, systematic study of the presidential impact on key votes and new laws from Eisenhower to Bush, 1953–2004 (Beckmann, 2010), shows the sequence of success. Presidents maximize impact when they vigorously exploit early-game agenda setting and end-game vote lobbying. Both are necessary to increase their odds of success. The picture is one of sustained and consistent White House action, beginning with clear policy aims.

A president cannot project weakness by reaching out and singing Kumbaya with his enemies, let alone by holding lengthy graduate seminars on TV with them. Reinforcing this belief in the magic of reaching out was a penchant for perpetual preemptive compromises in the legislative process. For example, during the early fight for a robust public alternative to commercial-provider dominance of health care, Obama repeated in one short paragraph that he favors a public option but is open to alternatives and that there are many good ideas that should be considered, that he draws no lines in the sand. If a president does this often enough, the vultures, sensing weakness, will close in, and his party and core voters will desert him. This formula for failure has become ever more significant for the first year or two of governing since money, the media, and the dealignment of the electorate became more significant.

Alan Abramowitz (2010: table 7) provides indirect evidence of this "Presidential referendum effect." Voters have increasingly viewed individual House and Senate contests as referenda on the performance of the president and the national parties. For instance, the average correlations between voters' evaluation of the president's job performance and their House and Senate votes over the past four decades have increased markedly. By decades, for the House the correlation went up steadily from .31 in 1972–1980 to .51 in 2002–2008; the Senate even more, from .28 to .57. So, as Obama's job rating plunged in 2010, his capacity to influence Congress will plunge with it, unless one assumes that politicians ignore their constituents. The Wall Street Journal/NBC News poll reported August 11, 2010, that "working class whites" (meaning whites without a college education) who helped the Democrats win big victories in both Houses in 2006 had moved to a Republican majority when asked which party they want to control Congress. The worst news for the Democrats – consistent with my analysis of issue-specific opinion – is that the Democrats suffered large losses among these voters on such traditional Democratic issues as Social Security and the economy. All the more reason for presidents to lead strongly the first year of their tenure.

Weak White House leadership can be seen in the watered down health-care bill (Chapter 5), the similar financial reregulation bill (Chapter 6), the postponement of the energy bill while increasing subsidies for fossil fuels (Chapter 2), and the abandonment of the Employee Free Choice Act. Most important for understanding the extended jobless recovery (Chapter 6) is the meager aid to the states so that their tax increases, budget cutbacks (education, Medicaid, transportation, housing, child care, etc.), and job cuts in public employees (teachers, police, and fire department personnel, laid off or furloughed with benefits and wages reduced) almost entirely offset the positive effects of the federal stimulus package.

## 2. The U.S. Senate: Can the Broken Branch Be Restored?

Any hope of progress in restoring deliberative and more representative democracy and getting off the low road rests with what can be done to repair the "broken branch," Congress, especially the U.S. Senate. We have seen in Chapter 5 that the arcane rules of the Senate are one of the big reasons for the unique failure of the United States to achieve national health insurance. Specifically, how can a center-left coalition change the rules or work the rules and thereby improve the process of governance and restore a modicum of trust in government?

Abstruse Senate rules are embedded in a 1,600-page encyclopedia, "Senate Procedure, Precedents and Practices." Changing these rules or exploiting them not for obstruction but for governing in the public interest is difficult but not impossible. Binder and Smith (1997) note more than three dozen cases where Congress has passed laws requiring the Senate to vote in an expedited manner. My view is that given the current political complexion of the parties, a Democratic majority should make more frequent use of them. Here are the suggestions of an outsider deeply concerned about his government's paralysis. One strategy for achieving majority rule in the Senate is to use two procedures more often – *reconciliation* on taxes and spending (that covers most bills) *and amendments*, germane or not, for which debate cannot be stopped without 60 votes but which under certain circumstances can pass with 51 votes.

Reconciliation is an exception to the supermajority rule in the Senate. If the issue involves the budget, filibusters are out of order. Further, amendments, loosely defined as "germane," can be adopted by majority vote. President George W. Bush used this simple majority for his tax cuts and some social spending cuts (Sinclair, 2008b). And the Democrats, after a year of paralysis, finally used reconciliation to help pass their timid health-care reform in March 2010, tacking on direct student loans that bypassed banks as middlemen, a good thing for everyone but the banks.

A third option gets its name from Article I, Section 5 of the Constitution. This "constitutional option" is based on the commonsense observation that "Each House may determine the Rules of its Proceedings" means what it says. Therefore, any move to stop the Senate from considering its own rules at the beginning of a new Congress would be unconstitutional (Klein, 2010). Thus, the idea that it takes 67 votes to change the rules does not pass Constitutional muster. Determined Democrats with enough unity could change the filibuster rule by 51 votes. From 1953 to 1979 this option was threatened at least 10 times with the result of several compromises between the parties.

Another tactic to reduce paralysis is to start with *Democratic defiance against filibuster threats*. Carefully select a good policy that is likely to resonate among voters. Then tell the Republicans, "Go ahead and talk this bill to death. See if your marathon opposition is popular as you visibly prevent Medicare expansion to 55–64-year-olds from coming to a vote." If such challenges to obstruction are used repeatedly on critical issues drawn from a center-left agenda (where, as Chapter 4 has shown, the majority of voters are), and if the president and congressional leaders fight for clear policies with passion and persistence, these challenges to the filibuster threat have a good chance of succeeding for both policy and politics. This tactic does not preclude a long-range fight to modify the filibuster rules. But it might discourage the routine subversion of the Senate's deliberative functions and traditions.

Around 1970 extended debate-related problems affected 10 percent of major legislation. By the 1980s that figure rose to 27 percent. But after Democrats took control of the Senate and Republicans were in a minority these weapons of paralysis soared to 70 percent (Sinclair, 2008a). The filibuster was (mis)used more times during the eight years of the Clinton administration than in the entire history of the Senate. It became routine as the Republican weapon of choice against the Obama administration. Because of its routine use, the mere *threat* of a filibuster is as effective as an actual filibuster in stopping or watering down big reforms already compromised but passed in the House – for example, climate change, job creation, financial regulation, college aid (all tied up in the Senate after House passage as of January 29, 2010). Even a big Democratic majority in the House can be intimidated by the mere threat of a Senate filibuster: Why stick our necks out, say, on health care, more substantial funding for states in crises, labor-law reform, or serious investment in rapid intercity rail if there is a sure death-by-filibuster in the Senate?

Beyond the filibuster, other weapons of paralysis include the following (Schickler, 2001: 220–224 and citations therein):

- *Postcloture filibusters.* Here obstructionists can exploit a loophole in the Senate rules to force endless roll calls on amendments and procedural motions even after a 60-vote cloture has stopped a filibuster.
- *Hold.* As it evolved from the 1960s, this device of the hold has become a way for a single senator to prevent a bill or an appointment from ever coming up for debate or vote. It became an especially powerful weapon as time pressures and legislative overload on Senate leaders grew and as entrepreneurial Senators who owed little to their party or to the traditions of the Senate emerged.
- *Unanimous consent agreements.* In the absence of 60 votes for cloture, this can result in endless delays if one senator objects to proceeding under rules to which the leaders have agreed. Without strong presidential leadership and clear policy commitments, these rules can spell defeat for any major bills. This was apparent in the handling of the stimulus package of 2009 and in the watering down of health reform and financial reregulation of 2010. A handful of "moderates" remaining in both parties could exert blackmail power as they exacted a big price from the majority party leadership. Remember the three Republicans (one from Pennsylvania and two from Maine) who managed to cut $40 billion in desperately needed state aid out of the stimulus package; or the small minority of representatives and senators who deleted any public option from health care and thereby any bargaining power of government to rein in the medical-industrial complex; or financial reregulation that ended up as a cobweb of financial regulations and agencies easily gamed or evaded by the Wall Street oligarchs.

Many critics of Congress, concerned about partisanship and polarization, find the failure of the House to follow "regular order" – discussion, debate, negotiation, compromise – almost as subversive of democracy as the abuse of Senate rules (Mann and Ornstein, 2006: 170; Green and Burns, 2010). Those of us who see disciplined parties as essential for representative and deliberative democracy note that the vitality of all modern democracies, their legitimacy, their capacity to govern, depends on strong parties that represent real differences in values and interests. They can enact an agenda. We are therefore less worried about the House than the paralyzed Senate.

In the absence of a substantial center-left majority in Congress, without a president passionate about a party agenda, three policy areas where opposition interests and their lobbies are most powerful are likely to remain paralyzed: national health insurance, labor-law reform, and candidate and party access to the media.

## 3. National Health Insurance

Chapter 5's analysis of why the United States remains exceptional in health care and why its nonsystem costs far more and yields far less in real health has covered the ground. The main message for policy is that without a dominant public share of total costs (exceeding 65% or so), without a major assertion of the public interest over the commercial interests of the medical-industrial complex, without a global budget, without something like universal coverage, the game of cost shifting and risk selection will remain the main game in town. The result is increasing costs and a large population with no coverage or, under the reform bill adopted in 2010, an increasing number with inadequate or unstable coverage.

The bill that took so much political energy and more than a year to pass highlights the necessity of presidential leadership. The weak bill reflected a flawed White House strategy interacting with the obstacles of a radically decentralized federalism and Senate rules that from the first were used as rationale for Senate leadership to cave in. White House leadership with Senate leadership would work these rules for governing instead of using them as an overriding excuse to avoid a fight.[11]

The White House strategy played out over two years in this sequence. First Obama made an early campaign pledge not to have a mandate in health-care reform. Someone must have told him that Social Security and Medicare were mandates with compulsory contributions because that promise was after some months dropped. Then when it came time to govern, the White House strategy was to promise efficiency so debt would not explode. Obama and his economic and health-care advisers repeated over and over again that they plan to squeeze a third of a trillion out of Medicare and Medicaid. They attacked Medicare cost increases without comparing private costs for comparable service and coverage (see Figure 4). That scared seniors who, not hearing much about saving Social Security and Medicare in the 2008 election campaign, did not give Obama a November majority anyway and were deserting in droves leading into the congressional election of 2010. These frightened seniors were vulnerable to the GOP-orchestrated "death panel" charges and similar lies. And they vote.

The major flaw in White House strategy was the failure to grasp the models of success not only from all 18 of our sister democracies but from our own experience with Medicare. Instead of a simple expansion of the one large federal program where there is already wide public understanding and strong support as well as an administrative agency ready to go with low administrative costs, the administration went for two models where none of this prevails – Medicaid with its means-tested benefits derived from the British Poor Law of 1834 and the Massachusetts hybrid model with its exploding costs. The Patient Protection and Affordable Care Act of 2010 is a complicated patchwork of subsidies, mandates, regulations, and programs; it assumes that the existing system of employer-based, commercially dominated medical care will remain intact with new regulations to coax savings out of both private and public sectors. It is a bonanza for insurance companies; they stand to gain 30 million new customers with no federal government plan to compete with. It targets Medicare spending by cutting projected payments to hospitals and private insurers that contract with Medicare; it will set limits on the amount of overhead costs (good luck in policing this one for 1,300 insurance companies). It sets up an Independent Payment Advisory Board to recommend reforms to control Medicare spending and save more than $400 billion in projected Medicare costs over the next decade. A tax on "Cadillac plans" will go into effect in 2018. A minority of these are union-negotiated benefits with adequate coverage; most are large non-union employers who voluntarily provide adequate coverage to improve efficiency and reduce turnover and absenteeism. This pending tax is already an incentive for employers to reduce benefits. (For a detailed and balanced account of the possible gains and costs of the Affordable Care Act, see Oberlander and Marmor, 2010, an analysis somewhat more favorable to Obama's approach than mine.)

Most of the potential benefits of this bill do not start for at least three election cycles, 2014 to 2018. Thus, future congresses and presidents will have many opportunities to respond to the medical-industrial complex and its lobbyists and thereby undermine the regulations and increase the population uninsured. In the best of scenarios it is an administrative nightmare. The secretary of Health and Human Services must write thousands of pages of regulations to implement this law, all subject to congressional oversight and attack by the regulated industries and their friends in government (see Chapter 7, sec. 13). The impact of this bill on both the insured and uninsured is impossible to predict; it depends on age, income, employment, type of existing coverage, what state you live in, what that state does about the insurance exchanges it might or might not set up, and the administrative structure and staffing of the agencies that write the rules and attempt to implement them. The bill eliminated a robust federal public option and substituted a federal high-risk insurance pool as a stopgap until 2014 when insurance companies are supposed to accept all applicants. The HHS Office of Consumer Information and Insurance Oversight expects the program over its duration to cover only 350,000 of the 45 million uninsured Americans. Finally, for what it's worth, the office of the chief Medicare actuary (Sisko et al., 2010) estimates that with reform, national health spending, public and private, which accounted for 17.3 percent of GDP ($2.5 trillion) in 2009, will rise to 19.6 percent of GDP in 2019 ($4.6 trillion), with the private sector leading in cost explosion. Using the hybrid model of Massachusetts repeats on a grand scale the failure to reduce the power of insurance companies and thereby contain costs. The state treasurer of Massachusetts, Timothy Cahill, called his state's program "a fiscal train wreck" (*Wall Street Journal*, Mar. 26, 2010).

Many insurance companies had a simple response to the "requirement" that any new plan they write for individuals and small employers must at least begin to allow children to stay on their parent's insurance policies until age 26, to eliminate copayments for preventive care, and to provide consumers "basic protection." They notified consumers just before the midterm elections that they would raise premiums by as much as double digits starting in September. Copayments would rise not for preventive care but for other medical services. Further anticipatory hikes before 2014 are planned (*Wall Street Journal*, September 10, 2010). Similarly, Obama's declaration that "insurance companies will be banned forever from denying coverage to children with preexisting conditions" was met with the industry's reminder that nothing in the small print prevents them from increasing premiums to cover added costs and nothing requires them to write insurance for the child in the first place. Insurance companies also understand that no one knows what new Congresses, the courts, and possibly a new president will do before 2014 – plenty of time to shape things to their liking.[12]

Using Medicaid as the basis for most of the expansion of coverage was the worst mistake in White House strategy. This book has shown that any program targeted to lower-income families that is complex and visible will inspire strong political resistance and keep funding limited. The downside of Medicaid as a model for health-care reform is that, like American "welfare," it is administered by 50 states and thousands of local governments that must share the cost. (On average Medicaid takes about one-fifth of state budgets. Many of these states are near bankruptcy.) Political resistance comes from the inevitable inequities of programs that are visibly targeted to the poor via a stiff income and/or assets test; families in similar circumstances receive starkly different benefits. For instance, a working family that is near poor or just above the eligibility line is aware that the single mother next door receives food stamps, Medicaid, public assistance, maybe some child-care subsidies, and other benefits while it receives nothing. Even when the reform bill raises the ceiling for eligibility, Medicaid remains stigmatized and is resented by lower middle- and middle-income families who do not qualify (see Chapter 7, sec. 9; Chapter 2; Chapter 4).

Contrast Medicare: it is a universal, categorical benefit; anyone of a given age receives Social Security and Medicare. It is not charity; it is a social right. It is relatively simple to administer and explain; it has low overhead cost (Chapter 5). Along with Social Security, it is the most popular and efficient social program of the past half century. If the Obama administration had used it as a model, if it had marketed the three-word sound bite "Medicare for All" starting with "Medicare for More" and, early on, had spent every day elaborating that message and fighting for it, it would not be in the shaky position it was as it approached the 2010 election; nor would it be giving health-care reform a bad name in the years ahead.

If the politics and economics of Medicaid were not so negative, the addition of millions of people to Medicaid eligibility would be a good move in the effort to expand access to health services and reduce poverty. But its downside is overwhelming. If instead Medicare were expanded to additional age categories (children, 55–64-year-olds), it could at the same time absorb the large and little-known component of Medicaid that is now the only long-term public program in the United States, Medicaid for the frail elderly and nonelderly, the "permanently" disabled. That part of Medicaid is now something of a challenge to the nonpoor. Upper-middle-class folks needing expensive extended care, with the advice of estate planners and tax accountants, declare themselves paupers in order to qualify for the best long-term care in their state. Folding this into Medicare would eliminate that practice and, along with reform of disability insurance, ultimately permit a reorientation toward rehabilitation of the young-old handicapped (Chapter 5). In time, as we moved toward "Medicare for Everyone," Medicaid could then be phased out entirely, along with the administrative apparatus in each state.

These errors in tactics and strategy were compounded by much talk about making Medicare more efficient. Echoing general attacks on government, the cry was, "waste, fraud, and abuse." The solution is to improve Medicare delivery and outcomes: pay doctors and hospitals on the basis of quality; fund research on best clinical practices; set up a Medicare Innovation Center to test payment reform. This resembles previous efficiency reforms under Presidents Reagan and G. H. W. Bush, a period when HMOs were said to be the road to cost savings. It all sounds good on paper, but with more than half the system private and commercial, the cost-shifting game will continue. As the chief Medicare actuary guesstimates, so will the march of the United States to 20 percent of GDP by 2019.

In the months leading up to the 2010 bill, a barrage of criticisms of the cost of Medicare and exhortation to take action to improve its efficiency poured out of the White House. Obama and his planners and advisers who articulated this theme deserve the label "techno-utopians." They are technological enthusiasts who have discovered economics, cost-benefit analysis, and "evidence-based medicine" without understanding their limits. Utopian aspirations are sometimes needed to avoid a slide of expectations to the bottom. Utopian conviction about technological fixes, however, has long been an American obsession. It diverts attention from the need for presidential leadership to build political coalitions around clear public policies that tackle root causes of cost explosions. Public bargaining power that can reduce the dominance of insurance industry and other parts of the medical-industrial complex must be the center of reform (Chapter 5). Singling out the alleged inefficiencies of Medicare not only ignores the problem of countervailing power but is often based on shaky research. Again we have assertions that are, to be kind, short on the relevant comparative data. In June 2009 President Obama pressed his staff and key senators to read a *New Yorker* article along this line. Drawing on a study by two Dartmouth economists, Dr. Gawande of Harvard claims in this attack on Medicare costs that the private-public distinction makes no difference, that the root of the troubles is instead excessive medical tests and procedures – too many doctors enriching themselves. He ignores commercial-sector games – risk selection and cost shifting – and other pathologies of a dominant private sector. He is impressed with regional and local variation in costs – for example, expensive McAllen, Texas, vs. low-cost Rochester, Minnesota. The president's budget director, Peter Orszag, similarly claimed that "nearly 30% of Medicare costs could be saved without negatively affecting outcomes." But these studies seldom control adequately for type of patient and patient risks (e.g., McAllen has very high rates of obesity and alcoholism) and never systematically compare public costs with private. They are comparing apples and oranges. Further, their notion that less Medicare spending yields better health comes from looking at hospitalized patients who have died and then working backward to trace variations in spending on their care before death. In contrast, Michael Ong et al. (2009) analyzed all hospitalized Medicare patients with heart failure in six California teaching hospitals over four and a half years concentrating on their 180-day survival rates. They found that the highest-cost hospital had one-third fewer deaths than the one that spent the least and, more broadly, a strong positive relation between direct hospital costs and later (180-day) survival rates.[13] Although all the best quantitative studies try to control for variables relevant to health outcomes such as age, data on much of what is important are either hard to measure or unavailable.

However, the Dartmouth researchers accurately invoke overspecialization as a factor explaining our uniquely high total cost. If you have more surgeons, you will have more surgery. Specialists everywhere take pride in their craft, and it is a good thing they do. The problem instead is how the system is financed and the commercialization of a medical-industrial complex, resulting in the extreme ratio of high-paid specialists to low-paid primary-care physicians and the lavish use of expensive tests, procedures, and technology of dubious medical merit (Chapter 5).[14]

No one denies the extraordinary cost and inefficiencies of an American medical care system dominated by commercial interests. But singling out its most cost-effective sector, the public programs exemplified by Medicare and the VA as the culprit is, to say the least, misguided. Consider one of the most ridiculous and costly practices – the overuse of hospital emergency rooms by people without adequate or any health insurance. The first systematic quantitative study (Pitts et al., 2010) found that from 2001 to 2004 more than half of the 354 million doctor visits made each year for acute medical care – fevers, stomachaches, coughs – are not with a patient's primary care physician. More than a quarter take place in emergency rooms, including almost all of the visits made on weekends and after office hours. Among the tens of millions of those acute-care patients without health insurance, more than half ended up in emergency rooms, the most ineffective and inefficient setting possible (e.g., there is seldom any follow-up care). Exhortation to practice efficiently cannot solve such problems; only universal coverage that guarantees access to care as a social right and operates within a global budget will work.

The Recovery Act of 2009 allocated $1.1 billion for comparative effectiveness research. By August 2010 it became clear that $27 billion in federal stimulus money would become available to help physicians and hospitals computerize patient records. Insurers such as United Health Group, Quality Systems, and Humana were responding to the efficiency dreams of the White House by joining a feeding frenzy. They see a new source of profit in manufacturing and selling IT equipment and services to compensate for any possible decrease under the new law in profits from collecting premiums and managing claims. That is what a commercial enterprise is supposed to do. We should pause, however, and ask, What should the public authority be doing? As I suggested 40 years ago, information technology cannot substitute for the intuitive knowledge of physicians in the critical task of differential diagnosis (Chapter 5; Wilensky, 1968: 149–150). The experienced primary-care physician takes the time to listen to the patient, whom she has followed in the past. If she has her eyes glued to the screen during the clinical encounter, as occurs with some of the younger practitioners, she cannot pay attention to the clues provided by conversation and apply the wisdom that comes from long experience. Treatment alternatives, once a correct diagnosis is made, are another matter. Here information technology tapping into the latest consensus can help the physician choose an effective therapeutic strategy. And computerized records can help to coordinate care and improve patient understanding of prevention and treatment of illness. Techno-utopians, however, overestimate the state of biomedical knowledge and underestimate its rapid change. No efficiency board can substitute for clinical experience on the scene adapted to the particular patient.[15]

The appointment of Dr. Donald Berwick of the Harvard Medical School as the administrator of the Centers for Medicare and Medicaid Services reflects both the techno-utopian mentality and the distortion of lessons from abroad. Professor Berwick (2008) suggests that we look to the United Kingdom as our model. Unfortunately, as I have shown, the United Kingdom's National Health Service is an extreme in organization, lean spending, and poor performance, a case that points to the upper limit of a good thing. It has long starved its NHS (although the Labour government increased public health-care spending per capita up to below average); it is the only rich democracy that relies almost entirely on direct government delivery of health services; it has too many primary-care physicians and not enough specialists (the opposite of the U.S. extreme) with poor communication between the two; and, with the United States and Ireland, is one of the three worst health performers among 19 rich democracies (Tables 8 and 9).

As Oberlander and Marmor observe (2010: 62) and as my comparative research shows, no other rich democracy puts great emphasis on computerized medical records and best practice research or pays providers on the basis of relative quality. Britain is a partial exception that is no comfort to technological enthusiasts; their exhortations regarding quality improvements failed to enhance health performance or reduce costs. The myth that other rich democracies have achieved good health at relatively low cost because of their widespread application of best-practices research and other technological breakthroughs rests on enthusiasm without evidence. The most commonly cited cases are the United Kingdom, Germany, Canada, and Australia (e.g., Gail Wilensky's discussion, 2006). Two troubles with this are notable. First, timing: the small moves toward cost-benefit analysis and advice came long after these countries achieved universal coverage through national health insurance; in no way can their edge over the United States in health performance be attributed to the application of best-practices research and its high-tech cousins. Germany set up its Institute for Quality and Efficiency in 2003; Canada began a coordinated drug review, not binding, in 2003. The United Kingdom's National Institute for Health and Clinical Excellence (NICE) set up in 1999 initiates and conducts evaluations of all types of medical technologies that have large health or budgetary impact. The second notable trouble with these observations is that cost-benefit analysis has nothing to do with the relative health performance of these countries. Comparison of changes in real health from 1980 to 2005 (see Chapter 5) yields this picture: the United Kingdom and Germany are below average in health performance. Germany, after structural reforms from 1981 to 1992 that reduced the bargaining power of drug firms and providers, moved up from a rank of 17th among 19 rich democracies to 12th. The United Kingdom, the poster child for technological enthusiasts, moved down from well below average in health performance (ranked 13th) to the bottom (ranked 17th of 19 cases). Australia, as we have seen, is a deviant case that moved sharply up in its health performance (from 11th to 3rd), not because of any marked change in spending or health-care provision or evidence-based medicine but because of the selective immigration of millions of highly educated, healthy populations. Canada, after adopting national health insurance, moved up toward the top (5th in 1980 to 3rd in relative performance in 2005).

Why the financing and organization of health care in all the other countries leads to both relatively low total cost and better performance than the United States – without any Efficiency Boards or even much cost-benefit analysis – is explained in Chapter 5. For the reasons listed there, health care is a more serious fiscal problem for the United States, and even less predictable than pension costs. Short of comprehensive, universal national health insurance with global budgets, or politically unacceptable cuts in needed services, this problem cannot be solved. Unlike pensions, the problems of adequate health-care financing and delivery do not yield to small incremental changes and cannot wait decades before major system reforms are made.

In sum, a flawed White House strategy interacting with a radically decentralized federalism and a GOP that has moved to the radical right and abuses Senate rules with abandon to paralyze government all doomed a move toward national health insurance. Is the 2010 bill better than nothing? Probably. But it is the very model of a missed opportunity with the great danger of a backlash and reversals in the years ahead.

## 4. Labor Law Reform

If this book shows nothing else it demonstrates the key role of inclusive, coordinated unions and strong labor federations in moving politics to the center-left. It also shows that accommodative industrial relations that integrate workers and unions into managerial decision making enhance productivity and economic performance (Chapters 3, 6, and 7). Finally, as one of the largest broad-based mediating associations, the labor movement is essential to the vitality of democracy – a force that counters mass-society tendencies and limits the impact of wedge issues in politics.

As with health insurance, a major shift in the political landscape would be necessary to improve the fairness of American labor law. Again a U.S.-Canadian comparison is suggestive. As Bruce (1989) and Wilensky (2002: 675ff.) have shown, neither differences in political culture nor contrasts in public attitudes toward unions can explain why Canada and the United States, starting from nearly identical low union densities 1945–1965, subsequently followed contrasting trajectories. U.S. union density declined from about a third to the current 14 percent, whereas Canadian unions – in the face of public attitudes less favorable to unions than those of the United States – climbed to more than a third. Canadian labor law, almost the antithesis of U.S. law, provides the lion's share of the explanation. In brief, and most important, union certification procedures are automatic and quick in Quebec and among federal employees if the union gives evidence that more than 50 percent signed cards; in British Columbia, Manitoba, and New Brunswick 55 percent must sign the card. If only a minority sign, an election is held promptly after a petition is filed. There is no chance for a long employer intimidation campaign. Canadian law also prohibits the use of permanent striker replacements, although Ontario has modified this. Provinces covering 80 percent of the labor force provide for "interest arbitration" of first contracts to prevent bad-faith bargaining. Finally, labor boards are more powerful in Canada and hear more cases more quickly than in the United States (Abraham and Voos, 1996).[16]

It is obvious that Canadian-style labor-law reform would make a difference for labor prospects in the United States. Students of industrial relations agree on the minimum steps needed to restore fairness: update and expand the coverage of labor relations statutes; strengthen protection for workers' right to organize; speed up certification elections and/or use a card check; give workers the same access to union spokespersons as they have to management spokespersons during certification campaigns; issue prompt injunctions to remedy discrimination against employees during organizing campaigns or first-contract negotiations; assist employers and newly certified unions to achieve first contracts through an upgraded dispute-resolution system. Most students of labor relations also consider an outright ban on employers' practice of hiring replacements for strikers essential to preserve a balance of power in collective bargaining. Combined with new resources labor is already committing to organizing, which at least slowed the slide in union density, this agenda would go far toward revitalizing the labor movement.[17]

As we have seen in Chapter 7, the Employee Free Choice Act contained three of these steps toward restoring the right to organize and bargain collectively – majority signup certification, increased penalties for illegal conduct by employers, and first contract arbitration. The bill passed the House 241 to 185 in 2007 but succumbed to a threat of filibuster in the Senate. In 2009–2010 it never came to a vote in either branch. Like national health insurance, a substantial shift in the political terrain is a prerequisite for labor law reform.

### 5. What Should Be Done about Money and the Media in Politics?

Current debate about money in politics and the evil influence of "special interests" exemplifies a solution in search of a problem. The *New York Times* labels "soft money" "sewer money"; Common Cause advocates still more limits on campaign contributions and, like politicians of every persuasion, rails against the "special interests." What is wrong with money in politics is not that there is too much of it. Under current conditions – without public funding, without candidate and party access to free media – very large sums are necessary to engage in any competitive campaign. It is fruitless to bemoan the size of expenditures without attending to the causes: political money is not visible enough, it is not as widely distributed as it should be, and large sums are necessary to run for office (cf. Ornstein, 1992; Jacobsen, 1993). Finally, what is wrong with ritual complaints about special interests is that groups vary hugely in their specialness; some foster wider civic attachments, others do not. Special or nonspecial, their capacity to influence government is indispensable to the vitality of democracy (Wilensky, 2002: chs. 3 and 11).

If the problem to be solved is to restore the representative and deliberative aspects of American politics, to raise the quality of campaign discourse, and to involve more voters in the process, we must focus first on politicians' access to the mass media and other increasingly costly means of communication with voters, both during election campaigns and year round. Second, we must think of ways to strengthen political parties. Regarding money, to reach voters in large political units such as congressional districts and most states, let alone the whole country, politicians must have very large sums. That is why, when confronted with limitations on spending, they invent "soft money" and political-action committees (PACs) that can buy media messages on issues. Soft money is individual and group contributions to state and local parties that are neither limited nor disclosed. The money moves between states and the national parties, too. It is usually spent on voter registration and get-out-the vote drives, polling, and party ads coordinated with national campaigns. It is the only money that gives both national and state parties leverage over candidate selection.[18] A mounting problem for party viability is the proliferation of self-selected entrepreneurial candidates (often weak or incompetent candidates) with their own money machines and separate campaigns. When and if these folks reach the Senate or House, they owe little to the national or state parties. This intensifies the already big problem of aggregating interests and accommodating clashing ideologies in order to govern.

Eliminating PACs and soft money without finding other means of campaign finance would not only further weaken political parties but would make political action difficult both for narrowly focused interest groups (corporations with a product focus, the gun lobby) and for broadly based interest groups such as labor, churches, and many multi-issue voluntary associations. Efforts to remove money from the system have, in fact, resulted in elaborate and opaque rules that are unenforceable, coupled with the inevitable phony charges of "corruption"; they do nothing to increase access to the media, increase the competitiveness of elections, cut the time politicians devote to money raising, or strengthen parties.

Among the small steps that might help (these are adapted from Norman Ornstein, who has long and persuasively advocated such reforms): enact a tax credit for small in-state individual contributions to candidates and parties, say up to $250 a year. Create incentives for candidates to raise this "good," "rank-and-file" money by federal matching funds for all such money raised over a threshold of $30,000. The tax credit for small contributions could be financed at least in part by a 10 percent fee for contributions more than $1,000 – another incentive to broaden the campaign base. If these two reforms were enacted, accountability could be enhanced by timely (48-hour) mandatory disclosure of the source of all contributions more than $1,000, including PAC money. A robust system of disclosure using the Internet would require funding a strengthened enforcement and disclosure arm of the Federal Election Commission. Finally, to enable challengers to surmount the campaign-finance barrier that now discourages many good candidates, double individual contribution limits from the present $2,400 per election for federal candidates and double the present limit of $30,000 per calendar year for political parties. Incidentally, indexing these ceilings to inflation would prevent the erosion that would trigger repeated combat over the same issue.

Of all the political reforms that would strengthen democracy, the most difficult to achieve is political party and candidate access to the broadcast media (Wilensky, 2002: chs. 3 and 11 describe in detail the ways other democracies have achieved this goal). The United States is unique in forcing its politicians into a continuous, enervating scramble for money to buy media access; all other rich democracies make plenty of room for party leaders and candidates to speak for themselves at public expense. It is significant that whenever a campaign finance reform bill reaches bipartisan sponsorship in Congress, it has already been stripped of provisions to provide free TV time for federal candidates. For obvious reasons, Congress is supersensitive to broadcast industry opposition.

When Commerce Secretary Herbert Hoover addressed one of a series of national radio conferences leading to the Radio Act of 1927 and to the predecessor to the FCC, the Federal Radio Commission, he put the issue plainly: "It is unthinkable that we should allow so great a possibility for service to be drowned in advertising chatter.... There is in all of this the necessity to establish public rights over the ether roads.... There must be no national regret that we have parted with a great national asset" (Hoover, 1952: 140–141). Similarly the Communications Act of 1934 granted broadcasters free and exclusive use of the public airwaves in return for a pledge to serve the "public interest, convenience, and necessity." Yet industry has been very successful not only in escaping from public-interest obligations but in obtaining subsidy for commercial needs. In 1997 the government doubled the amount of spectrum space it licensed to broadcasters; estimates of the value go as high as $70 billion, all for free – a generous dose of corporate welfare. Throughout, the powers of the FCC to regulate broadcasters in the public interest have been severely limited. (For detailed enumeration, see Hilliard, 1991: 29–41, 66ff.) It has the power to lift the license of a broadcaster who fails to fulfill public-interest obligations, but its admonitions and fines are largely ineffective.

Even assuming an administration that wants to assert the public interest, expand access, and offset media power, it is not easy to craft regulatory regimes that would do the job. Those who favor free air time and/or format requirements to improve the discourse in campaigns, redress the imbalance between incumbents and challengers, and overcome the necessity of endless money-chasing to buy sound bites (mostly attack ads) must solve several difficult problems. How many candidates get how much time? How should it be divided between candidates and parties? If the government requires all stations to give minimum time to parties and to thousands of candidates in hundreds of districts, what formula can account for the wide differences in media costs, market reach, and political realities in different electoral jurisdictions? Do the reforms apply to radio, as well as television? What about cable, which is not licensed by the federal government? If the loss of audience is substantial when candidates use the time, if all that happens is an increase in Netflix's movie rental profits, what has been accomplished? Will format requirements violate constitutional free speech provisions? Political scientists have offered practical proposals that answer these questions. For instance:

- *Mandate free prime time for qualified parties* in the two months preceding presidential and congressional elections and/or provide *public subsidies to buy that time*. Let parties choose what to air, as is done in most other democracies. The party allocations could reflect the share of seats in the House or, if minor parties are to be accommodated, the percentage of popular vote in presidential elections above a nontrivial threshold. This would strengthen parties and reduce the exclusively candidate-centered elections. *Format requirements*: Time minimums (to overcome the sound bite/attack ad pathology) and personal appearance by the candidates (to promote accountability for the tone of the message). This is less politically feasible than the following:
- *Create a "broadcast bank" or national political time bank* consisting of minutes of television and radio time on all broadcast outlets.[19] At the beginning of each election cycle every station must contribute two hours of prime advertising time to the bank. The Federal Election Commission (FEC) will disperse vouchers from the bank to candidates to purchase political ads. Half the vouchers go directly to general election candidates for the U.S. House and Senate who have raised over a threshold amount from small donors in their district or state. The other half goes to major (and qualifying minor) parties, which are free to

distribute vouchers to candidates of their choice for any office. Candidates who do not use their vouchers can trade them in to their party for other resources such as phone banks or direct mail. *Format requirements* (like those in several sister democracies): No message can be less than 60 seconds; the candidate must appear on screen for the duration and for radio use his or her own voice. The aim, again, is to overcome the worst excesses of nearly anonymous attack ads. *Financing*: The two hours each station contributes are assigned a monetary value based on market rates where it originated; the vouchers are denominated in dollars, not time. Candidates and parties can use vouchers at any station they wish. After the election, the bank reimburses stations that redeemed more than two hours' worth of free time with proceeds it collects from stations that redeemed fewer. This ensures that all stations bear an equitable burden and maximizes user flexibility. A ceiling of $500 million per two-year election cycle – the estimated value of the political time sold in 1995–1996 – was then appropriate. That figure escalated to as much as $3 billion for TV alone in the 2007–2008 cycle (Campaign Media Analysis Group, 2010). Hagen and Kolodny (2008) suggest that CMAG's estimate is much inflated, but no one doubts that media buys are on an upward curve. A ceiling of $1 billion per two-year cycle is perhaps more realistic now.

All of these political reforms could be financed in two ways, each contributing to an upgrading of campaigns, without utopian spending limits that do not work, without deadening the participation of mediating associations so essential to the democratic process: (1) a tax on PAC contributions to candidates and parties; and (2) a tax on television and radio advertising revenues. The fastest-rising cost of campaigning is those ads, which are increasingly profitable for the stations. The tens of millions of dollars so raised could be put into a trust fund to help pay for the tax credit for small contributions. The rationale is straightforward: those who benefit from the current system should pay a reasonable price to improve it.

## F. A MORE FEASIBLE PART OF THE AGENDA

I see eight public-policy shifts that can be accomplished without a huge Senate Democratic majority or a resurgence of Republican moderates in the Congress. They include a family policy and Social Security reform, an active labor-market policy (ALMP), education reform, a national service corps, reduction in poverty and inequality, immigration reform, and less surely, financial reregulation, and a major shift toward alternative energy sources and environmental protection. They would, however, likely require Democratic control of both houses of Congress and the presidency. Coalitions favoring most of these policies are already evident in the behavior of past presidents or one or the other branch of past Congresses or reforms adopted by some states. Most have been successfully implemented by all, most, or a few of the 19 rich democracies, as this entire book has shown. Several are the policies that, if adapted to American circumstances, are transferable from abroad. Together these policies and programs would reduce poverty and inequality and their associated pathologies (e.g., violent crime); they would lessen political polarization in government, making it difficult to mobilize the middle mass against the poor as with the right-wing use of the race card and immigration. Much of this agenda is a restatement of the obvious, but reminders are often useful. Two are especially ripe for transfer from abroad – a family policy and an active labor-market policy.

## 1. Family Policy and Social Security

Chapter 5 gave a detailed account of what other rich democracies have done to enhance family stability and well-being through direct government action. "Family policy" embraces a wide range of programs designed to assure the care of children, increase gender equality, and maximize choices in balancing the demands of work and family for everyone. It functions to (1) *replace or supplement household income* (e.g., family or child allowances, rent supplements and housing assistance, and pensions with flexible retirement); (2) *offer services to families* (e.g., family-planning services, family counseling, and child care, including preschools, day-care centers, before-school and after-school leisure centers, short workdays for parents, parental leave, paid and unpaid, leave for parents when their children are sick); or (3) *serve in lieu of the family* (e.g., home help or long-term care for the frail elderly and supplementary meals programs).

Three findings are especially relevant for the United States as it moves toward a sensible family policy. First these are universal, categorical programs that avoid heavy means testing or targeting to "the truly needy." If the benefits are income-related, the income tests are simple – a declaration at point of service or a tax return. Also they do not kick in at very low levels; benefits are typically reduced gradually as income brackets climb. For instance day-care places are free or almost free for a substantial portion of the population and copayments increase with increasing income, but no one family pays the full cost. Second, countries that have innovative and expansive policies spend very little on means-tested public assistance; there is a strong inverse relationship between scores on my family policy index and spending on means-tested programs. The reasons: a family policy reduces poverty without an intrusive, expensive apparatus of harassment of the poor; and because its benefits are widely shared, it is easier to fund. In contrast, public assistance targeted to the nonworking nonaged poor facilitates the mobilization of the middle mass against such symbolic targets as "welfare cheats." Further evidence of this trade-off is the finding in Chapter 5 that public spending on pensions (including survivors' and disability insurance), family allowances, work injury, and, to a lesser extent, health care constitutes a package that is inversely related to spending on public assistance and higher education. The third finding is that in no rich democracy is there a war between the generations about any of this. In multivariate analysis two of the strongest predictors of an expansive, innovative family policy are the percent over 65 and women working. In the United States as elsewhere, the aged make common cause with their adult children, not merely about pensions and flexible retirement but also about paid parental leave and public day care. The politics of family policy are integrative.

Needless to say, these lush cash transfers and services delivered by the family-policy leaders – Sweden, France, Belgium, Norway, and Finland – are expensive. But they are so popular that funding for them is politically feasible. And the alternatives – social problems that come from family breakup and population aging without a family policy – are both costly and severe. Family policy pays off in the long run in poverty-reduction, productivity increases of working parents, a better life for the aged, and the improved supervision, education, and cognitive development of children. That coalitions for family policy already exist in the United States is evident in small steps already taken in recent Congresses and proposals made by recent presidents. Most notable are the Family and Medical Leave Act and successive increases in the Earned Income Tax Credit (EITC), which uses a simple, confidential income- and family-composition test administered by the IRS (Chapter 7). The EITC has reduced the rate of poverty among working families; if expanded greatly, it would have a major impact. Other steps were blocked. For instance, proposals for publicly subsidized child care have passed one or the other branch of Congress or have appeared in presidential State of the Union addresses.[20]

As we have seen in Chapter 5, public pensions and related programs are areas where in 2006 the United States ranked 13th of 18 rich democracies in pension generosity (net and gross earnings replacement rates). It has also relied on unstable and now rapidly declining privately provided pensions. However, Social Security remains intact despite recurrent and ongoing attempts to privatize it. That in 1983 we successfully took small incremental steps to assure its financing, that such other countries as Finland have created flexible retirement systems to reduce long-run costs and reverse the decline in labor-force participation among the elderly, suggests that we are capable of the necessary incremental changes to solve this noncrisis.

There is much casual comment that the existing Social Security and Medicare systems have done little to reduce poverty. In fact, these universalistic programs for all the aged and their health have been the most successful poverty reduction programs of the past half century. In 1965, 30 percent of the officially defined poor were over 65. By 2000 that figure had fallen to one in eight. The main cause is expanded coverage and benefits for Social Security and Medicare. Pension checks obviously reduce the number of "pretransfer poor." But half of Medicare and 70 percent of Medicaid also go to those who would have been poor without those programs (Glennerster, 2000: 16). Any policy that protects these programs prevents their recipients from sinking into poverty.

## 2. An Active Labor-Market Policy

In Chapter 7, I define the idea of an active labor-market policy (ALMP) and note that labor-market researchers have listed 21 types of programs under the label ALMP, of which 17 fit the definition very well.

We have seen that on average from 2000 to 2006 the fragmented and decentralized political economies have invested very little as a share of GDP in ALMP – 0.40 percent. The United States ranks last at 0.15 percent, less than it spent in the mid-1980s. Along with the United Kingdom, it is at the bottom in passive expenditures as well, measured by generosity in coverage and size of unemployment cash benefits.

Is the U.S. lag because of the merit of recurrent claims that such programs as training, retraining, direct job creation, a strong labor-market board for placement and related services, and rehabilitation are ineffective, a waste of money? Elsewhere, I have reviewed evidence on their effectiveness (Chapter 6; 1985; 1992a). Even the United States has adopted many active programs from the Job Corps to wage and training subsidies, but the funding is too meager and their average quality too limited to have much national impact. If we add the armed forces' excellent training effort to the current U.S. civilian effort, it would still be feeble.

To make major progress here we would have to get over the research evaluation industry's obsession with cost-benefit analysis focused on one narrow part of one program – neat, well designed, quantitative, and misleading. We literally study these programs to death. As I suggested in reviewing such research on Head Start and the Job Corps (1985), and as I have shown throughout this book, there is an interdependence of policies that the leading countries in upgrading the labor force have long understood. As Henry Aaron (1978: 156–157) put it in assessing research in the war on poverty:

Improved education and training may be ineffective in increasing earning capacity unless steps are also taken to change the mix of available jobs, and efforts to change the mix of available jobs may fail if low-wage workers lack training and education. Either taken alone might fail, when both together might succeed. Research and experimentation would detect the failures but have no way to indicate the hypothetical potential success. A rather vague assumption of such an interrelatedness marked early political rhetoric about the War on Poverty but was wholly absent from the precise, but partial, analyses of its effectiveness performed by social scientists.

Like family policy, the cross-national transferability of ALMP is easier than most policy areas for the same reason: coalitions of the center Right and center Left have often formed around the evidence of the effectiveness of these programs or at least around their general appeal as a way to expand equality of opportunity and productivity. Because these programs are not exclusively targeted to the "undeserving poor" but to many groups – displaced workers in their prime, entire distressed communities, as well as hard-to-employ young, minorities, handicapped, single mothers, displaced homemakers, and older men – they do not set up a backlash against funding. Because they ease the shock of industrial readjustment, they can dampen labor's opposition to free trade. Because the training components of ALMP have been most successful with women, they supplement a family policy in reducing the feminization of poverty, so prominent in American society.

In short, an ALMP for the United States that is serious and feasible would combine job creation; apprenticeship training; incentives for on-the-job training and retraining; work-study programs to ease the transition from school to work; much better vocational counseling in high schools with continuous follow-up for two or three years; remedial programs to increase basic literacy and improve work habits and attitudes; a much strengthened placement service to increase efficiency in matching job seekers and job vacancies for everyone including compulsory notification of job vacancies or layoffs; and mobility allowances, relocation assistance and rent supplements tied to mobility for workers trapped in depressed areas and industries.

### 3. Reversing the Erosion of the U.S. Lead in Education: The Question of "Education vs. Training"

A memorable change must be made in the system of education, and knowledge must become so general as to raise the lower ranks of society nearer to the higher.

(John Adams, Correspondence, 1786)

Chapter 7, sec. 8, has traced the dramatic decline in K–12 performance since the late 1960s and the more recent erosion of higher education. It describes the historical roots of both our previous lead at every level of education and our current slump, first in primary and secondary education and now in postsecondary education. The reasons for these trends, so devastating for our economic, political, and social future, are there elaborated at length. Here are a few suggestions about how the United States can regain its historic lead.

#### *First, Upgrade K–12*
It is no mystery why the primary and secondary schools of other democracies now perform at a much higher level than ours. They pay their teachers more relative to other professionals and respect them more. They spend more of their budgets on academic resources – libraries and books, writing materials, computers, lab equipment. They insist on national standards for performance, they train and educate their teachers in subjects to be taught and give them more autonomy in the classroom. Both principals and teachers expect a higher level of performance from students and comprehensive tests measure that performance. The evaluation process is seldom confined to machine-graded multiple-choice questions; no country puts such tests at the center of their curriculum. Teachers are given time to confer with one another and plan their work; professional development is valued. The school year and school day tend to be longer among the better performers. Many of the other affluent democracies also make sure that children 0–4 are ready for school by funding a family policy that fosters their cognitive and emotional development.

This picture of our sister democracies' K–12 equivalents is approximated by most upper-middle-class public and private schools in the United States. The U.S. problem is that the other four-fifths suffer from mediocre to disgraceful schools, both public and commercial. When discussing this problem, many politicians and some academics argue that no big change is possible without privatizing the system, using vouchers or charter schools or both to give parents "choice." They often add a second reform strategy: break the power of teachers' unions. Compared to public schools, charter schools are typically run with public money but are subject to fewer regulations; they enroll disproportionately fewer students who are non-English-speaking or have disabilities. For these reasons alone, they should outperform the public schools. Similarly, public funding of vouchers to promote school choice, which are typically used in nonpublic sectarian schools, also escape regulations of public schools. The advocates of charters and vouchers claim that competition would shock the public schools into better performance; a rising tide would lift all boats.

None of this happened. The evidence shows that if we compare the performance of private and public schools of similar social composition, privatizing is no solution to the problem of upgrading standards even if it did not drain funds from public schools. Similar comparison of the performance of charter schools and public schools shows the same results – either no difference or an edge for the public schools. With rare exceptions, no amount of evidence will change the minds of ideologues on either side.[21]

One of the most comprehensive studies (CREDO, 2009) concludes that the majority of the more than 4,700 charter schools nationwide are no better and in many cases worse than local public schools when measured by growth in achievement on standardized tests of reading and math. The study matched students for socioeconomic status, English proficiency, and participation in special education and school lunch programs. Fewer than one-fifth of charter schools nationally offered a better education, measured by standardized growth scores, than comparable public schools. Almost half offered an equivalent education and more than one-third (37%) were "significantly worse" in math. The researchers found a smaller but significant edge for public schools in reading. "This study," the Stanford researchers conclude, "reveals in unmistakable terms that, in the aggregate, charter students are not faring as well as their traditional public school counterparts" (p. 6). Finally, Diane Ravitch (2010a; cf. Ravitch 2010b) reviews the record of academic achievement in the two cities where "choice" programs, both vouchers and charters, have been in effect the longest, Milwaukee (since 1990) and Cleveland (since 1995). Systematic evaluations show that in both cities students in voucher schools and/or charter schools make no greater gains in performance than students in public schools.

A more intensive study of 23 charter schools in Chicago funded by the Renaissance Schools Fund compared carefully matched public schools on the percentage of students who met or exceeded standards on the Illinois State Achievement Test of reading and math (Schanzenbach, 2009). Charter school students compared to students who stayed in their neighborhood public schools improved about the same year to year. There were almost no statistically significant differences.

Celebrities, philanthropists, the media, and now President Obama with federal billions rally around the successful minority of charter schools as their justification for funding the movement. The media frenzy culminated in a documentary film in September 2010, "Waiting for 'Superman,'" touting charter schools and other ways to escape public schools. Charter school and voucher advocates accent "choice" and competition; they claim that in a free market for education parents will remove students from bad schools in favor of good ones. Unfortunately, like a free market for health care (Chapter 5), it is an illusion.

Regarding unions, cross-national comparison shows that in countries with superior K–12 performance teachers are more highly unionized, one reason for the higher relative income and respect they have achieved.[22] And, in fact, there is no unified teachers' union resistance to the performance pay and the school accountability proposals necessary to upgrade standards: the American Federation of Teachers has long supported both; the larger National Education Association recently if reluctantly joined. In debates about reform it has become a popular sport not only to blame unions but to bash teachers for not shaping up, when in fact we have dumped our unsolved social problems on them – uncushioned family breakup, unsupervised children unprepared for learning or orderly behavior, rising poverty rates with related deficiencies in child nutrition and health, increasing racial tensions and neighborhood violence spilling over into schools. Then, while we self-righteously proclaim that our teachers are failing us, we decrease both the moral and financial support for instructional services and let the buildings in which they work deteriorate.

In education reform it would help to recognize that we do know a good deal about how to educate the young from our own past and lessons from abroad – the list on the first page of this section. If we paid attention to these basics, we might be less vulnerable to fads and fashions in education inspired by ideologies of the Left and Right. The Left says adopt informal quota systems for the deprived, avoid standards or grades or tests and other competitive devices because they discriminate against minorities or they make deprived kids feel bad. The Right says teachers and their unions are the enemy, do away with seniority and tenure; embrace charter schools, or privatization, or home schooling, or all three; stop throwing money at the schools, let the market work for parental choice.

In no other rich democracy are comprehensive tests used as a weapon against teachers' job security or opportunities for professional development. Decades of neglect means that the United States faces a choice: either we reward teachers with professional autonomy, a professional income befitting their education level, and opportunities for further education in subjects they teach; or we suffer a persistent teacher shortage, expansion of class size, and teacher turnover and early retirement combined with a continual descent in the recruitment pool – teachers for some time have come from roughly the bottom half of college graduates.[23] Standardized tests have their place in evaluating schools, administrators, teachers, and, above all, students. But they should never dominate the entire learning process, not just because they inspire "teaching to the test," not just because they divert student attention away from subject matter, but mainly because they do not capture much of the abilities and interests important in learning: student interest in reading as a road to knowledge; an ability to understand what they read; analytical writing; effective oral communication; the capacity to solve problems (e.g., knowing when a problem calls for quantitative analysis); the ability to move between the concrete and the abstract; the capacity to evaluate the reliability of sources; not to mention the grasp of particular subjects, for which tests have some validity.

The high-stakes examination movement took hold from the mid-1990s until now. To graduate, high-school students must pass a test early in their high-school career, or failing that, take it over again later. The practice spread from 13 states in 1996 to 22 states in 2006. So far, analysis of the effect of these exit exams is negative: little impact on the general high-school graduation rate; and, most disturbing, the tests increased the dropout rate for blacks and for the growing number of poor districts, whatever their racial composition (Goldin and Katz, 2008: 344–345). The bipartisan "No Child Left Behind" bill of 2002 promoted by Bush requires every school district to test all students in grades three to eight and reduces federal funding for schools, school districts, and states that fail to show progress. Test results must be classified by race, and even if a school shows test progress on average, if it has not reduced the racial gap, it suffers penalties. Then, under the Obama administration the slogan changed to "Race to the Top." The administration dangled $4.35 billion in competitive federal grants for innovative experiments in raising test scores and retaining good teachers. President Obama and Secretary of Education Duncan encouraged states to base teacher salaries in part on student test scores and praised model charter schools.[24] Lest anyone miss the thrust of these themes (that unions and incompetent teachers are the main barriers to education progress), President Obama displayed genuine enthusiasm for a school superintendent in a low-performing Rhode Island school district who took bold action to bypass union resistance to more hours with less pay: he fired all of the teachers and staff in the only high school in the district and hired all new personnel.

The effects of these major reforms were predictable: disadvantaged schools obviously have greater difficulty demonstrating test progress, so they tailor their curriculum to match the tests.[25] Many schools gamed the system to avoid losing funds: they disguised the number of students who dropped out, they cheated by sharing answers with students while administering the test, or simply corrected inaccurate answers. Even some schools in well-off neighborhoods moved toward "teaching to the test," sacrificing student practice in such old-fashioned activities as reading and writing. At the state level where control over tests is lodged, officials either lower the bar for passing the tests or dumb down the tests themselves. For these reasons the big reforms and their aim of improved test scores have had little or no relation to student learning.

Both "No Child Left Behind" and "Race to the Top" find inspiration in the notion that "scientifically based research" will guide schools to better performance. Like the techno-utopians in the "best practices" movement in health-care reform, the most ardent education reformers exaggerate the knowledge base about school performance and the possibilities of applying social and psychological sciences in the real world of teachers and students on the ground.

The problem with all this is the absence of a little common sense. If these tests are designed to measure the mastery of subject matter tied to common-core courses, that has been prominent in good schools for decades. Unhappily, effective national standards on such content have eluded us.[26] Facing this fact and noting the growing variation among states as some weakened their subject-matter standards to avoid penalties under "No Child Left Behind," in 2009 the Governors Association and the Council of Chief State School Officers convened English and math experts to produce common standards for what students should learn each year from K–12. The standards, like pre-1960s standards, were sensible. This step, if funding permits its implementation (after the deep economic crisis passes?), could restore an emphasis on mastery of subject matter with tests focused on course content.[27]

If, however, a one-shot high-stakes test is to be used for teacher or student evaluation for permanent tracking of the student or job tenure of the teacher, it will be counterproductive. Among rich democracies in the first half of the 20th century, many used one high-stakes test to track students in or out of an academic vs. vocational education as early as age 13, with no second chance, casting the die for their educational and occupational fate for decades ahead. Today, however, few have retained this rigidity, and of those, most are in South and Central Europe (Pastore, 2007). The United States should not adopt what has been abandoned by most of the good educational performers in Western Europe.

If student test performance is to be used for teacher evaluation there is one way to improve school quality and be fair to teachers at the same time: evaluate student progress over a long time, use peer-review systems with apprentice-like help and supervision, and take account of the huge variety of school inputs – type of student, type of home background. Punishing individual teachers for slow progress on badly designed student tests in blackboard jungle schools in slum neighborhoods with impoverished students who suffer from poor nutrition, no discipline or father in the home, no conventional success models – all that makes no sense. Given our decades of neglect of K–12 and urban centers, what these teachers need is hazard pay, help in keeping order, smaller class size, special tutors and teacher assistants, opportunities for graduate work in subjects to be taught, and a principal who is a moral leader and disciplinarian who has the right to remove violent children from the school. High-stake tests, dumbed down or not, do nothing to improve the quality of education.

One little noticed downside of the use of tests to rank teachers from excellent to poor and get rid of the poorly ranked is well known to students of incentive systems in complex organizations. Individual rewards for individual performance create destructive competition in which no one has incentive to share know-how with anyone in the workgroup. Collective rewards, in contrast, encourage cooperation, information sharing, and mutual help for improvement – especially important in the challenging task of educating the young. These recurrent findings from a half century of research on work behavior are naturally ignored by the ideologues who dominate school reform debates.

If teachers are given a chance to share their concerns, time to discuss improvements in teaching and student learning with their peers, and more influence over curriculum decisions, they can take control of failing schools and turn them around. Illustrations come from case studies of such success in 15 public high schools in five states and Washington, D.C. (AGI, 2009). Consider Brockton High School, the largest public school in Massachusetts. Of its 4,000 students, more than half were black, about 27 percent white, 12 percent Hispanic, and about two-thirds from households in poverty (pp. 57–74). In 1999 this was a failing school by any measure: one in three of the students dropped out; three of four students failed the statewide exit exam for high-school graduation. In 2001 a teacher, Dr. Susan Szachowicz, together with the head of the English department, began meeting with interested colleagues on Saturdays to brainstorm on ideas for improving Brockton High. It was soon known as the "school restructuring committee." The principal stood aside but did not interfere. The consensus that emerged among teachers was "Get back to basics – reading, writing, speaking, reasoning" – core learning skills. "Literacy charts" with details on key elements of each of the four skills were posted in every classroom. The greatest emphasis was on writing. The restructuring committee put together a guide for their 300 fellow teachers on what good writing was; teachers then trained in small groups. Reluctant teachers were offered collegial help. The teacher committee then persuaded every department head, every teacher, to assign writing and reading as well as projects in speaking and reasoning in every class, even gym, on a sustained schedule. If after all this a teacher could not fit the program, fellow teachers would suggest he or she leave.

Results were dramatic and quick. Within a year, improvement in scores on the statewide exam outpaced improvement in any other school. Within a few years, by 2008, Brockton achievement gains from 8th grade to 10th grade outpaced 90 percent of Massachusetts schools. In-school course exams confirmed the turnaround. As an incidental benefit, Dr. Szachowicz became associate principal. The lesson for school reformers is to respect the experience and autonomy of teachers, and tap what they know about reading, writing, and numeracy. And if they themselves require more education, make opportunities available. By the way, many teachers at Brockton expressed contempt for the high-stake tests of "No Child Left Behind": too much "drill and kill," not enough learning.

The misuse of standardized tests to punish teachers and lagging schools is one big mistake. At the other extreme is the popular notion that lower expectations will improve our schools. Much of the dumbing down of K–12 content is based on a destructive assumption that we must start with "where the students are." They absorb gargantuan amounts of TV and radio, maybe 40 hours a week, play incessant video games online, are addicted to YouTube, and show no interest in or capacity to read and write – those are "boring." Great. Meet them where they are, pandering to their untutored tastes by giving them better video games, bringing comic books, corporate in-school advertising, TV, and the Internet into the classroom, and swing with the tide. Start where they are – and end where they are. Expect little, get little. To expect little from deprived kids, to set no standards of achievement for them, should be seen as a form of child abuse. This formula for maintaining low standards, like grade inflation or automatic promotion, is a contributing cause of K–12 decline. Add it to the fundamental flaws listed already:

the decentralization of the system, decreasing moral and economic support for teachers, poor standards of teacher training and certification, inadequate and erratic funding of schools, no coherent curriculum, a short school day and year, an increase in class size, and vulnerability to intellectual fads and fashions.

That measures to overcome these deficiencies are possible with a popular and determined center-left leader and a legislature of the same party is suggested by the large increase of 16 percent for education in the first two budgets of Governor Gray Davis of California, 1999–2001. Included were incentives for professional development and tested school performance, incentives for teachers who agree to teach in hard-to-staff schools, and monitoring of student progress via a new Standardized Testing and Reporting (STAR) program. All the components of the center-left coalition, including teachers' unions, combined to give Davis his big victory. His campaign centered on K–12 reform. Business leaders added their voices in support.

### Changing Teachers' Education and Certification

To address the shortage and high turnover of teachers and their poor preparation, the United States needs to bypass or offset the influence of its schools of education (see Chapter 7 for details). One way is to follow the lead of Massachusetts: change teacher certification standards to require substantial hours of credit in an academic subject taught in high schools. New York adopted that requirement and much more.[28] Another way is to create numerous in-service training opportunities and teaching jobs for well-educated professionals in such fields as science, math, languages, music, and literature from the private or nonprofit sectors. These include retirees who want part-time jobs, career changers who would like to switch to K–12 teaching, and other outsiders who know their subjects. All this was part of Governor Davis's school reform program – that is, until the combination of the recession of 2001–2002 and the pathological political system of California inspired a recall movement and replaced him with "the terminator" of Hollywood fame, Governor Schwarzenegger (see Chapter 8 on direct democracy). There followed increasing budget deadlock as conflict between the Republican governor and the Democratic legislature escalated along with new paralyzing people's initiatives. Nevertheless, Gray Davis's educational reforms stayed in place. Before they were fully implemented in the spring of 2002, the test performance of California students in English and math was dismal. By 2009 there was substantial improvement in comprehensive statewide tests, including both these basic areas, for grades 2–11.[29] In seven years California moved from dismal before reforms to mediocre, by comparison with both its own past and our 19 rich democracies. If we look at data from the U.S. Census and the National Education Association, per enrolled pupil expenditure put California in the middle of all states in the mid-2000s, but it has likely dropped to the bottom as the state's finances crumbled. (NEA shows that California ranked 26th at \$9,539 per pupil in 2007–2008 but by 2009–2010 had declined to 44th at \$8,520, not far from Mississippi.)

A small Teach for America (TFA) program federally funded by Americorps has been in place for two decades. It attracts quite dedicated and bright young people but is too tiny to have much effect in upgrading national standards of teaching. Starting in 1990 with only 500 teachers, in the fall of 2010 it placed 4,500 teachers. Two facts suggest that TFA, if properly funded, would have a substantial effect. First is the extraordinary number of applicants – 46,000 in 2010 – a 10:1 ratio of applicants to placements. Second is their performance: studies comparing them with undercertified beginning teachers show that the TFA group has an edge in math but no difference in English (Decker, Mayer, and Glazerman, 2004: xiv). After experience and certification, the TFA teachers if they stay are more effective than other teachers. The problem is that these motivated young people turn over just as their non-TFA colleagues do, burned out from poor working conditions (Heilig and Jez, 2010). Of course, increasing starting pay and enhancing opportunities for professional development and promotion would increase the supply of above-average college graduates entering teaching.

In sum, there is nothing to prevent the United States from borrowing from abroad ideas about the organization, funding, and operation of preschool through secondary educational institutions, especially since the countries now outperforming us imported their models from America in the first place.[30]

## Postsecondary Education

We have seen in Chapter 7 that until recently U.S. colleges and universities led the world in excellence, diversity of curricula, basic research, and equality of opportunity. The reasons for the decline of the system at every level have been discussed there at length. What can be done to reverse the trend?

FUNDING. Unstable and declining funding lies at the root of trouble in postsecondary education, as is it does for K–12. Higher education is especially vulnerable because it is the largest discretionary component of the state budget. As diversified as it may seem, the core support of public universities and community colleges comes from state and local taxes, mainly the most painfully visible and unstable tax, property taxes on households, and to a lesser extent, income taxes, the next most visible and painful of all taxes. Chapter 4 shows why reliance on those two sources create sustained tax revolts. At the end of the book, I return to the need to diversify government revenue. Reduced funding per pupil in public institutions at every postsecondary level has undermined their quality, increased their tuition, and closed off educational opportunity for millions of least-affluent students.

Compared to public institutions, private universities and colleges have always charged higher fees and tuition, and raised more money from wealthy alumni, accumulating larger endowments, thereby retarding their decline during these recent years of crisis. Moreover they can at least in the short run ignore the budgeting decisions of state and local politicians; state universities are partly dependent on these political decisions. The private college and university advantage is reinforced by the current contrast in effective student-faculty ratios – typically 5 or 6 to 1 in liberal arts colleges and research-teaching institutions, as much as 25 or 30 to 1 in public institutions. Such contrasts in resources add up to an increasing advantage in balancing teaching and research.

All the more reason to be impressed with the achievements of the top public universities. Living in California with its dysfunctional government and populist politics, I have always viewed UC Berkeley as a miracle.

BALKANIZATION OF THE CURRICULUM. Higher education in the United States is so vast in size and variety that it is difficult to generalize about the content of curricula. Students of higher education agree, however, that the central tendency has been toward fewer language, science, and math requirements for graduation and, more generally, fewer required courses. The common core has been watered down or abandoned. In some institutions this has become a do-it-yourself curriculum, with little attention to coherence, sequence, or academic substance. Add to this a trend that is controversial among close observers but which I believe is widespread, the proliferation of more specialized niches. They are all interdisciplinary majors and range from the hard sciences and basic social sciences, most of them serious, to politicized majors based on race, ethnicity, gender or other presumed collective deprivation, majors devoted to affirming minority-group identity and solidarity. Examples of interdisciplinary niches that reflect a natural intellectual development and further a more diversified search for truth include biochemistry, geophysics, environmental sciences, political economy of industrial societies, contemporary civilization, and world civilizations. In contrast are more politicized majors created in the name of "diversity" or "multiculturalism" mainly based on bloodlines: ethnic studies, black studies, Native American studies, women's studies, gay-lesbian-bisexual-transgendered studies. Because every book or article assigned, every course added to the cafeteria of courses means some other book or course will be squeezed out, the trend undermines the concept of a liberal arts education, as well as any idea of achieving a multiyear core curriculum for all students. If an English department incorporates Derrida, Foucault, or Althusser into its curriculum, there will be less time devoted to the "Western" canon, from Chaucer, Shakespeare, Milton, and Swift to William Wordsworth, Jane Austen, Herman Melville, George Eliot, Mark Twain, Joseph Conrad, William Butler Yeats, and James Joyce. The rationale for avoiding such classics is that they do not speak to our time or (leaving aside Austen and Eliot) they are "dead white males." Yes, Shakespeare is a dead white male. So what? He lasts through centuries not because of his gender or genetic inheritance but because of his command of language and his insights into the human condition. Of course, the canon continually changes and the quest for new knowledge, fresh theoretical perspectives, is welcome not just in the sciences but in the humanities. But when women authors are properly included and we embrace literature from continents other than Europe, there is still the necessity of applying universal standards of literary worth. Resisting intellectual fads and fashions is still essential.

Most humanities and social-science departments have never succumbed to this "postmodernism" or "deconstruction."[31] Most have ignored the multiplication of majors and courses based on identity and ethnic or racial solidarity.

But enough do embrace these ideas to make a difference in their students' chances of transcending parochial bounds of family, class, ethnicity, and race. And, worse, the proliferation of these special niches blocks the student's understanding and appreciation of literature, art, music, history, and philosophy. The Balkanization of the curriculum is the higher-education match for the child-centered, expect-little norm of failing K–12 schools.

CASCADING IN REVERSE. Preschool and K–12 failures put downward pressure on postsecondary performance. We cannot have a decline in basic literacy and numeracy among high-school graduates without creating downward pressure on admissions, curriculum, and grading at colleges. We have already covered what must be done at preschool, primary, and secondary schools to reverse this drag.

THE GREAT AMERICAN RESEARCH UNIVERSITIES: WHY WORRY? These few research centers perform multiple missions – research, graduate instruction and tutorials, undergraduate teaching, service to government and industry, and contributions to the common good. Their central function, however, is to produce new knowledge. They are responsible for most of the research discoveries that have a major impact on our lives, among them the laser, the FM radio, the global positioning system, scientific agriculture (e.g., hybrid seed corn), climate forecasting models, vaccines to prevent diseases, the cure for childhood leukemia, the Pap smear, and a host of other medical discoveries. The social sciences and humanities at these research centers have greatly contributed to our understanding of social structure, culture, politics, and public policy – reflected in the content of every chapter of this book.[32] The faculty members of these top U.S. universities win most of the Nobel prizes in science and medicine. In short, great American research universities are engines of innovation and discovery.

When Jonathan Cole in his 616-page study of the contributions and problems of such universities presents a long analysis of their research achievements and economic payoffs (2009: chs. 5, 7–9), critics say that he exaggerates, that other institutions – industry, government, think tanks, research centers abroad – make important contributions to the economy and the fund of knowledge (Kirp, 2010). As we have seen in Chapter 6, studies of plant location in knowledge-heavy industries reveal a strong bias toward locating near research universities with their laboratory complexes and R&D advantages and their education, training, and development of executives, scientists, and technicians. This is evident in Silicon Valley south of San Francisco, Route 128 (Boston to Cambridge), and the Research Triangle in North Carolina. Similarly, AT&T laboratories, like many other corporate research operations, are lodged near Princeton. At the center of all are major university complexes, spinoff laboratories, and a large supply of educated researchers. Many of these innovations in both industry and government are rooted in university basic research and are done by products of university Ph.D. programs. Cole notes that companies begun by Stanford faculty and alums generated about $261 billion in worldwide sales in 2008 (Cole, 2009: 196). Finally, when we examine the loss of our lead in civilian R&D (Chapter 7, sec. 11), we can see that it parallels not only the rise of military R&D but also the erosion of our leading research universities. The three entities – research universities, government research centers, and private civilian R&D – are tightly connected.

While the economic payoff of world-class research universities is impressive, it is important to note that fundamental truths in science, humanities, and the arts often have no immediate practical applications. They are worthwhile as ends in themselves and as guides to ideas about the good life, as I suggested in my previous comment about the balkanization of the curriculum. Further, new knowledge with practical application is often an unanticipated effect of basic research at these universities, again undertaken in the persistent quest for new knowledge.

Among those who fund or write about higher education, there is a common notion that the research activities of leading universities drive out good teaching of undergraduate if not graduate students (the latest such critique is Hacker and Dreifus, 2010). In fact, "teaching" is made more lively by faculty enthusiastic about its research. Although peer review is perhaps the best evidence of this interplay of research and good teaching, student evaluations provide further confirmation. Students actually evaluate professors who are productive researchers as higher in teaching quality than less productive researchers (McCaughey, 2005: 88–97, a study of 24 select liberal-arts colleges and four research universities). Moreover, good undergraduate teaching cannot be measured by classroom contact hours, a measure popular among legislators debating education budgets. To classroom teaching we must add the guiding of both graduate and undergraduate students in labs and project offices and personal contact in any setting plus the usual faculty committees – admissions, recruitment, job placement and evaluation tasks, and more. It all adds up to an average 55–65 hour workweek.[33] Few professors resent the hours. The research-teaching enterprise is a source of intellectual stimulation and satisfaction matched in few other occupations.

Careful cultivation and generous funding for higher education from the 1930s to the 1990s have given America an impressive lead in research universities of top rank. In 2010, 8 of the world's best 10 research universities and 17 of the top 20 of the 1,000-plus ranked were in the United States. The 10-campus University of California alone accounted for 7 of the top 46 research universities and 3 of the top 14 in the world, with Berkeley leading the pack (Shanghai Ranking Consultancy, 2010).

As centers of independent thought devoted to free inquiry, these leading research universities are periodically under attack. The main source of hostility comes from groups, movements, and politicians who are suspicious of any new idea or simply operate in the old American tradition of populist, anti-intellectual, anti-"elitist" protest. Equally important are the budget police and the deficit hawks who oppose most government spending or intervention in "the" market. A weaker threat comes from within: a small minority of faculty members in these top universities believes that there is little difference between the university and a political party. They feel that it is appropriate to encourage student uprisings for causes they passionately embrace. One expression of this view is the occasional disruption of campus presentations by notable scholars or government officials who express unpopular opinions and are shouted down. Another is the few faculty who defend students who occupy buildings in a political demonstration that stops teaching and student entry. This intolerance, of course, violates the core of academic freedom, the idea that the university exists for free inquiry – discourse uninhibited by intimidation designed to stifle unpopular ideas.

As Jonathan Cole suggests, if university leaders had more courage, if they were more committed to the mission of the university as a center of independent thought, they would dig in against any behavior that restricts free inquiry and the dialogue essential to it, whether it comes from internal or external threats to academic freedom (2010: chs. 11–13 and 479ff., 494ff.). Academic leaders' weak response to recurrent external threats can be seen in their response to Cold War hysteria about loyalty and the recent post-9/11 war on terror. The latter is covered by Cole. I here summarize what I observed in the McCarthy era.

During the Cold War, at the peak of Joe McCarthy's attack on alleged Communists in government and academia, the leaders of Berkeley, Harvard, Yale, and many other universities caved in to political pressure. Harvard, for instance, collaborated with the FBI and CIA to gather secret "derogatory information" on faculty and staff. Earlier, in 1949, the University of California Regents adopted a loyalty oath and fired 31 faculty who were acknowledged not to be Communists but refused to sign. In contrast, President Hutchins of the University of Chicago showed exactly the kind of courage needed to ensure the survival of great American universities – from testifying vigorously and successfully against state legislation that would impose political criteria in hiring teachers to protecting the civil liberties of Chicago faculty under attack.

In 1953, I was sharing an office at Chicago with Val Lorwin, a leading labor historian and an expert on Belgian politics, who had been a State Department labor attaché in Paris and was now a nontenured professor at Chicago. In political orientation Lorwin had long been an anti-Communist social democrat. Of Senator McCarthy's list of 81 State Department employees alleged to be disloyal, only 1 ever came to a court, Lorwin. This fantastic affair was reminiscent of Kafka's *The Trial*. It took Lorwin and lawyers three and a half years to uncover the source of the anonymous accusation, a confused man who was a tenant of the Lorwins in the 1930s. That was the basis of an indictment for perjury – lying to a Loyalty Board about Communist connections during one of several loyalty-security investigations, after which Lorwin was cleared. As the court date approached, the university administration and its faculty closed ranks. They supplied advice from the Law School and held seminars for Lorwin on strategy for clearing his name. Many of the 90 people who had shown their courage by offering sworn testimony in the earlier administrative hearings were eager to testify for Lorwin in the expected criminal trial. Most were then employees of the government who knew what would happen to their careers if they testified and a miscarriage of justice resulted in Lorwin's conviction. When the case finally reached a court, the judge was enraged; he threw it out. He said the only perjury was in the Justice Department, not by Professor Lorwin, and forced the resignation of the department liar who resurrected the old anonymous accusation and obtained the indictment. Lorwin lost nearly four years of his life fighting a shadow.[34]

The case carries two lessons: one is the treachery of secret information; the other is that courageous leadership at a university under attack can bring good results.

### California: Killing the Goose that Laid the Golden Egg

Since 1960 California has shown the world how to combine excellence and equality of opportunity in its higher education. Many academic and political leaders played their part in creating this ingenious balance, including those from the Progressive Era, roughly 1900 to 1920 (Douglass, 2011). But the most important were academic leaders and politicians, including Clark Kerr and Governor Pat Brown, who in the late 1950s negotiated a compact between the public institutions and the state government that would permit an increase in enrollment, a controlled expansion in costs, and a formal division of labor among three types of postsecondary institutions. They consolidated a low-tuition three-tier system to accommodate all high-school graduates in the state: junior (now 112 "community" colleges with minimal entry requirements), state colleges (now 23 state universities), and the 9-campus research/teaching institution, the University of California (now 10 campuses). It is a forgiving, second-chance model, with much opportunity for students with motive and ability who start at community colleges to move up to state universities or the University of California. Transfers between the three levels for qualified students is relatively easy.[35] Not the least of their accomplishments was to institute statewide planning to end turf wars between the University of California and the growing number of state colleges aspiring to university status, each with its regional constituency among state legislators. High quality was protected by giving the University of California constitutional status, with an autonomous Board of Regents, a public trust that insulated it from legislative caprice.

For half a century this system accommodated vast majorities of young Californians and, at the graduate level, became the preferred destination for outstanding out-of-state and foreign students. It also demonstrated that an "elite" public university can contribute mightily to the economic and social well-being of the state and nation, that private universities with big endowments such as Harvard, Yale, or Princeton are not enough to educate all the talented young people, including those with limited means, who aspire to earn degrees, and that public universities, with state and federal support, can match them. Thus in the most reliable world ranking of quality in 2010 Berkeley is 2nd, UCLA 13th, and San Diego 14th, all stars in the pantheon of outstanding research-teaching universities. In fact, the University of California can boast that 7 of its 10 campuses are in the top 46 of the 1,000-plus ranked worldwide.[36] The achievement in equality of opportunity at the top of this system is remarkable. In 2010 4 out of 10 of the

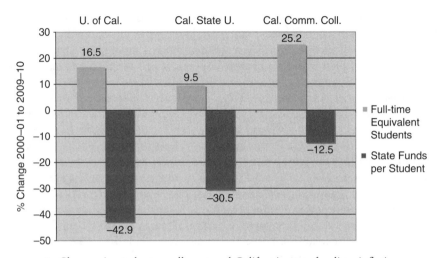

FIGURE 6. Changes in student enrollment and California state funding, inflation-adjusted, in the three-tier system, 2000–2001 to 2009–2010. *Source*: Glantz and Hays, 2009: table 1).

students at the University of California came from families with household incomes of less than $50,000. Half came from homes where English was not the primary language; a third were the first in their families to go to college.

It took decades to build this vibrant system and the great universities that lead it; it can be destroyed in 10 or 15 years. In real dollars, state support for each full-time equivalent student at the University of California declined by 43 percent from 1990 to 2010. The decline in per pupil state support for the state university system was 31 percent. The figure for state funding for the community colleges is a minus 13 percent. At all three levels enrollment continued to climb, although not to the levels specified by the Master Plan. Figure 6 tells the story in inflation-adjusted numbers.

State budget cuts for education at every level, begun in 2000–2001, accelerated in the Great Recession. Douglass (2010, fig. 2) shows the rank of California compared to all other states in the United States in the late 2000s on 10 indicators of funding and performance. They ranged from a best of 43rd in baccalaureate attainment of 18–24-year-olds to a worst of 50th in percent of 18–24-year-olds who enter a four-year institution and the ratio of students to teachers in K–12. On three of these criteria comparing the United States with 32 mostly developed countries, the United States ranked 10th to 15th. In short, while the United States has been declining relative to its competitors, California has moved from near the top of 50 states to near the bottom.

Glantz and Hays (2009: 2) estimate that the California cost for restoring the public higher-education system for all students who meet the standards specified in the Master Plan – to get back to the 2000–2001 level of access and quality while reducing student fees to 2000–2001 levels – would cost state taxpayers

$4.64 billion, less than $32 per median California taxpayer. This is an unlikely prospect during the continuing fiscal crisis.

In view of these draconian budget cuts, Berkeley, UCLA, and San Diego, along with the rest of postsecondary education, can no longer compete with other great universities that are busy raiding their best faculty. In 1984–1985, California public universities together received about 15 percent of the state's General Fund expenditures. For the 2009–2010 budget year, it was about 10 percent (Glantz and Hays, 2009).

Hardly an election goes by that fails to add nails to the pending budget coffin. In 2010 still more initiatives that limit taxing and spending passed. This time it was a proposition that will reduce funding of state and local services by redefining "fees" that can be passed with majority vote as "taxes" that require a two-thirds vote. Another people's choice that year prohibited taking local funds to help balance the budget (that initiative put another billion-dollar hole in the 2010–2011 budget). As we have seen in previous discussion of direct democracy, ballot-box budgeting borders on the insane.

California is not alone in this abandonment of higher education: Michigan, Wisconsin, Illinois, Arizona, and Florida are also well on the way to destroying their public universities (cf. Cole, 2009: 475–479, 142–143). This is a loss not only in the U.S. lead in innovation and discovery. Equally important, it is a loss in the long struggle for equality of opportunity. Top state universities have for decades expanded educational opportunities for able students who cannot afford the cost of outstanding private institutions. The average price of tuition and fees for in-state students at public four-year institutions in the school year of 2009–2010 had climbed to $7,605; add board and room and the total average cost was $16,140. Private nonprofit four-year colleges and universities, of course, charge much more: $27,293 just for tuition and fees; $36,993 total (College Board, 2010). Obviously these student cost increases squeeze out millions of qualified students whose families are in the lower two-thirds of the income distribution (see Chapter 7, sec. 3). The response to the lethal combination of decreases in state per pupil expenditures and sharp cuts in higher education budgets is clear: fewer students can afford to go to college; those who try depend increasingly on loans or loan-scholarship packages that state universities have more difficulty putting together. And, as before, these low- to medium-income students depend upon part-time work, opportunities for which have also declined. Dropout rates have increased. Public universities and colleges have cut programs, enlarged classes, instituted pay freezes and furloughs for faculty and staff, cut research institute budgets, squeezed savings out of administrative expenses, and in other ways have hunkered down. Without further substantial increases in student tuition and fees and a restoration of funding, they will have to reduce admissions radically, or, in time, go out of business as serious educational institutions.

Beyond the restoration of national economic growth, job creation, and reduced unemployment, and in view of the extraordinary collapse of state revenues, the only public policy that might offset the final destruction of public research-teaching universities is a big jump in federal government funding. The Obama administration and the 2009–2010 Congress took modest steps to slow the decline: they increased the federal share of direct aid to students in the form of Pell grants and veterans' benefits (now 44% of the $94 billion compared to 34% the previous year). Overall, they increased federal aid available to college students by nearly half to $145 billion (true, from a low base), and, in the most impressive step, made student loans cheaper by bypassing the banks as intermediaries – impressive because it required a fight against the most powerful lobby in Washington, the financial sector lobby (see Chapter 7, sec. 11). All this cannot offset the fiscal crisis of the states and their education systems. Despite these recent increases in student aid and in the budgets of NIH, NSF, and the Department of Energy, as well as the Obama reversal of the antiscientific bias of the Bush administration, these commendable efforts cannot offset the increase in the demand for those funds. Increased demand comes from drastic cutbacks in some leading research universities and all across the board in public support for colleges and universities. To make up for the fiscal crisis of the states and years of neglect of their education systems, the federal effort will have to be doubled or tripled.[37] The administration's measures do, however, point in the right direction.

The United States faces a choice: reverse the decline in public support for its world-class research universities or lose the economic engine of a good life, the basis of a good economy and a good society.

### *Education vs. Vocational Training?*

Much discussion of educational reform concerns the issue of how much specialized vocational education and general education are best. In Chapter 7 we have seen that the long-run trends have been toward the explicitly vocational. In this section I concentrate on four-year college degrees; later discussion covers community colleges, apprenticeships, and shorter-term technical training. I suggest that given the nature of modern work, the best vocational education is a good general education accenting basic literacy, numeracy, disciplined work habits, and the ability to solve new problems with all deliberate speed – a base for lifetime learning. Consider a few facts about modern work (details in Chapter 6):

- The average worker will hold a dozen jobs in a 45-year work life, most of them unrelated in function or status, many of them not now in existence (based on BLS, 2010c). Both schools and colleges cannot train for specific jobs or even most careers. Most jobs must be learned on the job.
- Increasingly, what the white-collar and professional and even skilled manual jobs require are general conceptual or cognitive abilities (what we have discussed under the labels reading, writing, speaking, reasoning) as well as human relations skills – skills not taught in any one department, skills that employers believe are acquired by college graduates, whatever their majors. Of course, if employers go to the pool of graduate and professional degree holders, they will favor relevant fields.
- Undergraduate degrees are poor predictors of occupational fate, although they certainly pay off in lifetime income. Data suggest that it is the exception

rather than the rule for a student to take an undergraduate degree (or even a first professional degree) in one field and remain there for the whole of his or her career. True, at least nine in ten of the graduates of medical and dental schools practice medicine or dentistry. And an undergraduate major in geology may lead to oil-field exploration and drilling. But the health fields are not typical; neither is geology. A large majority of undergraduate majors are not related to first jobs; even more are unrelated to jobs over the work life.

In short, a good general ("liberal arts") education as a base for lifetime learning is the best vocational education.

If I were a counselor talking with a college freshman or sophomore who had a sense of irrevocable commitment in her choice of a course or a college major, I would try to convey the following idea:

Even if you single-mindedly ignore every educational purpose beyond the vocational – education for the development of alert citizenship and critical thought, for making moral judgments, for the pursuit of knowledge, for the enhancement of capacities of appreciation and performance in the arts, for broader understanding of the individual in community and society – even if you ignore all that, you are badly advised if you think that every course, every curriculum can train you for a particular job. Most jobs are best learned on the job, and often can be learned no other way. Many students will go into jobs not now in existence and many jobs now in existence will be changed by the time the present crop of students is ready to move into them. Your capacity to *learn* a job quickly and do it effectively once you have learned it, your capacity to live a useful, healthy, and satisfying life, your ability to bounce back from reverses – this is where your education should count. So, keep your eye on the clusters of occupations your abilities, motives, and opportunities move you toward, but at the same time let your intellectual curiosity develop a bit – even if it takes you in "nonvocational" directions. In the end, this is the most practical way to play the game.

### Community Colleges: Overloaded and Underfunded

Community colleges are the underdogs of higher education. They epitomize the U.S. tendency to dump its severe social and labor-market problems on educational institutions that cannot solve them. In the fall of 2010 there were 1,173 community colleges in the United States serving nearly 7 million students and another 5 million on a noncredit basis (AACC, 2010). Nine in ten Americans live within 25 miles of one. Nearly half of all undergraduates in the United States attend a community college, most of them from lower socioeconomic backgrounds. These colleges accommodate most of the young high-school graduates from racial, ethnic, or other minority groups who go on to postsecondary education. Many students work, live, or have families in the area (data from AACC, 2010, and Ayers, 2010: 10).

Low costs were the main driver of enrollment in this system. In fall 2010 the average annual tuition and fees of community colleges were $2,713, compared to $7,605 for four-year public colleges (College Board, 2010). That made it affordable for millions, but, of course, many potential students cannot afford even that.

Community colleges have been assigned an impossible set of contradictory functions:

- *Tracking* – the first step upward to a baccalaureate. The earliest community college, Joliet Junior College, was established in 1901 to offer the first two years of a regular college. Graduates could then go for a baccalaureate at a place like the University of Chicago (Ayers, 2010: 10). By the 1970s other functions were added, and student enrollments accelerated until we see now an impossible overload, given the level of funding. Tracking to a baccalaureate can work only if the community college devotes itself mainly to college-level requirements in academic subjects. That is why the addition of a short-term vocational emphasis undermines the chance of student transfer.
- *Terminal vocational training of two years or less.* The aim is to supply local labor for local employers. This has increasingly been the function emphasized by government and industry.
- *Compensatory education.* Increasing time and resources are devoted to remedial reading, writing, and arithmetic to make up for the near collapse of K–12 and the lack of access to preschool preparation. Compensatory education is a major diversion from the original mission of college-level education. And it typically does not work anyway because of entering students' language deficiencies, whose early socialization was in families with multiple problems of poverty, malnutrition, ill health, and the absence of steady parental supervision – all of which combine to produce entrants who are functionally illiterate. For them, the community college is a terrifying place. Thus, the dropout rate in community colleges has steadily risen and is now 7 in 10.[38] We cannot expect postsecondary colleges and universities to make up for our neglect of preschool through high school.
- *Adult education.* An increasing portion of adults want either retraining for job change or courses that enrich their lives, or both. Community colleges, along with university extension services, are charged with meeting much of this demand.

Although the United States has piled more missions on top of the educational function community colleges once served, their funding has plunged while their enrollment climbed. Their faculty has suffered both decreasing security and fewer opportunities for shaping academic policy. In 2007 the U.S. Department of Education reported that 69 percent of community college faculty are part-timers and only 17 percent of the total are in tenure track positions. They work for relatively low pay. Without tenure, they typically lack authority over academic matters such as curriculum, recruitment, and evaluation of peers and even students. They cannot approximate any ideal of shared governance. They run scared, avoiding controversial material and discussion – easily pushed around by boss-administrators. With some variation, these colleges come close to the model of a factory run on command-and-control principles. (Cf. *Academe*, 2010.)

We have already covered the limits of a narrowly focused vocational training emphasis. Because community colleges are increasingly defined as vocational training institutions, it might help to suggest some limits that apply specifically to them. The first is that they already have too many missions to fulfill. The second is the model of training partly inspired by the White House promotion of private corporate–community college partnerships. President Obama, speaking at a Michigan community college July 13, 2009, was specific: "We'll put colleges and employers together to create programs that match curricula in the classroom with the needs of the boardroom .... We know that the most successful community colleges are those that partner with the private sector. We want to encourage more companies to work with schools to build these types of relationships" (White House Press Secretary, 2010). In 2010 the White House announced a new initiative, "Skills for America's Future." It aims to carry out the president's idea that these colleges should do more to meet the demands of local companies and work in close partnership with employers. The federal government will certify a list of "best practices." As of October 3, 2010 (*New York Times*), five employers had been named as partners – Gap, Inc., McDonald's, PG&E, Accenture, and United Technology. What is notable about that list is that they already have extensive in-house on-the-job training, not typical for American firms. (Compared to affluent democracies on the high road, turnover rates in the United States are very high so the typical manager is reluctant to put money in expensive training that will soon benefit his competitors.) Thus, if "Skills for America's Future" attracts the deviant companies that already invest heavily in training, it is unlikely to do more than shift industry costs to government and foundations. Moreover, in view of the short time-perspective of typical American managers, and especially their disinterest in investing in long-term development of their workers, the partnerships with community colleges are used mainly for short term, dead-end low-wage jobs or temps. Finally, the corporation with a local branch near a community college doubtless knows what jobs the local branch needs to fill now or for a couple years ahead but neither central headquarters nor the local unit thinks much about the skill mix of its medium to long term, say, 3 to 5 or 10 years ahead. That is why hiring managers prefer the products of a serious general education with bachelor's degrees (see Chapter 7, sec. 3). These more educated recruits can learn new jobs quickly and adapt to change more readily. In short, even if a community college devoted itself fully to job training and had the resources to overcome all the handicaps of entering students, its graduates would encounter the cascading effect of four-year college graduates displacing them (see Chapter 7, secs. 3 and 9).

These initiatives are typical of proposals from policy experts who know little about education, jobs, or careers and who do not grasp what is going on in community colleges overwhelmed by budget crunches, increased enrollment of marginally literate entrants, and huge dropout rates. "Skills for America's Future" is not a major contribution to rescuing community colleges. Nor is it the road to a strong active labor-market policy (ALMP) that would greatly improve job prospects for everyone. As we have seen in Chapter 7, an ALMP would constitute a serious approach to job training and job creation. It has the additional merit of political feasibility.

I do not argue that our community colleges cannot be important in job training. They are simply handicapped in that mission. If we look at countries that have been successful in job training, we find that they have a much more solid base to build on. In Continental Europe and Japan most vocational programs can assume that entrants are products of high-standard preschool through secondary school; the most outstanding invest heavily in apprentice programs or other, often lengthy work-study programs. They have adopted the many components of an active labor market policy (ALMP): job creation, including public subsidies for infrastructure projects timed for off-season construction or cyclical downturns in the demand for labor; wage subsidies to make up for shorter hours or lower wages in a recession and to encourage employers to retain and train workers; and vocational counseling in secondary schools drawing upon the resources of a strong labor-market board, with follow up of graduates the first year or two of transition from high school to work or further education. Sweden is the epitome of a comprehensive ALMP. Germany is outstanding in both ALMP and formal apprenticeship programs that go back centuries. Such training is a factor in Germany's success in exporting high-quality manufactured products since World War II (see Chapter 6 on the regulation of the labor market) while it keeps youth unemployment low compared to the rate in most other countries and no higher than it is for middle-aged workers. A final advantage of rich democracies with an ALMP is that their employers invest more in on-the-job training; in downturns they are loath to fire their well-trained workers. All this is nothing like job training in the United States. In short, there is no substitute for disciplined study of math, science, and equally important, writing, reading, reasoning, and speaking, on which job training can build.

In the present situation of the United States' neglect of education at every level, the greater the community college accent on short-term job training, the more its students will be tempted to see the cheaper for-profit virtual "universities" as a more attractive alternative, a road to a quick certificate or degree. Or they will remain unprepared for further academic work, the main avenue for occupational mobility.

### For-Profit "Virtual Education": The Latest Threat to Quality

In the past decade there has been an explosion of schools-for-profit that promise quick, easy courses leading to a B.A. or master's degree in record time through distance learning. They offer mostly technical and business degrees or programs for teachers on line. Enrollment growth rates for these enterprises are high – up to 68 percent per year.[39] The most popular of the online universities is Phoenix University, a wholly owned subsidiary of Apollo Group. Phoenix makes more than $1 billion a year in revenue. It claims a student body of 285,777 and an army of "instructors" numbering about 20,000. American Inter-Continental University, owned by Career Education Corporation, is also large and growing; it reports 124,730 students.

These electronic classrooms are the polar opposite of traditional classrooms. The student experience is comparable to watching a TV console, sending Tweets, or joining an online chat room. Virtual education is devoid of the living presence that characterizes the traditional classroom exchange, even in large classes – no tone of voice, no facial expression or gestures, no dialogue, no depth, no sustained contact, little or no intellectual challenge from either the professor or fellow students. Virtual students want directly useful information that pays off immediately in salable business or technical skills. They get by when they regurgitate that information.

Perhaps the greatest threat to quality education from the for-profits comes from what was the expanding market for teacher education before the Great Recession. A *Wall Street Journal* investigative reporter describes a virtual "Cambridge College" that found a niche in the teacher market:

> At Cambridge College, no entrance exam or minimum grade-point average is required to be admitted into the master's program in education. Most students complete half the coursework in a five-week summer program and graduate in about six months. Nearly every grade is an "A." And completing the program guarantees most students a pay increase in their teaching job. (Golden, 2003)

Phoenix University also entered the expanding national market for teacher degrees through distance education. Because opportunities for professional development and promotion are so important in recruitment and retention of talented teachers, virtual universities, by subverting teacher preparation, accelerate the race to the bottom for K–12.

Finally, these immensely profitable degree-delivering machines display a tendency toward fraud. In June 2010 the inspector general of the Department of Education reported that 70 percent of her fraud investigations were focused on the rapidly growing commercial school enterprises. They were caught for falsifying data on student attendance and eligibility requirements for student enrollment (a major source of profit from federal student aid). The report also found that these schools spent little money on teaching but lavish sums for recruitment, marketing, and administration (GAO, 2010). Many of the proprietary schools are blatantly fraudulent in their advertising – trucking schools with no trucks, computer skills classes with few computers and incompetent instructors.[40]

Only by regulating this industry, by increasing public funding of higher education, and by expanding opportunity from community colleges on up, reasserting education as a public good, can the United States reverse this trend toward the fake and the fraudulent.

### California: The Canary in the Coal Mine?

California postsecondary education, because of its size and because it pioneered an extraordinary three-tiered system, is a model of both success and a warning to the rest of the country about threats to its achievements of excellence and mass access. The population of the state is projected to grow from 37 million to 60 million by 2050.[41] Nationally, population growth and the goal of restoring America's previous lead in educational attainment and meeting the increased demand for educated labor require the United States to produce more than

8 million additional degrees. California's share would be about 1 million additional degrees (Douglass, 2010).

To grasp the crisis in higher education, we can begin with recent increases in enrollment and decreases in funding, from both the state and other sources – a bad combination for any educational institution. As Figure 6 shows, in the most recent decade, while enrollments climbed 17 percent in the University of California, 10 percent in the California state universities, and 23 percent in community colleges, real declines in state funds per student plunged. The decline for each of these levels was 43, 31, and 13 percent. California has virtually abandoned its world-class universities. In 1997–1998, the state funded 32 percent of the current operating budget of the University of California; in 2009–2010, it is only 18 percent (University of California, 1996; 2010).

While the United States awaits a recovery of its economy, some steps for structural reform and interim funding are possible. First, although California charges for student tuition, fees, and board and room remain among the lowest in the United States, the state system cannot return to the days when a California education was near free.[42] Beyond higher fees and tuition combined with greatly expanded subsidies and low-cost loans for less affluent students, there must be a clear understanding that out-of-state students both from the United States and abroad are welcome in larger numbers and, as now, will pay high tuition. Finally, with those steps, there is still need for a large infusion of funds from the federal government to support public education in every state.

To lessen the overload of functions among community colleges, some separation of missions could help overcome the mess we have created. J. A. Douglass (2010) suggests a reorganization along these lines:

- *A set of four-year institutions.* The aim would be to supplement the University of California and the state universities in the effort to restore the degree-achievement rates of the past and plan for expansion of the demand for educated labor in the years ahead. To encourage coordination and uniformly high standards, these four-year colleges could be pulled out from local district control (California has 72 community college districts) and report directly to the statewide community college chancellor.
- *A set of transfer-focused two-year institutions* that can concentrate on more serious training in basic literacy, numeracy, analytical skills, and the kind of vocational education that permits its graduates to achieve at least short-step job mobility and improve their capacity to adapt to change. In my view, these two-year colleges would eventually become part of an active labor-market policy, including work-study programs, when the federal government finds the will to act, moving us up from last among the 19 rich democracies in spending in this area (see Chapter 7, sec. 9).
- *A new California Open University* focused only on adult learners. Models of success from abroad range from England's Open University to the folk school traditions of Scandinavia. The growing demand for adult education reflects mass aspirations to enrich life or obtain training for career change.

Existing community colleges could assess their strength and limitations for each of these main missions and gradually specialize. However, the kind of long-range planning that created the three-tier system would be necessary to restructure it. That means strong leadership from the governor and the legislature.

## 4. Summary: What Is Wrong with Education and What to Do about It

Much of what is wrong with our schools at every level is what is wrong with our society: uncushioned family breakup; unsupervised children unprepared for learning or orderly behavior; an increasing rate of poverty and near poverty and growing social inequality; high rates of unemployment both official and hidden; a middle-income squeeze; concomitant deficiencies in child nutrition and health; the lack of national health insurance to deal with such problems; a continuing mortgage and foreclosure crisis; increasing racial tensions and neighborhood violence spilling over into schools – and more. In fact, systematic studies in both the United Kingdom and the United States show that about two-thirds of the variance in school performance can be explained by such inputs – the early socialization and continuing socialization of the child in family and neighborhood. Nevertheless, four strong in-school variables explain a great deal of good performance: higher per pupil expenditure; smaller class size; teacher quality and pay and opportunities and incentives for professional development; and longer school days and years (including summer learning opportunities). They interact to shape the whole school system but have most impact on disadvantaged students.[43]

Nothing in the comparative studies reviewed here suggests that charter schools or vouchers or bashing teachers and their unions will improve student learning or school performance. In fact, if public school teachers are brought into reform efforts, the chance for success improves. There are many cases like the Brockton, Massachusetts, high school where teachers themselves turned a failing school around. If we look abroad at better performing countries, we see much the same: strong unions and highly professional teachers enhance system performance.

Where the United States once led the world in higher education, that lead is severely threatened by funding cuts and an increasing demand for enrollment. The swift erosion of California's pioneering three-tier system, a stellar achievement in combining excellence with equality of opportunity, is the emblem of U.S. neglect from K–12 through Ph.D. The recent rise of for-profit distant learning enterprises, with awful completion rates and considerable fraud, is directly related to the vacuum created by the decline in postsecondary public education.

Further insight into what needs to be done to restore America's lead in education comes from good performing affluent democracies abroad. They learned how from us; we need to relearn the necessary steps from them. They pay their teachers more relative to other professionals and respect them more. They spend more of their budgets on academic resources. They have national standards for performance. They train and educate their teachers in subjects to be taught and give them more autonomy in the classroom. They expect a lot from their students and use comprehensive tests to measure that performance over time. Teachers are given time to confer with one another and plan their work; professional development is valued. The school year and school day tend to be much longer than schedules in the United States. Many of these countries have extensive preschool public programs that foster the cognitive and emotional development of 2–4-year-olds.

Finally, I return to a recurrent theme in this book, the interdependence of public policies. The immense cost of restoring our educational system to previous historical highs can be offset if we simultaneously do what is necessary to reduce poverty and inequality, adopt a family policy and an active labor-market policy, and create a national service corps. Any one of these would take some of the burden off our schools and colleges. Perhaps national service is a good place to begin.

### 5. A Large-Scale Voluntary Program of National Civic and Military Service

A greatly expanded AmeriCorps is the single policy shift that would do most to reduce mayhem, delinquency, and the Balkanization of the United States; it would also help to offset K–12 deficiencies and improve job training and mobility opportunities for many disadvantaged youths. It would increase college-completion rates. By moving young people from the path to prison (Chapter 7, sec. 10) onto the path to education and work, it would reduce our extraordinary rate of incarceration, the annual per capita cost of which exceeds the comparable AmeriCorps cost. Finally, it would represent a major investment in both physical and human capital.

National service should be seen as two alternatives, civilian or military service. The aim of both is to harness the energy, enthusiasm, and idealism of youth and direct them toward solving pressing social problems or serving defense needs. If large enough, it would do much to reestablish the crucial link between public benefits and civic obligation, and thereby restore a sense of community. There are plenty of successful precedents: the New Deal's Civilian Conservation Corps and current programs such as the Peace Corps, Vista, the Job Corps, and President Clinton's most ardently pursued reform, AmeriCorps, launched September 1994 as a three-year $1.5-billion program. Center Left and center Right combined to authorize AmeriCorps. However, by October 1999 only 150,000 volunteers had been enrolled, and Congress gave it a budget of $433.5 million, much less than the president requested and $15 million less than fiscal 1999. (For the rationale and detailed evaluation of such programs and their practical implementation, see Moskos, 1988; Sagawa and Halperin, 1993; and Perry et al., 1999. For a long history of bipartisan support for these programs, 1933–2004, see *Congressional Digest*, September 2006.)

The central exchange in an expanded AmeriCorps is this: young men and women agree to serve their community and nation for a fixed period in areas such as education (assist as tutors, mentors, child-care assistants, and coordinators of such services), health and human needs (help the elderly and frail to maintain their independence by home care and shopping assistance, assist in hospitals, mental institutions, church-based social services), the environment (conservation projects, park restoration), and public safety (enhance community policing, assist in rehabilitation projects). They serve at a quite low salary (the AmeriCorps started at $7,500 a year plus free health care). In return, the participant receives education vouchers for college, vocational education, or to pay off a college loan (this started at $4,725 per year of work). For military service as a citizen-soldier – on average exposing oneself to greater risks – the college benefit would be substantially larger. If both military and civilian vouchers were as generous as, say, the GI Bill, the participation rate would rise dramatically with the same benign effects.[44] On many projects, the civilian service can be combined with formal and informal learning on the job.

Beyond the gain in raising the civic consciousness of each generation of young people, an expanded national service corps also trains and educates them for their role in a modern economy while it brings them into contact with culturally diverse groups. We do not need to look abroad for models; the American armed forces – combining social integration and meritocracy – have been enormously successful at both tasks.

### 6. Reducing Poverty and Inequality

The only strategy for poverty reduction that will work, given the limited impact of the small incremental steps the United States has taken while poverty rates remained high, is to follow the lead of rich democracies that have reduced poverty (and inequality) to quite low levels. We have already elaborated each of these in Chapters 1, 7, and 8. Here is a reminder of a few highlights.

*First, make work pay.* Protect labor standards, including the right to organize. The aim is to avoid a race to the bottom in wages, working conditions, job security, and workers' voice. Beyond restoring the bargaining power of unions to offset the labor-crunch strategy of countries on the low road, the U.S. government can do more of what it has in the past done with small steps forward. Raise the minimum wage to its previous real value, with two or three years of exception for workers just entering the labor force or in on-the-job training. Expand the Earned Income Tax Credit (EITC); it has clearly reduced poverty among low-income workers. Again, adopt and fund an active labor-market policy (ALMP) that includes not just train- ing and retraining programs, but, recognizing that training without the prospect of work may fail, also job creation. That means such measures as direct government projects to meet urgent infrastructure and maintenance needs; wage subsidies and incentives for employers to retain and train workers in hard times; and job counseling with mobility allowances and rent supplements for displaced workers to help them relocate out of depressed areas, as well as work-study programs for high-school and community college students. (For discussion of 21 different types of ALMP programs and the relative effectiveness of several, see Wilensky, 1985.)

*Second, avoid stiff means-tested "welfare" programs characteristic of the United Kingdom, the United States, Canada, and Ireland. Instead adopt more universal, categorical programs of the welfare-state leaders, using simple, private income testing where appropriate* (*Chapter 1 and 3*). Means tests necessitate a bloated bureaucratic apparatus to investigate and harass the targeted poor or "truly needy." Because they are stigmatized, they are ineffective in reaching their targets as shown by low "take-up rates" of such programs as public assistance, food stamps, even Medicaid. They create a morass of multiple and overlapping programs, which leads to widespread inequities – families in similar circumstances receiving sharply contrasting benefits, some none at all. They seldom fit the heterogeneity of needs of the poor, even the welfare poor. Under some circumstances means-tested benefits create disincentives to work, although this flaw is much exaggerated. Finally, while they undermine the dignity of recipients and give political demagogues opportunities to use "welfare cheats" as scapegoats in political campaigns, they have a terrible record of poverty reduction. (For evidence, elaboration, and further citation, see Chapter 7, sec. 9, and Wilensky, 2002: ch. 8. For why "workfare" as a strategy for poverty reduction does not work, see pp. 311–327.)

*Third, adopt a family policy that improves the care of children, facilitates the achievement of parental balance between work and family obligations, increases gender equality, prevents the impoverishment of solo mothers and their children, while increasing female labor-force participation rates, thereby adding to economic growth.* A family policy includes government-subsidized, income-tested child care, before- and after-school programs, parental leave (paid and unpaid), and much more. Cross-national comparisons show that leaders in targeting the poor with stiff tests of income and assets are laggards in family policy, with the United States well toward the bottom of 19 rich democracies as a laggard (see Chapter 7, sec. 9; and Wilensky, 2002: ch. 7).

Making work pay, an active labor-market policy, a family policy, and other universalistic core programs of the welfare state are expensive. But poverty and a chaotic labor market are even more costly. Reducing poverty and the apparatus now used to monitor and investigate the poor and near-poor frees money for investment in more productive physical and human capital. These investments make all the other problems confronting the United States on the low road, such as a deteriorating education system, violent crime, and a world-beating incarceration rate, easier to solve.

## 7. Immigration Policy

Chapter 6 reviews extensive data on the economic and political effects of immigration, including national variation in nativism expressed in violence and voting. Migration from areas of economic despair and repression to areas of opportunity and hope are as old as poverty and persecution. In recent decades, rich democracies have been converging in their cultural and social diversity and their conflict centered on immigration. As we have seen, however, countries differ in their openness to economic migrants and political refugees and their policies toward social integration, as well as the intensity of their anti-immigrant mobilization.

As in all periods of massive immigration from the 1840s on, immigrants have made an important net contribution to the economic performance of the United States. Everyone recognizes their indispensability as unskilled and semiskilled workers in manufacturing, agriculture, construction, retail trades such as restaurants and hotels, household cleaning, child minding, and gardening. Leaving all that aside, it turns out that in 2010 in 14 of the 25 largest metropolitan areas, more than half the working immigrants held higher-paid jobs as professionals, technicians, and administrators (FPI, 2010).[45] It is true that some segments of the citizenry are short-term losers from the recent bursts of immigration from Latin America and the Caribbean. Most of the workers threatened, however, are themselves recent immigrants, legal and illegal, who have been in the United States for some years, or they are unskilled natives competing with illegals crossing the border last year or last month. It is a case where an oversupply of cheap immigrant labor is competing with an oversupply of cheap native labor – both trapped on the low road.

Across all 19 countries, the virulence of nativist sentiment and political action is greatest where the number and concentration of immigrants are heavy, the social distance between natives and strangers (in education, religion, language, ethnicity, and race) is great, and the instability of economic readjustment is most widely experienced. This combination is evident in Europe among Turks in Germany, North Africans in France and Italy, and Muslims everywhere. In the United States we see this combination mainly in states with the fastest growing Hispanic population, Arizona (of crackdown fame), Nevada, Colorado, New Mexico, Texas, and California.[46] Nativism is widespread in all countries. National differences in its expression, however, depend on the mobilizing structures of governments, parties, interest groups, social movements, and the media.

Finally, as I have shown, the main story is that in one or two generations, the children of immigrants evidence a trend toward assimilation as measured by education, workplace integration, and intermarriage rates. With the passing years, even the first generation shows signs of social integration, which varies by minority-group background and experience.

Immigration policy in the United States displays a cyclical quality with peaks of nativism to troughs of more tolerant acceptance in law and custom and back again. The peaks range from the nativist antebellum party, the Know-Nothings, to the 1882 Chinese Exclusion Act; from the 1924 immigration quota bill to the Japanese internment camps of World War II; and, finally, to today when the Republican Party's southern strategy under Reagan through Bush inspires the intense use of wedge issues in elections – playing the race card, the alien threat card, or the religion-moral-social card. These nativist movements and parties are at odds with both the recurrent need for immigrant labor and the values embedded in the Declaration of Independence ("all men are created equal" and denunciations of King George for restricting immigration to the colonies) or the message on the Statue of Liberty ("Give me your tired, your poor, Your huddled masses yearning to breathe free"). Those traditional American values are the first reason for some optimism that we can eventually reform the immigration laws.

The second reason for hope is that immigrant voters are increasing their political clout. The third reason is that Congress in the past few years has almost passed sensible comprehensive reform endorsed by both George W. Bush and proposed by Obama (Jencks, 2007; Tichenor, 2009; Marquez and Witte, 2009; Schrag, 2010; and citations in Chapter 6).

There are an estimated 11 million illegals in the United States. They came here for work and to a lesser extent for family reunification. When politicians suggest that we can round them up and deport them, it is pure demagoguery: the government and police cannot do it, and if they could, it would create havoc in both the labor market and families. Moreover, there are 5.5 million children of unauthorized parents in the United States. About three-quarters of these children are citizens born here; only 17 percent are unauthorized (Passel and Cohn, 2009). What do you do with these 5.5 million?

Recognizing reality, presidents and Congresses from the first and last bipartisan comprehensive bill, the Immigration and Reform Control Act of 1986 (Simpson and Mazzoli), to the narrowly defeated Bush reforms and the Obama proposals, which did not come to a vote, all embraced key components.

- An expanded guest worker program – visas for work
- Strict enforcement of employer sanctions to avoid a race to the bottom
- Earned citizenship – a path to naturalization for illegals through learning English and some American history and civics, paying fines and back taxes (or, most self-defeating because it deters millions from signing up, requirements to return to the home country and then return)

A fourth component of comprehensive reform was border control with increased mobile patrols and guards and more funding for fences and identity checks. Such measures were the price for reluctant politicians to vote for the bill. Though in the end, having achieved an emphasis on the border, a majority of Republican senators joined by 15 Democrats voted against the 2006 bill, enough to bury it in 2007 – 14 votes shy of the 60 needed to force a final vote. The "border control first" crowd either believed in the efficacy of policing and physical barriers or was merely pandering to the nativist sentiments of its constituents. In real life whenever the United States tried to tighten its 2,000-mile border with Mexico by fencing and policing, it did not reverse the increase in illegal crossings. ("Show me a 20′ fence and I'll show you a 21′ ladder.") What it did was raise the price racketeers extracted for a promise to deliver people across the border. It also increased the difficulty of success on a first try, encouraging multiple tries, while increasing the death rate of the migrants who got stranded on the way.

If increased border control is the price to pay for reluctant congressional votes and for countering nativist mass protests, there is a better way to meet the challenge and at the same time serve the well-being of all workers. Policing the border effectively means policing employers who hire illegals at substandard wages, often well below the legal minimum. Employer sanctions, used by almost all our 19 countries (Britain is an exception), vary in their effectiveness: vital to their success are adequate resources for enforcement, a secure identification system, links to broader strategies for controlling illegal migration and enforcing labor standards, and steps to prevent employer discrimination on the basis of immigrant status. The United States fails on all counts. Several European countries – Germany, France, and Switzerland – approximate them (M. Miller, 1987; Martin and Miller, 2000).

When employers claim that American workers do not want the jobs immigrants gladly take, they mean that native workers refuse to work at the low wage offered. When employers say that they hired an illegal unknowingly because the immigrant showed a fake ID, the employers have a point. Any comprehensive effort for regulating immigrant labor must start with a secure ID card. As Christopher Jencks suggests, if the Social Security Administration (SSA) were mandated to cooperate with Immigration and Customs Enforcement (ICE), it could replace the SSA ID card (routinely used to credit worker's retirement accounts with worker and employer contributions) with a tamper-proof card "including both a photo and information on whether the person was a citizen, a permanent resident authorized to work here, or a temporary resident to work here until some specific date" (2007: 50). Only with such a reliable ID card can stiff employer sanctions work. Once secure ID is in place, random inspections of workplaces as a deterrent against hiring illegals and violating labor laws can be reasonably carried out. And any court will assume that the employer who violates the law knew what he was doing.

Comprehensive reform embracing these four components is another demonstration of the interdependence of separate policies and was one rationale for the 1986 act and the bill endorsed by Bush (2006) and Obama's proposals (2008).[47]

Sympathetic critics of comprehensive reform argue that the failure to implement the 1986 reforms, especially employer sanctions, and the failure to reduce the flow of illegals, gave comprehensive reform a bad name. Implementation failures increased cynicism among voters and lawmakers and therefore made subsequent reform attempts more difficult. They believe that incremental strategies are the only option left (e.g., Marquez and Witte, 2009). In my view, any successful immigration reform cannot be achieved incrementally, one piece at a time. In fact, comprehensive reform is not just good policy but is more politically feasible. Different interests can each get something. Humanitarians, religious groups, and center-left activists get family visas, roads to citizenship, and enforceable employer sanctions, Social Darwinists and anti-immigration moderates get secure ID cards and more effort to control borders. Employers get a more regular labor supply and an increase in quotas for skilled, educated workers.[48]

Finally, the timing is right for the next 5 to 10 years. Aging of population and low birth rates combine to make it virtually certain that the United States will have a shortage of labor, accelerating over time. There is already a shortage of homegrown scientists and engineers. Assuming we are not mired in a jobless recovery for decades, shortages will develop at every level of skill. Comprehensive immigration reform will take account of this and can be one rationale for it.

How to promote cultural diversity and social cohesion at the same time is a challenge for all rich democracies (Chapter 6). The record shows that host-country language is the key to integration – occupational, educational, and social. It is a great irony that the United States, with a successful history of social integration of tens of millions of socially distant ethnic-religious-linguistic groups from 1900 to 1950s has more or less abandoned large-scale training in the host language. Language and citizenship training was the key to success not only of integration policy but of the education and social mobility of the immigrants. Promoting the heritage language and culture was secondary. For the next half century we have instead emphasized civil rights and multiculturalism, whereas Europe, trading places with us, has insisted that its immigrants learn the host-country language and take some civics lessons. In other words, we need to attend to our past success in teaching English to masses of immigrants at the peak immigration of the early 1900s to the 1950s. The United States should be concerned about a 30-year decline in English proficiency of full-time immigrant workers (age 25 and older). In 1980 or earlier only 33 percent were "limited English proficient" but by 2000–2005 that figure had climbed to 63 percent (Fix, 2009). Our sister democracies, borrowing from our past, have recognized that the host language is essential for integration, including promotion of adult language training to help break the intergenerational transfer of disadvantage.

This is no argument against learning foreign languages. To be fully bilingual or multilingual, as the citizens of many small European democracies are, is one thing; to be fluent in the immigrant's language but handicapped in the host language is entirely different. As part of recapturing our educational lead of the past, we should provide primary and early emphasis on learning English for both immigrant children and their parents. This could be part of a broader effort to expand learning opportunities to improve the prospects not only of immigrant populations but of the deprived lower half of the education ladder. As we have seen in our discussion of preschool through the Ph.D., increasing hours in education improves student performance. If we are unwilling to lengthen the school day and year, it is not beyond our grasp to set up homework centers, after-school classes, summer schools, remedial programs, and host-language classes to those in need, especially children who lack parental support at home and lag behind at school.

This is also no argument against studying diverse cultures. It is an argument to take both phrases in *E pluribus unum* seriously (it appears on our currency and the Seal of the United States) – "out of many," yes; but our immigration policies and often our schools have lost the meaning of "one." To learn the minimum of the English language and American history and government is not to insult minority languages and cultures; it *is* to recognize and celebrate our common heritage and values.

## 8. Energy Policy, Politics, and the Environment

Because Chapter 2 covers the problem and its history and evaluates alternative approaches to climate change in the United States and the other 18 rich democracies, this can be brief. The evidence shows that civilization as we know it cannot be sustained if we do not act now to substantially lower emissions of heat-trapping gases. In fact, the tipping point in climate change gives us only 40 to 60 years before irreversible planetary damage occurs – and that may overstate the time left. On the basis of the dismal history of international action, I have argued that to rely on binding and enforceable agreements among numerous countries to lower greenhouse gas emissions is a mistake. The nation-state remains the center of action on energy and the environment, as we can see from case studies of policy and politics in countries that have combined robust economic performance, energy efficiency, and marked reduction in carbon dioxide and other greenhouse gas emissions – for example, Denmark and Sweden.

A feasible energy policy for the United States would start with energy efficiency, the most cost-beneficial and most immediately effective step and the best of the green job creation strategies. This includes building retrofits, energy standards for new construction, time of use pricing that mandates installation of smart meters in both residential and commercial buildings, rapid urban transport and intercity rail, more investment in waste-to-energy projects. It means reducing our reliance on cars while we make them more efficient and invest in alternative rail and bus transportation. Equally important, it means gradually shifting subsidies away from fossil fuels and toward renewables such as biomass, wind, geothermal, solar, and waves.

What not to do is equally important. Research suggests that among the current subsidies that should be rejected as damaging the environment are supports for corn-based ethanol, the idea of "clean coal," and the myth that nuclear energy is not only safe in operation and the disposal of nuclear wastes but is also "clean." To cut through industry propaganda campaigns for all of these, we must pay attention to their *emissions over their life cycle and their costs in energy and natural resources.* The nuclear story in Chapter 2 pins this down. Nuclear energy plants do not directly emit greenhouse gases, but over their life cycle (of 24 years at full power and 30–40 years overall) total costs and indirect emissions are huge. The current cost of just one 1,000-megawatt nuclear plant is $6 to $8 billion. The life-cycle emissions include plant construction (always involving emissions from asphalt and cement plants that supply the building materials, roadways for heavy trucks to carry them), plant operation, uranium mining and milling and, most costly in $CO_2$ emissions, plant decommissioning. The environmental damage is heaviest at the beginning of plant construction and at the end of the cycle. More research of this kind on other energy sources would permit a more valid ranking of emissions.

The progress in research on the relative damage over the life cycle ("well to wheels") of various energy alternatives suggests a tentative rank order. Because carbon dioxide is the primary heat-trapping gas emission, the ranks are based on $CO_2$ per gallon of gasoline equivalent (Peña, 2008, figure 5) unless otherwise noted. The three groupings indicate largest differences from worst to best:

1. Coal, including coal-to-liquid fuel. Much the worst in damage, it accounts for about one-half of U.S. electricity production.
2. Oil. Ninety-five percent of transportation fuels in the United States are derived from petroleum. Although the production and use of a gallon of

fuel from crude oil releases only a little more than half the $CO_2$ per gallon of liquid fuel originating in coal, the two are the clear leaders in planetary harm (National Resources Defense Council, 2007).

3. Nuclear energy. (Cf. M. Jacobson, 2008; Sovacool, 2008; Goldemberg, 2009.)
4. Ethanol from corn.

--------------------

5. Hydroelectric power.
6. Biodiesel.
7. Ethanol from corn biomass with carbon capture and storage.

--------------------

7a. Wind, concentrated solar, tidal and wave power (see M. Jacobson, 2008: n. 179).
8. Ethanol from switchgrass.
9. Ethanol from switchgrass with carbon capture and storage. This is the only option that actually removes more $CO_2$ from the atmosphere than it emits over the life cycle.

As Chapter 2 suggests, perhaps the best of all the options among developed countries is ethanol from cellulosic biofuels based on dedicated energy crops such as straw and switchgrass that grow on abandoned land – perennials that grow from natural rainfall, create little or no erosion, and do not undercut the food supply.[49] Ethanol from corn is the polar opposite.

Note that this rank order ignores the lavish use of scarce water in producing some types of energy (natural gas via hydraulic fracturing); it ignores the clear and present danger of nuclear proliferation and security. And it assumes that we will do something about our archaic electrical grids. In short, we must act simultaneously on several fronts, taking care that gains from one policy are not offset by losses from another.

Any energy policy that is effective will gradually shift the enormous subsidies from fossil fuels and nuclear plants to more efficient uses of energy including government support for the current use and further development of cleaner energy sources. Reversing our decline in civilian R&D is an essential part of this development. As Chapter 7, sec. 11, and my discussion of research universities show, few important innovations have been accomplished without public investment. In fact, making a market through government subsidies and tax expenditures is customary for promising technologies.

If the U.S. government shifted even half of its subsidies and tax breaks away from these "private" government-supported firms in coal, oil, and nuclear, they would be forced to raise their prices and could no longer claim superior costs and benefits over clean energy sources. A level playing field would likely improve the prospects of renewables, bringing the price for clean energy down and speeding up market demand (Bower, 2010).

"Cap-and-trade" is the single most favorably discussed option for coping with energy pricing and emissions. Chapter 2 shows why this is folly. In theory, this "market-based solution" limits how much greenhouse gas (e.g., $CO_2$) producers can emit and lets them buy and sell emissions credits. In practice, three difficulties are fatal. First, in Europe where it has been tried since 1995 and in U.S. congressional proposals, producers can easily game the system. Carbon traders such as banks and brokers join the fun. Second, it is too complicated and costly to administer, regulate, and verify. Third, it puts a value on pollution. Contrast a straightforward carbon tax levied on producers upstream, not at the gas pump. It is simpler to explain, simpler to administer, regulate, and verify, much less subject to corporate gaming, and it offers no incentive to pollute. It is a basic incentive for efficient use of energy across the board – incentive to make cars, home appliances, homes, and workplaces more efficient while we free ourselves from dependence on oil from the Middle East and fund the necessary R&D to encourage innovation in the development of clean energy alternatives.

If the final argument for cap-and-trade is that whatever its deficiencies it is more politically feasible than a carbon tax, the record suggests that strong versions of both arouse passionate resistance from the industries and countries that produce the most greenhouse gases. So the fight might as well be for the best of the two.

The political record of recent attempts to move our resources to a more energy efficient economy and a more environmental friendly society is not encouraging. That is why I have listed this policy area as marginally feasible along with reregulation of the financial sector. By "marginally" I mean that progress requires only the addition of strong presidential leadership to a Democratic Party majority no larger than that in the 2009–2010 Congress, and with no move of the Republican Party toward "moderation." After all, there is much wider, organized support for environmental action than there is for, say, labor-law reform or free media access for parties and politicians, or even national health insurance.

An illustration of the recurrent political barriers to energy policies that address both energy efficiency and greenhouse gas emissions is the fate of good bills when they go through congressional procedures. In 2009 the House Committee on Energy and Commerce reported out the Waxman-Markey bill. By the time the energy industry lobbyists got through with the bill as it was being written, it gave large subsidies to nuclear, coal, oil, and gas and very little to alternatives. Further, it made its cap-and-trade provisions into a bonanza of free pollution permits – about 85 percent of them free and good for 10 years after its start in 2015. The watered-down bill passed the House by a narrow margin. (For a play-by-play account of the compromised bill, see Ryan Lizza, 2010.)[50] Although the energy industry lobby is only the third largest (in money spent), behind the medical-industrial and financial/real estate lobbies, it has been quite successful (CRP, 2009).

If, as seems likely, the Flat Earth crowd takes over the House in November 2010, there will be no serious action for at least two years.[51] This should not stop national debate and the mobilization of an increasingly effective environmental movement in another election cycle or two when the stars are in alignment (strong president, substantial Democratic majorities). When this happens, success would be possible with a little change in tactics and one big change in policy (move toward a simple carbon tax rather than a futile cap-and-trade policy). The tactical change is to begin with smaller committee compromises in the House, say, low to medium subsidies for carbon-emitting industries. And then, instead of *preemptive* compromises that end up even in the House with a near-worthless bill, trade a small beginning of a carbon tax – a line in the sand – in return for maintaining subsidies for the polluters to be phased out over time. The end product would be more effective than caving in to the polluters at the outset (see Chapter 2).

A promising step toward energy efficiency and reduction of GHG emissions that goes beyond the energy problem is a proposal reintroduced in the House of Representatives May 2009, the National Infrastructure Development Bank Act of 2009 (NIB). It would create and fund a bank that would direct public and private dollars toward infrastructure projects of national and regional significance. It would leverage private investments in critical needs in transportation, the environment, energy, and telecommunication, reversing the deterioration recorded in Chapter 7, sec. 8. The NIB would be authorized to provide loans and loan guarantees for large-scale projects. Included in the Obama budget and the budget resolution, it had wide support from a coalition ranging from the Chamber of Commerce and the construction industries to the AFL-CIO and the American Society of Civil Engineers (Ehrlich and Rohatyn, 2008; Rohatyn, 2009). If too much of this is devoted to roads and bridges, it could be self-defeating for the goal of cutting greenhouse gas emissions. But substantial funds for filling potholes and fixing dangerous bridges, vital for safety in their own right, is a small trade-off for the other components of such a bill. The auto-manufacturing and highway complex gets something; so does the public interest.

One White House tendency that favors better outcomes for research, including research on energy alternatives, is President Obama's rejection of the anti-science policies of Bush. For instance, Obama used his executive authority to permit federal funding of stem-cell research. Unhappily that was reversed again when a district court judge appointed by Reagan declared Obama's executive order unconstitutional.

## 9. Financial Reregulation

In 2010 it is too early to assess the impact of the effort to reregulate the financial sector. But some outcomes seem likely. The Dodd-Frank financial bill was the vehicle for reform. In 2008–2009 the financial sector associations and lobbyists spent $600 million to create a climate against reregulation and weaken the bill, with impressive success (Connor, 2010: 5). The final bill contains no serious structural reform to prevent recurrence of the banking crisis that triggered the worldwide Great Recession. The theme of "too big to fail" along with my analysis of "sure to fail" (Chapter 6) and the logical implication, "too big to survive," have been sidetracked.

In the end, Dodd-Frank is a cobweb of complexity and ambiguity that invites corporate gaming, agency capture, and revolving doors. Beyond deregulation, these are the problems that got us into the current mess (Chapters 6 and 7, sec. 12). The bill tells 11 government agencies to write 243 major rules (each one a large cluster of rules). It instructs them to conduct studies of many a topic (e.g., the SEC must study conflicts of interest in the rating agencies – in essence kicking that can down the road).

The small steps that tiptoe around the edges of the basic problems include new capital requirements for banks in the hope of curbing excess speculation in obscure derivatives; a ban on proprietary trading; a new consumer protection bureau, which, if staffed by consumer advocates, could limit lending abuses; the so called "Volcker Rule" limiting the ability of FDIC-insured institutions from operating hedge funds; strengthened regulations on investment advisers; and tighter oversight of the credit rating agencies.

The strongest obstacle to effectiveness of financial reregulation is the centralized power of a few large investment banks.[52] Their economic dominance of the financial sector is the problem of reshaping its structure (see Chapters 6 and 7). Dodd-Frank does nothing about that. In fact, we have already seen what the Wall Street oligarchs can do to elude this modest effort to change their behavior. For instance, the bill sets up an expanded authority to wind down a failing bank and avoid systemic risks. As Boone and Johnson (2010) suggest, however, there is a large loophole in the bill, a dangerous poison pill. All a bank or shadow bank has to do to escape that authority "is to grow so large that it is vital to not just the U.S. economy, but the entire international financial system." American legal requirements cannot apply to foreign countries. Thus, CEO Jamie Dimon of JP Morgan Chase and other powerful bankers have responded to Dodd-Frank by accelerating their already strong commitment to become bigger and more important to the world economy.

Other illustrations of gaming the system abound (*New York Times*, July 16, 2010). Faced with limits on debit card fees, Bank of America, Wells Fargo, and others have imposed fees on checking accounts. Faced with the demand that they trade derivatives more openly on regulated clearinghouses, Goldman Sachs and JP Morgan are building up their brokerage operations; they hope to make even more money by becoming matchmakers in the huge market for these toxic instruments. They can also move some of their derivative operations overseas. Faced with a bar on bets with their own money, banks respond by letting some of their traders continue derivative speculation as long as they work with clients, thereby escaping regulation. And so on. It does not help that the most powerful firms have armies of lawyers, traders, risk managers, and computer programmers to game a government regulatory regime that is understaffed and underfunded.[53]

There is a well-intentioned effort to regulate pay in the financial sector. About half of all revenue generated on Wall Street is paid out to employees as compensation. Among the incentives for top executives to engage in dangerous speculation, if not thievery, is the size and form of their compensation packages. Contrary to their favored image of the innovative entrepreneur taking risks to drive a robust economy, these financial elites are, in fact, among the most risk-averse folks in the world. This is evident in their pay packages, stock options, golden parachutes, long contracts specifying rewards for every contingency (mergers, buyouts, bankruptcies, and more). When things go wrong for a firm on Wall Street, its executives have little trouble moving sideways or up. Their counterparts in the more productive Silicon Valleys of the United States have similarly achieved contractual security. In other words, it is not only the American masses who seek security against the vagaries of the market; it is the American corporate elite as well. To top it off, if these bold entrepreneurs make too many bad bets, the government will rush to their rescue with large doses of corporate welfare – the bailouts, subsidies, and tax breaks that have accelerated in recent decades.

Regulating pay works only if you can make top decision makers suffer personal losses for short-term escalation of risks (Shiller, 2010; cf. French et al., 2010). The effort to regulate pay seems doomed.

I have earlier covered the problem of a revolving door and staffing regulatory agencies with ideologues dedicated to undermining the mission of their agencies. Because of the Rube Goldberg complexity of the bill and the mountain of rules to be written, regulators in these 11 agencies will necessarily be working with their private-sector counterparts. It can be a two-way capture. Regulating staff will try not to antagonize their most likely future employers; they will also pay attention to members of Congress who have received generous contributions from America's most powerful lobby and who want proposed regulations changed. Financial institutions will continue to hire staffers as advisers or directors.

Regarding foxes guarding the chicken coop, presidents so inclined can appoint regulators who do not believe in the aims of their agencies. Especially where so many specialized agencies are writing so many rules, the staffing of the agencies is crucial (Chapter 7, sec.12).

There is a good way to diminish these patterns of agency capture and the revolving door and at the same time increase government efficiency and morale: pay top civil servants in regulatory agencies higher salaries and reduce the number of political appointees. As the experience of Canada, the United Kingdom, and France shows, a well-paid, well-trained professional civil service increases agency efficiency, reduces corruption, and fosters honest advice. Some of our own experience is relevant: as Daniel Carpenter (2010) suggests in his history of one of the more effective agencies in the federal government, the Food and Drug Administration (FDA), if its professionals at every level are dedicated to protecting the agency's reputation for competence and vigilance, companies regulated will respect their authority and, except in brief periods when antiscientific fervor in high places prevails, government officials will respect their autonomy. Until Congress and the White House have a large majority of politicians and staffers who want to govern in the public interest, this improvement of the higher civil service will remain a dream. As it stands, it is amazing that our much-maligned government attracts more than a few excellent staffers and politicians dedicated to public service.

In sum, it may be essential to reach compromise to achieve passage of effective reregulation of the financial sector. But if we look to the model of the structural reforms of the New Deal that gave us more than half a century of reasonable banking practices – the Pecora investigation of abuses on Wall Street and major financial reforms of the 1930s – we will not compromise away the necessary components of financial reregulation. First, the economic dominance of the few megabanks is the problem of "too big to fail"; only structural reform can reverse this trend. As Peter Boone and Simon Johnson remind us (2010: 2), "Banks fail and massive banks fail massively." The other necessary reforms: set up an independent consumer protection agency covering banks, shadow banks, and nonbanks; rein in short-run speculation based on obscure derivatives; and, hardest of all, reduce the concentration of political power (see Chapter 6). Compromising these away is not "politics as the art of compromise." It is standing for little and fighting for less, especially if the new regulations are sure to fail and undercut future efforts at serious reform.

## 10. A Note on Tort Reform

The United States lacks channels for corporatist bargaining, which are alternatives to lawsuits and courts. So we have a load of lawyers and many nuisance suits. Scholars on the right, left, and center sometimes agree that nuisance suits could be reduced to good effect. But this is a case where something (legal redress) *is* better than nothing. And although the cost of free-swinging tort law for a few industries and occupations (obstetrics, the makers of football helmets) is very high, it is a small burden on total corporate budgets or the economy as a whole (Wilensky, 2002: 477–480). Small reforms might help if they do not threaten legal redress: first, follow the United Kingdom and many other countries that make losing lawyers pay the winner's legal fees and pay court costs. Second, replace "joint-and-several liability" with a fair-share rule; a defendant in a lawsuit would then be liable for the percentage of the final reward equal to her share of responsibility for the injury. These two reforms would go far in reducing nuisance suits. Such legislation is not high on the list of feasible reforms, however, because business lobbyists interacting with right-wing politicians undermine legal redress when crafting tort reform, leaving the average citizen defenseless against corporate wrongdoing or professional negligence.

## 11. Government Spending vs. Tax Breaks

There is much controversy about the economic effects of tax cuts vs. government spending (*Economist*, Sept. 24, 2009; Mankiw, 2008; Council of Economic Advisers, 2010). Most of it is ideological (starve the beast vs. expand government action), but among the more systematic researchers the disagreements are about how to measure fiscal multipliers under various economic conditions (whether the economy is in a recession or is running at or near full capacity) and how to take account of all the other variables that affect growth and employment. This book has shown that good answers must take account not only of the ups and downs of the economy but the precise types of taxes and types of spending. For instance, there is little doubt that in the Great Recession and the jobless recovery of 2009–2010 the fiscal multiplier for infrastructure investment is much more than that for tax cuts in both the short run and the long. In any slack economy, the types of productive social and labor-market spending discussed in Chapters 1, 3, 7, and 8 (education, health care, family policy, active labor-market policy, research and development, raising labor standards) foster economic growth because they stimulate spending by consumers and businesses. Christina Romer, chair of the Council of Economic Advisers for the first 20 months of the Obama administration, reported the consensus estimate of all the relevant agencies including the CBO, the CEA, and the Fed that a dollar of government spending results in a multiplier of 1.5 ($1.50) because it is spent on productive infrastructure and consumption. The estimate of the multiplier effect of a temporary tax cut was much lower – .4 and for a permanent tax cut, .8 (Council of Economic Advisers, 2010: table 3 and personal conversation with Romer). Chapter 7, sec. 11, shows that a dollar spent on military R&D yields much less in multiplier effect than a dollar spent on civilian R&D. Indeed, both American and cross-national data indicate that high total spending on defense subverts aggregate social spending for many years ahead. Of course, in the current crisis spending targeted to middle- and lower-income households will have a much larger immediate effect on growth compared to tax cuts benefiting high-income groups, who will spend little of their added tax breaks.

A final complication in assessing tax cuts vs. direct spending as a stimulus to growth and job creation is the effect of each on government revenue and debt. Paul Krugman puts it this way:[54]

If $100 billion in spending raises GDP by $150 billion, and the marginal tax rate is 1/3, $50 billion of the spending comes back in additional revenue. So bang for the buck – increases in GDP per dollar of added debt – is 3, not 1.5. Since the main concern about stimulus [in congressional debate] is that it will add to government debt, it's this bang for the buck measure, rather than the multiplier, that's relevant. And 3 sounds a lot better than 1.5.

In any case, it appears that the stimulus spending in the 2009 package, about one-third of which were tax cuts, although no doubt useful in preventing a slide into a 1930s' Depression, was not just too small; it was too short-lived to foster a robust recovery of jobs and growth. And without such stimulus debt will climb along with greater diversion of annual budgets from productive spending to interest payments on the debt, while misery for tens of millions of families will deepen. In our situation of 2010–2011 – an anemic, jobless recovery – tax cuts will have much less effect than spending on the human and physical infrastructure we have neglected for decades.

Democrats cannot outpace Republicans in their obsession with cutting taxes as Obama tried to do for most of his first two years and, of all times, three weeks before the 2010 election. The fate of Blue Dog Democrats in the 2010 congressional election is another indication that Republican Light is no viable strategy for center-left politics in the years ahead – unless Democrats wish to imitate Republican theology that tax cuts at any and all times not only spur economic prosperity but also increase government revenues, unless they also wish to disassemble government. Herbert Stein, former chairman of the Council of Economic Advisors under Presidents Nixon and Ford, called this tax-cut mania "punk supplysidism" – extreme to the point of being bizarre. Punk supplysidism or not, joining the tax-cut movement is neither good economics nor a good formula for a center-left coalition.

## G. HOW TO PAY FOR IT ALL: THE NEED FOR TAX BALANCE

The Grand Illusion of the Democratic Party is that the road to equality goes through progressive income taxes and especially taxes on the very rich and on business and property. Democrats could profit from the experience of the Social Democratic parties of Western Europe: as they lengthened their lists for job security, labor standards, and the welfare state, they found that income taxes and property taxes on households, the most painfully visible taxes invented, had reached their political limits in financing a center-left agenda. By "painfully visible" I mean taxes taken in one or two big bites from taxpayers who believe that they will not receive direct benefits in line with contributions. (Social Security taxes are moderately visible, but most citizens connect the tax with future benefits.) They diversified and broadened their tax base. No country has financed a center-left agenda without mass taxes.

A major finding in my own research on tax revolts in 19 countries shows that it is not the *level* of taxes that creates tax-welfare backlash but the *type* of taxes – property taxes on households and income taxes with their visibility and perceived pain. The Anglo-American democracies along with Denmark and Switzerland have specialized in these most unpopular taxes, with predictable political uproar. Conversely, consumption taxes (e.g., VAT, value-added tax) and social-security payroll taxes keep things cool; they have never triggered a sustained tax revolt. In the words of an old pop tune, "It ain't what you do, it's the way that you do it."

Democrats in the United States have long advocated a progressive tax system as ideal – fair, efficient, egalitarian, and poverty reducing. Leaving aside the fact that evasion and avoidance (and the time and resources devoted to tax games) mean that income taxes in action are not highly progressive, ignoring the fact that corporate taxes and taxes on the rich cannot yield huge sums, the main mistake is to believe that, by riveting one's attention on the tax side of the taxing/ spending equation, one can achieve much of anything on the center-left agenda. In fact, the most equalitarian and civilized democracies on the high road (see Table 2) have slightly regressive tax systems and highly progressive spending programs. *They are well on the way to the tax balance that permits stable public finance with least political fuss – less than a third of total revenues in progressive income taxes, a third in payroll taxes, almost a third in consumption taxes (e.g., VAT).* They avoid heavy property taxes on households like the plague. They design the VAT so that it is proportional or only mildly regressive by exempting some items (e.g., home-consumed food).

Further, the economic impact of VAT is consistently positive; social-security payroll taxes are positive in "normal" times (no recession). They both reduce demand and increase savings and investment; these effects outweigh a small initial inflationary effect of introducing a VAT (Wilensky, 2002: 453, 462, 483). Other taxes range from neutral to negative for growth, savings, investment, inflation control, and unemployment (Chapter 3; and Wilensky, 2002: ch. 12.)

Democrats who think that they must avoid the "T" word might note a 2006 shift away from the "something-for-nothing" plague: the National Conference of State Legislatures reports that voters passed only 1 of the 17 state measures that would have saddled legislators with arbitrary budget, taxation, and term-limit restraints, California style.[55] And, if we compare tax cuts with spending increases, not just for spending's bigger bang for the buck in a slack economy but for political effect, spending wins hands down. When the president repeatedly touted his tax cuts that were about a third of the stimulus package, neither his speeches nor the tax cuts penetrated the awareness of the public. In fact, on October 17, 2010, the *New York Times*, reviewing polls about these cuts, headlined the results: "From Obama, the Tax Cut Nobody Heard Of." Half of those surveyed thought that their taxes had stayed the same; a third thought their taxes had gone up. Contrast perceived threats of spending reductions in Social Security, Medicare, cutoffs in unemployment insurance, and fear of job and wage loss, most based on experience and reinforced by White House talk about health-care savings and fighting the debt – these have been mounting in voter concern for more than two years. (See also Chapter 4 on the politics of cutback budgeting.)

If American progressives believe that taxes buy civilization; that public spending for health, education, and the general welfare produces a more humane, equitable, and just society; if they also believe that a strong government is needed to curb the power, venality, and greed of private groups, then they would be well advised to advocate a 15-year plan for tiny incremental increases in social-security taxes on payroll and gradually phase in a European-style federal VAT (tax each business on the difference between sales to its customers and its purchases from other businesses). A responsible center Left would recognize that governments cannot persistently expand cash benefits and social services without increasing the tax take. It would accept the need for tax balance. My analysis (2002: ch. 10) shows that nowhere since World War II has the introduction of or modest increases in payroll taxes or the VAT created sustained tax-welfare backlash.

## H. COALITION POLITICS TO RESTORE THE PURSUIT OF A CENTER-LEFT AGENDA

A feasible agenda for moving the United States off the low road, from easiest politically to most difficult, includes a family policy together with social-security reform; an active labor-market policy (ALMP); a national civic and military service corps building upon Americorps; policies to restore our lead in education from K–12 to the Ph.D. (preschool and child care are part of a family policy); action to rebuild our physical infrastructure; comprehensive immigration reform; reducing poverty and inequality (all of the above are keys to reversing our high rate of poverty and the upward climb of wealth and income); and, less surely but no less important, action on energy and the environment and financial reregulation. Much more problematic are three policy domains that require strong coalitions that do not now exist: national health insurance; labor-law reform; and the restoration of representative and deliberative aspects of American democracy, beginning with an increase in party and candidate access to the broadcast media and other costly means of communicating with voters in campaigns if not year round.

I have explained why the Republican Party, with its radical shift to the right since the 1980s on all of these issues and its increasingly obstructionist role, cannot help; "bipartisanship" is a mirage. That is why I turned to the question of revitalizing the Democratic Party as the only channel that can begin to move the United States off the low road. Note especially my discussion of Table 11 comparing the economic, social, and political performance of the two major parties over time and the composition of a center-left coalition. Suggestions about how to overcome Senate paralysis are also relevant.

Happily the most feasible policies are interdependent bread-and-butter issues that could help to revitalize the Democratic Party – an active labor-market policy including not only training but also job creation, wage subsidies, an expanded earned-income tax credit, and many other ways to improve work opportunities, a family policy, education reform, and a national civic and military service corps. They accent universality of benefits and obligations, they avoid divisive means testing, they focus on jobs and the family. And there is no requirement that there be a revival of moderation in the Republican Party or that there be Johnson's two-to-one margin in the Senate. All of this could be done with strong presidential leadership and a Democratic margin in Congress no larger than that of 2009–2010.

The message from public opinion research since World War II is this: American voters do not grasp issues remote from their experience; they do not spend a lot of time worrying about monetary policy, the national debt, the multiplier effects of taxing vs. spending, Pentagon budgets, missile defense or any other foreign policy (unless a war directly affects their immediate family or if they believe that a trade agreement is outsourcing jobs). They do not understand White House seminars on the complexities of health-reform proposals that require an advanced degree to comprehend. But on the political economy close to home – people's pensions, disability insurance, the rising cost and declining coverage of their health care, the quality of their children's schools and the cost of college, their food and gas prices, their stagnant wages, the cost of their mortgage or rent, uncle Joe's loss of a job, the local plant shutdown, the personal bankruptcy of a neighbor, the threatened foreclosure on another's home – on these issues they have a laser-beam focus. It is not too much to hope that a Democratic president sometime in the next few election cycles will understand this and lead the next Democratic majority back to the issues that define the Party and inspire turnout, as happened in the congressional election of 1996 and the campaign of Bill Clinton in 1992 (Jobs, Jobs, Jobs).

Good policies, the center-left agenda, make good electoral strategies. Even the three most difficult policy clusters, starting with national health insurance, can be made simple in a three-word sound bite – "Medicare for All" (beginning with Medicare for more). Reforms of 2009–2010 represent a major missed opportunity but the issue will recur. Add two easier policy packages, "Work Should Pay" and "Make College Affordable." This is a trio of campaign messages rooted in good policies that, if repeated every day and spelled out, would help a center-left coalition achieve the dominance necessary for effective governing.

Because the agenda I have elaborated in this chapter accents universal benefits and responsibilities crosscutting minorities and majorities, the affluent and the nonaffluent; because it is family- and work-oriented and reflects popular sentiments; because it substitutes simple income-tests, where these are appropriate, for the divisive effects of means testing, it constitutes an alternative to affirmative action based on descent and family origin (race, religion, ethnicity, skin color). Racial-ethnic-religion-linguistic criteria for state allocation of rewards in a society with scores of minority groups undermine the coalition politics necessary to reduce poverty and inequality and enhance family well-being for all.

From a center-left standpoint, racial-ethnic preferences are a major trap. They arouse justified anger among majorities of the electorate, who become easy targets for demagogues who play the race card or nativist card.[56] They foster a debilitating competition for the status of historically most victimized, setting one minority against another. They use up so much political energy and passion among their defenders that there is little left for the promotion of a universalistic agenda and the coalition politics essential for its success.

This book has shown that wherever Democrats accent bread-and-butter issues, they overcome right-wing use of the race card and their exploitation of nativist fears. This is especially important for holding the Democrats and Democratic leaners in the white middle mass (high-school graduates and part-college workers, a majority of the electorate). These are the Reagan Democrats who periodically fill a vacuum left by the failure of the Democratic Party to speak to their concerns; these hard-pressed folks respond to divisive Republican appeals.

If race-based politics are subversive of the Democratic Party because they give their opponents an effective wedge issue, it is important to grasp its limitations for the Republicans as well. Since Goldwater devised the southern strategy and Reagan demonstrated its success, Republicans have done their best to become a regional party. Republicans are a juggernaut only where Democrats abdicate the political space. In fact, the only real realignment in American politics is in the 11 Confederate states where the Democratic reactionaries of old have been replaced by Republican counterparts. Leave aside the popular vote of 2000, which Gore won by more than one-half million (and the careful systematic research on the Florida case shows an electoral win as well [Chapter 4, note 4]). Consider the 2004 result: Bush won in the 11 Confederate states by a popular margin of 5.0 million. Kerry won in all other states by a margin of 2.0 million in a narrow electoral defeat.[57]

Of course, the radical Right, especially evangelicals and a random collection of protest voters, account for Republican successes not only in the South but in the Midwest and a few states with rapidly growing Latino populations (New Mexico, Oklahoma, Nevada, Arizona). That is almost entirely explained by a shift of something like 3 to 6 percent of the white middle majority – again the Democrats and Democratic leaners among high-school graduates and part-college folks – to the Republican candidates in the absence of Democratic bread-and-butter appeals (Wilensky, 2008).

From this analysis of the political landscape, the prospects for a center-left agenda and a coalition that can begin to move America off the low road, if not good for 2012 or 2014, look promising thereafter.

# Appendix: Concepts and Measures

## Consensual Democracies vs. Confrontational Democracies

See Wilensky, 1976: 21–25, 48, 50–51, for measures of degree of corporatism, and pp. 56–68 for measures of political effects; and Wilensky, 1983, for elaboration of the types of corporatism and their policy effects. For earlier theoretical work on the concept "corporatism," see Schmitter, 1974. My model of democratic corporatism accents four interrelated criteria: (1) bargaining channels for the interaction of strongly organized, usually centralized economic blocs, especially labor, employer, and professional associations with centralized or moderately centralized government obliged to consider their advice; (2) a blurring of old distinctions between public and private; (3) a broad scope of national bargaining going beyond labor-market issues and resulting in; (4) the integration of social and economic policy and a greater chance to reach consensus and implement policy. Germany is an ambiguous case of corporatism; Switzerland, a marginal case of corporatism without labor (see Wilensky, 1976: 51, and 1981: 379, n. 42; and Pempel and Tsunekawa, 1979). The numerical scores for corporatism used in regressions are slightly different from the types of corporatism in Tables 2, 7, and 8, especially for France, Japan, and Switzerland.

"Democracy" is a system in which people choose leaders through competitive elections made possible by a rule of law and freedom of association and related civil liberties (cf. Schumpeter, 1942: 250–302; Dahl, 1989). "Pluralism" is defined as a polity in which many relatively autonomous groups representing a real division of values and interests compete for power within a nation-state. All democracies are pluralist. But authoritarian regimes often have elements of pluralism; they tolerate a degree of autonomy for selected groups such as the church, the monarchy, the military, or industry. Pluralism is thus not the same as democracy. Finally, "democratic corporatism" is a subtype of democracy focused on differences among democracies in their national bargaining structures. It is distinguished from the authoritarian version of corporatism of Mussolini, Franco, or Peron. And, of course, both democracy and authoritarian regimes are distinguished from totalitarian systems, which aim to eliminate all independent associations, all zones of privacy – Nazi Germany, Stalinist USSR (Linz, 1975), North Korea.

## Cumulative Party Power

The concepts and measures of party power, duration, and continuity are elaborated in Wilensky, 1981 and 2002: fig. 2B.1 in appendix B. Focusing on the two mass-based parties with a long and continuous history, we first measured left party dominance and then used the identical procedure for gauging Catholic party dominance, producing a month-by-month, government-by-government score for every left and every Catholic party in the 19 countries from 1919 through 1976 whenever competitive politics prevailed. A long concept and coding memo is not included here, but the complexities are summarized in appendix B (2002). Party dominance is defined as a large amount of party power continuously exercised over a substantial period of time. We focus on three dimensions of dominance: (1) degree of control or influence left or Catholic parties have had in their countries' governments; (2) the number of times such parties have been thrown out; and (3) the total number of years of left or Catholic power. By keeping amount and continuity of power separate, we leave open the question of what counts most: the possession of power, however brief, or the continuity in office that permits program planning. By distinguishing between continuity as long duration and continuity as few interruptions of tenure, we can determine whether the sheer number of years in office is more important than security of tenure.

Parties are defined by their ideological stance, not by their social base or behavior in office: left parties (e.g., Social Democratic, Socialist, Labor) are committed to use the apparatus of the state to redistribute income, power, and status – an egalitarian ideology; Catholic parties (e.g., Christian Democratic, Social Christian, Christian Socialist) are anticollectivist, antiliberal (not fond of free markets), and draw on a traditional humanist concern with lower strata. We coded amount and duration of power in both executive and legislative bodies for every month of competitive politics from 1919 to 1976, for a measure of cumulative power (Wilensky, 1981). The shorter period 1946–1976 yields the same results. Michael Wallerstein (1989) independently updated and replicated this code for cumulative left party power adding 20 years and came up with the same rank order except for the United States (he counted the Democrats as non-left) and Israel (he dated its founding later than I did).

I am grateful to the late Val R. Lorwin and Arnold J. Heidenheimer for critical readings of an earlier, longer version of the section on cumulative party power and to the late Timothy L. McDaniel for his creative contribution to the coding.

## Types of Political Economy

To generate these five types in Tables 2, 3, 4, 6, 7, and 8, I combined cumulative mass party power with three types of national bargaining arrangements – democratic corporatism, corporatism without labor (Japan, France, and marginally Switzerland), and "least corporatist" (fragmented and decentralized political economies) described in the text. Thus, left corporatist, left-Catholic corporatist, Catholic corporatist, corporatist without labor, and least corporatist (i.e., most fragmented and decentralized). The concepts and measures are described in the text and further elaborated in Wilensky, 2002: ch. 2, and appendix B.

Among the systematic comparative analyses subsequent to my 1976, 1981, and 1983 publications are the collection of articles in Hall and Soskice, 2001, and Pontussen, 2005. A recent critique of that "Varieties of Capitalism" perspective is Streek, 2009. Too often these different perspectives are expressed as "schools" or "camps" at war, or at least incompatible. The varieties scholars take aim at modernization or convergence theory to emphasize differences among rich democracies. The critics find that wanting; they point to the dynamics of institutions and the importance of the state. The obvious need is to integrate these theories. In all my work I have used modernization theory to specify at least nine areas where continuing industrialization has posed problems all rich democracies confront (Wilensky, 2002: ch. 1) – for example, changing family structure and functions, the rise of mass higher education, and the ascendance of the media in culture and politics. Then I have used types of political economy to explain their contrasting responses to common problems, playing these theories against one another in empirical analysis to arrive at a more powerful analysis of the similarities and differences among equally rich democracies.

Students of the "varieties of capitalism" insofar as they stick to rich democracies are mislabeling their subject. For precision, I have avoided "capitalism" to describe market-oriented democracies; history is replete with authoritarian regimes that were market-oriented, "capitalist," but not democratic – for example, Tito's Yugoslavia, Pinochet's Chile, South Korea's military regime.

Moreover, I have found it necessary to integrate cumulative power and ideologies of political parties into contrasting national bargaining structures to generate types of political economy that explain the outcomes covered in this book. Such a strategy better captures the interplay of markets and politics. Finally, as I show in the text, despite all of these structural differences there is plenty of room for policy shifts that improve the well-being of people within each type of political economy.

## Electoral Systems

I = presence of proportional representation (PR) in national electoral system for first (lower) or only chamber 1945–1980; 0.5 = mixed proportionality-plurality; 0 = absence. The four parliamentary-plurality systems are Australia, Canada, New Zealand, and the United Kingdom; the ten parliamentary-PR systems are Sweden, Norway, Finland, Israel, Denmark, the Netherlands, Belgium, Austria, Italy, and Germany. Ambiguities include West Germany: list PR; mixed PR and plurality but almost entirely proportional in allocation of seats; two votes per voter. Japan: single nontransferable vote in multimember district makes minority representation possible; it is semiproportional. France IV 1946–1958 had list PR; France V 1958-on is mixed; national assembly is mixed majority-plurality with minimum of 12.5 percent for second ballot, where plurality rules; presidential majority by runoff if necessary. Ireland's system of a single transferable vote where voter ranks individual candidates makes it like PR. The United States is the purest case (and among rich democracies the only case) of presidential-plurality (Dahl, 1966; Rokkan, 1970; Wilensky, 1981; Bogdanor and Butler, 1983; Lijphart, 1984, 1990, 1991; Grofman and Lijphart, 1986). Politicians who negotiated the PR compromise typically avoided its pure forms: they set voting thresholds for legislative seats higher than the 1 percent or less of Israel and the Netherlands or the 2 percent of Denmark; they kept the number of candidates to be elected per district within reason; they used similar devices to discourage very minor parties and splinter movements. Major changes in electoral systems are rare. Among our 19 rich democracies, New Zealand in 1992–1993 is the only one that moved from the Westminster system of first-past-the-post, winner-take-all to a modified PR system, German-style.

## Exports as Percentage of GDP (Table 6)

For 1880–1939, data for Europe are from B. R. Mitchell, *European Historical Statistics 1750–1970* (New York: Columbia University Press, 1975); data for the United States, Canada, Australia and New Zealand are from B. R. Mitchell, *International Historical Statistics: The Americas and Australasia* (Detroit: Gale Research Co., 1983); data for Japan are from K. Ohkawa and H. Rosovky, *Japanese Economic Growth: Trend Acceleration in the Twentieth Century* (Stanford: Stanford University Press, 1973), Appendix Tables. Figures for Sweden, Australia, and Norway are as a percentage of GDP; for Switzerland, Germany, Belgium, the Netherlands, and Ireland as a percentage of Net National Product (= GNP minus maintenance and depreciation of capital stock); for New

Zealand as a percentage of aggregate personal income. The figures for 1950–1960 are averages of data for 1950, 1955, and 1960, all as a percentage of GNP. The 1950 data are from *Yearbook of International Trade Statistics 1974* (New York: UN, 1975) and the 1955 and 1960 data are from *Yearbook of International Trade Statistics 1987* (UN, 1989).

Averages cover fewer years for some countries. For Japan, only 1905–1913; for Switzerland, 1913 only; Canada 1880, 1890, 1900, 1910 only; and the Netherlands 1900–1913 only. The average for the Netherlands is above 100 percent for two reasons: it may include the large amount of reexports of primary products from the East Indies; and the denominator is Net National Product rather than GNP. In any case, monographic and historical literature confirms the early export dependence of the Netherlands.

For Denmark, 1921–1929; Belgium, 1924 and 1927; Austria, 1924–1929; Germany 1925–1929; Switzerland, 1924 and 1929; Canada, 1920 and 1926–1929; and Ireland, 1929 only. Belgium, 1930 and 1934–1939; Austria 1930–1937; Germany, 1930–1938; New Zealand, 1931–1939; and Ireland, 1931, 1933, and 1936.

## Projections of the Ratio of Workers to Retirees by Age in Figure 3 and Other Shaky Forecasts

These ratios for 2010 and 2050 are based on OECD data on the number of retirees aged 65+ (the population minus employment in this age grade) divided by the number of employed aged 15–64. The method used for both the short-run projection to 2010 and the long-run one to 2050: (1) take population projections from the UN Population Division, World Population Prospects (2008) for the 15–64 and 65+ age categories; (2) apply the participation rates for 2008 (use the OECD definition of labor force/population for a given age cohort). The short-run forecast is good: from 2008 actual to 2010 projected shows a correlation between the two of 0.99 if we remove the deviant Nordic cases of Finland, Norway, and Sweden.

As for long-run forecasts and projections, however, the assumptions they rest on are typically shaky. Although the worker-retiree ratios for 2010 and 2050 yield a similar rank order of trouble supporting the aging populations of rich democracies (Figure 3), they assume that the labor-force participation rate of 2008 remains stable for 42 years. Perhaps the UN projections of total population by age-grade are somewhat more reliable than the participation rates but the two together make a weak ratio. Or take the task of the actuaries of the Social Security Commission (Chapter 5). They are forced to go through the ritual of long-term predictions of the cost of OASDI as far ahead as 75 years. These costs, of course, depend not only on the percentage of eligible aged and how many of them work how many hours but also on rates of GDP real growth, inflation, unemployment, the employment practices of employers, the power and policies of unions, mass preferences for leisure over income, the political party and ideological composition of the government, the structure and politics of pensions and taxes, and more.

The label "ritual" is apt. In fact, the shaman of the primitive tribe may have a firmer anchor in reality than the actuaries and forecasters of modern societies. The shaman, with his rituals of curing illness, may actually have a few effective medicinal herbs at his command and make better predictions of the future course of disease among his followers than the predictions of the Congressional Budget Office of the cost of a 2,500-page medical reform bill as they "score" it over 10 years and longer.

A study of "The Failures of Forecasting" based on short-run forecasts of growth and inflation during 1987–1994 by high-status academic and commercial economists showed that they say more or less the same thing at the same time, that "the differences between all forecasts are trivial compared to the differences between all forecasts and what actually happens"; the forecasters are almost always wrong (Kay, 1996: 9). In other words, even short-run forecasts by these leading economists, to whom investors and government officials give great deference, take the form of collective delusions.

The main reason we engage in such rituals is the overriding need to make guesstimates of costs in situations of great ambiguity – to arrive at a decision rule.

## "Bank" Bailout Accounting 2009–2010

Estimates of government expenditures for the financial-system rescue after the meltdown of late 2008 vary greatly by the time of analysis, whether we count future commitments (e.g., loan guarantees, insurance against losses) and direct purchases of troubled assets such as mortgage securities and debt, and whether we include outlays and guarantees by both Treasury and the Federal Reserve. The *New York Times* (Sept. 14, 2009), the most inclusive summary, estimates that the total cost of bailouts will be $11.9 trillion, excluding a paltry $83 billion in loans to auto companies and their suppliers, including support through bankruptcy. The *Times* classification of costs follows:

| | |
|---|---|
| Help banks raise capital | $290 billion, direct aid.<br>    $3.2 trillion for short-term loan guarantees on bank debt and deposit accounts and insurance for Citicorp and Bank of America. |
| Get lending going again | Up to $2 trillion to provide cheap financing to investors to buy (1) troubled mortgage securities and (2) bonds backed by business and consumer loans. Aim: remove toxic mortgage derivatives from bank balance sheets. |
| Keep AIG afloat | $183 billion for direct investment in AIG lines of credit and purchases of troubled assets the company had guaranteed. Much of this went to AIG's trading partners. |
| Support the housing market | $1.9 trillion direct investments in Freddie Mac and Fannie Mae and a program to buy mortgage securities and debt from the companies.<br>    $50 billion for incentives to modify and refinance mortgages. |
| Get money markets moving | $4.8 trillion in guarantees to investors in money funds, short-term borrowing, loans for banks and investors to buy commercial paper. |

Those items add up to about $12 trillion, a couple of trillion short of the entire GDP of the United States. In contrast is the later estimate by economist Alan Blinder ("Government to the Economic Rescue," *Wall Street Journal*, June 16, 2010). He suggests that under TARP (Troubled Asset Relief Program) no more than $300 billion ever went to banks (including AIG). "The money," he argues, "went for loans and to purchase preferred stock; it was not 'spent.'" Further, much of it has been paid back with interest. In the end, he predicts, the net cost of TARP will probably be under $100 billion, a cheap way to forestall a financial cataclysm.

SourceWatch.org (2010) provides a recent estimate that falls between these two extremes; it confines analysis to TARP and housing subsidies. It concludes that TARP has disbursed about $360.4 billion as of March 31, 2010, of which $159 million is still outstanding. Total bailout, including TARP, loans, purchases, and subsidies to the housing market plus Fannie Mae and Freddie Mac, and liquidity loans to banks and financial companies, is estimated at $4.71 trillion disbursed with $2.01 trillion outstanding. The largest item in this disbursement figure is about $1.1 trillion in mortgage-backed securities purchased by the Federal Reserve.

Take your pick: inclusive and big; or exclusive, narrow, and small; or everything in between. The more important question is discussed in Chapter 8, especially the section on deregulation and reregulation: How can the deregulation fever, the root cause of the worst recession since the Great Depression, be reversed? And here, whatever the direct and indirect estimates of the bailout money may be, the issue remains, how to reduce the power of the large shadow banks in politics and the economy.

## Sources, Definitions, and Statistical Significance for Table 11. Differences in Economic, Social, and Political Performance under Democratic and Republican Presidents, 1946–2009

*Sources*: *DJIA* from Yahoo Finance; *Federal deficit* from U.S. Treasury Department & http://www.usgovernmentspending.com/federal_deficit_chart.html; *Unemployment* from Bureau of Labor Statistics, 2010a; *Real annual growth*, Bureau of Economic Analysis, 2010: table 1.1.1; *Inflation*, BLS (2010a); *Balance of payments*, U.S. Census Bureau, Foreign Trade Division, 2010; *Family poverty rate*, U.S. Census Bureau, 2010: table 13); *Family income inequality*, U.S. Census Bureau, 2010: table 5.2); *Violent crime rate*, Bureau of Justice Statistics, 2010; *Income growth by percentile*, Bartels, 2008; *Unionization*, Kenworthy, 2010; *Real Minimum Wage*, Kenworthy, 2010: 102). Cf. Bartels, 2008: ch. 8); *Senate Filibusters*, Sinclair, 2008a; Senate Web page, http://senate. gov; *Pork*, Citizens Against Government Waste, 2010.

*Notes and definitions*: *DJIA* is Dow Jones Industrial Average. DJIA growth is measured from first day of opening in year until first day of opening following year. *Federal deficit* covers fiscal year from October 1 previous calendar year and ends on September 30. Before 1976 year began on July 1 and ended on June 30. *Unemployment* is average annual seasonally adjusted unemployment rate (16 years and over, BLS Series ID LNS 14000000). *Inflation* is CPI-U, U.S. City Average (December to December change). To make inflation numbers fit presidential terms, I used CPI rather than the implicit price deflator for GDP. *Balance of payments* is the annual average percentage (exports-imports)/exports. *Family income inequality* is the share of aggregate income received by top fifth and bottom fifth families (families as of March of the following year). *Violent crimes* are murder and nonnegligent manslaughter, forcible rape, robbery, aggravated assault. Regarding *unionization*: for an explanation of union decline not captured by these partisan averages, see my Chapter 7. Regarding *pork*: the 2002–2003 FY has been given to the Republicans because of their control of the House and the split in the Senate. Removing that year from their total has a negligible effect on the average for the period.

*Statistical significance*: Eight results where Democratic presidents outperformed their Republican counterparts are statistically significant, using a *t*-test for difference in means, while the lone Republican result is not significant. The results, all one-tailed tests, show democratic outperformance for federal deficit, unemployment, violent crimes, income growth for 20th and 60th percentiles, and pork (all significant at $p < .1$, and balance of payments and average change in family poverty rate [$p < .01$]). In absolute number, the score in favor of Democrats is 15 to 1 in Table 11; using a *t*-test of the difference in means, the score of statistically significant results is 8 in favor of democrats and 0 in favor of Republicans.

# Notes

## Preface and Introduction

1. Altmeyer and Witte played key roles in formulating the Social Security Act of 1935. In 1934 President Roosevelt created the Committee on Economic Security (CES) to make recommendations that would a year later form the core of OASDI (Old Age, Survivors, and Disability Insurance). Altmeyer, assistant secretary of Labor at the time, was named chairman of the technical board of the CES. Witte, who by then had become chairman of the Department of Economics at the University of Wisconsin, was named executive director of the CES (Altmeyer, 1968: 7). Other scholarly voices calling for social insurance in the three decades before the New Deal included Isaac Max Rubinow, a physician who took political science courses at Columbia and became a leading comparative analyst of social insurance, especially job injury insurance, and who drafted AALL's standard health insurance bill; Paul Douglas, professor of economics at the University of Chicago, whose studies of wages, living standards, and working conditions led him to advocate family allowances and unemployment compensation and the elimination of demeaning welfare systems; and Abraham Epstein. All three published influential books on unemployment and social security (Douglas and Director, 1931; A. Epstein, 1933; Rubinow, 1913, 1916, 1934).

## Chapter 1. The Welfare State as the Center of Public Finance and Political Conflict

1. When dealing with the effects of "the" deficit or debt on any other economic outcome, there is great ambiguity in the concepts. Results, therefore, should be viewed with skepticism, and longer-term studies favored over shorter-term correlation-based pieces that may rely on changing definitions. The critical factor is how states and researchers label receipts and payments. For instance, see Kotlikoff, 2008, on the contrast between generational accounting and conventional accounting.
2. Comparable data on total housing subsidies of all kinds are very sparse. What we have on 12 of our 19 countries shows a close fit with the rest of social spending as a GNP share or per capita (Wilensky, 2002: appendix C, pp. 730–732). Higher education spending, however, because of its stronger meritocratic component, is generally negatively correlated with the rest of the welfare state, which is more egalitarian. Means-tested public-assistance spending has a similar pattern of negative correlations with

other social spending (2002: tables 6.Dl and 5.Cl). Social spending is defined broadly but differently by several major sources. They all yield roughly the same country rank order as what I use here (2002: 248, n. 5). Table 1 excludes education from social spending/GDP. That column is therefore a conservative estimate.

3. Unless otherwise indicated, the evidence for these assertions is in Wilensky, 2002: chs. 5, 7, and 12–16.

4. PPPs do not include the cost of nonmarket social goods and services, such as health care, education, and child care. In all of our consensual democracies, these are essentially provided as public goods or are much cheaper; they are an important part of the economic well-being of the population. The recent U.S. edge over most of Continental Europe by measures of PPPs obscures momentous differences in social and labor policies and expenditures.

5. Similarly, Joseph Stiglitz (2010: 37–38), Clinton's chairman of the Council of Economic Advisers, describes how he and Reich lost the argument about corporate welfare – generous subsidies and tax preferences for business – to the "Right" (Rubin and Larry Sommers, who also favored financial deregulation).

6. The specific effects of central bankers' autonomy and ideology interacting with the internationalization of finance are analyzed cross-nationally in Chapter 6.

7. For sources and rationale for measures in Table 2 and further discussion of results, see Wilensky, 2002: 432–50 and appendix G.

### Chapter 2. Energy Policy and Performance: The United States and the World

1. Reacting sympathetically to the EU Commission proposals for its 27 member nations, the Danish Energy Policy Statement of 2008 observes that those proposals, to say the least, are "challenging to provide for the complex interplay between a quota market, a sustainable energy certificate market, continued national subsidy schemes and the objective of more efficient competition across national borders" (Danish Ministry of Climate and Energy, 2008: 4). Trading systems require a detailed registry of emissions and a complicated system of accounting; they are difficult to understand.

2. This account is based on data from the Energy Information Administration, U.S. Department of Energy, available at http://www.eia.doe.gov/ and Swedish Ministry of Enterprise, Energy and Communications, 2007.

3. The next four paragraphs are based on Wilensky, 2002: 558–565, which provides a detailed account of nuclear policies and politics in France, Sweden, the United States, and Germany; and Jasper (1990), a member of our project who combined documentary sources and personal interviews with the main decision makers in these countries.

4. For skeptical analysis of the prospects for designing complex, tightly coupled technical systems that will never have accidents, see Perrow, 1984, and La Porte, 1978. La Porte is a student of high-hazard organizations with redundant systems designed to achieve near-perfect operational safety, among them aircraft carriers, nuclear power plants, and air traffic control systems. He believes that unless the U.S. nuclear industry and its regulatory agencies change their internal operational culture markedly, the dispersion of nuclear power and waste operations as a response to energy needs is extremely risky and that, in general, systems designed to be near error free cannot be sustained across successive management generations (personal conversation, Jan. 28, 2009).

5. There is much talk of nuclear fusion as the solution to problems of waste and safety. Dr. Jacque Bouchard, former director of nuclear engineering in the CEA and a prime mover in French nuclear development, notes an inside joke among nuclear scientists and

engineers: "Fusion is the future. And will remain the future." He sees no such development for the 21st century (Lecture, University of California, Berkeley, Feb. 26, 2009).

6. N. Lewis and D. Nocera (2006) estimate that to meet current rates of expansion of energy use with nuclear power would require the addition of a nuclear-power plant every 1.6 days. The current cost of building just one 1,000-megawatt nuclear plant is $6 billion to $8 billion. Since many plans call for twin units in one project, costs could be as high as $16 billion per plant (estimates by Cambridge Energy Research Associates, *Wall Street Journal*, Mar. 28, 2009: A3). Added to the building costs in the United States is the necessity of clean up from the past. In December 2008 the Energy Department's inspector general said that the department faces a "monumental task" in cleaning up the more than 1.5 million cubic feet of solid radioactive waste and 88 million gallons of radioactive liquid waste left over from half a century of nuclear defense and energy research across the country (*New York Times*, Feb. 14, 2009).

7. A rough test using EIA data on nuclear production as a percentage of total energy consumption in 2005 for all 19 rich democracies shows that the 10 top nuclear power producers (from 6.9% for Canada up to 38.8% for France) score an average production of alternative renewables as a fraction of total consumption of only 2.17%; the eight countries that have zero nuclear plus the Netherlands with 0.9% nuclear score better on renewables (geothermal, solar, wind, wood, and waste) – an average of 3.33%. There may be threshold effects: perhaps it takes a ratio of nuclear production to total consumption approaching about 35% to strongly undermine the renewables effort (France has been beyond that for 15 years, Sweden is as yet only about 30%). The other countries that have any nuclear power range from Canada's production/consumption ratio of 6.9% through United States' 8.1%, the United Kingdom's 8.8%, Germany's 10.7%, Japan's 13%, Finland and Switzerland's 17.9% each, to Belgium's 18.1%.

8. Advocates of "unconventional" natural gas claim that it, too, has a large world potential with a cost-benefit ratio far more favorable than that of nuclear energy. The complex technology involves both horizontal drilling to liberate shale gas and hydraulic fracturing where the producer injects a mixture of water and sand at high pressure to create multiple fractures throughout the rock, releasing the trapped gas to flow into the well (Yergin and Ineson, 2009). Although natural gas is cleaner than coal or oil and probably better than nuclear in cost and safety, its downside is substantial: the enormous use of scarce water and carcinogens in contaminated wastewater coughed up from some deeper wells.

9. All of the known or suspected cases of nation-states starting a secret nuclear weapons program, thus violating their Article II NPL commitments, were undertaken by nondemocratic governments (historically including North and South Korea, Libya, Iraq, Yugoslavia, Taiwan, Iran, and Syria), a few of which are highly vulnerable to terrorist attacks (Miller and Sagan, 2009: 11–12). Democratic or not, among current nuclear power states that lead in terrorist incidents are India, Pakistan, and Russia (p. 12, fig. 1). As Miller and Sagan indicate, the nuclear energy option poses five interrelated problems for international security: safety, sabotage, terrorist theft or purchase of a weapon or nuclear materials, nuclear proliferation, and destruction of nuclear facilities in a conventional war (pp. 126–137).

10. In April 2009 a coalition of business and environmental groups, the United States Climate Action Partnership, was making progress in watering down an environmental measure by two House Democratic leaders, the Waxman-Markey bill. The group includes Alcoa, DuPont, and GM; they pushed for a large number of free

pollution allowances in a cap-and-trade arrangement. By mid-May 2009, together with a group of southern and midwestern Democrats, coal, oil, and steel industry lobbyists succeeded in turning the House bill into a bonanza of free pollution permits. The final House bill barely passed in June with about 85% of the permits free and good for ten years after its start in 2015 (Doggett, 2009).

11. Until recently, Al Gore promoted a carbon tax. But when he was preparing for a new Kyoto at the Copenhagen climate and energy conference June 19, 2009 as a lead-in to the UN Climate Change Conference in December 2009 and was urging the Obama administration and Congress to act in 2009, he shifted to cap-and-trade as an important step worldwide (Vice President Gore, testimony, U.S. Senate Foreign Relations Committee, Jan. 28, 2009: 2). Like Gore, Paul Krugman later embraced cap-and-trade as better than nothing (*New York Times*, Apr. 11, 2010). Most of the potential signatories for an international protocol to replace Kyoto are already sold on the EU approach, whatever its merits. This is a case of the least effective as the enemy of the excellent. Under questioning in the Senate, Gore added that a carbon tax was good, too.

12. Geothermal basics: water is injected deep into the earth where it absorbs heat from the surrounding rock. As the fluid returns to the surface, that heat is used to generate electricity. The fluid is then reinjected. The system forms a closed loop. There are almost no emissions, it is entirely renewable, and takes less land than either solar or wind. The downside: more use of scarce water, more holes in the ground, more need for roads and trucks to service the holes (*The Future of Geothermal Energy*, 2006).

13. The next two paragraphs are based on Wilensky, 1965: xxiii.

14. For a detailed account of the formation, sustaining political coalition, and alternatives to the Interstate Highway System and the Highway Trust Fund, see Patachnik, 2000: 115–121.

15. To top it off, as of June 1, 2009, the federal government had spent $62 billion to salvage GM and Chrysler and see them through a downsizing in bankruptcy (*Wall Street Journal*, June 2, 2009). An additional $5 billion for the car suppliers was announced March 20, 2009. And in the 10 months before November 1, 2009, the government injected $15.3 billion in capital to save GMAC, the financial arm of GM. Auto bailout figures make the allocation to alternative transportation look trivial.

16. I am grateful to Chris Somerville, director of the Energy Biosciences Institute at Berkeley, for a detailed review of my assertions in the rest of this chapter and for helpful suggestions on the whole chapter.

17. Another similar and doubtful solution is electrolysis – converting electricity to hydrogen and then into fuel cells. The problem with this process is that you use one unit of very useful energy (electricity) to make a fractional unit of energy as fuel, a substantial energy loss. Then, as fuel cell advocates suggest, you would turn the hydrogen back into electricity with fuel cells and take another loss. So you pay a big price for fuel. When we add the hydrogen storage and transportation problems, the process yields little gain and much cost (Romm, 2004: 156). However, hydrogen used directly in gas turbines is straightforward and if we can develop effective geological sequestration, a big "if," it would be cost beneficial (personal communication from Chris Somerville).

18. Calculating GHG footprints for various fuel options is not easy. For instance, "emissions from the manufacture and use of fertilizer to produce a feed stock are usually included, but emissions related to the building of the fertilizer plant are generally not" (Peña, 2008: 3). Similarly, estimates of the environmental costs of

nuclear energy may include guesstimates of the cost of nuclear waste disposal and the cost of the regulatory regime, but never include the GHG emissions of the cement and asphalt plants that supply the building materials for these large plants (Sovacool, 2008). Also, current models probably underestimate the GHG emissions resulting from biofuel-related land use changes like those of corn-based ethanol (Peña, 2008: 11). My impression of the serious academic analysis of GHGs is that it typically errs on the side of caution, avoiding exaggeration.

19. The World Bank (2008) in an analysis of fluctuations in grain prices points to several forces at work in addition to subsidies for corn-based ethanol: among them depreciation of the dollar, growing world demand for grains, drought in Australia, and speculative commodities futures trading. My argument is that the corn-to-ethanol cycle uses much more scarce energy and land than alternative biofuels and plays its part in higher food prices. Finally, compared to gasoline, ethanol from maize emits 18% less $CO_2$, ethanol from sugars 91% less, and ethanol from cellulosics even less than sugars (Goldemberg, 2008: 4). Quantitative estimates of GHG emissions per gallon of gasoline equivalent show the clear superiority of ethanol from switchgrass and Brazilian sugarcane over all other biofuel pathways studied – gasoline, corn-based ethanol (even with carbon capture and storage), and biodiesel (Peña, 2008: 14, fig. 5). In fact, switchgrass is the only option that removes rather than adds emissions. These findings suggest that heavy U.S. subsidies for corn-based ethanol combined with our import duties on Brazilian sugarcane ethanol are, to say the least, counterproductive in the fight against global warming.

20. Aside from insulation and redesign, here is a relatively simple measure to improve building efficiency with a big payoff: make it mandatory to install smart meters in both residential and commercial buildings that permit time-of-use pricing of electricity so that the kilowatt cost of off-peak use is substantially lowered and the cost of peak period use is increased to above average. Both consumers and utilities gain from this GHG-reduction measure by stopping the huge subsidy of peak-period use. Lee Friedman (2009) presents the case for this type of energy efficiency and estimates that it would take about five years for widespread deployment. States such as California and Connecticut are already planning to install smart meters. Exceptions can be made for vulnerable groups such as the elderly or low-income families in apartment units without individual meters. Success of these measures depends largely on educating consumers about how they work ("What Utilities Have Learned from Smart Meter Tests," *Wall Street Journal*, Report on Energy, Feb. 22, 2010: R6).

21. There appears to be no imminent breakthrough for solar. Energy Secretary Steven Chu, like many other leading scientists, suggests that solar technology will have to get five times better than it is today to compete with other sources of energy, even clean energy alternatives (*New York Times*, Feb. 12, 2009). Wind technology, as Denmark demonstrates, is far ahead (see also "Technology Quarterly," *Economist*, Dec. 6, 2008: 22–25). A McKinsey study (2009: 27) analyzes the relative efficiency of various forms of GHG abatement in the United States, including building efficiency, solar, and wind. It concludes that an energy-efficiency push could limit greenhouse gas emissions by 2030 far more than renewable energy alternatives (saving more money than it costs) but that wind, while quite far behind building efficiency, is second and solar, third. All others, including nuclear, trail in the cost or savings per ton of carbon dioxide equivalents.

22. A scientist who was instrumental in developing Brazil's biofuel industry argues that deforestation in the Amazonia is a product of cattle breeding, not ethanol production

(Goldemberg, 2008: 5). Regarding the government's plan to halt deforestation, neither cattle ranchers and farmer/property developers nor environmentalists believe that Brazil can slow the destruction of the rainforest in less than two or three decades. By then, much of it will be gone; the fight today is over how fast deforestation will happen (*Economist*, June 13, 2009: 27–29). This is critical: deforestation greatly increases greenhouse gas emissions because trees convert $CO_2$ into oxygen, and the $CO_2$ is stored in the wood. Burning the wood releases that carbon into the atmosphere. Destruction of rainforests also means the loss of biodiversity. Developing countries such as Indonesia, Papua New Guinea, and others with impoverished populations in tropical areas – about 60 countries – have neither the resources nor the incentive to stop cutting down hardwood forests. Nor do they have the low-corruption governing structures to stop illegal logging, common in Brazil as well. It is their only livelihood (Stiglitz, 2006b: 179–180). Any international agreement must include compensation for maintaining their forests.

23. A similar problem confronts many high-tech industries from the makers not only of hybrid car batteries but of cell phones, laser-guided missiles, wind turbines, and more: the processing of the necessary rare-earth minerals will remain concentrated in China for years. Before mining of these rare elements in the United States and elsewhere can produce adequate supplies, China, with its stockpiles, will continue to dominate the market.

24. In the United States a start in this direction was 3.8% ($30 billion) of the $789.2 billion stimulus bill allocated to "modernization of the electric grid, advanced battery manufacturing and energy efficiency grants" (*Wall Street Journal*, Feb. 13, 2009).

## Chapter 3.  What Trade-Offs Are Good and Bad for the Economy? Domestic Structures and Policies That Permit Adaptation to Globalization

1. I explain these fateful differences in ch. 2 of *Rich Democracies* (2002). Ireland is the exception, until the mid-1990s the only one among the Anglo-American democracies that had PR. Japan, Germany, and France have mixed systems. Ireland was joined by New Zealand in the mid-1990s when a voters' revolt against a 10-year neoliberal experiment resulted in the adoption through referendum of PR, German style, the only shift from Westminster to PR on record.

2. In several cases PR was also inspired by the interaction of dominant ethnic-religious groups and competing minority groups as in the cases of Denmark's minority (in Schleswig-Holstein in 1855), or Ireland's minority Protestants. Less clearly, the extreme social heterogeneity of Israel and Switzerland moved them to adopt PR.

3. The reason some researchers find that trade dependence has a direct positive effect on economic performance (e.g., Brady, Beckfield, and Zhao, 2007) is that their regression equations overlook the time order of the forces at work: proportional representation leads to left and Catholic party power leading to consensual bargaining structures, which in turn lead to policies favorable both for economic performance and the well-being of people.

4. Huber and Stephens (1999: 18–21) outline a series of such trade-offs that are possible for corporatist democracies facing the financial turmoil and economic constraints of the late 1990s. These go beyond the standard trade-offs already prominent in the bargaining patterns of the past (discussed in Wilensky 2002: chs. 12 and 17): for example, wage moderation in return for commitments to invest capital domestically; lower payroll taxes in return for domestic investment commitments; a modest

widening of skill differentials to overcome the economic drag of radical wage compression (especially prevalent in Sweden) in return for skills training, job security, and so on (see chs. 1 and 12). The net effect of such trade-offs is to increase private and public savings and investment and hence real economic growth.

5. Economists studying the American slowdown in productivity experienced after 1973 attribute at least a fourth and as much as half of the slowdown to the lack of business investment (B. M. Friedman, 1989: 196 and 310, n. 11). However, they seldom consider industrial relations systems in a comparative context.

6. My finding that consumption taxes do not set off a wage-price spiral is supported by other studies showing that in 11 of 13 OECD countries surveyed, the introduction of the VAT "either had little effect on retail prices or simply resulted in a shift of the CPI trend line (one-time effect)" (Cnossen, 1991: 634 and 643). Cnossen also concludes that a VAT is superior to an income tax in promoting capital formation and economic growth, consistent with my findings (pp. 633–634, 643–644). See the similar finding for the United States 1955–1980 in Jorgenson and Yun, 1986.

7. By "tax-welfare backlash" I mean strong social-political movements and/or parties that emphasize antitax, anti–social spending, and antibureaucratic ideological themes and achieve electoral success for substantial periods. We coded our 19 countries on this idea (Wilensky, 2002: ch. 10). Highest scores are unrelated to the level of taxing and spending; they went to Denmark, a big spender (Glistrup and the Progress Party); the United States, a lean spender (Reagan to Bush and the Republicans); the United Kingdom, a middle-rank spender (Enoch Powell, Margaret Thatcher and the Tories); and Switzerland, a lean spender (from Schwarzenbach to Blocher). The country backlash rankings from the time when such candidates achieved success until now are remarkably steady as is their electoral base – middle-mass voters (people with only secondary-school certificates or a year or two of postsecondary vocational education but no baccalaureate, i.e., the merged "upper-working class" and "lower-middle class").

## Chapter 4. Retrenchment of the Welfare State? The Fate of "Cutback Budgeting" in Italy, France, Germany, the United States, the United Kingdom, and New Zealand

1. I am grateful for detailed comments on this account by Peter Haynes and Jack Vowles, a leading scholar of New Zealand politics.

2. From 1985 to 1992 real GDP growth per capita averaged 0.06%, almost zero (OECD, 1994: 92). Treasury people argue that without their reforms the New Zealand economy would have been worse, that reforms take time to have an effect, and that in the years since 1992 the New Zealand economy has improved. The counterargument: if an economy performs badly for a decade and recessions are deep, any improvement will look good; the record of the first decade of the neoliberal experiment is clear; only another 10 years of these policies would test their merits for economic performance, equality, political legitimacy, and the real welfare of New Zealanders. The voters, however, brought an end to the experiment.

3. Peter Saunders (1994: 19–20) shows a big acceleration of inequality in real disposable income from 1985–1986 to 1989–1990, mainly a redistribution from the middle to the top tenth of the distribution and then, with benefit cuts in the early 1990s, a sharp decrease in the real income of the poorest tenth.

4. Re Florida: Henry Brady of Berkeley and several Harvard colleagues did the definitive reanalysis of all available data. They found that Gore won that state (and hence the

Electoral College vote and the Presidency) by about ten thousand votes (Brady et al., 2001; cf. Wand et al., 2001). Bush lost the election but was appointed president by the disgraceful vote of the Supreme Court, 5 to 4.

5. My analysis based on surveys conducted by Knowledge Networks. The 2000 data came from an Internet panel comprised of a national random sample of households recruited by random digit dialing, who either have Internet access through their own computer or are given a Web-TV console in exchange for completing three or four surveys a month. N = 12,685. Data for 2004 are from the 2004 Presidential Election Survey commissioned by the Diane D. Blair Center of Southern Politics and Society and conducted by Knowledge Networks through its Internet Panel. N = 2,100. S. Hillygus of Harvard and T. Shields of the Blair Center kindly made these data available.

6. Using standard multivariate statistics on exit polls and one of the most thorough national postelection surveys, political scientists have shown that such "moral values" were at best very marginal in the 2004 outcome. Two of the several academics who analyzed this, D. S. Hillygus and T. G. Shields, summarize: opinions about gay marriage and abortion "had no effect on voter decision making among Independents, respondents in battleground states, or even among respondents with an anti-gay marriage initiative on the ballot.... Only in the South did either issue have an independent effect on vote choice, and even here the effect was minimal." Overwhelmingly what counted nationally as well as in the South were attitudes toward the economy, the Iraq war, and terrorism. (Of course, no one knows whether gay marriage was worth the 60,000-vote shift in Ohio that would have made Kerry president.) Sources include a symposium published in *P.S.: Political Science and Politics* 38, 2 (April 2005): especially 189–210. The most careful analysis is on pp. 201–209. Further citations are on p. 208.

7. I base these observations on documents and repeated interviews with Glistrup, Powell, and other politicians and party officials in these countries. Not all protest parties and mass discontents fit the idea of tax-welfare backlash. We sorted out the antitax, antisocial spending, antibureaucratic movements from the many environmental, peace, feminist, and civil rights movements that were rising at the same time, roughly 1965–1975 (Wilensky, 2002: 363–397). We could not separate nativist movements and parties from tax-welfare backlash parties because the latter, sooner or later, adopt nativist appeals (pp. 373–375). In short, while nativism is widespread among all rich democracies (see Chapter 6), only a few rank high on tax-welfare backlash; these few always combine hostility to taxing, spending, and government bureaucracy with hostility to socially distant minority groups.

## Chapter 5. Pensions Converge, U.S. Health Care Remains Unique

1. This account is based on documents supplied by the research scholar who directed the calculations and analysis carried out at the Finnish Centre for Pensions, Hannu Uusitalo. I am grateful for his comments.

2. The OECD study of this matter strongly advises against using tax-expenditure data for cross-national comparison and even cautions against aggregating tax breaks within one country (OECD, 1996; cf. Kraan, 2004). Problems include national variations in the treatment of the personal income tax unit and income tax allowances for marriage and children; different definitions and measures of "tax expenditures"; different benchmarks against which tax expenditures for pensions or depreciation allowances

are measured; and substantial, unknown interaction between different tax breaks. A clue to the effect of tax expenditures on U.S. rankings in both the GDP share of public pension spending (Table 6) and the private/public shares of health-care spending (Table 7) is U.S. government guesstimates of the size of such tax breaks. First consider the U.S. government's highest figure for 2006 (from Congress) for "net exclusion of pension contributions and earnings" – i.e., employer plans, individual retirement plans, Keogh plans, untaxed Social Security benefits, and exclusions of veterans' pensions. If we then assume that no other country has any tax expenditures and add the U.S. figure (about $140 billion) to column 1 of Table 6 (public pensions at 5.3% of GDP), we would increase U.S. spending to 6.4% of GDP, still below the average of each of the other four types of political economy, slightly ahead of only two countries (the Netherlands and Norway, both far more generous in their pension benefits than the United States). Regarding the effect of tax expenditures on the private/public shares of health-care spending in Table 8: the White House Federal Budget Estimates (2008) and the Congressional Estimates of Federal Tax Expenditures (2006) for all health-care tax breaks range from $115 to $150 billion. If we again assume the extreme case – take the highest estimate of all U.S. health care tax expenditures and assume that all of them go to "private" health-care providers, mainly employer-sponsored coverage – and further assume that no other rich democracy provides any tax breaks, then we would add $150 billion. That would boost the public share of health-care spending in recent years from 45% to less than 53%. In short, for the two most expensive and popular programs of the welfare state, the public share of the United States would remain relatively very low even if we adopt the highest estimates and ignore tax breaks abroad. Given dubious data and assumptions, such comparisons are foolish. There is no U.S. "Hidden Welfare State" for valid cross-national comparison.

3. In the first half year of 2009 the deficit of the U.S. Pension Benefit Guarantee Fund tripled. Surging bankruptcies of firms with pension obligations to 44 million workers who are covered by the PBGF resulted in a shortfall of $11 billion. The only reason the fund could continue payouts is that benefits are paid monthly over the lifetime of beneficiaries, so its assets will cover payouts for many years (*New York Times*, May 21, 2009).

4. Evidence for generalizations in this section are in my ch. 16 (2002) and citations therein. Among the best comparative studies of the organization, delivery, and real health effects of health-care systems are Hollingsworth, Hage, and Hanneman, 1990; Hollingsworth, Hanneman, and Hage, 1992; Evans and Stoddard, 1994; Heidenheimer, Heclo, and Adams, 1990; Mechanic and Rochefort, 1996; and OECD country studies, various years.

5. In constructing a real health index as part of our analysis of system outputs, I asked, "What health indicators could we expect to be affected by intervention of the medical community, indicators that could also be measured cross-nationally in all 19 countries?" We rejected numerous indicators for which knowledge about the effect of medical care is limited or dubious and cross-national comparability is insufficient (e.g., mental illness, Alzheimer's, peptic ulcers, multiple sclerosis, cirrhosis of the liver, and other ailments listed in Wilensky, 2002: ch. 16). We ended up with five dimensions of real health that themselves are intercorrelated: infant mortality rate per 1,000 live births; life expectancy at age 1 for males; the same for females; circulatory disease deaths per 100,000 aged 65–74; and deaths from pregnancy and childbirth complications per 100,000 females aged 25–34. Countries were ranked on each health

indicator using natural cutting points for a 4-point scale (0–3), and they were equally weighted. The summary scores ranged from Japan's 13.5 to the United States' 2.5 in Table 7. The country scores and ranks measure relative, not absolute, performance for the time period. Other studies using more numerous indicators report almost identical rankings for our 19 countries (e.g., WHO, 2000).

6. The number for increase in health spending per capita is inflated by the extreme case of Japan, whose spending increased by a whopping 730% (controlled for inflation) between the average of 1975 and 1980 and the average of 2000 and 2005. Without Japan, average spending increased by a factor of 2.3.

7. If we eliminate three deviant cases (Italy, Australia, and the United States), the importance of public spending as a source of good national health performance is confirmed by a moderate zero-order correlation (0.45) between per capita public spending and our real health index. For a roughly two-and-a-half-year lag of spending in relation to performance, Table 7 averages spending for 2000 and 2005 and focuses on 2005 for health outputs.

8. The hundreds of German prereform *Krankenkassen* are similar to the proposal of July 2009 in the U.S. Senate Finance Committee for a cobweb of nonprofit local cooperatives. Chapter 8 discusses the health-care reform effort of 2009.

9. A multiple regression study of prefecture reductions in infant mortality in Japan (whose rate of improvement was the best of our 19 countries, 1960–1980) found that public health nurses per 100,000 population represents the only significant medical intervention that is strongly correlated with reduced infant mortality (Morio, 1985).

### Chapter 6. The Impact of "Globalization": An Overview

This chapter is a revision and expansion of Wilensky, 2002: ch. 17, and a paper presented at the International Political Science Association 20th World Congress, Fukuoka, Japan, July 13, 2006. An early version was published in *Globalizzazione e sistemi di welfare*, ed. M. Ferrara (Torino: Edzioni della Fondazione G. Angelli, 1993), 41–63. I am grateful to John Talbott, Fred Schaffer, and Karen Adelberger for research assistance and to Betsy Carter and Bartholomew Watson for help in updating this chapter.

1. "A majority of international theorists . . . give priority to international explanation and employ theories of domestic politics only as needed to explain anomalies" (Moravcsik, 1993: 6).

2. Spain achieved dominance in the 16th and 17th centuries by relending money gained from silver taken out of Mexico and Peru; Holland's strength in the 17th century rested on profits from its colonial empire and from lending to Britain, Austria, and the Baltic countries. Pax Britannia in the 19th century rested not only on the Royal Navy but also on a flow of development capital to other countries; from 1870 to World War I Britain's net foreign investment averaged 5% of income. Later Germany and France deployed large amounts of capital, while during and after World War II the United States became a dominant lender through Lend-Lease, the Marshall Plan, the IMF, and the World Bank. Japan's net foreign investment in 1981 as a fraction of national income at 4%, had not yet reached Britain's 5% in its heyday (Friedman, 1989: 77–78, 81; Edelstein, 1982: ch. 2).

3. There is a difference, however, in the national response to defaults. In earlier periods international loans were sold to a wide range of bondholders, whereas now they are concentrated in the hands of top money-center banks, which makes defaults more visible and provokes more intervention by banks and governments (Eichengreen and Lindert, 1989: 2–3).

4. For example, in 1890 the foreign-born population in the United States as a percentage of total population was 14.8%; in 2007 it was 12.6% (Fix, 2009). The March 2002 Current Population Survey reported that 19 million of the 135 million employed U.S. workers were foreign born – i.e., 14.1%. The most popular destinations for migrants in 2010 were the United States, Russia, Germany, Canada, France, and Saudi Arabia (*Migration News*, Oct. 2009).

5. The argument that the white ethnic immigrants who entered the United States before World War I were much more easily integrated than later arriving Latinos and southern blacks who moved North misses the intense and sometimes violent hostility facing the white ethnics. For instance, at the turn of the century dominant Protestants in the Boston area despised the Italian Catholic newcomers as an alien *racial* stock. This is not to say that there are no variations in the ease of integration among ethnic and racial groups differently situated. It is a reminder that nativism and racism are not only centuries old but may be similar in their consequences. (For analysis of the fate of various types of minority groups, see Wilensky, 2002: 14–33, 713–715, 720, n. 10.)

6. According to Heinz Fassman and Rainer Münz (1994), of an estimated 14,160,000 migrants from East to West (including those from the GDR, ex-Yugoslavia, Poland, Soviet Union, and the Balkans) from 1950 to 1993, 68.1% landed in Germany, 8.1% in Israel, 6.6% in Turkey, 4.8% in the United States, and 12.8% in other countries (Austria, Scandinavia, France, United Kingdom, Canada, etc.).

7. Further, even before the welfare reform of 1996, permanent legal residents were effectively barred from receiving AFDC for three years following admission, and the three-year waiting period for legal immigrants' claims to SSI (Supplementary Security Income for poor retirees) was raised to five years in 1993. Legal permanent residents can be deported if they become public charges within five years of admission. Using welfare at any time increases the difficulty of later bringing relatives in. Thus, the image of recent immigrants as a welfare burden is misleading, although if we compare the percentage of households in which the head receives public assistance without controlling for age or condition, the immigrant percentage in 1990 was somewhat higher that the natives: Fix and Passel (1994: 63–67) calculate that 4.9% of pre-1980 entrants age 15 and older received some form of welfare in 1990 (SSI, AFDC, or other), vs. 4.2% of natives. But examining only working-age (15–64 year-old) naturalized and nonnaturalized immigrants from nonrefugee countries (Mexico, Philippines, India, etc.), they find that the 1980–1990 entrants are much less likely to be on the dole (2.8%) than comparable natives, 4.2% of whom receive "welfare." Refugees are typically in worse shape and take longer to adjust.

8. Huddle's (1993) is the worst. He not only fails to take account of any positive economic impact of immigrant businesses or consumer spending; he also massively understates revenue collected (e.g., he ignores about $50 billion of taxes immigrants paid in 1992) and omits the necessary comparisons with natives that show that they, too, receive more in services than they pay in taxes (Passel, 1994; Clark and Passel, 1993).

9. These three forces that encourage nativist protest action – economic deprivation, large numbers and concentration of immigrants, and great social distance between immigrants and natives – are the same as the forces that foster prejudice and the perception of group threat. See Quillian, 1995, for an analysis of Eurobarometer Survey no. 30 (Fall 1988) results on attitudes toward immigrants and racial minorities in 12 EEC countries. Individual characteristics had little impact on prejudice and explained none of the country differences. Economic conditions of the country, the

size of the minority group, and its social composition (e.g., non-EEC immigration) are the important variables shaping both levels of prejudice and the militancy of protest movements.

10. The Swedish naturalization rate has been consistently much higher than that of Germany. In 1991 naturalizations as a percentage of the stock of foreign population was 5.4% in Sweden, 2.7% in Germany (Guimezanes, 1994: 25). Ten years later, in 2001, naturalization in Sweden had increased to 7.6%, while it decreased in Germany to 2.4% (Migration Policy Institute, 2009).

11. The next six paragraphs draw on data developed in a 1993 term paper by my assistant, Karen Adelberger, from French and German surveys and recent literature. See also Wilensky, 1975: 57–59; 1976: 12–34; 2006.

12. One interpretation of the persistence of Le Pen and the FN is that they have moved from negative protest to positive issue-based campaigns. Nonna Mayer (2002: 41–57) breaks the FN into two voting groups, *ninistes* and *droitistes*, with the *ninistes* as the protest group, neither Right nor Left. That 20% of French voters chose Le Pen in the second round, with the election on the line, together with exit polls, Mayer argues, indicates that the FN has become less of a protest party and is increasingly normal, lasting, and positive. However, as I have shown in my comparative analysis of tax-welfare backlash, nativism is quite consistent with emphasis on welfare-state issues. Le Pen in early campaigns, for instance, not only whipped up hatred for minority groups; he called for increases in cherished French pensions and paid maternal leave for natives that would be denied his ethnic targets. The FN's message may have become broader, but it remains most interested in racial purity and cultural identity and the threat of immigrants to both (Wilensky, 2002: 365–367).

13. The failure of the far Right in Germany may reflect a common interchangeability of protest parties: 2005 saw the PDS (former East German Communists) score 8.0% of the constituency votes and 8.7% of the party list votes; it took 54 seats (cf. Zaslove, 2008).

14. For an account of German immigration debates, policies, and administrative practices, see Halfmann, 1995. Brubaker (1992) describes the evolution of French and German citizenship policies. Although Germany adopted a new legal immigration framework in place since January 2005, the change in law did not result in either a substantial increase in immigration or a departure from the self-image of a non-immigration country (Bauder, 2008: 95).

15. Alber (1994), using Eurobarometer surveys and data from Wiegand and Fuchs and Gerhards and Roller, devises an index of "rejection of foreigners" (respondents who say that there are too many foreigners in their country, that the presence of foreigners is disturbing, that the rights of foreigners should be restricted, and that asylum seekers should no longer be accepted). For 11 EC countries, this index of xenophobia correlates .82 with the percentage of foreigners from non-EC countries in each nation, underscoring the importance of numbers.

16. General restrictions on layoffs and individual dismissals imposed by collective bargaining and labor law are complemented by special job protections for vulnerable groups (e.g., pregnant women, the handicapped, draftees, older workers). If we add tenured public servants, about 20% of the total "dependent" work force is totally protected against ordinary dismissal.

17. Reviewing cross-national studies of Europe and North America on this point, ILO (1995) concludes that in terms of gross job destruction and creation, the most regulated European political economies are as flexible as the least regulated (e.g., the United States).

18. Of course, if labor costs get far out-of-line and the economy faces extraordinary burdens, as in Germany after unification, some industry leaders will press down on both job security and labor standards. Germany, however, did not become the "sick man of Europe" because of job stability, investment in worker training, and good wages; after 1989 it was done in by extremely heavy and continuing costs of absorbing East Germany – to this day taking 4% of GDP per year – and by the procyclical monetary policy of the Bundesbank (and today the similar policies of the European Central Bank). The very low number of annual hours of work in Germany may have been a contributing factor.

19. For a full account of the development and content of active labor-market policy in Germany and reasons for the lag in the United States, see Janoski, 1990. For a comparison of ALMP in six countries, see Schmid, Reissert, and Bruche, 1992.

20. A careful analysis of four decades of German export expansion 1953 to 1994 (Holtfrerich and Lindlar, 1995) confirms this observation. It concludes that even in the turbulent times of 1975–1989 German exports grew (in real terms) at an average yearly rate of 4.0%, an excellent record compared to other countries and the long-run past. From 1985 to 1990, Germany's trade surplus on the current account climbed to a remarkable 6% of GDP (p. 4). Even during the peak of the unification burden and a deep recession, 1990–1994, exports grew at an average yearly rate of 6.3%, including trade with East Germany (p. 5). The composition of these exports also remained exceptionally stable for the four decades – machinery, chemicals, automobiles, and transportation equipment – despite increased competition from low-cost producers using cheap labor (p. 18). Germany continues to excel in medium-tech products (as a percentage of value added to the entire economy) while matching Japan and the United States in high-tech production (pp. 20–23). In short, the German model, contrary to pronouncements of its death, held up well through thick and thin. The dark spot is the climb in unemployment, reflecting the rigidity of the Bundesbank in the early 1990s, when it engaged in a war against the inflation phantom. (See Chapter 5.) And, of course, the drastic decline of trade in the crisis of 2008–2010 hurt German and European as well as Asian exports.

21. The symbol of high-tech products and services is such high-growth centers as Silicon Valley (California), Route 128 (Boston-Cambridge), the Research Triangle Park (North Carolina), and federal facilities in space and defense around Cape Canaveral (Florida), Huntsville (Alabama), and Oak Ridge (Tennessee).

22. The U.S. Census Bureau creates 12 categories of retail sales people. If we aggregated them instead of sticking to the most detailed classifications, "retail sales" would be the largest fast-growing category in 1997, with 6,887,000 workers and a growth rate of 25% from 1983 to 1997.

23. If projected growth in 1994–2005 is preferred, the picture is even more low or no tech. The 16 occupations with the greatest percent increase (moderate estimates of 119% to 52% growth), in descending order of growth, are personal and home-care aides; home health aides; computer systems analysts, engineers, and scientists; electronic pagination systems workers; physical and corrective therapy assistants and aides; occupational therapy assistants and aides; physical therapists; residential counselors; human service workers; occupational therapists; manicurists; medical assistants; paralegals; medical records technicians; teachers in special education; and amusement and recreation attendants. The list is dominated by the medical-industrial complex discussed in Chapter 5. Again, only a couple of these can be seen as high tech. If we instead examine occupations with the largest total job openings

due to estimated growth and net replacement, the picture is the same (Jacobs, 1997: 166–174).

24. Incidentally and adding to the complications, a proposed $1.5 billion wind farm in Texas that applied to the feds for support under the stimulus package would create only 300 jobs in the United States but 2,000 jobs in China, where the wind turbines would be manufactured (Hindary et al., 2010: A22).

25. Kammen, Kapadia, and Fripp (2004) draw upon 13 independent reports and studies and develop a job creation model. Their research emphasizes what Chapter 2 has shown – the interdependence of many policies with a "comprehensive and coordinated energy policy that also supports energy efficiency and sustainable transportation." They assume that by 2020 electricity production remains the same as it was in 2002; they exclude learning effects as well as any jobs that come from manufacturing energy equipment for export. Their main conclusion: of the five scenarios they model (Table 3) – three with different mixes of renewables, one with fossil fuels as usual, one with 100% natural gas – the best average job creator is 85% biofuels, 14% wind energy, 1% solar PV (240,850 added jobs); next is 40% biomass, 55% wind energy, 5% solar (188,018 jobs); the third is 60% biomass, 37% wind, 3% solar (176,144 jobs). The other two create many fewer jobs: about 86,000 for fossil fuels as usual (half coal, half natural gas); or 84,000 with 100% natural gas. Winners in renewables in their view will likely far outnumber losers in the fossil-fuel sector.

26. By 1992 the 36,000 multinationals with over 170,000 affiliates abroad (only about 70,000 of which are in less developed countries) had reached a stock of foreign direct investment of about $1.9 trillion. By 1990 worldwide sales by foreign affiliates had reached $5.5 trillion; they became more important than the worldwide sum of exports (3.3 trillion in 1990) (Sauvant, Mallampally, and Economou, 1993: 37; UN, 1993: 37; Encarnation, 1993: 25). Regarding *employment*, most overseas employment by MNCs is in other industrialized countries, except for Japanese MNCs, whose expansion into Asia is concentrated in developing countries. In the early 1990s, however, with rapid growth and fewer restrictions, MNCs in Europe and North America and Japan alike expanded faster in Asia, Latin America, and the Caribbean. Although an estimate of worldwide employment by MNCs in parent firms and foreign affiliates was only 65 million (International Labor Office [ILO], 1992: 49), up from about 40 million in the mid 1970s (Parisotto, 1993: 34), the jobs are concentrated in rich countries. More than 9 in 10 of the MNCs are headquartered in industrialized countries – most of the biggest are in Japan, Germany, and the United States (Gold, 1993: 100) – and about 7 in 10 of the jobs created by their affiliates abroad are concentrated in the same affluent countries (ILO, 1992: 49). Still, these and more recent figures suggest that multinationals account for only a very small portion of employment in rich countries, perhaps no more than 10% (World Investment Report, 2008; OECD.stat, 2009–2010; BLS, 2001oa) and a tiny fraction of employment in less developed countries – around 1% (Sauvant et al., 1993: 37; calculations from World Investment Report, 2008: 9 and ILO, 2001) – whose *un*employed number is in the hundreds of millions. For a balanced analysis of the impact of MNCs on poor and developing countries, see Stiglitz, 2006: 187–210.

27. Bennett Harrison (1994: 165) describes another motive for adaptation – expand markets by strategic alliances – in his account of the 1990 Daimler-Benz and Mitsubishi agreement to engage in "intensive cooperation": Daimler gains access to Mitsubishi's prodigious knowledge of mechatronics (the wedding of mechanical and electrical engineering). What Mitsubishi gets from the alliance is Daimler's aid in blocking French and

Italian resistance to letting Japanese car makers into post-1992 Europe, and a connection to Europe's single largest and most commercially successful public-private partnership: the Airbus Industrie consortium that has made itself one of the world's three largest producers of civilian aircraft and a leader in airframe technology" (p. 165).

28. This adaptation of MNCs is also evident in U.S.-EU financial dispute management. Posner's (2006) five-case comparison of the regulation of financial services shows that American companies that operate in Europe under EU pressure changed their behavior to conform; they and U.S. financial authorities became more accommodative, less unilateral.

29. On trade as a nonlabor motive for direct foreign investment, see the *Economist's* "Survey of Multinationals," Mar. 27, 1993: 10. An American MNC like Intel enters an EC country to preempt potential trade barriers (to be in a position to cope if the community raises barriers against imported chips) and to counter competitors' moves (distract the rival, lower his profits, learn about his tactics and technology).

30. That foreign transplants are not looking for cheap, non-union labor is confirmed in a study comparing changes in foreign and domestic manufacturing investment across the 48 contiguous states for 1978–1985 (Grant and Hutchinson, 1996). Highly unionized states such as Pennsylvania and Ohio were more successful in attracting foreign firms than in preventing American firms from moving out to the South or abroad. Union avoidance was a much more frequent motive for American managers than among their European and Japanese counterparts, who were used to unions, investment in training, and worker participation. Even for Americans, however, union avoidance was less important in plant location than market demand (and the absence of recessions), tax policies, and federal revenue transfers (permitting states to invest in physical and human infrastructure).

31. A *Wall Street Journal* survey of capital flows based on World Bank data concludes that 10 of the 12 countries that receive the lion's share of foreign capital directed to the developing world are nonpoor; most are "upper-middle" in GNP per capita (*Wall Street Journal*, Sept. 18, 1997).

32. Personal communication from Andrew Martin, Sept. 2, 1997.

33. After 1998, the newly independent Bank of Japan choked off recovery and deepened deflation; it raised interest rates August 2000, with the same inappropriate effect as the earlier delay in tightening of 1989 from 2.5 to 3.25% (Vogel, 2006: 23, 27–28). In the prolonged crisis of the 1990s, the Ministry of Finance's commitment to fiscal balance reinforced the restrictive monetary policy of the Bank of Japan to deepen recessions at critical moments. MOF long maintained close ties with BOJ; MOF officials actually alternated with BOJ officials as the bank's governor until BOJ's recent autonomy. However the antiexpansionist policies of the 1990s were an aberration for the MOF, given its accommodative history for four decades of the Japanese miracle (pp. 48–50).

34. They are the HWWA-Institute for Economic Research in Hamburg; Ifo-Institute for Economic Research in Munich; Institute for the World Economy in Kiel; Institute for Economic Research in Halle; the Rhine-Westphalian Institute for Economic Research (RWI) in Essen; and the German Institute for Economic Research (DIW) in Berlin. A seventh more prominent source of independent analysis and forecasting is a group of professors on the Council of Economic Advisers completely independent of the government, located in Wissbaden.

35. If we exclude the former East Germany from these figures, the unemployment rate for West Germany is lower by just under one percentage point. The Bundesbank in late

1992 aimed to reduce inflation from 3.7% to 2%, while Germany was itself slipping into recession. Hans Tietmeyer, president of the Bundesbank since 1993, railed against the welfare state; an anti-inflation hawk, he favored a European Central Bank, if it could be a carbon copy of the Bundesbank (*Wall Street Journal*, Jan. 17, 1996: 1). Such a bank was established in January 1999.

36. Because fiscal stimulus policy in the United States, although rapid in its impact, must be approved by a slow-moving Congress, it is less effective in shaping recoveries than monetary policy (Romer and Romer 1994: 37–38, 55). Anticyclical increases in spending within the discretion of the executive (e.g., accelerating planned spending or tax refunds) are almost always small and so are their effects; the big changes plowing their way through Congress are typically mistimed or defeated (except for the popular extension of unemployment benefits). This may be an American quirk, however; in less paralyzed political economies, fiscal policy may have greater, speedier impact – that is, if central bankers cooperate.

37. James K. Galbraith's caustic analysis of Fed behavior as self-fulfilling prophecy based on incoherent theories concludes that Fed policy reduces to a syllogism: "Good times are followed by bad times; therefore good times must be prevented" (1994: 36). The syllogism in action has meant that since 1951, when the Fed was freed to conduct an independent monetary policy, all U.S. recessions, without exception, were preceded by a shift to a tight monetary policy (Friedman, 1989: 104).

38. Deane and Pringle (1994: 309–310, 324–325) point to an irony: at the very time the central banks' autonomy is increasing, their effectiveness in controlling inflation is being undermined by the large number of big private speculators in currency and arcane derivatives over which the central bankers have no control. Thus, central bankers' anti-inflation measures are likely to be even more exaggerated because moderate interest-rate increases are less and less effective. The authors also note that while New Zealand, with its strongly autonomous central bank (after 1989) achieved a low inflation rate by 1992–1993, Australia, with a controlled central bank, did just as well (pp. 339–340). Regarding limited knowledge of central bankers, in a rare admission, Fed Governor Donald Kohn said in December 2006, "In informal terms, we are uncertain about where the economy has been, where it is now and where it is going." Quoted in "Only Human: A Special Report on Central Banks and the World Economy," *Economist*, Oct. 20, 2007. This review of the causes of the credit crisis of summer 2007 is consistent with my suggestion that CBA puts too heavy a burden on monetary policy and subverts the countercyclical uses of fiscal policy.

39. The lack of global exchange-rate discipline fuels currency speculation, creates uncertainty for business firms, reduces economic growth, and encourages protectionism (as we saw in the passionate debates over NAFTA and GATT in 1994, the Mexican crisis of January 1995, and the protests against the WTO on the streets of Seattle, Genoa, and Prague). Some cross-national regime to prevent extreme volatility and misalignments among key currencies may be desirable – a more flexible successor to Bretton Woods. The rigidity of the ECB and the Euro, however, made currency devaluation impossible as a short-term solution to the 2009–2010 troubles of Spain and other big borrowers. Before the Great Recession, Spain was by all accounts a good economic performer; it was fiscally responsible and ran a high-wage, high-growth, high-export, low-debt economy with increasing standards of living widely shared. But rapid growth and inflation culminated in an extraordinary housing bubble – partly rooted in investment by foreign banks in construction, including seaside homes and resort development. (German and French banks loaned about $909 billion to Greece,

Portugal, Ireland, and Spain. Nearly half went to Spain according to September 30, 2009, figures from the Bank for International Settlements.) In the years before the bubble collapsed, Spain's spending and debt grew far out of line with other Eurozone countries, thereby making its exports uncompetitive in Euro prices. The Great Recession was the coup de gráce; unemployment and emergency spending soared, government revenue plunged along with Spanish bonds. The option of quick action reducing the value of the old pesata was closed; the rigidity of the Euro assured a prolonged slump and a long, painful recovery. The lesson is that the expansion of the Eurozone has ensnared the least rich countries on the periphery of the Eurozone so that they cannot reflate when the intense danger of deflation looms. Then their possible defaults become a threat to the entire financial system of the Continent – witness Greece and Portugal in April 2010.

40. For an insider's assessment of the "free market fundamentalism" that dominated policies of the Western financial community (IMF, World Bank, WTO, and central banks), see Stiglitz, 2002: 215–252, 11–22, 71ff. Such free-market ideology was the root of the deregulation and privatization measures that, in turn, created the Great Recession of 2007 on.

41. Both Argentina and Sweden illustrate the interaction of these types of crises. In Argentina in 2001–2002 the government defaulted on all of its debts; banks froze deposits indefinitely; the exchange rate (pesos/dollars) more than tripled overnight; prices went from deflation to inflation of at least 30%; real stock prices crashed by more than 30% (Reinhart and Rogoff, 2009: 251–252). In Sweden in 1983–1992 there was an interaction of financial deregulation and speculative bubbles, culminating in a severe banking crisis in 1991, currency fluctuations, and a credit squeeze – all brought on by changes in bargaining structures, party power and ideology, and policy mistakes (details in Wilensky, 2002: 110–114; cf. Huber and Stephens, 1996).

42. The National Bureau of Economic Research, the semiofficial scorer of duration of recessions, as of this writing May 16, 2010, had declared the beginning of the Great Recession December 2007 but had not declared the end. It defines a recession as a significant decline in economic activity spread across the economy lasting more than a few months and uses a variety of indicators. In this book I have used the unrealistic, very conservative rule of thumb that the Great Recession ended when the GDP growth stopped its negative slide in June or July of 2009. That ignores deteriorating labor markets and other indicators of mass misery in the long run. But I agree with those members of the NBER recession committee who noticed that the pain of this recession was so deep and widespread in 2010, that they resisted declaring the end.

43. Why was Ireland deviant in its good economic performance and productivity growth during the boom years of 2000–2007 (Tables 2 and 4) and equally exceptional in its poor performance in the bust – the earliest and worst recession in Europe, one of the deepest banking crises? A brief explanation: the earlier boom was driven by a remarkable influx of international capital in such export industries as information technology, medical equipment, and engineering services but especially in a construction industry dominated by large developers. Multinationals, including financial institutions, were encouraged to invest by lavish tax breaks and subsidies in land and infrastructure and easy lending. Ireland led in its dose of financial deregulation; in 2008 the Heritage Foundation declared Ireland the third "freest economy" in the world, behind only Hong Kong and Singapore. The result was the usual speculative credit and housing bubbles, bigger and broader than those in other rich democracies. Then the bubbles burst, taking with them much of the foreign capital that fueled the boom, putting

Ireland in a debt crisis like those of Greece, Portugal, and Spain. The "Celtic Tiger" was made of paper; the "Irish Miracle" fizzled. Ireland is deviant in many other ways, as well – in politics, religion, and demography (see Wilensky 2002: 125–126).

44. There is some evidence that a debt in excess of 90–100% of GDP may lower GDP growth by 1% per year in rich democracies or debt in excess of 35–40% of GDP may lower GDP growth even more among developing countries, though this remains controversial (Patillo, Ward, and Ricci, 2002). What is not controversial is that among rich democracies robust growth or even modest growth produces enough revenue to bring debt ratios down.

45. Judgment based on the work of economic historians and the small current breed of macroeconomists (e.g., Paul Krugman, 2009; Joseph Stiglitz; Simon Johnson) who have rediscovered the political and economic institutions that shape markets and have drawn upon the insights of previous generations – the influential labor economists of the early 20th century whom I list in the Preface, as well as Thorstein Veblen (1899, 1921), John Maynard Keynes (1936), Joseph Schumpeter (1942), Hyman Minsky (1957, 1963) and his mentor, Irving Fisher (1933), Charles Kindleberger (1958, 1973), George Stigler (1963, 1971), David Landes (1969), Albert Hirschman (1970, 1986), and Charles Lindblom (1977).

46. Countrywide and its home loan department, the largest mortgage lender during the housing bubble, is now a unit of Bank of America, the largest shadow bank in the United States. In June 2010 the Federal Trade Commission (FTC) fined Bank of America $108 million for the mortgage lender's lending practices – some of it predatory and legal, much of it straightforward corruption, violating its own contracts to pad fees and cheat mortgagees (*New York Times*, June 13, 2010). In court suits pending, it is clear that the investment banks who sold these loan pools to two Federal Home Loan Banks, among many other buyers, misrepresented actual loan characteristics in their pitch to investors. In disclosures filed with the SEC, about half of these derivatives involving some 525,000 mortgage loans in 156 pools sold by 10 investment banks from 2005 through 2007 were misrepresented (research by CoreLogic reported by Morgenson, 2010).

47. In July 2010 the SEC backed off. It diluted its serious fraud allegation against Goldman Sachs and instead settled out of court with a fine of $550 million on a lesser violation. The firm admitted no guilt. "Investors had expected any SEC fine in the case to be $1 billion or more" (*Wall Street Journal*, July 17, 2010). GS shares jumped up. Because Goldman Sachs is so large and profitable, the SEC fine is unlikely to hurt the company nor deter others from similar behavior. The fine is chump change compared to Goldman's bonus pool; it is even less than its depressed 2010 second-quarter profit.

48. The Fed chairman, Ben Bernanke, recognized this in his second term: the market plunge of 1,000 points and equally swift recovery May 6, 2010, he said, "was just a small indicator of how complex and chaotic, in the formal sense, these systems have become. Our financial system is so complicated and so interactive – so many sets of rules. What happened in the stock market is just a little example of how things can cascade or how technology can interact with market panic" (*New York Times*, May 16, 2010).

49. In mid-July 2010 Congress sent a 2,319-page bill to the president to sign. Why it is too early to know its effect is discussed in Chapter 8.

50. In 2010 the SEC and congressional investigators accused Goldman Sachs of duping its clients, stonewalling investigators, and betting against entire economies. In a bizarre liaison, Goldman was actually hired by BP to advise it on its public relations problems after BP's Gulf oil spill.

51. Critics of Bernanke's record note that he could have pricked the bubble by raising interest rates but instead continued Greenspan's policies, that as late as March 2007 he claimed that the problems of the subprime market would not have much impact on the economy and financial markets, and so on. However, unlike his counterparts in the EU and the European Central Bank, he later resisted the call for a preemptive fight against the inflation phantom. Unlike other Fed chairs, as a Princeton professor and serious scholar he was a student of the Great Depression and of Japanese deflation. Unless one thinks that biography is irrelevant as a guide to current behavior, his history should shape Fed policies positively even as his mission is constrained by FRB's charter, traditions, and the rest of his board and staff.

52. For chapter and verse on the deals Treasury and the Fed worked out, bank by bank, see S. Johnson, 2009; Stiglitz, 2010; Krugman, 2009.

53. MNCs evidence an additional non-labor-cost motive for direct foreign investment: an American multinational like Intel enters an EC country to preempt potential trade barriers (to be in a position to cope if the community raises barriers against imported chips) and to counter competitors' moves (distract the rival, lower his profits, learn about his tactics and technology) ("A Survey of Multinationals," *Economist*, Mar. 27, 1993: 10).

## Chapter 7. Low Road vs. High Road: American Exceptionalism?

1. These six countries share a decentralized, fragmented political economy. This book has shown that the least-corporatist, least-consensual democracies pursue common policies with the common outcomes captured by the inverse of Figure 5. Despite differences that look large when we compare two or three countries within this category (the United Kingdom or Canada vs. United States – presidential vs. parliamentary systems, a well-trained, well-paid, efficient civil service vs. its opposite), the more important differences that hold the six together fit the label, least corporatist.

2. In 1980 a remarkable 1 in 20 workers who favored unions were fired. Freeman and Medoff (1984: 232–233) estimate that this is about one case of NLRB-declared illegal discharge for every NLRB election. After President Reagan sent a signal by breaking the air traffic controllers PATCO strike in 1981, management militancy mounted. For example, the practice of breaking strikes and abandoning collective bargaining contracts by hiring permanent replacements accelerated after 1981 (LeRoy, 1995). An acceleration of the full range of employer intimidation, interrogation, and retaliation for union activity from 1986 to 2003 is documented in a comprehensive review of primary NLRB documents for a random sample of 1,004 NLRB certification elections and an in-depth survey of 562 of those elections (Bronfenbrenner, 2009).

3. Throughout this section, the following definitions should be kept in mind: *Income*: the increase in command over goods and services received by a person or other social unit (e.g., a corporation) during a particular time period. This includes earnings from work, property income, and transfers in cash or kind. *Earnings or pay*: income derived from work. This includes overtime, incentive pay, and fringe benefits. *Wages or salaries*: the basic rate of pay received per unit of time – hour, week, month. *Property*: a system of rights and duties, socially recognized and sanctioned, of persons and other social units (e.g., a corporation, the state) with respect to valued objects (tangible like a house, or intangible like an idea). *Wealth*: a stock of natural resources and previously produced goods in existence at one moment, such as land, structures, machinery, consumer goods, and business inventories, as well as any financial claims of individuals such as cash, stocks, government or corporate bands, and retirement claims. *Economic*

*inequality*: refers to all differentials in income, earnings or pay, wages, or salaries, property or wealth. It should be distinguished from *poverty*, which refers only to limited economic resources in the hands of persons or other social units below some absolute or relative minimum (Wilensky, 1978: 87; Wolff, 1995, 1987).

4. A long-standing pattern. Executive pay has been a far greater multiple of worker pay than in other developed countries. In 2005 the *Wall Street Journal* found that total CEO compensation in U.S. large firms was 475 times greater than the average worker's compensation. Compare the ratios they found for Japan, 11 times greater; France, 15; Canada, 20; Britain, 22 (*Wall Street Journal*, Jan. 21–22, 2006: A7). An earlier comparison of 12 rich democracies found that in 1997 the CEO/worker ratio was largest in the United States, Australia, and the United Kingdom; it was least, most egalitarian, in Japan, Switzerland, and Germany (Mishel, Bernstein, and Schmitt, 1999: 213, table 3.52). As usual, the fragmented, decentralized political economies shine in this measure and other indicators of inequality. (For a recent measure of household income inequality by type of political economy, see Table 2.) Can any of this be justified by the special talents of American executives? Even if we ignore the *Journal*'s annual review of top executive compensation from 1990 until now and their recurrent conclusion that it is either unrelated to corporate performance or negatively related, we can note that the success of Japanese export firms for decades did not suffer from the modest pay of their top executives. Auto manufacturers in Japan were hardly less productive than the Big Three of Detroit.

5. Dividing the 18 countries by high and low impact of taxes and transfers (the welfare state, not counting personal social services) on poverty, we find that 8 of the 9 with most reduced poverty (24% to 17% reduction) are corporatist democracies while 8 of the 9 with least impact (16.5% to 9.2%) are either fragmented, decentralized political economies, or corporatist without labor. Among the high scorers, the United Kingdom is the exception; among the low scorers, Australia is the exception, both near the median. The United States, again, achieves the very least impact on pretransfer, pretax poverty, with only 9.2% reduction (details on the U.S. welfare state in Chapter 1).

6. The survey was conducted in the first half of 2008 before the worst of the recession hit. Median wage was $8.02/hour, with three in four of those interviewed earning less than $10.00/hour. At that time the minimum wage was $7.15 in NY State, $7.50 in Illinois and $8.00 in California. Over two-thirds of those surveyed had experienced at least one pay-related violation in the previous workweek.

7. When I was living in Sweden in 1970, all these policies to balance the demands of work and family were already in place. They have since been strengthened. They were first adopted in the 1930s by the Social Democratic Party platform when young Alva Myrdal led the women's caucus inside the party.

8. Adding to the jobless recovery and the continued decline in household income in 2010 was an orchestrated campaign by right-wing governors and members of Congress to pin the state fiscal crisis on public-sector unions, the one area where union strength has increased since 1970. This took the form of severe work-force reductions in the states combined with efforts to cut or eliminate pensions and other negotiated benefits and, finally, laws to make collective bargaining illegal. At the end of 2010, there was even a Republican move in Washington to allow states to file some kind of bankruptcy as a way to abrogate union contracts and break public-sector unions. The myth that public employees' lavish benefits are the cause of our escalating troubles is belied by their total compensation, which is slightly below that of comparable private-sector employees of the same educational level and occupation.

9. The top six in hours in 1994 are the United States (1,994 hours), Japan (1,960), Canada (1,898), the United Kingdom (1,824), Italy (1,804), and France (1,638). Except for Italy, five of the six are decentralized fragmented political economies with little left-labor power or they are corporatist without labor (Japan, France). The bottom five – least working hours – are democratic corporatist: Norway (1,549), Germany (1,541), Denmark (1,573), the Netherlands (1,599), and Sweden (1,627).

10. Self-reports in surveys, based on a concept of the "labor force" – all those at work or who have been seeking work in the past four weeks before the interview. The official unemployment rate is those not at work but seeking work divided by the total labor force.

11. I could not find detailed enough comparisons of industrial accidents, occupational injuries, and illness in the 19 rich democracies to see how types of political economy shaped them. But my intensive 3-country comparison is consistent with the low-road idea. Sweden scored best (lowest) in rates of industrial accidents, Germany a close second, and the United States worst (most accidents) (Wilensky 2002: 546–550).

12. The full-blown demand for university graduates came quite late. Arnold Heidenheimer's analysis of policy thresholds for higher education and for social security shows that the year when university enrollment, both public and private, first constituted 10% of primary school enrollment was 1946 for the United States, 1968 for Sweden, 1973 for the United Kingdom, and 1975 for Germany (1981: 294–299). Elsewhere I have shown that spending on the welfare state (health, pensions, and other social policies) is inversely related to spending on higher education (1975: 3–7). The former is clearly and directly a contribution to absolute equality, the reduction of differences between the affluent and the poor, young and old, minority groups and majorities; higher education, in contrast, is a contribution to equality of opportunity – enhanced mobility for those judged to be potentially able or skilled.

13. Source is OECD (2010). The U.S. Census Bureau for 2008 puts the U.S. figure a bit higher at 52.8%, still far behind most rich democracies. OECD has missing data for Canada and Israel, while Irish numbers are suspiciously low (only 1% enrollment) and were also excluded. The Netherlands was excluded owing to 0% attendance at age three, though the number jumps to 99% at age four. That zero may be due to the unusually low female labor-force participation in Holland.

14. In the interest of full disclosure: in the late 1960s when a much larger percentage of graduating seniors aspired to be teachers, California changed the rules enough so liberal arts students could receive credit toward teacher certification for courses in the college directly related to the subject they wanted to teach such as English, science, math, history, social science. I was assigned to counsel these typically bright students on the new system. Many had already taken courses or explored the requirements in the Graduate School of Education, which was by no means in the lower ranks of such schools. They repeated such phrases as "Mickey Mouse courses" they could not stand; they bitterly complained about how the school was gaming the system so they would be overloaded if they did not give up some of their content courses. In a very few years the system collapsed. Periodic campuswide outside faculty evaluations recommended that the school be phased out. Fearing retaliation by a populist legislature, UCB's top administrators vetoed faculty phase-out recommendations; they prevented the battle from reaching beyond the campus. The only state-financed Graduate School of Education in Northern California survived and grew through thick and thin.

15. Germany joined the United States as deviant but only because of its 2000 shift from abundant apprenticeships to college prep courses in response to shifting demand. In time, Germany should join the rest as the college-bound increase, although some types of apprenticeship will likely grow with economic recovery and labor shortages.

16. The Earned Income Tax Credit (EITC) of the United States, adopted in 1975, requires only a short form in the tax return; the Treasury mails confidential checks to the working poor and near poor with no administrative discretion. The rules are national and clear. Successive increases in the EITC under President Clinton were one factor in the brief reduction of poverty from 1995 to 2000. Clinton's goal in signing the 1996 welfare reform bill was to remove "welfare" from politics as a wedge issue hurting Democrats.

17. Some of my colleagues argue that all these right-wing attacks on the welfare poor to mobilize resentment and race prejudice among white high-school and part-college folks in elections are a thing of the past. They acknowledge that baiting the welfare poor as living on a lifetime vacation plan on your hard-earned taxes was a major theme in Reagan's gubernatorial and presidential victories. But they say that's passé. These political scientists did not attend to the saturation media coverage by Meg Whitman, Republican candidate for governor of California in 2010 – many months of constant 24–7 commercials on undeserving people on welfare running away with the California budget and telling us that a crackdown on their growing numbers is necessary to restore fiscal responsibility. Whitman offered an almost word-for-word repetition of the antiwelfare, antitax, antibureaucratic sound bites of Ronald Reagan. In the same election cycle, Newt Gingrich described the Democrats as "the party of Food Stamps." Plus ça change …

18. OECD's definition of ALMP includes placement and related services, benefit administration, government-supported training in and out of the workplace, apprenticeship support, employment and recruitment incentives, rehabilitation and supported employment, direct job creation and startup incentives. OECD data on ALMP may underestimate the active effort of several countries. More intensive studies of a few cases (data from the late 1970s and early 1980s in Johannesson and Schmid, 1980; Wilensky, 1985; Janoski, 1990) show a higher GDP share than the OECD estimates indicate. For instance, the budgets and programs of Sweden suggest that its GDP share has fluctuated between 2% and 3% – almost equivalent to the U.S. Pentagon budget before George W. Bush (3% of GDP is now about $420 billion). The OECD average for 2000–2006 for Sweden is 1.44%, American equivalent to "only" about $202 billion a year spent on ALMP. Unless the ALMP double share in the intensive studies of circa 1980 is entirely explained by the subsequent 23 years of economic growth, the OECD's 1.44% for Sweden may be a bit low. OECD is handicapped in these hard-to-measure budget items: it must try to achieve cross-national comparability for 30 democracies.

19. Across 19 countries we could not measure family planning or counseling; or home-care help, supplementary meals, or institutional care for the aged. But case studies suggest that they tend to be related to what we could measure. For concepts and coding, detailed results, country by country, and citations to researchers who used the Index of Family Policy to replicate my findings with added measures and somewhat different samples and arrived at almost identical country rankings, see Wilensky, 2002: ch. 7. Wherever data permit, the analysis is an adaptation of regression techniques to my causal models using path diagrams. Such a model is tested for the causes of national variation in family policy (p. 280).

20. All of these effects of family policy are demonstrated in Wilensky, 2002: chs. 7 and 14.

21. The crackdown mentality – political slogans about "law 'n order" – had a not-so-incidental effect. It increased police and prosecutorial misconduct and incompetence, as suggested by the 1999 revelation by the Los Angeles police chief that dozens of people are known to have been framed by the police and by police confessions that at least two unarmed gang members were shot. Similar incidents of police abuse occurred across the country, most dramatically in New York, New Jersey, and Washington, D.C. Excessive zeal in pursuit of the bad guys is not typically corruption, where police join thieves, deal dope, or take bribes. Instead the police, operating in a dangerous environment, are responding to the sometimes-hysterical but always-consistent demand of the public, politicians, and prosecutors and their supervisors that they apprehend and help convict criminals. Stretching the truth to put a known bad actor away comes to be seen as righteous protection of the community. When the police prosecutors cross that line, as they have in Los Angeles, they may start down a slippery slope that ends with framing a suspect for murder.

22. What unemployment and poverty have in common as sources of violent crime is their effect on parents' capacity (little time and energy, few resources) and will (low morale, despair, pent-up frustration) to monitor children's or teenagers' behavior and punish them for deviance or reward them for good behavior (Hirschi, 1983). Such loss of authority is especially acute where the father is absent (family breakup) or loses his job (and appears to his children as a model of failure and weakness). In the tangle of pathologies that constitute American slums, the schools, too, have diminished capacity to monitor children's behavior. Conversely, social integration – the bonds of family, school, work, church, community – can in Durkheimian style protect the poor and/or the unemployed from crime and suicide. For supporting studies, see Wilensky, 2002: 510–515.

23. Until economists and others enter these demographic and social variables into their equations, we will not know whether these conclusions hold for more recent years.

## Chapter 8. Policy Implications for the United States: How to Get Off the Low Road

1. Owens and Wade (1986: 688) show that in 85 cases of lopsided spending in California between 1924 and 1984, one-sided negative spending prevailed in 29 of 32 (a 91% defeat rate) while one-sided positive spending won in 29 of 53 (55%). Because on average only one-third of all these initiatives pass, while 66% of referenda pass, and because Owens and Wade include 68 initiatives and only 17 mandatory referenda – yielding a weighted average usual passage rate of 40% – the climb to a 55% success rate for disproportionate proponent spending is impressive (Magleby, 1994: 250). Similar findings appear in an econometric study of California initiatives from 1976 to 1990 and Oregon initiatives from 1970 to 1990 (Banducci, 1998). There is some indication that propositions on hot-button issues of the populist right (tax and spending limitations, abortion, death penalty, crime, term limits, immigration) and populist left (campaign reform, affirmative action, term limits, environmental cleanup) require less money than initiatives of central concern to industry (regulation of private insurance or health care). In 1988, five California insurance initiatives evoked more than $101 million in campaign spending, overwhelmingly insurance-company money (Magleby, 1994: 242). Movement-type initiatives, in contrast, can command free airtime and even some volunteers. Hence, their spending is not so obscene.

Examples are anti-illegal immigrant Proposition 187 and the "three strikes" crime measure, where free national media coverage was prominent and total spending was well below the California average (Donovan et al. 1998: ch. 4).

2. Switzerland and the United States, however, different in their size, culture, economy, and politics, have one thing in common: they both achieve uniquely low voter turnout, lowest among our 19 democracies. But Switzerland, at least marginally, fits our category of corporatism without labor and has a consensual style of governing. The seven-member Federal Council that runs Switzerland – the grand coalition – has had almost the same party representation since 1959 (Klöti, 1991: 2, 15–16). There is a sizable labor movement and industrial peace. The government bans political advertising on television and imposes universal military service. In sharp contrast, the United States has a confrontational governing style, a weak labor movement, above-average industrial conflict, unrestricted media dominance of politics, no large integrative national service, and more big swings in politics and policy. The differences in size of population are huge. These institutional differences explain why the Swiss can indulge direct democracy without subverting consensual democracy. The U.S.-Swiss similarities that explain their common low turnout are their extraordinary frequency of elections, their radical use of the initiative and referenda, and the voter fatigue that both of these create (cf. Crewe, 1981; Jackman and Miller, 1995; Wilensky, 2002: 415–417).

3. Reinforcing this move of the political spectrum to the right is the increasing politicization of the judiciary. An adviser to President-elect Reagan's transition team told me that they were determined to go beyond the usual screening of candidates for top positions. They were extending the search to younger middle- and even lower-level appointees, especially for potential judiciary positions. The aim was to expand the pool of ideological loyalists who would be around for a very long time as actual or potential recruits for as many positions as possible. One result of this ambitious but careful planning can be seen today in the stable of Republicans judges at upper levels all the way to the Supreme Court. Of course, before Reagan, judicial decisions at federal district courts on up have often reflected the preferences of the presidents who appointed them and many a judge has surprised his sponsor by an independent or deviant stance (e.g., Earl Warren, David Souter). But party ideology as a criterion since Reagan has now gone to such an extreme that it is perhaps the best single predictor of important judicial decisions at the upper levels. Confirmation of this polarization appears in a longitudinal study of Supreme Court justices. Miles and Sunstein (2006) present trend data on increasing political polarization (1990–2004) finding that conservative appointees increasingly invalidated liberal agency decisions (e.g., EPA and the NLRB).

4. There is some disagreement among students of American politics regarding the polarization of the electorate. For instance, Abramowitz finds that party loyalty and voting the straight ticket in the U.S. Senate elections declined sharply from the 1950s to the 1970s, then climbed sharply from the 1980s to 2009 (2010: fig. 4). Throughout that period, however, many measures of political participation suggest a trend toward mass withdrawal from the system and more volatility in party attachments in the electorate (Wilensky, 2002: 402–420; Verba, Schlozman, and Brady, 1995; Reiter, 1989). For a summary of both sides of the dispute, see Wilensky, 2002: 398 ff. Both my cross-national analysis of 12 measures of party decline (410–415) in six nations and several other comparative analyses point to the United States as the textbook case of party dealignment. The United Kingdom is the runner-up.

5. Also contradicting the myth of the independent voter is Abramowitz (2010: fig. 4) who shows that party loyalty in Senate elections has increased. One caution is that, while

still the best predictor of voting preferences in both presidential and congressional elections, party loyalties are now more lightly held; the long-term trend is toward party dealignment in the electorate.

6. My analysis based on surveys conducted by Knowledge Networks. The 2000 data came from an Internet panel comprised of a national random sample of households recruited by random digit dialing, who either have Internet access through their own computer or are given a Web-TV console in exchange for completing three or four surveys a month. N = 12,685. Data for 2004 are from the 2004 Presidential Election Survey commissioned by the Diane D. Blair Center of Southern Politics and Society and conducted by Knowledge Networks through its Internet Panel. N = 2,100. S. Hillygus of Harvard and T. Shields of the Blair Center kindly made these data available.

7. The new myth that that the young are a new force in the Democratic Party who turned out in droves for Gore and Obama is belied by careful study of their turnout (Kaufmann, Petrocik, and Shaw, 2008). For 40 years (1971–2008) American National Election Studies have shown that the 18–24 year olds vote consistently less than any other age cohort. The youth turnout deficit averaged 20% in presidential elections. In 2004 it was 17%; in 2008 it was again 17%. In off years the gap is much wider. As I have repeatedly indicated (e.g., 2008), the dirty little secret of 2004 and 2008 is that the American electorate remains neither black, poor, young, college students, nor graduate and professional degree holders. Perhaps in the long run demographic shifts such as the growth of minority populations will change this, if their party preferences do not change, but the long run is far from here.

8. The stark difference that showed up in the exit polls for losing presidential candidate Kerry in 2004 underlines the importance of economic issues: union members who ranked bread-and-butter issues as important voted 76% Democratic; non-union voters concerned with "moral values" voted 11% Democratic (Francia, 2006: table 4). More relevant is that among respondents without a four-year college degree the economy/jobs/taxes combination was the central issue for 40% of union member voters compared to only 23% of similar non-union voters, who said those economic issues were "most important." And in the off-year Democratic victory of 2006 white working-class union voters favored Democratic candidates for Congress and governors by more than 60%. In contrast, white working-class non-union voters supported Republicans for governor (55% margin), Senate (53%), and the House (58%) (p. 29).

9. After the 2004 election many instant analysts argued that the wedge issues of abortion and gay marriage were critical in the defeat of John Kerry. Using standard multivariate statistics on exit polls and one of the most thorough national postelection surveys, political scientists have now shown that such "moral values" were at best very marginal in the 2004 outcome. Two of the several academics who analyzed this, D. S. Hillygus and T. G. Shields, summarize: opinions about gay marriage and abortion "had no effect on voter decision making among Independents, respondents in battleground states, or even among respondents with an anti-gay marriage initiative on the ballot. . . . Only in the South did either issue have an independent effect on vote choice, and even here the effect was minimal." Overwhelmingly what counted nationally as well as in the South were attitudes toward the economy, the Iraq war, and terrorism. (Of course, no one knows whether gay marriage was worth the 60,000-vote shift in Ohio that would have made Kerry president.) Sources include a symposium published in *P.S.: Political Science and Politics* 38, 2 (Apr. 2005): especially 189–210. The most careful analysis is on pp. 201–209. Further citations are on p. 208.

10. David Mayhew (1991), in a systematic study of the frequency of investigations and legislation passed from 1946 to 1990, concludes that party-divided government does not make a difference. His analysis, however, is based on issues that rose to the top and were voted up or down; it ignores what did not happen – issues not addressed, and bills that were passed in a watered-down form inadequately addressing core issues. Further, when Mayhew makes a stab at qualitative differences, his analysis shows big differences. He identifies 19 "historic bills" – bills that fundamentally changed federal policy, altered the political landscape, and left a lasting legacy. Here unified periods produced historic laws at twice the yearly rate of divided periods (.61 to .31). Finally, other studies that give more attention to qualitative differences (e.g., new policy vs. modification of existing policy), issues that never make the agenda, and passage rates as opposed to absolute number of laws show that divided government accomplishes much less (e.g., Light, 1981–1982: 68, 73, 79; Peterson, 1990: 210–212).

11. Some scholars (e.g., Oberlander and Marmor, 2010; Marmor, 2010) attribute presidential passivity to the Obama team's determination to avoid the mistakes of the failed Clinton health-care reform proposal of 1993–1994, a 1,342-page bill Clinton sent to Congress. This "do-the-opposite-of-Clinton" strategy, these close observers suggest, account for the president's refusal to propose anything specific and draw any lines in the sand. My view is that Clinton lacked anything like the Senate majority of either Johnson or Obama and, no matter what strategy he adopted, no matter how simple and short his proposal, any national health-care proposal would have crashed. The Obama White House drew the wrong lesson from the Clinton experience. Johnson's Medicare success after a bitter fight in the early 1960s was the relevant model, modified for the politics of 2008–2010. "Medicare for all" starting with "Medicare for more" was the likely fit (Wilensky, 2009). The struggle in the early 1960s fight included Kennedy on May 20, 1962, speaking to 20,000 people at a rally for a bill providing hospital care for the aged, 1 of 45 such rallies nationwide. He said that the bill was part of the "great unfinished business in this country." After two more months of fighting, the Kennedy bill was defeated in the Senate, where Kennedy, despite substantial numerical majorities, was facing a conservative coalition of southern Democrats and Republicans and the effort failed (cf. Oberlander, 2003: 28–29).

12. Nearly half of the savings promised in the reform bill come from reducing fees to providers and insurers who contract with Medicare. As the industry responds by upping premiums and reducing services (e.g., dental, vision, other), the social compact of Medicare between the healthy young and less-healthy older populations will be broken. That long-standing compact emphasized that both aging and illness are shared risks where everyone chips in for the health care we all now or eventually need. If insurers and providers continue to respond as they have, the net effect will be a transfer from the sick of any age to the younger well. The idea of shared risk, the basis of both Medicare and Social Security, will fade, while total costs continue to rise (cf. *Wall Street Journal*, July 26, 2010). In September 2010 the Centers for Medicare and Medicaid Services announced that it had reviewed 2,100 bids from privately run Medicare plans and had turned down 14.2% of them as charging excessive premiums (*Wall Street Journal*, Sept. 22, 2010). Several large insurers plan to stop selling individual policies to cover children because of regulations concerning preexisting conditions, thus continuing the cost-shifting and risk-selection games wherever hybrid public-private systems prevail.

13. The California study analyzed a total of 3,999 individuals hospitalized with a principal diagnosis of heart failure at six medical centers between January 1, 2001 and June 30, 2005. The researchers used multivariate risk-adjusted models for total hospital stays, total hospital direct costs, and mortality within 180 days after initial admission ("Looking Forward"). A subset of 1,639 individuals who died during the study period were analyzed with multivariate risk-adjusted models for total hospital days and total hospital direct costs within 180 days before death – the period other research shows can be attributed to processes of care ("Looking Back"). The Spearman rank-order correlation coefficients were –0.68 between mortality and hospital days and –0.93 between mortality and total direct costs. (See especially Ong et al., 2009: table 3.)

14. For example, the United States has 25.9 magnetic imaging machines per million people; the OECD countries have an average of 11. The United States uses them much more often: 91.2 times per 1,000 people per year compared to the OECD average of 39.1 (OECD Health Data, 2010). Similarly large differences between the U.S. and other countries appear when we confine averages to the subset of 11 rich democracies with data on machines and the 6 rich democracies with data on frequency of use. The CBO in 2009 estimated that population aging accounts for only about a quarter of future health-care inflation over the next few decades; the share in other rich democracies is about the same. Commercialization and the poor organization of health care are the main sources of uniquely American cost levels. Aging alone explains little (Chapter 5; cf. Relman, 2007).

15. Chapter and verse on why "evidence-based medicine" and the "best practices" movement neither improves health nor cuts costs comes from a former advocate who has become a full-fledged skeptic, Dr. Jerome Koopman. "Over the past decade," he writes, federal "choice architects" using research on comparative effectiveness "have repeatedly identified 'best practices,' only to have them shown to be ineffective or even deleterious" (2010: 13). Many of these best practices resulted in unanticipated, severe side effects such as heart attacks and deaths. In the real world of individual patients, the recipient of best practices may have multiple medical conditions or an illness that evolves over time – all missed by mandated "quality care." This leaves aside experts who, under political pressure or for funding advantage, issue standards congenial to the insurance and drug companies.

16. Some scholars argue that adversary legalism is much stronger in the United States and accounts for greater industrial conflict and union busting than in Canada (e.g., Kaufman, 2009). But, as I have shown (2002: 689–690), the load of lawyers and their use by contentious parties in the United States is a consequence of the lack of channels for consensual bargaining, not its cause.

17. The Worker Representation and Participation Survey makes it clear that U.S. employees want more voice in the workplace (Freeman and Rogers, 1999: 45, 69, 151, 156, 183). This 1994 survey was based on a national cross section of adults, age 18 or more, working in private companies or nonprofits with 25 or more employees (N = 2,408 plus 801 reinterviews). For all age, sex, race, occupation, education, and earnings groups, there is a large gap in the desire for participation and the current work situation. In non-union companies 66% of nonmanagerial workers believe that management would oppose a union drive either through information campaigns or harassment and threats. Most of the total sample want cooperative joint committees with some independent standing inside their companies, and about half want a union or something very close to a union; 32% of non-union, nonmanagerial

employees would vote union "if an election were held today." Among current union members, 90% would vote to keep their union if a new election were held today. Overall, 40% of respondents reported that they would vote union if a new election were held today. The "near-union" responses bring the figures to over 80% – adding those respondents who say that rather than a union they prefer cooperative programs including the right to elect representatives, access to company information, decisions by an outside arbitrator in cases of conflict, etc. These attitude surveys are validated by the growth of public-sector unionism. Where employees have a choice free of intimidation, where their preferences can be expressed in a legal context that constrains union-busting campaigns, they vote overwhelmingly for unions.

18. The Supreme Court Citizens United ruling of January 21, 2010, that corporations and unions can spend unlimited political money with no identification of sources has exacerbated the pre–Citizens United problem of visibility. In the 2010 election, corporations led the charge. They pooled enormous resources of big banks, insurance companies, and oil companies. Leaving aside the upward trend in candidate spending, spending by noncandidates has been climbing for several election cycles; the Supreme Court may have accelerated this somewhat. In any case "non-party, independent spending and electioneering" totals through mid-October soared from $32 million in 2006 to $85 million in 2008 and to $148 million in 2010. Counting candidates, party, and nonparty spending, the Campaign Finance Institute estimates the total at about $1.2 billion (for House races $808 million, for Senate campaigns $389 million) (CFI, 2010).

19. The following is paraphrased from proposals by Ornstein et al. (1997); and the Free TV For Straight Talk Coalition (1997). Cantor, Rutkus, and Greely (1997) review the role of the FCC, the history of congressional action, and legal and constitutional issues posed by these proposals; they conclude that there is no constitutional bar to their enactment.

20. In my *Rich Democracies* (2002: ch. 7) I recount the coalition politics that brought politicians of opposing persuasion together on this issue. Nine Republican senators joined Democrats to pass a childcare bill with modest funding, the ABC Bill of 1989. It died in a conference committee. Until we are willing to produce serious and sustained funding for training and paying child minders, nursery school teachers, and other educators and spread the benefit well beyond the poor, the child care that has become routine in most other rich democracies will elude us.

21. One exception is Diane Ravitch, a leading historian of American education, an activist-scholar who served as assistant secretary of education in the G. H. W. Bush administration. She changed her mind in the face of systematic evidence. In a recent book (2010a), Ravitch evaluates conflicting evidence on the most recent round of unsuccessful school reforms, including those she herself supported – universal testing and the promotion of charter schools. She provides a guide to various reform movements and their consequences.

22. Five studies comparing Japanese and American schools done in the 1980s showed sharp contrasts in the mastery of academic subject matter, habits of discipline, and preparation for lifetime learning among the general population. The average Japanese 18-year-old had an edge of about three years over his American age-mate in science and math; earlier in the elementary years, he or she had acquired an edge in languages, music, and art; and the Japanese gap between the well educated and the poorly educated was small compared to that in the United States. Today this picture remains about the same. In view of the current sport of blaming our poor K–12

performance on teachers' unions, it is notable that Japanese public schools are almost 100% unionized, deeply entrenched, and political. (For details, see Wilensky, 2002: 465–473 and table 12.10.) These are extreme cases, but comparisons of Western European schools with American schools yield a similar result with a somewhat lesser gap – and again, widespread unionization of teachers in the better performing countries.

23. The teacher shortage and greatest turnover occurs in poor districts with low-performing schools. When Chattanooga offered teachers in such schools $5,000 bonuses, free graduate school tuition, and mortgage assistance, vacancies dropped to near zero. More talented teachers, like other professionals, respond to such incentives. If the attack on tenure took the form of delaying tenure for, say, five instead of three years while offering beginning teachers decent pay with chances for professional development, the pool of top applicants would expand. Decent pay has eluded the United States. In 2009 the average salary for K–12 teachers was only $40,071. A teacher with a master's degree on average got an added $5,436 (Roza and Miller, 2009). In contrast, the average salary for all persons with a master's degree was $74,217. In other words, teachers with equivalent education, arguably facing a more difficult job than most, receive less than three-fifths of the general average (BLS, 2010a: table PINC-06).

24. In August 2010 the administration announced the 10 winning states for these grants from the $4.35 billion Race to the Top. They promised one or more of the following innovations: expand the number of charter schools they allow; tie teacher pay to student performance; overhaul low-performing schools, including plans to fire teachers and principals; and adopt common core standards (*Wall Street Journal*, Aug. 25, 2010).

25. One inner-city elementary school actually provided minute-by-minute scripts for their teachers (Perlstein, 2007) – a parody of the reformers' unanticipated effects.

26. The resistance to high national standards comes not mainly from average citizens, not from unions, and not from teachers, although some of the least competent see standards as a threat. It comes from the House Education and Labor Committee interacting with sectarian religious and political groups fighting over (1) the balance of federal, state, and local rights; and (2) equality of opportunity vs. "diversity" – i.e., equality of outcomes. Confronted with universal standards the right screams "states' rights," and "big government;" the left complains that higher uniform standards are racist in their effect. The left often implicitly adopts the condescending racist tone of the "bell curve": minorities are so backward that if we expect everyone to learn basics and if we toughen standards we will handicap blacks and other racial or ethnic minorities.

27. Since 2007 New York City has evaluated schools on how much each student knows at the end of each year compared with what she knew at the beginning, year after year.

28. Teachers in New York are required to have a dozen courses in their specialty in an accredited college and a year of student teaching before applying for a provisional license. To make the license permanent the teacher must earn a master's degree, work in the classroom for two years, and pass requisite exams. In contrast, most states rely on schools of education that may or may not be accredited or monitored. Many new hires have not even studied the subjects they teach (e.g., only about half of math teachers have an undergraduate degree in math). Poorly paid, poorly prepared, the new teachers are typically assigned to the least-prepared students, with little or no help or guidance. The latest commission sounding the alarm (they come at intervals

of 5 or 10 years) shows what we have known for a century – teachers' training and education, their pay and working conditions, and their experience are critical for school performance (Carroll and Foster, 2010). Data reported by this National Commission on Teaching and America's Future also indicate that the nation is losing experienced teachers "at an alarming rate" (pp. 10–12). A careful study of teacher retention in California public schools tracked teachers in their first seven years of employment in the 1990s (Reed, Reuben, and Barbour, 2006). It found that two variables were powerful in reducing high turnover of elementary school teachers ("leaving" = two consecutive years of no public school employment): professional development programs increased retention 26%; starting salary increases of $4,400 increased retention 17%. Such increased retention helped to raise student test scores and to increase the number of fully credentialed teachers.

29. On statewide tests taken by over 90% of the millions in grades 2–11 in the spring of 2002, the percentage of students scoring above "basic efficiency" (proficient or advanced) in the English/Language Arts Standard was 32.5%; failing scorers (below basic or far below) were 35%. In math the performance is similar: for grades 2–9 (the Mathematics Standards test, grades 2–7, and the General Mathematics test, grades 8–9) the percentage was 32.3 above basic and 38.1 below. Seven years later, in the spring of 2009, performance had improved substantially: English up from 32.5% above basic to 49.8% while the percentage scoring below basic went down from 35% to 22.4%. In math, the trend was up from 32.1 above basic to 54.4%. Below basic declined from 38.1% of test takers to 22%. Source: the California Department of Education at http://star.cde.ca.gov/. Even discounting the gaming of tests previously discussed, the upward trend is impressive.

30. If you think I have romanticized the past situation of teachers and their recruitment pool, consider the plans of the 1961 college graduating class. Spring 1961 interviews with a cross section of 33,982 graduating seniors in 135 colleges and universities reveal that three in four had plans to go on to graduate school (one in three counting on fall entry); that they were highly "professional," "intellectual," or service-motivated in their orientation (only 18% were planning careers in business, while 18% were heading for the arts and sciences, 7% for the traditional professions of law and medicine, and a whopping 33% for education); that *half* of all these seniors anticipated that one of their career activities would be teaching; that the typical student took a "liberal," not a "vocational" view of his or her education (J. Davis, 1964: 8–9,11–13). This is in sharp contrast to today's diminishing pool of talent with aspirations to teach.

31. For a satirical treatment of these tendencies in English departments and the Modern Language Association, see Crews, 2001. Since the 1960s these ideas have slowly migrated from sociology to anthropology to English departments. Happily, successive early enthusiasts in the social sciences have abandoned the cause, although their legacies remain in some departments.

32. For a thorough, definitive account of the nation's top research universities, see Cole, 2010. Cole, a leading scholar of the sociology of knowledge, was provost at Columbia University 1989–2003.

33. In earlier research on hours of work in various occupations and classes (Wilensky, 1961), I showed that professors and lawyers, especially solo lawyers, and advertising account executives averaged 55 hours per week. In one of the three leading universities at which I taught (Chicago, Michigan, and Berkeley), my impression of professorial hours was confirmed by systematic study. My department at Michigan studied its members' workload; it was more than 55 hours, and climbed with rank.

34. Senators Kefauver and Douglas offered to introduce a private bill to recompense Lorwin for his losses. Of tens of thousands who were victims of anonymous accusations, Lorwin was one of the rare cases who chose to fight, rather than resign. He thanked the senators and refused the offer unless others who had suffered political persecution could also be compensated. (For a detailed account of this case, see Wilensky 1967: 140–143.)

35. Full disclosure: my admiration for the California system may reflect my bias for the good taste of former chancellor and president Clark Kerr in actively hiring me in 1962 and my equal admiration for Governor Pat Brown, a politician who, with Kerr, formalized the three-tier system and fought for its adoption and implementation.

36. This "Academic Ranking of World Universities" (Shanghai Ranking Consultancy, 2010) ranks more than 1,000 universities. It emphasizes five fields: natural sciences and mathematics, engineering/technology and computer science, life and agricultural sciences, clinical medicine and pharmacy, and social sciences. In each, the criteria and weighting are alumni achievements (10%), medals awarded to faculty (15%, such as the Nobel or Fields medal), highly cited researchers (25%), publications (25%), and papers in the top 20% of field journals (25%).

37. There are three reasons why the United States cannot rely on private funds to restore its lead in higher education performance, let alone just stay above water. First, although some increase in tuition and fees may be essential, these can only be kept low enough for student access at or near the old rate by public funds. Second, as analysts of innovation in science and letters have shown, public funds are necessary to support both basic and applied research. Public funds in the past have come mainly from state and federal budgets, from direct funding, indirect support of students (loans and grants), research granting agencies using peer review such as NSF, NIH, the Energy Department, and, to a lesser extent, tax exempt foundations. Third, the essential liberal arts – one of the keys to past success – cannot survive without public funding (Newfeld, 2010). It is clear from previous discussions that squeezing research subverts good teaching in all fields, and without adequate support, the two deteriorate.

38. Following a cohort of California Community College students, Moore and Shulock (2010: 4) found that after six years, only 31% of the students had completed a certificate or associate degree or transferred to UC or CSU.

39. This account is largely based on Versluis, 2004; Golden, 2003; *New York Times*, Nov. 7, 2010.

40. Virtual universities' hustling customers for profit and their claims of degrees on the cheap attract many students with meager resources who are encouraged to take out loans they cannot pay back. When the Department of Education investigated 16 of the publicly traded companies in 2010, they found very low rates of graduation and a terrible loan repayment rate. Graduation rates are a good measure of performance. At the for-profit virtual University of Phoenix graduation was 9%, American Intercontinental, 38%; the weighted averaged for the 16 for-profit schools was 34%. In contrast, the 36 public colleges and universities studied had a weighted average of 67%. The loan repayment rate to federal aid programs gives the best picture of hardship. It is the percentage of federal debt repaid in fiscal year 2009 that was owed by students leaving or finishing school (entering repayment) in the prior 3.5 fiscal years. The loan repayment rates of students in the 16 for-profit virtual universities covered by the Education Department ranged from 25% to 52%; students in the seven largest for-profits averaged 34%. In contrast, the 36 public colleges

and universities studied had much higher loan repayment rates, a weighted average of 62%. Calculated from *New York Times*, Education Supplement, Nov. 7, 2010.

41. All such 40- or 50-year projections must be viewed with caution. For the limits of forecasting, see the Appendix.

42. Most rich democracies now value higher education enough to make colleges and universities near free, although some have made loans a larger part of the subsidy package (Guille, 2002). They make loan paybacks easier than the current practice in the United States: link paybacks to long-term earnings in the occupations graduates enter or to their income reported in tax returns. Loan forgiveness or free educational benefits through national service commitments is another good alternative. In the near future, it is unlikely that the United States will adopt these common Continental European or Japanese practices.

43. Among the most useful overviews of both the sources and effects of school performance are Sparks, 1999; Hannum and Buchmann, 2005; and Goldin and Katz, 2008: especially 346–352. On class size, see Fred Mosteller (1995; 1997) who conducted a large four-year experiment on the effect of both class size and the cost-effectiveness of teachers' aides in Tennessee schools from kindergarten through third grade. The researchers compared small classes (13 to 17 pupils), regular size (22–25 pupils), and regular size with a teacher's aide. Student performance on both standardized math and reading tests and curriculum-based tests was much improved in small classes, with greatest improvement among low-income and minority students. Most encouraging, a several-year follow-up found that gains from smaller class size persist in later grades when children were returned to regular-sized classes. Gains from aides did not persist. A cautionary note is sounded by Arthur Levine, former president of Teachers College, Columbia University (*New York Times*, Apr. 7, 1999). He points out that reducing class size in the United States would require funding another 15 to 20% increase in the number of teachers just as the nation is losing 2 million experienced public school teachers through retirement and, I would add, more through burnout. Thus, smaller class size (with necessary building space) and teacher pay and recruitment are intertwined.

44. A study of 1,000 men raised in poverty areas of Boston during the Great Depression found that military service was a turning point in their lives. Overseas duty, in-service schooling, and GI bill training and education at age 17 to 25 enhanced subsequent occupational achievement, job stability, and economic well-being independent of childhood differences and socioeconomic background. Benefits of the GI Bill were even larger for veterans with a delinquent past (Sampson and Laub, 1996).

45. One explanation for this influx of educated workers is national differences in equality discussed in Chapters 1 and 6. Richard Freeman (2006: 150) notes that the labor market is the least-developed part of globalization. Thus, highly paid workers move from Continental Europe where income and wage differences are small to the United States where dispersion of earnings and income is larger and taxes are lower.

46. In 2010 Arizona passed a law requiring police to check the immigration status of anyone "where reasonable suspicion exists" that the person is an illegal alien. This police-state style of law is probably unconstitutional. But it reflects the hysteria whipped up by politicians who see nativist sentiment as the road to power.

47. I leave out the two bills President Clinton passively signed; they were written by a Republican Congress and focused entirely on policing the border and punishing illegals. The first set the goal of adding 10,000 border patrol officers, expedited deportation, tightened asylum procedures, required financial sponsors for newcomers,

and established tough provisions for criminal and undocumented aliens. Under the slogan, "immigration yes, welfare no," the second bill barred noncitizens from a broad range of federal benefits (Tichenor, 2009: 10–12).

48. Although I do not agree with their conclusion about legislative strategy, Marquez and Witte (2009) provide a useful overview of attempts to reform immigration law since the last successful bipartisan Hart-Cellars Act of 1965. Their study shows the political lineup in both House and Senate votes, 21 interest groups and their positions on core issues – *admissions* (ceilings, family reunification, guest workers, skilled workers), *enforcement* (IDs, local government action, verification, barriers), and *integration* (social services and health care, amnesty or paths to citizenship). After 1965, partisan differences in Congress were the most important variables shaping votes on these issues. In 2010 a comprehensive reform covering all four of the necessary components in the text discussion was introduced by Senator Menendez (D-NJ) and Leahy (D-VT).

49. Mark Jacobson (2008) uses a much more inclusive index for nine electric power sources and two liquid fuel options. His index compares their effects on global warming emissions ($CO_2$), air pollution mortality (premature deaths), and several other lesser-weighted indicators (e.g., operating reliability, water consumed, footprint area on land or water). His list matches the ranks in my text closely and adds wind-powered battery electric vehicles (BEVs), concentrated solar-powered BEVs, and geothermal-powered BEVs among his best four of eleven ranked. He ranks nuclear-powered BEVs and coal with carbon-capture-powered BEVs as ninth and tenth worst of his eleven. The reason he ranks "corn and cellulosics" together as the very worst is that his focus is on the world (areas occupied by poor or developing countries where abandoned land is scarce and the damage to the environment and food supply and price is great just as it is for corn-based ethanol in the United States). But rich countries can produce biomass for energy on the abundant land that has already been converted, already abandoned.

50. Even Waxman-Markey was too much for the Senate. It died there. President Obama did nothing to rally public opinion on the issue. Instead, he announced that he would open up new areas to offshore drilling, thereby undermining Senate negotiations.

51. These folks who deny any human cause of climate change are no longer marginal. They include the top leaders of the Republican Party. For instance, in 2009 John Boehner (R-OH), who is likely to be House Speaker, said on ABC-TV, "The idea that carbon dioxide is a carcinogen, that it is harmful to our environment, is almost comical." Similar sentiments have been voiced by other top Republicans such as Representative Issa (R-CA), who says we should stop persecuting corporate America and instead investigate climate-change scientists, and Joe Barton (R-TX) who apologized to the CEO of BP for the Obama's administration's "shakedown" of the company. As we have seen in Chapters 2 and 7, a substantial minority of voters follow their lead.

52. In 2009 the top five players accounted for 40% of industry revenues, up from 25% in 2006; they all are global in their reach. In the absence of structural reform, big banks in just a few years have become megabanks.

53. Consistent with this picture is much systematic research that shows that the very rich and corporate oligarchies but not public opinion shape policy changes, especially international economic policies and especially in U.S. Senate roll-call votes. (For an overview of this research, see Winters and Page, 2009.)

54. Available at: http://krugman.blogs.nytimes.com/2009/01/13/bang-for-the-buck-wonkish/.

55. In the decentralized federalism of the United States, with the spread of the initiative and referendum and the increasing volatility of the electorate, 1996, a year of Democratic sweep, could be followed by successive party swings in the states, with periodic mobilization of the antitax, antispend activists. We have already seen three such swings in rapid succession – 2006, 2008, and almost surely 2010. All the more reason for more stable federal funding, including a national VAT.

56. For a review of evidence in dozens of studies that show the strong effects of both implicit and explicit racial messages in politics, see Mendelberg, 2008.

57. President Obama's strategists at times have suggested that he can count on increased black turnout to achieve a string of victories in the South, especially in such states as Georgia, North Carolina, and even Mississippi. This is fantasy. In fact, as Thomas F. Schallar shows (2006; *New York Times*, July 1, 2008), black voter turnout in the South is already high. In the 11 states of the old Confederacy, they were 17.9% of the age-eligible population in 2004 and 17.9% of the actual voters. More importantly, blacks go to the polls more often than comparable whites. And most important, the more blacks in a southern state, the more likely the white voters are to vote Republican. There is little, if any, net gain in a Democratic southern strategy. The 50-state strategy of the Democratic Party is based on the same flaws as a Democratic southern strategy – it exaggerates the potential of the old Confederacy.

# Bibliography

AACC. "American Association of Community Colleges, 2010 Fact Sheet." Washington, DC: American Association of Community Colleges, 2010.

Aaron, Henry J. *Politics and the Professors: The Great Society in Perspective.* Washington, DC: Brookings Institution, 1978.

Abo, Tetsuo, ed. *Hybrid Factory: The Japanese Production System in the United States.* New York: Oxford University Press, 1994.

Aboud, Leila, and Stephen Power. "U.S. Aims to Skirt Flaws in European's Carbon Limits." *Wall Street Journal,* May 30, 2008, A4.

Abowd, John M., and Richard B. Freeman, eds. *Immigration, Trade and the Labor Market.* Chicago: University of Chicago Press, 1991a.

"Introduction and Summary." In *Immigration, Trade and the Labor Market,* ed. John M. Abowd and Richard B. Freeman, 1–25. Chicago: University of Chicago Press, 1991b.

Abraham, Seven E., and Paula B. Voos. "Changes in Canadian Labor Law and U.S. Labor Law Reform." Forty-eighth annual proceedings of the Industrial Relations Research Association, San Francisco, 1996.

Abramowitz, Alan I. "U.S Senate Elections in a Polarized Era." Paper presented at the conference on the Changing Senate: 1960–2010, Dole Institute, University of Kansas, March 25–26, 2010.

*Academe.* Special Issue, "Casualties of the 21st Century Community College." 96, 3 (May–June 2010).

AGI. "How High Schools Become Exemplary." Achievement Gap Initiative at Harvard University 2009 Conference Report. Cambridge, MA, 2009.

Aguilar, Soledad, et al. "Summary of the Eleventh Conference of the Parties to the UN Framework Convention on Climate Change (UNFCCC) and First Conference of the Parties Serving as the Meeting of the Parties to the Kyoto Protocol." *Earth Negotiations Bulletin,* December 12, 2005.

Ahearne, Alan G., William L. Griever, and Francis E. Warnock. "Information Costs and Home Bias: An Analysis of US Holdings of Foreign Equities." *Journal of International Economics* 62 (2004): 313–336.

Ajami, Riad A., and David A. Ricks. "Motives of Non-American Firms Investing in the United States." *Journal of International Business Studies* 12, 3 (1981): 25–34.

Akerlof, George, and Janet Yellen, eds. *Efficiency Wage Models of the Labor Market.* Orlando, FL: Academic Press, 1986.

Alber, Jens. "Recent Developments in the German Welfare State: Basic Continuity or a Paradigm Shift?" In *Changing Patterns of Social Protection*, ed. Neil Gilbert and Rebecca Van Voorhis, 9–74. New Brunswick, NJ: Transaction, 2003.

"Towards Explaining Anti-foreign Violence in Germany." Lecture at the Center for European Studies, Harvard University, March 17, 1994.

Alesina, Alberto. "Macroeconomics and Politics." In *NBER Macroeconomic Annual 1988*, ed. Stanley Fischer, 13–51. Cambridge, MA: MIT Press, 1988.

Alesina, Alberto, and Lawrence H. Summers. "Central Bank Independence and Macroeconomic Performance: Some Comparative Evidence." *Journal of Money, Credit, and Banking* 25, 2 (1993): 151–162.

Almeida, Beth, and Ilana Boivie. "The Staying Power of Pensions in the Public Sector." *California Public Employee Relations Journal* (CPER) 195 (May 2009): 5–11.

Altmeyer, Arthur J. *The Formative Years of Social Security.* Madison: University of Wisconsin Press, 1968.

*American Community Survey.* United States Census Bureau. 2005. Available at http://www.census.gov/acs/www/index.html.

An, Feng, and Amanda Sauer. "Comparison of Passenger Vehicle Fuel Economy and GHG Emission Standards around the World." Prepared for the Pew Center on Global Climate Change, December 2004.

Applebaum, E., A. Bernhardt, R. J. Murnane, eds. *Low-Wage America: How Employers Are Reshaping Opportunity in the Workplace.* New York: Russell Sage Foundation, 2003.

ASCE. "2009 Report Card for America's Infrastructure." Washington, DC: American Society of Civil Engineers, 2009.

Atkinson, A. B. "The Welfare. State and Economic Performance." Centre for Economics and Related Disciplines Discussion Paper No. WSP/109. London School of Economics, 1995.

Auer, Peter, and Christoph F. Büchtemann. "Arbeitsrechtliche De-Regulierung durch Erleichterung befristeter Arbeitsvertrate? Erfahrungen in der Bundesrepublik Deutschland und in Frankreigh." *Internationale Chronik zur Arbeitsmarktpolitik* 38 (1989): 1–6.

Autor, David H., Frank Levy, and Richard J. Murnane. "The Skill Content of Recent Technological Change: An Empirical Exploration." *Quarterly Journal of Economics* 188, 8 (November 2003): 1279–1333.

Ayers, David F. "Putting the Community Back into the College." *Academei*, May–June 2010. Available at http://www.aaup.org/AAUP/pubsres/academe/2010/MJ/.

Baccaro, Lucio, and Diego Rei. "Institutional Determinants of Unemployment in OECD Countries: A Time Series Cross-Section Analysis (1960–98)." International Institution for Labour Studies Discussion Paper, DP/160/2005. International Institute for Labour Studies, Geneva, 2005.

Bailey, Paul, Aurelio Parisotto, and Geoffrey Renshaw, eds. *Multinationals and Employment: The Global Economy of the 1990s.* Geneva: International Labor Office, 1993.

Baker, Dean, Andrew Glyn, David R. Howell, and John Schmitt. "Labor Market Institutions and Unemployment: A Critical Assessment of the Cross-Country Evidence." In *Fighting Unemployment: The Limits of Free Market Orthodoxy*, ed. D. R. Howell, ch. 3. Oxford: Oxford University Press, 2005.

Banducci, Susan. "Direct Legislation: When Is It Used and When Does It Pass? In *Citizens as Legislators: Direct Democracy in the American States*, ed. Shaun Bowler, Todd Donovan, and Caroline Torbert. Columbus: Ohio State University Press, 1998.

Bank of International Settlements. "Semiannual OTC derivatives statistics." 2009. Available at http://www.bis.org/statistics/derstats.htm.

Bardhan, Ashok, and Cynthia Kroll. "The New Wave of Outsourcing." Fisher Center for Real Estate & Urban Economics Working Paper No. 1103. University of California, Berkeley, 2003.

Bartels, Larry M. *Unequal Democracy: The Political Economy of the New Gilded Age.* Princeton: Princeton University Press, 2008.

Bauder, Harald. "Media Discourse and the New German Immigration Law." *Journal of Ethnic and Migration Studies* 34, 1 (January 2008): 95–112.

Baumol, William J., Sue Anne Batey Blackman, and Edward N. Wolff. *Productivity and American Leadership: The Long View.* Cambridge, MA: MIT Press, 1989.

Beckmann, Matthew N. *Pushing the Agenda: Presidential Leadership in US Lawmaking, 1953–2004.* Cambridge: Cambridge University Press, 2010.

Berkman, Michael B., Julianna Sandell Pacheco, and Eric Plutzer. "Evolution and Creationism in America's Classrooms: A National Portrait." *PLoS Biology* 6, 5 (May 2008): 920–924.

Bernhardt, Annette, Ruth Milkman, Nik Theodore, Doublas Heckathorn, Mirabai Auer, James DeFilippis, Ana Luz Gonzalez, Victor Narro, Jason Perelshteyn, Diana Polson, and Michael Spiller. "Broken Laws, Unprotected Workers: Violations of Employment and Labor Laws in America's Cities." Center for Urban Economic Development, National Employment Law Project, and UCLA Institute, for Research on Labor and Employment. 2009.

Berwick, Donald M. "A Transatlantic Review of the NSH at 60." *Physicians for a National Health Program.* Available at www.pnhp.org.

Binder, Sarah A., and Steven S. Smith. *Politics or Principle? Filibustering in the United States Senate.* Washington, DC: Brookings Institution, 1997.

Blackman, W. *Swiss Banking in an International Context.* London: Macmillan, 1989.

Blanchflower, David G., and Richard B. Freeman. "Unionism in the United States and Other Advanced OECD Countries." *Industrial Relations* 31, 1 (1992): 438–460.

Blau, Francine D., and Lawrence M. Kahn. "Swimming Upstream: Trends in the Gender Wage Differential in the 1980s." *Journal of Labor Economics* 15, 1 (1997): 1–42.

"Wage Structure and Gender Earnings Differentials: An International Comparison." *Economica* 63 (May 1996): S29–S62.

Blinder, Alan S. "Offshoring: The Next Industrial Revolution?" *Foreign Affairs*, March–April 2006, 113–128.

"On the Measurability of Offshorability." October 2009. Voxeu.org. Available at http://www.voxeu.org/index.php?q=node/4072.

Blinder, Alan S., and Alan B. Krueger. "Alternative Measures of Offshorability: A Survey Approach." NBER Working Paper 15287. August 2009.

Bloemraad, Irene, Anna Korteweb, and Gökce Yurdakul. "Citizenship and Immigration: Multiculturalism, Assimilation, and Challenges to the Nation-State." *Annual Review of Sociology* 34 (2008): 8.1–8.27.

Blome, Agnes, Wolfgang Keck, and Jens Alber. *Family and the Welfare State in Europe: Intergenerational Relations in Ageing Societies.* London: Edward Elgar, 2009.

Bodenhorn, Karen A., and Lee D. Kemper. *Spending for Health. Living Well 3.* California Center for Health Improvement, 1997.

Bogdanor, Vernon. "Conclusion: Electoral Systems and Party Systems." In *Democracy and Elections: Electoral Systems and Their Political Consequences*, ed. Vernon Bogdanor and David Butler, 247–262. Cambridge: Cambridge University Press, 1983.

Bogdanor, Vernon, and David Butler, eds. *Democracy and Elections: Electoral Systems and Their Political Consequences*. Cambridge: Cambridge University Press, 1983.

Bohringer, Cristoph, Alfred Voß, and Thomas F. Rutherford. "Global $CO_2$ Emissions and Unilateral Action: Policy Implications of Induced Trade Effects." *International Journal of Global Energy Issues* 11, 1/2/3/4 (1998): 18–22.

Boone, Peter, and Simon Johnson. "Way Too Big to Fail." *New Republic*, November 11, 2010, 20–21.

Borjas, George J. *Friends of Strangers: The Impact of Immigrants on the U.S. Economy*. New York: Basic Books, 1990.

"National Origin and Skills of Immigrants in the Postwar Period." In *Immigration and the Work Force: Economic Consequences for the United States and Source Areas*, ed. George J. Borjas and Richard B. Freeman, 17–47. Chicago: University of Chicago Press, 1992.

Borjas, George J., and Richard B. Freeman. "Introduction and Summary." In *Immigration and the Work Force: Economic Consequences for the United States and Source Areas*, ed. George J. Borjas and Richard B. Freeman, 1–15. Chicago: University of Chicago Press, 1992.

Borjas, George J., Richard B. Freeman, and Lawrence F. Katz. "On the Labor Market Effects of Immigration and Trade." In *Immigration and the Work Force: Economic Consequences for the United States and Source Areas*, ed. George J. Borjas and Richard B. Freeman. Chicago: University of Chicago Press, 1992.

Bower, Tom. *Oil, Money, Politics and Power in the 21st Century*. New York: Grand Central, 2010.

Brady, David, Jason Beckfield, and Martin Seeleib-Kaiser. "Economic Globalization and the Welfare State in Affluent Democracies, 1975–2001." *American Sociological Review* 70 (December 2005): 921–948.

Brady, David, Jason Beckfield, and Wei Zhao. "The Consequences of Economic Globalization for Affluent Democracies." *Annual Review of Sociology* 33 (2007): 313–334.

Brady, Henry E., Michael Herron, Walter Mebane, Jasjeet Sekhon, Kenneth Shotts, and Jonathan Wand. "Law and Data: The Butterfly Ballot Episode." *PS: Political Science and Politics* 34, 1 (March 2001): 59–69.

Bronfenbrenner, Kate. "No Holds Barred: The Intensification of Employer Opposition to Organizing." Briefing paper No. 235. Economic Policy Institute, Washington, DC, May 20, 2009.

Brookings Papers on Economy Activity. "Comments and Discussion." Brookings Institute, Washington, DC, 2005: 270–284.

Brown, Claire, and Greg Linden. *Chips and Change: How Crisis Reshapes the Semiconductor Industry*. Cambridge, MA: MIT Press, 2009.

Brubaker, Rogers. *Citizenship and Nationhood in France and Germany*. Cambridge, MA: Harvard University Press, 1992.

Bruce, Peter. "Political Parties and Labor Legislation in Canada and the United States." *Industrial Relations* 28, 2 (Spring 1989): 115–141.

Büchtemann, Christoph F. "Leaving Employment: Patterns in EC Countries." Discussion paper FSI-1991. Berlin, WZB, 1991.

"More Jobs through Less Employment Protection? Evidence for West Germany." *Labour* 3 (Winter 1989): 23–56.

Büchtemann, Christoph F., and N. Meager. "Leaving Employment: Patterns in EC Countries." Discussion paper FSI-1991. Berlin, WZB, 1991.

Burdekin, Richard C. K., and Thomas D. Willet. "Central Bank Reform: The Federal Reserve in International Perspective." *Public Budgeting and Financial Management* 3, 3 (1991): 619–649.

Bureau of Economic Analysis. "National Economic Accounts." 2010.

"Summary Estimates for Multinational Companies: Employment, Sales, and Capital Expenditures for 2007." News Release, April 17, 2009.

Bureau of Justice Statistics. "Violent Crime Statistics." 2010.

Bureau of Labor Statistics. "Current Population Survey, February 1996: Displaced Workers, Job Tenure, and Occupational Mobility." December 1996.

"Current Population Survey, Unemployment." 2010a. Available at http://www.bls.gov/cps/.

"Job Openings and Labor Turnover (JOLT) Survey, May 2010." July 13, 2010b.

"Median Years of Tenure." Bureau of Labor Statistics, 2010c. Available at http://www.bls.gov/news.release/tenure.t01.htm.

Burke, James, Gerald Epstein, and Minsik Choi. "Rising Foreign Outsourcing and Employment Losses in U.S. Manufacturing, 1987–2002." PERI Working Paper Series No. 89. 2004.

Business Monitor International Online Database. 2008. Available at http://www.businessmonitor.com.

California Postsecondary Education Commission. "Quick Data: College Going Rates and Student Migration." 2010. Available at http://www.cpec.ca.gov/StudentData/CollegeGoingRates.asp.

Cameron, David R. "On the Limits of the Public Economy." *Annals* 459 (1982): 46–62.

"Social Democracy, Corporatism, Labor Quiescence, and the Representation of Economic Interest in Advanced Capitalist Society." In *Order and Conflict in Contemporary Capitalism*, ed. John H. Goldthorpe, 143–178. New York: Oxford University Press, 1984.

Campaign Media Analysis Group. "Spending on Political and Issue-Advocacy TV Commercials." Washington, DC: Campaign Media Analysis Group, 2010.

Cancian, Maria, and Sheldon Danzinger, eds. *Changing Poverty, Changing Policies.* New York: Russell Sage, 2009.

Cantor, Joseph E., Denise S. Rutkus, and Kevin B. Greely. *Free and Reduced-Rate Television Time for Political Candidates.* Washington, DC: Library of Congress, Congressional Research Service, 1997. 97-680 GOV.

Carlin, W., and D. Soskice. *Macroeconomics and the Wage Bargain.* Oxford: Oxford University Press, 1990.

Carpenter, Daniel. *Reputation and Power: Organization Image and Pharmaceutical Regulation at the FDA.* Princeton: Princeton University Press, 2010.

Carroll, T. G., and E. Foster. "Who Will Teach? Experience Matters." Washington, DC: National Commission on Teaching and America's Future, 2010.

Carter, Luther J. *Nuclear Imperatives and Public Trust: Dealing with Radioactive Waste.* Washington, DC: Resources for the Future, 1987.

Cascio, Wayne. "Decency Means More than 'Always Low Prices': A Comparison of Costco to Wal-Mart's Sam's Club." *Academy of Management Perspectives* 49 (August 2006): 26–37.

Castells, Manuel. *Towards the Informational City.* Working Paper 430. Institute of Urban and Regional Development, University of California, Berkeley, 1984.

Castells, Manuel, and Yuko Aoyama. "Paths towards the Informational Society: Employment Structure in G-7 Countries, 1920–1990." *International Labour Review* 133, 1 (1994): 5–33.

Cayrol, Roland. *The 2002 French Elections: A Drama in Five Acts.* Washington, DC: Brookings Institute Center on the United States and France, 2002.

CBO, Department of Commerce, Bureau of Economic Analysis, Office of Management and Budget. "Discretionary Outlays, 1968 to 2007, as a Percentage of Gross Domestic Product." 2008a. Available at http://www.cbo.gov/budget/historical.shtml.

"Discretionary Outlays, 1968 to 2007, in Billions of Dollars." 2008b. Available at: http://www.cbo.gov/budget/historical.shtml.

Cerny, Philip G. "The Dynamics of Financial Globalization: Technology, Market Structure, and Policy Response." *Policy Sciences* 27 (1994): 319–342.

CFI. "Election-Related Spending by Political Committees and Non-Profits Up 40% in 2010." Report prepared for a conference on the Impact of Citizens United jointly sponsored by the Campaign Finance Institute and the University of Virginia's Miller Center of Public Affairs, October 18, 2010.

Chambers, Clarke A. *Seedtime of Reform: American Social Service and Social Action, 1918–1933.* Minneapolis: University of Minnesota Press, 1963.

Chamon, Marcos, Paolo Mauro, and Yohei Okawa. "Mass Ownership in the Emerging Market Giants." *Economic Policy* (April 2008): 243–296.

Citizens Against Government Waste. "Congressional Pig Book." Various years. Available at http://www.cagw.org/reports/pig-book/.

Citrin, Jack, and Isaac Martin, eds. *After the Tax Revolt: California's Proposition 13 Turns Thirty.* Berkeley: Berkeley Public Policy Press, 2009.

Citrin, Jack, and Matthew Wring. "Defining the Circle of We: American Identity and Immigration Policy." *Forum* 7, 3 (October 2009): article 6.

Clark, Colin. *The Conditions of Economic Progress.* London: Macmillan, 1940.

Clark, Rebecca L., and Jeffery S. Passel. *How Much Do Immigrants Pay in Taxes? Evidence from Los Angeles County.* Program for Research on Immigration Policy. Washington, DC: Urban Institute, 1993.

Cnossen, Sijbren. "Consumption Taxes and International Competitiveness: The OECD Experience." Statement before the Committee on Ways and Means, Hearings on Factors Affecting U.S. International Competitiveness, U.S. House of Representatives, Washington, DC, June 20, 1991.

Cohan, William. "You're Welcome Wall Street." *New York Times*, Op-Ed, April 20, 2010.

Cohen, Wilbur J., and Robert J. Lampman. Introduction to *The Development of the Social Security Act*, ed. Edwin E. Witte. Madison: University of Wisconsin Press, 1962.

Cole, Jonathan R. *The Great American University: Its Rise to Preeminence, Its Indispensable National Role, and Why It Must Be Protected.* New York: Public Affairs, 2009.

College Board. "Trends in College Pricing, 2010." Trends in Higher Education Series, College Board Advocacy and Policy Center, 2010. Full report available at http://trends.collegeboard.org.

Collinson, Sarah. *Europe and International Migration.* London: Pinter Publishing, 1993.

Congressional Estimates of Federal Tax Expenditures. "Estimates of Federal Tax Expenditures for Fiscal Years 2005–2009." *Joint Committee on Taxation*, 2006.

Connor, Kevin. "Big Bank Takeover: How Too-Big-To-Fail's Army of Lobbyists Has Captured Washington." Institute For America's Future, Washington, DC, 2010.

Cook, Brian J., Jacque L. Emel, and Roger E. Kasperson. "Problem of Politics or Technique? Insights from Waste-Management Strategies in Sweden and France." *Policy Studies Review* 10, 4 (1991–92): 103–113.

Cooke, William N., and Deborah S. Noble. "Industrial Relations Systems and US Foreign Direct Investment Abroad." *British Journal of Industrial Relations* 36, 4 (1998): 581–609.

Council of Economic Advisers. "The American of Recovery and Reinvestment Act of 2009, Fourth Quarterly Report." July 14, 2010.

CREDO. "Multiple Choice: Charter Performance in 16 States." Center for Research on Education Outcomes, Stanford, 2009.

Crewe, Ivor. "Electoral Participation." In *Democracy at the Polls: A Comparative Study of Competitive National Elections*, ed. David Butler, Howard R. Penniman, and Austin Ranney, 216–263. Washington, DC: American Enterprise Institute, 1981.

Crews, Frederick. *Postmodern Pooh*. Evanston: Northwestern University Press, 2001.

Croucher, Richard, and Michael Brookes. "German Employers' Inputs to Employee Skills Development." *Industrial Relations: A Journal of Economy and Society* 48, 2 (April 2009): 231–236.

CRP. "Ranked Sectors Lobbying." Center for Responsive Politics. 2009. Available at http://www.opensecrets.org/lobby/top.php?showYear=2009&indexType=c.

CRS Report RL32292. "Offshoring (a.k.a. Offshore Outsourcing) and Job Insecurity among U.S. Workers." By Linda Levine, Congressional Research Service. August 6, 2007.

Cukierman, Alex. *Central Bank Strategy, Credibility, and Independence: Theory and Evidence*. Cambridge, MA.: MIT Press, 1992.

Cukierman, Alex, Pantelis Kalaitzidakis, Lawrence H. Summers, and Steven B. Webb. "Central Bank Independence, Growth, Investment, and Real Rates." Vol. 39. Carnegie-Rochester Conference Series on Public Policy, 1993.

Dahl, Robert A. *Democracy and Its Critics*. New Haven: Yale University Press, 1989.

*The New American Political (Dis)order*. Berkeley: University of California, Institute of Governmental Studies Press, 1994.

"Some Explanations." In *Political Oppositions in Western Democracies*, ed. R. A. Dahl, 348–386. New Haven: Yale University Press, 1966.

Danish Energy Agency. "Energy Policy Statement 2008: The Report of the Minister of Climate and Energy Pursuant to the Danish Act on Energy Policy Measures." 2008. Available at www.ens.dk.

Danish Ministry of Climate and Energy. "The Danish Example – towards an Energy Efficient and Climate Friendly Economy." April 22, 2008.

Dark, Taylor E., III. "Prospects for Labor Law Reform." *Perspectives on Work*, Summer 2008–Winter 2009, 23–26.

Davidson, William H. "The Location of Foreign Direct Investment Activity: Country Characteristics and Experience Effects." *Journal of International Business Studies* 11 (1980): 9–22.

Davis, James A. *Great Aspirations: The Graduate School Plans of America's College Seniors*. Chicago: Aldine, 1964.

Davis, Natalie Z. "Poor Relief, Humanism, and Heresy: The Case of Lyon." *Studies in Medieval and Renaissance History* 5 (1968): 215–275.

Deane, Marjorie, and Robert Pringle. *The Central Banks*. London: Hamish Hamilton, 1994.

Decker, Paul T., Daniel P. Mayer, and Steven Glazerman. "The Effects of Teach for America on Students: Findings from a National Evaluation." *Mathematica Policy Research*, June 9, 2004.

Dickens, William T., and Jonathan Leonard. "Accounting for the Decline in Union Membership, 1950–1980." *Industrial and Labor Relations Review* 38, 3 (April) 1985: 323–334.

Dickens, Richard, and Abigail McKnight. "Assimilation of Migrants into the British Labour Market." LSE Case Paper no. 133. October 2008.

Doggett, Tom. "Shell Says U.S. Oil Refiners Need More $CO_2$ Permits." Reuters, July 8, 2009.

Donovan, Too, Shaun Bowler, David McCaun, and Ken Fernandez. "Contending Players and Strategies: Opposition Advantages in Initiative Campaigns." In *Citizens as Legislators: Direct Democracy in the American States*, ed. Shaun Bowler, Todd Donovan, and Caroline Torbert, ch. 4. Columbus: Ohio State University Press, 1998.

Dore, Ronald. *Flexible Rigidities: Industrial Policy and Structural Adjustment in the Japanese Economy, 1970–80*. London: Athlone, 1986.

Douglas, Paul H., and Aaron Director. *The Problem of Unemployment*. New York: Macmillan, 1931.

Douglass, John Aubrey. "Re-imagining California Higher Education." Center for Studies in Higher Education, Research & Occasional Paper Series, CSHE 14.10. October 2010.

"Revisionist Reflections on California's Master Plan @ 50." *California Journal of Politics and Policy* 3, 1 (2011): article 1. Available at http://www.bepress.com/cjpp/vol3/iss1/1.

Drezner, Daniel W. "Globalization and Policy Convergence." *International Studies Review* 3, 1 (2001): 53–78.

Dunning, John H. "The Eclectic Paradigm of International Production: An Update and Some Possible Extensions." *Journal of International Business Studies* 19, 1 (1988): 1–32.

"Trade, Location of Economic Activity, and the Multinational Enterprise: A Search for an Eclectic Paradigm." In *The International Allocation of Economic Activity*, ed. Bertil Ohlin, Per-Ove Hesselborn, and Per Magnus Wijkman. London: Macmillan, 1977.

Ebbinghaus, Bernhard. *Reforming Early Retirement in Europe, Japan, and the USA*. Oxford: Oxford University Press, 2006.

*Economist.* "Rushing on by Road, Rail and Car." February 14, 2008.

"Is Sarkozy a Closet Socialist?" November 15, 2008.

"A Survey of Multinationals." March 27, 1993.

Edelstein, Michael. *Overseas Investment in the Age of High Imperialism: The United Kingdom, 1850–1914*. New York: Columbia University Press, 1982.

Ehrlich, Everett, and Felix G. Rohatyn. "A New Bank to Save Our Infrastructure." *New York Review of Books* 55, 15 (October 9, 2008).

EIA. "International Energy Statistics." Energy Information Administration. 2009. Available at http://www.eia.gov/cfapps/ipdbproject/IEDIndex3.cfm.

Eichengreen, Barry, and Peter H. Lindert, eds. *The International Debt Crisis in Historical Perspective*. Cambridge, MA: MIT Press, 1989.

Eichengreen, Barry, and Kevin H. O'Rourke. "A Tale of Two Depressions: What Do the New Data Tell Us." VOX EU, February 2010 update. Available at http://www.voxeu.org/index.php?q=node/3421.

Eisenhower, Dwight D. "Letter to Edgar Newton Eisenhower." 1954. The Presidential Papers of Dwight David Eisenhower, doc. no. 1147. Available at http://www.eisenhowermemorial.org.

Emerson, Michael. "Regulation or Deregulation of the Labour Market: Policy Regimes for the Recruitment and Dismissal of Employees in the Industrialized Countries." *European Economic Review* 32, 4 (1988): 775–817.

Encarnation, Dennis J. "A Common Evolution? A Comparison of United States and Japanese Transnational Corporations." *Transnational Corporations* 2, 1 (1993): 7–32.

Energy and Environment News (E&E News). "Agriculture: Corn Prices Soar to New Record." January 14, 2008.

Enrich, David, and Damian Paletta. "Finance Reform Falters as Shock of '08 Fades." *Wall Street Journal*, September 9, 2009.

Environmental Protection Agency. "Inventory of U.S. Greenhouse Gas Emissions and Sinks: 1990–2006." April 15, 2008.

Epstein, Abraham. *Insecurity: A Challenge to America*. New York: Smith and Haas, 1933.

Epstein, Gerald. "Political Economy and Comparative Central Banking." *Review of Radical Political Economics* 24 (1992): 1–30.

Esman, Milton J. "The Political Fallout of International Migration." *Diaspora* 2, 1 (1992): 3–41.

Esping-Andersen, Gosta. *Politics against Markets*. Princeton: Princeton University Press, 1985.

Evans, Peter. *Dependent Development: The Alliance of Multinational, State and Local Capital in Brazil*. Princeton: Princeton University Press, 1979.

"The Eclipse of the State? Reflections on Stateness in an Era of Globalization." *World Politics* 50, 1 (Oct. 1997): 62–87.

Evans, Robert G., and Gregory L. Stoddart. "Producing Health, Consuming Health Care." In *The Nation's Health*, ed. Philip R. Lee and Carroll L. Estes, 14–33. 4th ed. Boston: Jones and Bartlett, 1994.

Fassmann, Heinz, and Rainer Münz. "European East-West Migration 1945–1992." *International Migration Review* 28 (1994): 520–538.

FDIC. "Quarterly Banking Profile." Federal Deposit Insurance Corporation. 2010. Available at http://www2.fdic.gov/qbp/.

Federal Reserve System. "Balance Sheet of Households and Nonprofit Organizations." 2010. Available at http://www.federalreserve.gov/releases/z1/current/accessible/b100.htm.

Ferguson, Niall. "Europe between Brussels and Byzantium: Some Thoughts on European Integration." Institute of European Studies Working Paper No. PRI-6. University of California, Berkeley, November 1, 2003. Available at http://ies.berkeley.edu/pubs/workingpapers/ayo304.html#7.

Fiorina, Morris P., with Samuel J. Abrams. *Disconnect: The Breakdown of Representation in American Politics*. Norman: University of Oklahoma Press, 2009.

Fiorina, Morris P., with Matthew Levendusky. "Disconnected: The Political Class versus the People." In *Red and Blue Nation*, ed. Pietro S. Nivola and David W. Brady, 49–71. Washington, DC: Brookings Institution Press and the Hoover Institution, 2006.

Fisher, Irving. "The Debt-Deflation Theory of Great Depressions." *Econometrica* 1, 4 (October 1933): 337–357.

Fix, Michael. "Immigration and Language." Unpublished paper and tables presented at conference on Language Acquisition and Immigrant Integration: Comparing European and U.S. Experiences, University of California, Berkeley, May 4, 2009.

Fix, Michael, and Jeffrey S. Passel. *Immigration and Immigrants: Setting the Record Straight*. Washington, DC: Urban Institute, 1994.

Flaherty, Sean. "Strike Activity and Productivity Change: The U.S. Auto Industry." *Industrial Relations* 26 (1987a): 174–185.

"Strike Activity, Worker Militancy, and Productivity Change in Manufacturing, 1961–1981." *Industrial and Labor Relations Review* 40 (1987b): 585–600.

Flanagan, Robert J. "Has Management Strangled U.S. Unions?" *Journal of Labor Research* 26, 1 (Winter 2005): 33–63.

*Globalization and Working Conditions.* Oxford: Oxford University Press, 2006.

Flora, Peter, ed. *Growth to Limits: The Western European Welfare States since World War II.* Berlin: Walter de Gruyter, 1986.

Flora, Peter, and Arnold J. Heidenheimer, eds. *The Development of Welfare States in Europe and America.* New Brunswick, NJ: Transaction, 1981.

Fogarty, Michael Patrick. *Christian Democracy in Western Europe, 1820–1953.* London: Routledge and Paul: 1957.

*Foreign Policy Magazine.* "The FP Index: Ranking the Rich – Hooray for High Gas Prices." September–October 2008.

FPI. "Across the Spectrum: The Wide-Range of Jobs Immigrants Do." Fiscal Policy Institute, April, 2010.

Francia, Peter L. *The Future of Organized Labor in American Politics.* New York: Columbia University Press, 2006.

Frears, John. *Parties and Voters in France.* New York: St. Martin's Press, 1991.

Free TV For Straight Talk Coalition. Proposal for a National Time Bank. Free TV For Straight Talk Coalition, 1997.

Freeman, Gary P. "Can Liberal States Control Unwanted Migration?" *Annals of the American Academy of Political and Social Science* 534 (1994): 17–30.

Freeman, Richard B. *America Works: The Exceptional U.S. Labor Market.* New York: Russell Sage Foundation, 2007.

"People Flows in Globalization." *Journal of Economic Perspectives* 20, 2 (Spring 2006): 145–170.

*When Earnings Diverge: Causes, Consequences, and Cures for the New Inequality in the U.S.* Washington, DC: National Policy Association, 1997.

Freeman, Richard B., and James L. Medoff. *What Do Unions Do?* New York: Basic Books, 1984.

Freeman, Richard B., and Joel Rogers. *What Workers Want.* Ithaca, NY: Cornell University Press; New York: Russell Sage Foundation, 1999.

French, Kenneth R., et al. *The Squam Lake Report.* Princeton: Princeton University Press, 2010.

Friedman, Benjamin M. *Day of Reckoning: The Consequences of American Economic Policy.* New York: Vintage Books, 1989.

Friedman, Lee S. "The Importance of Marginal Cost Electricity Pricing to the Success of Greenhouse Gas Reduction Programs." Paper presented at the annual research conference of the Association for Public Policy Analysis and Management, November 2009. Available at http://gsppi.berkeley.edu/faculty/lfriedman/lee-s-friedman.

*The Future of Geothermal Energy: Impact of Enhanced Geothermal Systems (EGS) on the United States in the 21st Century.* MIT-led interdisciplinary panel, 2006. Available at http://www1.eere.energy.gov/geothermal/egs_technology.html.

Galbraith, James K. "Self-Fulfilling Prophets: Inflated Zeal at the Federal Reserve." *American Prospect* 18 (Summer 1994): 31–39.

GAO. "For-Profit Colleges: Undercover Testing Finds Colleges Encouraged Fraud and Engaged in Deceptive and Questionable Marketing Practices." United States Government Accountability Office, GAO-10-948T, August 4, 2010.

Gardner, Bruce. "Fuel Ethanol Subsidies and Farm Price Support." *Journal of Agricultural & Food Industrial Organization* 5, 2 (2007): article 4.

Garner, Alan C. "Offshoring in the Service Sector: Economic Impact and Policy Issues." Federal Reserve Bank of Kansas City, *Economic Review*, third quarter, 2004.

Gauld, Robin. "One Country, Four Systems: Comparing Changing Health Policies in New Zealand." *International Political Science Review* 24, 2 (2003): 199–218.

Gautié, Jérôme, and John Schmitt, eds. *Low Wage Work in the Wealthy World*. New York: Russell Sage Foundation, 2010.

Giaimo, Susan. "Health Care Reform in Britain and Germany: Recasting the Political Bargain with the Medical Profession." *Governance: An International Journal of Policy and Administration* 8, 3 (July 1995): 354–379.

Glantz, Stanton A., and Eric Hays. "Financial Options for Restoring Quality and Access to Public Higher Education in California." Working Paper. Council of UC Faculty Associations, December 10, 2009.

Glennerster, Howard. "United States Poverty Studies and Measurement: The Past 25 Years." CASE paper 42. London School of Economics, 2000.

Global Energy Network Institute. "A Case Study of Energy Policy in Denmark." 2008. Available at http://www.geni.horg/.

Gold, David. "World Investment Report 1993: Transnational Corporations and Integrated International Production. An Executive Summary." *Transnational Corporations* 2, 2 (1993): 99–123.

Goldemberg, José. "Nuclear Energy in Developing Countries." *Daedalus* 138, 4 (Fall 2009): 71–80.

"The Challenge of Biofuels." *Energy and Environmental Science* 1 (2008): 523–525.

Golden, Daniel. "Quick Studies." *Wall Street Journal*, September 22, 2003.

Goldin, Claudia, and Lawrence Katz. *Race between Education and Technology*. Cambridge, MA: Harvard University Press, 2008.

Gottschalk, Peter, and Timothy M. Smeeding. "Cross-National Comparisons of Earnings and Income Inequality." *Journal of Economic Literature* 35 (June 1997a): 633–687.

"Empirical Evidence on Income Inequality in Industrialized Countries." Luxembourg Income Study Working Paper No. 154. Maxwell School of Citizenship and Public Affairs, Syracuse University, 1997b.

"Empirical Evidence on Income Inequality in Industrialized Countries." Luxembourg Income Study Working Paper No. 154. February 1999.

Gore, Al. "Statement to the Senate Foreign Relations Committee." January 28, 2009. Available at http://blog.algore.com/2009/01/statement_to_the_senate_foreig.html.

Gourevitch, Peter. *Politics in Hard Times: Comparative Responses to International Economic Crises*. Ithaca, NY: Cornell University Press, 1986.

Grant, Don Sherman, II, and Richard Hutchinson. "Global Smokestack Chasing: A Comparison of the State-Level Determinants of Foreign and Domestic Manufacturing Investment." *Social Problems* 43, 1 (1996): 21–38.

Green, Donald. "Industrialization and the Engineering Ascendancy: A Comparative Study of American and Russian Engineering Elites, 1870–1920." Ph.D. dissertation, University of California at Berkeley, 1972.

Green, Matthew, and Daniel Burns. "What Might Bring Order Back to the House?" *PS: Political Science and Politics* 43 (2010): 223–226.

Greenberg, Stanley B. "The Mythology of Centrism: Why Clinton and Blair Really Won." *American Prospect*, no. 34 (September–October 1997): 42–44.

Greenwald, Bruce C., and Judd Kahn. *The Irrational Fear That Someone in China Will Take Your Job*. Hoboken, NJ: John Wiley and Sons, 2009.

Greve, B. "The Hidden Welfare State, Tax Expenditure and Social Policy: A Comparative Overview." *Scandinavian Journal of Social Welfare* 3 (1994): 203–211.

Grilli, Vittorio, Donato Masciandaro, and Guido Tabellini. "Political and Monetary Institutions and Public Financial Policies in the Industrial Countries." *Economic Policy* 13 (1991): 341–392.

Grofman, Bernard, and Arend Lijphart, eds. *Electoral Laws and Their Political Consequences*. New York: Agathon Press, 1986.

Guille, Marianne. "Student Loans: A Solution for Europe?" *European Journal of Education* 37, 4 (2002): 417–431.

Guimezanes, Nicole. "What Laws for Naturalization?" *OECD Observer* 188 (1994): 24–26.

Hacker, Andrew, and Claudia Dreifus. *Higher Education? How Colleges Are Wasting Our Money and Failing Our Kids – and What We Can Do about It*. New York: Henry Holt, 2010.

Hacker, Jacob S. "The Case for Public Plan Choice in National Health Reform: Key to Cost Control and Quality Coverage." *Institute for America's Future*, 2008.

Hacker, Jacob S., and Elisabeth Jacobs. "The Rising Instability of American Family Incomes, 1969–2004: Evidence from the Panel Study of Income Dynamics." Economic Policy Institute Briefing Paper No. 213. May 29, 2008.

Hacker, Jacob S., and Paul Pierson. *Off Center: The Republican Revolution and the Erosion of American Democracy*. New Haven: Yale University Press, 2005.

Hagen, Michael G., and Robin Kolodny. "Finding the Cost of Campaign Advertising." *Forum* 6, 1 (2008): article 11.

Hakovirta, Harto. "The Global Refugee Problem: A Model and Its Application." *International Political Science Review* 14 (1993): 35–57.

Halfmann, Jost. "Two Discourses of Citizenship in Germany: The Difference between Public Debate and Administrative Practice." In *The Postwar Transformation of Germany: Democracy, Prosperity and Nationhood*. Center for German and European Studies. Berkeley: University of California, 1995.

Hall, Peter A. "Central Bank Independence and Coordinated Wage Bargaining: Their Interaction in Germany and Europe." *German Politics and Society* 31 (Spring 1994): 1–23.

Hall, Peter A., and David Soskice, eds. *Varieties of Capitalism: The Institutional Foundations of Comparative Advantage*. Oxford: Oxford University Press, 2001.

Hallet, Andrew Hughes, John Lewis, and Jürgen von Hagen. *Fiscal Policy in Europe, 1991–2003: An Evidence-Based Analysis*. Washington, DC: Center for Economic Policy Research, 2003.

Handler, Joel F. *The Poverty of Welfare Reform*. New Haven: Yale University Press, 1995.

Hannum, Emily, and C. Buchmann. "Global Educational Expansion and Socio-economic Development: An Assessment of Finds from the Social Sciences." *World Development* 33, 3 (2005): 333–354.

Hansen, J., Mki Sato, P. Kharecha, D. Beerling, R. Berner, V. Masson-Delmotte, M. Pagani, M. Raymo, D. Royer, and J. Zachos. "Target Atmospheric $CO_2$: Where Should Humanity Aim?" *Open Atmospheric Science Journal* 2 (2008): 217–231.

Harrison, Bennett. *Lean and Mean: The Changing Landscape of Corporate Power in the Age of Flexibility*. New York: Basic Books, 1994.

Heclo, Hugh. *Modern Social Politics in Britain and Sweden.* New Haven: Yale University Press, 1974.

Heidenheimer, Arnold J. "Education and Social Security Entitlements in Europe and America." In *The Development of Welfare States in Europe and America,* ed. Peter Flora and Arnold J. Heidenheimer, 269–304. New Brunswick, NJ: Transaction, 1981.

Heidenheimer, Arnold J., Hugh Heclo, and Carolyn Teich Adams. *Comparative Public Policy: The Politics of Social Choice in America, Europe, and Japan.* 3rd ed. New York: St. Martin's Press, 1990.

Heilig, Julian Vasquez, and Su Jin Jez. "Teach for America: A Review of the Evidence." Great Lakes Center for Education Research and Practice, June 2010.

Heisenberg, Dorothee. "The Institution of 'Consensus' in the European Union: Formal versus Informal Decision-Making in the Council." *European Journal of Political Research* 44 (2005): 65–90.

Held, David, and Anthony McGrew. *Globalization/Anti-Globalization: Beyond the Great Divide.* 2nd ed. Malden, MA: Polity Press, 2007.

Hemerijck, Anton, and Maurizio Ferrera. "Welfare Reform in the Shadow of the EMU." In *Euro and Europeans,* ed. Andrew Martin and George Ross. Cambridge: Cambridge University Press, 2004.

Hicks, Raymond. "Globalization and Central Bank Independence: A Partisan Explanation." Working Paper 2006–03. Niehaus Center for Globalization and Governance. 2006.

Hilliard, Robert L. *The Federal Communications Commission: A Primer.* Boston: Focal Press, 1991.

Hillygus, D. S., and T. G. Shields. "Moral Issues and Voter Decision Making in the 2004 Presidential Election." *PS: Political Science and Politics* 38, 2 (April 2005): 201–209.

Hindary, Leo, Jr., et al. "FDR Had It Right: If the Economy Is Going to Come Back, We Need to Buy – and Make – American." *American Prospect* (January–February 2010): A21–23.

Hirst, Paul, and Grahame Thompson. *Globalization in Question: The International Economy and Possibilities of Governance.* Cambridge: Policy Press, 1996.

Hirschi, Travis. "Crime and Family Policy." *Journal of Contemporary Studies* 6, 1 (1983): 3–16.

Hirschman, Albert. *Exit, Voice, and Loyalty: Responses to Decline in Firms, Organizations, and States.* Cambridge, MA: Harvard University Press, 1970.

*Rival Views of Market Society and Other Recent Essays.* New York: Viking, 1986.

Hodson, Randy. "Individual Voice on the Shop Floor: The Role of Unions." *Social Forces* 74, 4 (June 1997): 1183–1212.

"Worker Resistance: An Underdeveloped Concept in the Sociology of Work." *Economic and Industrial Democracy* 16, 1 (February 1995): 79–110.

Hollifield, James F. *Immigrants, Markets, and States: The Political Economy of Postwar Europe.* Cambridge, MA: Harvard University Press, 1992.

Hollingsworth, J. Rogers, Jerald Hage, and Robert Hanneman. *State Intervention in Medical Care: Consequences for Britain, France, Sweden, and the United States.* Ithaca, NY: Cornell University Press, 1990.

Hollingsworth, J. Rogers, Robert Hanneman, and Jerald Hage. "The Effect of Human Capital and State Intervention on the Performance of Medical Delivery Systems." Unpublished manuscript, University of Wisconsin, Madison, University of California, Riverside, and University of Maryland, College Park, 1992.

Hollingsworth, J. Rogers, Philippe C. Schmitter, and Wolfgang Streeck, eds. *Governing Capitalist Economies: Performance and Control of Economic Sectors*. New York: Oxford University Press, 1994.

Holtfrerich, Carl-Ludwig, and Ludger Lindlar. "Four Decades of German Export Expansion: an Enduring Success Story?" Paper presented at a conference on The Postwar Transformation of Germany, Center for German and European Studies, University of California, Berkeley, November 30–December 2, 1995.

Hoover, Herbert. *The Memoirs of Herbert Hoover: The Cabinet and the Presidency, 1920–1933*. New York: Macmillan, 1952.

Houghton, J., S. Weatherwax, and J. Ferrell. "Breaking the Biological Barriers to Cellusosic Ethanol: A Joint Research Agenda." A research roadmap resulting from the biomass to biofuels workshop sponsored by the Office of Science and Office of Energy Efficiency and Renewable Energy, U.S. Department of Energy, December 7–9, 2005, Rockville, Maryland. 2006.

Howard, Christopher. *The Hidden Welfare State: Tax Expenditures and Social Policy in the United States*. Princeton: Princeton University Press, 1999.

Howell, David R., Dean Baker, Andrew Glyn, and John Schimitt. "Are Protective Labor Market Institutions at the Root of Unemployment? A Critical Review of the Evidence." *Capitalism and Society* 2, 1 (2007): 1–71.

Huber, Evelyne, and John D. Stephens. "Internationalization and the Social Democratic Welfare State: Crisis and Future Prospects." Paper delivered at the conference on Challenges to Labor: Integration, Employment and Bargaining in Scandinavia and the United States, Berkeley, March 21–22, 1996.

"Welfare State and Production Regimes in the Era of Retrenchment." School of Social Sciences, Institute for Advanced Study, Occasional Paper 1 (1999): 1–29.

Huddle, Donald. *The Costs of Immigration: Executive Summary*. Carrying Capacity Network, 1993.

Huh, Kil, and Lori Grange. "Green Data: What Do We Really Know about the Green Economy?" *Pathways*, Fall 2009, 23–27.

Hyman, Richard. "Industrial Relations in Western Europe: An Era of Ambiguity?" *European Journal of Industrial Relations* 1, 1 (1994): 47–62.

IAEA. Power Reactor Information System database. 2009. Available at http://www.iaea.or.at/programmes/a2/.

Intergovernmental Panel on Climate Change. "Common Reporting Framework." 1996.

International Council on Clean Transportation. "Fuel Economy Standards and GHG Standard Charts." Updated January 2009.

International Energy Agency. *Energy Policies of IEA Countries – Sweden*. Paris: International Energy Agency, 2008.

International Labour Office. *World Labour Report*. Geneva: International Labour Office, 1992.

International Labour Organization. *ILO's World Employment Report, 2001*. Geneva, 2001.

*World Employment, 1995: An ILO Report*. Geneva, 1995.

Iversen, Torben, and Thomas R. Cusack. "The Causes of Welfare State Expansion: Deindustrialization or Globalization?" *World Politics* 52 (April 2000): 313–349.

Jackman, Robert W., and Ross A. Miller. "Voter Turnout in the Industrial Democracies during the 1980s." *Comparative Political Studies* 27, 4 (1995): 467–492.

Jacobs, Lawrence R. "Politics of America's Supply State: Health Reform and Technology." *Health Affairs* (Summer 1995): 144–146.

Jacobson, Gary. "The Misallocation of Resources in House Campaigns." In *Congress Reconsidered*, ed. Lawrence C. Dodd and Bruce I. Oppenheimer, 115–140. 5th ed. Washington, DC: Congressional Quarterly Press, 1993.

Jacobson, Mark Z. "Review of Solutions to Global Warming, Air Pollution, and Energy Security." Department of Civil and Environmental Engineering, Stanford University, Stanford, 2008. Available at http://www.stanford.edu/group/efmh/jacobson/EnergyEnvRevo908.pdf&sa=U&ei=5cReTt7FMq_RiAKF8IyzBQ&ved=0CBwQFjAC&usg=AFQjCNH WIULnOq4slKbI6psxTaM3jC8DlQ.

Janoski, Thomas. *The Political Economy of Unemployment: Active Labor Market Policy in West Germany, and the United States*. Berkeley: University of California Press, 1990.

Janowitz, Morris. *The Professional Solider: A Social and Political Portrait*. New York: Macmillan, 1961.

Jasper, James M. *Nuclear Politics: Energy and the State in the United States, Sweden, and France*. Princeton: Princeton University Press, 1990.

Jay, Michael. 2008. "Combating Climate Change: An International Cooperation Framework beyond 2012." June 29, 2008. A consensus paper by legislators from the G8 and +5 countries, presented by Lord Michael Jay for GLOBE International.

Jencks, Christopher. "The Immigration Charade." *New York Review of Books*, September 27, 2007, 49–52.

Jensen J. Bradford, and Lori G. Kletzner. "Tradeable Services: Understanding the Scope and Impact of Services Offshoring." *Brookings Trade Forum 2005* (2006): 75–133.

Johanneson, Jan, and Gunther Schmid. "The Development of Labour Market Policy in Sweden and in Germany: Competing or Convergent Models to Combat Unemployment?" *European Political Research* 8 (1980): 387–406.

Johnson, Chalmers. *MITI and the Japanese Miracle*. Stanford: Stanford University Press, 1982.

Johnson, Simon. "The Quiet Coup." *Atlantic*, May 2009.

Jorgenson, Dale W., and Kun-Young Yun. "Tax Policy and Capital Allocation." *Scandinavian Journal of Economics* 88, 2 (1986): 355–377.

Kagan, Robert A. *Adversarial Legalism: The American Way of Law*. Cambridge, MA: Harvard University Press, 2003.

Kammen, Daniel M., Kamal Kapadia, and Matthias Fripp. *Putting Renewables to Work: How Many Jobs Can the Clean Energy Industry Create?* Renewables and Appropriate Energy Laboratory Report, University of California, Berkeley, 2004. Available at http://socrates.berkeley.edu/~rael/papers.html.

Kammen, Daniel M., and Gregory F. Nemet. "Reversing the Incredible Shrinking Energy R&D Budget." *Issues in Science and Technology* 22, 1 (Fall 2005).

Karier, Thomas. "U.S. Foreign Production and Unions." *Industrial Relations* 34, 1 (1995): 107–118.

Katzenstein, Peter J. *Small States in World Markets: Industrial Policy in Europe*. Ithaca, NY: Cornell University Press, 1985.

Kaufman, Jason. *The Origins of Canadian and American Political Differences*. Cambridge, MA: Harvard University Press, 2009.

Kaufmann, Karen M., John R. Petrocik, and Daron R. Shaw. *Unconventional Wisdom: Facts and Myths about American Voters*. New York: Oxford University Press, 2008.

Kay, John. "The Failures of Forecasting." In *The Business of Economics*, ch. 2. Oxford: Oxford University Press, 1996.

Keating, Michael, and Liesbet Hooghe. "Bypassing the Nation-State? Regions and the EU Policy Process." In *European Union: Power and Policy-Making*, ed. Jeremy Richardson, 269–286. New York: Routledge, 2005.

Keck, Wolfgang, and Agnes Blome. "Is There a Generational Cleavage in Europe? Age-Specific Perceptions of Elderly Care and of the Pension System." In *Handbook of Quality of Life in the Enlarged European Union*, ed. Jens Alber, Tony Fahey, and Chiara Saraceno, 73–99. London: Routledge, 2008.

Kenworthy, Lane. "How Much Do Presidents Influence Income Inequality?" *Challenge* 53, 2 (March–April 2010): 90–112.

Keohane, Robert O., and Joseph S. Nye Jr. *Introduction to Governance in a Globalizing World*, ed. Joseph S. Nye Jr. and John D. Donahue. Washington, DC: Brookings Institution Press, 2000.

Keohane, Robert O., and Joseph S. Nye. "Transnational Relations and World Politics: A Conclusion." *International Organization* 25, 3 (1971): 721–748.

*Power and Interdependence: World Politics in Transition*. Boston: Little, Brown, 1977.

Keynes, John Maynard. *The General Theory of Employment, Interest and Money*. 1936. Available at http://www.newschool.edu/nssr/het/texts/keynes/gtcont.htm.

*The Means to Prosperity*. London: Macmillan, 1933.

Kirp, David L. "The Great School Delusion." *American Prospect*, April 2010.

Kitschelt, Herbert. "Industrial Governance Structures, Innovation Strategies, and the Case of Japan." *International Organization* 45, 4 (October 1991): 453–493.

Klein, Ezra. "How to End the Filibuster with 51 Votes." *Washington Post*, July 27, 2010.

Kletzer, Lori. "Measuring Tradable Services and the Task Content of Offshorable Service Jobs." Information draft for NBER-CRIW preconference on Labor in the New Economy. 2007.

Kliesch, James, and Therese Langer. "Plug-in Hybrids: An Environmental and Economic Performance Outlook." American Council for an Energy-Efficient Economy Report No. T061. September 2006.

Klöti, Ulrich. "Small States in an Interdependent World." Paper presented at the World Congress of the International Political Science Association, Buenos Aires, July 21–25, 1991.

Klotz, Robert. "Positive Spin: Senate Campaigning on the Web." *PS: Political Science and Politics* 30, 3 (1997): 482–486.

Kochan, Thomas A., Michal Smith, John C. Wells, and James B. Rebitzer. "Human Resource Strategies and Contingent Workers: The Case of Safety and Health in the Petrochemical Industry." *Human Resource Management* 33, 1 (1994): 55–77.

Kollmeyer, Christopher. "Consequences of North-South Trade for Affluent Countries: A New Application of Unequal Exchange Theory." *Review of International Political Economy* 16, 5: 803–826.

Koopman, Jerome. "Health Care: Who Knows Best?" *New York Review of Books* 52, 2 (February 11, 2010): 12–15.

Korpi, Walter. *The Working Class in Welfare Capitalism*. London: Routledge & Kegan Paul, 1978.

Kotlikoff, Laurence J. "The Emperor's Dangerous Clothes." *Economists' Voice* 5, 2 (April 2008): article 3. Available at www.bepress.com/ev.

Kraan, Dirk-Jan. "Off-Budget and Tax Expenditures." *OECD Journal on Budgeting* 4, 1 (2004): 121–142.

Kreile, Michael. "West Germany: The Dynamics of Expansion." In *Between Power and Plenty*, ed. Peter Katzenstein, 191–224. Madison: University of Wisconsin Press, 1978.

Krohn, Steven. "Swedish Green Certificate Plans Could Halt Wind." European Wind Energy Association, 2003.

Krueger, Alan B. "How Computers Have Changed the Wage Structure: Evidence From Microdata, 1984–89." *Quarterly Journal of Economics* 108, 1 (February 1993).

"When It Comes to Income Inequality, More Than Just Market Forces Are at Work." *New York Times*, April 4, 2002.

Krugman, Paul. "Reckonings, Sins of Emissions." *New York Times*, November 29, 2000.

*The Return of Depression Economics and the Crisis of 2008*. New York: W. W. Norton, 2009.

Kudrle, Robert T., and Theodore R. Marmor. "The Development of Welfare States in North America." In *The Development of Welfare States in Europe and America*, ed. Peter Flora and Arnold Heidenheimer, 81–121. New Brunswick, NJ: Transaction, 1981.

La Porte, Todd. "Nuclear Waste: Increasing Scale and Sociopolitical Impacts." *Science* 201, 4350 (July 7, 1978): 22–28.

Lackner, Klaus S., and Jeffrey D. Sachs. "A Robust Strategy for Sustainable Energy." *Brookings Papers on Economic Activity* 2 (2005).

Lange, Peter. "The Politics of the Social Dimension." In *Euro-Politics: Institutions and Policymaking in the European Community*, ed. Alberta M. Sbragia, 225–256. Washington, DC: Brookings Institution, 1992.

Lascher, Edward L., Jr., and John L. Korey. "The Myth of the Independent Voter, California Style." *California Journal of Politics and Policy* 3, 1 (2011): article 2. Available at http://www.bepress.com/cjpp/vol3/iss1/2.

LeRoy, Michael H. "The Changing Character of Strikes Involving Permanent Striker Replacements, 1935–1990." *Journal of Labor Research* 16, 4 (1995): 423–438.

Lester, Richard K., and Robert Rosner. "The Growth of Nuclear Power: Drivers and Constraints." *Daedalus* 138, 4 (Fall, 2009): 19–30.

Levine, Arthur. "Dueling Goals for Education." *New York Times*, April 7, 1999, sec. A, 21.

Levy, Frank, and Richard J. Murnane. *The New Division of Labor: How Computers Are Creating the Next Job Market*. Princeton: Princeton University Press, 2004.

"U.S. Earnings Levels and Earnings Inequality: A Review of Recent Trends and Proposed Explanations." *Journal of Economic Literature* 30, 3 (1992): 1333–1381.

Levy, Jonah. "The State Also Rises: The Roots of Contemporary State Activism." In *The State after Statism*, ed. Jonah Levy. Cambridge, MA: Harvard University Press, 2006.

Lewis, N., and D. Nocera. "Powering the Planet: Chemical Challenges in Solar Energy Utilization." *PNAS* 103, 43 (October 24, 2006): 15729–15735.

Lewis-Beck, Michael S., Charles Tien, and Richard Nadeau. "Obama's Missed Landslide: A Racial Cost?" *PS: Political Science and Politics* 43 (2010): 69–76.

Lieberson, Stanley. *A Piece of the Pie: Blacks and White Immigrants since 1880*. Berkeley: University of California Press, 1980.

Light, Paul C. "Passing Nonincremental Policy: Presidential Influence in Congress, Kennedy to Carter." *Congress and the Presidency* 9, 1 (1981–1982): 61–82.

Lijphart, Arend. "Constitutional Choices for New Democracies." *Journal of Democracy* 2, 1 (Winter 1991): 70–84.

*Democracies: Patterns of Majoritarian and Consensus Government in Twenty-One Countries*. New Haven: Yale University Press, 1984.

"The Political Consequences of Electoral Laws, 1945–85." *American Political Science Review* 84, 2 (1990): 481–496.

Lincoln, James R., Harold R. Kerbo, and Elke Wittenhagen. "Japanese Companies in Germany: A Case Study in Cross-Cultural Management." *Industrial Relations: A Journal of Economy and Society* 34, 3 (1995): 417–440.

Lindblom, Charles E. *Politics and Markets: The World's Political-Economic Systems.* New York: Basic Books, 1977.

Lindert, Peter H. *Growing Public: Social Spending and Economic Growth since the Eighteenth Century.* Vols. 1–2. Cambridge: Cambridge University Press, 2004.

Linz, Juan. "Totalitarian and Authoritarian Regimes." In *Handbook of Political Science*, ed. Nelson Polsby and F. Greenstein, 3:175–411. Reading, MA: Addison Wesley, 1975.

Lizza, Ryan. "As the World Burns." *New Yorker*, October 11, 2010, 70–83.

Lubove, Roy. *The Struggle for Social Security, 1900–1935.* Cambridge, MA: Harvard University Press, 1968.

Lynch, Julia, and Mikko Myrskyla. "Always the Third Rail? Pension Income and Policy Preferences in European Democracies." *Comparative Political Studies* 42, 8 (August 2009): 1068–1097.

MacKay, Charles. *Extraordinary Popular Delusions and the Madness of Crowds. With a foreword by Andrew Tobias. 1841.* New York: Harmony Books, 1980.

Madison, James. "Federalist Papers No.10." 1787. Available at http://www.constitution.org/fed/federa10.htm.

Magleby, David B. "Direct Legislation in the American State." In *Referendums around the World: The Growing Use of Direct Democracy*, ed. David Butler and Austin Ranney, 218–257. Washington, DC: American Enterprise Institute, 1994.

Management Information Services. "Analysis of Federal Expenditures for Energy Development." Prepared for the Nuclear Energy Institute, Washington, DC, September 2008.

Mankiw, Gregory. "Spending and Tax Multipliers." December 11, 2008. Available at http://gregmankiw.blogspot.com/2008/12/spending-and-tax-multipliers.html.

"One Answer to Global Warming: A New Tax." *New York Times*, September 16, 2007.

Mann, Catherine. "This Is Bangalore Calling: Hang Up or Speed Dial?" Federal Reserve Bank of Cleveland Working Paper. 2005.

Mann, Thomas E., and Norman J. Ornstein. *The Broken Branch: How Congress Is Failing America and How to Get It Back on Track.* New York: Oxford University Press, 2006.

Marmor, Theodore R. "American Health Care Policy and Politics." In *The Fragmentation of U.S. Health Care*, ed. Einer Elhauge, 343–388. Oxford: Oxford University Press, 2010.

Marquez, Benjamin, and John F. Witte. "Immigration Reform: Strategies for Legislative Action." *Forum* 7, 3 (2009): article 2.

Martin, Andrew, and George Ross. "European Integration and the Europeanization of Labor." In *Transnational Cooperation among Labor Unions*, ed. Michael E. Gordon and Lowell Turner, 120–149. Ithaca, NY: ILR Press/Cornell University Press, 2000.

Martin, Philip L. "Immigration and Integration: Challenges for 1990s." *Unpublished manuscript*, 1993.

"The Migration Issue." *Migration World* 20, 5 (1992): 10–15.

Martin, Philip L., Manolo Abella, and Christiane Kuptsch. *Managing Labor Migration in the Twenty-First Century.* New Haven: Yale University Press, 2006.

Martin, Philip L., and Elizabeth Midgley. "Immigration to the United States: Journey to an Uncertain Destination." *Population Bulletin* 49, 2 (1994): 1–47.

Martin, Philip L., and Mark Miller. "Employer Sanctions: French, German, and US Experiences." International Labour Office, International Migration Papers 36. September 2000.

Mattila, Mikko and Jan-Erik Lane. "Why Unanimity in the Council." *European Union Politics* 2, 1 (2001): 31–52.

Maxfield, Sylvia. *The International Political Economy of Central Banking in Developing Countries.* Princeton: Princeton University Press, 1997.

Mayer, Nonna. *Ces Français qui votent Le Pen.* Paris: Flammarion, 2002.

Mayhew, David R. *Divided We Govern: Party Control, Lawmaking, and Investigations, 1946–1990.* New Haven: Yale University Press, 1991.

McAlinden, Sean P., Kim Hill, and Bernard Swiecki. "Economic Contribution of the Automotive Industry to the U.S. Economy – An Update." A study prepared for the Alliance of Automobile Manufacturers by the Center for Automotive Research. 2003. Available at http://www.cargroup.org/pdfs/Alliance-Final.pdf.

McCaughey, Robert A. "Scholars and Teachers Revisited: In Continued Defense of College Faculty Who Publish." American Council of Learned Societies, *ACLS Occasional Paper* 59 (2005): 88–97.

McCormick, John. *The European Superpower.* New York: Palgrave Macmillan, 2007.

Mechanic, David. "Professional Judgment and the Rationing of Medical Care." *University of Pennsylvania Law Review* 140, 5 (May 1992): 1713–1754.

Mechanic, David, and David A. Rochefort. "Comparative Medical Systems." *Annual Review of Sociology* 22, 2 (1996): 239–270.

Mendelberg, Tali. "Racial Priming Revived." *Perspectives of Politics* 6, 1 (March 2008): 109–123.

Metcalf, Gilbert E. "Designing a Carbon Tax to Reduce U. S. Greenhouse Gas Emissions." NBER Working Paper No. 14375. National Bureau of Economic Research, October 2008.

Metcalf, Gilbert E., Sergey Paltsev, John M. Reilly, Henry D. Jacoby, and Jennifer Holak. "Analysis of U.S. Greenhouse Gas Tax Proposals." MIT Joint Program on the Science and Policy of Global Change Report No. 160. Massachusetts Institute of Technology, 2008.

Meyer, Niels I. "Learning from Wind Energy Policy in the EU: Lessons from Denmark, Sweden and Spain." *European Environment* 17 (2007): 347–362.

*Migration News.* "Foreigners Still under Attack in Germany." 1, 7 (August 1994). Available at http://migration.ucdavis.edu/mn/more.php?id=398_0_4_0.

"UN Migration, WB Remittances." 15, 4 (October 2009). Available at http://www.migration.ucdavis.edu/mn/more.php?id=3563_0_5_0.

Migration Policy Institute. "Immigration Data Hub." Available at http://www.migrationinformation.org/datahub/.

Miles, Thomas J., and Cass Sunstein. "Do Judges Make Regulatory Policy? An Empirical Investigation of Chevron." AEI Brookings Joint Center for Regulatory Studies, Working Paper 06-15. May 2006.

Miller, Mark J. *Employer Sanctions in Western European Countries.* Staten Island, NY: Center for Migration Studies, 1987.

Miller, Steven E., and Scott D. Sagan. "Alternative Nuclear Futures." In vol. 1 of *The Global Nuclear Future. Daedalus* 139, 1 (Fall 2010): 126–137.

"Nuclear Power without Nuclear Proliferation?" *Daedalus* 138, 4 (Fall, 2009): 7–30.

Mintz, Alex, and Chi Huang. "Guns versus Butter: The Indirect Link." *American Journal of Political Science* 35 (1991): 738–757.

Mishel, Lawrence, Jared Bernstein, and Sylvia Allegretto. *The State of Working America: 2006–07.* Ithaca, NY: ILR Press, Cornell University Press, 2007.

Mishel, Lawrence, Jared Bernstein, and John Schmitt. *The State of Working America: 1998–99.* Ithaca, NY: ILR Press, Cornell University Press, 1999.

Moore, Colleen, and Nancy Shulock. "Divided We Fail: Improving Completion and Closing Racial Gaps in California's Community Colleges." Institution for Higher Education and Leadership and Policy, October 2010.

Moskos, Charles C. *A Call to Civic Service: National Service for Country and Community.* New York: Free Press, 1988.

"Racial Integration in the Armed Forces." *American Journal of Sociology* 72, 2 (1966): 132–148.

Mosteller, Frederick. "The Tennessee Study of Class Size in the Early School Grades." *Future of Children* 5, 2 (1995): 113–127.

"The Tennessee Study of Class Size in the Early School Grades." *Bulletin of the AAAS* 1, 7 (May, 1997): 14–26.

Moravcsik, Andrew. "Introduction: Integrating International and Domestic Theories of International Bargaining." In *Double-Edged Diplomacy*, ed. P. B. Evans, H. K. Jacobson, and R. D. Putnam, 3–42. Berkeley: University of California Press, 1993.

Morgenson, Gretchen. "The Inflatable Loan Pool." *New York Times*, June 20, 2010, B1.

Morio, Shinsuke. "Quantitative Relationship between Infant Mortality and Social Factors." *Yonago Acta Medica* 28, 1 (1985): 8–37.

Muller, Thomas. *Immigrants and the American City.* New York: New York University Press, 1993.

Myles, John, and Jill Quadagno. "Recent Trends in Pension Reform: A Comparative View." Paper presented at the conference on Reform of the Retirement Income Systems, Queen's University, February 1–2, 1996.

Nader, Ralph, and Toby Heaps. "We Need a Global Carbon Tax." *Wall Street Journal*, December 3, 2008.

National Resources Defense Council. *Why Liquid Coal Is Not a Viable Option to Move America beyond Oil.* Washington, DC: NRDC, February 2007.

Nee, Victor, Jimy M. Sanders, and Scott Sernau. "Job Transitions in an Immigrant Metropolis: Ethnic Boundaries and the Mixed Economy." *American Sociological Review* 59 (1994): 849–872.

Newfeld, Christopher. "Avoiding the Coming Higher Education Wars." *Academe* 96, 3 (May–June 2010): 39–42.

*New York Times.* "China's Route Forward." January 23, 2009.

Ngongo, Kypa Ngoyi, Nicola Nante, Laurent Chenet, and Martin McKee. "What Has Contributed to the Change in Life Expectancy in Italy between 1980 and 1992?" *Health Policy* 48 (1999): 1–12.

Nickell, Stephen J. "Unemployment and Labor Market Rigidities: Europe versus North America." *Journal of Economic Perspectives* 11, 3 (Summer 1997): 55–74.

Nickell, Stephen J. "Unemployment: Questions and Some Answers." *Economic Journal* 108, 448 (May 1998): 802–816.

Niemelä, Heikki, and Kari Salminen. "State or Corporations: Trends of Pension Policy in Scandinavia." *Politiika* 35, 4 (January 1994).

Noiriel, Gérard. "Difficulties in French Historical Research on Immigration." In *Immigrants in Two Democracies: French and American Experience*, ed. Donald L. Horowitz and Gérard Noiriel, 66–79. New York: New York University Press, 1992.

Nørregaard, John, and Jeffrey Owens. "Taxing Profits in a Global Economy." *OECD Observer* 175 (1992): 35–38.

Norsworthy, J. R., and Craig A. Zabala. "Worker Attitudes, Worker Behavior, and Productivity in the U.S. Automobile Industry, 1959–1976." *Industrial and Labor Relations Review* 38 (1985): 557.

Oberlander, Jonathan. *The Political Life of Medicare*. Chicago: University of Chicago Press, 2003.

Oberlander, Jonathan, and Theodore R. Marmor. "The Health Bill Explained at Last." *New York Review of Books*, August 19, 2010.

Obama, Barrack, and Joseph Biden. "Energy and Environment Plan." 2008. Available at http://change.gov/agenda/energy_and_environment_agenda/.

OECD. "Country Reports: Graduate Contributions to Higher Education." *Paris: OECD*, 2004.

"Country Reports: Thematic Review of Migrant Education." *Paris: OECD*, 2008b.

*Detailed Tables*. Vol. 2, *National Accounts, 1978–1990*. Paris: OECD, 1992.

*Implementing the OECD Jobs Strategy: Lessons From Member Countries*. Paris: OECD, 1997.

*Indicators of Employment Protection*. Paris: OECD, 2010. Available at www.oecd.org/employmentprotection.

*Labour Force Statistics*. Paris: OECD, 2009. Available at: http://webnet.oecd.org/wbos/.

*Labour Market Flexibility: Trends in Enterprises*. Paris: OECD, 1989.

*Main Aggregates*. Vol. 1, *National Accounts of OECD Countries*. Paris: OECD, 1974.

*Main Economic Indicators*. Paris: OECD, 2008a.

*National Accounts*. Vol. 1. Paris: OECD, 1994.

*National Accounts Statistics of OECD Countries*. Paris: OECD, various years.

*OECD Employment Outlook, 2003: Towards More and Better Jobs*. Paris: OECD, 2003.

*Tax Expenditures: Recent Experiences*. Paris: OECD, 1996.

*Youth Unemployment*. Paris: OECD, 1978.

OECD.stat 2009–2010. Available at http://stats.oecd.org.

Ong, Michael K., *et al*. "Looking Forward, Looking Back: Assessing Variations in Hospital Resource Use and Outcomes for Elderly Patients with Heart Failure." *Circulation: Cardiovascular Quality and Outcomes* 2 (2009): 548–557.

Ornstein, Norman J. "Money in Politics: Campaign Finance Reform." *Current*, October 1992, 10–14.

Ornstein, Norman J., Thomas E. Mann, Paul Taylor, Michael J. Malbin, and Anthony Corrado Jr. "Five Ideas for Practical Campaign Reform." League of Women Voters Education Fund, July 21, 1997.

Overbye, Einar. "Convergence in Policy Outcomes: Social Security Systems in Perspective." *Journal of Public Policy* 14, 2 (1994): 147–174.

Owens, John, and Larry L. Wade. "Campaign Spending on California Ballot Propositions, 1924–1984: Trends and Voting Effects." *Western Political Quarterly* 39, 4 (1986): 675–689.

Page, Andrew, Stephen Begg, Richard Taylor, and Alan D. Lopez. "Global Comparative Assessments of Life Expectancy: The Impact of Migration with Reference to Australia." *Bulletin of the World Health Organization* 85 (2007): 474–481.

Paltsev, Sergey, John M. Reilly, Henry D. Jacoby, Angelo C. Gurgel, Gilbert E. Metcalf, Andrei P. Sokolov, and Jennifer F. Holak. "Assessment of U.S. Cap-and-Trade Proposals." MIT Joint Program on the Science and Policy of Global Change Report No. 146. Massachusetts Institute of Technology, 2007.

Parisotto, Aurelio. "Direct Employment in Multi-national Enterprises in Industrialized and Developing Countries in the 1980s: Main Characteristics and Recent Trends." In *Multinationals and Employment: The Global Economy of the 1990s*, ed. Paul Bailey, Aurelio Parisotto, and Geoffrey Renshaw, 33–68. Geneva: International Labour Office, 1993.

Passel, Jeffery S. *Immigrants and Taxes: A Reappraisal of Huddle's "The Cost of Immigrants." Program for Research on Immigration Policy*. Washington, DC: Urban Institute, 1994.

Passel, Jeffery S., and D'Vera Cohn. "A Portrait of Unauthorized Immigrants in the United States." Washington, DC: Pew Hispanic Center, 2009.

Pastore, Francesco. "Employment and Education Policy for Young People in the EU: What Can New Member States Learn from Old Member States?" IZA DP No. 3209, December 2007.

Patashnik, Eric M. *Putting Trust in the U.S. Budget*. Cambridge: Cambridge University Press, 2000.

Pattilo, Catherine A., Helene Poirson Ward, and Luca A. Ricci. "External Debt and Growth." International Monetary Fund WP/02/69. April 2002.

Pauly, Louis. *Who Elected the Bankers?* Ithaca, NY: Cornell University Press, 1997.

Pempel, T. J., and Keiichi Tsunekawa. "Corporatism without Labor?" In *Trends toward Corporatist Intermediation*, ed. Gerhard Lehmbruch and Philippe C. Schmitter, 231–270. Beverly Hills, CA: Sage, 1979.

Peña, Naomi. "Biofuels for Transportation: A Climate Perspective." Pew Center on Global Climate Change, June 2008.

Perlstein, Linda. *Tested: One American School Struggles to Make the Grade*. New York: Henry Holt, 2007.

Perrow, Charles. *Normal Accidents*. New York: Basic Books, 1984.

Perry, James L., Ann Marie Thomson, Mary Tschirrhart, Debra Mesch, and Geunjoo Lee. "Inside a Swiss Army Knife: An Assessment of AmeriCorps." *Journal of Public Administration Research and Theory* 9, 2 (April 1999): 225–250.

Persson, Torsten, and Guido Tabellini. "Is Inequality Harmful for Growth?" *American Economic Review* 84, 3 (June, 1994): 600–621.

Peterson, Mark A. *Legislating Together: The White House and Capitol Hill from Eisenhower to Reagan*. Cambridge, MA: Harvard University Press, 1990.

Pew Center on the States. "One in 100: Behind Bars in America 2008." Washington, DC: Pew Charitable Trust, 2008.

Phelps-Brown, Henry. *The Inequality of Pay*. Oxford: Oxford University Press, 1979.

Piketty, Thomas, and Emmanuel Saez. "Income Inequality in the United States, 1913–1998." *Quarterly Journal of Economics* 118, 1 (February 2003): 1–39.

Pierson, Paul. *Dismantling the Welfare State? Reagan, Thatcher, and the Politics of Retrenchment*. Cambridge: Cambridge University Press, 1994.

*The New Politics of the Welfare State*. Oxford: Oxford University Press, 2001.

Pil, Frits K., and John Paul MacDuffie. "Japanese and Local Influences on the Transfer of Work Practices at Japanese Transplants." Paper presented at the 48th annual meeting of the Industrial Relations Association, San Francisco, January 5–7, 1996.

Pimentel, David, and Ted W. Patzek. "Ethanol Production Using Corn, Switchgrass, and Wood; Biodiesel Production Using Soybean and Sunflower." *Natural Resources Research* 14, 1 (March 2005): 65–76.

Pitts, Stephen R., Emily R. Carrier, Eugene C. Rich, and Arthur L. Kellermann. "Where Americans Get Acute Care: Increasingly, It's Not at Their Doctor's Office." *Health*

*Affairs*, 2010. Available at http://content.healthaffairs.org/cgi/content/abstract/29/9/ 1620.

Plender, Richard. "EU Immigration and Asylum Policy – The Hague Programme and the Way Forward." *ERA Forum* 9, 2 (2008): 301–325.

Pollin, Robert, Heidi Garrett-Peltier, James Heintz, and Helen Scharber. *Green Recovery: A Programme to Create Good Jobs and Start Building a Low-Carbon Economy.* Washington, DC: Center for American Progress, 2008.

Pontusson, Jonas. *Inequality and Prosperity: Social Europe vs. Liberal America.* Ithaca, NY: Cornell University Press, 2005.

Posner, Elliot. "The New Transatlantic Regulatory Relations in Financial Services." Paper presented at the first annual Garnet Conference, University of Amsterdam, September 27–29, 2006.

Pulliam, Susan, Kara Scannell, Aaron Lucchetti, and Serena Ng. "SEC and Prosecutors Cast Wider Net in Mortgage Investigation." *Wall Street Journal*, May 13, 2010.

Prasad, Monica. "On Carbon, Tax and Don't Spend." *New York Times*, March 25, 2008.

Presser, Harriet. *Working in a 24/7 Economy: Challenges for American Families.* New York: Russell Sage Foundation, 2003.

PriceWaterhouseCoopers. "The Economic Impacts of the Oil and Natural Gas Industry on the U.S. Economy: Employment, Labor Income, and Value Added." Prepared for the American Petroleum Institute, September 8, 2009.

Pryor, Frederic L., and David L. Schaffer. *Who's Not Working and Why: Employment, Cognitive Skills, Wages, and the Changing U.S. Labor Market.* Cambridge: Cambridge University Press, 1999.

Quillian, Lincoln. "Prejudice as a Response to Perceived Group Threat: Population Composition and Anti-immigrant and Racial Prejudice in Europe." *American Sociological Review* 60 (1995): 586–611.

Rasmussen, B. "Power Production from the Wind." In *Wind Energy in Denmark*, Report from the Danish Ministry of Energy. Copenhagen, 1987.

Ravitch, Diane. "Resegregation." *New Republic*, October 14, 2010b, 40–43.

*The Death and Life of the Great American School System: How Testing and Choice Are Undermining Education.* New York: Basic Books, 2010a.

Reed, Deborah, Kim Reuben, and Elisa Barbour. *Retention of New Teachers in California. Public Policy Institute of California*, 2006. Available at www.ppic.org.

Reich, Robert B. *Locked in the Cabinet.* New York: Alfred A. Knopf, 1997.

Reiche, D., and M. Bechberger. "Policy Differences in the Promotion of Renewable Energies in the EU Member States." *Energy Policy* 32 (2004): 843–849.

Reinhart, Carmen M., and Kenneth S. Rogoff. *This Time Is Different: Eight Centuries of Financial Folly.* Princeton: Princeton University Press, 2009.

Reiter, Howard L. "Party Decline in the West: A Skeptic's View." *Journal of Theoretical Politics* 1, 3 (1989): 325–348.

Relman, Arnold S. *A Second Opinion: Rescuing America's Health Care.* New York: Public Affairs, 2007.

Reuters. "Norway, Sweden Aim to Unify Renewable Power Scheme." June 27, 2008.

Roberts, David. "The Truth about Green Jobs." *Mother Jones*, November–December 2008. Available at http://www.motherjones.com/print/15547.

Rodrik, Dani. *Has Globalization Gone Too Far?* Washington, DC: Institute For International Economics, March 1997.

Rogers, Joel. "Divide and Conquer: Further Reflections on the Distinctive Character of American Labor Laws." *Wisconsin Law Review* 1 (1990): 1147.

Rohatyn, Felix. *Bold Endeavors: How Our Government Built America, and Why It Must Rebuild Now.* New York: Simon and Schuster, 2009.

Rokkan, Stein. *Citizens, Elections, Parties.* Oslo: Universitetsforlaget, 1970.

Romer, Christina D. "Putting Americans Back to Work." *Wall Street Journal,* December 2, 2009, A25.

Romer, Christina D., and David H. Romer. "Does Monetary Policy Matter? A New Test in the Spirit of Friedman and Schwartz." *NBER Macroeconomics Annual 1989* (1989): 121–170.

"What Ends Recessions?" *NBER Macroeconomics Annual 9* (1994): 13–57.

Romm, Joseph J. *The Hype about Hydrogen.* Washington, DC: Island Press, 2004.

Roza, Marguerite, and Raegen Miller. "Separation of Degrees: State-By-State Analysis of Teacher Compensation for Master's Degrees." *Schools in Crisis: Making Ends Meet Rapid Response Brief.* Seattle: Center of Reinventing Public Education, 2009.

Rubinow, Isaac Max. Social Insurance with Special Reference to American Conditions. New York: H. Holt, 1913.

*Standards of Health Insurance.* New York: Holt, 1916.

*The Quest for Social Security.* New York: Holt, 1934.

Runge, Ford C., and Benjamin Senauer. "How Biofuels Could Starve the Poor." *Foreign Affairs* 86, 3 (May–June 2007).

Sachs, Jeffrey. "Putting a Price on Carbon: An Emissions Cap or a Tax?" *Environment* 360 (May 7, 2009). Available at http://e360.yale.edu/content/feature.msp?id=2148.

Sagawa, Shirley, and Samuel Halperin, eds. *Visions of Service: The Future of the National and Community Service Act.* Washington, DC: National Women's Law Center and American Youth Policy Forum, 1993.

Samaras, Constantine, and Kyle Meisterling. "Life Cycle Assessment of Greenhouse Gas Emissions from Plug-in Hybrid Vehicles: Implications for Policy." *Environmental Science and Technology* 42, 9 (2008): 3170–3176.

Sampson, Robert J., and John H. Laub. "Socioeconomic Achievement in the Life Course of Disadvantaged Men: Military Service as a Turning Point, circa 1940–1965." *American Sociological Review* 61 (June 1996): 347–367.

Sassen, Saskia. *The Mobility of Capital and Labor: A Study in International Investment and Labor Flow.* Cambridge: Cambridge University Press, 1988.

Saunders, Peter. "Rising on the Tasman Tide: Income Inequality in the 1980s." Discussion Paper No. 49. Social Policy Research Centre, the University of New South Wales, June 1994.

Sauvant, Karl P., Padma Mallampally, and Persephone Economou. "Foreign Direct Investment and International Migration." *Transnational Corporations* 2, 1 (1993): 33–69.

Savage, James D. "Budgetary Collective Action Problems: Convergence and Compliance under the Maastricht Treaty on European Union." *Public Administration Review* 61, 1 (January–February 2001): 43–53.

Scarr, Sandra. "Child Care Research, Social Values and Public Policy." *Bulletin of the American Academy of Arts and Sciences* 50, 1 (1996): 28–45.

Schaller, Thomas F. *Whistling Past Dixie.* New York: Simon and Schuster, 2006.

Schanzenbach, Diane Whitmore, et al. "Renaissance Schools Fund-Supported Schools: Early Outcomes, Challenges, and Opportunities." *SRI International and Consortium on Chicago School Research,* 2009.

Schickler, Eric. *Disjointed Pluralism: Institutional Innovation and the Development of the U.S. Congress.* Princeton: Princeton University Press, 2001.

Schlesinger, William. "Carbon Trading." *Science* 314 (November 24, 2006): 1217.
Schlozman, Kay Lehman, Sidney Verba, and Henry E. Brady. "Weapon of the Strong? Participatory Inequality and the Internet." *Perspectives on Politics* 8, 2 (2010): 487–509.
Schmid, Günter, Bernd Reissert, and Gert Bruche. *Unemployment Insurance and Active Labor Market Policy: An International Comparison of Financing Systems*. Detroit: Wayne State University Press, 1992.
Schmitter, Phillipe. "Still the Century of Corporatism." In *The New Corporatism: Social-Political Structures in the Iberian World*, ed. F. B. Pike and T. Stritch, 85–131. Notre Dame, IN: University of Notre Dame Press, 1974.
Schrag, Peter. *Not Fit for Our Society: Immigration and Nativism in America*. Berkeley: University of California Press, 2010.
*Paradise Lost: California's Experience, America's Future*. Berkeley: University of California Press, 1999.
"The Populist Road to Hell: Term Limits in California." *American Prospect*, no. 24 (1996): 24–30.
Schulten, Thorsten. "European Works Councils: Prospects for a New System of European Industrial Relations." *European Journal of Industrial Relations* 2, 3 (1996): 303–324.
Schumpeter, Joseph A. *Capitalism, Socialism, and Democracy*. New York: Harper and Brothers, 1942.
Schwartz, Christine R. "Earnings Inequality and the Changing Association between Spouses Earnings." *American Journal of Sociology* 115, 5 (2010): 1524–1557.
Schweizerische Nationalbank. *Das Schweizerische Bankwesen im Jahre 1992*. Vol. 77. Zürich: Schweizerische Nationalbank, 1993.
Sferza, Serenella. "What's Left of the Left? More Than One Would Think." *Daedalus* 128, 2 (Spring 1999): 101–126.
Shanghai Ranking Consultancy. "Academic Ranking of World Universities, 2010." 2010. Available at http://www.arwu.org/.
Shaw, David. "Revolution in Cyberspace; Digital Age Poses the Riddle of Dividing or Uniting Society." *Los Angeles Times*, June 15, 1997, A26.
Shiller, Robert J. "Help Prevent a Sequel. Delay Some Pay." *New York Times*, June 20, 2010.
Shonfield, Andrew. *Modern Capitalism: The Changing Balance of Public and Private Power*. London: Oxford University Press, 1965.
Simonnot, Philippe. *Les nucleocrates*. Grenoble: Presses Universitaires de Grenoble, 1978.
Sinclair, Barbara. "Leading the New Majorities." *PS: Political Science and Politics* (January 2008b): 89–93.
"The New World of U.S. Senators." In *Congress Reconsidered*, ed. Lawrence C. Dodd and Bruce I. Oppenheimer, ch. 1. 9th ed. Washington, DC: CQ Press, 2008a.
Singelmann, Joachim. *From Agriculture to Services: The Transformation of Industrial Employment*. Beverly Hills, CA: Sage, 1978.
Sisko, Andrea M., Christopher J. Truffer, Sean P. Keehan, John A. Poisal, M. Kent Clemens, and Andrew J. Madison. "National Health Spending Projections: The Estimated Impact of Reform through 2019." *Health Affairs*. Available at http://content.health-affairs.org/cgi/content/abstract/hlthaff.2010.0788v1.
Skolnick, Jerome H. "Making Sense of the Crime Decline." *Newsday*, February 2, 1997, G8, G15.
Smeeding, Timothy M. "The Gap between Rich and Poor: A Cross-National Perspective for Why Inequality Matters and What Policy Can Do to Alleviate It." National

Institute of Population and Social Security Research Working Paper. Tokyo, March 21, 2001.

"Differences in Higher Education: Investments, Costs, and Outcomes." *La Follette Policy Report* 8, 2 (Spring 2009): 1–4. School of Public Affairs, University of Wisconsin, Madison.

Smith, Marshall S. "Education Reform: A Report Card." *AAAS Bulletin* 56, 2 (Winter 2003): 38–54.

Social Security Administration. "The 1995 Annual Report of the Board of Trustees of the Federal Old-Age and Survivors Insurance and Federal Disability Trust Funds." U.S. Government Printing Office, September, 1995. Available at http://www.ssa.gov/history/reports/trust/1995/.

"Summary of the 1983 Annual Report of the Board of Trustees of the Federal Old-Age and Survivors Insurance and Federal Disability Trust Funds." Office of the Actuary, June 24, 1983.

"The 2009 Annual Report of the Board of Trustees of the Federal Old-Age and Survivors Insurance and Federal Disability Trust Funds." House Document 111–41. U.S. Government Printing Office, May 12, 2009.

Sokolski, Henry. "Toward Nuclear Weapons Capability for All?" Washington, DC: New Nuclear Age Foundation, 2008.

Solomon, Susan, Gian-Kasper Plattner, Reto Knutti, and Pierre Friedlingstein. "Irreversible Climate Change Due to Carbon Dioxide Emissions." *Proceedings of the National Academy of Sciences in the United States* 106, 6 (February 10, 2009): 1704–1709.

Somerville, Chris. "Biofuels." *Current Biology* 17, 4 (2007): R115–R119.

Soskice, David, and Ronald Schettkat. "West German Labor Market Institutions and East German Transformation." In *Labor and an Integrated Europe*, ed. Lloyd Ulman, Barry Eichengreen, and William T. Dickens, 102–127. Washington, DC: Brookings Institution, 1993.

Sovacool, Benjamin K. "Valuing the Greenhouse Gas Emissions from Nuclear Power: A Critical Survey." *Energy Policy* 36 (2008): 2950–2963.

Sparkes, Jo. "Schools, Education and Social Exclusion." Centre for Analysis of Social Exclusion, CASE paper 29. November 1999.

Stein, Herbert. "Professor Knight's Law of Talk." *Wall Street Journal*, October 14, 1981, 28.

Stephens, Robert. "Radical Tax Reform in New Zealand." *Fiscal Studies* 14, 3 (1993): 45–63.

*Stern Review on the Economics of Climate Change*. Report headed by Sir Nicholas Stern for HM Treasury, 2006. Available at http://www.hm-treasury.gov.uk/sternreview_index.htm.

Stigler, George. *Capital and Rates of Return in Manufacturing Industries*. National Bureau of Economic Research. Princeton: Princeton University Press, 1963.

"The Theory of Economic Regulation." *Bell Journal of Economics and Management Science* 3 (1971): 3–18.

Stiglitz, Joseph E. *Globalization and Its Discontents*. New York: W. W. Norton, 2002.

"A New Agenda for Global Warming." *Economists' Voice* 3, 7 (2006a): article 3.

*Making Globalization Work*. New York: W. W. Norton, 2006b.

*Freefall: America, Free Markets, and the Sinking of the World Economy*. New York: W. W. Norton, 2010a.

"Government Failure vs. Market Failure: Principles of Regulation." In *Government and Markets: Toward a New Theory of Regulation*, ed. Edward J. Balleisen and David A. Moss, 13–51. Cambridge: Cambridge University Press, 2010b.

Storm, Servaas, and C. W. M. Naastepad. "Labor Market Regulation and Productivity Growth: Evidence for Twenty OECD Countries (1984–2004)." *Industrial Relations: A Journal of Economy and Society* 48, 4 (2009): 629–654.

Strange, Susan. *The Retreat of the State: The Diffusion of Power in the World Economy.* Cambridge: Cambridge University Press, 1996.

Streeck, Wolfgang. "More Uncertainties: German Unions Facing 1992." *Industrial Relations* 30, 3 (1991): 317–347.

*Reforming Capitalism: Institutional Change in the German Political Economy.* Oxford: Oxford University Press, 2009.

Swedish Ministry of Enterprise, Energy and Communications. "Energy Policy." September 25, 2007.

Swedish Ministry of Sustainable Development. "Fact Sheet." May 2006.

Taylor-Gooby, Peter, ed. *Welfare States under Pressure.* London: Sage, 2001.

Thompson, G. "The Supranational Regionalization of the International Financial System." Paper prepared for Garnet Conference on Global Financial and Monetary Governance, the EU, and Emerging Market Economies, Amsterdam, September 28–30, 2006.

Tichenor, Daniel J. "Navigating an American Minefield: The Politics of Illegal Immigration." *Forum* 7, 3 (2009): article 1.

Timmersfeld, Andrea. "Chancen und Perspektiven europäischer Kollektivverhandlunger." Dissertation, Trier, 1992.

Turner, Lowell. "Beyond National Unionism? Cross-National Labor Collaboration in the European Community." Paper presented at the American Political Science Association annual meeting, Washington, DC, September 2–5, 1993b.

"The Europeanization of Labor: Structure before Action." *European Journal of Industrial Relations* 2, 3 (November 1996): 325–344.

*Fighting for Partnership: Labor and Politics in Unified Germany.* Ithaca, NY: Cornell University Press, 1998.

"Prospects for Worker Participation in Management." In *Labor and an Integrated Europe,* ed. Lloyd Ulman, Barry Eichengreen, and William T. Dickens. Washington, DC: Brookings Institutions, 1993a.

UCTAD. *World Investment Report, 2007.* New York: United Nations Publishing Division, 2007.

UN. *Conference on Trade and Development.* New York: United Nations, 1993.

*International Migrant Stock.* New York: UN Population Division, 2002.

"International Tables." *Yearbook of National Accounts Statistics.* Geneva: UN International Division, various years.

*World Population Prospects.* New York: UN Population Division, 2006, 2008, 2009.

*Yearbook of International Trade Statistics, 1987.* New York: United Nations, 1989.

University of California. "1997–1998 Budget for Current Operations." Office of the President, October 1996.

"2010–2011 Budget for Current Operations, Budget Detail." Office of the President, 2010.

U.S. Census Bureau. Current Population Survey, 2009 Annual Social and Economic Supplement. 2009. Available at http://www.census.gov/hhes/www/cpstables/032009/pov/new06_100_01.htm.

Current Population Survey, Annual Social and Economic Supplements, 2010.

U.S. Census Bureau, Foreign Trade Division. "Balance of Payments." 2010.

U.S. Department of Agriculture. *Economic Research Service.* 2009. Data available at http://www.ers.usda.gov/Data/.

U.S. Department of Labor, Bureau of Labor Statistics. *Employment and Earnings* 31, 1 (January 1984).

*Employment and Earnings* 45, 1 (January 1998).

U.S. Department of Labor Employee Benefits Security Administration. "Private Pension Plan Bulletin: Abstract of 2005 Form 5500 Annual Reports." *Private Pension Plan Bulletin* 12 (October 2009).

U.S. House of Representatives. Hearing on the American Clean Energy and Security Act of 2009, Day 4. Rep. Ed Markey, Chair, Subcommittee on Energy and Environment, Committee on Energy and Commerce. Washington, DC, April 24, 2009.

Veblen, Thorstein. *The Engineers and the Price System.* New York: Viking Press, 1921.

*The Theory of the Leisure Class: An Economic Study in the Evolution of Institutions.* New York: Modern Library, 1934 (1899).

Verba, Sidney, Kay Lehman Scholzman, and Henry Brady. *Voice and Equality: Civic Voluntarism in American Politics.* Cambridge,MA: Harvard University Press, 1995.

Visser, Jelle. "The Strength of Union Movements in Advanced Capitalist Democracies – Social and Organizational Variations." In *The Future of Movements*, ed. Marino Regini, 17–52. London: Sage, 1992.

"Union Membership in 24 Countries." *Monthly Labor Review* 129 (2006): 38–49.

Vogel, Steven K. *Freer Markets, More Rules: Regulatory Reform in Advanced Industrial Countries.* Ithaca,NY: Cornell University Press, 1996.

*Japan Remodeled: How Government and Industry Are Reforming Japanese Capitalism.* Ithaca, NY: Cornell University Press, 2006.

von Hagen, Jürgen. "Budgeting Procedures and Fiscal Performance in the European Communities." DG II Economic Papers No. 96. Commission of the European Communities, 1992.

"Fiscal Discipline and Growth in Euroland: Experiences with the Stability and Growth Pact." ZEI Working Paper B 06. University of Bonn, 2003.

Vowles, Jack, and Peter Aimer. *Voter's Vengeance: The 1990 Election in New Zealand and the Fate of the Fourth Labour Government.* Auckland: Auckland University Press, 1993.

Wallerstein, Immanuel. *The Modern World System: Capitalist Agriculture and the Origins of the World Economy in the Sixteenth Century.* New York: Academic Press, 1974.

"Union Organization in Advanced Industrial Democracies." *American Political Science Review* 83, 2 (1989): 481–501.

*Wall Street Journal.* "Obama's Pick to Head SEC Has Record of Being a Regulator with a Light Touch." January 15, 2009.

Wand, Jonathan N., Kenneth W. Shotts, Jasjeet S. Sekhon, Walter R. Mebane Jr., Michael C. Herron, and Henry E. Brady. "The Butterfly Did It: The Aberrant Vote for Buchanan in Palm Beach County, Florida." *American Political Science Review* 95, 4 (2001): 791–810.

Ward, Michael D., and David R. Davis. "Sizing Up the Peace Dividend: Economic Growth and Military Spending in the United States, 1948–1996." *American Political Science Review* 86, 3 (1992): 748–755.

Wasylenko, Michael, and Theresa McGuire. "Jobs and Taxes: The Effect of Business Climate on States' Employment Growth Rates." *National Tax Journal* 38 (1985): 497–511.

Weiss, Andrew. *Efficiency Wages: Models of Unemployment, Layoffs, and Wage Dispersion.* Princeton: Princeton University Press, 1990.

Western, Bruce. "A Comparative Study of Working-Class Disorganization: Union Decline in Eighteen Advanced Capitalist Countries." *American Sociological Review* 60 (1995): 179–201.

"Postwar Unionization in Eighteen Advanced Capitalist Countries." *American Sociological Review* 58 (April 1993): 266–282.

Western, Bruce, and Katherine Beckett. "How Unregulated Is the U.S. Labor Market?" *American Journal of Sociology* 104, 4 (1999): 1030–1060.

Western, Bruce, and Becky Pettit. "Incarceration and Social Inequality." *Daedalus* 139, 3 (Summer 2010): 8–30.

Whiteford, Peter, and Edward Whitehouse. "Pension Challenges and Pension Reforms in OECD Countries." *Oxford Review of Economic Policy* 22, 1 (2006): 78–94.

White House Federal Budget Estimates. "Budget of the Federal Government, Fiscal Year 2009." Executive Office of the President, Office of Management and Budget, 2008.

White House Press Secretary. "Remarks by the President on the American Graduation Initiative." The White House, July 14, 2010.

Wildeman, Christopher. "Parental Imprisonment, the Prison Boom, and the Concentration of Childhood Disadvantages." *Demography* 46, 2 (2009): 265–280.

Wilensky, Gail. "Developing a Center for Comparative Effectiveness Information." *Health Affairs* 25, 6 (2006): w572–w585.

Wilensky, Harold L. "Active Labor-Market Policy: Its Content, Effectiveness, and Odd Relation to Evaluation Research." In *Social Research and Social Reform*, ed. Colin Crouch and Anthony Heath, 315–350. Oxford: Oxford University Press, 1992a.

"Careers, Counseling, and the Curriculum." *Journal of Human Resources* 2 (Winter 1967b): 19–40.

"The Great American Job Creation Machine in Comparative Perspective." *Industrial Relations: A Journal of Economy and Society* 31, 3 (1992b): 473–488.

"Is There a Crisis of the Welfare State?" In *Handbook of Public Policy*, ed. B. Guy Peters and Jon Pierre, 201–217. Thousand Oaks, CA: Sage Publications, 2006.

"Leftism, Catholicism, and Democratic Corporatism: The Role of Political Parties in Welfare State Development." In *The Development of Welfare States in Europe and America*, ed. P. Flora and A. J. Heidenheimer, 345–382. New Brunswick, NJ: Transaction, 1981.

"The Moonlighter: A Product of Relative Deprivation." *Industrial Relations* 8, 1 (October 1963): 105–124.

*The "New Corporatism," Centralization and the Welfare State.* London: Sage Publications, 1976.

"Nothing Fails Like Success: The Evaluation-Research Industry and Labor-Market Policy." *Industrial Relations: A Journal of Economy and Society* 24, 1 (1985): 1–19. See also Symposium on Active Labor Market Policy, edited by Wilensky, this issue.

*Organizational Intelligence: Knowledge and Policy in Government and Industry.* New York: Basic Books, 1967a.

"The Political Economy of Income Distribution: Issues in the Analysis of Government Approaches to the Reduction of Inequality." In *Major Social Issues: A Multi-disciplinary View*, ed. Milton J. Yinger and S. J. Cutler, 87–108. New York: Free Press, 1978.

"Political Legitimacy and Consensus: Missing Variables in the Assessment of Social Policy." In *Evaluating the Welfare State: Social and Political Perspectives*, ed. S. E. Spiro and E. Yuchtman-Yaar, 51–74. New York: Academic Press, 1983.

"The Problems and Prospects of the Welfare State." In *Industrial Society and Social Welfare*, enlarged ed., ed. Harold L. Wilensky and Charles N. Lebeaux, v–lii. New York: Free Press-Macmillan, 1965.

*Rich Democracies: Political Economy, Public Policy, and Performance.* Berkeley: University of California Press, 2002.

"2008: Democratic Sweep or Near Miss?" *Huffington Post*, July 15, 2008. Available at http://www.huffingtonpost.com/harold-l-wilensky/.

"The Uneven Distribution of Leisure: The Impact of Economic Growth on 'Free Time.'" *Social Problems* 9, 1 (Summer 1961): 32–56.

"U.S. Health Care and Real Health in Comparative Perspective: Lessons from Abroad." *Forum* 7, 2 (2009): article 7.

*The Welfare State and Equality: Structural and Ideological Roots of Public Expenditures*. Berkeley: University of California Press, 1975.

"Women's Work: Economic Growth, Ideology, and Social Structure." *Industrial Relations: A Journal of Economy and Society* 7 (1968): 235–248.

Wilensky, Harold L., and Charles N. Lebeaux. *Industrial Society and Social Welfare: The Impact of Industrialization on the Supply and Organization of Social Welfare Services in the United States*. New York: Russell Sage Foundation, 1958.

Wilensky, Harold L., and Lowell Turner. *Democratic Corporatism and Policy Linkages: The Interdependence of Industrial, Labor-Market, Incomes, and Social Policies in Eight Countries*. Research Monograph Series No. 69. Institute of International Studies, University of California, Berkeley, 1987.

Winters, Jeffrey A., and Benjamin I. Page. "Oligarchy in the United States?" *Perspectives on Politics* 7, 4 (December 2009): 731–744.

Wolff, Edward N. "Estimates of Household Wealth Inequality in the United States, 1962–83." *Review of Income and Wealth*, ser. 33 (September 1987): 231–256.

"Recent Trends in Asset Ownership." In *Assets for the Poor: The Benefits of Spreading Asset Ownership*, ed. Thomas M. Shapiro and Edward N. Wolff. New York: Russell Sage, 2001.

"Recent Trends in Household Wealth in the United States: Rising Debt and the Middle-Class Squeeze – an Update to 2007." Levy Economics Institute of Bard College, W.P 589. March 2010.

*Top Heavy: A Study of the Increasing Inequality of Wealth in America*. Twentieth Century Fund Report. New York: Twentieth Century Fund Press, 1995.

*Top Heavy: A Study of Increasing Inequality of Wealth in America*. Updated and expanded ed. New York: New Press, 1996.

Woodward, Douglas P., and Norman J. Glickman. "Regional and Local Determinants of Foreign Firm Location in the United States." In *Industry, Location and Public Policy*, ed. Henry W. Herzog Jr. and Alan M. Schlottmann, 190–217. Knoxville: University of Tennessee, 1991.

World Bank. "G8 Hokkaido-Toyako Summit – Double Jeopardy: Responding to High Food and Fuel Prices." 2008. Available from http://web.worldbank.org/WBSITE/EXTERNAL/NEWS/0,, contentMDK:21827681~pagePK:64257043~piPK:437376~t-heSitePK:4607,00.html.

World Health Organization. "Health Systems: Improving Performance." The World Health Report, 2000.

"The World Health Report, 2000 – Health Systems: Improving Performance." WHO, 2008.

World Investment Report. "The World Investment Report, 2008." New York: UNCTAD, 2008.

World Resources Institute. "Climate Analysis Indicators Tool." 2008. Available at http://cait.wri.org/.

Versluis, Arthur. "Virtual Education and the Race to the Bottom." *Academic Questions* 17, 3 (2004): 38–51.

Yahoo Finance. Available at http://finance.yahoo.com/q?s=%5EDJI.

Yergin, Daniel, and Robert Ineson. "America's Natural Gas Revolution." Wall Street Journal, November 3, 2009.

Zaslove, Andrej. "Here to Stay? Populism as a New Party Type." *European Review* 16, 3 (2008): 319–336.

Zedillo, Ernesto. "Carbon Prices, Not Quotas." *Forbes*, March 24, 2008. Available at www.forbes.com/columnists/forbes/2008/0324/035.html.

Zimring, Franklin E. *The Great American Crime Decline.* Cary, NC: Oxford University Press, 2006.

Zingales, Luigi. "Why Paulson Is Wrong." *Economist Voice* 5, 5 (2008): article 2.

Zysman, John. *Governments, Markets, and Growth: Finance and the Politics of Industrial Change.* Ithaca, NY: Cornell University Press, 1983.

# Index

AACC, 243
AALL (American Association for Labor
  Legislation), xvii, 277n1
Aaron, Henry, 226
ABC Bill (1989), 304n20
Abella, Manolo, 91
Abo, Tetsuo, 119, 120
abortion. *See* wedge issues
Abowd, Leila, 94, 95, 96, 119, 121
Abraham, Seven E., 219
Abramowitz, Alan, 196, 209, 300–301nn4,5
active labor-market policy (ALMP)
  definition, 53
  and economic performance, 5, 53
  and education, 245
  and low road, 176, 178–80
  and political economy types, 179–80, 298n18
  and poverty reduction, 226, 251
  and U.S. policy implications, 225–27, 245,
    246, 267
Adams, John, 227
AEC (Atomic Energy Commission) (United
  States), 23–24
affirmative action, 172
aged
  and family policies, 224–25
  and health care/health insurance, 212–13
  and job protection, 167
  and welfare state, 57
  *See also* retirement systems
agency capture, 148, 188–89, 262
AGI, 232
Aguilar, Soledad, 28
Ahearne, Alan G., 90
Aimer, Peter, 61
Ajami, Riad A., 121
Akerlof, George, 104
Alber, Jens, 59, 96, 97, 98, 288n15
Alesina, Alberto, 124, 131

Allegretto, Sylvia, 10
Almeida, Beth, 178
alternative energy. *See* biofuels; renewable
  energy
Altmeyer, Arthur J., xvii, 277n1
American Association for Labor Legislation
  (AALL), xvii, 277n1
American Concord Coalition, 62
American Recovery and Reinvestment Act
  (2009) (United States), 217
  and automobile dependence, 32
  benefits of, 137
  and energy policy, 282n24, 289–90n24
  and tax cuts, 264, 266
American Society of Civil Engineers (ASCE),
  170
AmeriCorps, 250–51
An, Feng, 31
Andrews, John B., xvii
Aoyama, Yuko, 111
Applebaum, E., 163
Argentina, 293n41
ASCE (American Society of Civil Engineers),
  170
Atkinson, A. B., 52
Atomic Energy Commission (AEC) (United
  States), 23–24
Auer, Peter, 101
Australia, 96, 178, 218, 292n38
Austria, 80
automobile dependence, 30–35, 32, 280n15
Autor, David H., 108
Ayers, David F., 243, 244

baby boom, 173–74
Baccaro, Lucio, 105
Baker, Dean, 105
Ball, Robert, 69
Banducci, Susan, 194

343